RELIGIOUS DOCTRINES IN THE MAHĀBHĀRATA

Religious Doctrines in the Mahābhārata

Nicholas Sutton

MOTILAL BANARSIDASS PUBLISHERS
PRIVATE LIMITED • DELHI

First Edition: Delhi, 2000

ISBN: 81-208-1700-1 (Cloth)
ISBN: 81-208-1702-8 (Paper)

MOTILAL BANARSIDASS

236 Sri Ranga, 9th Main III Block, Jayanagar, Bangalore 560 011
41 U.A. Bungalow Road, Jawahar Nagar, Delhi 110 007
8 Mahalaxmi Chamber, Warden Road, Mumbai 400 026
120 Royapettah High Road, Mylapore, Chennai 600 004
Sanas Plaza, 1302 Baji Rao Road, Pune 411 002
8 Camac Street, Calcutta 700 017
Ashok Rajpath, Patna 800 004
Chowk, Varanasi 221 001

PRINTED IN INDIA
BY JAINENDRA PRAKASH JAIN AT SHRI JAINENDRA PRESS,
A-45 NARAINA, PHASE I, NEW DELHI 110 028
AND PUBLISHED BY NARENDRA PRAKASH JAIN FOR
MOTILAL BANARSIDASS PUBLISHERS PRIVATE LMITED,
BUNGALOW ROAD, DELHI 110 007

CONTENTS

INTRODUCTION

1. Background Details

The *Mahābhārata* is a huge monument of Hindu literature. It is generally designated as an 'epic' by Western writers along with the *Rāmāyaṇa* of Vālmīki, which is shorter, of a different style and does not contain the extensive didactic material that is such a notable feature of the *Mahābhārata*. In the West the term epic generally refers to a work which recounts heroic deeds and while this is undoubtedly true of the *Mahābhārata*, within the Hindu tradition it is recognised primarily as a religious text with the status of scripture. It tells of the acts of Kṛṣṇa, the Deity manifest on earth, it portrays the behaviour of the righteous and of the wicked and it contains numerous didactic passages, including the *Bhagavad-gītā*, expounding religious doctrines of various types. Therefore although the term epic is retained, the primary understanding of the text is as an authoritative religious literature of crucial significance to the Hindu tradition.

The authorship of the *Mahābhārata* has been the subject of much debate. The traditional view is that it is the work of Vyāsa, who in later Hinduism is identified as an incarnation of Viṣṇu appearing to compile and arrange the Vedas and other sacred works. Much of the earlier Western work on the epic followed a text-critical approach in seeking to establish an original *Mahābhārata* which might be distinguished from later accretions included within the work as it stands today. Despite the shortcomings and subjectivity of text-critical methods, most contemporary Western scholars accept the view of Hopkins[1] that the *Mahābhārata* is not the work of one author but is a composite collection of pieces from different times loosely held together in a final epical form. It is notable, however, that more recent work has tended to move towards the view that the form the text now holds is not random, but is the careful composition of a final redactor or redactors.[2]

In van Buitenen's opinion the original story on which the epic is based was composed in the 8th or 9th century B.C., but is now irrecoverable.[3] This was reworked into the present form so that, "the old and new are inextricably bound together"[4] probably not much before 400 B.C. to form the oldest parts of the text as it is known today. These oldest sections comprise the basis of the narrative which has been subjected to subsequent reworkings and interpolations. The long didactic passages were added to the epic over the ensuing centuries to leave the text in its final form probably around 300 A.D. Again according to van Buitenen, "In particular, the didactic portions of what has been called the pseudo-epic were added to very late, perhaps as late as the fourth century A.D.".[5]

Chronologically, the *Mahābhārata* spans what is arguably the most significant period in the development of the Hindu tradition when the ideas of the Vedic orthodoxy were confronting new philosophies of a radically ascetic nature. It also contains the earliest expressions of the non-Vedic devotional theism which was to become so significant during the first millenium AD, and has had such a profound effect on subsequent Hindu thought.[6] Thus the text embodies the traditional Vedic stress on *yajña*, the social regulations and ritual duties of *dharma-śāstra*, the ascetic paths to salvation, and devotion to the Supreme Gods, Viṣṇu and Śiva.

2. Summary of the Contents of the *Mahābhārata*

The epic is divided into eighteen major sections, known as *parvans*, each with a title that relates approximately to its contents. Each *parvan* is subdivided into chapters made up of verses composed in various metres, usually in the *śloka* form, but also in *triṣṭubhs* and other less common metres as well as occasional prose passages. There are also sub-*parvans* into which the longer major *parvans* are divided of which the entire epic contains one hundred. In the usual form of verse reference, however, the sub-*parvans* are ignored, so that the sequence runs *parvan*-chapter-verse, which I have presented throughout in the standard form as, for example, 12.125.13.

The *Mahābhārata* begins with the *Ādi-parvan, ādiḥ* meaning beginning or first. Its 225 chapters first present the cycle of myths leading up to King Janamejaya's snake sacrifice at which the *Mahābhārata* is first spoken by Vaiśaṁpāyana, a disciple of Vyāsa. After this introduction, it proceeds to tell of the origins of the

Pāṇḍava brothers and their cousins the Kauravas, the marriage of the Pāṇḍavas to Draupadī and of the roots of the conflict between them that is the main theme of the central narrative.

The *Sabhā-parvan* (72 chapters) takes the narrative further by recounting how the kingdom was divided between the two branches of the family and how the great *Rājasūya* sacrifice was performed by Yudhiṣṭhira and the Pāṇḍavas. It tells of the envy of Duryodhana and the Kauravas and finally of the gambling match at which Yudhiṣṭhira loses everything to the Kauravas, the Pāṇḍavas are exiled to the forest, and Draupadī is insulted. The *Vana-parvan* (229 chapters) whilst recounting numerous adventures that befall the Pāṇḍavas during their exile in the forest, also contains a number of notable didactic interludes in which various teachers give religious and philosophical instructions to the main characters. The *Virāṭa-parvan* (67 chapters) describes how the Pāṇḍavas pass their final year of exile living incognito at the court of King Virāṭa. Here the drama is not punctuated by didactic passages as in the *Vana*.

The *Udyoga-parvan* (197 chapters) describes the preparations for war with lengthy debates in both camps over what course of action is righteous and how success is gained in life. It is in this *parvan* that Kṛṣṇa begins to play a prominent role as the controller of events. The *Bhīṣma-parvan* (117 chapters) describes the initial drawing up of the armies at Kurukṣetra and contains the *Bhagavad-gītā,* in which Kṛṣṇa convinces Arjuna that it is right for him to wage war. The battle is then described up to the point at which Arjuna shoots down Bhīṣma, the Kaurava general.

The *Droṇa-parvan* (173 chapters) takes the story of the battle further, up to the point at which Droṇa is slain by Dhṛṣṭadyumna, and the *Karṇa-parvan* (69 chapters) concentrates specifically on the conflict between Arjuna and Karṇa. The *Śalya-parvan* (64 chapters) tells of the final stages of the battle in which Yudhiṣṭhira kills his uncle, Śalya, and Bhīma puts an end to Duryodhana in single combat. The *Sauptika-parvan* (18 chapters) describes the massacre in the Pāṇḍava camp by three survivors from the Kaurava host, and the *Strī-parvan* (27 chapters) describes the lamentations of women whose husbands and sons have fallen on the battlefield and the attempts of the survivors to understand philosophically the catastrophe that has taken place.

The *Śānti-parvan* (353 chapters) is comprised of numerous

didactic treatises covering a range of religious and philosophical perspectives. It opens with the victorious Yudhiṣṭhira lamenting over the suffering he has caused and wishing to abandon the kingdom he has won to take up the life of an ascetic. There follows a lengthy debate on the proper duty of a king, before everybody returns to the battlefield where the fallen Bhīṣma gives more detailed instructions on this subject. This section is known as the *Rāja-dharma.* Bhīṣma then presents the *Mokṣa-dharma,* teachings on the subject of salvation in the form of various loosely connected treatises based mainly on the ideas of Sāṁkhya and Yoga. The *parvan* concludes with an exposition on devotion to the Deity Nārāyaṇa known as the *Nārāyaṇīya-parvan.*

The *Anuśāsana-parvan* (154 chapters) contains a passage teaching devotion to Śiva and then returns to Bhīṣma instructing Yudhiṣṭhira. Here the teachings take the form of *dharma-śāstra,* or social regulations, as well as describing ritual acts that bring reward in the afterlife. The *Aśvamedhika-parvan* (96 chapters) then narrates how the Pāṇḍavas executed a horse sacrifice to atone for the sins incurred by killing others in battle. Much of the *parvan,* however, consists of teachings from Kṛṣṇa to Arjuna (chapters 16 to 50) similar to those of the *Mokṣa-dharma,* including the three chapters known as the *Anugītā* (16-18).

The *Āśramavāsika-parvan* (47 chapters) describes the final meeting of the surviving characters when the Pāṇḍavas go to visit the elders of the family who have now renounced the world and are practising religious austerities in the forest. The *Mausala-parvan* (9 chapters) tells of the destruction of Kṛṣṇa's own race, the Yadus, through civil strife, and the departure of Kṛṣṇa from this world. The *Mahāprasthānika-parvan* (3 chapters) describes the deaths of the Pāṇḍavas and of Draupadī after they have given up their kingdom and journeyed to the Himalayas. The final *parvan,* the *Svargārohaṇa* (5 chapters), depicts the major characters of the epic residing amongst the gods in heaven.

This brief outline gives no more than the barest insight into an extremely complex text, but does offer some preliminary indication of what material is where, and also a broad guide to the division between didactic and narrative passages, though it must be borne in mind that the epic has a tendency to slip into didactic mode at virtually any point in its progression. The huge difference in size between the various *parvans* may seem to indicate the absence of any overall plan, but the fact that there are eighteen *parvans* probably reveals the work of a final redactor, as this number matches the chapters of the *Bhagavad-gītā* which Esnoul[7] recognises as significant in the compilation of the *Nārāyaṇīya*.

3. The Aims of the Present Study

This study of the *Mahābhārata* focuses above all on the religious teachings and philosophical doctrines that it propounds. Whilst acknowledging the importance of text critical studies, it is not my aim to pursue the numerous questions they raise, although use will be made of the work done in this field when it sheds light on doctrinal development. The specific aims are as follows:-

(1) The first task of this study, and arguably the most important, is one of cataloguing.[8] The *Mahābhārata* is a vast literary work containing different ideas from various religious tendencies. Anyone embarking on any form of study of the epic is faced with the daunting prospect of initially tracing the particular material relevant to their work. Van Buitenen points to the reason why so few Western scholars have worked with the *Mahābhārata* as being that, ". . . the text is so dismally intractable. Its sheer size is really forbidding."[9] It is my hope that the present work will contribute to some extent to the easing of these difficulties, at least where matters of religious doctrine are concerned, by indicating the extent to which the epic discusses particular ideas and the main passages in which such discussion is to be found.

(2) I have in addition set myself the task of interpretation and explanation. This involves attempting to highlight the significance and meaning of specific passages and showing the way in which different doctrinal tendencies interact with each other in the text. I have tried to point out the major themes of epic thought with their specific beliefs and ideas. Some attempt has also been made to provide a historical context by suggesting both Vedic and non-Vedic antecedents, and also pointing out how the epic itself provides antecedents for later Hindu beliefs, especially those of the *Purāṇas* and the medieval devotional sects. I have throughout sought to demonstrate unity of thought where it exists and also highlight the doctrinal tensions explored by the text as well as the background and possible solutions where disunity and dissonance are apparent.

(3) In the interpretation of epic thought, I have attempted to

demonstrate that it is possible to consider the *Mahābhārata* as a whole, including all its various elements, whilst at the same time admitting that various passages express quite different perspectives. I have not argued that the same values and beliefs prevail throughout the epic, as it is apparent that any such thesis is demonstrably inaccurate. This lack of overall continuity, despite the obvious difficulties it presents, does not, however, mean that consideration of the epic as a unitary work is impossible and I hope that the present study goes some way towards demonstrating that this is so.

(4) For me the most interesting aspect of epic studies is that pursued most frequently by Indian scholars in trying to incorporate the ideas it expresses into contemporary ideological debates. I am certain that the questions confronted by the *Mahābhārata* are of continuing relevance in shaping the values of our global culture. I have pursued this interest sparingly in this work and only where the topic under discussion obviously lends itself to such considerations, but it is a path that I feel may be profitably followed where time and space allow a fuller exploration.

4. Critical and Structural Approaches

Whilst recognising the contribution of historical criticism to the understanding of epic thought, I have not drawn distinctions between different passages on that basis. Hopkins, for example, chooses to refer to what he sees as later additions to the central narrative as the 'pseudo-epic',[10] while more recently Laine has spoken of the *Nārāyaṇīya* as 'in the epic but not of it'.[11] My decision not to follow such an approach is based partly on the fact that historical text criticism is an inexact science frequently displaying circular logic[12] and subjective appreciations of the text to the extent that it is virtually impossible to find precise agreement between any of the authorities. More fundamentally, however, I consider that criticism of this type offers only a partial insight into a text, and will always fall short of providing a complete understanding. Here I would refer to Brevard Childs' much maligned 'canonical method'[13] which does not deny the validity of historical criticism, but argues from another perspective that a text may be recognised as having a unity by dint of its being appreciated as such by the tradition in which it is venerated.

The point is particularly apt when considering a text such as the *Mahābhārata.* Although Western scholars have quite legitimately recognised different historical levels a within the epic, the fact cannot be ignored that for over 1,500 years the Hindu tradition has regarded the text as having a distinctive unitary form. Therefore, although historical criticism will assist our understanding of the epic's doctrines, when it comes to defining what is the *Mahābhārata* there can be little hesitation in accepting that it is the work of eighteen *parvans* that has been recognised as such for centuries by the tradition in which it was formed.

I have chosen to approach the study by topic rather than by reviewing portions of the text in succession, posing questions in the form of "What does the epic teach about . . . ?" My primary concern has constantly been to establish and understand what the text is teaching, for in its final form I have no doubt that it is a strongly didactic work. Exclusive stress on a critical understanding tells us many facts surrounding a literary work, but not the message the text itself is attempting to convey. My overriding aim has been to focus on the message and I have referred to text-critical scholarship only when it provides insights that help to illuminate the nature of that message.

Where critical methods are permitted to prevail in isolation, there is an inevitable danger of taking all types of apparent contradiction as being evidence of different textual levels and thereby glossing over some of the more subtle and dialectical teachings that the text is exploring. This criticism is strongly argued by M. Biardeau, who writes, "On parle trop facilement de contradiction quand on n'est pas sur de comprendre la logique d'un chapitre".[14] It is only too obvious that Western thought, and especially Western religious thought, is far more uncomfortable with formulaic dissonance in establishing doctrines than is that of the Hindu tradition. There are identifiable historical, theological and possibly cultural reasons why this is so, but here I wish only to point out that where a Western scholar may recognise a clear doctrinal contradiction and seek immediate recourse to a critical theory, Indian thought may recognise a subtle approach to the resolution of a complex issue that cannot be simplistically resolved by a unidimensional creed, or perhaps even remain unaware of any contradiction. This does of course render the task of establishing epic doctrines all the more complex, for van Buitenen does not overstate the case by much when he writes, "The epic is a series of precisely stated problems imprecisely and therefore inconclusively resolved, every inconclusive solution raising a new problem, until the very end, when the question remains whose is heaven and whose is hell?"[15]

Whilst the approach of reviewing the text under selected topics may be regarded as structuralist, I have not followed Biardeau, Dumézil and others in allowing myself to indulge in excessive theorising as to a possible sub-meaning lying beneath the overt statements of the *Mahābhārata.* Here I must admit to a degree of frustration at the manner in which the direct assertions of the epic have been ignored, whilst detailed studies have been devoted to the unearthing of encoded messages found concealed beneath the text. I do not believe that the *Mahābhārata*'s teachings are concealed in any form of symbolic code, especially one that has only been penetrated by twentieth century Western scholarship.

As a result, my approach to understanding the epic's teachings involves as close a study of the text as space and time allow, and particular emphasis on the didactic rather than the purely narrative portions of the text. When Greg Bailey writes, "what is implicit in the narrative material is made explicit in the didactic mode",[16] he seems to imply that there is complete continuity of thought between the various sections of the epic. This is surely an overstatement, for a very large part of the didactus is concerned with the attainment of *mokṣa,* an idea that is of little significance in the narrative.[17]

An immediate objection to the method of approach I have outlined must be that in selecting certain topics to consider and certain questions with which to address the text a cultural imposition is inevitable, for the questions have been selected by myself rather than by the text and are those that preoccupy our culture rather than that of the authors. From the outset I have been very aware of this objection; for a number of reasons, however, I do not believe that it is insurmountable.

Firstly, a number earlier works, a notable example being that by Wendy O'Flaherty on the subject of evil, have shown that a question that is recognisable as arising from one culture may be put to the traditions of another with results that do full justice to both the question and the tradition. Secondly, alongside the distinctive features of cultural traditions, I believe that a bond of commonality resting on the underlying human experience must also be acknowledged. Thus although differences of experience, based on history and culture, may lead to different issues coming to the fore in particular times and places, simultaneously the common experience of human life means that identical problems are confronted in radically different historical and cultural environments. A detailed study of the epic reveals, for example, that although concepts such as *dharma* are alien to the contemporary Western world view, the underlying preoccupation with right action is one that is always relevant.

It is, of course, essential that the text be allowed to speak in its own terms and follow its own preoccupations in answering the questions raised. Thus the topics considered must be broad enough to allow for a cross-cultural analysis. Obviously, to discuss how the epic understands the nature of the trinity or the unique magnificence of Allah is inappropriate, but to investigate its teachings on the nature of God will provide valid insights into the theism it propounds. The process adopted is in effect that described by Heestermann when he writes of, ". . . the patient and sometimes fruitless task of listening to facts and documents for their own sake, without burdening them with our contemporary concerns. Not infrequently, they then appear of their own accord to be not all that remote from our problems."[18]

Finally, I remain unconvinced that arguments stressing the insurmountable nature of cultural incommensurability have not been shaped to some extent by an underlying Christian agenda. Contemporary Christian thought faces the dilemma of maintaining the uniqueness of the revelation of its own tradition whilst avoiding the appearance of an unfashionably supremacist attitude towards other faiths. The idea of cultural incommensurability provides a means by which the view of Christ's uniqueness can be maintained without having to lay stress on the concomitant idca that all other revelations are false or inferior. There is thus grounds for suspicion that stress on incommensurability is at least in part polemical.

5. The *Bhagavad-gītā*

In analysing the religious teachings of the *Mahābhārata,* I have made extensive, perhaps even excessive, use of the *Bhagavad-gītā.* There are several reasons why this should be so. Above all, I would contend that the *Gītā* is the principal didactic passage of the epic in which the preoccupations of both the narrative and the bulk of the didactus are directly confronted. Here, almost uniquely, the theism of the narrative, centring on Kṛṣṇa and its concern with *dharma* are set alongside the Sāṁkhya and Yoga teachings characteristic of the *Mokṣa-dharma*. Thus the *Gītā* is to be recognised as the one passage which deals thoroughly with the major questions that the text as a whole explores, and that Laine is therefore substantially correct when he asserts that the *Gītā* is, "the source for our understanding of the theology of the Mahābhārata."[19] Western scholars, to some extent following the Hindu tradition here, have frequently sought to understand the *Bhagavad-gītā* in isolation from its epical context, seeing it as an interpolation that relates only marginally to the epic as a whole. More recently several writers have recognised the fallacy of this view,[20] urging that consideration of its location in the *Mahābhārata* is essential for a proper understanding of the doctrines of the *Gītā*. A secondary aim of the present work is to demonstrate how the *Gītā*'s teachings are closely related to the overall thought of the epic, especially in terms of its attempt at reconciling the *Mahābhārata*'s major doctrinal tendencies of *pravṛtti* and *nivṛtti*.

6. Use of the Critical Edition

I have chosen to work from the text of the Critical Edition of the *Mahābhārata* and have only occasionally referred to verses or passages excluded from it. This decision is justified on a number of grounds, not least the authority of van Buitenen who speaks of, ". . . a general sense of satisfaction that the text presented by the critical edition from Poona is the best attainable", and again, "the meticulous reading that a word-by-word translation demands has borne out, to my own satisfaction, the excellence of the established text."[21] From a practical point of view it seems essential that studies of the epic should have one recognised version to refer to and there can be little doubt that the Critical Edition is the best available to fit that function. It should not be overlooked that this edition of the text has been produced by Indian scholars, albeit influenced by Western ideas, rather than its being an external imposition onto the religious literature of the Hindu tradition.

I am aware of Biardeau's attitude towards the Critical Edition, which she sees as based on unsound technique and as eliminating material that is essential for a complete understanding of the text.[22]

It is almost axiomatic that structuralist scholars should feel uncomfortable with a version of the epic produced solely on the basis of text-critical methods. Furthermore, Biardeau has a particular interest in ensuring that the excluded passages are not wholly dismissed; her studies are notable for the common themes she finds in 'epico-Purāṇic' thought, and it is the case that the passages of the *Mahābhārata* which come closest to Purāṇic material are frequently those which the Critical Edition excludes.[23] These arguments against the Critical Edition do, however, carry weight, for some of the excluded passages contain well-known and much-revered episodes traditionally related to the *Mahābhārata*.[24] Furthermore, even if they are not to be accepted as truly a part of the text, such passages are important in revealing how the tradition understood the epic in the early part of its history.

7. Translations

Any textual study of the *Mahābhārata* must work closely with the Sanskrit original and include translations of relevant passages. The translations presented throughout this work are my own. I have tried as far as possible to offer a literal representation in English of the author's words and meanings, though at some points I have lapsed into summarisation. This was done when a word for word examination was not considered essential and limitations of time and space made it impractical. The study includes numerous Sanskrit quotations for the benefit of those familiar with the language. Such quotations are presented when the original wording is judged to be of particular significance, when the Sanskrit allows for more than one interpretation, when a translation cannot do full justice to the precise meaning intended or sometimes merely because a particular turn of phrase appealed to me and I wished to share it with the reader.

8. Problems and Shortcomings of the Present Study

Previous non-critical work on the epic has either focused on particular passages or else taken the structuralist approach of pursuing specific themes and ideas, often tracing them through epics, *Purāṇas* and oral traditions. The former approach has the merit of being able to deal thoroughly with the passage under discussion,[25] but by its very nature is able to offer only a limited understanding of the epic as a whole. The structuralists, on the other hand, attempt to draw conclusions about the complete work by discovering the unifying themes that run through the entire text, but they are almost invariably guilty of a selective use of material in constructing a case that appears thoroughly convincing only when alternative passages are overlooked.

I have tried as scrupulously as possible to be non-selective and to examine all passages pertaining to a particular topic, or where this is impossible a genuine cross-section of material. The obvious difficulty with a study of this type is that pointed out by Brockington, who writes, "The biggest problem that any interpreter of the *Mbh* has to face is quite simply the scale of the work."[26] There is so much material within the epic, and such a range of ideas represented, that the mere location of relevant passages and the recognition of their perspective presents a daunting obstacle.

Moreover, the complexity and variegatedness of the material is such that each of the topics examined could have been pursued in much greater depth than the perimeters of the present study allow. It is a question of how strong a lens one should use; whether to examine all possible details on a particular subject or else to move back a little and attempt to observe the wider context. It would undoubtedly have been possible to present a work of equal length on, for example, epic soteriology. Such a study would have allowed for a more thorough examination of relevant material, but would have suffered because of its isolation from the overall philosophical and religious context, for, as Ninian Smart puts it, ". . . each central concept comes not in utter nakedness, but trailing clouds of doctrine".[27] When a broader approach is adopted a more complete understanding is made possible, but it is unavoidable that certain relevant passages and even specific doctrines will be discussed in a cursory manner, or even occasionally overlooked completely.

Such limitations are frustrating, but must be accepted as an inevitable feature of epic studies; the over-abundance of material is something one has to come to terms with and find the most effective means of confronting. One has to recognise that it is impossible to present the final word on any aspect of the *Mahābhārata* and much of what is offered here does no more than indicate lines of approach which may be followed up in greater depth at a later stage. I have experienced all too often the difficulties of scanning such a huge text in the search for specific ideas and I hope that this work will be of assistance to those who undertake any future study. I hope that it will also be of use to anyone interested in religious thought and serve to highlight the contribution offered by Hindu literature in confronting the great questions that beset humanity age after age.

Notes

1. Hopkins, E.W. *The Great Epic of India,* Calcutta, 1969 (1st Ed 1901), pp. 398-402.
2. See, for example, Hacker P., *Kleine Schriften,* Wiesbaden, 1978, p. 170, van Buitenen, J.A.B., *Mahābhārata, Volume 1, The Book of the Beginning,* Chicago, 1973, p. xvi, and Biardeau M., *Le Mahābhārata, Volume 2,* Paris, 1986, p. 27.
3. van Buitenen, 1973, p. xxiv.
4. Ibid, p. xxv.
5. Ibid.
6. Biardeau states that the *Mahābhārata* signifies the foundation of *bhakti* in India.
7. Esnoul, A-M. *Nārāyaṇīya Parvan du Mahābhārata,* Paris, 1979, p. 20.
8. Bailey is dismissive of cataloguing as a form of scholarship (Bailey, G. *The Mythology of Brahmā,* Delhi, 1983, p. xiv). This is an opinion I cannot share. To my mind a major weakness of much modern work on the epic is excessive theorising based on inadequate textual study. Whatever theories one may arrive at about a text must be supported by a thorough discussion of the material contained in that text; therefore cataloguing is an essential preliminary to any study.
9. van Buitenen 1973, p. xxxi.
10. Hopkins 1969, p. 46.
11. Laine, J.W. *Visions of God: Narratives of Theophany in the Mahābhārata,* Doctoral Thesis, Vienna, 1989, p. 152.
12. The tendency in form criticism is always to convert hypotheses into criteria. A hypothesis about the structure of a text is arrived at through textual analysis and then further analysis is presented with the hypothesis used as the major criterion for deciding the status of particular passages.
13. Childs, B. *Introduction to the Old Testament as Scripture,* London, 1979.
14. Biardeau 1986, p. 326.
15. van Buitenen, J.A.B. *Studies in Indian Literature and Philosophy,* Ludo Rocher Ed, Delhi, 1988, p. 314.
16. Bailey, G. 'Suffering in the Mahābhārata: Draupadī and Yudhiṣṭhira' in *Suffering: Indian Perspectives,* K.N. Tiwari Ed, Delhi, 1986, p. 39.
17. *Mokṣa* is discussed in the narrative only during interludes in which sages such as Sanat-sujāta appear on the scene and give teachings. These incidents are largely unconnected with the central story.
18. Heesterman, J.C. *The Inner Conflict of Tradition, Essays in Indian Ritual, Kingship and Society,* Chicago, 1985, p. 129.
19. Laine 1989, p. 123.
20. Hiltebeitel, A. *The Ritual of Battle, Krishna in the Mahābhārata,* Ithaca, 1976,

p. 122; Pusalker, A.D. *Studies in the Epics and Purāṇas of India*, Bombay, 1963, p. 135.

21. van Buitenen 1973, p. xxxi
22. Biardeau, M. 'Some more Considerations about Textual Criticism', *Purāṇa* 10,2, 1968, pp. 115-123.
23. Biardeau and Scheuer are, for example, reluctant to accept the editing out of a verse from the *Vana* which refers to Viṣṇu and Śiva as being the same Deity as this provides the main support for their theories about the role of the two Deities in the epic.
24. Note, for example, the stories of Kṛṣṇa's providing an unlimited length of cloth to keep Draupadī covered and Arjuna's rejection of Urvaśī's amorous advances.
25. See, for example, Laine's work on theophanies and van Buitenen's essays on epic Sāṁkhya.
26. Brockington, J. 'The Epic View of the Gods', *Shadow*, Vol. 9, 1992, p.3.
27. Smart, N. *The Science of Religion and the Sociology of Knowledge: Some Methodological Questions*, Princeton, 1977, p. 25.

Chapter 1

BACKGROUND TO AND MAJOR THEMES OF EPIC THOUGHT

1. Introduction

In this chapter I propose to provide a background to the subsequent discussion of the *Mahābhārata*'s religious and ethical teachings by attempting to establish the principal concerns that faced its authors and the ideological climate in which they worked. In addition, it would seem appropriate at this point to present a preliminary outline of the major themes of epic thought.

The epic period was clearly one of transition in which new ideas emerged and perhaps older non-Āryan religious beliefs were absorbed into the developing tradition. According to Pandé, the *Mahābhārata*, "reflects the contradictions of an age of transition when an old aristocratic and ritual order was yielding place to a new order in which lawless tyranny, social miscegenation, religious scepticism, and heterodoxy were emerging as significant features."[1] This view is confirmed by Frauwallner who concludes, "The period of epic philosophy shows, therefore, the typical features of a transitional period."[2]

The epic does not reflect the views of an established orthodoxy, but rather recognises the validity of varying ideas. This eclecticism is not, however, without limit and the text is not prepared to follow the Buddhists and Jains in their complete dismissal of the Vedic belief system. It is unlikely that these changes were sought from without; the epic is clearly the work of *brāhmaṇas* who recognised both the validity of non Vedic ideas and also the need to preserve the central core of orthodox belief and practice.

2. The Epic Period

To find a *sitz im leben* for any religious work is problematic. It is only too easy to lapse into a circular mode of reasoning wherein we construct a hypothetical environment for the authors based on textual evidence, and then take that hypothesis back to the text as the key to its comprehension, setting in motion a spiral of insubstantial conjecture. Thus efforts in this direction must be cautious and their limitations recognised.

With regard to the *Mahābhārata,* we have little hard historical or archaeological evidence to employ and most of what is conjectured about the period in question is derived from the religious works themselves. Nonetheless, certain significant observations can be made that will be of value in understanding the text. It is reasonable to observe that the societies reflected by the Vedas and by the epic are of a substantially different nature. The religion of the *Ṛgveda* is that of an aristocratic, tribal society with its wealth based on agriculture and especially animal husbandry. Vedic religion reflects this in its focus on pacifying a pantheon of gods who to a large extent personify natural forces. *Yajñas* are to be performed by kings or tribal leaders under the direction of a developed priest class. The *yajñas* are to bring prosperity to earth and produce harmony in nature by nourishing the gods with the offerings that are made through the fire.

The society we find in the *Mahābhārata* is different in many ways. Although descriptions of the conflict in the *Virāṭa* and of Duryodhana's trip to see the Pāṇḍavas' distress in the *Vana* reveal the continuing importance of animal husbandry, the society of the *Mahābhārata* is clearly substantially urban. According to Brockington[3] the rise of large monarchical states in the Ganges basin and the concomitant decline in tribalism sparked a greater sense of individualism which is reflected in the changing religious environment of the period.[4]

The archaeological discoveries at Harappa and Mahenjo-daro have revealed the complex urban society of the pre-Āryan inhabitants of India, but one can only speculate as to the forces that moved the tribal Āryans toward the urban culture we find in the epics. Again according to Pandé, ". . . it may be assumed that it was an age in which the towns had clearly emerged . . . including merchants and craftsmen, kings and officials."[5] In an urban environment tribal structures disintegrate and a trend towards greater individualism becomes apparent. The total dependence on natural forces is less obvious in an urban society, though famine and disease, as well maintaining social order, remain prominent concerns. Thus the tribal religion of the Āryans based on *yajña* may have become less relevant as a result of these social changes. A different form of religion would have been demanded pertaining to the individual rather than to the tribe and its chieftain. On at least two occasions in the *Mahābhārata,* Yudhiṣṭhira urges that *yajña* is unsuitable because it can be performed only by the rich and asks Bhīṣma what religious practices are suitable for common people:

> *na te śakyā daridreṇa yajñāḥ prāptuṁ pitāmaha*
> *bahūpakaraṇā yajñā nānā-saṁbhāra-vistarāḥ*
>
> *pārthivai rāja-putrair vā śakyāḥ prāptuṁ pitāmaha*
> *nārthan yūnair avaguṇair ekātmabhir asaṁhataiḥ*
>
> *yo daridrair api vidhiḥ śakyaḥ prāptum sadā bhavet*
> *tulyo yajña-phalair etais tan me brūhi pitāmaha*
>
> 'But, grandfather, *yajñas* cannot be performed by those who are poor. For *yajñas* a large number of varied implements must be collected. They may performed by monarchs or the sons of kings, O grandfather, but not by those who are not wealthy, who lack the higher qualities, or by those who are isolated without close contacts. Tell me, grandfather, of that discipline which allows results equal to those derived from *yajña* to be obtained by those who are poor.' (13.110.2-4)

This is not to say that the epic seeks to gainsay the importance of *yajña* and Vedic beliefs in general (though some passages certainly display such a tendency) for the execution of such rituals has a prominent place in both the narrative and didactic portions of the text. There is a clear recognition, however, that as long as they do not oppose the most basic premises of Vedic belief and practice alternative ideas are to be endorsed and pursued..

The integration of the beliefs of the indigenous peoples of India with those of the Āryans is a factor about which we can do little more than speculate. There are certainly indications from the Indus Valley culture and from references in the Vedas to worshippers of the phallus that substantial elements of their belief systems came to be included within the *corpus* of Hindu doctrine. For Frauwallner, the theistic element in epic thought is, ". . . above all to be traced to the fact that an indigenous element penetrates more and more strongly into the layer of the Āryan immigrants."[6] It is thus not unreasonable to conjecture that after a period of invasion, the Āryans adopted a more settled way of life and their own culture and beliefs became integrated with those of the indigenous population. As a result non-Vedic ideas entered the orthodox belief system and this process is represented in the doctrines and ideas presented by the *Mahābhārata*.

A major feature of the religious transformation that took place in the epic period was the appearance of a variety of ascetic sects. These espoused world-denying philosophies and sought salvation through renunciation, wisdom and spiritual practice. Such philosophies stood in marked contrast to the worldliness of the Vedas and most of these sects included a critique of such religion as a part of their teachings. Not all of them, however, completely rejected the Vedas and it is the works of those who adopted this more moderate posture that are represented in the epic. The *Mahābhārata* gives us very little by way of description of the actual schools and *āśramas* in which these doctrines and practices were taught, but van Buitenen offers an attempt at a reconstruction of the likely milieu:

> There must have existed scores and scores of more or less isolated little centres where parallel doctrines were being evolved out of a common source. Occasional meetings at pilgrimages and festivals, reports from other and remote *āśramas* brought by wandering ascetics, polemic encounters with other preachers must have resulted in a laborious process of partial renovation and conversation, more precise definitions of doctrines and eclecticism, readjustments of terminology etc.[7]

van Buitenen further expresses the view that the treatises contained within the *Mokṣa-dharma* were originally composed for the purpose of instructing novitiates in the specific doctrines of particular *āśramas*.[8]

Thus, in summation, the epic period is characterised by social change in which the tribal Āryan warrior bands in North India adopted a more settled and partially urban lifestyle, began to replace tribal structures with monarchical states and integrated their communities with the indigenous populations. These social transitions are reflected in the religious ideas expressed by the *Mahābhārata.* The Vedic religion of the Āryans is not wholly abandoned, but new and radically different systems of thought are accepted into the overall belief system. In addition to the social values based on *dharma-śāstra,* a new set of values appears stressing renunciation, world-denial, and the abandonment of society. It is with these contending beliefs and value systems as well as with the revered orthodoxy of the Vedas that the creators of the epic are working in their shaping of the doctrines the text propounds.

The arrival of these new ideas, which to a greater or lesser degree rejected the previous orthodoxy, must have created a climate of religious uncertainty in which any belief was open to challenge. According to Friedhelm Hardy:

> Such a this-wordly attitude was shattered by new developments which may well be regarded as a religious revolution. New and baffling forms of religious experience were propagated by homeless mendicants, and eventually two major trends emerged out of the fertile chaos which this 'revolution' had created.[9]

According to Hardy these 'two major trends' were Buddhism and Upaniṣadic Vedānta, but it is apparent from the range of material contained in the *Mahābhārata* that the new doctrines that persisted into the epic period were of a diverse nature. Amongst the new sects that appeared the most strident in rejecting the previous orthodoxy appear to have been the Buddhists, the Jains and the Ājīvakas, all of whom dismissed the Vedas as works of men and condemned animal sacrifices as violent, cruel and immoral. The doctrine of *ahiṁsā,* non-harming, so prominent in both Buddhism and Jainism is in clear opposition to the Vedic *yajñas.* The *Mahābhārata* never goes this far, and whilst advocating new ideas, particularly those of Sāṁkhya, Yoga and Bhakti, it will not countenance the assault on the revelatory status of the Vedas that was current. Those who deny the Vedas are designated as *nāstikas,* or atheists, and are roundly condemned. In the *Śānti,* for example, Bhīṣma narrates how Indra in the form of a jackal gives the reasons for his low birth:

aham āsaṁ paṇḍitako haituko veda-nindakaḥ
anvīkṣikīṁ tarka-vidyām anurakto nirarthikām

hetu-vādān pravaditā vaktā saṁsatsu hetumat
ākroṣṭā cābhivaktā ca brahma-yajñeṣu vai dvijān

nāstikaḥ sarva-śaṅkī ca mūrkhaḥ paṇḍita-mānikaḥ
tasyeyaṁ phala-nirvṛttiḥ sṛgālatvaṁ mama dvija

'I was a learned scholar who favoured reason and rejected the Vedas, devoted to the worthless sciences of logic and speculative reasoning. In assemblies of learned men I was an eloquent speaker employing reason and logic, decrying the recitation of the Vedas and speaking arrogantly to the *brāhmaṇas.* I was an atheist, doubtful of everything, a fool who thought himself a great scholar. This present position of mine as a jackal is the result I have gained from this, O *brāhmaṇa.*' (12.173.45-47)

Thus we see within the epic the attempt to break with and yet still sustain the orthodoxy of the past. New ideas had to be admitted but a certain caution is apparent, the fear of *nāstikyam* or atheism. In the *Anuśāsana,* we read of King Nimi's introducing worship of ancestors through the offering of *piṇḍa.* After performing the rite (13.91.17) he expresses his fear of being cursed by *brāhmaṇas* for introducing a new mode of worship, before his fears are removed by Atri who assures Nimi that the ceremony had been ordained by Brahmā at the beginning of creation. This story surely reveals something of the tensions arising when new processes and ideas were being integrated into a previously established orthodoxy.

3. Complexities and Contradictions

This integration of various strands of belief–Vedic orthodoxy, non-Āryan traditions, and newer ideas forged out of a changing social structure–provides the background to the ideas explored by the authors of the *Mahābhārata.* The epic, however, falls far short of producing what would be understood in the West as a coherent doctrinal system. There are clear tensions and contradictions within the text, but whilst recognising these certain observations are called for by way of justification.

Firstly, Western thought reacts more strongly than does that of the East to any hint of contradiction. The *Mahābhārata* authors are clearly aware of the tensions they are confronting, but are reluctant to resort to any simplistic formulae that may make for an easy doctrine, but have little depth of understanding. Furthermore, the epic period is characterised by the lack of any central authority which is able to dictate orthodox doctrines. In contrast the means to reach the truth is accepted as being discussion amongst masters of wisdom. For this reason any final readactor would have seen no difficulty in including the different views of different schools of thought within the text. Religious truth is acknowledged as complex, *dharma* is subtle and hard to define, and therefore different opinions must be listened to, for they may express the truth in a different manner.

The teachings of the epic thus suggest the environment of a weakened orthodoxy being challenged and possibly overthrown by alternative doctrines. Frequently in the text it is observed that different opinions are held even amongst the wise. Aśvatthāman states:

> *puruṣe puruṣe buddhiḥ sā sā bhavati śobhanā*
> *tuṣyanti ca pṛthak sarve prajñayā te svayā svayā*
>
> 'Intelligence appears differently in different men. They all take delight in their own different understanding of things.' (10.3.3)

The Vedas are not regarded as a clear arbiter of true doctrine, for though they are not denied, their conclusions are seen as contradictory:

> *yad idaṁ veda-vacanaṁ loka-vāde virudhyate*
> *pramāṇe cāpramāṇe ca viruddhe śāstratā kutaḥ*
>
> 'In the opinion of the world the words of the Vedas are contradictory. How can there be scriptural authority over whether something is a true conclusion or not when such contradiction exists?' (12.234.10).

Finally, Hinduism has long recognised that one religious doctrine cannot be appropriate for all types of person. The doctrine of the transmigration of souls allows for gradual elevation towards salvation rather than an all or nothing test in this life. Thus a variety of beliefs can be tolerated because they cater for various levels of spiritual development. Within society different standards of behaviour are demanded from the different *varṇas*, thus creating an ethical hierarchy that permits for one group what is forbidden to another. Similarly, the teachers of *mokṣa-dharma* claim that their beliefs and practices are superior to ritual religious acts, but they accept and urge that their way is open only to the most spiritually advanced, and should be kept secret from most people for whom such doctrines will be a disturbance. Thus Vasiṣṭha informs Janaka:

> *etair guṇair hīnatame na deyam*
> *etat paraṁ brahma viśuddham āhuḥ*
> *na śreyasā yokṣyati tādṛśe kṛtaṁ*
> *dharma-pravaktāram apātra-dānāt*

> 'It is said that where such good qualities are not found in a person this knowledge of the supreme *brahman*, which is most pure, is not to be given. Nothing good will arise if these religious truths are proclaimed to such a person who is an unsuitable receptacle for them.' (12.296.35)

Clearly where different doctrines and values are expressed within one work tensions are bound to occur. In the narrative such tension primarily takes the form of conflicts and debates between principal characters over what is the right course of action. Thus we find bitter arguments between Yudhiṣṭhira, Bhīma and Draupadī over when it is proper to wage war, and the *Bhagavad-gītā* itself is a debate between Kṛṣṇa and Arjuna over whether it is righteous to kill social superiors in battle. Frequently these debates do not produce clear-cut conclusions; we are not shown that one path is right and the other wrong. Yudhiṣṭhira is portrayed as the most virtuous of all the characters, and yet his opposition to warfare and royal obligations is countered by others such as Arjuna, Kuntī, Vidura and Vyāsa who are equally sagacious and fully on the side of virtue. Again the conclusion we are left with is that religious truth is complex and subtle, and can accommodate paradox and a variety of overlapping ideas. In the didactus, dissonance arises from the fact that a prominent feature of the teachings on salvation is the rejection of the value system that underlies social *dharma*. All forms of worldly action, and animal sacrifice in particular, are condemned as materialistic and hence barriers to absolute emancipation.

The tolerance of different doctrines thus displayed by the epic is not, however, without limits. The *Mahābhārata* embraces ideas which challenge the previous orthodoxy, but will not allow those which reject it completely, thereby establishing for itself a position somewhere in the middle ground with regard to the religious transformations taking place in the epic period. In Chapter 211 of the *Śānti*, for example, we find a polemical attack on Buddhist doctrines, and the Sāṁkhya treatises of the *Mokṣa-dharma* typically present themselves not as rejecting the Vedas, but as providing the true meaning of Vedic instruction which is by nature subtle and ambiguous. On this basis the ascetic critics of Vedic ritual are able to defend themselves against criticism that their views are those of *nāstikas*.

4. Major Themes in Epic Thought

Concluding his study of the myths of Brahmā, Greg Bailey writes, "From its incipient period Hinduism (as opposed to Brāhmanism, the prevailing religious ethos of the Vedas) has been constituted of three fundamental features."[10] These he goes on to define as the value systems centred on *pravṛtti*, *nivṛtti* and *bhakti*. This threefold division provides a useful basis for the understanding of the main themes of epic thought and the relationship which exists between them.

Under the heading of *pravṛtti* are to be included all beliefs and practices concerned with worldly existence. This includes the fables, the stories of animals that impart lessons on proper conduct,[11] and direct instructions on similar topics, the *nīti* delivered by Vidura and other sagacious characters.[12] The *Anuśāsana* in particular contains long sections describing ritual acts that guarantee success in this world, either prosperity in the present life or else elevation to the domain of the gods after death. Most of these acts take the form of different types of charity to be offered to *brāhmaṇas*, but occasionally we find injunctions that come close to 'folk' Hinduism urging that one should make offerings to *rākṣasas, yakṣas, uragas, gandharvas* and other lesser divine beings in order to gain prosperity, harm one's enemies, remain free of disease, gain favour with women, or beget numerous offspring.[13]

Closer to the core of the epic's *pravṛtti* values, however, is the concept of *sva-dharma,* expressed in terms of the duty dictated to each individual on the basis of the social class or *varṇa* into which he is born. Each of the four *varṇas* has a social function to fulfil and has specific rules of conduct and modes of life that circumscribe the behaviour of its members. Strict adherence to such prescriptions constitutes the proper *sva-dharma* of each individual. Appropriate action of this type lies at the very heart of the ethics of *pravṛtti.*

In the *Mahābhārata,* the understanding of *sva-dharma* is closely related to the execution of the Vedic sacrificial ceremony, the *yajña,* though the linkage is somewhat artificial. *Pravṛtti* values focus on the ordered placement of each category of beings within the creation and the interrelationship between them. Amongst men, the *vaiśyas* and *śūdras* provide wealth and service for the *kṣatriyas* who in turn sustain and protect the *brāhmaṇas.* The *brāhmaṇas* and *kṣatriyas* together execute the *yajñas* which provide nourishment for the gods who reciprocally ensure that the earth provides food for humanity. The *yajña* is also regarded as a means of atonement for sins committed in the course of dharmic duty (as when Yudhiṣṭhira is advised to execute a horse sacrifice after the battle) so that the individual may reap the eschatological reward of enjoying an afterlife of heavenly delights amongst the gods.

The value system designated by the epic as *nivṛtti* stands in marked contrast to the world-affirming beliefs characteristic of the *pravṛtti* tendency. In the *Mahābhārata, nivṛtti* is represented by the Sāṁkhya doctrines and Yoga teachings set forth in the *Mokṣa-dharma* and the *Aśvamedhika,* and in the didactic interludes of the *Vana.* Here the value of *sva-dharma* is denied on the grounds that it pertains to continued existence in this world, while the highest goal to be striven after is complete salvation from material existence. The nature of life in this world is characterised primarily by suffering; therefore one should abandon worldly life and renounce all aspirations for sensual enjoyment. Instead one should try to understand the true spiritual identity of the self, for the joy that comes from such realisation is unlimited and the eschatological result takes one beyond all forms of rebirth.

Clearly these two value systems embody substantially divergent views of life and much of the ideological tension in the *Mahābhārata* arises as a result of this dissonance. Furthermore, there is a double tension within the text. Even within the *pravṛtti* tendency there is a tension between stress on the ritualised behaviour of *sva-dharma* and the notion of virtue with which it may sometimes conflict. This tension is expressed in the epic primarily through the different views expressed by the central characters in the numerous debates on the question of right action.

The dissonance between the values of *pravṛtti* and *nivṛtti* is, however, even more stark and surfaces in most of the major doctrinal questions that the epic confronts. In terms of eschatology, whilst both tendencies accept the notion of transmigration of souls, the final goal sought through *pravṛtti* is *svarga-loka*, the heaven of the gods, but *nivṛtti* dismisses that domain as impermanent and seeks instead eternal salvation from this world. Likewise, two forms of soteriology are urged for the attaining of these different goals, one involving worldly action in accordance with *sva-dharma*, and the other demanding the abandonment of human society for a life of renunciation, asceticism and meditation.

The ethics of the two tendencies also display notable divergences. The teachings on *mokṣa-dharma* repeatedly urge tolerance, restraint, self-control and non-violence, whereas for a *kṣatriya* the very opposite is demanded, for as a warrior and ruler he must be aggressive, self-interested to some degree, and never seek to avoid violence in opposing enemies, punishing wrongdoers, and also in the performance of *yajñas*. There is also a different perspective on the nature of the individual's *varṇa*. From the point of view of *pravṛtti*, the individual is born into a particular *varṇa* and his duty is determined for life by that designation in terms of the appropriate *sva-dharma*. Where *nivṛtti* is taught, however, and also in the views expressed by Yudhiṣṭhira, a more fluid attitude prevails. The notion of *varṇa* is not denied here, but it is qualities and propensities that are stressed as the decisive criteria.

In terms of causality, *nivṛtti* emphasises the absolute control of destiny over human existence, thereby indicating that action in this world has no real meaning for it cannot change the preordained outcome of events. Therefore tolerance of misfortune is called for and the imperative is towards transcending material life rather than attempting to adjust circumstances within it. From the standpoint of *pravṛtti* such a world view is unacceptable, for the ideology of *pravṛtti* is based on the efficacy of actions in producing desired results. Therefore, whilst the force of destiny is not wholly denied, it is repeatedly urged that human endeavour is effective in shaping events, interacting with destiny, and also that destiny itself is not blind but is shaped by an individual's previous actions.

A fundamental difference between the two tendencies is that *pravṛtti* embodies an essentially social view of religious life in which the individual is allotted a specific position in the created order with a clearly defined relationship to all other beings. The values associated with *nivṛtti* define the human being in an entirely different way, not purely in relation to the social and created order but as an individual who exists only in relation to himself. Thus the *mokṣa-dharmin* is not obliged to adhere to his dharmic duties but has an obligation only to himself to attain the highest form of spiritual realisation.

The *Mahābhārata* thus contains within its teachings two quite distinctive and largely irreconcilable religious tendencies, and hence it is hardly surprising that much of its doctrinal exposition centres on tension and contradiction. The third major doctrinal strand the epic expounds is that of *bhakti*, devotion to an all-powerful Deity. The view of the world from the perspective of *bhakti* is radically different from that of the Vedas or *Upaniṣads*. Here the universe is created and controlled by one Supreme Deity, known in the epic as Nārāyaṇa or Śiva, who sets the cosmic order in motion with *dharma* as its manifestation on earth. Creation, destruction, rebirth and destiny are recognised not as blind forces of nature, but as subject to the will of a Supreme Controller whose grace may be invoked through worship and devotion. Whereas the Vedic pantheon, of which Viṣṇu and Śiva are a part, acts from a position within the cosmos and may be affected by disturbances to its order, the great Deities of *bhakti* are transcendent beings; they are not created as an aspect of this world, but intervene from a position apart to maintain the harmony that creation sets in motion. The epic narrative recounts the story of such an intervention, as Nārāyaṇa appears on earth in the guise of Kṛṣṇa to ensure that *dharma* is sustained and the threat to the gods and the earth is removed.

How then does *bhakti* stand in relation to *pravṛtti* and *nivṛtti*, which, as we have seen, represent divergent value systems? In effect, *bhakti* does not seek to deny or oppose either system, but rather to draw in both and incorporate them into its own system, though because of the distinctions between the two this is not always possible. In terms of eschatology, for example, *bhakti* primarily adopts the position of *nivṛtti* by offering the devotee absolute salvation, though it is the grace of the Deity that allows such salvation rather than the individual's own efforts. Sāṁkhya, especially in the *Gītā* and *Nārāyaṇīya* becomes a theistic doctrine with the Deity represented as the Unmanifest from which all the elements of matter emerge and also being identified with the transcendent self which in Sāṁkhya is rigidly distinguished from matter. Likewise, Yoga is understood as a devotional act with meditation being concentrated not just on the individual soul, but on the Deity who is within.[14]

Although it thus accepts the values of *nivṛtti* and crucially the imperative towards salvation, *bhakti* is also able to accept the values of *pravṛtti*. The Deity is the creator of the universe and hence his concern is to ensure that the harmony he has engendered is not overturned. On earth this harmony is represented by *sva-dharma*, the ordered placement of all beings and the proper execution of the duty and function allotted to each. Therefore the appearance of Viṣṇu in this world stems from the need to preserve the gods and *dharma*, both of which are primary elements of *pravṛtti* that are virtually irrelevant to *nivṛtti*. Furthermore, the *Bhagavad-gītā* draws *sva-dharma* into the realm of *bhakti* by teaching that dharmic duty is not to be performed in pursuit of material reward but as a form of *yoga* and more specifically an act of devotion which pleases the Deity and thereby invokes his grace. Similarly, the ritual of *yajña* is not rejected in *bhakti*, but is reappraised as a means by which Viṣṇu[15] and also Śiva[16] may be worshipped. Even the Vedic pantheon is not dismissed for the gods are restyled as devotees and assistants of the Supreme Deity and worship of these lesser gods is recognised as an indirect form of devotion to him.[17]

The tendency of *bhakti* is not to deny different forms of religion, but to include them within its overall purview as different means by which the Deity may be worshipped. Thus it is able to move between *pravṛtti* and *nivṛtti* without seeing itself to be in conflict with either. In the *Nārāyaṇīya*,[18] it is asserted that worship of ancestors, gods, teachers, guests, cows, *brāhmaṇas*, and the earth is in fact worship of Nārāyaṇa, and later in the same treatise, Vyāsa states:

eṣa veda-nidhiḥ śrīmān eṣa vai tapaso nidhiḥ
eṣa yogaś ca sāṁkyhaṁ ca brahma cāgryaṁ harir vibhuḥ

'The mighty Hari (Nārāyaṇa) is the repository of the Vedas and also the repository of religious austerity. He is Yoga, he is Sāṁkhya, and he is the highest *brahman.*' (12.335.74)

By drawing the conflicting views of *pravṛtti* and *nivṛtti* into its own value system, *bhakti* places itself in a position from which a reconciliation of the two becomes possible, and the key passage in which this synthesis is attempted is the *Bhagavad-gītā.* Actions based on *sva-dharma* are judged as non-binding in the sense of generating future *karma* so long as they are performed without desire for material gain. Such actions are placed on the same footing as the Yoga techniques of *mokṣa-dharma,* for the acts demanded by *sva-dharma* are to be understood as expressions of devotion to the Deity and hence a path towards ultimate salvation. Through this new perspective on dharmic action practices central to *pravṛtti* are redesignated as techniques of *mokṣa-dharma,* referred to as *karma-yoga,* and thereby are no longer excluded from *nivṛtti.*

5. Summary and Conclusions

It is apparent that the religious beliefs espoused and explored by the epic mark a notable progression from those of earlier works in the Hindu tradition. It is important, however, to understand that the process is very much one of development as opposed divergence, for the major themes of Vedic and Upaniṣadic thought are identifiable in the epic, though often in a modified or reinterpreted form. Epic thought, drawing on such antecedents, also provides the basis for much that is prominent in the subsequent development of Hinduism, perhaps most notably in its definition of the roles of Viṣṇu and Śiva as Supreme Deity and the notion of *bhakti.*

The ideological tensions highlighted by the text in both its narrative and didactic portions have also persisted into later developments of the tradition. The tension between *pravṛtti* and *nivṛtti* reemerges continually in Hindu thought in countless disputes. Even the assassination of Gandhi by Hindu extremists may be viewed as another chapter in the tension between Yudhiṣṭhira's virtue and his opponents' stress on rigid caste *dharma.* The same tension is apparent in the way that Hindu families view the decision of any of their members to adopt *saṁnyāsa* and seek salvation. Although *mokṣa* is the highest goal, still it is seen, as for example in the lives of Caitanya[19] and Rāmānuja,[20] that the abandoning of family duties for a life of renunciation was rarely welcomed.

There has emerged, moreover, a deep-seated antagonism between the tendencies of *bhakti* and *nivṛtti*, for a personal God is central to one view but largely irrelevant to the other. One mode of synthesis is offered by the *Gītā*, but the two tendencies fit ill together and in later Hinduism each has tended to interpret the *Gītā* according to its own beliefs, with devotional and non-devotional schools of thought remaining distinct and antagonistic.

Cautious suggestions may be made as to the *sitz im leben* out of which the *Mahābhārata* arose. The 'epic period' from 400B.C. to 200A.D. is one in which monarchical states have largely replaced the Āryan tribal aristocracy, as the Āryans became culturally and racially mixed with the indigenous peoples of North India. The Vedic religion of the Āryans was no longer appropriate for this evolving society, and thus it was either redefined to meet new conditions or else abandoned completely.

The *Mahābhārata* presents the ideology of *brāhmaṇas* of various persuasions, all of whom are attempting the redefinition of traditional beliefs under the influence of non-Āryan and mystical ideas. Emerging from a period of religious transition in which various diverse ideas were current, the epic does not present one coherent system of thought but rather embodies and seeks to synthesise several divergent tendencies. These are primarily the ascetic tradition referred to as *nivṛtti* which denies the validity of this world and seeks absolute release, the path of *dharma* or *pravṛtti* which inherits many of the values of Vedic belief and stresses the importance of ritualised forms of human conduct, and finally *bhakti* which seeks to draw into its domain all other beliefs and practices by reinterpreting them as acts of devotion to the great Deities it venerates.

The differing beliefs and practices of these broad tendencies inevitably produce tensions and apparent contradictions. The epic rarely seeks to establish a clearcut answer, at least in terms of Western logic, to the apparent difficulties raised by such divergent beliefs. It firstly accepts and allows that different forms of religion are required for different types of individuals. It is also apparent that the epic does not view questions of doctrine as matters that can be resolved with a simple definition of faith. Religious truths and the paths of right action are subtle matters viewed in different ways by men of wisdom. Therefore rather than constantly seeking to define, one should hear from authorities and seek wisdom through meditation and reflection in order to approach a comprehension that is substantially beyond the grasp of the mental faculties alone.

When reviewed from a Western perspective, such an approach may be frustrating, particularly when a study is concentrating primarily on questions of doctrine. It is apparent, however, that in all religious thought some element of paradox is unavoidable for the divine rarely submits itself to mundane logic. It is thus perhaps one of the strengths of epic thought that it accepts the necessity of paradox without constantly resorting to the inadequate formulations of a credal system.

Notes

1. Pandé, G.C. 'The Socio-Cultural Milieu of the Mahābhārata: An Age of Change', in *Mahābhārata Revisited,* R.N. Dandekar Ed, New Delhi, 1990, p. 123.
2. Frauwallner, E. *History of Indian Philosophy,* Volume 1, V.M. Bedeker trans, Delhi, 1973, p. 116.
3. Brockington, J.L. *The Sacred Thread: Hinduism in its Continuity and Diversity,* Edinburgh, 1981, p. 76.
4. Heesterman, however, points out that one should not overemphasise the collapse of tribal loyalties which clearly remained a prominent feature of monarchical states. Texts such as the *Kautilya-artha-śāstra,* 3-2cBC, reflect the attempt to graft monarchical institutions onto tribal systems rather than being statements of the existing nature of monarchical states. (Heesterman, J.C. *The Inner Conflict of Tradition, Essays in Indian Ritual, Kingship and Society,* Chicago, 1985, p. 130).
5. Pandé 1990, p.125.
6. Frauwallner 1973, p. 16
7. van Buitenen, J.A.B. *Studies in Indian Literature and Philosophy,* Ludo Rocher Ed, Delhi, 1988, p. 98.
8. Ibid, p. 98
9. Hardy, F. *Viraha Bhakti. The Early History of Kṛṣṇa Devotion in South India,* Delhi, 1983, p. 14.
10. Bailey, G. *The Mythology of Brahmā,* Delhi, 1983, p. 235.
11. See, for example, Chapters 112, 113 and 136 of the *Śānti.*
12. See, for example, Chapters 33 to 41 of the *Udyoga.*
13. See, for example, Chapters 101 and 109 of the *Anuśāsana.*
14. The *Bhagavad-gītā,* for example, states;

ananya-cetāḥ satataṁ yo māṁ smarati nityaśaḥ
tasyāhaṁ sulabhaḥ pārtha nitya-yuktasya yoginaḥ
'For a *yogin* who always remembers me with his mind constantly fixed on no other thing and who repeatedly engages in such practice, I am very easily attained. (8.14)

15. See, for example, 12.327.48-52 of the *Nārāyaṇīya* and 5.29 of the *Gītā*.
16. See, for example, 10.18.23.
17. See, for example, 9.23 of the *Gītā*.
18. According to the *Nārāyaṇīya*:
ye yajanti pitṝn devān gurūṁś caivātithīṁs tathā
gāś caiva dvija-mukhyāṁś ca pṛthivīṁ mātaraṁ tathā
karmaṇā manasā vācā viṣṇum eva yajanti te
'Those who worship the ancestors, gods, teachers, guests, cows, *brāhmaṇas*, or Mother Earth with their deeds, thoughts and words in truth worship Viṣṇu himself.' (12.333.24)
19. *Caitanya-caritāmṛta*, translation and commentary by AC Bhaktivedanta Swami Prabhupada in 17 volumes, Los Angeles, 1975.
20. *Life of Rāmānujācārya*, Naimiṣaraṇya dasa, Veda Books, Jarna, 1989.

CHAPTER 2

THE *MAHĀBHĀRATA*'S TEACHINGS ON THE STATUS OF SCRIPTURE

1. Introduction

The *Mahābhārata* is aware of a variety of other authoritative works and makes frequent reference to them. The attitude of the epic towards these texts varies in accordance with the religious tendency that a specific passage is expressing. Not only is the *Mahābhārata* aware of the revealed and authoritative nature of other literature, but it makes similar claims about its own status as a work that should be respected, listened to and revered. In the past much scholarly endeavour has been put into establishing the relationship between the *Mahābhārata* and other texts, sometimes reaching a consensus, but frequently disagreement that is strongly expressed. A major problem here arises from the different times at which individual sections of the epic were compiled and included. Whilst a specific passage, or even verse, may display awareness of another text, it cannot be concluded on that basis that the epic as a whole knows the work, thus creating ample scope for scholarly disagreement on the subject.

2. Review of Works Referred to by the *Mahābhārata*

(i) The Vedas

The Vedas are mentioned throughout the *Mahābhārata*, in hundreds of passages. They are usually referred in the plural as the Vedas, but the terms *āgama* and *śruti* are also employed. They are also referred to by name as the *Ṛk*, *Sāma*, *Yajuṣ*, and *Atharva*. The status of the *Atharva* is less well established; in some passages it is omitted from the list[1] whilst in others it is included.[2] There are also references to the three Vedas, which again exclude the *Atharva*. It may be that passages which include the *Atharva* can be taken as later, but there is no conclusive evidence to support such an idea. The attitude of the *Mahābhārata* to the Vedas is a key aspect of its understanding of scriptural authority and is dealt with in detail below.

(ii) The *Upaniṣads*

The *Mahābhārata* alludes frequently to the *Upaniṣads*, generally in the plural, but does not mention any of them by name; the references are non-specific and it is thus hard to determine how well the authors knew the *Upaniṣads*. A sample of the passages in question illustrates the point. After Bhīṣma is felled from his chariot, it is stated that he practised the *yoga* of the Great *Upaniṣad*–*mahopaniṣadaṁ caiva yogam āsthāya vīryavān* (6.114.112). In Chapter 236 of the *Śānti*, Bhīṣma describes the four stages of life, the *āśramas*. When he comes to the fourth, that of complete renunciation, he introduces it as the *dharma* that is based on the *Upaniṣads–caturthas copaniṣado dharmaḥ sādhāraṇaḥ smṛtaḥ* (12.236.15). Such passages reveal a general understanding of the *Upaniṣads* as teaching a philosophical doctrine that aims at *mokṣa*. From Chapter 306 of the *Śānti*, which describes how the Vedas and *Upaniṣads* are instilled into the heart of Yājñavalkya by the Sun God, it is apparent that the *Upaniṣads* are accepted as a part of the Vedas and are thus *śruti* rather than *smṛti*.

If such references display a general rather than specific knowledge of the *Upaniṣads*, then certain sections of the text do reveal a more detailed acquaintance. Hopkins, drawing on the earlier work of Holtzmann, has cited passages wherein the epic directly quotes the *Śvetāśvatara*, *Kaṭha* and *Maitri Upaniṣads*, most frequently in the teachings of Sanat-Sujāta, in the *Bhagavad-gītā* and in the *Mokṣa-dharma*.[3] It is noteworthy that the two *Upaniṣads* most frequently quoted in the *Bhagavad-gītā* and *Mokṣa-dharma* are the *Kaṭha* and the *Śvetāśvatara*, both of which are noted by Larson as expressing the earliest forms of Sāṁkhya.[4] It is reasonable to conclude that the authors of *Mahābhārata* were aware of the *Upaniṣads* as a body of literature teaching *mokṣa-dharma*, and that the authors of certain passages had detailed knowledge of individual *Upaniṣads*.

(iii) The *Vedānta-sūtras*

The *Vedānta-sūtras*, accredited to Bādarāyaṇa, present an exposition of Vedānta philosophy that has been variously interpreted by different commentators. According to Kane, all parts of the *Mahābhārata* are earlier than the *Vedānta-sūtras,* and he gives evidence to show that Śaṁkara was of the same opinion.[5] References in the *Mahābhārata* are less frequent than to the *Upaniṣads,* and usually speak in the plural of the *Vedāntas.* In Chapter 230 of the *Śānti,* for example, Vyāsa discusses whether acts are to be performed or abandoned. He praises *tapas,* austerity, saying that by such means one becomes that which creates the world and is the lord of all beings (10). In verse 11, he adds that what one becomes through penance is concealed in the Vedas but is made evident in the *Vedāntas* through methodical practice of *yoga–vedānteṣu punar vyaktaṁ krama-yogena lakṣyate.* The passage is a difficult one, but the reference to *Vedāntas* as teachings offering instruction on the subject of *brahman* is clear.

In Chapter 290, which glorifies Sāṁkhya, this world is compared to a fearful ocean in which the acceptance of Vedānta–*vedānta-gamana*–is an island (68), presumably that offers refuge. In Chapter 16 of the *Anuśāsana,* Tandin, while offering prayers to Śiva, states, *yaṁ ca veda-vido vedyaṁ vedānteṣu pratiṣṭhitam*–Śiva is the object of knowledge contained in the *Vedāntas* for knowers of the Vedas (44).

The *Bhagavad-gītā* has two interesting references to Vedānta, in 13.4 and 15.15. In 13.4, Kṛṣṇa says the teaching he is going to impart is given by many *ṛṣis* in various hymns and also by the aphorisms of the *Brahma-sūtras–brahma-sūtra-padaiḥ*–another name for the *Vedānta-sūtras.* Kane has argued that here the *Gītā* is not referring to the *Vedānta-sūtras* of Bādarāyaṇa,[6] but to earlier works of Bādari, Auḍulomi, and Āśmarathya.[7] The existence of such earlier works that were known as *Brahma-sūtras* would seem to be enough to throw doubt on the identity of the work referred to by the *Bhagavad-gītā.* In 15.15, Kṛṣṇa claims that he is to be known from all the Vedas–*vedaiś ca sarvair aham eva vedyaḥ*–that he is the creator of Vedānta–*vedānta-kṛt*–and that he has knowledge of the Vedas–*veda-vit.* From these and other references it is apparent that some of the authors of the *Mahābhārata* were aware of Vedānta as a doctrine, and of literary works and *sūtras* which expounded that doctrine. The precise nature of those texts is unclear, although it appears that they existed in the form of aphorisms, as do the extant *Vedānta-sūtras* of Bādarāyaṇa.

(iv) Pañcarātra Literature

Direct references to *Pañcarātra* are found only in the *Nārāyaṇīya.* The followers of Pañcarātra were an early Vaiṣṇava sect, whose literature concentrates on the worship of Viṣṇu in the form of images in temples. Chapter 323 of the *Śānti* gives a description of Śvetadvīpa, a domain inhabited by devotees of Nārāyaṇa whom they worship through their knowledge of Pañcarātra—*pañca-kāla-jña* (42). In Chapter 326, Nārāyaṇa explains that he is the creator and sustainer of all the worlds. At the conclusion of the passage, Bhīṣma refers to these doctrines as a great *Upaniṣad,* in harmony with the four Vedas and with Sāṁkhya, and spoken of as Pañcarātra –*pañcarātrānuśabditam* (100). Pañcarātra is authentic because it was spoken by the mouth of Nārāyaṇa–*nārāyaṇa-mukhodgītam*–to Nārada who repeated it to others in the assembly of Brahmā (101). In 12.336.76, Vaiśaṁpāyana expresses the opinion that Pañcarātra is the same doctrine as Sāṁkhya and Yoga and as that taught in the Vedas and *Āraṇyakas.* In Chapter, 337, he refers to various religious groups (59f) who each follow their own scriptures, be it Sāṁkhya, Yoga, the Vedas, or Pañcarātra. The creator of Pañcarātra is the Lord himself (63), and those who worship Hari in that way enter into him (67).

The most prominent of the extant Pañcarātra scriptures is the *Sātvata-saṁhitā,* and in the opinion of Dasgupta this is referred to in 12.322.[8] There Bhīṣma describes King Uparicara's worship of Nārāyaṇa. Verse 24 describes Uparicara as a knower of Pañcarātra, while the rituals he performed are called *sātvata* (19) and came originally from Sūrya, the Sun God. These references indicate that the author of the *Nārāyaṇīya* was a follower of Pañcarātra and, according to Bhandarkar, the *Nārāyaṇīya* itself should be regarded as an early Pañcarātra work.[9] There are no conclusive references to extant Pañcarātra scriptures, though it is clear that the doctrines expressed display similarities to those given in extant works, particularly the *Sātvata-saṁhitā* which the author may have known.

(v) Dharma *Śāstras*

The *dharma-śāstras* are a body of literature that have existed from an early time delineating Hindu law and the codes of behaviour required from all levels of society, notably the different *varṇas* and castes, and the *āśramas* that form the stages of life for the twice-born. Sections of the *Śānti* and the *Anuśāsana* are themselves *dharma-śāstra* in which Bhīṣma instructs Yudhiṣṭhira on his duties as a king and the form of social organisation that he should encourage and enforce. *Dharma-śāstras* are usually referred to in the *Mahābhārata* in general terms, without specific texts being mentioned. In 12.25.13, Vyāsa tells Yudhiṣṭhira that a king must be guided by *dharma-śāstra* if he is to avoid sin. In 13.9.6, Bhīṣma informs him that pious acts produce no good result for one who has made a promise of a gift and not fulfilled it, and that those who know *dharma-śāstra* confirm that this is so—*api codāharantīmaṁ dharma-śāstra-vido janāḥ*.

The best known of the extant *dharma-śāstras* is the *Manu-smṛti*. Its relationship with the *Mahābhārata* has been extensively discussed by Kane, Buhler, Hopkins and others with differing conclusions being drawn. Max Mueller has found 250 verses that are common to both the *Mahābhārata* and *Manu-smṛti*,[10] while Buhler reckons there to be 260.[11] Much discussion has been devoted to the question of which text drew on the other but I do not propose to recapitulate this debate in any detail.

The *Manu-smṛti* makes reference to several texts, but does not mention the *Mahābhārata* or refer to any incident or character in the epic narrative.[12] The *Mahābhārata*, however, does on several occasions refer to Manu as a compiler of *dharma-śāstra*.[13] Hopkins admits only that the *Manu-smṛti* was known to the compiler of the *Anuśāsana*,[14] while Buhler extends this to the *Śānti* also,[15] both concluding that references in other sections are derived from an amorphous body of dharma-śāstric material loosely ascribed to Manu. Definite conclusions are impossible, but the most reasonable opinion seems to be that of Kane, who concludes:

> Long before the 4th century B.C. there was a work on Dharmaśāstra composed by or attributed to Svāyaṁbhuva Manu. This work was most probably in verse. There was another work on Rāja-dharma attributed to Prācetasa Manu which was also prior to the 4th century B.C. It is not unlikely that instead of there being two works there was one comprehensive work embodying rules on dharma as well as on politics . . . The Mahābhārata also (particularly in the earlier portions) probably refers to the same. This work was the original kernel of the present Manusmṛti. Then between 2nd century B.C. and 2nd century A.D the Manusmṛti was finally recast probably by Bhṛgu.[16]

(vi) Sāṁkhya and Yoga *Śāstras*

The *Mahābhārata* includes lengthy discourses on Sāṁkhya and Yoga, and refers to texts that propound these doctrines as the *sāṁkhya-śāstras* and the *yoga-śāstras*. In Chapter 289 of the *Śānti*, Yudhiṣṭhira asks Bhīṣma about the differences between Sāṁkhya and Yoga. Bhīṣma gives his opinion that both are positive spiritual paths, but differ in that followers of Yoga accept the existence of God while followers of Sāṁkhya do not (3), and that Yoga conclusions are derived from direct perception - *pratyakṣa* - while those of Sāṁkhya are based on scripture - *śāstra-viniścayāḥ*. He concludes, however (9), that both systems are equal in purity, compassion to all beings, and vows, and that if practised according to their *śāstras* they lead to the highest goal (8).

The principal extant *sāṁkhya-śāstra* is the *Sāṁkhya-kārikā*, attributed to Īśvarakṛṣṇa, and probably composed in the fifth century A.D. The *Mahābhārata* predates this work by several centuries and naturally makes no reference to it; the *sāṁkhya-śāstras* referred to are thus in all likelihood treatises very similar, or even identical, to those included within the *Mokṣa-dharma* itself. The major extant exposition of Yoga doctrine is the *Yoga-sūtras* of Patañjali, which attained its final form in the 3rd century A.D. The *Mahābhārata* makes no reference to this work or to its author and in 12.337.60 states, *hiraṇyagarbho yogasya vettā nānyaḥ purātanaḥ*, the ancient Hiraṇyagarbha, and no-one else, is the teacher of Yoga. Thus it may be concluded that the authors of the *Mokṣa-dharma* were aware of texts that expounded the doctrines of Sāṁkhya and Yoga, and probably used them as source material.

(vii) *Purāṇas*

The eighteen major *Purāṇas* known today are generally accepted as having been composed later than the *Mahābhārata*, during a period ranging from the second to the tenth centuries A.D. It is clear, however, that literatures known as *Purāṇas* have been in existence from a very early date. Even one of the earliest *Upaniṣads*, the *Chāndogya*, asserts that *Purāṇa* and *Itihāsa* are the fifth Veda (7.1.2-4). The *Mahābhārata* makes numerous references to *Purāṇa* throughout its text. From 1.102.18 we learn that Pāṇḍu and Dhṛtarāṣṭra became learned in *Itihāsas* and *Purāṇas*. In 12.43.6, Yudhiṣṭhira, glorifying Kṛṣṇa as a manifestation of Viṣṇu, says that in *Purāṇa–purāṇe*–it is stated that he has appeared seven times from the womb of Aditi. In 12.86.8, Bhīṣma, giving instructions on the appointment of ministers, states that amongst them there should be one *sūta* who is learned in the *Purāṇas*. In Chapter 201, when Yudhiṣṭhira asks about the seven original sages, Bhīṣma gives their names and cites *Purāṇa* as the authority, again in the singular, *purāṇe*. In 12.283.7, Parāśara states that he has heard from *Purāṇa* that in previous ages men were righteous; 12.321.24 states that in the Vedas and *Purāṇas–sa-purāṇeṣu*–Nārāyaṇa is glorified as the original creator, controller and basis of the world; in 13.16.18, Tandin says that *Śiva* is described by the knowers of *Purāṇa–purāṇa-jñaih*–as having three forms.

The above provides a small sample of the numerous references to *Purāṇa* in the *Mahābhārata*. The references are general and it is impossible to determine the relationship between these texts and the extant *Purāṇas*. All that can be said is that they appear to cover some of the same topics, and it is likely that the extant *Purāṇas* are based to some extent on the literatures known to the authors of the *Mahābhārata*. The frequent reference to *Purāṇa* in the singular lends weight to Kane's[17] surmise that originally there was only one work that was later subdivided.

Finally, two passages in the epic must be noted which appear to mention specific *Purāṇas*. In Chapter 189 of the *Vana*, Mārkaṇḍeya instructs Yudhiṣṭhira about the characteristics of the four *yugas*. At the conclusion, in verse 14, he describes this instruction as, *vāyu-proktam anusmṛtya purāṇam ṛṣi-saṁstutam*–recounted from the *Purāṇa* spoken by Vāyu that is praised by *ṛṣis*. Then in 3.185.53, at the conclusion of his narration of the story of Maṭsya, Mārkaṇḍeya says, *ity etan mātsyakaṁ nāma purāṇaṁ parikīrtitam* - this which is named the *Matsya Purāṇa* has thus been recounted. The reference to the *Vāyu Purāṇa* is too imprecise for any direct comparison, although the early verses of 3.189 bear no resemblance to anything found in the extant text of that work. The reference to a *Matsya Purāṇa* in 3.185 is even more vague, and may be referring only to the story that has just been narrated. The two verses in question do, however, give some indication that there were individual *Purāṇas* with specific names known to the authors of the *Mahābhārata*.

(viii) Other Literatures

The *Mahābhārata* makes reference to a variety of other works. The *Vedāṅgas*, which were compiled between the eighth and fourth centuries B.C, are mentioned on a number of occasions[18] but never in a specific manner that discusses their contents. There is also mention of the *Dhanurveda,*[19] the science of warfare, the *Āyurveda,*[20] the science of medicine and the *Jyotirveda,*[21] the science of astronomy and astrology.

The *Āranyakas* are mentioned in 12.330.32 and 12.336.36, while 12.306 gives the story of the compilation of the *Śatapatha-brāhmaṇa* by Yājñavalkya. Links between the *Mahābhārata* and the *Rāmāyaṇa* have been discussed at length by several writers, the general conclusion being that most of the *Mahābhārata* is earlier. Hopkins differs from this conclusion, noting that there are four *Mahābhārata* passages that refer to the *Rāmāyaṇa.*[22] Of these one is from the *Harivaṁśa,* while 12.57.40 refers to a work called *Rāma-carita* by an author known as Bhārgava, and the verse quoted from it is not found in the extant *Rāmāyaṇa.* 7.118.48, however, clearly states, *śloko vālmīkinā bhuvi* and then quotes verse 29 of Chapter 81 of the *Yuddha-kāṇḍa.* Similarly, in 3.147.11 Bhīma cites the *Rāmāyaṇa* by name as describing the greatness of Hanumān. It is apparent that the *Mahābhārata* is aware of the story of the *Rāmāyaṇa,* and includes a version of it within its text as well as the encounter between Bhīma and his brother Hanumān referred to above. The evidence of two verses, however, is inadequate to conclude that the authors of *Mahābhārata* knew the extant *Rāmāyaṇa* and it is more likely that they drew upon earlier Rāma material as did the Vālmīki *Rāmāyaṇa* itself.

(ix) Conclusions

It is apparent from this brief analysis that the authors of the *Mahābhārata* were aware of a variety of other literatures and cited them as authoritative. However, they evidently do not feel the need to cite scriptural authority for all doctrinal statements, and a large number of the references are made almost in passing. The *Mahābhārata* does not feel the need to support its statements with scriptural authority for it sees itself as authoritative in its own right. The vast majority of references to other texts are found in the *Śānti* and *Anuśāsana.* It may be concluded that this is the case because these two sections are later than the rest of the epic, but equally it must be recognised that reference to other works is more likely to occur in the course of moral and religious discourse than in the straightforward telling of a narrative story.

3. The *Mahābhārata*'s View of its Own Status

As noted above, despite the numerous references to other works found in the didactic sections, the *Mahābhārata* does not feel the necessity of justifying all its assertions on the basis of previous authority. From the beginning, the *Mahābhārata* states that it is to be accepted as equal to the Vedas. In 1.1.205, it calls itself *kārṣṇaṁ vedam,* the Veda of the dark one, Vyāsa. Verses 208 and 209 of the same chapter tell how the gods once weighed the four Vedas against the *Mahābhārata* and found that the latter was superior in greatness and in gravity–*mahattve ca gurutve ca dhriyamāṇaṁ tato 'dhikam.* 1.56.15 states:

> *idaṁ hi vedaiḥ samitaṁ pavitram api cottamam*
> *śrāvyamāṇām uttamaṁ cedaṁ purāṇam ṛṣi-saṁstutam*
>
> 'This work which is equal to the Vedas, is excellent and most pure. This *Purāṇa,* praised by *ṛṣis,* is the best of all things that may be heard.'

1.56.17 again describes the *Mahābhārata* as, *kārṣṇaṁ vedam imam,* this Veda of Vyāsa, and in verse 21, it describes itself as, *artha-śāstram idaṁ puṇyaṁ,* this auspicious scripture relating to personal gain, *dharma-śāstram idam param,* this best of all scriptures concerning religious duties, and *mokṣa-śāstram idam,* this scripture that teaches the way to salvation. In the epic's concluding words, it is stated, *itihāsam imaṁ puṇyaṁ mahārthaṁ veda-samitam,* this holy narrative is of great importance and equal to the Vedas (18.5.43).

The difference between *śruti* and *smṛti* is that *śruti* is the eternal Veda, not the compilation of any mortal being, while *smṛti* is literature composed by various sages on the basis of their spiritual insights. Therefore *śruti* is regarded as superior to the *smṛti.* The *Mahābhārata,* although it claims to be the work of Vyāsa, overrules the possibility of any lesser status being ascribed to it by elevating its author beyond the realm of ordinary men. This is done in two ways. Firstly, Vyāsa is presented as a personality with powers far beyond those of most mortals. He has divine insight that enables him to gain knowledge of all things in all times. 1.56.21 states that the *Mahābhārata* was spoken by Vyāsa whose intelligence is unlimited–*vyāsenāmita-buddhinā.* In 18.5.31-33, Vyāsa is described as follows:

puṇyo 'yam itihāsākhyaḥ pavitraṁ cedam uttamam
kṛṣṇena muninā vipra niyataṁ satya-vādinā

sarva-jñena vidhi-jñena dharma-jñānavatā satā
atīndriyeṇa śucinā tapasā bhavitātmanā

aiśvarye vartatā caiva sāṁkhya-yoga-vidā tathā
naika-tantra-vibuddhena dṛṣṭvā divyena cakṣuṣā

'This work, known as a history, is sacred, pure and excellent. O *brāhmaṇa,* it was composed by the sage Kṛṣṇa (Vyāsa), whose speech is truthful. He knows all things, and all religious principles, he is learned in *dharma,* and righteous. He can perceive things beyond the senses, he is pure, and because of his penance his heart is faultless. He is also endowed with mystic potency and is learned in Sāṁkhya and Yoga. Having comprehended many sciences, he beheld (what has been described) through his divine vision.'

The *Nārāyaṇīya* raises Vyāsa's status even higher, so that he is no longer a being of this world but an incarnation of Nārāyaṇa, as he is in the *Purāṇas.* Therefore he is not limited like ordinary men, but knows all things, past, present and future (12.337.49). The *smṛti* literature composed by Vyāsa is to be accepted as being as authoritative as the Vedas, for both are divinely revealed by the Supreme who is beyond the blemishes of this world. Thus, although the *Mahābhārata* is composed by a man, Vyāsa, he is not limited by the normal human restraints of intellect, he receives direct revelation from Nārāyaṇa, as did the seers of the Veda, or he may even be understood as Nārāyaṇa himself appearing as an expansion to impart spiritual knowledge and arrange the Vedas. On this basis Vaiśaṁpāyana states that Vyāsa instructed his disciples in the Vedas with the *Mahābhārata* as the fifth - *vedān adhyāpayāmāsa mahābhārata-pañcamān* (12.327.18).[23]

There are in addition a number of statements regarding the great benefits, material and spiritual, that may be gained from studying the *Mahābhārata.* Such study is not merely a means of understanding theological or philosophical doctrines, but is in itself a religious act and brings appropriate results. In particular, study of the *Mahābhārata* is referred to as being an act of atonement–*prāyaścittam*–that removes sins. 1.1.191 states:

> *bhāratādhyayanāt puṇyād api pādam adhīyataḥ*
> *śraddadhānasya pūyante sarva-pāpāny aśeṣataḥ*
>
> 'All sins are completely cleansed from one who, with faith, learns even one line during the sacred act of studying the *Mahābhārata*.'

Similarly, 1.2.235 describes the *Mahābhārata* as *pāpa-haram*, destroying all sins, 1.56.23 states that a man who hears the *Mahābhārata* quickly crosses beyond all sin committed with body, words or mind, and verse 31 of the same chapter says that one who knows its true meaning–*niruktam*–is freed from all sins–*sarva-pāpaiḥ pramucyate*. The concluding chapter also stresses that one hearing or reciting the *Mahābhārata* is *pāpa-nirmuktaḥ*, free from sin (18.5.44), and that daily recital removes any contamination that may have been gathered by the senses or the mind during that day (37).

Beyond mere atonement for sins, hearing or recital also brings more concrete benefits. Chapter 56 of the *Ādi*, which serves as a second introduction, mentions some of these as follows: *mahīṁ vijayate sarvām śatrūṁś cāpi parājayet*, he conquers all the earth and vanquishes his enemies (19), *putrāḥ śuśruṣavaḥ santi preśyāś ca priya-kāriṇaḥ*, the sons and servants of one who hears it become well-behaved (22), *nāsti vyādhi-bhayaṁ teṣāṁ para-loka-bhayaṁ kutaḥ*, there is no fear of disease nor of one's fate in the next world (24). A wise man who causes *brāhmaṇas* to hear it destroys his sins, attains heaven–*jita-svargaḥ*–and reaches the level of salvation–*brahma-bhūyaṁ sa gacchati* (1.56.28). The offerings of *śrāddha* made to the ancestors are perfect when accompanied by recitation of the *Mahābhārata* (1.56.29 and 18.5.36). One desiring heaven or victory in battle can attain success by hearing the *Mahābhārata*, and a pregnant woman gets a good child by the same means (18.5.40).

Thus various results can be gained from hearing or reciting the *Mahābhārata* which may be summarised as being of four types:

1. All sins and the reactions to them are removed and atoned for.
2. Success in one's life and worldly endeavours can be gained.
3. After death one can obtain happiness by elevation to the realm of the gods, *svarga-loka*.

4. It appears that salvation or *mokṣa* may be gained in the same way for 1.56.28, referring to the hearer, states, *brahma-bhūyaṁ sa gacchati*, 18.5.35 says, *brahma-bhūyāya gacchati*, and 12.326. 116-117 says that one who hears or recites that chapter becomes an inhabitant of the abode of Nārāyaṇa, Śvetadvīpa.

4. The *Mahābhārata*'s View of the Vedas and Previous Scriptures

The attitude of the *Mahābhārata* to the Vedas is ambiguous, seeking as it does to preserve the traditional authority and yet to propound elements of non-Vedic thought. Here the dichotomy within the epic between the values of *pravṛtti* and *nivṛtti* is a significant factor. The world-affirming nature of Vedic belief is substantially incorporated into the value system of *pravṛtti*. *Sva-dharma* is not a legitimately Vedic notion, but in the epic Veda and *dharma-śāstra* are regarded as virtually identical in representing orthodox belief and practice, and the connection between *sva-dharma* and *yajña* is emphasised. Hence *pravṛtti* values include a positive attitude towards the Vedas and lay stress on their integrity and authoritative nature.

The perspective of *nivṛtti* is different. There is a clear ideological conflict between the Vedic world view and the world-denying values of the epic's teachings on *mokṣa-dharma*; consequently the values of *nivṛtti* include a much less enthusiastic view of the Vedas and Vedic beliefs. It is important to note, however, that nowhere in the epic are the Vedas utterly condemned after the manner of the Buddhists, Jains and Ājīvakas. The *ācāryas* of the Sāṁkhya schools whose ideas are contained in the *Mahābhārata* are often critical of those who adhere to Vedic ritual, but always they stop short of denying the revealed status of the Vedas, and thereby maintain their position within the broad limits of an eclectic orthodoxy. It is appropriate at this point to examine how the epic expresses these contrasting attitudes towards the Vedas.

(i) Teachings that Stress the Authority of the Vedas

a) The *Mahābhārata* contains a number of passages that reaffirm the divine origin of the Vedas and tell of their being imparted by Nārāyaṇa himself as a part of the creation process. In the *Nārāyaṇīya*, Chapter 335 of the *Śānti* tells how Nārāyaṇa creates the universe through his agent Brahmā. Nārāyaṇa also generates two *asuras*,

Madhu and Kaitabha, who find Brahmā creating the Vedas–*sṛjantaṁ prathamaṁ vedāṁs* (25). They seize the Vedas from Brahmā who then prays to Nārāyaṇa for help, as he is powerless without them:

> *vedā me paramaṁ cakṣur vedā me paramaṁ balam*
> *vedā me paramaṁ dhāma vedā me brahma cottamam*
>
> 'The Vedas are my supreme vision, the Vedas are my supreme power, the Vedas are my supreme resting place, and the Vedas are my ultimate spiritual energy' (12.335.29).

Nārāyaṇa kills Madhu and Kaitabha and returns the Vedas to Brahmā who is then able to continue his work of creation. This narrative confirms the belief that the Vedas are not merely works of men, or even gods or sages, but are eternal and essential for the existence of the world.

Other passages confirm the belief that the Vedas are eternal and nowhere is this understanding rejected or challenged. In 9.44.11, in listing the celestial beings who attended the investiture of Skanda, Vaiśaṁpāyana includes, *vedāś caiva sanātanāḥ* - and also the eternal Vedas. In 12.224, Vyāsa praises the practice of rigorous austerity, and in verse 55 asserts that it is as a result of such *tapas* that *ṛṣis* are able to study the Vedas that were generated in the beginning by the self-born–*svayaṁbhuvā*. 12.327.30 makes the assertion that for the perfection of all the world Brahmā generated the Vedas, *vedāṅgas, yajñas* and *yajñāṅgas*. The *Bhagavad-gītā*, in stressing the necessity of *yajña*, also asserts that the Vedas come from the imperishable–*brahmākṣaraṁ samudbhavam* (3.15).

b) The *Mahābhārata* repeatedly refutes the notion that reason or logic can be superior to faith in scriptural revelation. The Vedas are divinely inspired and higher than human logic; hence they must remain authoritative. In Chapter 49 of the *Karṇa*, after a bitter quarrel between them, Arjuna threatens to kill Yudhiṣṭhira. Kṛṣṇa, who is present throughout, criticises Arjuna for making such a vow and condemns him as fool (17). As a part of this criticism, Kṛṣṇa states that what is right or wrong action is to be understood not from one's own opinion but from the *śruti*. "Everything can be understood from the *śruti*," he insists, "but you do not know such things"–*śrutena jñāyate sarvaṁ tac ca tvaṁ nāvabudhyase* (18).

In 12.173.45-48, Indra states that one who teaches on the basis of logic, thinking himself very learned–*paṇḍita-mānikaḥ*–and criticises the Vedas–*veda-nindakaḥ*–is doomed to take birth as a jackal. In 12.140.1-2, Yudhiṣṭhira rejects parts of Bhīṣma's teaching on *rāja-dharma*, as vile and false. Bhīṣma replies to this criticism by arguing that his teachings are based on the Vedas–*āgamāt*–and the wisdom taught by the learned. He urges that only fools and evil-doers–*mandāḥ . . . nara-pāpiṣṭhāḥ* (12, 13), place their own wisdom above that of the *śāstras*. Such wrongdoers criticise and find fault with scripture–*parimuṣṇanti śāstrāṇi śāstra-doṣānudarśinaḥ* (14). They look upon wisdom as a commodity to profit from–*vidyā-vaṇijaḥ*–and are just like evil spirits of the night–*rākṣasān iva* (15).

In Chapter 25 of the *Anuśāsana*, Yudhiṣṭhira asks Bhīṣma to list sins which are equal in wickedness to the killing of a *brāhmaṇa*. Citing Vyāsa as his authority, Bhīṣma asserts that one such sin is that of criticising the *śruti* or the *śāstras* compiled by saints–*yaḥ pravṛttāṁ śrutiṁ samyak śāstraṁ vā munibhiḥ kṛtam dūṣayati* (8). In Chapter 37, he states that a *brāhmaṇa* is not to be respected if he teaches that the Vedas are not authoritative–*aprāmāṇyaṁ vedānām*–or if he transgresses against *śāstra–śāstrāṇāṁ cātilaṅghanam.* Such a *brāhmaṇa* who is a critic of the Vedas is learned only in his own estimation. Following logic and reason, he seeks victory in debate in assemblies of learned men. He is condemned as a childish fool barking at others like a dog or looking to bite them as he attempts to destroy the authority of *śruti, smṛti* and *Purāṇa* (16).

In Chapter 147, Bhīṣma again condemns the *prājña-mānins* who rely only on reason–*hetu-vād*–and direct perception–*pratyakṣa*–doubting the authority of scripture. In verse 9, Yudhiṣṭhira asks about the best source of knowledge, whether it is perception, inference, the precept of those who are perfect, or learning from the Vedas–*āgama-pūrvakāḥ*. Bhīṣma replies that knowledge gained from any of the first three must be subject to doubt, and therefore true contentment is gained only by those who keep the *āgamas* as their intelligence–*ya evāgama-buddhayaḥ* (13). Those who give up the Vedas–*śruta-tyāga-parāyaṇāḥ*–are fools and haters of dharma–*mandāḥ . . . dharma-vidveṣiṇaḥ* (12).

The *Bhagavad-gītā* also condemns those who abandon *śāstra* for their own opinions. 16.23-24 states:

> *yaḥ śāstra-vidhim utsṛjya vartate kāma-kārataḥ*
> *na sa siddhiṁ avāpnoti na sukhaṁ na parāṁ gatim*

tasmāc chāstraṁ pramāṇaṁ te kāryākārya-vyavasthitau
jñātvā śāstra-vidhānoktaṁ karma kartum ihārhasi

'One who abandons the injunctions of scripture and lives according to his own desire never obtains perfection, happiness or the highest goal. Therefore, having understood the version of scripture in determining what acts should or should not be performed, you should perform your duty in this world according to the injunctions of the scriptures.'

The reassertion of Vedic and śāstric authority is a theme that is found throughout the *Mahābhārata.* Those who reject this authority are condemned as foolish, wicked and destroyers of religion. Such criticism seems to be levelled at the various anti-Vedic sects and also at *paṇḍitas* who engaged in logical debate to establish themselves as authorities in their own right, disregarding the existing Vedic authority.

c) Study and recitation of the Vedas are presented as a part of a *brāhmaṇa*'s dharmic duty, and are accepted by all parties, notably by Yudhiṣṭhira, as auspicious activities. Where *sva-dharma* is advocated, the duties of a *brāhmaṇa* always include studying and reciting the Vedas; by such activities a *brāhmaṇa* will gain success both in this world and the next. Reflecting the stress on the appropriate *dharma* for each *varṇa,* the *Mahābhārata* asserts that *śūdras* must neither recite the Vedas nor be instructed in them. Describing to Janamejaya the high state of civilization in a previous age, Vaiśampāyana gives as evidence of this the fact that *brāhmaṇas* never recited the Vedas in the presence of *śūdras–na ca śūdra-samābhyāśe vedān uccārayanty uta* (1.58.18). Similarly, in Chapter 10 of the *Anuśāsana,* we are given the story of a *brāhmaṇa* who taught the Vedas to a pious *śūdra* and had to suffer in hell for this misdeed.

In the *Vana,* there are many descriptions of the purity and beauty of the Pāṇḍavas' forest abode. The melodic chanting of Vedic hymns by the *brāhmaṇas* in Yudhiṣṭhira's retinue harmonises with the naturally auspicious setting of the unsullied forest. In Chapter 1, we are told of the Pāṇḍavas' first night in exile surrounded by *brāhmaṇas* who constantly enunciate the sacred sounds of the Vedas (42). 3.27.3-4 states:

> *yajuṣām ṛcāṁ ca sāmnāṁ ca gadyānāṁ caiva sarvaśaḥ*
> *āsīd uccāryamāṇānāṁ nisvano hṛdayaṁgamaḥ*
>
> *jyāghoṣaḥ pāṇḍaveyānāṁ brahma-ghoṣaś ca dhīmatām*
> *saṁsṛṣṭaṁ brahmaṇā kṣatraṁ bhūya eva vyarocata*
>
> 'There was constant recital of the *Ṛk*, *Sāma* and *Yajur* Vedas, and other auspicious sounds. The sounds of this chanting moved the heart.
>
> The sound of the Pāṇḍavas' bow strings and the Vedic recitations of the wise men combined together, and this mixing of the ways of *brāhmaṇas* and *kṣatriyas* was very pleasing.'

During the forest exile, the Pāṇḍavas are visited by a sage named Lomaśa who recounts to them the story of how the Kālakeyas, a race of *asuras*, afflicted the earth. Because of their depradations the *brāhmaṇas* were unable to perform their duties–*niḥsvādhyāya-vaṣaṭ-kāraṃ naṣṭa-yajñotsava-kriyam*–of Vedic study, pronouncing 'Vaṣaṭ' (to conclude *yajñas*), and performing *yajñas* and religious festivals (3.100.11); as a result the earth became bereft of its natural energy–*nirutsāham*. Here we have a reassertion of the Vedic belief that *yajña* nourishes the gods and sustains the cosmic order; Lomaśa extends the concept to include other brahminical practices, including study of the Vedas.

From the passages of the *Śānti* in which Bhīṣma discusses the *sva-dharma* of a *brāhmaṇa*, it is clear that study of the Vedas is to be regarded as one of the most important duties for a *brāhmaṇa*. In Chapter 37, Vyāsa describes the best type of *brāhmaṇa* to whom a *kṣatriya* should give charity. Verse 38 states that a gift may be given to an unlearned *brāhmaṇa* out of compassion, but there is no gain for the giver thereby. The next verse, which also appears in the *Manu-smṛti* (2.157), explains this:

> *yathā dārumayo hastī yathā carmamayo mṛgaḥ*
> *brāhmaṇaś cānadhīyānas trayas te nāma-dhārakāḥ*
>
> 'Like an elephant made of wood, or a deer made of leather, a *brāhmaṇa* who has no knowledge of the three Vedas is such in name only.' (12.37.39)

The *Bhagavad-gītā* contains some notable passages critical of those who follow Vedic rites, yet it recognises *svādhyāyaḥ* as a religious practice. In 4.28, Kṛṣṇa describes all religious acts performed by *yatis* fixed in their vows as *yajñas* and therein includes *svādhyāya-jñāna-yajñaḥ*, the sacrifice of gaining knowledge through study. Similarly, in 8.28 he lists acts that lead to *puṇya-phalam*, an auspicious result, as *veda, yajña, tapa,* and *dravya*–study of Veda, sacrificial rites, austerity and charity—noting that the *yogin* is bereft of the results of none of these.

(ii) Teachings that Include Criticisms of the Vedas

The above references serve to demonstrate that there is a substantial strand of thought within the epic that opposes tendencies to denigrate the Vedas, and those sects and teachers who questioned their divine origin. Whilst most of such support for the Vedas is from the perspective of *pravṛtti*, it is apparent that even the epic's teachings on Sāṁkhya, reflecting the values of *nivṛtti*, also provides endorsement, albeit sometimes qualified, of Vedic authority. There is, however, a notable tendency within certain passages of the text to level criticism at the Vedic rituals, and more particularly at those religionists who regard the Vedic literatures as no more than prescriptions for complex rituals that bring material prosperity. Naturally this criticism is made overwhelmingly from the standpoint of *nivṛtti* and is thus to be found in the later chapters of the *Śānti*, in the *Aśvamedhika*, and in the *Bhagavad-gītā*.

The primary criticism of the Vedas and the religious practices they teach parallels the transcendence of *sva-dharma* that *mokṣa-dharma* repeatedly urges. The followers of the Vedas are righteous in that they adhere to the prescribed rules of *dharma*, but the goals they seek, either in this life or the next, are essentially materialistic. The Vedas provide the means for success in this world but, crucially for *mokṣa-dharma*, they do not offer the means of salvation. In Chapter 194 of the *Śānti*, Bṛhaspati puts questions to Manu. He insists that he has studied the *Ṛk. Sāma* and *Yajur* Vedas, as well as various other hymns and treatises on astronomy and grammar (8), but now wishes to understand topics that are not revealed in the Vedas–*yan mantra-śabdair akṛta-prakāśaṁ tad ucyatāṁ me bhagavan yathāvat* (4). Despite his study of the Vedas, he has no knowledge of the nature or source of created beings–*bhūta-prakṛtiṁ na vedmi* (8). In verses 10 to 24, Manu gives instructions on gaining salvation through the renunciation of material acts, and explains that the

Vedas are a part of the process of performing activities and for this reason cannot to lead one to *mokṣa.* Verse 16 notes:

> *guṇātmakaṁ karma vadanti vedās*
> *tasmāt mantrā mantra-mūlaṁ hi karma*
>
> 'The Vedas themselves say that acts have the attributes of the three material strands. Therefore the Vedic *mantras* must have similar qualities, for acts are based on these *mantras.*' (1.194.16)

In Kṛṣṇa's teachings to Arjuna in the *Aśvamedhika,* he presents a discourse on the higher states of spiritual realisation through the mouth of a renounced *brāhmaṇa.* The most elevated state of realisation is attained by a true *saṁnyāsin,* and is described as follows:

> *na tatra kramate buddhir nendriyāṇi na devatāḥ*
> *vedā yajñāś ca lokāś ca na tapo na parākramaḥ*
>
> 'The intellect, the senses and the gods are not active in that state. Neither are the Vedas, *yajñas,* the heavens of this world, austerity or religious vows.' (14.46.48)

The conclusion is that the final state of salvation takes one completely beyond all the features of this world and its religious practices, and that includes the religion of the Vedas.

This attitude towards the Vedas is characteristic of *nivṛtti,* as expressed in the *Mokṣa-dharma.* The scriptural status of the Vedas is not wholly denied, but they are overtly included amongst the features of this world that are to be renounced and transcended. It is somewhat surprising that the most thoroughgoing rejection of the Vedas in the *Mahābhārata* is to be found in the *Bhagavad-gītā.* Despite his repeated stress on not abandoning *dharma* for the sake of *mokṣa,* Kṛṣṇa is unrestrained in his criticism of those who interpret the Vedas in a world-affirming manner:

> *yām imāṁ puṣpitāṁ vācaṁ pravadanty avipaścitaḥ*
> *veda-vāda-ratāḥ pārtha nānyad astīti vādinaḥ*
>
> *kāmātmānaḥ svarga-parā janma-karma-phala-pradām*
> *kriyā-viśeṣa-bahulāṁ bhogaiśvarya-gatiṁ prati*

bhogaiśvarya-prasaktānāṁ tayāpahṛta-cetasām
vyavasāyātmikā buddhiḥ samādhau na vidhīyate

trai-guṇya-viṣayā vedā nistrai-guṇyo bhavārjuna
nirdvandvo nitya-sattva-stho niryoga-kṣema ātmavān

yāvān artha udapāne sarvataḥ samplutodake
tāvān sarveṣu vedeṣu brāhmaṇasya vijānataḥ

'O Pārtha, foolish persons who do not see clearly and who are attached to the teachings of the Vedas speak flowery words, and say that there is nothing beyond them.

With their hearts filled with desire, seeking the heavens of the gods, they perform many grand rituals that bring good rebirth, activities and rewards in terms of opulence and enjoyment.

For those attached to enjoyment and opulence, and bewildered by such things, the determined intelligence in spiritual consciousness does not arise.

The Vedas deal with subjects within the purview of the three *guṇas*, but you should rise above such things, Arjuna, being free from duality, fixed in higher consciousness, free from ideas of gain and sustenance, and devoted to spiritual matters.

All the uses of a small pond are served by a great lake. Similarly all the purposes of the Vedas have been realised by a *brāhmaṇa* who has true knowledge.' (2.42-46)

Kṛṣṇa is outspoken here in condemning those who rigidly follow the Vedic rituals. He seems to be attacking an entrenched orthodox faction who will allow the validity of nothing except the traditional Vedic religion which has no concept of *mokṣa*. This faction may be the followers of the Mimāṁsa school of philosophy, whose doctrines were very like those criticised here. According to the *Gītā*, such persons never attain the higher levels of spiritual realisation, for the Vedas and the rituals they prescribe deal exclusively with material things. The Vedas are thus an obstacle–*śruti-vipratipannā*–that must be overcome by the aspiring seeker after salvation (2.53).

This view is not unique to the second chapter. 6.44 mentions that one practising *yoga* goes beyond the Vedas–*sabda-brahmātivartate*.

In Chapter 11, after the revelation of the *viśva-rūpa*, Kṛṣṇa tells Arjuna that such a vision can be gained only by *bhakti* (54) and not by penance, by the Vedas, by charity, or by worship–*nāhaṁ vedair na tapasā na dānena na cejyayā; śakya evaṁ vidho draṣṭum,* (11.53).

Another criticism levelled at the Vedas is that their teachings are contradictory, particularly their prescribing various ways of action whilst condemning acts as leading to bondage in this world. In the arguments over Yudhiṣṭhira's desire to renounce the kingdom after the battle, he rejects his critics who have cited Vedic authority by arguing:

> *vedāhaṁ tāta śāstrāṇi aparāṇi parāṇi ca*
> *ubhayaṁ veda-vacanaṁ kuru karma tyajeti ca*
>
> *ākulāni ca śāstrāṇi hetubhiś citritāni ca*
> *niścayaś caiva yan mātro vedāhaṁ taṁ yathā vidhi*
>
> 'I know both superior and inferior scriptures. The words of the Vedas say that one should perform acts and renounce acts.
> The scriptures are confusing and they are embellished by various modes of reasoning. I know the full conclusion that is given in scripture.' (12.19.1-2)

The reference to recommending both the execution and the renunciation of acts would appear to be based on the understanding that both *pravṛtti* and *nivṛtti* are contained in the *śruti*, possibly indicating the distinctive views of the ritual portions of the Vedas and the mysticism of the *Upaniṣads.* Following a similar line to Kṛṣṇa in 2.46 of the *Gītā,* Yudhiṣṭhira is here arguing that there is a mode of wisdom that is beyond the vicissitudes of scriptural argument, and that one who has transcended worldly attachments naturally understands the truth. This is an important element in the *Mahābhārata*'s view of scripture and will be discussed more thoroughly below For the moment we may recognise the criticism of the Vedic teachings that they present different conclusions, and hence cause confusion to those who study them.

This point is reiterated as one of the persistent criticisms of the Vedas found in the *Mokṣa-dharma.* Śuka says to Vyāsa in 12.234.10-11 that in the opinion of the world the statements of the Vedas are contradictory–*yad idaṁ veda-vacanaṁ loka-vāde viruddhyate*–and that he should therefore tell him conclusively how *mokṣa* and prescribed acts can be reconciled–*karmaṇāṁ avirodhena katham etat pravartate.* Speeches of this type seem to act as prefaces for certain passages of teaching on *mokṣa-dharma.* The questioner states that scriptures are contradictory and therefore a conclusive version is required from the speaker to clarify matters. In this way there is a subtle move, without outright rejection, to demonstrate that the treatises of the *Mokṣa-dharma,* in contrast to the confusions and contradictions of the Vedas and other *śāstras,* are providing a definite exposition of philosophical truth.

The *Mahābhārata* thus reasserts the authenticity of the Vedas as authoritative texts, divinely revealed and eternally existing. It opposes logicians who stress reason over revelation and heterodox groups who deny the authority of the Vedas. Throughout the epic, the *brāhmaṇas* are praised and elevated, and study and recitation of the Vedas are presented as an essential part of the *sva-dharma* of a *brāhmaṇa.* Passages that teach from the perspective of *nivṛtti* are, however, less enthusiastic about the Vedas, which are noted as espousing religious ideas that pertain only to gain and progress within this world and therefore must be transcended in the search for salvation. The Vedas are also regarded as contradictory, making it difficult for a person to judge conclusively from them what path he should follow. The *Mokṣa-dharma* does not go so far as to deny the status of the Vedas as sacred texts, but sees them as a stage of religious progress that one must go beyond. The most severe criticism is found in epic Sāṁkhya, which here strays close to heterodoxy. Most notable are the criticisms of the Vedas found in the *Gītā* which condemns an unbending orthodoxy of sensual materialists who will not allow that there is any higher path than material gain derived from complex rituals.

5. The Notion of Wisdom as opposed to Scriptural Learning

In passages where *nivṛtti* is the dominant value system, it is urged that while *śāstras* may dictate behaviour the key to salvation is detachment through wisdom. The brahminical duty of *svādhyāya* may bring success and prosperity in this world but not necessarily *jñāna,* the spiritual wisdom that is the foundation of salvation. *Jñāna* is the superior insight that recognises the true identity of the self as different from matter–*anyo'ham* (12.259.19) in *Sāṁkhya* terms–and thereby detaches the individual from desire. Therefore *jñāna* is far more than just adherence to a doctrine that may be learned from the practice of *svādhyāya*; it is rather a transformed state of consciousness wherein one's entire functional self-identity is changed from body to soul. It is notable, therefore, that although Vedic study is proscribed for non-*brāhmaṇas*, the wisdom of *mokṣa-dharma* may be gained and taught by those born in the lower orders of society, as demonstrated by the examples of Tulādhara (12.253-256) and the wise hunter (3.198-206).

One who has such *jñāna* may transcend the ordinances of the Vedas, for his consciousness, purified by wisdom, naturally directs him towards right action and he has no interest in the results that accrue to the Vedic ritualist. Thus for one who follows *mokṣa-dharma*, scripture is not taken as absolute authority as it must be for the orthodox Muslim or Christian. In Chapter 43 of the *Udyoga*, Dhṛtarāṣṭra receives instructions from Sanat-Sujāta, whose teachings, based on Upaniṣadic monism rather than Sāṁkhya, urge renunciation and condemn desire and ignorance. According to Sanat-Sujāta, salvation comes from knowledge, but this emancipating *jñāna* does not arise from study of the Vedas–*nainaṁ sāmāny ṛco vāpi na yajūṁṣi vicakṣaṇa trāyante karmaṇaḥ pāpāt* (5.43.2). The point that true knowledge is a state of consciousness which must be realised and not merely learned is made clearly and succinctly later in the chapter.

na vedānāṁ veditā kaścid asti
kaścid vedān budhyate vāpi rājan
yo veda vedān na sa veda vedyaṁ
satye sthito yas tu sa veda vedyam

'There is no-one who is a knower of the Vedas, or else there may be one who knows the Vedas, O king. One who knows the Vedas does not know the object of knowledge, but one who is fixed in truth knows the object of knowledge.' (5.43.31)

Up to this point, the discussion has concentrated on the different perspectives on the Vedas presented by the tendencies of *pravṛtti* and *nivṛtti*. The understanding of the Vedas from the point of view of *bhakti* may be recognised as covering both views.

The Vedas are understood as being intimately related to *dharma*, laying down the ritual basis of human life which culminates in the world-sustaining *yajña*. The Deity is the creator and sustainer of the cosmic order and therefore he acts to preserve the Vedas, as the creation story in the *Nārāyaṇīya* makes clear (12.335). At the same time, the exponents of *bhakti* cannot accept that the Vedas offer the highest path to be followed by seekers of salvation. In the *Bhagavad-gītā*, after the display of the *viśva-rūpa*, Kṛṣṇa tells Arjuna.

> *nāhaṁ vedair na tapasā na dānena na cejyayā*
> *śakya evaṁ vidho draṣṭuṁ dṛṣṭavān asi māṁ yathā*
>
> *bhaktyā tv ananyayā śakya aham evaṁ vidho 'rjuna*
> *jñātuṁ draṣṭuṁ ca tattvena praveṣṭuṁ ca parantapa*
>
> 'Not by the Vedas, not by penance, not by charity, nor by worship is it possible to see me like this as you are seeing me.
>
> But only through undivided devotion, Arjuna, is it possible to know me, to see me and truly enter into me, O destroyer of enemies.' (11.53-54).

The point is reiterated as a part of the conclusion of the *Gītā*,

> *bhaktyā mām abhijānāti yāvān yaś cāsmi tattvataḥ*
> *tato māṁ tattvato jñātvā viśate tad anantaram*
>
> 'One truly understands me as I am through devotion, and having gained true knowledge of me, he then enters into me.' (18.55)

The concept of *jñāna*, be it attained from self-realisation or by the grace of the Deity, does not, however, indicate that such teachings reject the value of scripture altogether. The *Mokṣa-dharma* and the *Bhagavad-gītā* are clearly didactic scriptures in which questions of doctrine are posed and answered to guide the listener towards salvation. In the *Bhagavad-gītā*, Kṛṣṇa claims that the teachings he is imparting are themselves *jñāna* and are the means by which *mokṣa* may be attained:

śrī bhagavān uvāca
idaṁ tu te guhyatamaṁ pravakṣyāmy anasūyave
jñanaṁ vijñāna-sahitaṁ yaj jñātvā mokṣyase 'śubhāt

'I shall instruct you, who are free from envy, in this most secret of all wisdom along with its practical application. When this is understood, you will be freed from all impurity.' (9.1)

Yet hearing and understanding these esoteric doctrines is just the beginning stage, a preliminary to realisation and absorption of a radically different view of life. True *jñāna* is this alternative perspective, and therefore the ability to recite and philosophically comprehend doctrines and creeds is merely the beginning of the process.

6. Reinterpretation of the Vedas

The view of the Vedas expressed in the *Mokṣa-dharma* and *Bhagavad-gītā* that has been considered up to this point is that the Vedas, *śāstras, āgamas,* and *Vedāṅgas* are a part of this world and hence must be transcended on the path to salvation. However, an alternative view expressed by the text claims that the Vedas have a hidden esoteric meaning that indicates the way to *mokṣa* rather than material gain. The *Mahābhārata* attempts no exegesis of specific passages in pursuit of this notion, but merely makes the general claim that when properly understood by one who is wise or advanced in *yoga,* the Vedas also teach *mokṣa-dharma.*

In Chapter 238 of the *Śānti,* Vyāsa instructs his son Śuka on the subject of *adhyātma,* knowledge of the true self. In verse 13, concluding the discourse, Vyāsa states that this instruction which is a *śāstra–śāstram idaṁ putrānuśāsanam*–is the secret of, or is concealed in, all the Vedas–*rahasyaṁ sarva-vedānām.* He then explains:

dharmākhyāneṣu sarveṣu satyākhyāneṣu yad vasu
daśedam ṛk-sahasrāṇi nirmathyāmṛtam uddhṛtam

'All works on *dharma,* and all those based on truth, as well as ten thousand hymns of the *Ṛgveda* have been churned to extract this nectar.' (12.238.14)

Here the word *nirmathya* meaning to churn or rub, often in the sense of producing butter from milk or fire from wood, could be taken as a euphemism for a mode of exegesis, or the sense may be that these literatures have been studied exhaustively for the conclusions taught to be arrived at. In either sense the idea of a hidden meaning is apparent from the word *rahasyam* in verse 13, and this secret has been extracted by Vyāsa's acute insight.

In Chapter 291, King Karālajanaka asks Vasiṣṭha about the supreme eternal *brahman–param brahma-sanātanam*–from which one never returns (1). In reply Vasiṣṭha instructs the king in Sāṁkhya; in Chapter 293, vs 12-21, the king objects to Vasiṣṭha's teachings, arguing that matter and spirit, *prakṛti* and *puruṣa*, are united and interdependent and citing the Vedas as authority for this assertion–*evam etad dvija-śreṣṭha veda-śāstreṣu paṭhyate* (17). Vasiṣṭha's response to this is significant:

yad etad uktaṁ bhavatā veda-śāstra-nidarśanam
evam etad yathā caitan na gṛhṇāti tathā bhavān

dhāryate hi tvayā grantha ubhayor veda-śāstrayoḥ
na tu granthasya tattva-jño yathāvat tvaṁ nareśvara

yo hi vede ca śāstre ca grantha-dhāraṇa-tat-paraḥ
na ca granthārtha-tattva-jñas tasya tad dhāraṇaṁ vṛthā

bhāraṁ sa vahate tasya granthasyārthaṁ na vetti yaḥ
yas tu granthārtha-tattva-jño nāsya granthāgamo vṛthā

'What has been spoken by you regarding the Vedas and *śāstras* is so, but you do not take the texts as they should be taken.

You merely carry the words of both the Vedas and *śāstras,* but you do not properly understand the meaning of the text, O king.

One who bears just the words of the Vedas and *śāstras* but does not understand the true meaning and purpose of the text bears a burden uselessly.

One who does not know the true purpose of the text does indeed carry a heavy burden, but for one who knows

> the true meaning of the text the burden is never useless.' (12.293.22-25)

Vasiṣṭha admits that Karālajanaka knows the text of the Vedas, but he indicates that there is a deeper purpose contained therein. This *granthārtha-tattvam* is indicated later in the same chapter (29) to be the knowledge of Sāṁkhya and Yoga that Vasiṣṭha proceeds to impart. His sense thus seems to be that the same concepts of *mokṣa-dharma* are found in the Vedas and *śāstras,* but are not apparent through a superficial reading and may only be grasped by comprehension of the true, though apparently concealed, meaning.

The same point is reiterated in the teachings of Yājñavalkya to King Janaka, beginning from Chapter 298. In Chapter 306, following his lengthy discourse, he explains that he reached these conclusions after being enlightened in the Vedas and *Upaniṣads* by Sūrya, the Sun God. In verse 46, he recommends that all the Vedas should be studied and their rites observed. He then defines the *vedārtham,* the true aim of the Vedas, as knowing that from which all fallible beings take birth and die (47). If all the five Vedas (presumably this includes the *Purāṇas* and *Itihāsas*) and their branches are studied but one does not realise this true object of Vedic knowledge–*veda-vedyam*–then his study is simply a burden-*veda-bhāra-vaho hi saḥ* (48). If one churns ass's milk he will gain filth and not ghee, and similarly one who churns the Vedas but does not understand their object gains only the burden of his foolish ignorance (49-50). Again we have a teacher of Sāṁkhya claiming not to deny the Vedas but that his doctrines are the true conclusion of the Vedas, recognised within them only by those who are able to properly comprehend such wisdom. The fools will see only the superficial meaning and thus gain nothing from their efforts but the burden of study.

Passages which extol the notion of *bhakti* to both Śiva and Viṣṇu maintain a similar view, asserting that the true message of the Vedas aims at the glorification of either of the two Deities. Again there is no hint of genuine textual exegesis, simply the claim that this is the true object of the Vedas. In Chapter 47 of the *Śānti,* Bhīṣma adores Kṛṣṇa as the Supreme Being who is Viṣṇu himself. In verse 16 he states:

yaṁ vākeṣv anuvākeṣu niṣatsūpaniṣatsu ca
gṛṇanti satya-karmāṇaṁ satyaṁ satyeṣu sāmasu

'It is you whom in the *Vāks, Anuvāks, Niṣats* and *Upaniṣads* they declare to be true in action, and in the *Sāmas* to be the truth amongst all truths.'

In Chapter 321, at the beginning of the *Nārāyaṇīya,* Nārada praises Nārāyaṇa as the one whom the Vedas and *Purāṇas* glorify as the unborn, ever-existing, immortal sustainer, who has no equal (24). The Vedas and the scriptures for the different *āśramas,* though differing in their views, all speak with devotion of Nārāyaṇa (41). In Chapter 328, when Arjuna asks Kṛṣṇa, as Viṣṇu, about his names that are glorified by *maharṣis,* the latter replies by giving a list of scriptures–the *Ṛgveda, Yajurveda, Sāmaveda* and *Atharvaveda, Purāṇa* and *Upaniṣad,* the *Jyotis,* the *Āyurveda,* the Sāṁkhya and Yoga *śāstras*–in all of which the many names of the Deity are praised by great saints–*bahūni mama nāmāni kīrtitāni maharṣibhiḥ.*

These passages do not refer to a secret hermeneutic that reveals a hidden meaning in scriptural texts, but they do indicate an attempt to represent essentially non-Vedic doctrines as the real purpose of the Vedas. The point is summed up concisely in the *Bhagavad-gītā* wherein Kṛṣṇa explicitly asserts, "It is I who am known through all the Vedas"–*vedaiś ca sarvair aham eva vedyaḥ* (15.15). Even a casual acquaintance with the Vedas is sufficient for one to be aware that neither Kṛṣṇa nor Viṣṇu is the primary object of their devotions. Therefore Kṛṣṇa's statement must be taken as indicating that there is some other meaning or interpretation of the texts that reveals himself as their true object.

There are in addition several passages in the *Anuśāsana* that claim that Śiva is the true subject of the Vedas, most notably in the prayers of Tandin in Chapter 16. Here verse 44 states that it is Śiva whom the knowers of the Vedas comprehend, and who is indicated in the *Vedāntas*–*yaṁ ca veda-vido vedyaṁ vedānteṣu pratiṣṭhitam.* He is praised by the hymns of the *Ṛgveda,* the priests who recite the *Yajurveda* regard him as the object of the ritual (48), while the knowers of the *Sāmaveda* glorify him with their chanting of hymns–*sāmabhir yaṁ gāyanti sāmagāḥ śuddha-buddhayaḥ.* Tandin is making the same claim as noted above with regard to Viṣṇu, that the object of his devotion, Śiva, is the Supreme Spirit of all the world and is thus the sole object of all Vedic teachings.

7. Summary and Conclusions

1. A number of previous scriptural works are known to the authors of different passages of the epic. These are referred to at various times, but rarely directly quoted or cited as authority. The complex nature of the final text of the *Mahābhārata* makes all critical work on the relationship between the epic and other texts extremely problematical.

2. In the *Mahābhārata* we do not find the concept of canonicity as understood in a Christian sense. This lack of a hard dividing line in the consideration of scriptural texts works in two ways. On the one hand, virtually any literature, be it the Vedas, *Upaniṣads, Dharma-śāstras,* or works on Sāṁkhya, Yoga, astronomy or medicine, are taken as authoritative in a religious sense, for there is no evidence of any notion of secular literature. On the other hand, the authority ascribed by the *Mahābhārata* to these works is notably limited. They are viewed as relative rather than absolute, and hence subject to criticism and radical reinterpretation.

3. The distinction between *śruti* and *smṛti* is noted and sustained; *śruti* is eternal and divinely revealed while *smṛti* is the inspired composition of a man of wisdom. This does not, however, indicate any higher status being ascribed to *śruti,* and hence while the *Bhagavad-gītā* is critical of the *veda-vāda,* it describes its own teachings as the highest scripture–*uttamaṁ śāstram.* Similarly, the *Mahābhārata* does not refer to itself as *śruti* yet makes clear in several passages that it regards itself as the best of all scriptures, surpassing even the Vedas.

4. It is accepted within the *Mahābhārata* that there are different levels of religious attainment and different rites and practices appropriate for those at different levels. This perspective applies also to scripture, for those levels of religion, or *āśramas,* will each have their own scriptures, sometimes teaching different doctrines. This appears acceptable as long as the Vedas are not openly denied. Thus there is no universal gospel appropriate for all people, and it is made clear that certain teachings should be kept secret from the majority of the population lest they threaten social stability.

5. Where *pravṛtti* is stressed, the Vedas are regarded as the traditional, unchallengeable authority. The notion of *sva-dharma* is, however, somewhat removed from Vedic ideology and the epic's

attempt to equate *dharma* and *dharma-śāstra* with the injunctions of the Vedas is something of an imposition. Nonetheless, within the value system of *pravṛtti*, one who objects to *sva-dharma* is condemned as a denier of the Vedas and hence a *nāstika* or non-believer.

6. Teachings based on *nivṛtti* accept the concept of different levels of religion, and view the Vedas accordingly. The Vedas are related to creation, and hence to religious practices leading to success within the world rather than transcending it to gain salvation. The means of transcendence is *jñāna*, a state of continual awareness of one's true identity as a non-material being. Acquiring *jñāna* is not simply a matter of extensive study, but is to be achieved through self-discipline, practice and realisation. While one line of thought teaches that the rituals of the Vedas are to be transcended, another indicates that the Vedas also teach *mokṣa-dharma*, but that this teaching is secret or concealed and is apparent only to one who understands the true object of the Vedas.

7. The *Nārāyaṇīya* claims that *bhakti-śāstras*, such as those teaching Pañcarātra doctrines, are revealed by Nārāyaṇa himself, and therefore are as authoritative as *śruti*. Teachings stressing *bhakti* claim that the true object of the Vedas is Viṣṇu or Śiva, though presumably this understanding of the texts is possible only for one who is a devotee and therefore has true vision as to the inner meaning of the texts.

Notes

1. As, for example, in 9.17 of the *Bhagavad-gītā* and 12.230.8
2. As, for example, in 12.328.8
3. Hopkins, E.W. *The Great Epic of India*, Calcutta, 1969 (1st Ed 1901) p. 27.
4. Larson, G.J. *Classical Sāṁkhya, An Interpretation of its History and Meaning*, Delhi, 1969, p. 9.
5. Kane, P.V. *History of Dharma-śāstra*, Poona, 1968, p. 354.
6. Ibid, pp. 1173-1174.
7. This view is supported by Dasgupta who is of the opinion that the reference is either an interpolation or else is to be understood as referring to a work other than the *Brahma-sūtras* of Bādārayaṇa. (Dasgupta, S. *A History of Indian Philosophy*, Vol 2, Cambridge, 1973, p. 549).
8. Ibid, p. 21
9. Bhandarkar, R.G. *Vaiṣṇavism, Śaivism and Minor Religious Systems*, New York, 1980, p. 12.
10. Cited by Kane 1968, p. 315.

11. *The Laws of Manu,* translated by G. Bühler, Delhi, 1982.
12. Kane 1968, p. 344.
13. See, for example, 12.322.41-*asmāt pravakṣyate dharmān manuḥ svāyambhuvaḥ svayam,* 3.178.30-*asminn eva mati-dvaidhe manuḥ svāyambhuvo 'bravīt,* and 5.40.10-*gṛhe sthāpayitavyāni dhanyāni manur abravīt.*
14. Hopkins 1969, p. 21.
15. Cited by Kane 1968, p. 335.
16. Ibid, p. 344.
17. Ibid, p. 408.
18. See, for example, 12.321.24
19. See, for example, 1.102.17
20. See, for example, 12.330.22
21. See, for example, 12.328.8
22. Hopkins 1969, p. 61.
23. The notion of the *Purāṇas* and histories being the fifth Veda is an ancient one traceable as far back as the *Chāndogya Upaniṣad* (7.1.2-4) which states, *itihāśa-purāṇaḥ pañcamo vedānām.*

Chapter 3

RELIGIOUS ORGANISATION IN THE *MAHĀBHĀRATA*

1. Introduction

The question of whether an individual can act on his religious beliefs alone or whether it is required that he participate as a member of a group of believers is an important aspect of any religious doctrine. A number of questions are raised by such considerations: is it possible to contact the divine through one's own spiritual endeavours or is the gulf so wide that a church or individual is required to act as intercessor. Where a religious doctrine is not wholly individualistic, the relationship between those who adhere to it and society as a whole is a further issue that must be addressed. This involves consideration of the structure of such a community, which may range from a loose association of like-thinking individuals to a rigid hierarchy with strictly enforced regulations. Relations between spiritual and secular authorities, their separation or conjunction, raise further questions that religious traditions have sought to resolve in various ways over the centuries.

From a Western perspective, Hinduism is typically viewed as a faith firmly rooted in community, with the individual strictly regulated by the duties imposed upon him by his position within a caste-based social system. This social system is enforced by religious belief, for it is ordained by scripture and tradition. Whilst there is no Hindu 'Church' in the Christian sense, with a complex organisation and hierarchy there are specific sects, with unique beliefs and practices, which come closer to the concept of a 'Church'. Very few, however, have evolved any form of 'high ecclesiology' that demands membership as a prerequisite for salvation.

In terms of mediation between man and the divine, this role is occasionally taken by the *guru,* especially in tantric sects. More often, however, the *guru's* role is limited to that of teaching the scriptures and performing family rituals. The modern state of India has sought to imitate the Western model of a secular state, but traditionally the organisation of state and society were supposed to be based on the religious injunctions of *dharma-sāstra* (though it is probable that such teachings merely legitimated an evolving social order) and thus there was no theoretical division between the religious and the secular.

2. The *Mahābhārata's* Teachings on Social Structure

(i) The Four *Varṇas*

The position of the individual in society is viewed by the *Mahābhārata* as a religious issue, and is one of the major questions explored by the text. Yudhiṣṭhira's reluctance to perform his duty as a *kṣatriya* by encountering his political foes in war frequently focuses the narrative on the subject of an individual's social duties, whilst the numerous passages of the didactus which consider the tensions between *pravṛtti* and *nivṛtti* similarly concern themselves with this point. The system that Yudhiṣṭhira struggles to come to terms with is that of the four *varṇas* or social classes. From a Western perspective, the maintenance of such a social order is hardly religion, any more than the maintenance of feudalism was in medieval Europe. Nonetheless, for the *Mahābhārata,* or at least for those passages that teach *sva-dharma,* adherence to social obligations is an essential feature of religious life.

The system of the four *varṇas,* prescribed by the *dharma-śāstras,* is endowed with the same orthodox status as the Vedas. It is not the concoction of man, but the will of the divine as to how society should be structured, as Kṛṣṇa makes clear when he states, *cātur-varṇyaṁ mayā sṛṣṭam*–the four *varṇas* are created by me (*Bhagavad-gītā* 4.13). The *Mahābhārata* itself claims to be *dharma-śāstra* (1.56.21), and in various passages outlines the duties of these four orders in a manner similar to that of the *Manu-smṛti.*[1] In the earlier chapters of the *Śānti,* it is urged that correct adherence to social duties is the proper way of religious life leading to prosperity on earth and elevation to a higher sphere after death. In 12.25.22-33, Vyāsa tells Yudhiṣṭhira the story of King Hayagrīva who performed his duties as a *kṣatriya,* notably fighting heroically in battle and executing *yajñas,* and as a result gained the heaven of the gods after death–*hayagrīvo modate svarga-loke* (29). Bhīṣma further states that Viṣṇu is satisfied by proper execution of social duties (12.63.9), thereby confirming the teachings of Kṛṣṇa in the *Gītā.*

It is well known that in contemporary Hindu society there are no longer just four *varṇas,* but hundreds of different castes of varying social positions. The usual Hindu view is that these castes arose from the intermingling of the *varṇas.* If a mixed liaison occurred, then the offspring was assigned to a new social grouping that was different from that of either the father or mother. Thus numerous castes proliferated from the four original *varṇas* of the perfect Vedic society. Historically, however, it is far more likely that most castes emerged from occupational guilds or from tribal peoples being integrated into the social structure of Hindu kingdoms. The epic narrative and almost all the teachings on *sva-dharma* reflect the view of society as being divided into four *varṇas* only, *brāhmaṇas, kṣatriyas, vaiśyas* and *śūdras.* The *Anuśāsana,* however, in Chapters 47 to 49, recognises other castes and offers regulations for their coexistence in society. These other castes are presented as arising from mixed liaisons and these passages from the *Anuśāsana* reflect strong condemnation of any such trend, while in the *Rāja-dharma,* the death penalty is recommended for anyone causing the mixing of *varṇas,*

> *rājño vadhaṁ cikīrṣed yas tasya citro vadho bhavet*
> *ājīvakasya stenasya varṇa-saṁkarakasya ca*
>
> 'There should be death by various means for one who attempts to cause the death of the king, for one belonging to the Ājīvaka sect, for a thief, and for one who causes mixing of *varṇas*' (12.86.21).

(ii) *Sva-dharma* as an Individual's Inherent Nature

Up to this point the nature of *sva-dharma* has been considered as if it consisted of no more than the prescribed regulations of a religious system. An individual's *dharma,* however, is much more than a set of duties or pattern of life that he is obliged to follow. It is rather something that is a part of his very nature in this lifetime. Thus he has no real choice about acting in a certain way as a *brāhmaṇa, kṣatriya, vaiśya* or *śūdra.* Viewed from this perspective, Yudhiṣṭhira's refusal to fight is not merely a dereliction of religious duty, but a violation of nature. Kṛṣṇa views Arjuna's decision to abandon his *sva-dharma* in similar light, arguing not just that he ought to perform his duty but also that his inherent nature as a *kṣatriya* will compel him to act in such a way.

> *svabhāva-jena kaunteya nibaddhaḥ svena karmaṇā*
> *kartuṁ necchasi yan mohā kariṣyasy avaśo'pi tat*
>
> 'Bound by your own actions that are born from your nature you will be forced to perform that which you do not wish to do because of illusion. (18.60)

This intensely deterministic view of *dharma* is not, however, without mitigation. Arjuna is also told that he should act as he sees fit, as if he does indeed have a choice, and Yudhiṣṭhira repeatedly displays an individualistic attitude towards the strictures imposed by his *varṇa.*

There is furthermore a recognition that there are outsiders who neither accept any form of *sva-dharma* nor acknowledge the social order of four *varṇas.* These are either members of sects who reject the traditional orthodoxy, referred to as *nāstikas,* or tribes who do not conform to Vedic and dharma-śāstric norms. The most graphic illustration of the latter case is found in the quarrel between Karṇa and Śalya in Chapters 27 to 30 of the *Karṇa.* Therein Karṇa savagely defames Śalya's people, the Madrakas, condemning their disregard for the regulations of religious life. The term he uses is *mleccha,* defined by Monier-Williams as, 'a foreigner, barbarian, non-Āryan, man of an outcast race, any person who does not speak Sanskrit and does not conform to the usual Hindu institutions':[2]

> *madrakāḥ sindhu-sauvīrā dharmaṁ vidyuḥ kathaṁ tv iha*
> *pāpa-deśodbhavā mlecchā dharmāṇām avicakṣaṇāḥ*
>
> 'But how can the Madrakaṣ and Sindhu-Sauvīras know about *dharma* in this regard, *mlecchas* that they are, born in a sinful land, ignorant of the branches of *dharma.*' (8.27.91)

(iii) The Hierarchy of the Social Order

Within the social order prescribed by the *Mahābhārata* there is a clear hierarchy and ruling elite. The *vaiśyas* are the merchants and agriculturalists who provide taxes to finance the kingdom, while the *śūdras* are the labourers, artisans and performing artists. There appear also to have been slaves kept by kings,[3] though details of this institution are vague and are never discussed in any of the epic's dharma-śāstric passages. Above the *vaiśyas* and *śūdras* are the *kṣatriyas,* the kings and warriors, and the *brāhmaṇas,* the priests who perform *yajñas* on behalf of the kings. This hierarchical social system of four *varṇas* is enforced by tradition, religious legitimation, and also, where necessary, by physical compulsion. The *Rāja-dharma* makes it clear that it is the king's duty to force all the citizens of his kingdom to live according to the regulations of *sva-dharma.* Thus Bhīṣma instructs Yudhiṣṭhira, *daṇḍa-nītiḥ sva-dharmebhyaś cāturvarṇyaṁ niyacchati* - the science of punishment regulates the four *varṇas* in terms of their prescribed duties (12.70.3).

The *brāhmaṇas* and *kṣatriyas* together form the ruling elite of society, but it must be emphasised that the distinction between them is primarily one of function within a religious system rather than between distinctive religious and secular social institutions. The *brāhmaṇas* have a role in the administration of the state by acting as advisors to the *kṣatriyas,*

sva-dharma-paritṛptāya yo na vitta-paro bhavet
yo rājānaṁ nayed buddhyā sarvataḥ paripūrṇayā

brāhmaṇo hi kule jātaḥ kṛta-prajño vinīta-vāk
śreyo nayati rājānaṁ bruvaṁś citrāṁ sarasvatīm

rājā carati yaṁ dharmaṁ brāhmaṇena nidarśitam
śuśrūṣur anahaṁvādī kṣatra-dharma-vrate sthitaḥ

'Such (a *brāhmaṇa*), who in order to satisfy his own *dharma* has no desire for wealth, should guide the king completely in all matters through his intellect.

> Born in a good family, the wise, modestly-spoken *brāhmaṇa* guides the king towards prosperity, speaking in a manner that is clear and eloquent:
>
> The king follows his proper duty, instructed by the *brāhmaṇa,* listening carefully, without presumption, fixed in the regulations of *kṣatriya-dharma.*' (12.73.15-17)

In his final instructions to Yudhiṣṭhira on how to rule the kingdom, Dhṛtarāṣtra gives the same advice, urging that he should have as ministers *brāhmaṇas* who are endowed with wisdom–*mantrinaś caiva kurvīthā dvijān vidyā-viśāradān* (15.9.20).

Neither is the king merely a secular administrator and protector of the kingdom. His royal duty is his *sva-dharma,* and hence an act of religious significance, and he is also the performer of *yajñas* which satisfy and nourish the gods–*devā . . . yajñam evopajīvanti* (12.73.21)–and thereby bring prosperity to the kingdom. Performance of *yajña* is an essential part of *rāja-dharma,* dependent on cooperation between *brāhmaṇas* and *kṣatriyas,* for the well-being of the kingdom depends upon it. Therefore Bhīṣma says, in concluding the story of King Mucukunda, that the greatest success is obtained in ruling a kingdom when there is cooperation between the king and the *brāhmaṇas* (12.75.21-22).

A prominent feature of the teachings of the *Mahābhārata* is the repeated stress placed on the injunction that *kṣatriyas* must respect, honour and provide for the *brāhmaṇas.* Time and again throughout the text this point is reiterated through the example of the Pāṇḍavas in the narrative, through instructive stories about righteous kings, and through repeated instructions from Bhīṣma and other teachers of *rāja-dharma.*,Of equal significance is the injunction that *brāhmaṇas* are not to gain materially from their elevated position in society, but are to remain renounced and aloof from the acquirement of riches.[1]

The *Rāja-dharma* is insistent that recognition and privelege must be allowed to the community of *brāhmaṇas.* They are to be neither punished for misdeeds (12.56.22) nor taxed even in times of emergency (12.72.22). The one rule of kingship that can never be transgressed, even when a king is faced with the most pressing danger, is that he must always serve *brāhmaṇas,* for this is the height of purity–*brāhmaṇān eva seveta . . . pavitraṁ hy etad uttamam* (12.140.35). The very last instruction given by Bhīṣma before he passes away after months of lying wounded on the battlefield reemphasises the respect that must be paid to *brāhmaṇas.*

> *brāhmaṇāś caiva te nityaṁ prājñāś caiva viseṣataḥ*
> *ācāryā ṛtvijaś caiva pūjanīyā narādhipa*
>
> 'O lord of men, the *brāhmaṇas,* and especially those who are wise, the teachers and the priests at *yajñas,* should always be worshipped by you.' (13.153.50)

At certain points it is even suggested that the *brāhmaṇas* have divine status. In Chapter 136 of the *Anuśāsana,* Yudhiṣṭhira asks Bhīṣma who should be worshipped and respected. Predictably, Bhīṣma replies that it is the *brāhmaṇas,* and then launches into a eulogy of that *varṇa,* saying they are the refuge of all people but can bring destruction when angered. In verses 21-23, he concludes by saying that like a fire a *brāhmaṇa* can never be tainted by wicked deeds and even if ignorant is to be considered as a god–*avidvāṁś caiva vidvāṁs ca brāhmaṇo daivataṁ mahat.* Again, in 14.50.12, Kṛṣṇa, instructing Arjuna, refers to the *brāhmaṇas* as, *ete viśvakṛto viprāḥ* - the creators of the world.

It is tempting to guess at the actual social order that underlay the brahminical view of an ideally structured society presented in the *Mahābhārata.* The continual emphasis on the respect that must be offered by kings to *brāhmaṇas* suggests that the position of the latter was somewhat less secure than the authors of the epic would have liked. Historically, the rise in significance of the heterodox sects, paralleled by a decline in the importance of *yajña* and the Vedic religion in general, may well have meant that the traditional *brāhmaṇa* communities were under pressure in the epic period, and that the teachings noted above are part of an attempt by the *brāhmaṇas* to reassert their authority. Interesting as such speculations may be, they can be considered no more than conjecture; taken at face value it is apparent that the *Mahābhārata* considers the status of the *brāhmaṇas* essential for the maintenance of a proper social order that reflects the traditional values revealed in the Vedas and made explicit in the *dharma-śāstras.*

Several writers have argued that the *Mahābhārata* narrative indicates underlying conflict between the *brāhmaṇas* and *kṣatriyas.* Grierson contends that the account of the struggle between the Pāṇḍavas and Kauravas is based on historical conflict between *brāhmaṇas* and *kṣatriyas,* and that this tension underlies much of the epic.[5] Pargiter sought to isolate two strands of Sanskrit literature, one representing a *kṣatriya* tradition and the other that of the *brāhmaṇas,* which reflect ongoing conflicts between the two superior *varṇas.*[6] The evidence for such theories is inadequate to render their conclusions anything more than speculation, however, and in this regard Pusalker's warning is apposite,

> . . . some stray quarrels between individual kings and their priests do not warrant the inference of a fight between the Church and the State, which European scholars are always prone to draw on the analogy of similar eternal quarrels in their own country.[7]

Heesterman further argues that stories of *brāhmaṇa/kṣatriya* conflict have nothing to do with social tensions, but are in fact resonances of the agonistic form of the pre-classical *yajña,* an essential element of which was the opposition between the performer and a rival faction.[8]

On the other hand, it is reasonable to presume, the nature of power being what it is, that relations between two factions within a ruling élite would not always be harmonious, and the *Mahābhārata* does provide evidence suggesting such conflict. Firstly, the repeated stress on respect for *brāhmaṇas* within the *Rāja-dharma* arouses suspicion that from the brahminical perspective kings did not have sufficient regard for their status. Secondly, within the epic certain instances of such conflict are recounted. Most notable here is the character of Paraśurāma, who appears regularly throughout the story. The fullest account of his activities appears in Chapters 115 to 117 of the *Vana.* Paraśurāma is a *brāhmaṇa* who becomes a warrior when his father is first insulted and then murdered by the King of the Haihayas, Kārtavīrya Arjuna, and his sons. In the ensuing conflict twenty-one generations of *kṣatriyas* are destroyed, and even during the epic's central narrative, Rāma makes appearances still apparently nursing a grudge against the ruling order.

Another notable episode takes place during Draupadī's *svayaṁvara.* There Arjuna, disguised as a *brāhmaṇa,* defeats all the kings in an archery contest and wins the hand of Draupadī. At this, the defeated monarchs rise up to express their rage that a royal princess should be married to a *brāhmaṇa,* displaying an attitude towards *brāhmaṇas* that is far removed from that recommended by

Bhīṣma in the *Śānti.* They wish to kill Drupada for offering his daughter to a *brāhmaṇa,* whom they consider unqualified even to attend such a *svayaṁvara* (1.180.10). All the *brāhmaṇas,* waving their deer skins and water pots, then prepare to fight the kings, but are restrained by Arjuna and Bhīma (1.181.1-2) who proceed to defeat all their opponents by themselves. Only after they have been routed do the *kṣatriyas* conclude, somewhat disingenuously, that even though they have given offence, *brāhmaṇas* should always be protected (1.181.31).

(iv) Conclusions

1. The values of *pravṛtti* dictate that society should be divided into four *varṇas,* though the *Anuśāsana* indicates that sub-*varṇas* with their own codes of practice have come into being through mixing of the main *varṇas.* The two upper *varṇas* form a ruling élite and ideally should work together to ensure that the material, spiritual and moral well-being of the whole of society is maintained.
2. No rigid distinction is observed between secular and spiritual spheres of life. Society should be structured and governed in accordance with divinely ordained regulations and guided by *brāhmaṇas* who are endowed with superior wisdom. Within the ruling élite, the *kṣatriyas* must make it their highest duty to revere, serve and maintain the *brāhmaṇas.* The *brāhmaṇas* are the true owners of all land, but allow the *kṣatriyas* to enjoy the wealth while they themselves abjure all desire for power and riches.
3. One suspects that the presentation of an ideal community offered by the *Mahābhārata* is reflective more of theory than practice. There are indications, particularly from the story of Paraśurāma, that relations between *brāhmaṇas* and *kṣatriyas* were not always harmonious. There is historical evidence, however, notably the example of Candragupta Maurya and Cānakya, to show that the system advocated in the epic did function to some extent in practice as well.
4. By properly fulfilling his duties in accordance with the regulations of *sva-dharma,* the individual gains success both in this world and the next, through prosperity here and then elevation to *svarga-loka* or rebirth in a superior *varṇa.*
5. Peoples, tribes and individuals who do not accept the prescribed

social order are condemned and despised as a lower type of human being.

6. The society described in the *Mahābhārata* is not an 'ecclesia' in the classical Christian sense. There is no sense of mission and no imperative felt to spread the message or enlarge the community. Neither is there any concept of the community and its hierarchy acting in the role of mediator between man and the divine. The beliefs underpinning the social order are essentially eudaemonistic. If the individual acts in the appropriate manner the result is guaranteed, without intrusion from any concept of grace. A personal God is involved only as the creator of the cosmic order which is represented in human society as *dharma,* as its preserver in times of crisis and where the concept of *sva-dharma* is drawn into the realm of *bhakti,* notably in the teachings of the *Bhagavad-gītā.*

3. Communal Religious Practice and Worship

Though society as a whole is thus to be structured in accordance with divine injunction, the didactic passages of the epic place little stress on communal religious practice. *Yajñas* are performed by the *kṣatriyas* and *brāhmaṇas* together, but there is no instruction for the whole community to come together on such occasions. The function of the *yajña* in nourishing the gods and sustaining the order of the universe is achieved without any need for mass participation. From Chapter 30 of the *Sabhā,* which describes the preparations for the *Rājasūya yajña,* we learn that *vaiśyas* and *śūdras* were invited to the ceremony–*viśaś ca mānyāñ śūdrāṁś ca sarvān ānayateti ca* (41). This may indicate that the whole community assembled to witness the performance of a *yajña,* but the absence of any injunction to this effect in the didactic passages on *sva-dharma* must make one cautious about pressing the point too far. The reasonable conclusion is that if such assemblies did take place, they were not considered essential for the successful conclusion of a *yajña.* This is certainly the view of Heesterman who is emphatic that the classical form of Vedic *yajña* was an individual act: "First, though the ritual is a regeneration of the universe, it is not communal, but a strictly private celebration, centring on the single yajamāna who is the sole beneficiary."[9]

It is also instructive to note the infrequency of references either to the worship of images or construction of temples. Brockington notes that inscriptional evidence shows that there were temples dedicated to Kṛṣṇa in Mathurā in the second century A.D.,[10] while Pusalker puts the date as early as the second century B.C.[11] According to Bharadvāja, a temple dedicated to Vāsudeva and Saṁkarṣaṇa discovered at Nagarī and dated at between 350 and 250 B.C, is the oldest yet discovered,[12] while Krishna Moorthy states that the Besnagar Pillar inscription reveals that there was a Kṛṣṇa temple in Vidiśa in the second century B.C.[13]

Such archaeological evidence reveals that temples did exist during the epic period, although not how widespread they were. The paucity of references in the epic indicates that temple worship in this early period was confined to a relatively small number of locations, although there is a possibility that it was a practice begun amongst the less orthodox devotional sects and hence not encouraged by the authors of the *Mahābhārata.* Brockington sees temple worship as taking the place of *yajña,* with the symbolic continuity expressed in the design of early temples which was based on the sacrificial arena in which the *yajña* was performed.[14]

The *Mahābhārata* provides virtually no evidence of any such development taking place during the epic period. Kings who have riches are urged to perform *yajñas* and never once in any of the teachings on *rāja-dharma* to construct temples for the worship of gods or their images. At the beginning of the *Śānti,* for example, when Yudhiṣṭhira proposes to renounce the kingdom and go to the forest to live as a hermit, Arjuna praises wealth as it enables one to perform religious acts (12.8.13-20). That he is referring to *yajña* here is made clear from 12.8.27–*yaṣṭavyaṁ caiva yatnataḥ*– and there is no hint of temple building as a religious act for the wealthy. The *Nārāyaṇīya* is clearly influenced by the ideas of the Pañcarātras, a sect whose main religious practice is known from later texts to have been the worship of images in temples. Even there, however, we find no instructions on image worship, apart from a passing reference in the *Anugītā* (14.18.8.), nor any reference to temples.

Thus it is safe to assert that worship of images and gods in temples is not recognised by the *Mahābhārata* as a feature of the religion it expounds. There are, however, a few passages to be noted that suggest that the authors were at least aware of such practices. In the *Vana,* where Mārkaṇḍeya tells the Pāṇḍavas of the terrible conditions at the end of the Kali age, he makes the point that the places of the gods–*deva-sthāneṣu*–will be desecrated and the surface of the earth will no longer be decorated by the houses of the gods–*na deva-gṛha-bhūṣitā* (3.188.65-66). In Chapter 108 of the *Bhīṣma,* Droṇa describes to his son, Aśvatthāman, the omens that presage the fall of Bhīṣma. In verse 11 he says,

> *devatāyatana-sthāś ca kauravendrasya devatāḥ*
> *kampante ca hasante ca nṛtyanti ca rudanti ca* .
>
> 'The images of the gods of the King of the Kauravas, situated in the house of the gods, tremble, laugh, dance and cry.'

Devatāḥ here almost certainly refers to images of gods and *devatāyatana* must mean the abode of such images, for it is virtually impossible to conceive of any alternative meaning. The same phrase, *devatāyatanāni,* is used in 12.232.26 in a list of places wherein *yoga* exercises should be practised. Chapter 10 of the *Anuśāsana* relates the story of a *śūdra* who was instructed in the Vedas. Describing his spiritual inclinations, it mentions that he went to the forest and built an *āśrama,* part of which consisted of *devatāyatanāni.*

There are also references to *gṛha-devatās,* household gods, suggesting that images were worshipped by individual families within the home. Chapters 101 to 103 of the *Anuśāsana* contain a discussion of the offering of lamps, fruits, flowers, food, and incense, items that in temple worship are presented as offerings to the deities. In Chapter 101, however, it is urged that such offerings be made to the gods, *yakṣas, uragas,* and *rākṣasas*–the lower celestial beings that must be propitiated (58). It is also stated that a household shines with beauty when the first portion of food is offered to the *gṛha-devatās*–*jvalaty aharato veśma yāś cāsya gṛha-devatāḥ* (13.101.63).

It thus appears that offerings such as those made in temples were known to the authors of the *Mahābhārata.* In the *Bhagavad-gītā,* Kṛṣṇa urges Arjuna, in a verse which according to Dasgupta, "undoubtedly refers to image-worship",[15] that he should be worshipped in this manner,

> *patraṁ puṣpaṁ phalaṁ toyaṁ yo me bhaktyā prayacchati*
> *tad ahaṁ bhakty-upahṛtam aśnāmi prayatātmanaḥ*

> 'One offers me with devotion a leaf, a flower, a fruit, and water. I accept that devotional offering from one who is righteous at heart.' (9.26)

The scarcity of such references, however, especially when compared to the stress on *yajña*, indicates that large-scale communal worship of this type was not widespread, and that the progression from *yajña* to temple indicated by Brockington was still in its beginning stages. Where there is reference to *devatāyatanāni*, houses of the gods, it seems more likely that these were the worship places of individual households, as are found in many Hindu homes today, rather than places of communal worship. It is surely significant that there is no injunction anywhere in the epic for the wealthy to construct large temples; always the command is to use wealth for *yajña*. Of course the version of the *Mahābhārata* may reflect the aspiration of the authors rather than historical reality, but from a doctrinal perspective it must be asserted that temple worship is unimportant or even unknown to the epic. Duties are performed by each section of society, and *yajña* is the duty of *brāhmaṇas* and *kṣatriyas*. There is no apparent religious function that calls for the communal assembly of all members of society for worship.

4. Religious Organisation from the Perspective of *Nivṛtti*

The social structure based on four *varṇas* is challenged by the ideas of *mokṣa-dharma* which urge a withdrawal from society in order to search for salvation. Those who practise *sva-dharma* are not offered salvation as a goal,[16] but only prosperity in this life and a superior rebirth in the next. Therefore *mokṣa-dharma* entails the abandonment of community and the individual's position within it. This is clearly confirmed in Chapter 266 of the *Śānti*, where Bhīṣma admits that it is a different path, just as the path to the eastern ocean is different from that to the west (4).

Despite the conventional wisdom that Hinduism is a communal religion, the way to salvation given by the *Mahābhārata* is wholly individualistic. The institution of *āśramas*, dividing a *brāhmaṇa*'s life into four stages, can be seen as an attempt at integrating the institution of four *varṇas* with renunciation and the search for *mokṣa*. As described in Chapters 61 and 62 of the *Śānti*, a *brāhmaṇa* is first a student or *brahmacārin*, then a householder or *gṛhastha*, then a forest dweller or *vanaprastha*, and finally a complete renunciant or *saṁnyāsin.* This integration of renunciation and *mokṣa-dharma* with conventional *sva-dharma* does not, however, make the quest for salvation any the less individualistic and it is clear that while the *pravṛtti* view may be that *mokṣa-dharma* is for *brāhmaṇas* is the last stage of life, this notion is not shared by the exponents of *nivṛtti.*

It is noteworthy that while teachings on *sva-dharma* dictate a rigid delineation of *varṇas* based on birth alone, the teachers of *mokṣa-dharma* take a more flexible view. One's *varṇa* is not just a matter of birth but depends on individual qualities and tendencies. 12.182.8, for example, states that if a *śūdra* has the qualities of a *brāhmaṇa,* then he should be taken as such and vice-versa, while Vyāsa instructs his son that no man or woman is disqualified from the practice of *yoga* merely on the basis of their position in the social hierarchy (12.232.32). *Nivṛtti* views the individual as a spiritual entity separate from the body and hence, despite the apparent designations of *varṇa,* or even species, each individual being is essentially equal. The *Bhagavad-gītā* asserts,

> *vidyā-vinaya-sampanne brāhmaṇe gavi hastini*
> *śuni caiva śva-pāke ca paṇḍitāḥ sama-darśinaḥ*
>
> 'The wise men view equally a *brāhmaṇa* who is mild and learned, a cow, an elephant, a dog, and one who eats the flesh of dogs.' (5.18)

The individual pursuing *mokṣa-dharma* in effect renounces his membership of society in his attempt to transcend all material designations. Even the Vedas, the hallmark of orthodox belief, are abandoned, their rituals, priests and social forms irrelevant in the quest for salvation.

There is no question here of any mediation through God's representative body on earth to grant the individual salvation. *Mokṣa-dharma* centres on the transformation of the consciousness of the individual, away from attachment and desire towards *jñāna,* the realisation of the self as transcendent to the world of matter. Thus while *sva-dharma* is essentially religious practice within a community, salvation is gained by the individual alone contacting the divine through self-transformation. There is no reference to any 'community of believers' in *mokṣa-dharma,* and the practioner of *yoga* is urged to eschew all contact with other people:

> *yogī yuñjīta satatam ātmānaṁ rahasi sthitaḥ*
> *ekākī yata-cittātmā nirāśīr aparigrahaḥ*
>
> 'The practitioner of *yoga* must constantly engage himself in *yoga* in a deserted place, living alone, controlling his mind and self, without desire and without possessions.' (*Bhg.* 6.10)

It is true that there are apparently ascetics living in the forest in communities, such as those encountered in the stories of Nala and Damayanti (3.61), Śakuntalā (1.63-69), and Savitrī (3.277-283), but these are never portrayed as a sect of *mokṣa-dharmins.* Theorising as to the sources of the treatises of the *Mokṣa-dharma,* van Buitenen offers a picture of different schools and *āśramas* in which Sāṁkhya and Yoga were taught to novitiates.[17] The accuracy of this picture must remain a matter of conjecture, but it is noteworthy that the passages themselves make virtually no reference to *āśramas* of this type and appear to attach little importance to membership of or adherence to any such group. Clearly, there is no question of organisation for the purpose of mission, for *mokṣa-dharma* is to be practised only by a very few individuals who are uniquely qualified, and membership of any sect or group is never presented as a prerequisite for gaining salvation.

(i) The Position of the *Guru* as Mediator

In some of the later Hindu sects the *guru* takes the role of mediator between man and the Deity. There is no concept here of a divinely empowered community or body, but an individual by his own specific powers is able to elevate his disciple towards *mokṣa.* In the *Mahābhārata,* there is frequent reference to the role of *guru,* but never as a transcendent mediator. In the epic, the *guru* is a performer of auspicious rituals, as Dhaumya is for the Pāṇḍavas, or the imparter of different forms of knowledge, as Droṇa is to the Pāṇḍavas and Kauravas in teaching the science of warfare.

It is the duty of a *brāhmaṇa* boy to study the Vedas from a *guru* as a celibate student or *brāhmacārin.* This institution is well illustrated by the story of Uttaṅka's devotion to his *guru,* narrated in Chapter 3 of the *Ādi.* In Chapter 234 of the *Śānti,* Vyāsa instructs that a *brahmacārin* should live at the house of his *guru,* or his *guru*'s son, and render menial service to them in return for the teachings in the Vedas that he is given (16-29). This formal relationship exists within the context of *sva-dharma* for *brāhmaṇas,* but the role of a *guru* as an imparter of the wisdom that is the basis of *mokṣa-dharma* is also apparent in the *Śānti,* wherein one teacher after another is introduced giving instructions on *mokṣa* to one or more disciples, and one of the longer treatises takes the form of a discussion between *guru* and disciple (chs. 203-210). In the *Bhagavad-gītā,* Kṛṣṇa tells Arjuna,

> *tad viddhi praṇipātena paripraśnena sevayā*
> *upadekṣyanti te jñānaṁ jñāninas tattva-darśinaḥ*
>
> *yaj jñātvā na punar moham evaṁ yāsyasi pāṇḍava*
> *yena bhūtāny aśeṣāṇi drakṣyasy ātmany atho mayi*
>
> 'You should understand this by humble submission, by enquiry and by service. The wise who see the truth will give wisdom to you.
>
> Having understood this wisdom, by which you will see all beings in the self, that is to say in me, you will never again fall prey to illusion.' (4.34-35)

In Chapter 44 of the *Udyoga,* Sanat-sujāta makes the same point to Dhṛtarāṣṭra, saying that by serving their *gurus* and living an austere life, *brahmacārins* gain *mokṣa* (3-8). Clearly then the role of a *guru* is important both in the *sva-dharma* of a *brāhmaṇa* and in the practice of *mokṣa-dharma.* In neither case, however, does the *guru* take the role of mediator or intercessor. For a *brāhmaṇa* he imparts the Vedic teachings that allow the individual to practise his *sva-dharma.* For the practitioner of *mokṣa-dharma* he imparts the ideas, and possibly the *yoga* practices, that form the basis of the individual's quest for *jñāna,* the transformation of consciousness that brings salvation. At no point do we find the *guru* using his own power to transform the consciousness as an external agent. *Mokṣa-dharma* is a religion for the individual with no mediator and the *guru* does no more than provide the philosophical basis that is the beginning point of the individual's personal quest.

(ii) The *Bhagavad-gītā* and Religious Organisation

It has been noted before that the *Bhagavad-gītā* teaches a form of *mokṣa-dharma* that does not entail renunciation of dharmic duties.

The doctrine of *niṣkāma-karma,* central to the *Gītā,* dictates that social obligations should be carried on, but without desire for consequent personal gain, to ensure that society flourishes and to set a proper example for the mass of the people for whom *mokṣa-dharma* is forbidden. The goal of the *Bhagavad-gītā* is primarily *mokṣa,* although certain passages do appear to focus on worldly success.[18] The *Gītā* does not, however, accept that the quest for *mokṣa* necessitates a total disregard for community. This idea of *niṣkāma-karma* is not unique to the *Bhagavad-gītā* and is expressed in other parts of the *Mahābhārata,* notably by Arjuna in Chapter 16 of the *Śānti,* by Vyāsa in Chapter 26, and by Janaka, a king cited by Kṛṣṇa to illustrate his teachings (*Bhg.* 3.20), in Chapters 268 and 312.

It should not be misunderstood, however, that Kṛṣṇa is teaching that salvation is reached as the end result of dharmic action. The key to *mokṣa* remains either the transformation of one's consciousness, or else the grace of God bestowed upon an individual devotee. In the *Gītā,* Kṛṣṇa does not advocate *sva-dharma* in accordance with *pravṛtti* values. He argues that social duties must be performed, but the stress is on detachment and never seeking personal gain through any action. Dharmic duty is reinterpreted in the *Gītā* as a form of *yoga* executed by the individual, so that the individualistic quest for *mokṣa* takes place even within the context of social organisation.

The teachings of the *Bhagavad-gītā* are aimed at the individual rather than any community or sect. The soteriology it espouses illustrates this very clearly. The individual is urged to remain within society and perform his duties as dictated by *dharma. Mokṣa,* however, is sought not on a communal level, but is attained through the individual within the community achieving a higher awareness of spiritual identity. The duties of *sva-dharma* can lead to *mokṣa* only if they are performed as devotional acts dedicated to Kṛṣṇa, thereby invoking his grace, or as acts of *yoga* through which the individual may transform his consciousness. This is made clear in verses 42 to 46 of Chapter 18 wherein Kṛṣṇa first briefly explains the duties and dispositions expected of each *varṇa,* and then in verse 45 states that a man can obtain perfection by performing such duties. In verse 46 it is explained how this takcs place:

yataḥ pravṛttir bhūtānāṁ yena sarvam idaṁ tatam ·
sva-karmaṇā tam abhyarcya siddhiṁ vindati mānavaḥ

'Having worshipped that one who is the origin of all beings and by whom all this is pervaded by performing his own duties, a person gains perfection.'

In the *Bhagavad-gītā,* the doctrine of *niṣkāma-karma,* duty performed without desire for personal gain, thus shades into that of *bhakti,* for dharmic duties are to be performed for the satisfaction of the Supreme Being. *Bhakti* in the *Gītā,* like *yoga,* is the action and disposition of an individual, and there is little or no reference to any sect or community of devotees within the text. 10.9 refers to devotees conversing and joyfully sharing their experiences of devotion–*bodhayantaḥ parasparam, kathayantaś ca*–but there is nothing to indicate any form of religious organisation. In 9.13-14, where the activities of a devotee are described, it is in terms of an individual rather than a community and in the final teachings on devotion, Kṛṣṇa instructs that the individual can establish his own relationship of surrender with the Deity and then need have no further recourse to any form of *dharma.*

sarva-dharmān parityajya mām ekaṁ śaraṇaṁ vraja
ahaṁ tvā sarva-pāpebhyo mokṣayiṣyāmi mā śucaḥ

'Having given up all forms of *dharma,* find shelter with me alone. I will deliver you from all sins, do not fear.' (18.66)

Here Arjuna is urged to abandon the communal religion that is his *dharma* and as an individual depend on the grace of God. Normally the abandonment of *dharma* is a great sin and produces evil results, but here the devotee is assured that the grace of the Deity will deliver him. Thus, although Kṛṣṇa stresses the importance of *sva-dharma,* the path to *mokṣa* he espouses is not a communal one. The instruction is for the individual on the individualist path of *mokṣa-dharma* as to how he should interact with the community and its religious order to ensure that society is not harmed by his striving for salvation.

There is little or no reference to mission in the *Gītā,* although 18.68 might possibly be construed as such,

ya idaṁ paramaṁ guhyaṁ mad-bhakteṣv abhidhāsyati
bhaktiṁ mayi parāṁ kṛtvā mām evaiṣyaty asaṁśayaḥ

'One who explains this supreme secret to my devotees, having performed pure devotion unto me, will come to me without fail.'

This can hardly be taken as urging the development of an organisation to spread the message, and is more in line with 10.9 in seeing devotees interacting on an informal basis. In any case, ideas of mission seem to be ruled out by the previous verse which orders that the *Gītā* should not be taught to those who are not devotees, who are not reverential in hearing, or to those who are envious. As we have seen, this is an injunction typically applied to teachings on *mokṣa-dharma.*

5. Religious Organisation from the Perspective of *Bhakti*

(i) Introduction

In neither *sva-dharma* nor *mokṣa-dharma* is there any need for a mediator between man and the divine. The execution of *sva-dharma* is typically performed without reference to the Deity, and, as in Mimāṁsa thought, can be atheistic, remaining as no more than adherence to a set of laws that brings a result when followed. The question of the Law Maker, or of direct approaches to Him to gain the same or a better result, does not arise. The practice of *mokṣa-dharma* is likewise essentially non-theistic, for the individual executes the process of self-transformation without the necessity of appealing to any external divinity. *Bhakti,* however, is different in that it seeks salvation from an external source, the Deity–Viṣṇu or Śiva–whose grace will deliver individuals who surrender to Him. It is on the basis of such theology that the notion of a mediator or intercessor between man and the divine is likely to be introduced. The idea that the gulf between man and God is so vast that the Deity can only be approached through a mediating body of individual is certainly the basis of Christian ecclesiology. Therefore, in the epic, parallel notions are most likely to be found where the doctrines of *bhakti* are stressed.

Ideas on *bhakti* in the *Mahābhārata* are found throughout the text, but are expressed particularly in the following passages: 1. In the narrative where the divine presence of Kṛṣṇa is noted as a principal element in the story. 2. In the *Bhagavad-gītā.* 3. In the *Nārāyaṇīya.* 4. In various passages, most notably in the *Anuśāsana,* where Śiva is glorified.

(ii) Devotion to Kṛṣṇa in the Narrative

A prominent feature of the epic narrative is the presence of Kṛṣṇa. He is Viṣṇu, the Supreme Deity, descended to earth to ensure that events unfold towards the preservation of *dharma* and the success of the gods. There is, however, no reference at all within the narrative to any Kṛṣṇaite sect and no hint of instruction that one should become a member of any such group. Despite Kṛṣṇa's divine status, he remains a very approachable Deity. He is God in all respects, and yet even flawed characters such as Bhīma, Dhṛtarāṣṭra, or Karṇa are able to meet him face to face without need for mediation. There is thus no indication of a great divide between man and God which necessitates recourse to any type of intercessor in the expression of an individual's devotion.

(iii) The *Bhagavad-gītā*

In the *Bhagavad-gītā,* Kṛṣṇa tells Arjuna that worshipping him is the most direct means of gaining *mokṣa.* The *bhakti* that is taught therein is strictly individualistic, a one-to-one relationship between the votary and the Deity. In some passages, devotees worshipping Kṛṣṇa are referred to in the plural (9.13-14, 10.10-11, or 10.9) and this may be seen as implying groups of devotees communing together in some way. There is, however, nothing at all to indicate the existence of the Vāsudeva-Kṛṣṇa cult referred to by Bhandarkar,[19] nor to suggest that the author felt that adherence to a particular sect was important. Later devotional sects, such as the Śaivite Liṅgāyats[20] and the followers of Rāmānanda,[21] opposed the caste system and allowed individuals of different castes to worship together. The *Bhagavad-gītā,* however, reaffirms the importance of the system of four *varṇas* and urges the devotee of Kṛṣṇa to remain fixed in the duties of his *varṇa,* executing such obligations as acts of devotion. In Chapter 9, the *Gītā* specifically addresses the question of the status of the *varṇas* in relation to the worship of the Deity.

> *māṁ hi pārtha vyapāśritya ye 'pi syuḥ pāpa-yonayaḥ*
> *striyo vaiśyās tathā śūdrās te 'pi yānti parāṁ gatim*

> *kiṁ punar brāhmaṇāh puṇyā bhaktā rājarṣayas tathā*
> *anityam asukhaṁ lokam imaṁ prāpya bhajasva mām*
>
> 'Having surrendered to me, even those who have taken degraded births, women, *vaiśyas* and *śūdras*, also attain the highest goal.
>
> How much more so then for the *brāhmaṇas*, the righteous, the devotees, and saintly kings. Having reached this temporary miserable world, you must worship me.' (9.32-33)

The *Gītā* clearly does not advocate the formation of any sect outside the social order of the four *varṇas*. *Bhakti* is devotion from the individual who remains within the system. It is accepted that *brāhmaṇas* and *kṣatriyas* are superior by disposition, but *bhakti* enables even those of lower birth to gain *mokṣa* through the grace of Kṛṣṇa.

(iv) The *Nārāyaṇīya*

The *Nārāyaṇīya* makes several references to the Pañcarātra mode of worship, and from this one may infer that the author approved of a Pañcarātra sect or may even have been a member. The descriptions of Śvetadvīpa (chs. 323 and 325), the heaven for the devotees of Viṣṇu, reveal the notion of a community of devotees living and worshipping together, although this does not necessarily imply a recommendation that such a community should be formed here on earth. In contrast to the typically exclusivist outlook of sectarian movements, the *Nārāyaṇīya* displays a notably inclusivist perspective. Devotees of Śiva are not condemned outright, for Śiva is the same as Viṣṇu (12.328. 13-26) and worship of Śiva is the same as worship of Nārāyaṇa (20). Likewise, the followers of Sāṁkhya and Yoga are approved of for they are also worshipping Nārāyaṇa in their own way (12.327.24), as are the followers of the Vedas (12.321.40). Where descriptions of the qualities of the devotees are given it is in terms of the individual rather than a community of believers (12.326. 18-21) and no injunction is found for the individual to perform his worship within the context of any such community or sect.

Direct contact with the Deity is possible for the individual but only for one who has specific qualities. That this is a one-to-one process without the need for a mediator or membership of any community is made apparent by the contrasting fortunes of the sages, Ekata, Dvita, and Trita, and Nārada. Chapter 323 describes the visit of the three sages to Śvetadvīpa to see Nārāyaṇa. Despite years of penance they are still unable to behold the Deity whose effulgence blinds them (28). After further penance they return and are able to see the inhabitants of Śvetadvīpa, who worship Nārāyaṇa according to Pañcarātra (42), but not the object of their devotion. The key to direct vision of Nārāyaṇa is revealed in verse 48, *na sa śakyo abhaktena draṣṭuṁ devaḥ kathaṁcana*–for one who is not a devotee, it is impossible to see the Deity.

Nārada, on the other hand, is granted direct contact with Nārāyaṇa (12.326.1) and it is made explicit that this is because, in contrast to the three sages, he has devotion for the Deity (11-14). In 12.322.3-4, Nārada gives a list of the excellent deeds and qualities–*viśeṣaiḥ*–that have made him pure and thus qualified to see Nārāyaṇa. The need for a mediator is thereby obviated, for the individual is able to purify himself by his acts to the point where he is able to see the Deity directly, although the text makes it clear that the crucial quality mentioned in Nārada's list is, *taṁ cādi-devaṁ satataṁ prapannaḥ*–constant surrender to that original Deity.

12.323.34 indicates that all the devotees in Śvetadvīpa are of equal status–*na tatrābhyadhikaḥ kaścit sarve te sama-tejasaḥ*–and there is none of the emphasis on the duties of *sva-dharma* found in the devotional thought of the *Bhagavad-gītā*. This may indicate that the followers of Pañcarātra were less committed to *sva-dharma*, although in the prose verses of Chapter 329, the *brāhmaṇas* are praised as the first created by Nārāyaṇa and superior to the *kṣatriyas* and all other types of person (5.10). The *Nārāyaṇīya* thus recommends the Pañcarātra system of worship and has little to say about the importance of dharmic duty in expressing devotion to Nārāyaṇa. This may indicate sectarian tendencies but the text does not at any point recommend adherence to any sect or community of believers as a part of the path of devotion.

(v) Passages Teaching Devotion to Śiva

Within the *Mahābhārata* there are several passages that glorify Śiva and praise the path of devotion to him. Notable here are the encounters of Arjuna with Śiva (3.39-41; 7.57 and 172-173) and Chapters 14 to 18 of the *Anuśāsana*, which describe Kṛṣṇa's devotion to Śiva. Elsewhere, reference is made to Pāśupātas and

Kapālikas, both Śaivite sects (12.337.58 and 12.237.7), but in neither case is the reference favourable and there is no evidence whatsoever that the passages of Śiva *bhakti* come from such a source. Chapter 15 of the *Anuśāsana* gives a description of Kṛṣṇa's initiation into the worship of Śiva by Upamanyu. This consists of instruction in certain *mantras*, the continual repetition of which grants the reciter direct vision of the Deity. The initiation referred to by Kṛṣṇa in 13.15.4 thus appears to be no more than the transmission of wisdom from a mature devotee of Śiva to an aspiring devotee. Again we find little interest in any structured group or any concept of mediation in the teachings delivered in this passage.

13.14.177 describes the ecstasy of the devotee on encountering Śiva; in 13.14.188 Kṛṣṇa asks his *guru* if he will be allowed to see Śiva directly and is told that this is possible; 13.16.19 states that Śiva is known by the wise within themselves; and 13.16.38-40 states that though Śiva is unknown to gods, *asuras* and men, he reveals himself by his grace to one who is devoted to him. The *guru* who initiates the devotee into worshipping Śiva is thus not a mediator, and initiation does not involve adherence to a particular group or sect. When the instructions given as a part of the initiation process are accepted and put into practice, direct contact between the individual and the Deity will ensue. Neither sin nor the human condition is an insurmountable barrier to such contact. Śiva's grace is such that if he wishes to reveal himself to one who has found his favour, nothing can prevent this. With such an understanding of the disposition of the Deity, it is apparent that there is no necessity within a theological scheme for adherence to a particular sect or organised group of devotees.

(v) Conclusions

Bhakti offers a path to salvation that entails intervention from a Supreme Deity into the existence of the individual. Within the *Mahābhārata* we find no stress on the formation of sects or communities of devotees or communal worship of the Deity. The *Bhagavad-gītā* teaches that *bhakti* is to be practised within the context of the orthodox social structure based on the four *varṇas*, though its stress remains on transcending this world. The *Nārāyaṇīya* places far less emphasis on *sva-dharma* and affirms the ideas of the Pañcarātra sect, though it stops short of urging the necessity of adherence to this group. In fact nowhere in the *Mahābhārata* is there any instruction for the individual to be a member of any religious order apart from the traditional structures of *sva-dharma.* The Deity, Śiva, Viṣṇu or Kṛṣṇa, is not a remote figure only to be reached through an intercessor, and humanity is not viewed as inherently flawed and thus constitutionally separated from God. Human beings can perfect themselves in order to see God directly, or else the grace of God is such that any obstacles to such contact may be overcome without recourse to a mediating body or individual.

6. Summary and Conclusions

1. The following questions are raised by consideration of religious organisation:- a) Does a doctrinal value system necessitate membership of a specific group which shares its beliefs, and the acceptance of the strictures and hierarchy imposed by such a group. b) If such a sect or community exists, how do its power structure and regulations relate to those of the state. c) Is the attainment of the earthly or eschatological results offered by the doctrine dependent upon membership of the community and participation in its activities, or is the doctrine to be accepted and acted upon independently by an individual. d) Is there the necessity of a mediating individual or body to span the gulf between the human and divine spheres of existence. e) Does the imperative of mission necessitate the existence of an organisation of believers to accomplish such work.

2. *Pravṛtti* values stress the regulation of society in accordance with divinely ordained rules, or *dharma*, and recognise a distinction between those who accept this orthodoxy and outsiders who do not participate in the social order based on four *varṇas.* This social structure is governed by a ruling élite of *brāhmaṇas* and *kṣatriyas* who together guide society and enforce the acceptance of the prescribed social order. There is thus no division between secular and spiritual authority. Neither the community as a whole nor its élite functions as a mediator, it merely provides a structure within which individuals can live correctly and thereby gain prosperity in this life and higher rebirth in the next; it also ensures stability, order and prosperity for society as a whole. There is no concept of mission within this social order and the organisation is not designed to achieve any such objective.

3. The values of *nivṛtti* represent an individualistic perspective and conceive of no necessity of community, structure or hierarchy. On the contrary, adherence to social duties in the traditional order is to be given up, as the community along with all other material designations is to be transcended. There is no mediating body conceived of, for the divine exists within each individual and is contacted when the individual transforms his own consciousness. The *guru* offers instructions in the esoteric philosophy and practices that can bring the individual to salvation, but he is not a mediator. There is no necessity for mission, for the teachings on *mokṣa-dharma* are only for the very few individuals who are qualified to follow them and are to be kept secret from the mass of the people. In the *Bhagavad-gītā*'s teachings, the individual is urged to remain in his position in the social order but to transcend it within his consciousness.

4. Where *bhakti* to Viṣṇu or Śiva is taught, the individual is urged to seek salvation through the grace of an external Deity. There are references to sects of believers, but no details of structure or hierarchy and no injunction on the necessity of submitting oneself to the rule of any such sect. Teachers give instruction on the greatness of the Deity and the methods of worship, and sometimes initiation, but they do not act as mediators. The disciple worships the Deity as instructed and thereby obtains the grace of the Deity. He is then able to perceive the Deity directly. There is no insurmountable barrier between God and humanity, for the individual can perfect himself through devotion, and the grace of Viṣṇu or Śiva is such that direct, one-to-one contact takes place. Mission does not play a role in such teachings, though this path is open to all levels of society (*Bhg* 9.32-33), and hence there is no discussion of organisation for such activities.

Notes

1. See, for example, Chapters 60-63 of the *Śānti*.
2. M. Monier-Williams, *A Sanskrit-English Dictionary*, Motilal Banarsidass, Delhi, 1976. p. 837.
3. See, for example, 12.61.1, 12.254.38, and 15.20.3.
4. See, for example, Nārada's eulogy of *brāhmaṇas* in Chapter 32 of the *Anuśāsana*.
5. Cited by Pusalker, A.D. *Studies in the Epics and Purāṇas of India*, Bombay, 1963, p. 9.
6. Ibid, p. 6.

7. Ibid, p. 64.
8. Heesterman, J.C. *The Inner Conflict of Tradition, Essays in Indian Ritual, Kingship and Society,* Chicago, 1985, p. 152.
9. Ibid, p. 27.
10. Brockington, J.L. *The Sacred Thread: Hinduism in its Continuity and Diversity,* Edinburgh, 1981, p. 60.
11. Pusalker 1963, p. 89.
12. Bharadvaja, R. *A Philosophical Study of the Concept of Viṣṇu in the Purāṇas,* New Delhi, 1981, p. 363.
13. Moorthy, K. 'Socio-Cultural Milieu in the Mahābhārata', In *Mahābhārata Revisited,* R.N. Dandekar Ed, New Delhi, 1990, p. 143.
14. Brockington 1981, p. 201.
15. Dasgupta, S. *A History of Indian Philosophy,* Vol 2, Cambridge, 1973, p. 546.
16. Except in the teachings of the *Gītā* which makes the practice of *sva-dharma* a form of *yoga.*
17. van Buitenen, J.A.B. *Studies in Indian Literature and Philosophy,* Ludo Rocher Ed, Delhi, 1988, p. 98.
18. See, for example, 2.31-38, 11.33.
19. Bhandarkar, R.G. *Vaiṣṇavism, Śaivism and Minor Religious Systems,* New York, 1980, p. 30. Bhandarkar also sees the references in verses such as 10.9 to devotees worshipping together as significant:-"There is to be observed here one special characteristic of the Bhakti school, and that is that the devotees meet together, enlighten each other as to the nature of God and contribute by discourses on him to each other's elevation and gratification. This is almost a characteristic mark of Bhaktas as distinguished from the Yogins who have to go through their exercises singly and in solitude." (Bhandarkar 1980, p. 20)
20. Ibid, p. 134.
21. Ibid, p. 66.

CHAPTER 4

EPIC SOTERIOLOGY

1. Introduction

In conducting a review of epic soteriology I propose first to examine the text's understanding of this world, for soteriology implies the recognition of an undesirable status from which one seeks salvation. Having examined the situation from which one is urged to seek release, I will then turn to the various means offered by the epic through which salvation may be attained. According to Ninian Smart these may be categorised as 'self-help', 'other-help', or more commonly a mixture of both.[1] 'Other-help' is prominent in theistic theology where it frequently takes the form of a doctrine of grace. This is certainly true of Christianity, for example, though, with the exception of extreme Calvinist theology, some action is required by the individual or group in the form of rituals or good works. 'Self-help' is naturally predominant in non-theistic belief systems which teach techniques of personal transformation as a means to salvation.

The text of the *Mahābhārata* is dominated by soteriological ideas. The persistence of the individual after death is taken for granted by all the characters in the narrative and all actions are performed in light of the necessity of preparing for the life after death. In the epic we find the Vedic concepts of heaven and hell as reward or punishment for good and bad deeds mixing with the Upaniṣadic and Sāṁkhya ideas of *saṁsāra,* repeated birth and death, and salvation from this cycle. These two soteriological perspectives represent the alternative value systems of *pravṛtti* and *nivṛtti,* one seeking success within the creation and the other looking for release from it. The idea of heaven and hell is to some extent at odds with the law of *karma* and repeated rebirth, but a blatant contradiction is avoided by stressing that both heaven and hell are temporary states and a part of the vast journey of life and death through one creation after another.

Within the narrative, we find the characters preoccupied with acting in accordance with *dharma*, for that will ensure that after death they enter *svarga-loka*, the heaven of the gods. This understanding of action in accordance with *dharma* is based on *pravṛtti* and its soteriological aspect centres on gaining sensual rewards after death in a higher world. The *Mokṣa-dharma*, as the name suggests, is devoted entirely to the subject of soteriology, not in terms of attaining the enjoyments of *svarga-loka*, but the quest for complete and eternal salvation from all types of birth and death. The *Mokṣa-dharma* is made up of a series of treatises on this subject containing elements of Upaniṣadic Vedānta, but predominated by Sāṁkhya ideas which the text links with *yoga*-practice. Each section has its own approach and perspective, some of them obscure, and hence there are difficulties in presenting an overall doctrine of salvation. Clearly the attempt must be to trace the broad themes that predominate, whilst avoiding the danger of becoming enmeshed in the subtle variations of Sāṁkhya philosophy.

Outside the *Mokṣa-dharma* the way to salvation is described by various teachers in the narrative and by Kṛṣṇa in the *Aśvamedhika* and the *Bhagavad-gītā*. The relationship between *bhakti* and soteriology is more complex as *bhakti* is linked to both *pravṛtti* and *nivṛtti*. Where the Deity is the leader of a pantheon of gods whose mission is to preserve *dharma*, *bhakti* is linked to *pravṛtti* and recognises *svarga-loka* as the eschatological goal. In the *Gītā* and *Nārāyaṇīya*, however, *mokṣa* is stressed and *bhakti* becomes a means of invoking the grace of the Deity which serves to deliver the worshipper from the cycle of birth and death.

2. Definition of the Problem of Life in this World

(i) *Pravṛtti*

Pravṛtti seeks success in this world in terms of prosperity on earth and a desirable rebirth after death, ideally in the realm of the gods. Thus *pravṛtti* is primarily world-affirming and provides the means by which the negative features of life may be removed and replaced by an existence of constant enjoyment. It is accepted that life is a mixture of happiness and misery, but when dharmic action is pursued the misery is obviated and the happiness increased, even to the point where one may reside amongst the gods for a vast span of life enjoying a variety of sensual pleasures. Thus there is nothing fundamentally wrong with life in this world and it is debatable as to how far *pravṛtti* embodies a legitimate form of soteriology. Essentially it argues that life can be improved by proper action, and when proper action is pursued to the highest degree then the balance between happiness and distress moves overwhelmingly towards the former. The process of affecting this change may be recognised as a form of soteriology, although it never offers or seeks complete deliverance from material life.

(ii) *Nivṛtti*

Teachings on *mokṣa-dharma* take a much more negative view of life in this world. Stress is laid on the miseries of worldly existence wherein decay, old age, disease and death are inevitable. This view is evident not just from didactic passages, but is the message of the entire epic narrative. After their victory, the Pāṇḍavas are portrayed as being in a perpetual state of misery, wracked by feelings of regret and loss and finding no pleasure in the kingdom they have won. The message here, however, seems to be that *dharma* may not initially bring happiness, but one must have faith and understand that the rewards are more frequently reaped in the afterlife. Thus the conclusion to the narrative may be identified as a reflection on the nature of *pravṛtti* rather than an assertion of the *nivṛtti* world view.

It is in the didactus that a negative view of the world is expressed most vehemently, as one teacher after another urges renunciation of worldly aspirations. At the beginning of the *Vana*, we find Śaunaka, a teacher of Sāṁkhya and Yoga, addressing the Pāṇḍavas who have just been banished to the forest. His teaching centres on renunciation of desire as the means to overcome the misfortunes of life. In 3.2.15, he states that every day those who are fools are afflicted by thousands of causes of sorrow and hundreds of causes of fear. Sorrow here is caused by disease, contact with undesirable events, hard labour and unfulfilled desires–*vyādher aniṣṭa-saṁsparśāc cchramād iṣṭa-vivarjanāt* (21). In life we develop affection for various things but this affection is the cause of misery and fear–*sneha-mūlāni duḥkhāni sneha-jāni bhayāni ca* (27). Affection leads to desire and because of desire one is led toward sin and the misery that ensues from it (34). Even those who possess wealth find no joy, for they live in constant fear of losing what they have and thus also suffer misery (40-41).

At the end of the battle, we have the *Strī-parvan* in which the women come to the battlefield and lament piteously over their fallen loved ones. This lamentation leads to reflection on the miseries of life. In Chapter 5, Vidura gives the allegory of the *brāhmaṇa* in the forest to illustrate the miserable plight of the individual in this world. In a frightful forest, full of savage creatures, the *brāhmaṇa* fled here and there in fear. After seeing a terrifying female figure, he fell into a pit and was caught by creepers so that he hung there head downwards, looking at a huge snake at the bottom of the pit. A large elephant with six faces and twelve legs stood above but bees had made a nest there from which honey dripped, some of which the *brāhmaṇa* was able to taste though never enough to satisfy him. Black and white mice knawed at the creepers that held him, but still he maintained hope in life.

The parable is explained in Chapter 6. The *brāhmaṇa* is the living being on his journey through life which is the dreadful forest in which the savage beasts are diseases and the terrible woman is old age. The pit is the body, the snake is time, and the creeper in which he is tangled is the desire for life. The elephant is the passing year with its six seasons, and the black and white mice are the days and nights that gradually take life away. The bees are our desires and the drops of honey are the pleasures we enjoy in life. Those who are wise see life in this way and seek to break free from this bondage. In Chapter 7, Vidura continues to expound in the same manner on the misery of earthly existence, stressing the fact that disease and old age destroy all hopes, taking away beauty and life itself.

The negativity of the view of life expressed by Vidura in these chapters is extreme for the *Mahābhārata,* and even here falls short of the horror of the flesh that is found in some Buddhist works. Nonetheless, a negative view of life is fundamental to *mokṣa-dharma.* There is great suffering to be endured here and now but worse may follow for one may be forced to take birth as an animal or else undergo terrible tortures in the purgatories presided over by the God of the Dead.[2] Even the loving relationships we form in this world are condemned as causes of entanglement. They can bring no real happiness, for absolute separation is inevitable at death. Vyāsa describes human relations as follows:

naivāsya kaścid bhavitā nāyaṁ bhavati kasyacit
pathi saṁgatam evedaṁ dāra-bandhu-suhṛd-gaṇaiḥ

> 'Nobody belongs to any individual, and the individual does not belong to anybody else. The meeting with wife, relatives, and friends is just like a temporary companionship on the road.' (12.28.39)

Tulādhara makes the same point in 12.254.23-24, but he compares human relationships to the coming together and separation of twigs and grass on a flowing river. In this world, people find pleasure and comfort in their friends, family and relatives but the teachings here dismiss such attachments as temporary, relating only to one lifetime and ultimately sources of misery and obstacles to salvation.

This stress on the suffering and misery that characterise existence in this world is found throughout the *Mokṣa-dharma* and is continued in the *Aśvamedhika,* in Kṛṣṇa' a teachings to Arjuna. In the *Anugītā,* Kṛṣṇa states that nowhere in this world is there permanent happiness. Again and again, there is death and then birth once more and each time there is more misery due to previous acts (14.16.28-36). In Chapter 44, Kṛṣṇa stresses once again the misery of living in this world. All happiness ends in sorrow and from sorrow comes happiness once more–*sukhasyāntaḥ sadā duḥkhaṁ duḥkhasyāntaḥ sadā sukham* (17). There is no permanence here; all associations end in separation, all life ends in death, all that is achieved is destroyed in the end–*sarvaṁ kṛtaṁ vināśāntam*–and for all who take birth, death is a certainty–*jātasya maraṇaṁ dhruvam.*

Nivṛtti does not deny the possibility of attaining *svarga-loka,* but argues that this is only a temporary solution to the sufferings of this world. In Chapters 246 and 247 of the *Vana,* Vyāsa narrates to the Pāṇḍavas the story of Mudgala who is offered a position in *svarga-loka* but declines when he is told of the faults of such a position by a messenger from the gods. These are discussed in verses 27-33 of Chapter 247. In the abode of the gods one cannot accrue merit through pious acts and hence that which has been amassed in the previous life on earth is gradually diminished through enjoyment in heaven (28). Thus the individual is eventually forced to fall from *svarga-loka* back to earth. Suffering arises both from regret at having lost one's position with the gods and, prior to the fall, fear of what is about to happen fills with dread those who see their celestial garlands gradually beginning to fade–*pramlāneṣu ca mālyeṣu tataḥ pipatiṣor bhayam* (31). In 12.9.34,

Yudhiṣṭhira, pursuing the same theme, rhetorically asks who would want such a position in *svarga-loka* when even gods and great *ṛṣis* fall down from their positions above. His point has been illustrated earlier by the stories of Nahuṣa (3.177) and Yayāti (5.118-121), both of whom were righteous kings elevated to live amongst the gods and then cast down because of pride.

Indra himself admits that although some beings gain greater happiness than others, nobody in this world is fully contented–*naikānta-sukham eveha kvacit paśyāmi kasyacit* (12.173.22). Having gained wealth a man wants power and having gained power he wishes to become a god; having become a god, he then wants to become Indra himself. Thus whatever one's position, however elevated, there is still no contentment even when all one's goals are attained–*na tṛptiḥ priyalābhe 'sti tṛṣṇā nādbhiḥ praśāmyati* (25). Elevation to *svarga-loka* is most stridently dismissed by Bhīṣma in Chapter 191. There he briefly describes the domains of the different gods with their fabulous mansions and aerial chariots but concludes, *ete vai nirayās tāta sthānasya paramātmanaḥ*–my son, these are certainly hells (compared to) the position of the Supreme Soul (6).

(iii) The Causes of Rebirth

Thus from the perspective of *nivṛtti*, the problem that necessitates the quest for salvation is that this world is full of suffering due to repeated death, decay and disease. Solutions from the perspective of *pravṛtti* that entail seeking elevated rebirth within this world are not dismissed as wholly useless, but even when they are at their most effective and offer admission to the realm of the gods, still they provide an inadequate solution to the problem. Many passages in the *Mahābhārata* claim to offer a genuine solution and path to salvation, but few if any look at the original cause of the problem. Questions such as, Why are we here? How did we get here? How did this situation come into being? remain unposed and unanswered. The question as to what keeps us here now is explained and discussed at some length, but not the origin of our existence in this world.

This absence of speculation as to the origins of the soul's entanglement with matter is probably due to the epic's understanding of time and creation. The world is regarded as eternal although subject to an unending cycle of creation and annihilation in which all beings are withdrawn and then emerge once more to continue the cycle of rebirth. Against such a background of eternal existence, questions of when, how and why lose much of their pertinence. In addition, it is important to appreciate that the ideas on *mokṣa* presented in the epic are above all practical. The imperative is on finding the means to gain salvation, and a theoretical understanding of the history of existence is a secondary concern.

The problem of material existence is thus not presented in historical terms. The cause of our misery here is a non-temporal phenomenon; it is the continual covering of ignorance, illusion and misidentification that keeps the soul bound to the unending progress of *saṁsāra.* The Sāṁkhya ideas that dominate the teachings on *mokṣa-dharma* centre on the understanding of the self as different from matter–*anyo 'ham,* I am different (12.295.19). The ignorance that is the barrier to salvation is the failure to appreciate this true identity, and seeing the self and self-interest in terms of the body and senses. In this state of ignorance one accepts the fortunes of the body, its dualities and miseries, as one's own and thus undergoes suffering.

The idea of ignorance as the cause of bondage in this world is a prominent theme of the *Mokṣa-dharma.* In Chapter 292 of the *Śānti,* this topic is discussed at length by Vasiṣṭha. In reality the self has nothing to do with the actions of the body and senses, but because of illusion, one regards the different bodies occupied in the cycle of rebirth as oneself, and their good fortune and distress as one's own. Even the religious acts and *yajñas* one performs have nothing to do with the self, and neither does one's position in the social order as *brāhmaṇa, kṣatriya, vaiśya* and *śūdra* (19-26). Because of this attachment to the body, and the dualities of its existence in terms pleasure and misery, the transcendent *ātman* remains entangled in matter (29) and misidentifies itself with a succession of bodily forms. In the concluding verses (45-48), Vasiṣṭha summarises the nature of the illusion as follows: the soul, though without senses, thinks he is the doer; though beyond death, he thinks that he dies; though separate from the body, he regards himself as the body; and though unborn, as having taken birth–*akṣetraḥ kṣetram ātmānam asargaḥ sargam ātmanaḥ* (47). One who has no intelligence, though indestructible, thinks that he can be destroyed–*akṣaraḥ kṣaram ātmānam abuddhis tv abhimanyate* (48).

The consequence of this ignorance in terms of salvation is given by Vasiṣṭha in the first verse of Chapter 293:

> *evam apratibuddhatvād abuddha-jana-sevanāt*
> *sarga-koṭi-sahasrāṇi patanāntāni gacchati*
>
> 'Thus, due to absence of intelligence and association with those who have no intelligence, one undergoes thousands of millions of births, all of which end in destruction.' (12.293.1)

Here in a nutshell Vasiṣṭha defines the reason for the bondage of the self in matter. It is ignorance of its true identity that keeps the *ātman* bound, and hence it follows that the way to salvation is the search for true knowledge of the self.

Frauwallner elaborates on this theme by identifying two separate causes of bondage: "Indeed there stand two original causes for the bondage of the soul–ignorance and desire–one beside the other."[3] There is no intrinsic conflict of doctrine here, however, for desire is the result of ignorance. Misidentifying the body as the true self leads the individual to seek to gratify this illusory identity by providing pleasure through the senses. At the same time this desire acts to obscure the process of acquiring the knowledge which would overcome the ignorance that is the cause of desire. Again according Frauwallner, ". . . the contact of the sense organs with the sense objects causes the disquiet and the turbidity of knowledge, impairs consequently the ability for knowledge and hinders the attainment of the Delivering Insight."[4] Hence both ignorance and desire may legitimately be regarded as causes of the soul's imprisonment in this world, but there is no contradiction in this for both are features of the same situation, each fostering and sustaining the other.

(iv) The Problem of Existence from a *Bhakti* Perspective

In theistic soteriology, especially that with a tendency towards mysticism, the problem of existence is sometimes expressed not in terms of the misery and perversion of life here, but rather the suffering of the devotee in a state of separation from the Deity. In Hindu thought, the later *bhakti* sects, which derived many of their ideas from the *Bhāgavata Purāṇa*, developed a similar perspective. In their writings, Jayadeva, Caṇḍidāsa, and Caitanya all laid great stress on the attitude of Rādhā, the beloved of Kṛṣṇa, who seeks nothing at all from the Deity except to be engaged in her loving relationship with him. In this mood the devotee prays that he does not care about the suffering that may engulf him in this world, and has no desire for *mokṣa* so long as he may remain a devoted servant of the Lord. In the *Mahābhārata,* this perspective is found only in a very embryonic form and then, notably, in passages expressing devotion to Śiva. The teachings on *bhakti* centre on the greatness, power and majesty of the Deity, on the need to worship the Deity, and on the power of the Deity to deliver his devotee.

For the epic, *bhakti* is a means of gaining salvation by invoking the grace of the all-powerful Supreme God. It is important to note how the devotional teachings of the *Gītā* and the *Nārāyaṇīya* are closely linked with Sāṁkhya and share the imperative of Sāṁkhya towards salvation. The problem of human existence may thus be taken as being essentially the same as that discussed above in relation to the perspective of *nivṛtti. Bhakti* shares the values of *pravṛtti* and *nivṛtti,* stressing both *dharma* and *mokṣa.* Both the *Gītā* and the *Nārāyaṇīya,* however, clearly accept the view of *nivṛtti* that the highest goal to be sought is complete salvation from rebirth in this world and thus share the negative world view of *nivṛtti,* regarding the world as a place of suffering wherein the *ātman* is held captive–*anityam asukhaṁ lokam imam* (Bhg 9.33). In *bhakti* the means of gaining salvation is different, for the concept of grace is introduced, and possibly the goal is different for it is seen as the Deity himself or even his abode, but the view of the problem remains the same.

3. Attainment of *Svarga-loka*

(i) *Dharma* and Morality

The highest goal to be attained in the view of *pravṛtti* is a position amongst the gods after death, and the ethics of *pravṛtti* offer a range of pious acts leading to elevation to *svarga-loka.* Essentially, this domain is attained through morality and adherence to the prescribed rules of *sva-dharma.* Thus the *Bhagavad-gītā* describes the heavens of the gods as, *puṇya-kṛtāṁ lokān* (6.41), the worlds of those who act righteously.

The text contains many discussions of various acts through

which *svarga-loka* is gained. That morality plays an important part in this process is apparent from a number of passages. In Chapter 111 of the *Ādi*, we are told that Pāṇḍu gained the domain of the gods through hearing without pride, self control and conquest of the senses–*śuśrūṣur anahaṁvādī saṁyatātmā jitendriyaḥ svargaṁ gantuṁ parākrāntaḥ* (2). In Chapter 178 of the *Vana*, Yudhiṣṭhira asks Nahuṣa how one gains the highest abode–*gatir uttamā* (1). To this Nahuṣa replies,

> *pātre dattvā priyaṇy uktvā satyam uktvā ca bhārata*
> *ahiṁsā nirataḥ svargaṁ gacched iti matir mama*
>
> 'Having given charity, spoken pleasing words, and spoken the truth, one who does no injury to any being may go to *svarga-loka*. That is my opinion.' (3.178.2)

In verse 9, Nahuṣa states that one is elevated to *svarga-loka* by his own actions–*sva-karmabhiḥ*–and in verse 10, this is elaborated upon by his statement that charity, endeavour and non-injury are acts that lead to this goal–*dānabhir atandritaḥ/ahiṁsārtha-samāyuktaiḥ kāraṇaiḥ svargam aśnute.* In 12.127.8-10, Yama, questioned by Gautama, gives his version of how a person attains worlds that are wonderful to behold. He mentions austerity, purity, devotion to the religion of truth–*satya-dharma-ratena*–serving one's mother and father, performing *aśvamedha yajñas,* and giving charity to the priests.

In the *Droṇa,* following the death of her son Abhimanyu, Subhadrā laments and prays that because of his heroic death he may now pass on to the realm of the gods. As a part of this lament, she makes reference to the various acts and ways of life by which such success may be attained in the afterlife (7.55.20-31) and hence provides us with a more complete understanding of this form of soteriology.

Residence in heaven is given as being the reward of the following types of person: of those who perform *yajñas* where charity is given–*yajvanām dāna-śīlānām*–of self-controlled *brāhmaṇas*–*brāhmaṇānāṁ kṛtātmanām*–of those who practise celibacy–*carita-brahmacaryāṇām*–and those who bathe at pilgrimage sites–*puṇya-tīrthāvagāhinām* (20); of those who are grateful–*kṛta-jñānām*–generous–*vadānyānām*–and hear from their teachers–*guru-śuśrūṣiṇām*–and of those who give thousands of gifts to their teacher–*sahasra-*

dakṣiṇānām (21); of those heroes who never retreat from battle–*yudhyamānānāṁ śūrāṇām anivartiṇām*–and of those who die in battle having slain their enemies–*hatvārīn nihatānām* (22); of those who give thousands of cows in charity–*go-sahasra-pradātṝṇām*–give charity at sacrifices–*kratu-dānām*–or give away pleasant houses–*naiveśikaṁ cābhimataṁ dadatām* (23); wise men who are celibate and firm in their vows go there–*brahmacaryeṇa . . . munayaḥ saṁśita-vratāḥ*–and women who take only one husband–*eka-patnyaḥ* (24).

This is the domain gained by kings through their righteous conduct–*rājñāṁ sucaritaiḥ*–of those who piously follow the duties of the four *āśramas*–*catur-āśramiṇāṁ puṇyaiḥ*–and of those who are pure because of careful adherence to their duties–*pāvitānāṁ surakṣitaiḥ* (25); of those who are compassionate to the poor–*dīnānukampinām*–of those who always share their goods with others–*satataṁ saṁvibhāginām*–and of those who never speak harshly of others–*paiśunyāc ca nivṛttānām* (26); of those who follow vows–*vratinām*–of those who adhere to *dharma*–*dharma-śīlānām*–of those who hear from their teachers–*guru-śuśrūṣiṇām*–and who never fail to provide for guests–*amoghātithinām* (27); of those wise men who approach their wives only at the time when conception is likely–*ṛtu-kāle svakāṁ patnīṁ gacchatām manasvinām*–and never indulge sexually with the wives of others–*na cānya-dāra-sevīnām* (28).

Those who are free from envy, and equal to all beings go there–*sāmnā ye sarva-bhūtāni gacchanti gata-matsarāḥ*–(to the abode), of those who never wound others–*nāruṁtudānām*–and are forgiving–*kṣamiṇām* (29); of those who abstain from honey, meat, liquor, pride and falsehood–*madhu-māṁsa-nivṛttānāṁ madād dambhāt tathānṛtat*–and have given up acts that cause pain to others–*paropatāpa-tyaktānām* (30); and of those who are humble–*hrīmantaḥ*–learned in all scriptures–*sarva-śāstra-jñāḥ*–satisfied with wisdom–*jñāna-tṛptāḥ*–and have control over the senses–*jitendriyāḥ*. Subhadrā prays that her son may reach the same abode that such saintly persons attain–*yāṁ gatiṁ sādhavo yānti tāṁ gatiṁ vraja putraka* (31).

This passage gives a valuable insight into the means that are advocated for gaining a position in *svarga-loka*, a combination of morality, religious rituals, and adherence to social duties. It appears that most of the above righteous acts are for *kṣatriyas* and *brāhmaṇas* and that the lower orders are largely excluded, though against this view can be cited the statement of Parāśara,

sarve varṇā dharma-kāryāṇi samyak
kṛtvā rājan satya-vākyāni coktvā
tyaktvādharmaṁ dāruṇaṁ jīva-loke
yānti svargaṁ nātra kāryo vicāraḥ

'O king, all the *varṇas,* having properly performed their religious duties, having spoken only words that are true, and having given up irreligion and harshness in this world, go to *svarga-loka.* On this there is no need for further deliberation' (12.285.39).[5]

Other passages lay stress on ritual acts and austerities for gaining entrance to the world of the gods. In Chapters 80 to 83 of the *Vana,* Pulastya describes to the Pāṇḍavas holy places, *tīrthas,* and the rituals, such as fasting and giving charity, that should be performed in each one. The results of such pilgrimages are given precisely in terms of different regions of *svarga-loka* being attained for so many thousands of years, or as being equal to the result attained in *svarga-loka* by performing different kinds of *yajña.*

It is also stated that elevation to *svarga-loka* may be gained through austerity and harsh penances. In 3.106.40, Lomaśa tells the Pāṇḍavas that their ancestor Dilīpa went to the third region of *svarga-loka–tri-divaḥ*–by success in his austerities–*tapaḥ siddhi-samāyogātsaḥ.* The same idea is conveyed by Indra to Srucāvatī, the daughter of Bharadvāja, who is living as an ascetic at the *tīrtha* named Badarapācana,

yāni sthānāni divyāṇi vibuddhānāṁ śubhānane
tapasā tāni prāpyāni tapomūlaṁ mahatsukham

iha kṛtvā tapo ghoraṁ dehaṁ saṁnyasya mānavāḥ
devatvaṁ yānti kalyāṇi śṛṇu cedaṁ vaco mama

'O beautiful one, these celestial places of the gods are attained by penance. Penance is the root of great happiness. .

Having performed terrible penances here in this world, human beings attain the status of gods when they give up their bodies. Noble lady, hear this statement of mine.' (9.47.14-15)

Another means of gaining the celestial world is the recitation of sacred works, though it should be noted that in the passages where this is stated it is mainly to glorify the text referred to rather than give teachings on how *svarga-loka* may be gained. Thus in the *Vana,* after Mārkaṇḍeya has narrated the story of Matsya and Manu, he concludes by stating that a man who listens daily to that ancient history will go to heaven–*svarga-lokam iyān naraḥ* (3.185.54). Similarly, in the first chapter of the *Ādi,* Sūta states that a man who listens daily to the *Mahābhārata* with faith gains long life, fame, and a place in heaven–*sa dīrgham āyuḥ kīrtiṁ ca svar-gatiṁ cāpnuyān naraḥ* (1.1.207).

Finally, it must be noted that the *Mahābhārata* also teaches that *satī,* ritual suicide after the death of her husband, is a means by which a woman may follow him to heaven. This is implicit in the story of the pigeon and the hunter, told by Bhīṣma in Chapters 141 to 145 of the *Śānti.* In Chapter 144, the pigeon's wife cries out, *pati-hīnāpi kā nārī satī jīvitum utsahet,* what righteous woman would continue to live when her husband is slain. She then casts herself onto the fire that is burning her husband's body and is transported to *svarga-loka* with her husband in a celestial chariot. Again in the *Āśramavāsika,* having brought those slain in the battle down to earth in their heavenly forms, Vyāsa instructs the wives of these dead warriors that they should drown themselves so that they may return to heaven with them (15.41.17-19).

(ii) The *Anuśāsana-parvan*

The subject of gaining admission into heaven is discussed most exhaustively in the *Anuśāsana* and is a major theme of the teachings presented therein. Different sections of the *Anuśāsana* give different pious acts that bring rewards in the afterlife, and also describe ritualised means and times most appropriate for executing these acts. Charity, for example, is stressed as a means of gaining *svarga-loka,* but the proper times and recipients of charity are an important part of obtaining the desired result.

The ways of reaching heaven given in the *Anuśāsana* may be summarised as follows. In Chapters 26 and 27, different *tīrthas* are described, as well as the ritual behaviour such as bathing, celibacy and fasting that should be performed in each, and the reward in heaven that will be obtained thereby. In Chapter 57, Bhīṣma tells Yudhiṣṭhira of different penances–eating only fruit, sleeping on the bare ground, bathing three times daily in cold water–by which *svarga-loka* is gained. He also briefly discusses different kinds of gifts which should be given in charity. Chapters 61 to 65 give a description of how food should be given to the most worthy *brāhmaṇas* and also of the ritual manner and time at which such gifts should be made. Chapters 70 to 73 describe how and to whom gifts of cows should be made if one is to be with the gods in the afterlife, and mentions that the heaven gained thereby is higher than that gained by those who give food. Chapter 74 argues that *svarga-loka* may be reached by one who always shows restraint–*damaḥ*–in his dealings, by properly performing the duties of one's *varṇa* (19-21), by executing *yajñas* (29), and by accepting a vow of celibacy (36-39).

In Chapters 75 to 78, Bhīṣma on Yudhiṣṭhira's request, returns to the subject of giving cows in charity and in Chapter 78 states that the duration of one's stay in *svarga-loka* is dependent on the number and especially the quality and breed of the cows that are given. In Chapter 109, various fasts and vows are prescribed. These are given differently for each *varṇa* and the duration of one's existence in heaven is dependent on the duration of the fast that is undertaken. Chapters 116 and 117 discuss the merits of not eating flesh and the reward in heaven available for those who refrain from such food. In Chapter 124, Bhīṣma describes how women may get to heaven by serving their husbands with faith and devotion. In Chapter 132, Śiva tells Umā of the ethical behaviour for which one is rewarded in the celestial regions. The ideas here are very similar to those expressed by Subhadrā in the *Droṇa*–not injuring others, compassion, not coveting others' property or lusting after their wives, being content with what one has, charity, penance, speaking the truth, never being deceitful, welcoming guests, promoting good-will, and not speaking harshly. In Chapter 133, he continues by stressing respect for *brāhmaṇas*, charity, and being liberal by nature (1-9), before moving on to discuss those who will punished in hell after death.

It is thus clear that *svarga-loka* is gained by righteous living in this world. There is no concept of grace here that would contradict or override a strictly eudaemonistic perspective. The passages discussed above give us a comprehensive picture of what the authors of the epic considered a righteous lifestyle to be in terms of moral behaviour. Those who adhere to this pattern are promised rewards after death in the realm of the gods, while those who disobey and disregard the teachings are threatened with punishments in the hells of Yama.

(iii) *Śrāddha* Rites performed for Ancestors

From the *Mahābhārata* we also learn that ancestors can be sustained in their heavenly existence by the activities of their descendants. It is unclear whether this is in *svarga-loka* itself or in some other domain. This idea is central to the story of the birth of Astika who stops the snake *yajña* at which the *Mahābhārata* is spoken by Vaiśaṁpāyana. In Chapter 41 of the *Ādi*, the sage Jaratkāru sees his ancestors hanging upside down on the point of descending into hell, having fallen from heaven–*lokāt puṇyād iha bhraṣṭāḥ* (16)–because their descendant is an ascetic who will beget no offspring. At their request, Jaratkāru marries the daughter of the King of the Snakes and begets Astika as his son. There is no reference to descendants performing any ceremonies or making offerings on behalf of their ancestors, and it appears that the perpetuation of the male line is sufficient to preserve their status. A similar story is narrated by Lomaśa to the Pāṇḍavas (3.94), here with the sage Agastya seeing his ancestors suspended in a pit. Once again this sight is the impetus for the sage to marry and beget a son and again no reference is made to any ritual.

The story of King Yayāti, narrated by Nārada to the assembly of the Kauravas (5.118-121) also involves the role of descendants in preserving their ancestor's position with the gods. By his excellent rule, King Yayāti is elevated to *svarga-loka* at death, but destroys all the merit due to him by displaying arrogance amongst the gods. Cast down to earth once more, he encounters four of his grandsons and is restored to his celestial position when each of them offers him a portion of the merit they have accrued from their own righteous acts. Mādhavī, the daughter of Yayāti, tells him that his grandsons will save him, for this is an ancient practice–*ime tvāṁ tārayiṣyanti diṣṭam etat purātanam* (5.119.23)–presumably referring once again to the idea of descendants preserving the position of their ancestors in the afterlife.

In the *Āśramavāsika,* when Dhṛtarāṣṭra is about to depart to the forest, he asks Yudhiṣṭhira for money so that he can make offerings to benefit his relatives who died in the battle and here there is specific mention of *śrāddha* offerings–*śrāddham icchati dātum*

(15.17.4). The offerings are not made solely for the benefit of Dhṛtarāṣṭra's ancestors or relatives, but also for Droṇa and all of Dhṛtarāṣṭra's dead sons and allies–*putrāṇāṁ caiva sarveṣāṁ ye cāsya suhṛdo hatāḥ*. It is interesting that Bhīma opposes any such gift on behalf of Duryodhana and his brothers, urging that they should be allowed to fall down from one miserable position to another–*kaṣṭāt kaṣṭataraṁ yāntu sarve duryodhanādayaḥ*–implying that the *śrāddha* offering is required to retain the status in *svarga-loka* gained by death in battle. In Chapter 20, when Dhṛtarāṣṭra performs the *śrāddha* offerings, they take the form of charitable gifts such as gold, food, slaves, clothing, chariots and land made to *brāhmaṇas* and the most worthy *ṛṣis–brāhmaṇān ṛṣi-sattamān* (2)–on the full moon day of the month of Kārtika (15.19.15). As each gift is made a particular person among those slain in the battle is named as the desired beneficiary of this pious act (15.20.5).

The idea of those still living performing pious acts on behalf of those departed is thus quite clearly established in the narrative. This is not a form of ancestor worship or placation of the spirits of the dead, but is a duty of all male descendants that is purely for the benefit of the ancestors. In Chapters 87 to 92 of the *Anuśāsana*, there is a detailed discussion of the *śrāddha* rites and the offerings that should be made. Here, however, there is a difference in that the benefit of such offerings is enjoyed not solely by the ancestors but also by the offerer here on earth. Chapter 87 describes the benefits gained by one who makes a *śrāddha* offering to the *pitṛs*, forefathers, depending on the day of the waxing moon on which the ceremony is performed. Thus, for example, if the offering is made on the fifth day one will be blessed with sons, and if made on the eighth day, one's business will flourish. Chapter 88 describes different types of food, including different types of flesh and even that of the cow, that may be offered in the *śrāddha* ceremony, and how long the *pitṛs* remain pleased after each type of offering. At the end of Chapter 88, in verses 12 to 15, there is a passage attributed by Bhīṣma to Sanatkumāra, which states that a *śrāddha* offering should be made on the anniversary of the death of one's father–*piṭr-kṣaye*–under the constellation of Māgha, beneath a banyan tree in the city of Gayā. To this day Gayā, in Bihar state, is the primary place of pilgrimage to which sons travel to make *śrāddha* offerings on behalf of their deceased parents.

Chapter 89 describes the benefits that come to those who make *śrāddha* offerings under different astronomical constellations, and in Chapter 90, Bhīṣma outlines the qualities of the righteous *brāhmaṇas* to whom the offerings should be given and also the degraded *brāhmaṇas* who should not be made recipients. Persons who are not *brāhmaṇas* should also be fed at a *śrāddha* ceremony, and these should not be friends or relatives, or persons who criticise *brāhmaṇas*. If offerings are made to deceitful persons, the giver's ancestors may fall down from heaven–*teṣāṁ pretān pātayed devayānāt* (13.90.41). Chapter 91 tells of the origin of the *śrāddha* ceremony, how it was initiated by King Nimi and approved by Brahmā himself. It then discusses again different types of food that should and should not be offered. Chapter 92 concludes Bhīṣma's discourse on *śrāddha* rites, describing how Agni agreed to transport offerings made into a fire up to the *pitṛs* in heaven. At rivers one should offer water to one's ancestors, friends and relatives (16-18), and once every two weeks (19) the ceremony must be performed. One who makes offerings to the *pitṛs* gains prosperity, long life, strength and wealth (19) while the ancestors are delivered by this action of their relative (21).

The emphasis in the *Anuśāsana* is quite different from in the passages considered above taken from the narrative. Clearly in the stories of Jaratkāru, Agastya, Yayāti, and in the passage describing Dhṛtarāṣṭra's offerings, the stress is on benefitting the *pitṛs* and sustaining their elevated position in the afterlife. There is little attention paid there to ritual; Jaratkāru and Agastya merely beget a son to continue the line, the four grandsons bestow upon Yayāti a portion of the merit from their righteous acts, and Dhṛtarāṣṭra gives charity to *brāhmaṇas*. The chapters of the *Anuśāsana* may more legitimately be considered as ancestor worship for greater emphasis is placed there on the benefits in this world that accrue to one who performs the *śrāddha* rites. That the offerings are meant to sustain the *pitṛs* seems almost taken for granted. There is greater emphasis placed here on ritual, as is typical of the *Anuśāsana,* than in the earlier passages which indicate that the mere perpetuation of the line is sufficient. In either case it can be recognised that one's position in *svarga-loka* is dependent to some extent on the actions of one's relatives and descendants here on earth.

(iv) The Means of Gaining *Svarga-loka* for *Kṣatriyas*

Most of the major characters in the *Mahābhārata* are *kṣatriyas* and the teachings given deal especially with the means for *kṣatriyas* to attain *svarga-loka* after death. Above all it is stressed that they must rule their kingdoms righteously, protecting and not oppressing the citizens, respecting the *brāhmaṇas*, performing *yajñas* and sustaining order. In Chapter 25 of the *Śānti*, Vyāsa cites the example of King Hayagrīva who ruled his kingdom righteously, fought heroically against his enemies, performed many *yajñas* at which charity was given to the priests and as a result was able to enjoy in heaven in the afterlife. In Chapter 70, Yudhiṣṭhira is told that a king may create any one of the four *yugas* in his kingdom by the efficacy of his rule and if he is righteous enough to create the conditions of the *Kṛtayuga* during his reign then he will certainly reach *svarga-loka–kṛtasya karaṇād rājā svargam atyantam aśnute* (26).

Throughout the text the point is repeatedly made that whatever else he does in life, if a *kṣatriya* dies in battle he will reach heaven after death. Thus even the most sinful of the characters, those dominated by asuric qualities, are found enjoying heavenly delights in the epic's final *parvan*. When Yudhiṣṭhira enters heaven and sees the elevated status of Duryodhana, he protests against this apparent injustice. He says to Nārada that he does not wish to remain in the same place as Duryodhana, who was always greedy and lacking in foresight–*nāhaṁ duryodhanena vai sahitaḥ kāmaye lokāḷ lubdhenādīrgha-darśinā* (18.1.7). Yudhiṣṭhira then refers to Duryodhana's sinful deeds, but Nārada tells him that in heaven all enemities must cease–*niruddhaṁ cāpi nasyati* (11). Duryodhana is now worshipped by those who dwell in *svarga-loka* because he offered his own body as a sacrifice in battle–*yuddhe hutvātmanas tanum* (14)–and is worthy of his position because he followed the *dharma* of *kṣatriyas* by showing no fear in a position that was most fearful–*bhaye mahati yo'bhīto babhūva* (15). Despite his many sins Duryodhana's heroic death has entitled him to an honourable position in *svarga-loka.*

Yudhiṣṭhira is dissatisfied with Nārada's explanation and cannot accept that one who has lived so wickedly should be rewarded so greatly. This difference of perspective between Nārada and Yudhiṣṭhira, both of whom speak with authoritative voices, represents an ongoing tension within the values of *pravṛtti.*

Soteriologically, it has been noted both morality and social duties of a ritual nature are accepted as means by which a position in heaven may be attained. In the *Svargārohaṇa* especially this tension is brought to the fore with the constant moralist openly condemning the rewards granted to those who adhered to *sva-dharma* but had no respect for morality. The question is posed but remains unanswered; it is recognised that the righteous will find the precedence of ritual over morality difficult to accept, but such is the nature of *dharma* in which harmony with the cosmic order is of equal significance to natural virtue.

4. The Path to Complete Salvation–*Mokṣa-Dharma*

(i) Introduction

Within the epic lengthy sections of the text are devoted to the subject of gaining salvation. Chapters 168 to 352 of the *Śānti*, the *Mokṣa-dharma*, are dedicated to this subject as is a substantial section of the *Aśvamedhika* and a number of earlier passages in the narrative in which various wise men instruct the major protagonists. It is these passages of the epic that enunciate the ideals of *nivṛtti* and the soteriology they present is based on this perspective.

The *Mokṣa-dharma* is made up of a series of *Upaniṣad*-like discourses each of which is worthy of detailed scrutiny to highlight the more or less unique perspective that it brings, but within the context of the present work such an attempt is clearly not possible. Rather the aim must be to look for the broad themes that unite the individual sections. In examining this complex topic I propose to utilise a view of soteriology that examines the subject under the following major headings:- 1. Rituals 2. Techniques 3. Ethics 4. Religious Organisation 5. Doctrines and 6. Grace. Some of these headings will require lengthy discussion and some of them very little, dependent of course on the nature of epic soteriology. Even if it is found that the teachings completely ignore one of these ways to salvation, that very absence is certainly noteworthy in attempting to establish a complete analysis of epic thought.

(ii) Ritual

It was noted earlier that the rituals of *yajña*, fasting, charity and pilgrimage play a significant role in reaching *svarga-loka*. In the teachings on *mokṣa-dharma*, however, such rituals have little or no significance. The *Mokṣa-dharma* is frequently critical of religious ritual, urging that such practice is based on ignorance. The Vedic rituals are of no value in gaining *mokṣa* and are in fact obstacles on the path, for the practitioner is striving after reward within this world rather than liberation from it. Bhīṣma therefore states that only those who are ignorant of Sāṁkhya wisdom perform *yajñas* and make pilgrimages–*tena tīrthāni yajñāś ca sevitavyāvipaścitā* (12.306.101). By *yajñas*, penances, acts of self-control and accepting vows men may attain heaven but they fall down again to earth–*divaṁ samāsādya patanti bhūmau* (103). The position of the unmanifest can never be gained by study of the Vedas, by penances, or by *yajñas–na svādhyāyais tapobhir vā yajñair vā kuru-nandana labhate 'vyakta-saṁsthānam* (102). Thus the rituals that lead to *svarga-loka* are dismissed as useless in the attempt to gain salvation.

(iii) Techniques and Practices

Under this heading are included practices that are almost exclusively 'self-help'. They are means that individuals can adopt to transform their consciousness and thereby become free from the ignorance that prevents salvation. If the problem that keeps us tied to this world is ignorance of our true identity, then the solution must be its antithesis, knowledge. This knowledge involves wholesale transformation of self-identity.

The *Mahābhārata* has clearly drawn on Upaniṣadic antecedents, but its teachings are distinguished from those of the *Upaniṣads* by the predominance of Sāṁkhya ideas that are present in the *Upaniṣads* only in the most embryonic forms. Although Sāṁkhya analyses matter as being composed of 24 elements, it is essentially a dualist doctrine for it insists on an emphatic distinction between matter and the inner self, the *ātman, puruṣa* or *kṣetrajña.* Its soteriological technique involves the transferral of self-identity from the body and senses to the *ātman.* The first phase of this transformation is the withdrawal from material identification. For this to be achieved all aspirations for pleasure and satisfaction through experience of the material elements must be given up. Thus the Sāṁkhya method of gaining salvation is characterised by asceticism and withdrawal from the world.

This stress on renunciation is reiterated throughout the teachings on *mokṣa-dharma.* In Chapter 2 of the *Vana,* Śaunaka instructs Yudhiṣṭhira that it is hankering–*tṛṣṇā*–that is the cause of sin and irreligion (34). Only those who give up desire can ever find happiness–*tāṁ tṛṣṇāṁ tyajataḥ sukham* (35). In the *Udyoga,* Sanatsujāta, who teaches Vedānta doctrines based on the *Kaṭha* and other *Upaniṣads,*[6] likewise urges that desires for worldly enjoyment must be abandoned. Men cannot conquer death because they desire to enjoy the results of their actions and thus are held captive by their acts (5.42.8). It is lust and anger that bind one to death and hence one who rises above such urges is able to go beyond death–*dhīrās tu dhairyeṇa taranti mṛtyum* (12). The removal of desire is a concomitant of the *jñāna* that is the key to *mokṣa* and hence death can only be conquered by one who has transcended sensual aspirations.

The *Mokṣa-dharma* also accepts this premise, and makes the transcendence of desire a vital element in the means of gaining salvation. In Chapter 197 of the *Śānti,* Manu uses the allegory of clear water to illustrate the point. When water is still and clear it is transparent and in the same way when the senses are stilled one is able to see by means of knowledge that which is the object of knowledge–*tadvat prasannendriyavāñ jñeyaṁ jñānena paśyati* (2). But as one can see nothing within disturbed water so when the senses are disturbed one can no longer perceive the object of knowledge–*tathendriyākulī-bhāve jñeyaṁ jñāne na paśyati* (3). In Chapter 207, a part of the instructions given by a *guru* to his disciple, it is argued that *brahmacārya,* celibacy, is the way to gain *brahman–brahmacāryam iti smṛtam . . . tena yānti parāṁ gatim* (7). In Chapter 208, the disciple is instructed on the lifestyle of one who seeks salvation. He should give up all desires and live happily on whatever he gets by begging, without any attachment–*bhikṣur nirapekṣaś caret sukham* (3). He should wander alone, eat sparingly, execute austerities and control his senses–*vivikta-cārī laghvāśī tapasvī niyatendriyaḥ* (15).

Virtually every teacher in the *Mokṣa-dharma* makes the point that to gain salvation, desire for material enjoyment has to be abandoned. There is never any palatable compromise whereby one is able to enjoy the pleasures of this world and yet somehow still gain *mokṣa.* The ideas of *buddhi-yoga* and *niṣkāma-karma* of the *Bhagavad-gītā* are not expounded at any length in the *Mokṣa-dharma* and in fact are dismissed by the female ascetic, Sulabhā, in her teachings to Janaka (12.308.127-177). In any case, although it urges the practitioner to remain in his position in society rather than withdraw to a life of mendicancy, the *Gītā* still teaches that sensual enjoyment must be abandoned. The only different is that *buddhi-yoga* teaches that desire can be transcended whilst the individual continues to perform his social duties. In the quest for *mokṣa* no-one can be the servant of two masters. One who seeks permanent liberation from the cycle of rebirth must give up the aspirations for happiness that are common in human society. For this reason it is made plain that the quest for salvation is only for those few who are most spiritually elevated and that these teachings are a disturbance for the mass of the people and nothing more.

It is important to recognise how the *Mokṣa-dharma* repeatedly links Sāṁkhya with Yoga. A clear pattern may be detected whereby the nature of existence is presented on the basis of Sāṁkhya followed by an exposition on the *yoga* practice that will enable the individual to perceive these truths. As with virtually any assertion about the structure of the *Mokṣa-dharma*, this is not absolute but it is undoubtedly a significant trend that is also found in the *Bhagavad-gītā.* The earliest known expositions of Sāṁkhya are found in the *Mokṣa-dharma*, though they fall short of being systematic presentations. The enumeration of the elements of matter and the stress on the difference between the soul and *prakṛti* are the central themes, but these are mixed with monistic speculation on the oneness of the soul and *brahman*, characteristic of Vedānta.

Bearing all these points in mind, it is still possible to attempt to identify a distinctive epic soteriology. Sāṁkhya is a technique of gaining salvation, and as the technique is that of 'knowing', *jñāna* is the essential key to *mokṣa.* Chapter 289 of the *Śānti* is particularly significant for an understanding of epic Sāṁkhya for therein Bhīṣma discusses the features that distinguish it from Yoga. He concludes in verse 9 that the two are in essence the same–*tulyam*–and that the only difference is in their scriptures or doctrines–*darśanaṁ na samaṁ tayoḥ* (9). He defines the distinctive doctrines of Sāṁkhya as follows,

> *vadanti kāraṇaṁ cedaṁ sāṁkhyāḥ samyag dvijātayaḥ*
> *vijñāyeha gatīḥ sarvā virakto viṣayeṣu yaḥ*
>
> *ūrdhvaṁ sa dehāt suvyaktaṁ vimucyed iti nānyathā*
> *etad āhur mahāprājñāḥ sāṁkhyaṁ vai mokṣa-darśanam*

'The twice-born followers of Sāṁkhya then put forward the argument that one who is detached from sensual pleasures and has knowledge of all states of being, on leaving the body is clearly seen as liberated. It cannot be otherwise. Those who are very wise say that this doctrine of salvation is Sāṁkhya.' (12.289.4-5)

In Chapter 294, a part of the Sāṁkhya teachings of Vasiṣṭha, the same point is made, but the nature of the knowledge being referred to is made more specific. Vasiṣṭha states that the followers of Sāṁkhya teach that matter is composed of twenty-four elements–*tattvāni ca caturviṁśat parisāṁkhyāya tattvataḥ*–but that which is beyond these elements is the twenty-fifth–*nistattvataḥ pañcaviṁśakaḥ* (42). Vasiṣṭha then defines the knowledge that is the key to salvation,

pañcaviṁśo 'prabuddhātmā 'budhyamāna iti smṛtaḥ
yadā tu budhyate "tmānaṁ tadā bhavati kevalaḥ

'The twenty-fifth element is known as the self which does not have its intelligence awakened. But when the self is perceived then it is alone (and free from contact with matter). (12.294.43)

He concludes in verses 45 to 49 by asserting that those who absorb this knowledge escape from the control of matter and become liberated, while those in ignorance remain here.

The word Sāṁkhya means a calculation, analysis or, according to Edgerton,[7] differentiation. Matter, designated as *prakṛti* in later Sāṁkhya but often referred to as *sattva* or *pradhāna* in the *Mahābhārata,* is analysed as being composed of twenty-four elements. The listings vary between the treatises of the *Mokṣa-dharma,* and occasionally the number sixteen is reached rather than twenty-four, but typically they include the five elements—earth, water, fire, air and space—the five senses—smell, taste, touch, hearing and sight—the five objects of the senses—scent, flavour, feel, sound and form—and the organs of action—speech, legs, arms, anus and genitals; in addition there is mind, intelligence, self-awareness (*manas, buddhi, ahaṁkāra*) and the *mahat,* the great element from which all else has been created. The elements included in such enumerations differ slightly between passages, but twenty-four is the usual number arrived at.

The soul is defined as the true self which is entirely different from the twenty-four elements of matter. It is only because of ignorance and misidentification that the soul is controlled by matter and when one reaches a state of full knowledge of the distinction between the elements of matter and the soul, then matter no longer has any control. This is *mokṣa.* Sāṁkhya salvation is thus based on a dualist view of existence, and it is realisation of the dualism that is the key to *mokṣa.* This knowing should not, however, be misinterpreted as salvation through the comprehension of a doctrine. It is realisation and identification with the soul. Far beyond the mere academic comprehension of philosophical truths, Sāṁkhya *mokṣa* means to no longer live as if one were the body that is comprised of gross matter or even the mind and intelligence that are matter of a more subtle kind.

Material aims in the form of sensual pleasures, prestige, power, and even elevated rebirth are useless goals in the Sāṁkhya view for they pertain only to something that is not oneself. Thus in Chapter 206, for example, we find the *guru* teaching his disciple that knowledge has sensual desire as its antithesis for desire only exists where true knowledge is absent. It was noted earlier that asceticism and withdrawal from the world were prominent themes in the *Mahābhārata's* teachings on salvation. When the Sāṁkhya perspective is understood it becomes clear why there is no possibility of any reconciliation between enjoying material pleasures and finding salvation through the Sāṁkhya technique of absorbing knowledge.

Although the *Mokṣa-dharma* is dominated by Sāṁkhya, the *Mahābhārata* also draws upon the Vedāntic concepts first enunciated in the *Upaniṣads.* From a soteriological perspective the ideas of Sāṁkhya and Vedānta are markedly similar. Crucially in both systems it is knowledge that is the key to *mokṣa.* It is the nature of that knowledge that differentiates Vedānta from Sāṁkhya, for it is based on a monism that sees all things as one, and recognises the variety in this world as illusion. While Sāṁkhya identifies distinctive categories in its analysis of matter and does not see *mokṣa* in monistic terms, in Vedānta the key doctrine is expressed as, *sarvaṁ khalv idaṁ brahma*–all is *brahman* alone, and the illusion that binds the *ātman* to this world is the misidentification of the self as an individual separate from *brahman,* the totality of all existence. Hence, *tat tvam asi*–you are that–is another key aphorism in the *vedānta-jñāna* that leads to *mokṣa.*

The teachings of Sanat-sujāta to Dhṛtarāṣṭra are clearly based on Vedānta rather than Sāṁkhya. The *jñāna* that Sanat-sujāta stresses as the means to remove all miseries reveals that the *ātman* is one with *brahman,* the Supreme Spirit. Thus he says, *abhyāvarteta brahmāsya antarātmani vai śritam*–you must turn towards that *brahman* situated within the self (5.33.44). Sanat-sujāta instructs that one should take to *yoga* practice for *yogins* gain true vision. This vision enables them to see that the Supreme is situated within themselves. In Chapter 45, he repeatedly stresses that what the *yogins* perceive is the Supreme Brahman that is all-pervasive and exists in all things, repeating the refrain, *yoginas taṁ prapaśyanti bhagavantaṁ sanātanam*–the *yogins* see that eternal Worshipful One.

Thus within the *Mahābhārata* the teachings that tend towards Sāṁkhya and those that are based more on Vedāntic ideas (though the distinction is frequently blurred) both contain the notion that salvation is attained through realised knowledge. Both also recognise that practical means may be employed in attaining such realisation, and hence both are typically linked with techniques that aim at absorbing and realising *jñāna.* It is such techniques that are referred to as Yoga.

Yoga is an ancient practice, perhaps even predating the Āryan invasion, that probably originated as a means of gaining magical power. Unlike Sāṁkhya, Yoga is referred to in numerous *Upaniṣads* although, notably, it is the *Kaṭha* and *Śvetāśvatara* that have the most thorough expositions. Within the epic narrative, we find various characters practising *yoga,* usually in conjunction with harsh austerity, in order to gain power to defeat their enemies but, as Frauwallner notes,[8] this is clearly distinct from the practice of *yoga* as a part of the quest for salvation. Jayadratha gains the power to defeat four of the Pāṇḍavas thereby, and Ambā is granted her wish for vengeance against Bhīṣma. Within the didactic passages, however, Yoga is recognised primarily as a soteriological technique and the magical powers gained are warned against as a distraction. The narrative also recognises the soteriological function of Yoga, as the death of Droṇa reveals, but in the context of the power struggle it is describing it is more often the former function that predominates.

The *Mokṣa-dharma* frequently refers to Yoga in conjunction with Sāṁkhya as a powerful means of gaining salvation. Sāṁkhya is the process of gaining salvation through knowledge and Yoga is the discipline by which one may detach oneself from this world and gain the knowledge that brings *mokṣa.* It is important to note that both Yoga and Sāṁkhya have at their heart the idea that knowledge is the key that can unlock the door to salvation and it is this common ground that links them together. Yoga is the means, through its techniques of meditation and turning one's vision inwards, by which the soul may be perceived as independent of the body. Thus it allows direct perception of the *sāṁkhya-jñāna* that frees the *ātman* from its bondage to matter and to material actions and their results.

In order to understand the *Mahābhārata*'s view of Yoga, in terms of both its practice and its purpose, I propose to attempt a brief survey of the chapters of the *Mokṣa-dharma* in which Yoga is specifically discussed.

(a) *Bhīṣma's Teachings in Chapters* 188 *to* 190

In Chapter 187 of the *Śānti,* Yudhiṣṭhira asks Bhīṣma to explain to him that which is known as *adhyātma.* Under this heading, Bhīṣma gives a discourse on the nature of the soul as different from matter in terms that reflect the influence of Sāṁkhya, though without specific reference. In Chapter 188, he goes on without interruption to introduce the topic of *yoga* meditation, which he says is of four types–*hanta vakṣyāmi te pārtha dhyāna-yogaṁ catur-vidham.* Verse 2 illustrates the links between Yoga and *jñāna* by stating that the *yogins* are *jñāna-tṛptāḥ,* satisfied with knowledge. Verse 3 makes it clear that Yoga, like Sāṁkhya, is a means of gaining salvation, stating that *yogins* are free from the faults of rebirth and never come back again–*nāvartante punaḥ pārtha muktāḥ saṁsāra-doṣataḥ.*

Bhīṣma stresses that the *yogin* should live in a solitary place, restrain his senses from any form of indulgence, and remain rapt in meditation. The result of this is happiness that is unobtainable through either destiny or endeavour. The process of meditation is joyful for the *yogins* to perform, and through it they gain salvation from which there is no return–*gacchanti yogino hy evaṁ nirvāṇaṁ tan nirāmayam* (22).

In Chapter 189, Bhīṣma discusses the process of meditation known as *japa,* which involves audible recitation of a *mantra.* The technique is different but the aim is still to withdraw the senses and bring the mind under control (13). Chanting the assigned or beneficial *mantra–japan vai saṁhitāṁ hitām*–the *yogin* meditates on *brahman–tad dhiyā dhyāyati brahma* (14)–but gives up the practice when he enters the stage of *samādhi* or total absorption in meditation. Again the conclusion of this discourse is notably soteriological. When he is fully tranquil within and free from contamination the *yogin* attains immortality in a purified state–*amṛtaṁ virajaḥ śuddham ātmānaṁ pratipadyate* (21). In Chapter 190, Bhīṣma expresses the opinion that *japa* is an inferior *yoga* technique and that if he falls short in his endeavours, acts with pride or desire for material results, the *jāpaka* will go to hell–*nirayaṁ sa nigacchati* (3). The explanation for this is given in verse 13; *japa* is certainly a praiseworthy practice–*praśastaṁ jāpakatvam*–but those who fail in their endeavours experience many hells because it is a technique lacking proper knowledge–*duṣprajñānena nirayā bahavaḥ samudāhṛtāḥ*.

(b) *The Yoga Practised by Ikṣvāku and a Brāhmaṇa*

Chapter 192 contains the story of a *brāhmaṇa* and King Ikṣvāku, both of whom endeavour to gain salvation through Yoga. The *brāhmaṇa* recites *japa* in the form of a *mantra* or *saṁhitā* and gains *mokṣa* thereby. Having given the results of his *japa* to the king, the *brāhmaṇa* then begins to practise a different type of *yoga* with him. Verse 16 of Chapter 193 describes how they engaged in breathing exercises to regulate and control the airs of life that circulate within the body. The two breaths in which the soul is thought to reside, the *prāṇa* and *apāṇa*, are raised from the abdomen to a point between the eyebrows (17) while their concentration is fixed on the tip of the nose. Their bodies are motionless, their vision steady, their minds completely fixed–*niśceṣṭābhyāṁ śarīrābhyāṁ sthira-dṛṣṭī samāhitau* (18). In this state the *ātman* is moved to the head–*tathādhāya mūrdhny ātmānam*–and then the effulgent soul of the *brāhmaṇa* bursts upwards from his head and ascends to the highest part of heaven–*tālu-deśam athoddālya . . . jagāma tridivaṁ tadā* (19). From there both the *brāhmaṇa* and Ikṣvāku gain *mokṣa* by entering into the god Brahmā–*brahmāṇaṁ prāviśat tadā* (20).

(c) *Vyāsa's Teachings to Śuka*

Chapter 228 contains a detailed discourse on Yoga delivered by Vyāsa to his son Śuka. In verse 1 he states that *jñāna* is the raft that can deliver one who is cast up and down on the ocean of life. The wise can deliver others, but the ignorant cannot even save themselves. Having thus laid stress on *jñāna*, Vyāsa begins his discourse on Yoga as the means to gain that knowledge. In this chapter Yoga is combined with Sāṁkhya for Yoga is the means by which the soul, here designated by the Sāṁkhya term *kṣetrajña*, is able to break through the elements of matter to which it is bound by ignorance. The method of *yoga* taught here is *dhāraṇa*, concentration of the mind on one object. Verse 13 states that there are seven basic kinds of *dhāraṇa* directed through each of the senses so that sometimes the mind is fixed on a sound, sometimes on a taste, sometimes on a sight etc.

By such practice, the *yogin* is able to project his vision through the covering elements of matter defined by Sāṁkhya, and thus gradually begin to perceive the soul within as it becomes more clearly apparent in its nature as *brahman–aśuklaṁ cetasaḥ saukṣmyaṁ brahmaṇo 'sya vai* (20). The *yogin* will then gain tremendous power, like that of the gods, being able to make the world tremble with just his toe or hand. But it is through giving up all worldly aspirations, controlling his senses and never harming other beings that the follower of Sāṁkhya is liberated by this technique–*īdṛk sāṁkhyo vimucyate* (36-37). In this chapter Yoga is presented as a facet of Sāṁkhya from which it is inseparable. Again the soteriological conclusion to the discourse is noteworthy as the object of all that has been previously discussed–*evaṁ bhavati nirdvaṁdvo brahmaṇaṁ cādhigacchati*, thus he is free from duality, and attains *brahman* (38).

In Chapter 231, Vyāsa, according to his own statement, teaches Śuka further on the basis of Sāṁkhya, and in Chapter 232 turns to Yoga once more. The formula for this introduction is familiar and significant: I have taught you on the basis of Sāṁkhya logic–*sāṁkhya-nyāyena*–now hear about *yoga* practice. This *yoga* is defined in verse 2 as the concentrating together of the mind, intelligence and senses and meditating on the *ātman*. The *yogin* should be peaceful and restrained and find pleasure in the *ātman*. He must withdraw the senses from their objects and live a renounced life, pure, without indulgence, and equal to all (3-12). At dawn and dusk he should concentrate the mind by means of the self–*dhārayen mana ātmanā* (13)–and thus restrain the mind and senses. When the senses and mind are still, the *yogin* is able to perceive *brahman* (17) or the *ātman* which is everywhere and pervades all things (18). After engaging in such practice for a measured time, the *yogin* attains equality with the imperishable–*gacched akṣara-sāmyatām* (20). Magical powers will come to him, but he must turn away from them and continue his practice–*tāṁs tattva-vid anādṛtya svātmanaiva nivartayet* (22). The process is then repeated before reaching the soteriological conclusion; whatever his birth or social status, one who follows this path can reach the highest goal–*etena mārgeṇa gacchetāṁ paramāṁ gatim* (32).

The *yoga* practice described in this chapter aims at the concentration of perception on the self within. There is no reference here to breath control or raising the airs of life to the upper parts of the body. In addition, it is apparent that the *yoga* described in Chapter 232, despite the introductory verse, is based on Vedānta rather than Sāṁkhya. *Mokṣa* is still gained by the knowledge that is acquired through *yoga* perception, but it is a monist form of *jñāna* recognising the self within as equal to the one all-pervading spirit that is the key that opens the door to salvation.

(d) *Bhīṣma's Teachings in Chapter* 289

Chapter 289 is important in understanding the *Mahābhārata*'s teachings on both Sāṁkhya and Yoga. Here Yudhiṣṭhira specifically asks Bhīṣma what the differences are between these two paths to salvation. Bhīṣma starts by saying that the followers of Sāṁkhya and Yoga each think that their own way is superior. It is implied in verse 3 that the followers of Yoga criticise Sāṁkhya because it is non-theistic–*anīśvaraḥ kathaṁ mucyed iti . . . vadanti kāraṇaiḥ śreṣṭhyaṁ yogāḥ*.

In verses 4 and 5, Bhīṣma gives the Sāṁkhya version; by knowing all the features of the world, one who becomes dissociated from all objects of sensual enjoyment is clearly liberated after giving up his body–*vijñāyeha gatīḥ sarvā virakto viṣayeṣu yaḥ: ūrdhvaṁ sa dehāt suvyaktaṁ vimucyed.* Hopkins is convinced that these and other passages reveal conclusively that Sāṁkhya and Yoga were originally two distinct systems and that the 'pseudo-epic's' endeavour to draw them together is an artificial imposition based only on their common soteriological objective'.[9] Hopkins has here missed several points. First, he has failed to grasp that both Sāṁkhya and Yoga are essentially soteriological systems, and hence if the soteriological ground is common the two must be closely linked. Furthermore, the notion that theism is central to Yoga cannot be sustained, for, as is apparent from the passages examined above, the Deity plays no role in the execution of yogic techniques. In soteriological terms, Yoga does not embody any doctrine of grace from the *Īśvara,* or Deity, revealed either within or without. Yoga, Like Sāṁkhya, is a 'self-help' technique based on the efforts of the individual to absorb knowledge and on these grounds it is reasonable to accept the epic's repeated assertions of the close connections between Sāṁkhya and Yoga.

Bhīṣma then states that he approves of both Sāṁkhya and Yoga and that either may be adopted. Yoga depends on direct perception while Sāṁkhya is based on the evidence of scripture–*pratyakṣa-hetavo yogāḥ sāṁkhyāḥ śāstra-viniścayaḥ* (7). This may again appear to be a major difference of approach, but the point is that the *sāṁkhyas* gain their knowledge of the difference of the self from matter from scripture, while the *yogins* directly perceive the transcendent soul through meditation. The actual knowledge and its soteriological goal remain the same.

Bhīṣma states again that both systems are acceptable in his opinion, and in the opinion of the best of men, in terms of their truth–*tattve*–and their knowledge–*jñāne.* If followed according to their scriptures, they will lead one to salvation–*anuṣṭhite yathā-śāstraṁ nayetāṁ paramāṁ gatim* (8). Both entail equal purity and compassion to all beings–*tulyaṁ śaucaṁ tayor yuktaṁ dayā bhūteṣu ca*–and both are equal in adhering to vows–*vratānāṁ dhāraṇaṁ tulyam* (9). The final phrase of verse 9–*darśanaṁ na samaṁ tayoḥ*–seems to refer back to the differences of doctrine mentioned in verses 3 and 4. Bhīṣma, however, clearly does not think that this apparent theism of Yoga and atheism of Sāṁkhya is crucial, and the key here is again soteriological. If the theism of Yoga entailed a doctrine of salvation through grace then that would make the two systems essentially different, but a review of the teachings on Yoga reveals that this is not the case.

In verse 10, further elucidation is sought by Yudhiṣṭhira on why the doctrines should differ when other facets of the two systems are identical–*tulyaṁ na darśanaṁ kasmāt.* Bhīṣma's reply seems not to address the question, for he then begins a discourse on Yoga alone. It is noteworthy that the ensuing description of the means by which *yogins* attain salvation is markedly antithetical to any concept of grace, for the entire passage centres on the power of the *yogin.* This great power enables the *yogin* both to dominate this world by his supernatural potency and to break free from material existence and gain salvation. As an accomplished archer can hit a target, so the *yogin* reaches *mokṣa–yuktaḥ samyak tathā yogī mokṣaṁ prāpnoti* (31).

In verses 32 to 41, Bhīṣma stresses that *yoga* practice will bring salvation, though the exercises themselves are here referred to only briefly. Verse 33 mentions the purification of the self through fixed control–*ayamātmānaṁ . . . niścalam*–and 37 elaborates on this slightly by mentioning inner concentration. The *yogin* remains immovable with his self, or perhaps consciousness, having entered into the self–*āveśyātmani cātmānaṁ yogī tiṣṭhati yo 'calaḥ* (38)–and thereby removes all sins to reach the topmost goal. By uniting the subtle self with the self–*ātmanā sūkṣmam ātmānaṁ yuṅkte*–in various parts of the body the *yogin* burns to ashes all reactions to his previous acts–*sa śīghram amala-prajñaḥ karma dagdhvā śubhāśubham* (41). Then, if he desires it, he may attain salvation. The point here is that rebirth ensues as the reactions to previous acts inevitably bear their fruits. If these reactions are destroyed by the power of *yoga* one is no longer compelled to exist in this world to live out his self-generated destiny.

Yudhiṣṭhira then inquires about how a *yogin* must live whilst executing his vows. Bhīṣma replies by describing the harsh lifestyle that is required of one who seeks success on this path (43-62). He must fast for long periods, never touch meat, remain celibate and give up worldly attachments. For this reason very few people are able to follow the *yoga* system, which is like the edge of a razor (55). One who is successful in Yoga is able to enter any of the gods listed in verses 58 to 61. The final verse, 62, states that this teaching relates to the all-powerful Deity–*deve mahā-vīrya-matau*–and that the great one who has conquered all forms of *yoga* is able to make Nārāyaṇa his very self–*yogān sa sarvān abhibhūya martyān nārāyaṇātmā kurute mahātmā.* This reference to Nārāyaṇa may be connected with Bhīṣma's earlier assertion that Yoga demands the acceptance of *Īśvara* or God, but it must be recognised that in the *yoga* teachings presented no role whatsoever is ascribed to the Deity.

(e) *Vasiṣṭha's Teachings to Karālajanaka*

In Chapter 294, King Karālajanaka questions Vasiṣṭha, saying that he has not fully understood the latter's previous discourse because he is unsure on the issue of oneness and multiplicity. The question itself is interesting because the matter about which the king seeks clarification seems to be that on which the major division between Sāṁkhya and Vedānta rests. At the end of his question he states that he wishes to know about Sāṁkhya and Yoga in full (5).

Vasiṣṭha replies by dealing first with Yoga (6-24) and then with Sāṁkhya (25-49). He begins by pointing out what has become apparent from previous passages, that there are two types of *yoga* meditation taught by those who know the Vedas–*tac cāpi dvi-vidhaṁ dhyānam āhur veda-vido janāḥ* (7).[10] One involves concentration of the mind on one point and the other the regulation of breath–*ekāgratā ca manasaḥ prāṇayāmas tathaiva ca* (8). The discourse that follows focuses primarily on concentrating the mind on the self within. First the senses must be withdrawn from their objects (10) and then by twenty-two methods the mind must be fixed on that which is beyond the twenty-four elements–*daśa-dvādaśabhir vāpi catur-viṁśāt paraṁ tataḥ*. That is the *ātman* which is never subject to decay and may be known by these methods–*taiś cātmā satataṁ jñeyaḥ* (12). Free from attachments, eating what comes of its own accord, and controlling the senses–*vimuktaḥ sarva-saṅgebhyo labdhvāhāro jitendriyaḥ*–the *yogin* must concentrate his mind on the self at dawn and at dusk–*pūrva-rātre pare caiva dhārayeta mano "tmani* (13). Perfection in Yoga comes when the mind is fixed on this one point and all the senses are rendered inactive (14-18).

Verse 19 claims that through Yoga the knower becomes that which is to be known, the soul within–*hṛdaya-stho 'natarātmeti jñeyo jñaḥ*. This *ātman* is perceived by great souls who have reached *brahman*. It is smaller than the smallest thing–*aṇubhyo 'ṇu*–and is within all beings–*antaḥ sarva-bhūteṣu* (22). The *ātman* is the creator of the world and may be perceived beyond the great darkness in a state where darkness does not exist–*mahatas tamasas tāta pāre tiṣṭhann atāmasaḥ* (23). Vasiṣṭha concludes his discussion of Yoga by saying that through this technique the *yogins* are able to perceive the ageless, supreme *ātman*–*evaṁ paśyaṁ prapaśyanti ātmānam ajaraṁ param* (25).

Significant here is the fact that Yoga is presented as a means of gaining knowledge through direct perception. This refers back to Bhīṣma's statement in Chapter 289 that Yoga utilises *pratyakṣa*, direct perception, while Sāṁkhya is based on the version of scripture. Here it is plain that Yoga is a means of gaining direct perception of the transcendent *ātman* described by the Sāṁkhya scriptures. In the *yoga* system described by Vasiṣṭha there is little to suggest a theistic perspective. It may be construed from the words *loka-kṛt* in verse 23 that the *ātman* is to be equated with *īśvara,* but this is only hinted at and no elaboration ensues or is requested by Karālajanaka.

(f) *The Teachings of Yājñavalkya*

The teachings of Yājñavalkya which follow those of Vasiṣṭha also deal with the subject of Sāṁkhya and Yoga. In Chapter 303, he discusses the difference of the *puruṣa* from *prakṛti,* and concludes by saying,

> *sāṁkhya-darśanam etat te parisaṁkhyātam uttamam*
> *evaṁ hi parisaṁkhyāya sāṁkhyāḥ kevalatāṁ gatāḥ*
>
> *ye tu anye tattva-kuśalās teṣām etan nidarśanam*
> *ataḥ paraṁ pravakṣyāmi yogānām api darśanam*
>
> 'This most excellent analysis, the doctrine of Sāṁkhya, (has now been imparted) to you. By such analysis the *sāṁkhyas* gain a state of separateness from matter.
>
> But there are others who are experts in the truth; this is their teaching. Hence I shall now expound on the excellent doctrine of those who follow Yoga.' (12.303.20-21)

In Chapter 304, Yājñavalkya makes the interesting statement that there is no *jñāna* like that of the *sāṁkhyas* and no power like that of the *yogins–nāsti sāṁkhya-samaṁ jñānaṁ nāsti yoga-samaṁ balam* (2). Men of small intelligence see them as separate–*pṛthak pṛthak*–but Yājñavalkya sees them as one system–*vayaṁ tu rājan paśyāma ekam* (3). Verses 5 and 6 are obscure but according to the commentator indicate that by practising the techniques of breath control the *yogin* gains the magical power to wander in all directions at will. In the Vedas an eightfold *yoga* is described by the wise–*aṣṭa-guṇitaṁ yogam* (7). This verse provides some link with the later *Yoga-sūtras* of Patañjali which also refer to *aṣṭāṅga-yoga,* a *yoga* of eight limbs.

Yājñavalkya gives a brief description of *prāṇāyāma,* referring to twelve ways of impelling the breath at the beginning of the night and twelve ways to be practised in the early morning (10-11). He then moves on to *dhāraṇa*; the senses are to be withdrawn back into the mind–*manasy abhiniveśya ha* (14)–the mind into *ahaṁkāra*, *ahaṁkāra* into the intelligence, and intelligence into *prakṛti*, the original source of the material elements. It is to be noted that this *yoga* technique is based on Sāṁkhya and is in effect a reversal of the Sāṁkhya concept of the evolution of the elements in the process of creation. The idea seems to be that Yoga reverses the process by which the *ātman* becomes ensheathed in these elements and thereby held in bondage; thus the connection here between Yoga and Sāṁkhya is very close. Like a lamp in a place where no wind blows, the *yogin* cannot be disturbed. He is as firm as a rock and even the loud sounds of musical instruments cannot break his concentration (22). The conclusion of the discourse takes the usual soteriological form. One who practises *yoga* is able to perceive the supreme unchanging *brahman* and having given up his body, he becomes free from matter and is alone–*etena kevalaṁ yāti tyaktvā deham asākṣikam* (25).

The discourse of Yājñavalkya displays the typical features noted in earlier chapters on the same subject. Yoga is linked with Sāṁkhya by the declaration that they are essentially the same system, though the stress in Yoga is on the power that it brings both whilst existing in this world and in forcing one's way to salvation. The two types of *yoga*, breath control and concentration, are described briefly and the ultimate goal of the techniques is presented as *mokṣa* in the conclusion of the discourse. There is no reference to theistic beliefs and no hint of the identification of the *ātman* with Viṣṇu or Nārāyaṇa. Again the perspective can only be described as non-theistic, and the apparent distinction between Sāṁkhya and Yoga based on Chapter 289 cannot be sustained here.

The passages reviewed above are by no means the only references to Yoga found in the *Mahābhārata*, but they represent the principal sections of the epic in which teachings on Yoga are disseminated. There are clearly some differences of perspective between individual passages but these are of a minor nature and throughout a basic continuity of thought prevails. Yoga is repeatedly linked to Sāṁkhya as a means of directly perceiving the knowledge of the soul expounded in Sāṁkhya doctrine. This knowledge is the key to salvation and soteriology is at the very heart of Yoga as it is with Sāṁkhya.

(iv) Ethics

Ethics plays a very important part in the *Mahābhārata*'s religious ideas and the characters of the narrative are clearly drawn to illustrate ethical traits. With regard to soteriology, the key role of ethics in the attainment of *svarga-loka* has already been noted. In looking at the relationship between ethics and salvation, however, the issue is more complex. It is apparent that *mokṣa* is not gained as a reward for living in accordance with ethical precepts but through *jñāna*. Some passages even indicate that all notions of ethics are a part of this world and are hence to be transcended in reaching *mokṣa*. Right and wrong pertain to actions in this world and thus lose their relevance for one who is able to go beyond it. Righteous and wicked deeds bring pleasant or unpleasant results but one who seeks *mokṣa* wants no results at all and hence must transcend both:

> *puṇya-pāpa-mayaṁ dehaṁ kṣapayan karma-saṁcayāt*
> *kṣīna-dehaḥ punar dehī brahmatvam upagacchati*
>
> 'The body is derived from piety and sin, from the accumulation of various acts, but the embodied soul which can transcend bodily existence attains the level of *brahman*.' (12.267.37)

Nonetheless, within the teachings on salvation emphasis is placed on right action. The ethics of *mokṣa-dharma* are a world-renouncing belief system that opposes all aspirations for sensual enjoyment and seeks only the happiness of inner contemplation. The recognition of the connection between *mokṣa* and proper behaviour is shown by the teachings of Sanat-sujāta. In Chapter 43 of the *Udyoga*, he presents an ethical treatise which discusses the acts that must be followed and avoided by one seeking salvation (7-22). Only one who renounces the wicked qualities he refers to and seeks the good will find happiness–*mukto hy etaiḥ sukhī bhavet* (21). The notion of right action is based on dissociation from the world and giving up greed, anger, enmity and all forms of sensual desire, for immortality is found in self-restraint, in renunciation and in careful vigilance–*damas tyāgo 'pramādaś ca eteṣv amṛtam āhitam* (14).

Discourses of this type make up a substantial part of the

teachings of the *Mokṣa-dharma,* revealing that right action is recognised as a vital part of the process of gaining salvation. Chapter 222 of the *Śānti,* for example, presents teachings from the sage Jaigiṣavya to the effect that salvation is gained by living a lifestyle based on renunciation and adhering strictly to an appropriate ethical code. There is no reference here to Sāṁkhya or Yoga although Bhīṣma's recitation of this treatise comes in response to a question specifically on the subject of the lifestyle of one seeking salvation.

Right action, based on renunciation, not harming other beings, and not retaliating when insults and injuries are received is thus a central feature of the prescribed path to salvation, but is it then an alternative to the techniques of Sāṁkhya and Yoga discussed previously? It is apparent from the text that this is not the case and that ethical conduct is an integral part of these systems. *Sāṁkhya-jñāna* stresses the distinction of *puruṣa* from *prakṛti* and thus only one in ignorance of this wisdom seeks pleasure through the senses. Desire is both the antithesis of *sāṁkhya-jñāna,* in that it reflects the view that the body is the self, and also the basis of unethical action. Ethics is both a sign of knowledge and a means of gaining it by restraining the senses. One does not harm others or retaliate for injuries received because to do so is to acknowledge the perspective of ignorance and identify the self with the body.

This antithesis between knowledge and desire that lies at the heart of the ethics of *mokṣa-dharma,* is expressed in Chapter 206 of the *Śānti,* wherein the unnamed *guru* says to his disciple, *mānavā jñāna-saṁmohāt tataḥ kāmaṁ prayānti vai*–because of bewilderment of knowledge men seek to satisfy desires (3). From such desires come anger, greed and bewilderment, and then pride and egotism, different actions, affection, happiness and distress, and rebirth in various species. Thus when *jñāna* is absent, desire is manifest and in desire are the roots of unrighteous behaviour. When *jñāna* is present, desire is conquered and the ethics of *mokṣa-dharma* automatically prevail. In Chapter 266, Bhīṣma stresses that virtue is not in itself the way to *mokṣa* and eventually must also be transcended. But it is a part of the path because lust, anger, greed and other bad qualities are impediments to Yoga. These are removed by ethical conduct and then the soteriological techniques can be successfully undertaken.

It is thus correct to conclude that ethics are an essential part of epic soteriology. The role of ethics, however, must be correctly understood. It is very different from that postulated in certain forms of Christian theology wherein it is conceived that at death one's righteous and wicked deeds are weighed against each other and on the basis of the ensuing judgement one is assessed as worthy of either damnation or the gift of grace which brings salvation. In the passages discussed above, ethics have nothing to do with grace or gaining the favour of an external Deity, but are a part of the techniques of Sāṁkhya and Yoga. In this sense they do not even appeal to some absolute morality ordained by higher authority, as is the case with *sva-dharma* which is supposed to be delineated by Vedic decree. In *mokṣa-dharma* ethics are followed not because they are essentially 'right' but because they are efficacious in bringing detachment from desire. Desire depends on the illusion that the self is material and if desire is constrained by right conduct the illusion falls away and *jñāna* prevails. *Jñāna* is always the key to salvation and the ethics of *mokṣa-dharma* must be understood in this context.

(v) Religious Organisation

In Chapter 3, the links between religious organisation and soteriology have been discussed at some length and I do not propose to repeat that discussion here. Suffice to say that the way of *mokṣa* is wholly individualistic and no significance is ascribed to adherence to sect, church or religious community. In the doctrines of *mokṣa-dharma* even the traditional view of who is a *brāhmaṇa* is challenged to allow it to include any person who is spiritually advanced. The concept of salvation through the mediation of an individual or body on earth is also absent from the doctrines of Sāṁkhya and Yoga taught by the epic.

(vi) Comprehension of a True Doctrine

It may appear that the attainment of salvation through *jñāna* in Sāṁkhya, Vedānta and Yoga should be placed in this category. The discussion of the nature of *jñāna* in Chapter 2 revealed, however, that the knowledge that brings salvation goes far beyond the comprehension of a philosophical or theological system. It involves a total transformation of self-identity, as the doctrine is not only learned but lived by moment by moment. Intellectual understanding of the doctrine is only the very preliminary stage of the technique and hence it is wrong to conclude that the epic teaches that *mokṣa* can be gained in such a way.

(vii) Grace

The concept of grace implies a powerful external agent able to overcome the circumstances that bind the individual to his unwanted position in this world. Hence this form of soteriology is typically linked to a theistic perspective; it demands a being or beings beyond man intervening in the world to expedite the process of salvation. The epic narrative is based on a theistic understanding of the world, for events are dominated by the controlling figure of Kṛṣṇa. The text makes it clear that all the events leading up to the battle at Kurukṣetra are a part of the plan of Viṣṇu, but the reason for Kṛṣṇa's descent is not a soteriological one. The mission of the *avatāra* is to sustain *dharma*, to protect the righteous and to ensure that they are able to rule the earth in accordance with dharmic principles.

The *Bhagavad-gītā*, as will be discussed below, is primarily a soteriological treatise and at several points Kṛṣṇa stresses his own role in this soteriology. It may be argued that the *Gītā* is the theological essence of the *Mahābhārata* and that the entire narrative can only be understood in light of it. If this is the case then the *avatāra* is to some extent a soteriological phenomenon but this is not apparent where his descent is discussed elsewhere, nor in the opening verses of Chapter 4 which deal specifically with this subject.[11]

Within the *Mokṣa-dharma*, outside of the *Nārāyaṇīya*, grace is largely ignored as a path to salvation and the Sāṁkhya ideas presented in the *Mokṣa-dharma* are substantially non-theistic. There are occasional references to Viṣṇu or Nārāyaṇa but the concept of a Supreme Deity remains irrelevent to the fundamental doctrine for there is no hint in the text that *jñāna* may be bestowed on a deserving individual through the intervention of an external Deity.

In the *Mahābhārata*, grace is stressed only in passages that discuss *bhakti* to either Śiva or Nārāyaṇa/Viṣṇu. In the *Nārāyaṇīya*, much of the text is devoted to glorification of Viṣṇu and descriptions of his worship. There is, however, a clear soteriological theme in the text and here we find grace as a key element. At the beginning of Chapter 321 of the *Śānti*, Yudhiṣṭhira asks Bhīṣma which deity should be worshipped–*devatāṁ kāṁ yajeta*–by one seeking perfection–*ya icchet siddhim* (1). That the inquiry relates to both *svarga-loka* and salvation is made clear by the next verse–*kuto hy asya dhruvaḥ svargaḥ kuto niḥśreyasaṁ param.* It is significant to note that Yudhiṣṭhira's inquiries that preface the *Nārāyaṇīya* contain a soteriological element reinforced by a further question in verse 3–*muktaś ca kāṁ gatiṁ gacchen mokṣaś caiva kim ātmakaḥ,* what destination do the liberated souls attain and what is the essence of salvation?

Bhīṣma replies initially by saying that this question is a secret matter that cannot be explained without the grace of God–*ṛte deva-prasādāt*–or the development of knowledge–*jñānāgamena vā* (6). There then follows an account of Nārada's meeting with the two *ṛṣis,* Nara and Nārāyaṇa. Questioned by Nārada as to whom they offer *yajñas* to, the *ṛṣi* Nārāyaṇa, who is a form of the Deity Nārāyaṇa, replies with an explanation of theistic Sāṁkhya. The Supreme God is equated with the indwelling soul, referred to by the Sāṁkhya term *kṣetrajña–sa hy antarātmā bhūtānāṁ kṣetrajñaś ceti kathyate* (29). Verse 38 gives the Sāṁkhya view of salvation, saying that those who have gone beyond the material attributes are liberated–*kalāḥ pañca-daśa tyaktvā te muktā iti niścayaḥ.* The end reached by the liberated is *brahman* and that is known as *kṣetrajña–muktānām tu gatir brahman kṣetrajña iti kalpitaḥ* (39). He is perceived by the *yoga* of knowledge–*dṛśyate jñāna-yogena*–and having known that *ātman* the two *ṛṣis* constantly worship him–*evaṁ jñātvā tam ātmānaṁ pūjayāvaḥ sanātanam* (40). All the Vedas and modes of life–*āśramas*–worship him with devotion–*bhaktyā saṁpūjayanti*–and it is he who grants the results of their worship–*gatiṁ caiṣāṁ dadāti saḥ* (41). But those who worship him here without deviation–*ye tu tad bhāvitā loke ekāntitvaṁ samāsthitāḥ* – gain a higher result for they enter into him–*etad abhyadhikaṁ teṣāṁ yat te taṁ praviśanty uta* (42).

Thus in the opening chapter of the *Nārāyaṇīya,* we find a presentation of a theistic form of Sāṁkhya which equates the inner soul with the Deity. As with earlier Sāṁkhya treatises the object is soteriological but here the element of grace is introduced. The *ṛṣis* claim that they worship the *kṣetrjña* with devotion (the key words here are the verb *pūj* and the noun *bhakti*) and that the *kṣetrajña* bestows results on those who worship him.

The *Nārāyaṇīya* contains long passages glorifying Nārāyaṇa and extolling his pastimes and *avatāras.* Much of this description does not touch upon the issue of soteriology but what is apparent throughout is the prevalent influence of Sāṁkhya. Chapter 326 contains a typical Sāṁkhya description of the self as the transcendent element beyond the other twenty-four (20-26) but this is equated with Vāsudeva, another name of Nārāyaṇa, and in verse 67 of Chapter 327, Nārāyaṇa states that he is the *kṣetrajña.* In Chapter 332, we have a description of gaining *mokṣa* by entering the forms of Nārāyaṇa–Vāsudeva, Saṁkarṣaṇa, Pradyumna, and Aniruddha, and it is stated that this is the path gained by followers of Sāṁkhya as well as the devotees–*viśanti vipra-pravarāḥ sāṁkhyā bhāgavataiḥ saha* (16).

It is in Chapter 336 that the *Nārāyaṇīya* turns specifically to the issue of *mokṣa.* Janamejaya opens the chapter with an apparent summary of the previous teachings. The Lord accepts all worship offered to him in accordance with the proper rules–*viddhi-prayuktām.* Verses 2 and 3 seem to compare the process of gaining knowledge with worship of the Deity in terms of their bringing salvation. Those who have transcended the reactions to their good and evil deeds–*puṇya-pāpa-vivarjitāḥ*–and have the ancient wisdom that is handed down–*pāramparyāgatāḥ*–go to the fourth destination, the supreme person–*caturthyāṁ caiva te gatyāṁ gacchanti puruṣottamam*–but those fixed in single-minded devotion achieve the highest position–*ekāntinas tu puruṣā gacchanti paramaṁ padam.* The verses are obscure but I take them to mean that those who follow Sāṁkhya attain the fourth form of Nārāyaṇa referred to in Pañcarātric doctrine (Vāsudeva, Saṁkarṣaṇa, Pradyumna, and Aniruddha) by a gradual process, while the devotees immediately attain the highest destination.

In reply to Janamejaya's questions about the religion of devotion, Vaiśaṁpāyana reminds him of the *Bhagavad-gītā* that he has heard earlier. This is interesting in itself, for it shows that the *Nārāyaṇīya* recognises the *Gītā* as a treatise on *bhakti,* something which the other stated recapitulation in the *Anugītā* does not do. He then gives a history of how the doctrines and practices of *bhakti* were introduced by Nārāyaṇa himself and how they were passed down from one teacher to another. In verse 62, Janamejaya asks why some *brāhmaṇas* take to other doctrines and practices and ignore those of *bhakti.* Vaiśaṁpāyana replies that persons are influenced to follow different religious processes by the *guṇas* that predominate in their personality. Those in whom *sattva* prevails are the best for they seek salvation (64) and understand the Supreme Person, for salvation is dependent on Nārāyaṇa–*nārāyaṇa-paro mokṣaḥ* (65). Thinking always of that Supreme Person, the worshipper of Nārāyaṇa gains wisdom–*manīṣitaṁ ca prāpnoti . . . ekānta-bhaktiḥ* (66). Hari gives the desired result to wise renunciants who have no desires and are seeking salvation. That person upon whom Viṣṇu bestows his glance–*yaṁ paśyen madhusūdanaḥ*–is known as a *sāttvika* and becomes fixed in salvation–*bhaven mokṣe ca niścitaḥ* (68).

This religion is equal to Sāṁkhya and Yoga–*sāṁkhya-yogena tulyaḥ*–for by following it one gains the supreme destination in salvation that has Nārāyaṇa as its very self–*nārāyaṇātmake mokṣe tato yānti parāṁ gatim* (69). Verse 70 is important as it clearly establishes the necessity of grace in gaining salvation.

> *nārāyaṇena dṛṣṭaś ca pratibuddho bhavet pumān*
> *evam ātmecchayā rājan pratibuddho na jāyate*
>
> 'The person who is seen by Nārāyaṇa becomes awakened. Thus one does not become awakened merely by one's own desire.' (12.336.70)

Persons who engage in the religion of *pravṛtti,* which seeks material pleasure as its goal, are wedded to the lower *guṇas, rajas* and *tamas,* and Hari does not behold them directly–*nāvekṣati hariḥ svayam* (71). The demiurge, Brahmā, who creates under the supervision of Viṣṇu, sees those who act under the influence of *rajas* and *tamas.*

This passage, which is the main soteriological teaching of the *Nārāyaṇīya,* reveals that the doctrines of *bhakti* also have salvation as their goal. Throughout the text we have noted the influence of Sāṁkhya and it can be concluded that the Sāṁkhya stress on *mokṣa* has also been absorbed. The new element here, however, is that of grace. The verses cited above emphasise that *mokṣa* is made possible by the mercy of Viṣṇu, referred to in terms of his glance upon the devotee. The concept of grace here is apparently not unconditional, for verse 71 indicates that the glance falls upon those who are qualified by their adherence to the religious path that involves renunciation of desire. As verse 70 makes plain, we are here confronted with an 'other-help' means of salvation which sharply distinguishes *bhakti* from the 'self-help' techniques of Sāṁkhya and Yoga discussed earlier.

Within the narrative, passages that glorify Śiva as the Supreme Deity (for example 7.172-173; 10.6-7) consist mainly of prayers extolling him as the all-powerful Lord and contain virtually nothing that can enlighten us about the soteriology of Śiva-*bhakti*. Chapters 14 to 18 of the *Anuśāsana* may be recognised as the Śaivite equivalent of the *Nārāyaṇīya* in the *Mahābhārata*. The passage is based around the story of Kṛṣṇa's worship of Śiva in order to get a son, Sambā, who was born of his wife, Jāmbavatī.

In Chapter 14, *Kṛṣṇa* describes how he went to the Himalayas to worship Śiva in order to obtain a son. There he meets the sage Upamanyu who tells him of the greatness of Śiva and how he first became a devotee. Having offered prayers to Śiva for many years, Upamanyu was visited by Indra, the lord of the gods, who offered him any boon he desired. Upamanyu's response to this offer is interesting from a soteriological perspective. In verse 95, he states that if it is the will of Paśupati (Śiva), he is willing to become a worm or a tree but if it is not obtained by the mercy of Paśupati–*apaśupati-vara-prasāda-jāḥ*–then he has no wish even to rule the entire universe. As long as he has not received the mercy of Śiva, he will continue to bear the old age, death, rebirth and miseries that are brought about by the body–*tāvaj jarā-maraṇa-janma-śatābhighātair duḥkhāni deha-vihitāni samudvahāmi* (97)–for without pleasing Rudra no-one can attain real peace.

Already we can detect a change in tone here. In the *Nārāyaṇīya*, with its close ties to Sāṁkhya, *mokṣa* was the desired goal of worship but here the worship and devotion are indicated as ends in themselves. In verse 104, Upamanyu states that he is willing to accept either a blessing or a curse from Śiva but wants nothing at all from any other deity. The idea of selfless devotion is being introduced here, a concept absent from the less emotional perspective of the *Nārāyaṇīya*. Soteriologically, it moves the emphasis away from salvation as the grace of the Deity becomes an end in itself rather than the means of winning liberation. In verse 187, when Śiva finally manifests himself and offers a boon, all that is requested by Upamanyu is that his devotion may remain undiminished–*bhaktir bhavatu me nityaṁ śāśvatī tvayi śaṁkara* (187).

The idea of gaining *mokṣa* through grace is not, however, entirely ignored in this passage. There is also an awareness of Sāṁkhya, but little attempt to make use of its ideas. In Chapter

14, verse 154 praises Śiva as the *puruṣa* in Sāṁkhya teaching–*sāṁkhye puruṣa ucyase*–and 155 as the one indivisible object for yogins–*yogināṁ niṣkalaḥ śivaḥ*. In Chapter 15, he is glorified as the *kṣetrajña*, the *puruṣa* in the hearts of all beings and the real object of Yoga (40-43). Chapter 16 states that all those who seek *mokṣa* in truth seek Śiva alone and that it is because of his grace that the result desired is granted or denied–*tvat prasādād hi labhyante na labhyante 'nyathā vibho* (63-65).

In Chapter 17, the text returns to the idea that *bhakti* is an end in itself. The greatest among men praise Śiva with hymns through many births, notably without any apparent concern for salvation–*āstikāḥ śraddhadhānā ca bahubhir janmabhiḥ stavaiḥ* (156). Awake, asleep or walking on the road, they are satisfied and take delight in singing the glories of Śiva–*stuvanti stūyamānāś ca tuṣyanti ca ramanti ca*–even though they pass through millions of births on the cycle of *saṁsāra*–*janma-koṭi-sahasreṣu nānā-saṁsāra-yoniṣu* (157). Only by the grace of Śiva can such devotion be found amongst men–*tasya . . . prasādena bhaktir utpadyate nṛṇām*–and through it they gain the highest perfection–*yayā yānti parāṁ siddhim* (160). Śiva is merciful to those who surrender to him and delivers them from the cycle of rebirth–*prapanna-vatsalo devaḥ saṁsārāt tān samuddharet* (161). No other god but Śiva is able to grant this boon of salvation from endless rebirth.

It may be noted that Hardy is of the opinion that the idea of *bhakti* for its own sake and the absence of any fear of *karma* that goes with it is the result of a South Indian input into Sanskrit thought.[12] Unless it is a later interpolation, this passage indicates, however, that the Sanskrit tradition was aware of and propagated this type of devotional thought from a relatively early date, notably in relation to Śiva. The difference of emphasis in this passage is clearly evident. The text is aware of Sāṁkhya and Yoga but displays no desire to incorporate their doctrines into its teachings on *bhakti*. Śiva is the Lord of these systems and he grants the results gained by their practitioners; apart from this there seems little interest. Again in contrast to the *Nārāyaṇīya*, there is less emphasis on salvation as the goal to be gained through *bhakti*. *Nārāyaṇa-bhakti* sees itself as related to Sāṁkhya and Yoga and able to grant the same salvation that these systems urge their practitioners towards. In the Śiva-*bhakti*, however, we find that devotion is an end in itself and not merely a parallel technique to Sāṁkhya and Yoga. Śiva does grant *mokṣa* through his grace, but crucially the devotee does not pray for or apparently seek such a boon through his worship. He does not mind the misery of repeated rebirth so long as he can remain fixed in his devotion.

This shift away from the quest for *mokṣa* is a theological readjustment that comes to full fruition in the medieval *bhakti* sects devoted to both Śiva and Viṣṇu. For the Alvars, for the followers of *Śiva-siddhānta* and the Śaivite poets such as Mānikkavācakar, for Rāmānuja in his understanding of full surrender[13] and for Caitanya in his emotional expressions of unrestricted love for Kṛṣṇa, there was no question of gaining a reward for acts of devotion. *Bhakti* was both the means and the end, an unstoppable surge of love from the devotee to the Deity. This type of devotion is not found in the *Nārāyaṇīya* or the *Bhagavad-gītā*, but perhaps this treatise on devotion to Śiva in the *Anuśāsana* contains the first written expression of the new form of emotional *bhakti.*

5. The Soteriology of the *Bhagavad-Gītā*

(i) Introduction

I have previously insisted on treating the *Gītā* as an integral part of the *Mahābhārata*, for it both elucidates and is elucidated by its context. This principle is not to be sacrificed here but because soteriology has such an important place in epic doctrines and because the *Gītā* is such a vital passage of the *Mahābhārata* it is necessary at this point to allow for a more detailed analysis of the *Gītā*'s ideas.

The *Bhagavad-gītā* draws directly upon Vedic concepts, Upaniṣadic Vedānta, Sāṁkhya, Yoga, *bhakti* and *dharma-śāstra*, and from these more or less diverse strands of thought attempts to put forward something approaching a coherent doctrinal system that is religious more than philosophical and practical more than speculative. The key issue it addresses is how to gain salvation and specifically how to gain salvation whilst not breaking all contact with worldly affairs.

(ii) Svarga-loka

Svarga-loka is paid scant attention by the *Gītā*. In 2.2, Kṛṣṇa tells Arjuna that his decision to renounce violence will not lead to heaven and this point is elaborated upon in 31 to 37 of the same chapter. Here Arjuna is urged to fight on the basis of *kṣatriya-dharma* and is reminded that *kṣatriyas* who die bravely in battle go to *svarga-loka* after death. In 9.20-21, Kṛṣṇa states that after worshipping him with *yajñas–māṁ . . . yajñair iṣṭvā*–those who follow the three Vedas, drink Soma and are cleansed of their sins may enter *svarga-loka–trai-vidyā . . . soma-pāḥ pūta-pāpa . . . svar-gatiṁ prārthayante.* There they enjoy the pleasures of the gods–*aśnanti divyān divi deva-bhogān.* Verse 21 gives the criticism of rebirth in *svarga-loka* found elsewhere in the *Mahābhārata,*[14] that it is temporary and when the results of one's piety have been enjoyed there one must return to this world–*kṣīṇe puṇye martya-lokaṁ viśanti.* Elsewhere, both 7.23 and 9.25 assert that the worshippers of the gods go to the gods, and 6.41 mentions that unsuccessful *yogins* enjoy in heaven before resuming their endeavours in this world. These somewhat passing references serve only to reinforce what has been noted elsewhere in the text. Those who die in battle, live piously, perform *yajñas* and worship the gods gain *svarga-loka* after death. This heaven is a domain in which one can enjoy great sensual pleasure without sin but residence there is not eternal and eventually the cycle of *saṁsāra* must be resumed.

(iii) The Impetus Towards Salvation

Several passages from the epic have previously been noted which stress the misery of life in this world. The eternal self transmigrates through different bodily forms enjoying and suffering the results of previous actions in a combination in which misery predominates. Dasgupta is quite emphatic that the *Gītā* does not teach a negative view of this world, stating, ". . . a description of the evils of this worldly life does not form any part of the contents of the *Gītā.* The *Gītā* has no pessimistic tendency."[15] This opinion, however, is shaped to some extent by the author's desire to demonstrate the absence of any Buddhist influence on the *Gītā,* and is to be regarded as an overstatement. Despite the emphasis on dharmic action there is little to suggest that life here and now is to be regarded as anything but a source of misery that must be transcended. The *Gītā*'s stress on gaining freedom from birth and death clearly implies an acceptance of the Sāṁkhya view that material existence is characterised by suffering and is not the true state of the soul.

Whilst this view seems to be taken as accepted wisdom, at certain points it is stated directly. In 8.15, Kṛṣṇa teaches that one who has reached him never again has to accept rebirth which is, *duḥkhālayam aśāśvatam*–temporary and full of suffering. In 9.33, he refers to, *anityam asukhaṁ lokam imam*–this world which is impermanent and without happiness. 5.22 reasserts the doctrines of the *Mokṣa-dharma* in teaching the inadequacy of any pleasure gained through the senses:

> *ye hi saṁsparśa-jā bhogā duḥkha-yonaya eva te*
> *ādy-antavantaḥ kaunteya na teṣu ramate budhaḥ*
>
> 'Those pleasures that arise from contact with the senses are in actuality the roots of misery. Because they have a beginning and an end the wise man does not seek pleasure in them.' (5.22)

Later Kṛṣṇa refers to recognising the fault of worldly life due to the misery of birth, death, ageing and disease–*janma-mṛtyu-jarā-vyādhi-duḥkha-doṣānudarśanam*–as one of the elements of wisdom (13.9), and describes salvation as gaining freedom from the misery of birth, death and ageing–*janma-mṛtyu-jarā-duḥkhair vimukto 'mṛtam aśnute* (14.20). Though the *Gītā* does not contain any sustained teaching on the miseries of life in this world, it is thus apparent that it accepts the negative perspective of Sāṁkhya expressed more fully elsewhere in the *Mahābhārata.*

(iv) The Means of Gaining Salvation

It has been noted that the soteriological doctrines of the *Mokṣa-dharma* are based primarily on Sāṁkhya which is closely linked with the practices of Yoga. The *Bhagavad-gītā* draws on Upaniṣadic wisdom but its doctrines are substantially based on *Sāṁkhya* thought, again recognising the connection between such ideas and practices it calls Yoga. The truly unique element in the *Gītā* is its thorough integration of *bhakti* with the Sāṁkhya and Yoga ideas it teaches.

The teachings described by Kṛṣṇa as Sāṁkhya contain few of the concepts central to classical Sāṁkhya. What is stressed, however, in 2.11-30, is the difference between the soul and the body, and it is this idea that is the Sāṁkhya referred to in 2.39. This dualistic view of the individual is revealed in 2.13 which refers to the *deha* and *dehin*, the body and the embodied, and in 2.22, where the transmigration of the embodied soul is compared to the changing of clothes. As is characteristic of the Sāṁkhya teachings previously referred to, the understanding of the transcendence of the soul over matter is accompanied by a mood of renunciation and aloofness from the world. This does not necessarily entail the lifestyle of a hermit, though this is indicated in Chapter 6, for the *Gītā* urges the maintenance of one's social position in accordance with *sva-dharma.* There is, however, stress throughout on abandoning sensual pleasures, living in the world but remaining aloof and unattached to its fluctuating fortunes. 2.14 states that happiness and distress are always coming and going–*āgamāpāyinaḥ*–and that one should therefore learn to tolerate changing fortunes–*tāṁs titikṣasva.*

Chapter 2 follows a pattern familiar from the *Mokṣa-dharma.* Having given the dualist Sāṁkhya doctrines, Kṛṣṇa states that he will instruct Arjuna in the practice of *yoga.*

> *eṣā te 'bhihitā sāṁkhye buddhir yoge tv imāṁ śṛṇu*
> *buddhyā yukto yayā pārtha karma-bandhaṁ prahāsyasi*
>
> 'This Sāṁkhya has been described to you, now hear about the *yoga* of the intelligence (*buddhi-yoga*). By this engagement of the intelligence, O son of Pṛthā, you will be freed from the bondage of actions.' (2.39)

The term Sāṁkhya does not refer to the teachings of verses 31 to 38, which deal somewhat aberrantly with *sva-dharma,* but to the ideas contained in 11 to 30 and possibly 38 as well. Verses 40 and 41 introduce the *yoga* instruction that will follow but in verses 42 to 46 there is an apparent change of subject, introducing criticism of excessively orthodox doctrines which urge that there is nothing more than the rituals of the Vedas in religious life. It may appear that this passage is another aberration but this is not the case for the critique is relevant to the *yoga* that Kṛṣṇa is teaching here.

In 47 to 51, Kṛṣṇa finally enunciates the *yoga* that he introduced in 39 but this *buddhi-yoga* is different from the *yoga* practices discussed in the *Mokṣa-dharma.* It involves neither *dhāraṇa* nor *prāṇāyāma* but is *niṣkāma-karma,* the performance of social duties without attachment to the results. The critique of Vedic rituals in 42 to 46 was relevant because that is *sakāma-karma,* performance of duties with a desire for reward, and Kṛṣṇa wishes to distinguish the *buddhi-yoga* he is expounding from such practices. Verse 47 states that Arjuna should perform his duty–*karmaṇye vādhikāraste*– but must not expect the results–*mā phaleṣu kadācana*–and should never be attached to abandoning his duty–*mā te saṅgo 'stv akarmaṇi*. Fixed in *yoga*, he should perform his duties but without any attachment–*saṅgaṁ tyaktvā*; he should be equal in success and failure for such equanimity is called *yoga* (48). Through this *buddhi-yoga* one should give up lower acts (i.e. acts that seek sensual pleasure as a result), surrendering to the intelligence–*buddhau śaraṇam anviccha*–for only those who are avaricious seek the rewards of action–*kṛpaṇāḥ phala-hetavaḥ* (49). One who practises this *buddhi-yoga* removes the reactions to his pious and evil deeds; therefore one should practise *yoga*, for *yoga* is the correct means of performing one's duties–*yogaḥ karmasu kauśalam* (50).

Verse 51, concluding the passage, is notable because it demonstrates the soteriological purpose of the *yoga* Kṛṣṇa is teaching. Again the pattern is familiar, Sāṁkhya doctrine, *yoga* practice, and soteriological result.

> *karma-jaṁ buddhi-yuktā hi phalaṁ tyaktvā manīṣiṇaḥ*
> *janma-bandha-vinirmuktāḥ padaṁ gacchanty anāmayam*
>
> 'The wise who engage in *buddhi-yoga*, having given up rewards that may be derived from ritual actions, are free from the bondage of repeated rebirth and attain a status beyond all faults.' (2.51)

The teaching of *niṣkāma-karma* as a soteriological technique is a recurring theme in the *Gītā* which it is now possible to contextualise. The pattern of following Sāṁkhya teachings with a description of *yoga* practice is found in the *Gītā* as well as the *Mokṣa-dharma*. *Niṣkāma-karma* is taught by Kṛṣṇa as a form of *yoga* that, like *dhāraṇa* or *prāṇāyāma*, is based on Sāṁkhya and is a soteriological technique leading to *mokṣa*. That it is not merely a means of psychological adjustment to alleviate Arjuna's tension is apparent from the beginning. As early as 2.15, Kṛṣṇa states that one who remains equal in happiness and distress will gain immortality–*sama-duḥkha-sukhaṁ dhīraṁ so 'mṛtatvāya kalpate*–and the same point is reiterated at the end of the chapter in verses 71 and 72. By teaching this type of *yoga* the *avatāra* is able to achieve his goal of sustaining *sva-dharma* on earth whilst stressing *mokṣa-dharma*. It is this attempt at a reconciliation of the tensions between *pravṛtti* and *nivṛtti* that makes the *Gītā* so important for an understanding of the epic as a whole.

It has previously been asserted that the teachings of the *Gītā* are based substantially on the doctrines of early Sāṁkhya.[16] From 2.39, 3.3, and 5.4/5 it is apparent that the *Gītā* regards the *jñāna* that it is imparting as *sāṁkhya-jñāna*, associated with practices it refers to as *yoga*. The text also contains teachings that are more obviously those of a Sāṁkhya school. Verses 4 and 5 of Chapter 7 contain a characteristic listing of elements, though without the familiar numbers of 24 and 25 being arrived at. Because of its presentation of theistic Sāṁkhya, this passage will be dealt with more fully below under the heading of *bhakti*.

Chapter 13 is recognisable from the *Mokṣa-dharma* as being a Sāṁkhya treatise. It opens with definitions of the terms *kṣetra* and *kṣetrajña*; the former is the body, or matter, and the latter is the soul within. In verse 3, Kṛṣṇa claims that he is the *kṣetrajña* in all bodies–*kṣetrajñaṁ cāpi māṁ viddhi sarva-kṣetreṣu bhārata*. This idea of the identification of the self within with the Deity was noted especially in the *Nārāyaṇīya* where Sāṁkhya and *bhakti* are closely linked. Verses 6 and 7 contain a listing of the elements of matter, concluding with the words, *etat kṣetraṁ samāsena*–this is the field (matter) in summary. Verses 8 to 12 give a list of the qualities and attributes of one who has gained *jñāna*, based on the world-renouncing ethics of Sāṁkhya familiar from the *Mokṣa-dharma*.

In verse 13, Kṛṣṇa announces that he will now speak of the soul which is *brahman*, without beginning and dependent on Kṛṣṇa–*anādi mat-paraṁ brahma*. The soul is everywhere in all bodies, above all attributes of matter, subtle and imperceptible. Verse 17 is interesting in that it appears to deny the later Sāṁkhya doctrine of the eternal plurality of souls and tend back towards monism, *avibhaktaṁ ca bhūteṣu vibhaktam iva ca sthitam*–(the soul) is undivided in all beings, yet situated as if it were divided. It is the light of all that is light, it is knowledge, it is the known, it is attained by knowledge and it is in the heart of all beings–*jñānaṁ jñeyaṁ jñāna-gamyaṁ hṛdi sarvasya viṣṭhitam* (18). In verses 19 to 23, the differentiation between the soul and matter, characteristic of Sāṁkhya, is stressed again.

In 24, the basic Sāṁkhya doctrines having now been set forth, the discussion turns towards soteriology. One who knows this wisdom regarding the soul and matter will never again take birth. In verse 25, we have reference to the *yoga* practices that can bring this knowledge. Some perceive the soul through meditation some through the *yoga* of Sāṁkhya and others through the *yoga* of action. Here there are three techniques listed which give the knowledge of the self that frees the soul from rebirth. These are meditation, the realisation of Sāṁkhya doctrine and the disinterested action the *Gītā* has stressed throughout. In verse 26, those who gain wisdom from the *śruti,* presumably here the *Upaniṣads,* are also included amongst those who have knowledge of the soul.

The chapter concludes by reasserting that those who imbibe this wisdom gain immortality. One who sees the world in this way truly sees (29) and will go to the highest destination–*tato yāti parāṁ gatim* (30). Verse 31 again seems to display a monist tendency in the text, for it describes the wisdom that brings salvation as seeing the diverse living beings situated as one–*yadā bhūta-pṛthag-bhāvam eka-stham anupaśyati*–though it could also mean that all individual souls are of the same nature despite the diversity of material forms. In either case, the conclusion is that one who realises this gains *brahman–brahma sampadyate tadā.* The final verse provides a summary of the teachings that have gone before, again revealing the soteriological context,

> *kṣetra-kṣetrajñayor evam antaraṁ jñāna-cakṣuṣā*
> *bhūta-prakṛti-mokṣaṁ ca ye vidur yānti te param*
>
> 'Those who thus perceive with the eye of knowledge the difference between matter and the conscious self, and the way of salvation from matter for the living being—they attain the supreme end.' (13.34)

The ideas here are similar to those encountered in the *Mokṣa-dharma* and other passages of the *Mahābhārata.* Salvation is attained through realisation of the philosophy of Sāṁkhya which distinguishes the true self from matter. Elsewhere, the same point is made regarding *jñāna,* though the influence of Sāṁkhya is less pronounced. Chapter 4 teaches that *jñāna* is the way to salvation. After describing various religious practices and rituals as *yajñas,* Kṛṣṇa states in verses 30 and 32 that one who knows these attains the eternal *brahman* and is liberated–*evaṁ jñātvā vimokṣyase.* Through Yoga the laws of *karma* are transcended and by *jñāna* doubts are destroyed; actions cannot bind one who has thus realised the true self–*ātmavantaṁ na karmāṇi nibadhnanti* (41). The chapter concludes with Arjuna being ordered to arise, steady in *yoga*, having cut through with the sword of wisdom the doubts that have arisen in his heart.

In this passage the soteriological references are more oblique than in Chapters 13 and 14 which are more obviously based on Sāṁkhya. Nonetheless, the assertion in verses 37 and 41 that *jñāna* inhibits reactions arising from acts is linked to the quest for salvation. The wisdom referred to here is not designated as Sāṁkhya and is described briefly only in 35 but the link with Yoga follows a pattern found elsewhere in the *Gītā* and the *Mahābhārata* usually indicative of Sāṁkhya. The *yoga* referred to in verse 42, on which Arjuna must base his determination to fight, is clearly the *buddhi-yoga* of Chapter 2 and there Kṛṣṇa based his teachings on doctrines designated as Sāṁkhya.

(v) *Yoga* in the *Bhagavad-gītā*

The previous discussion has demonstrated that the *Gītā*, like the *Mokṣa-dharma*, recognises *sāṁkhya-jñāna* as the key to salvation and regards the techniques of Yoga as the means of imbibing such wisdom. Unique to the *Gītā*, however, is the understanding of desireless action as one of the techniques to be employed. In the *Mokṣa-dharma*, Yoga typically means either the discipline of breath control, *prāṇāyāma*, or that of inner concentration, *dhāraṇa*. Despite its stress on desireless action, these other two techniques of *yoga* are not ignored by the *Bhagavad-gītā*. Control of the bodily airs is first mentioned in 4.29 in the list of religious practices that Kṛṣṇa is describing as *yajñas*. Chapter 5 offers Sāṁkhya teachings on the transcendence of the soul and speaks of *yoga* in terms of *niṣkāma-karma* but in verses 27 and 28 refers specifically to concentration and breath control.

The short passage serves as an introduction to the more extensive treatment of the subject in Chapters 6 and 8. Chapter 6 opens with a reassertion of *niṣkāma-karma*, laying stress on equanimity and the elimination of material desire. Verses 10 to 15 then describe the practices of *yoga*, specifically here the *dhāraṇa* method of concentration. Free of desires, the *yogin* must reside in a lonely place, controlling his mind and fixing it on one point–*ekākī yata-cittātmā* (10). Sitting on a firm seat of *kuśa* grass and deer skin, controlling the activities of the mind and senses, he must practise this *yoga* to purify the self–*yuñjyād yogam ātma-viśuddhaye* (11-12). With his body, head and neck in an even line he must concentrate on the tip of the nose, ignoring everything else. At peace, free of fear, celibate, controlling his mind and fixing it on Kṛṣṇa–*manaḥ saṁyamya mac-cittaḥ*–the *yogin* sits devoted to the Deity–*yukta āsīta mat-paraḥ* (14). The passage concludes by stating that the *yogin* who engages in this practice gains the peace of supreme salvation that is Kṛṣṇa's position–*śāntiṁ nirvāṇa-paramāṁ mat-saṁsthām adhigacchati* (15).

Verses 16 to 32 recapitulate and expand somewhat on what has gone before. The *yogin* should be moderate in his eating and sleeping, and when he has controlled his mind and fixed it on the soul–*ātmany evāvatiṣṭhate*–untouched by desire, he has gained success in *yoga*–*yukta ity ucyate tadā* (18). When, through *yoga* practice, he perceives the soul he experiences a joy that is beyond anything known through the senses and he cannot be deviated from that experience (20-21). The mind must be fixed on the soul and not allowed to wander–*ātma-saṁsthaṁ manaḥ kṛtvā na kiñcid api cintayet* (25).

Verse 27 reminds us once more of the goal of salvation gained through *yoga*. The *yogin* whose mind is stilled finds the ultimate joy; he attains a spiritual existence free of contamination and devoid of the passions of this world–*upaiti śānta-rajasaṁ brahma-bhūtam akalmaṣam*. In touch with the eternal spiritual nature–*brahma-saṁsparśam*–he enjoys unlimited pleasure (28). With equal vision he sees the *ātman* in all beings and all beings in the *ātman* (29). One who thus sees Kṛṣṇa everywhere and all things in Kṛṣṇa is never lost to the Deity, for one who worships Kṛṣṇa alone in all beings is a *yogin* in Kṛṣṇa–*sa yogī mayi vartate* (31). The greatest *yogin* is one who in both happiness and distress maintains the equanimity that allows him to perceive the *ātman* existing everywhere (32).

The teachings presented in Chapter 6, though making initial reference to *karma-yoga*, deal with *dhāraṇa* and ignore the technique of breath control, referred to in 4.29 and 5.27. It is relevant to recall here the statement of Bhīṣma in Chapter 289 of the *Śānti* that Yoga reveals through direct perception what the followers of Sāṁkhya learn from their scriptures. In verses 29 and 30 here, Kṛṣṇa says that *yogins* are able to see the transcendent self in all beings, an insight that confirms the dualist doctrine taught by

Sāṁkhya. Here also the Deity is identified with the *ātman*; this idea is found occasionally in the *Mokṣa-dharma*, but is stressed only in the *Nārāyaṇīya*. There the teachers of the doctrines of devotion to Nārāyaṇa use Sāṁkhya concepts and assert that the *kṣetrajña*, the soul within, is none other than Nārāyaṇa himself whom they worship. This doctrine is reflected in the *Gītā*'s teachings on Yoga in Chapter 6.

Chapter 8 presents a further description of *yoga* practice, but the emphasis and technique are notably different. Here the discussion is even more clearly soteriological, for it arises from Arjuna's question as to how Kṛṣṇa may be known at the time of death (2) which arose in turn from Kṛṣṇa's statement in 7.30 that those who have control over their minds think of him as they die. Repeatedly in the course of the chapter we find this emphasis on one's state of mind at the time of death as the key to *mokṣa*. Verse 5 states that one who remembers Kṛṣṇa when leaving the body, will attain his nature–*prayāti mad-bhāvam*–though it should be noted that in verse 4, Kṛṣṇa identifies himself with the soul in all bodies. Whatever the mind is fixed upon at death dictates the destination of the soul (6) and therefore the *yoga* instructions in this chapter are concerned with controlling the mind at the point of death.

Verses 7 and 8 urge that the mind should be fixed on Kṛṣṇa at all times. This is the means of gaining salvation which is expressed as going to Kṛṣṇa–*mām evaiṣyasi* and *paramaṁ puruṣaṁ divyaṁ yāti*. Verse 9 describes the self within on whom the consciousness should be fixed. It is ancient and wise, and is the controller–*kaviṁ purāṇam anuśāsitaram*–more minute than the smallest thing, the sustainer of all, of inconceivable form, effulgent and beyond all darkness. At the time of death the air of life–*prāṇa*–should be fixed between the eyebrows, with the mind steady and fixed in devotion by the power of *yoga–bhaktyā yukto yoga-balena*. One who does this goes to that divine supreme being–*sa taṁ paraṁ puruṣam upaiti divyam* (10). Kṛṣṇa then states that what he will speak of now is that which the Vedic seers describe, the renunciants enter, and those who practise celibacy are seeking (11).

In verse 12, he refers to *yoga-dhāraṇa*, describing it as controlling the gates of the body–*sarva-dvārāṇi saṁyamya*–fixing the mind on the heart and raising the life air to the head–*mūrdhny ādhāyātmanaḥ prāṇam*. One who does this, chants the syllable *oṁ* and remembers Kṛṣṇa while leaving his body attains the supreme goal (13). For the *yogin* who always remembers Kṛṣṇa with undeviating attention, he is easily attained and having reached that supreme perfection there is no more rebirth–*punar janma . . . nāpnuvanti,* and, *mām upetya . . . punar janma na vidyate* (15-16). Verses 17 to 19 describe the repeated generation and annihilation of all beings that persists in an eternal cycle. Beyond this is another dimension of existence that is never destroyed, the domain of Kṛṣṇa from which there is no return–*yaṁ prāpya na nivartante tad dhāma, paramaṁ mama* (21).

Verses 23 to 26 form a curious passage somewhat unrelated to what has gone before, describing the times of the solar year and lunar month during which a *yogin* should leave his body if he is to attain *mokṣa.*[17] Aware of such matters, *yogins* are not confused–*naite sṛtī pārtha jānan yogī muhyati kaścana* (27)–and therefore at all times Arjuna should practise *yoga.* The *yogin* gains a result which surpasses that which comes from following the Vedas, performing *yajñas* and penances, or giving gifts in charity, for the *yogin* attains the original position that is above all else–*yogī paraṁ sthānam upaiti cādyam* (28).

Clearly the *yoga* described in Chapter 8 differs considerably from the that presented in Chapter 6 and they may represent the independent views of different schools. Although both have a marked soteriological objective, this is more pronounced in Chapter 8 which stresses in almost every verse that the goal is complete salvation. The technique of *yoga* involves control of the airs in the body and raising the *prāṇa* to the head, as well as concentration on the soul within, particularly at the time of death, while Chapter 6 dealt exclusively with the practice of concentration. The teachings of Chapter 8 are most notable, however, because of the dominant influence of *bhakti.* The instructions on *yoga* given here are linked with ideas of devotion to a degree that is unique not just in the *Gītā* but the entire *Mahābhārata.* The transcendent soul is Kṛṣṇa himself, meditation on the soul is a form of devotion to Kṛṣṇa and salvation means gaining the position, nature or domain of Kṛṣṇa. Elsewhere in the epic, and to a certain extent in Chapter 6, this link between Yoga and *bhakti* is touched on briefly but only in Chapter 8 of the *Gītā* is it made such a central feature of *yoga* teachings.

It is also significant to note the connection between the deaths of Bhīṣma and Droṇa in the narrative and the teachings on *yoga* in this chapter. When Droṇa gives up his life (7.165.39) after hearing of the death of his son Aśvatthāman, he does so after fixing his consciousness in a trance of yogic concentration in the manner referred to in verses 12 and 13. The death of Bhīṣma, on the other hand, is delayed for many days so that he may depart the world while the sun is taking its northerly course, in accordance with the teachings of verses 23 to 25, allowing him the time to impart his extensive instructions to Yudhiṣṭhira.

(vi) Salvation and *Bhakti* in the *Bhagavad-gītā*

The influence of Sāṁkhya in the *Bhagavad-gītā*, especially with regard to its teachings on salvation, has already been discussed. In this the *Gītā* is akin to the *Mokṣa-dharma* but its presentation of theistic Sāṁkhya, and the central role ascribed to the Deity in its *yoga* teachings, is unique in the *Mahābhārata*. In verses 4 and 5 of Chapter 7, we have a listing of the elements of matter and the distinction of the living being from them typical of Sāṁkhya thought. Verse 6 asserts that this combination should be understood as the source of all beings–*etad yonīni bhūtāni sarvānīti upadhāraya*–but that Kṛṣṇa himself is the source and the destruction of all existence–*ahaṁ kṛtsnasya jagataḥ prabhavaḥ pralayas tathā.* There is nothing else beyond him–*mattaḥ parataraṁ nānyat kiñcid asti*–and all this world rests on him as jewels are held in place on a thread–*mayi sarvam idaṁ protaṁ sūtre maṇi-gaṇā iva* (7). This passage thus teaches a form of Sāṁkhya that lists the elements of matter and differentiates the soul from them, but also includes the theistic view that the world consisting of spirit and matter is derived from, sustained, and wound up by the Deity who is Kṛṣṇa himself.

Significantly from a soteriological perspective, verse 14 introduces the concept of grace into the discussion. Here salvation is not gained merely through knowledge of the situation described but by surrender to the Deity.

> *daivī hy eṣā guṇa-mayī mama māyā duratyayā*
> *mām eva ye prapadyante māyām etāṁ taranti te*
>
> 'This divine illusion of mine, composed of the three *guṇas*, is very difficult to go beyond. Those who surrender to me cross beyond this illusion.' (7.14)

The Sāṁkhya teachings of Chapters 13 and 14 are closer to those found in the *Mokṣa-dharma*, in that they lack a clear theistic dimension. Such a perspective is not completely absent, however, even here. In verse 11 of Chapter 13, Kṛṣṇa lists among the factors that comprise true wisdom, *mayi cānanya-yogena bhaktir avyabhicāriṇī*–undeviating devotion to me through constant practice of *yoga.* In verse 13, he states, that the knowable–*jñeyam*–is dependent upon him, the beginningless *brahman,* beyond existence and non-existence–*anādi mat-paraṁ brahma na sat tan nāsad ucyate.* In verse 19, Kṛṣṇa tells Arjuna that, having understood these doctrines regarding the self and matter, his devotee will attain his nature–*mad-bhakta etad vijñāya mad-bhāvāyopapadyate.*

In verses 3 and 4 of Chapter 14, Kṛṣṇa ascribes to himself the central role in the process of creation through which all living beings come into existence. For all the different forms of life which arise here, Kṛṣṇa claims that he is the seed-giving father–*ahaṁ bīja-pradaḥ pitā* (4). Finally, after what is essentially a Sāṁkhya discourse on the nature of the three *guṇas,* he concludes by stating.

> *māṁ ca yo 'vyabhicāreṇa bhakti-yogena sevate*
> *sa guṇān samatītyaitān brahma-bhūyāya kalpate*
>
> *brahmaṇo hi pratiṣṭhāham amṛtasyāvyayasya ca*
> *śāśvatasya ca dharmasya sukhasyaikāntikasya ca*
>
> 'One who serves me through unswerving devotional *yoga* gains the transcendent status of *brahman,* having gone beyond these *guṇas.*
>
> I am the basis of this *brahman,* which is immortal, unchanging, and eternal, the one joyful true status of existence.' (14.26-27)

These references are significant in revealing how the Sāṁkhya of the *Bhagavad-gītā* displays a theistic perspective that is distinctive from the *Mokṣa-dharma.* The teachings on *yoga* given in Chapters 6 and 8 have likewise been noted as unique in the role that Kṛṣṇa ascribes to himself as the Deity. Chapter 8 in particular is thoroughly theistic in its presentation of Yoga and in Chapter 6, verses 14, 30 and 31 are to be noted as conveying the idea that the soul within, the object of the technique, is none other than Kṛṣṇa himself. In the final two verses of that chapter, Kṛṣṇa presents a 'ladder' that places *jñāna* above penances, actions above *jñāna,* and Yoga above actions. This point is then further elaborated upon.

yogīnām api sarveṣāṁ mad-gatenāntar-ātmanā
śraddhāvān bhajate yo māṁ sa me yuktatamo mataḥ

'In my opinion, of all the *yogins*, one who worships me with faith, seeking me within himself—he is best of all in the execution of *yoga*.' (6.47)

Such assertions regarding the preeminence of *bhakti* are characteristic of the *Gītā*'s unique perspective on Yoga and demonstrate the text's consistent tendency towards theism and devotion.

The *Bhagavad-gītā* is also distinct from the treatises of the *Mokṣa-dharma* in its presentation of *niṣkāma-karma, buddhi-yoga,* alongside *dhāraṇa* and *prāṇāyāma* as prescribed action leading to *mokṣa.* This type of *yoga* is again linked to *bhakti.* In 10.10, Kṛṣṇa refers to *buddhi-yoga* as a gift of grace which enables his devotees to attain him–*dadāmi buddhi-yogaṁ taṁ yena mām upayānti te*–though here the term probably refers to the mood of renunciation rather than detached action. In Chapters 2, 3, 4, 5 and 6, *niṣkāma-karma* is presented as the performance of dharmic duty without sensual desires and without seeking material gain as a result. In Chapter 9, this concept is linked to *bhakti* as the work without material desire becomes work as an act of devotion for the pleasure of Kṛṣṇa. In 9.25, Kṛṣṇa tells Arjuna that those who worship him will come to him–*yānti mad-yājino 'pi mām.* If offerings of leaves, flowers, fruits, or water are made with devotion, he will accept them–*tad ahaṁ bhakty-upahṛtam aśnāmi* (9.26). The next two verses then teach the devotional form of *niṣkāma-karma* as a *yoga* that leads to salvation:

yat karoṣi yad aśnāsi yaj juhoṣi dadāsi yat
yat tapasyasi kaunteya tat kuruṣva mad-arpaṇam

śubhāśubha-phalair evaṁ mokṣyase karma-bandhanaiḥ
sannyāsa-yoga-yuktātmā vimukto mām upaiṣyasi

'O Son of Kuntī, whatever acts you perform, whatever you eat, whatever sacrifices you offer, whatever charity you give, and whatever penance you undertake, do it as an offering to me.

By doing so, you will be freed from the bondage that

> arises from actions, with their auspicious and inauspicious results. Attaining salvation by engaging in this *yoga* of renunciation, you will come to me. (9.27-28)

The same point is confirmed in 12.6, in Kṛṣṇa's description of devotional practice–*ye tu sarvāṇi karmāṇi mayi sannyasya*–and in 18.46, which again describes how perfection is attained by worshipping the Deity through prescribed acts–*sva-karmaṇā tam abhyarcya siddhiṁ vindati mānavaḥ.*

The *Gītā* stresses knowledge–*jñāna*–as the way to salvation in Chapter 4, but this concept is also critiqued and appraised from the perspective of *bhakti,* especially where Kṛṣṇa is identified with the *ātman* that is the object of knowledge. On the basis of this doctrine, it is stated that knowledge of Kṛṣṇa leads to *mokṣa,* while the usual Sāṁkhya idea is that knowledge of the soul brings salvation. Thus 4.9 asserts:

> *janma karma ca me divyam evaṁ yo vetti tattvataḥ*
> *tyaktvā dehaṁ punar janma naiti mām eti so 'rjuna*
>
> 'One who knows in truth of my divine birth and activities does not take rebirth on leaving his body, but goes to me, Arjuna.' (4.9)

Here it is knowledge of Kṛṣṇa the *avatāra* rather than Kṛṣṇa the self within that brings salvation from rebirth, a concept even further removed from the usual Sāṁkhya notion. In verse 14, Kṛṣṇa says that he is never bound by his acts, and one who understands him thus is likewise liberated from the bondage of action–*iti māṁ yo 'bhijānāti karmabhir na sa badhyate*–and a similar idea is expressed in 5.29–*jñātvā māṁ śāntim ṛcchati.* In Chapter 7, the *jñānin* is given as the best of those who worship Kṛṣṇa–*teṣāṁ jñānī nitya-yukta eka-bhaktir viśiṣyate* (7.17). After passing through many births, one who has gained *jñāna* eventually surrenders to Kṛṣṇa–*jñānavān māṁ prapadyate*–realising that he is everything–*vāsudevaḥ sarvaṁ iti*–but such a great one is very rare–*sa mahātmā sudurlabhaḥ* (7.19).

Thus it can be demonstrated that the soteriological teachings of the *Gītā,* despite their links with the Sāṁkhya and Yoga of the *Mokṣa-dharma,* are distinctive because of the pervasive influence of the ideology of devotion. In the *Gītā*'s theistic Sāṁkhya, Kṛṣṇa becomes the supreme element controlling and sustaining the entire system; the *yoga* practices of *dhāraṇa* and *prāṇāyāma* aim at realising him as the self within; *buddhi-yoga* becomes not just action without desire, but prescribed action as worship of the Deity; and *jñāna*, whether it be distinctively Sāṁkhya or otherwise, becomes realisation of Kṛṣṇa as the Supreme Deity and the self within.

Chapter 9 describes the worship of Kṛṣṇa that leads to salvation. Verses 26 to 28 introduce the devotional element into *niṣkāma-karma* and in 29 we find a clear indication of the concept of grace. Kṛṣṇa is equal to all beings but still those who worship him with devotion are in him and he is in them–*ye bhajanti tu māṁ bhaktyā mayi te teṣu cāpy aham* (29). Even a wrongdoer is to be considered a saint if he worships Kṛṣṇa, for he will soon become a righteous soul and attain unending peace–*kṣipraṁ bhavati dharmātmā śaśvac-chāntiṁ nigacchati* (31). Even those of lower births who surrender to Kṛṣṇa gain the supreme destination–*te 'pi yānti parāṁ gatim* (32). Arjuna is therefore urged to fix his mind on Kṛṣṇa, be his devotee, worship him, and bow down before him–*man-manā bhava mad-bhakto mad-yājī māṁ namaskuru,* through such devotion he will come to Kṛṣṇa who is the self within–*māṁ evaiṣyasi yuktvaisvam ātmānaṁ mat-parāyanaḥ* (34).

Chapter 12, which follows the display of the *viśva-rūpa,* opens with Arjuna asking which are the best practitioners of *yoga,* the devotees who worship Kṛṣṇa as just described, or those who revere the eternal unmanifest–*ye cāpy akṣaram avyaktam.* The question itself is significant for it recognises a differentiation between the non-theistic doctrines of Sāṁkhya, Vedānta and Yoga encountered elsewhere in the *Mahābhārata,* and the devotional ideas prominent in the *Bhagavad-gītā.*

Kṛṣṇa's reply is unequivocal. Those who fix their minds on him and are always in engaged in worship with faith are the best of *yogins.* Those who worship the imperceptible, unlimited, unmanifest–*akṣaram anirdeśyam avyaktam*–which is all-pervading, inconceivable steady and unchanging, and are attached to the welfare of all beings, also attain Kṛṣṇa–*te prāpnuvanti mām eva* (4). Their path, however, is fraught with difficulty and causes sorrow–*kleśo 'dhikataras teṣām . . . avyaktā hi gatir duḥkhaṁ dehavadbhir avāpyate* (5). In contrast, the way to salvation found by the devotees is much easier for they are liberated through the grace of the Deity. They surrender all their actions to Kṛṣṇa–*ye tu sarvāṇi karmāṇi mayi sannyasya*–and worship him through fixing their *yoga* meditation on him without deviation–*ananyenaiva yogena māṁ dhyāyanta upāsate* (6). For such devotees he is the saviour from the ocean of death and rebirth–*teṣām ahaṁ samuddhartā mṛtyu-saṁsāra-sāgarāt bhavāmi* (7). Grace is thus the easy path to salvation, for devotion calls into play the strength of an external Deity who can easily lift them from their bondage in this world. Those who ignore the personal, God, and instead seek the unmanifest, unknowable feature of the divine, may also gain salvation, but because they depend on their own strength their path is very difficult.

This short chapter concentrates primarily on outlining the various practices that may be undertaken as expressions of devotion to Kṛṣṇa, and on describing the qualities that are found in such a devotee. The qualities of the devotee are virtually identical to those given in the *Mokṣa-dharma* in descriptions of persons who have gained perfection in Sāṁkhya or Yoga. There is also a marked similarity with the description of the *yogin* in Chapter 6, with several phrases common to both.[18] The devotional thought of this chapter is clearly based on the values of the world-denying ethical system of *nivṛtti* and demonstrates again the absence of any world-affirming perspective in the *Gītā*'s devotional ideology. Soteriologically, the important points to note here are first Kṛṣṇa's repeated stress on the love he feels for his devotees which he reciprocates with them, and secondly the introduction of the concept of grace. The way to salvation through the unmanifest is not denied but is shown to be far more difficult than that of devotion to a personal God, for here Kṛṣṇa himself intervenes out of love to deliver his devotee from the cycle of birth and death.

It is significant that this theme is taken up again in the concluding teachings in Chapter 18, in verses 61 to 66. The final verse of this short passage is well-known for its stress on grace and the protection offered by Kṛṣṇa in delivering salvation to those devoted to him:

> *sarva-dharmān parityajya mām ekaṁ śaraṇaṁ vraja*
> *ahaṁ tvā sarva-pāpebhyo mokṣayiṣyāmi mā śucaḥ*
>
> 'Having given up all prescribed religious duties, find shelter in me alone. I will deliver you from all your sinful deeds. Do not be afraid.' (18.66)

Thus the doctrine of salvation through devotion, surrender and grace is restated as the final teaching of the *Gītā*. The grace offered is not unconditional in a Calvinist sense for it is invoked by devotional acts and sentiments. As the *īśvara* in the hearts of all beings, Kṛṣṇa is equally disposed to all but when he is served with devotion his love and compassion are aroused. Because of his affection for those beings devoted to him, he is moved to bestow grace and deliver the *bhaktas* from this world. Such a thoroughgoing exposition of the concept of grace as the best means of salvation is not found in the *Mokṣa-dharma* and is a unique statement of the *Bhagavad-gītā*.

The most prominent doctrine of salvation found in the *Gītā* is *bhakti*, though Sāṁkhya, *jñāna* and various types of *yoga* are also discussed and recommended. The *Nārāyaṇīya*, the epic's other major presentation of Vaiṣṇava doctrines, is based on early Pañcarātra teachings but there is no evidence of Pañcarātra ideas in the *Gītā*. This absence is notable and indicates that the *Gītā*, and probably the present form of the narrative, expresses the doctrines of non-or pre-Pañcarātric Vaiṣṇavism.[19] Like the *Nārāyaṇīya*, the *Gītā* bases much of its speculation on Sāṁkhya but its more philosophical approach, as opposed to the *Nārāyaṇīya*'s preoccupation with glorification of the Deity, show again a different background. The variances in the non-theistic doctrines of the *Mokṣa-dharma* indicate that works from separate schools of Sāṁkhya and Yoga are represented. It would appear that the same conclusion must be reached regarding the *Bhagavad-gītā* and the *Nārāyaṇīya*, to the effect that two distinct schools of Vaiṣṇava *bhakti* are represented by these works, the latter based on Pañcarātra and stressing worship of Nārāyaṇa, the former non-Pañcarātric, closer to Vedic orthodoxy, and emphasising the worship of Kṛṣṇa above all other paths.

6. Summary and Conclusions

A consideration of epic soteriology highlights once again the fundamental dichotomy between the ideals of *pravṛtti* and *nivṛtti*. *Pravṛtti* is concerned primarily with this world and regards success within the material sphere as the goal of existence. It is therefore questionable as to whether *pravṛtti* truly contains any notion of soteriology. Within the epic, the idea of the transmigration of the self is combined with the Vedic belief in elevation to the domain of the gods after death. Hence there is no imperative towards escaping from this world entirely but rather towards the elevation of one's status within it through rebirth in an exalted position either amongst the gods or within human society.

Pravṛtti advocates a number of methods by which such a goal may be attained. Principal amongst these is adherence to the social duties ascribed to an individual by his *sva-dharma*. *Brāhmaṇas, kṣatriyas, vaiśyas* and *śūdraṣ* all have a specific social function to fulfil and duties to perform in pursuit of that function. By acceptance of such obligations one is guaranteed a desirable future rebirth. The ideal of *sva-dharma* embraces and interacts with a conventional understanding of morality and the text frequently highlights tensions between ritual and moral ethics. The conclusion seems to be that both sva-dharmic and moral actions are efficacious in securing a desired position in the afterlife, though difficulties may arise in attempting to harmonise the two paths of action. The *Mahābhārata*, and the *Anuśāsana* in particular, also offers a series of ritual actions that guarantee the practitioner rebirth amongst the gods. Such acts include penance, pilgrimage, charity of specific kinds, fasts and sacrificial ceremonies. Furthermore, one's position in paradise can be sustained by the actions of one's descendants who can perform *śrāddha* rites for this purpose.

Nivṛtti takes a far more negative view of this world and seeks complete emancipation from it. The cycle of rebirth with its concomitants of old age, disease and death is viewed as a cycle of misery and even existence amongst the gods is dismissed as temporary and fraught with anxiety because of one's impending return to the human sphere. Therefore, under the heading of *mokṣa-dharma*, the epic prescribes various techniques which enable the transcendent self to avoid further rebirth. Central to such techniques is the notion of *jñāna*, the realised wisdom that allows one to perceive one's true identity as a spiritual entity completely separate from matter and from the body, mind and senses through which it is currently forced to operate. This wisdom is based on the philosophy of Sāṁkhya which stresses a rigid differentiation between the true self and the elements of which the material creation is comprised. Based on this view, the individual is urged to renounce his connections with the world, including his dharmic duties, and to abandon all aspirations and endeavours for worldly pleasure. Realisation of *sāṁkhya-jñāna* is far more than comprehension of philosophical logic and hence techniques of *yoga* involving controlled breathing and inner concentration may be employed in order to gain direct perception of the self. When one realises this spiritual identity, salvation is gained and after death there is no further rebirth.

Bhakti draws into its own purview the values of both *pravṛtti* and *nivṛtti*. Thus the narrative repeatedly illustrates the exercising of the will of both Viṣṇu and Śiva so that *dharma* may be preserved on earth and the position of the gods sustained in heaven. In this way *bhakti* endorses *pravṛtti* and thereby recognises the validity of the aspiration for higher rebirth that *pravṛtti* aims at. In other passages, however, notably the *Nārāyaṇīya* and the *Bhagavad-gītā*, the perspective of *nivṛtti* is embraced as being essentially that of *bhakti*. The *Nārāyaṇīya* espouses many of the central notions of Sāṁkhya and recognises *mokṣa* as the final goal of spiritual endeavours. Here, however, *bhakti* with its stress on an all-powerful Deity introduces a further element into epic soteriology, that of grace. The Sāṁkhya view of this world as a place of misery is endorsed as is the notion of *mokṣa* as liberation from rebirth but here devotional practices and worship are recommended as the best path to achieving this for thereby the grace of the Deity is invoked and he acts to deliver his votary from rebirth. The passage dedicated to Śiva at the beginning of the *Anuśāsana* is interesting in that it appears to embody a later understanding of salvation. Here *bhakti* is no longer a means to an end but is an end in itself as the worshipper, in an emotional state of devotion, cares for nothing except his relationship of love with the Deity.

The soteriology of the *Bhagavad-gītā* includes ideas based on both *nivṛtti* and *bhakti*, but the aspirations for elevated rebirth of *pravṛtti* are substantially rejected. Here less emphasis is placed on the miseries of rebirth in this world, though a world-denying ethos is sustained. Thus Arjuna is urged to seek complete salvation and offered various techniques for achieving this goal. The wisdom of Sāṁkhya, differentiating the soul from matter, is asserted as a central doctrine and different *yoga* practices are presented by means of which this *jñāna* may be realised. To the concentration and breath control referred to elsewhere, Kṛṣṇa adds a *karma-yoga* which is the execution of sva-dharmic duty without desire for material gain in an apparent attempt to reconcile social duties with the quest for salvation. The *bhakti* of the *Gītā* emphasises the power of the Deity to deliver his devotee from the cycle of rebirth and several verses make it clear that this path is both the easiest and most elevated of all.

It is thus possible to recognise the manner in which the major strands or religious thought in the *Mahābhārata* produce their own soteriologies, based largely on their own views of this world. The perspective of *pravṛtti* which dominates the narrative and is there linked to *bhakti* is critiqued and rejected in various didactic interludes in which the values of *nivṛtti* are seen to demand a more genuine soteriology based on a negative view of worldly life. *Bhakti* is able to absorb this imperative, accepting the fundamental problems of worldly life and offering grace as the best means of gaining salvation. At the same time *bhakti* is unwilling to abandon completely its links with *pravṛtti* and thus in the *Gītā* it converts dharmic duty into a form of *yoga* and in the *Nārāyaṇīya* accepts that both paths are valid though *nivṛtti* is superior.

Notes

1. Ninian Smart, 'Soteriology: An Overview', Article in *The Encyclopaedia of Religion,* Vol 13, New York, 1987, pp. 418-423.
2. See 12. 146.16-18 and 12.306.26-37.
3. Frauwallner, E. *History of Indian Philosophy,* Volume 1, V.M. Bedeker trans, Delhi, 1973, pp. 87-88.
4. Ibid, p. 88.
5. See also 5.40.23-26 wherein Vidura explicitly states that the members of all four *varṇas* can attain *svarga-loka* through the proper execution of their duties.
6. Hopkins, E.W. *The Great Epic of India,* Calcutta, 1969 (1st Ed 1901), p. 31.
7. Edgerton, F. 'The Meaning of Sāṁkhya and Yoga', *American Journal of Philosophy* XLV, No. 177, 1924, p. 6.
8. "But the ascetic who gathers in himself magic fervour through fasts and self-mortification is, in spite of its contact with Yoga in some particulars, separated far by a gap from a Yogin who strives to see the highest in his restful inner composure." (Frauwallner 1973, p. 106)
9. Hopkins 1969, pp. 130-134.
10. This appears to be a very obvious attempt to assert the orthodoxy and enhance the status of Yoga teachings by stressing that Yoga is included in the Vedas.
11. It is noteworthy, however, that the *Padma Purāṇa* (6.269.53) adds the granting of salvation to the functions of the *avatāras* given by the *Gītā* (Bharadvāja, K. *A Philosophical Study of the Concept of Viṣṇu in the Purāṇas,* New Delhi, 1981, p. 324).
12. Hardy, F. *Viraha Bhakti, The Early History of Kṛṣṇa Devotion in South India,* Delhi, 1983, pp. 448-449. Hardy further argues that emotional love of God, "is typical

only of the Kṛṣṇa religion, and though found in other theistic streams, its roots are exclusively in Kṛṣṇaism." (Ibid, p. 7)
Again one must either regard the passage from the *Anuśāsana* as late or else recognise the existence of emotional *bhakti* in early Śaivism.

13. Bharadvāja cites the *Śaraṇāgati-gadyam* of Rāmānuja as referring to two types of *bhakti, parā* which is *bhakti* as a means to an end and *paramā* in which *bhakti* is regarded as an end in itself. Nimbarka, in V9 of his *Daśa-ślokī*, expresses the same idea, referring to the two types of *bhakti as parā* and *aparā* (Bharadvāja 1981, p. 319).
14. As in the story of Mudgala, in Chapter 247 of the *Vana.*
15. Dasgupta, S. *A History of Indian Philosophy,* Vol 2, Cambridge, 1973 (1st Ed, 1922), p. 521.
16. I find it hard to agree with Dasgupta that Sāṁkhya in the *Gītā* should be understood as indicating no more than wisdom or renunciation (Ibid, p. 457). Some of the more complex features of Epic Sāṁkhya are absent, but the essential idea of gaining salvation through realisation of the distinction of the self from matter is at its heart in contrast to the Vedāntic notion of gaining salvation through the realisation of oneness. Dasgupta's preoccupation with denying Buddhist influences on the *Gītā* may be a factor in his stress on the differences between the ideas of the *Gītā* and those of the *Mokṣadharma.*
17. Frauwallner cites the *Chāndogya Upaniṣad* (5.3-10) and the *Bṛhadāraṇyaka* (6.2) as the basis for this passage (Frauwallner 1973, p. 40). Dasgupta likewise refers to 5.10 of the *Chāndogya* and opines that the passage offers an eschatology inconsistent with other teachings of the *Gītā* (Dasgupta 1973, p. 521).
18. Compare especially 12.18 and 6.7.
19. In the opinion of Bhandarkar, the *Gītā* expresses the beliefs of an early devotional sect dedicated to Vāsudeva-Kṛṣṇa (Bhandarkar, R.G. *Vaiṣṇavavism, Śaivism and Minor Religious Systems,* New York, 1980, pps. 8-12).

CHAPTER 5

EPIC THEISM: THE NATURE OF GOD

1. Introduction

(i) Theism and Non-theism in Epic Thought

Within the Hindu tradition theistic and non-theistic thought have for centuries existed side by side and both tendencies are represented in the *Mahābhārata.* Here the key factor is the way that *bhakti* interacts with the contrasting views of *pravṛtti* and *nivṛtti. Pravṛtti* reaffirms the major features of Vedic thought, stressing the role of right action both in sustaining the order of creation and in gaining success in this world for the individual and for society. The gods are central to this world view and the universal system it postulates, receiving the results of human ritual action and bestowing in return the resources required by humanity. They are, however, essentially 'within' the system rather than being its external creators and controllers.

Where epic theism is linked to *pravṛtti,* the Deity is presented as the creator, sustainer and destroyer of the universal order who acts in this world to ensure that *dharma* is maintained. Thus the narrative tells of the appearance of Nārāyaṇa as Kṛṣṇa to achieve his goal of perpetuating the desired equilibrium in creation. The actual prosecution of dharmic action, however, makes little or no reference to the Deity except in the teachings of the *Bhagavad-gītā.* Such action, including the ritual of *yajña,* is performed without reference to God and without any sense of devotion. *Bhakti* thus intervenes into the sphere of *pravṛtti* only in presenting a creator and controller of the universal system who acts to set it in motion, set it aright when problems arise, and finally bring it to a close. The perspective of *nivṛtti* is represented primarily by teachings on Sāṁkhya and Yoga through which the individual transforms his self-identity. Again this religious endeavour is typically presented without reference to any form of Deity.

The above discussion provides a context for understanding the significance of theism in epic thought. The narrative tells the story of a disruption to the cosmic order due to *asuras* being born as kings on earth. Here the role of the Deity is prominent for he accepts the duty of maintaining dharmic order and thus Kṛṣṇa plays a leading role in the narrative, manipulating events towards the desired outcome of dharmic normality. In passages which directly teach the proper execution of dharmic duty, however, there is a notable absence of theistic emphasis. Where *nivṛtti* is central, much of the didactic material is essentially non-theistic; only in specific passages which teach theistic Sāṁkhya and devotional Yoga does the Supreme Deity play an important role in the doctrines of *nivṛtti*.

The result is that though the *Mahābhārata* is regarded as the earliest known text of Vaiṣṇava theism,[1] the greater part of its didactus is non-theistic. The teachings of the righteous hunter (3.198-206), Śaunaka (3.2.60-79), Sanat-sujāta (5.41-45) and Vidura (5.34-40) all display no concern whatsoever with theism or devotion. In the *Śānti*, Bhīṣma prefaces his extensive teachings with words of homage to Kṛṣṇa and Narāyaṇa, but the forms of *dharma* that he then discourses upon pay virtually no attention to any notion of God. The Anuśāsana contains extensive teachings on ritual acts that bring a desirable result in this world and the next but the gaining of such results is described virtually as an automatic process, without reference to the Deity as the gracious rewarder or bestower of benedictions. Thus although it is accurate to identify the epic as a Vaiṣṇava work, it must be recognised that it contains extensive teachings based on the non-theistic tendencies of *pravṛtti* and *nivṛtti*.

(ii) Theism in the Narrative

The epic Deity is typically presented as Viṣṇu or Nārāyaṇa, although in some passages Śiva appears in this role. It may be possible to attempt to draw conclusions regarding the differences of nature and status between Nārāyaṇa, Viṣṇu and Kṛṣṇa, and certain passages clearly prefer one name and one aspect of the Deity. Overall, however, it is impossible to draw firm conclusions and for most of the epic Nārāyaṇa and Viṣṇu, along with other names such as Hari and Janārdana, appear to be used interchangeably as designations for the same Deity. It has also been argued that the *Bhagavad-gītā* is devoted to Kṛṣṇa as a Deity in his own right.[2] Within the context of the *Mahābhārata*, however, this view cannot be sustained and therefore I have chosen to regard all passages on the basis of the predominant epic view that Kṛṣṇa is a manifestation of Viṣṇu and that no distinction is to be drawn between Viṣṇu and Nārāyaṇa.

The epic recounts the story of a fratricidal conflict between two branches of the Kuru dynasty, the political intrigues and betrayals, the massive conflict of the final battle and the triumph of the rightful heirs to the kingdom. At the same time the audience is made aware of the cosmic dimension of the conflict. Chapter 58 of the *Ādi* relates how, after the slaughter of the ruling dynasties by Paraśurāma, the *brāhmaṇas* begot sons by *kṣatriya* women and these sons ruled the earth according to the *dharma* of the four *varṇas*. In verse 25, we are told that the *asuras*, deprived of their opulence by the victorious gods, took birth on earth desiring sovereignty in this sphere. These *asuras*, taking on the identities of belligerent warrior kings, became a great burden to the earth and the Earth Goddess approached Brahmā, the first-born of the gods.

In verse 47, Brahmā instructs the gods to take birth in the ruling dynasties on earth so that they can combat the disruptive influence of the *asuras*. The gods then approach Nārāyaṇa and request that he also appear and lead them in this mission. Nārāyaṇa agrees to this request. In Chapter 61, we are informed that Nārāyaṇa has appeared on earth as the son of Vasudeva, one of the leaders of the Yadu dynasty, related by marriage to the Kurus and particularly the righteous Pāṇḍava faction in the dynastic dispute (90). This description of the descent of Nārāyaṇa is repeated by Bhīṣma to Duryodhana in 6.61.14f without any notable change of detail or emphasis.

This account establishes that Kṛṣṇa's mission on earth is to remove the asuric burden and reestablish the principles of *dharma*. The narrative is thus to be understood both on its human level and also from this cosmic perspective. The events that unfold are directed by Kṛṣṇa, the son of Vasudeva and Devakī, to bring about the result desired by the gods. Repeatedly, and throughout its duration, the text draws attention to the fact that Kṛṣṇa is none other than Nārāyaṇa, an assertion confirmed by virtually all the leading characters–Arjuna (3.13.10-20), Dhaumya (3.86.21-24), Yudhiṣṭhira (7.59.8-13), Mārkaṇḍeya (3.187.54), Dhṛtarāṣṭra (5.22.10), Saṁjaya (5.46.82), Kuntī (5.88.103), Bhīṣma (6.61.14f), Nārada (2.33.10-20), Vidura (7.9.72), Karṇa (8.22.49) and even Duryodhana (9.64.28). These examples are typical rather than exhaustive, for the understanding of Kṛṣṇa as the Supreme Deity directing events is fundamental to the narrative and the authors, or at least the final redactors, wish to sustain the audience's awareness of it.

Kṛṣṇa's mission is to be achieved by establishing Yudhiṣṭhira, the Dharmarāja, on the throne of the kingdom and by destroying the asuric kings who are a burden to the earth. Thus he seeks the victory of the Pāṇḍavas through a massive conflict in which almost all the kings of the earth will die. The narrative moves inexorably to this conclusion with Kṛṣṇa sometimes to the fore and sometimes in the background. At times the triumph of *dharma* and the slaughter of the kings is ascribed to fate but it is clear that this is not a blind force. Kṛṣṇa, the Supreme Deity, is directing events toward this conclusion and his will cannot be checked by man or god.

The role of Kṛṣṇa in the narrative is especially prominent in the preparations for war and in the battle itself. In the *Udyoga*, he is present in the Pāṇḍava camp as the most vociferous and persuasive of those in favour of war, notably in Chapters 30 and 71. He dispels Yudhiṣṭhira's doubts about the righteousness of violence and is even more vehement than Bhīma in urging that Duryodhana must be confronted in battle. In Chapter 73, with Arjuna and Bhīma apparently in agreement with Yudhiṣṭhira that peace is better than war, Kṛṣṇa is quick to remind Bhīma of his previous vows of revenge and chides him for his lack of manliness–*puṁstvaṁ klība ivātmani* (17)–his trembling heart and faltering mind which lead him to look for peace–*tasmāt praśamam icchasi* (18). As a result of this pressure from Kṛṣṇa, Bhīma regains his resolve and events resume their course towards the outcome sought by the Deity. Even whilst acting as a peace envoy from the Pāṇḍavas, Kṛṣṇa is aware that Duryodhana will accept no compromise and the endeavour serves only to strengthen Yudhiṣṭhira's faltering resolve towards conflict. Despite this apparent endeavour to avoid war it is clear that Kṛṣṇa never truly deviates from directing events towards a violent conclusion and the episode merely emphasises the righteousness of the Pāṇḍavas and the asuric qualities of Duryodhana's party.

Having thus ensured that a conflict of mass destruction will take place, Kṛṣṇa's next task is to ensure that the Pāṇḍavas will gain victory by killing all their adversaries. Throughout the extensive descriptions of warfare in the *Bhīṣma, Droṇa, Karṇa* and *Śalya,* Kṛṣṇa in his role as Parthasārathi, the charioteer of Arjuna, controls the course of events to achieve the result he desires. The downfall of Bhīṣma is engineered by Kṛṣṇa; he saves Arjuna from the Vaiṣṇava weapon (7.28.16f); he urges Ghaṭotkaca to attack Karṇa so that the latter's *śakti* weapon will be drawn from him (7.147); he enables Arjuna to kill Jayadratha by altering the movements of the sun; he persuades Yudhiṣṭhira to tell a lie so that Droṇa may be vanquished (7.164.98); he protects the Pāṇḍava host from Aśvatthāman's Nārāyaṇa weapon (7.170); he urges Arjuna to kill Karṇa when the latter dismounts from his chariot (8.67, though in the Critical Edition he does no more than dismiss Karṇa's plea for *dharma* to prevail in the fight); and he indicates to Bhīma that Duryodhana should be defeated by an unchivalrous blow on the thigh (9.57.5).

(iii) The Lack of Consistency in Epic Theism

Brockington has argued that epic theism is inconsistent and displays characteristics which tend towards both 'polytheism' and 'that form of classical Hinduism where one Deity is regarded as supreme.'[3] His point here is an important one for it is clear that the *Mahābhārata* contains a variety of perspectives, probably from different periods and religious viewpoints. Although the epic displays clear monotheistic tendencies, the Vedic pantheon also has a prominent role and individual gods are at times extolled with prayers and narrations of their mythologies. Furthermore, while Viṣṇu and Śiva are typically presented in their position as the Supreme Deity, aloof and transcendent, a number of passages portray them in their Vedic role as leading members of the pantheon who are definitely a part of the cosmic order rather than transcendent controllers of it.

A few examples will demonstrate that the monotheistic perspective is not consistently expressed throughout the epic. In 1.59.16, it is asserted, based on the traditional Ṛgvedic teaching, that Viṣṇu is one of the Āditya gods, the twelfth son of Aditi–*viṣṇur dvādaśa ucyate*–though it is stressed that he is the greatest of them–*sa sarveṣāṁ ādityānāṁ guṇādhikaḥ.* In 2.11.32, as a part of the description of the great assembly halls of the gods given by Nārada, it is mentioned that Nārāyaṇa is one of the gods in the entourage of Brahmā. 3.195.5-6 relates how the *asura* Dhundhu, having attained boons from Brahmā, oppressed all the gods including their leader Viṣṇu–*babādha sarvān asakṛd devān viṣṇuṁ ca vai bhṛśam.* The description of the *tīrthas* in the *Vana* refers to the abode of Viṣṇu not as a transcendent realm, but as one of the heavens that may be attained by pilgrimage.[4] In 9.44.4, we find Viṣṇu as one of the pantheon of gods come to pay reverence to Skanda who has just been appointed commander of the celestial host in their battle with the *asuras.*

Such references are incompatible with the concept of Viṣṇu as a monotheistic Deity but within the *Mahābhārata* they are the exception rather than the rule. Their lack of congruence with the epic's prevailing theistic perspective appears to demonstrate the reluctance of the authors to revise or discard traditional myth and wisdom, even where it conflicts with the major theological tendency of the text. On this basis I have chosen to regard such passages as an aberrant feature of the theistic teachings of the epic. Their presence and significance must be noted, particularly with regard to the inconsistency of doctrine they represent, but when the topic of epic theism is considered the main focus should be directed towards the predominant doctrinal perspective which regards Nārāyaṇa and Śiva as the Supreme Deity of epic monotheism.

This predominant tendency, in contrast to the references noted above, glorifies Nārāyaṇa and his manifestation as Kṛṣṇa as the one Supreme Deity. Whilst the narrative depicts Kṛṣṇa as the controller of all things, the numerous hymns of praise offered to Nārāyaṇa at various stages of the epic clearly indicate that he is the one God who repeatedly creates, controls, sustains and annihilates this world. In the opening chapter of *Ādi*, Sūta offers a prayer to Viṣṇu before beginning his recital of the text,

ādyaṁ puruṣam īśānaṁ puruhūtaṁ puruṣṭutam
ṛtam ekākṣaraṁ brahma vyaktāvyaktaṁ sanātanam

asac ca sac caiva ca yad viśvaṁ sad asataḥ param
parāvarāṇaṁ sraṣṭāraṁ purāṇaṁ param avyayam

maṅgalyaṁ maṅgalaṁ viṣṇuṁ vareṇyam anaghaṁ śucim
namaskṛtya hṛṣīkeśaṁ carācara-guruṁ harim

maharṣeḥ pūjitasyeha sarva-loke mahātmanaḥ
pravakṣyāmi mataṁ kṛtsnaṁ vyāsasyāmita-tejasaḥ

'Having bowed before the first of all beings, the controller, who is beseeched and prayed to, who is the one unchanging truth, *brahman*, who is both the manifest and unmanifest and is eternal, who is both existence and non-existence, who is everything and is yet beyond existence and non-existence, the ancient one, supreme and immutable, the creator of all things superior and inferior, to the most exalted, auspicious Viṣṇu, who is auspiciousness itself, pure and untainted, Hṛṣīkeśa, Hari, the guide of both moving and unmoving beings, I will now impart all the teachings of the unlimitedly potent Vyāsa, the exalted sage, the great soul who is worshipped everywhere in the world.' (1.1.20-23)

From this statement at the very beginning of the epic it is apparent that we are no longer dealing with the leader of a pantheon of gods but have moved into the sphere of monotheistic thought wherein a Supreme Deity, whose omnipotence is beyond question or challenge, has complete mastery over all creation. This theological notion is the major theme of epic theism and is expressed repeatedly throughout the narrative, in the *Bhagavad-gītā* and *Nārāyaṇīya,* and also in the passages that extol the supremacy of Śiva. The central focus of all these passages is the omnipotence of the Supreme Deity, and their significance is that they establish the monotheistic doctrine of the *Mahābhārata* in a manner that has had a profound influence on the subsequent Hindu tradition.

2. The Iconography of Nārāyaṇa in the *Mahābhārata*

(i) Introduction

In the Hindu tradition the progression from polytheism to monotheism did not entail the abandonment of a prominent iconography as the concept of a Supreme Deity developed. It is true to say that as monotheistic doctrines expanded and became more firmly established in the Purāṇic and medieval period, so the iconography of the Deity became more pronounced in religious texts, religious art and in the images of the Deity worshipped in the temples that appeared throughout India during the first millennium of the Common Era.

Hindu monotheism differs radically from that of Islam, Judaism and Christianity. Iconography marks a major, though by no means the only, feature of this distinction and its extravagant influence on the monotheistic Hindu sects has frequently been used by the adherents of other faiths as the focus of attempts to decry and belittle the significance of this tendency in Hinduism. To the Western religious mind iconography is a feature of polytheism and a primitive religious view. The Western Deity typically lacks a specific form, though in baroque artistic representations he is sometimes portrayed as an elderly person peering down from the clouds or as an effulgent triangle containing the letters of the tetragrammation. Islam, Judaism and Protestant Christianity have all anathematised plastic portrayals of their Deity, as it appears to reduce their God to the level of some lesser divine being. That a developed iconography is not incompatible with monotheistic theology is apparent from the rich Hindu tradition. Notably the teachings of Rāmānuja display a combination of sophisticated monotheism with adoration for a God whose form is described in detail and whose image is venerated in numerous places of worship.

By the time of the later *Purāṇas* the exact iconography of Viṣṇu was well-established. Typically he is described or represented as beautiful to behold, of a dark complexion, with four arms that carry his four symbols, the conch, lotus, disc and mace. His consort is Śrī or Lakṣmī, the Goddess of Prosperity, his carrier is the mighty bird, Garuḍa, and his bed is the celestial serpent known as Ananta or Śeṣa. His eyes are long, like lotus petals, he dresses in yellow garments and wears a helmet or crown on his head; his chest bears the gem known as the Kaustubha and has a white mark called *Śrī-vatsa* representing his connection with the goddess.

A review of relevant passages reveals that in the *Mahābhārata* this iconography is present but in a less developed and notably more restrained form than is found in the *Purāṇas*. Typically the emphasis is placed on the supremacy of Viṣṇu, his creation of and dominion over the world, and on his all-pervasive nature. Epic theism ascribes a cosmic identity to the Vedic god, Viṣṇu, and it is likely that this reinterpretation would tend to place less emphasis on the non-cosmic aspect of the divine that iconography represents. Later Vaiṣṇava *bhakti* offers a more personal understanding of the Deity and it is against this background that the increased emphasis on iconography is to be understood.

(ii) The Consort of Viṣṇu

The Goddess Śrī plays a prominent role in the *Mahābhārata* for she appears on earth as Draupadī, the wife of the Pāṇḍavas, and thereby symbolises the royal sovereignty that is theirs by right.[5] In addition, she appears in the *Śānti* discussing with Indra and Bali why, as prosperity, she attaches herself to different people at different times (chs 218 and 221). Hiltebeitel has noted the problem posed by Śrī becoming the wife of the Pāṇḍavas, for as the consort of Nārāyaṇa she would be expected to appear as Rukminī, the first wife of Kṛṣṇa.[6] Certain passages, rejected by the Critical Edition as interpolations, do in fact make this adjustment by referring to Rukminī as Śrī and Draupadī as Śacī, the consort of Indra. It is likely that such passages were added to the text at a later date when Śrī was widely known as the consort of Viṣṇu but that this relationship was unknown in the epic period and hence the marriage of Draupadī to the Pāṇḍavas posed no difficulties. Throughout the text of the Critical Edition I can find no reference to Śrī being the consort of Nārāyaṇa, who stands as a Deity alone and largely detached from human-like sentiment.[7] Even the *Nārāyaṇīya,* which comes closest to Purāṇic thought, makes no reference to Nārāyaṇa having Śrī as his consort.

(iii) Garuḍa, The Carrier of Viṣṇu

Garuḍa is referred to in the *Mahābhārata* as the carrier of Viṣṇu but only in occasional references and the Deity is usually portrayed without any carrier. Chapters 18 to 30 of the *Ādi* recount the story of the birth of Garuḍa and how he came to be the enemy of his cousins, the serpents. In Chapter 29, Garuḍa encounters Nārāyaṇa whilst returning from seizing the nectar of the gods (12). Pleased with the bird's endeavours, the Deity grants him the boon of immortality and freedom from old age (14). Garuḍa than offers

Viṣṇu a boon in return and the Deity requests that he become his carrier (16) and always remain as the symbol on his banner. In this brief interlude in the story of Garuḍa Nārāyaṇa appears more as the leader of the gods and less as the cosmic Deity presented elsewhere in the epic. Apart from this passage. I can find only two other references to Garuḍa as the carrier of Viṣṇu. Chapter 103 of the *Udyoga* gives the story of the humbling of Garuḍa by Viṣṇu when the former became proud because of his ability to bear the Supreme Deity, and in the *Nārāyaṇīya* (12.324.30-39), Viṣṇu dispatches Garuḍa to deliver his devotee, King Vasu, from the pit in which he is being punished. In all three of these passages the portrayal of Viṣṇu tends towards a more anthropomorphic perspective, somewhat at odds with the descriptions of the cosmic Deity. In the epic as a whole it is correct to assert that the text does not recognise Viṣṇu as having either a consort or a carrier.

(iv) Bodily Complexion

In the *Mahābhārata,* it is only Kṛṣṇa, as his name indicates, who is described as a having a dark bodily hue, though the name is also occasionally applied to Viṣṇu. Thus in 12.51.8, when Bhīṣma prays, *atasipuṣpa-saṁkāśaṁ pīta-vāsaṁ samacyutam/vapur hy anumimīm aste meghasyeva savidyutaḥ*–dressed in yellow garments the colour of an Atasi flower, your body resembles a dark cloud surrounded by lightning–he is addressing Kṛṣṇa rather than Nārāyaṇa of whom he is a specific manifestation.

Brahmā's prayers to Nārāyaṇa refer to the Deity as *harikeśa,* having fair hair (6.61.47), while the *Viṣṇu-sahasra-nāma-stotram* describes him as being *suvarṇa-varṇa* and *hemāṅga*–golden coloured and having golden limbs (13.135.92); Mārkaṇḍeya describes Nārāyaṇa's manifestation as a child as *atasī-puṣpa-varṇābhaḥ* (3.186.86), being similar in colour to the (yellow) Atasi flower, and Bhīṣma glorifies Viṣṇu as *hiraṇya-varṇam,* having a golden hue (12.47.43). In the *Nārāyaṇīya,* Vaiśaṁpāyana describes Viṣṇu as *ravi-varṇam*–having a complexion like the sun (12. 334.16) and in Kṛṣṇa's explanation of the meanings of his names, he states, *varṇaś ca me hariśreṣṭhas tasmād dharir ahaṁ smṛtaḥ*–and my complexion is of the purest gold; therefore I am known as Hari (12.330.3). Where the same chapter later states, *kṛṣṇo varṇaś ca me yasmāt tasmāt kṛṣṇo 'ham arjuna*–because of my dark complexion I am Kṛṣṇa, O Arjuna (12.330.14)–I take this again to be a reference to the *avatāra* rather than Viṣṇu himself, a view reinforced by the insertion of the vocative, *arjuna*. As these are the only references in the Critical Edition it is apparent that only slight attention is devoted to the question and this in itself is significant. What evidence there is suggests that the idea of Viṣṇu having a dark complexion is later than the epic and is probably based on the appearance of Kṛṣṇa. What references there are suggest that the epic authors understood the form of the Deity to be of a golden hue.

(v) The Four Symbols of Viṣṇu

The Purāṇic descriptions of Viṣṇu refer to him as having four arms, the hands of which each hold a particular symbol, the conch, lotus, disc and club. The *Mahābhārata* is aware of this feature of the Deity but it is less firmly established than in the later literature. In the *Rāmopakhyāna,* Brahmā tells the gods of the appearance of the *avatāra* Rāma by stating, *tad-artham avatīrṇo 'sau man-niyogāc catur-bhujaḥ*–for this purpose the four-armed one has descended because of my appeal (3.260.5). In 5.64.15, Saṁjaya, describing his departure from the Pāṇḍava camp, refers to Kṛṣṇa as *catur-bhūjaṁ harim*-Hari with four arms, while the *Viṣṇu-sahasra-nāma-stotram* gives *catur-bhuja*(13.135.28) and *catur-bāhu* (13.135.95) as names of Viṣṇu. The *Bhagavad-gītā* contains an obscure reference to the four-armed feature of the Deity at the conclusion of Chapter 11, following the display of the *viśva-rūpa.* Terrified by this manifestation of divine power, Arjuna requests that Kṛṣṇa return once more to his form wearing a helmet, with club and disc in hand–*kirītinaṁ gadinaṁ cakra-hastam*–and having four arms–*tenaiva rūpena catur-bhujena* (11.46). This apparent description of Kṛṣṇa as being four-armed is unusual and no explanation for it is given. Within the *Nārāyaṇīya* no reference is to be found to any description of the Deity as having four arms.

Mention of the symbols of Nārāyaṇa occurs more frequently, though the idea of the conch, lotus, disc and club in the four hands is absent. Notably, there is no reference to Viṣṇu carrying a lotus flower. When the gods decide to approach Nārāyaṇa to request that he relieve the burden of the earth, he is referred to as *cakra-gadā-pāṇiḥ*–having a disc and club in his hands (1.58.50). In Chapter 187 of the *Vana,* in which the Deity describes himself to Mārkaṇḍeya, there is no reference to his having four arms but in verse 38 he states, *ahaṁ nārāyaṇo nāma śaṅkha-cakra-gadādharaḥ*–I am named Nārāyaṇa, the bearer of the conchshell, disc and club. 5.103.35 describes Viṣṇu as *cakra-gadādhara*, the bearer of disc and club, the thousands of forms of Viṣṇu manifested by Śiva in the *Sauptika* are referred to as *śaṅkha-cakra-gadādharāḥ*, bearing conch, disc and mace, and the same phrase is used by Brahmā in the story of the appearance of the *avatāra* narrated by Bhīṣma (6.62.14). The *Nārāyaṇīya* makes no reference to these features, but the *Viṣṇu-sahasra-nāma-stotram* gives *cakra-gadādhara* (13.135.71), *śaṅkha-bhṛt* (13.135.120), and *gadādhara* (13.135.120) as names of the Deity. Viṣṇu is also described as bearing a bow known as Śārṅga–*śārṅga-dhanur-dharaḥ* (6.6145), *śārṅga-dhanvanaḥ* (12.200.6), *śārṅga-dhanvā* (13.135.120)–but this is usually referred to alone and not in connection with other symbols, a reference in the prayers of Yudhiṣṭhira–*śārṅga-cakra-pāṇiḥ* (12.43.16)–being the exception. The *Mahābhārata* thus knows of Viṣṇu as being four-armed and carrying the conch, disc and club, but it is left to later iconographers to combine these two features and add the lotus flower to produce the classical Purāṇic description.

(vi) The Kaustubha and the Śrīvatsa

The beautiful Kaustubha gem worn by Viṣṇu is a common element in the Purāṇic descriptions of the form of the Deity. The *Mahābhārata* is aware of it but again references are infrequent. In the narration of the churning of the Milk Ocean in Chapter 16 of the *Ādi*, various persons, beasts and objects produced from the churning are given. Among these are mentioned the goddess Śrī and the Kaustubha gem. Whilst no connection is made between the goddess and Nārāyaṇa, it is mentioned that the Kaustubha is found on his chest,

> *kaustubhaś ca maṇir divya utpanno 'mṛta-saṁbhavaḥ*
> *marīci-vikacaḥ śrīmān nārāyaṇa-urogataḥ*
>
> 'And then the divine Kaustubha gem arose, produced from nectar. Its radiant beauty shines forth from its place on the chest of Nārāyaṇa.' (1.16.35)

The only other reference to the Kaustubha gem is in the *Bhīṣma*, in Bhīṣma's description to Duryodhana of the descent of Kṛṣṇa as a manifestation of Nārāyaṇa. In Chapter 62, citing Brahmā's address to the gods, he refers to Viṣṇu as *kirīta-kaustubha-dharaṁ mitrānām abhaya-karam*–wearing a crown and the Kaustubha gem, freeing his friends from fear (22).

In the *Purāṇas*, the *śrīvatsa* is described either as a curl of white hair or a white line on the chest of Viṣṇu. Both of these are connected with Śrī, who in some stories takes these forms to remain always in contact with her consort. The epic is aware of the emblem on the chest of Nārāyaṇa but no specific connection with the goddess is made. The *Nārāyaṇīya* gives two different stories of how Viṣṇu came to bear this mark. 12.329.42 tells of how Ganges water, splashed onto the chest of Viṣṇu by the *ṛṣi* Bharadvāja, left a mark that must presumably be the *śrīvatsa*, though it is not named as such. In Chapter 330, Kṛṣṇa tells Arjuna of a fight between Śiva and the *ṛṣis* Nara and Nārāyaṇa who are forms of Viṣṇu. In the course of the conflict, Nārāyaṇa is struck on the chest by a lance thrown by Śiva (44) and when peace is restored he tells Śiva that the mark made by the weapon will stay on his chest as the *śrīvatsa–adya prabhṛti śrīvatsaḥ śūlāṅko 'yam* (65). These two stories are notable first because they demonstrate the *Nārāyaṇīya*'s awareness of the *śrīvatsa*, secondly because they stand in contrast to Purāṇic explanations of the feature and thirdly because they ignore any relation to the goddess Śrī.

Elsewhere, Mārkaṇḍeya refers to Nārāyaṇa as *śrī-vatsa-kṛta-lakṣaṇaḥ* and *śrī-vatsa-dhārī*, the one who is marked by the *śrīvatsa* and the one who bears the *śrīvatsa* (3.186.86,87); in Chapter 81 of the *Udyoga*, where Vaiśaṁpāyana is again asserting the divinity of Kṛṣṇa, he describes him as, *taṁ sarva-guṇa-saṁpannaṁ śrīvatsa-kṛta-lakṣaṇam*–that one who possesses all good qualities and bears the mark of *śrīvatsa* (36); Brahmā refers to *Nārāyaṇa* as *Śrī-vatsāṅkam*–marked by the *Śrīvatsa* (6.62.20); the *Viṣṇu-sahasra-nāma-stotram* (13.135.77) gives *śrī-vatsa-vakṣāḥ*–having the *śrīvatsa* on his chest–as a name of Viṣṇu; and in the *Nārāyaṇīya*, Vaiśaṁpāyana describes the Deity as *śrī-vatsāṅkaṁ vibhūṣanam*–decorated by the mark of *śrīvatsa* (12.331.12). Whilst the *Mahābhārata* is thus aware of the *śrīvatsa*, no description of it is given and no connection is made with the goddess Śrī. As it stands, it is no more than a mark on the chest indicating that auspiciousness and prosperity attend upon Nārāyaṇa.

(vii) The Personal Features of Viṣṇu

The commonest reference to the appearance of Nārāyaṇa is to the fact that his eyes are long like the petals of a lotus. Bhīṣma (6.63.12, 12.47.62, 12.51.9), Vaiśaṁpāyana (2.33.13), Brahmā (12.335.40), the inhabitants of Śvetadvīpa (12.323.99) and Yudhiṣṭhira (12.43.3, 12.200.1) all refer to the Deity as *puṇḍarīkākṣa.* Mārkaṇḍeya (3.186.14) describes him as *pṛthu-dīrghākṣa*–having broad, long eyes; when the gods pray for Viṣṇu to descend, he is described as *pṛthu-cārvañciteksaṇaḥ*–having beautiful, broad, curved eyes (1.58.50), while Brahmā's prayers speak of Nārāyaṇa as *viśālākṣa*–having large eyes (6.61.44, 60, 62). The *Viṣṇu-sahasra-nāma-statram* includes *puṣkarākṣa* (13.135.18, 72) *puṇḍarīkākṣa* (25), and *aravindākṣa* (41), all meaning having eyes like lotuses, as well as *mahākṣa,* large-eyed (41), and *sulocana,* having beautiful eyes (98). In addition, the *Stotram* has *sundara* (98), *suruci* (107), both meaning beautiful, and *puṣpa-hāsa,* having a smile, or perhaps teeth, like flowers (115). It is perhaps indicative of an aversion to iconography that in 5.68.6, Saṁjaya explains the term *puṇḍarīkākṣa* in a way very different from the obvious meaning. There it is stated that *puṇḍarīka* means 'abode'–*dhāman*–and that *akṣa* means indestructible–*akṣara*–thus rendering the meaning as one who has an indestructible abode rather than one who has eyes like lotus petals.

The dress of the Deity is never described in detail. Apart from his wearing a crown or helmet–*kirīṭa* (6.62.22)–the only reference is to his clothing being yellow in colour–*pīta-vāsas* (1.58.50, 3.186.14), *hari-vāsaḥ* (6.61.47), and *atasi-puṣpa-saṁkāśaṁ pīta-vāsam,* having yellow garments the colour of an Atasi flower (12.47.60, 12.51.8). Apart from the name Kuṇḍalin, meaning a wearer of earrings, in the *Viṣṇu-sahasra-nāma-stotram* there is no reference to any of the ornamentation, necklaces or flower-garlands characteristic of Purāṇic descriptions.

(viii) Overview

The *Mahābhārata* narrative is a Vaiṣṇava text describing the intervention of the Deity to restore *dharma* on earth and sustain the control of the gods in the heavens. A notable feature of the text, particularly when compared to later Vaiṣṇava literature, is the restrained nature of the iconography. Nowhere within the epic is to be found a passage that deals exclusively with the form and appearance of Viṣṇu, the stress repeatedly being placed on the all-pervasive nature of the Deity, on his majesty, his creative acts, his dominance, his control and his sustenance of all things in this world. References to his form and appearance are found scattered within such descriptions but are never the central theme of the prayer or glorification. Where they occur, such references are substantially in accordance with the descriptions of the *Purāṇas* but are less developed. Hence a process of expansion is to be recognised in the development of the Hindu devotional tradition, rather than any new or radical departure.

Throughout the *Mahābhārata* the personalised features of Viṣṇu are displayed primarily through his manifestation as Kṛṣṇa. The Supreme Deity himself generally remains transcendent and aloof, although this is not the case when he is portrayed as the leader of the Vedic pantheon. He is often only a short step philosophically from the Upaniṣadic *brahman*, a concept more than a person. Clearly epic Vaiṣṇavism is aware of the iconographic features of the Deity but compared to the *Purāṇas* these are markedly curtailed and not central to the mode of exaltation of Viṣṇu that the work as a whole seeks to press.

Theologically, the attempt to ascribe a particular form to the Deity in a monotheistic doctrine is problematic. It is hard to conceive how the notion of form can be reconciled with a being who is omnipotent, unlimited and all-pervasive. It is clear that epic theism is based both on an extension of Vedic polytheism and also on philosophical ideas of the nature of transcendence. Iconographic features are connected with a more personal and intimate form of devotion but the *bhakti* of the epic is of an austere nature and the Deity it is aimed at is typically a remote being, beyond the range of human conception. The question of whether Viṣṇu has a particular form and appearance is left in the background. There is no denial and yet it is the universal aspect of the Deity that is repeatedly emphasised. The different facets of epic theism lead to a paradox epitomised by the words of the *Bhagavad-gītā* wherein Arjuna, after beholding the divinity of Kṛṣṇa, addresses his friend as *ananta-rūpa,* one whose form has no end. If there is no end to the Supreme Being then it would seem that there can be no form except one that is an illusory display for the benefit of living beings, but on this issue the epic declines to speculate further.[8]

3. The Concept of *Avatāra* in the *Mahābhārata*

(i) Introduction

The idea of *avatāra* is central to classical Vaiṣṇavism. The doctrine teaches that at various times Viṣṇu descends to this world in a particular form to achieve his purpose. This may be to deliver teachings, to restore *dharma* when it is neglected, or most frequently to aid the gods in their perpetual struggle with the *asuras*. The *Mahābhārata* includes the earliest notions of *avatāra* found in the Hindu tradition and the concept is central to the narrative which describes how Viṣṇu descended to earth to bring victory to the Pāṇḍavas and annihilate the asuric kings.

The epic's view of *avatāra* is, however, far less developed than that of some of the later *Purāṇas*. The *Bhāgavata Purāṇa* considers virtually any form assumed by Viṣṇu to be an *avatāra* and is therefore able to produce extensive lists of such manifestations. This is not the case in the epic which has a more limited understanding of the concept and in fact never once in the Critical Edition uses the term *avatāra*. Viṣṇu assumes a variety of forms and guises, in the manner of the Vedic gods, without any apparent connection with the doctrine of *avatāra* and it is only in the later tradition that the idea was extended to include all such manifestations. In this progression one may recognise again the development of Hindu theism away from early Vedic ideas towards the later stages of Hindu monotheism. In examining the *Mahābhārata*'s ideas on this subject I propose to divide the study under three headings:- 1. *Avatāras* referred to by the text. 2. The doctrine of *avatāra*. 3. The divinity of Kṛṣṇa, the epic's principal *avatāra*.

(ii) *Avatāras* of Viṣṇu Referred to by the *Mahābhārata*

In the Vaiṣṇava *Purāṇas*, the *avatāras* of Viṣṇu are described at great length, with many chapters devoted to the legends that surround them. Hindu tradition commonly refers to ten *avatāras*, which are listed in the *Liṅga Purāṇa* as, 1. Matsya, the fish, 2. Kūrma, the tortoise, 3. Varāha, the boar, 4. Nara-siṁha, the man-lion, 5. Vāmana, the dwarf, 6. Rāma, the son of Jamadagni, 7. Rāma, the son of Daśaratha, 8. Kṛṣṇa, 9. Buddha, and 10. Kalki, the final *avatāra*.[9] The *Garuḍa Purāṇa* also lists ten *avatāras*,[10] but includes Baladeva, the brother of Kṛṣṇa, at the expense of Vāmana, while Jayadeva, a twelfth century Bengali poet, includes Baladeva but omits Kṛṣṇa.[11] The *Bhāgavata Purāṇa* takes the understanding of *avatāra* far beyond these ten and includes in the lists it gives in 1.3 and 2.7 the Kumāra sages, Nārada, the *ṛṣis* Nara and Nārāyaṇa, Dattātreya, Yajña, King Ṛṣabha, King Pṛthu, Dhanvantari, Kapila, Hayaśiras and Haṁsa, the goose. 1.3.26 of the *Purāṇa* states that there are in fact innumerable *avatāras* descending repeatedly throughout all time.

The *Mahābhārata*'s *avatāra* doctrine is far less developed than this, and the epic is aware of fewer individual *avatāras*. The Critical Edition appears to know only Kṛṣṇa, Baladeva, Rāma Dāśarathi, Vāmana, Varāha, and Nara-siṁha. The only extended *avatāra* myth in the epic is the *Rāmopakhyāna*, narrated by Mārkaṇḍeya to the Pāṇḍavas in Chapters 258 to 275 of the *Vana*. Nara-siṁha and Vāmana are referred to only in passing, while Varāha is described in one chapter of the *Śānti*. Thus there is a clear difference of emphasis between the epic and the *Bhāgavata Purāṇa*.[12] For the *Bhāgavata*, the *avatāra* myths are central to the glorification of Viṣṇu, whilst the *Mahābhārata* only very occasionally strays into such discourse.

In examining the epic's treatment of individual *avatāras*, I have used the *Bhāgavata Purāṇa* for comparison because it is in this work that the notion of *avatāra* reaches a fully developed form. The following characters referred to by the epic are regarded as *avatāras* by the *Bhāgavata*.

1. Kṛṣṇa is at the heart of *Mahābhārata* and will be discussed in detail below.

2. Baladeva, the brother of Kṛṣṇa, plays only a marginal role in the narrative as, for example, in the kidnapping of Subhadrā and the slaying of Duryodhana, and there is little emphasis placed on his divine status. In Chapter 61 of the *Ādi*, he is mentioned as a part of the divine serpent Śeṣa, the bed of Nārāyaṇa–*śeṣasyāṁśas tu nāgasya baladevo mahā-balaḥ* (1.61.91). This is confirmed in the *Mausala*, which describes how Baladeva leaves this world in the form of a huge white serpent with a thousand heads (16.5.12-13). That Śeṣa is himself viewed as a form of Viṣṇu is apparent from Brahmā's prayers for the descent of Nārāyaṇa which glorify the Deity as a mighty serpent–*mahoragaḥ* (6.61.47). Later Brahmā states that Nārāyaṇa created the divine Śeṣa, who is unlimited–*śeṣaṁ cākalpayad devam anantam iti yo viduḥ*–and who bears the earth with all its mountains and all creatures (6.63.10-11). The

identity of Baladeva as a part of Viṣṇu is confirmed again in the *Ādi,* in the story of the five previous Indras born as the Pāṇḍavas to be the husbands of Śrī. After giving Śiva his permission for this arrangement, Nārāyaṇa takes one white and one black hair from his head and these enter the wombs of Devakī and Rohiṇī to be born on earth as Kṛṣṇa and Baladeva,

tau cāpi keśau viśatāṁ yadūnāṁ
kule striyau rohiṇīṁ devakīṁ ca
tayor eko baladevo babhūva
kṛṣṇo dvitīyaḥ keśavaḥ saṁbabhūva

'And those two hairs entered Rohiṇī and Devakī, two women of the Yadu tribe. One of them became Baladeva, and through the other Keśava (Viṣṇu) became Kṛṣṇa.' (1.189.31)

While these passages, and also the *Viṣṇu-sahasra-nāma-stotram* which includes Halāyudha, a name of Baladeva (13.135.73), confirm the status of Baladeva as a form of Viṣṇu, within the narrative he does little to contribute to the mission of the *avatāra.* Indeed, though he does not oppose the purposes of Kṛṣṇa he seems to have little awareness of the divine mission as, for example, in his display of anger at the killing of Duryodhana, to whom he is partial. The position of Baladeva within the epic is paradoxical in that he descends to earth with Kṛṣṇa as a form of Viṣṇu and yet contributes little or nothing to expediting the purpose of the divine mission.

3. Rāma Dāśarathi, the hero of the other great Hindu epic, is known to the *Mahābhārata* as a manifestation of Viṣṇu. In Bhīma's meeting with Hanumān, the monkey chieftain who is a major character in the *Rāmāyaṇa,* the life of Rāma is discussed. In his brief summary of the story (3.147.23-41), Hanumān refers to Rāma as, *viṣṇur mānuṣa-rūpeṇa* (28)–Viṣṇu in a human form. A longer recital of the life of Rāma is given by Mārkaṇḍeya later in the *Vana,* in Chapters 258 to 275. Throughout this narration, Rāma behaves as if he were no more than an ordinary mortal and several times appears subject to human limitation. The introduction, however, makes it clear that he is Viṣṇu himself. The King of the Rākṣasas, Rāvaṇa, gains a boon from Brahmā that he will never be defeated by any of the higher beings in the universe (3.259.25). Therefore, in a manner that obviously parallels the descent of Nārāyaṇa in

the *Ādi* and the *Bhīṣma*, all the gods appear on earth as monkeys or bears while Viṣṇu, at the request of Brahmā, appears as a man:

> *tad-artham avatīrṇo 'sau man-niyogāc catur-bhujaḥ*
> *viṣṇuḥ praharatāṁ śreṣṭhaḥ sa karmaitat kariṣyati*
>
> 'For this purpose the four-armed Viṣṇu, the best of warriors, has descended at my demand and he will perform this deed.' (3.260.5)

Rāma is cited as a name of Viṣṇu in the *Sahasra-nāma-stotram* (13.135.56) and he is included in the short list of *avatāras* found in the *Nārāyaṇīya*. Therein addressing Nārada, the Deity announces that at the juncture of the Tretā and Dvāpara *yugas* he will become Rāma Dāśarathi, the ruler of the world–*rāmo dāśarathir bhūtvā bhaviṣyāmi jagat-patiḥ*–and will slay Rāvaṇa, the terrible Lord of the Rākṣasas (12.326.78-82).

4. Nara-siṁha, the man-lion, whose exploits are described in Book 7 of the *Bhāgavata Purāṇa*, is referred to in the *Mahābhārata* only in passing. The epic is aware of his mission to slay the *asura* Hiraṇyakaśipu but his protection of Prahlāda appears to be unknown. In the story of Agastya narrated by Lomaśa, the gods approach Nārāyaṇa out of fear of the Kālahilya *asuras*. Referring to previous occasions when the Deity had protected the earth, the gods mention the *avatāras*, Varāha, Vāmana, and Nara-siṁha–*narasiṁhaṁ vapuḥ kṛtvā* (3.100.20)–the latter as the slayer of Hiraṇyakaśipu. In the *Bhīṣma*, when Bhīṣma is requested by Duryodhana to speak further about Vāsudeva, he mentions three *avatāras*–*varāhaś caiva siṁhaś 'ca trivikrama-gatiḥ prabhuḥ* (6.63.13). Here it is to be presumed that *siṁha*, the lion, refers to Nara-siṁha. The *Droṇa* (7.164.146) likens Dhṛṣṭadyumna in the act of slaying Droṇa to the form of Viṣṇu as he smote Hiraṇyakaśipu–*yathā rūpaṁ paraṁ viṣṇor hiraṇykaśipor vadhe,* though without explicitly referring to Nara-siṁha. In the *Nārāyaṇīya* Nara-siṁha is mentioned in the list of *avatāras* in Chapter 326, though only in one verse, 73, which describes him as the killer of Hiraṇyakaśipu. Chapter 337 mentions that Nārāyaṇa will take the forms of Varāha, Vāmana, Nara-siṁha, and of a man–*vārāhaṁ nārā-siṁhaṁ ca vāmanaṁ mānuṣaṁ tathā* (36)–but no further details are given. The *Sahasra-nāma-stotram* also records Nara-siṁha (13.135.16) as a name of Viṣṇu.

5. Vāmana, the dwarf, is described in Book 8 of the *Bhāgavata Purāṇa.* The story recounted there tells of how Bali, the king of the *asuras,* conquered *svarga-loka* from the gods. Viṣṇu then took the form of a dwarf-*brāhmaṇa,* the son of Aditi and brother of Indra, and begged three steps of land from Bali. When this request was granted the Deity covered the entire universe with his three paces, thereby restoring sovereignty to the gods.

In Pulastya's description of pilgrimage sites, he refers to a place known as Vāmanaka, where one should bathe in Viṣṇu's footprint-*tatra viṣṇu-pade snātvā*-and worship Vāmana-*arcayitvā ca vāmanam* (3.81.87). The prayers of the gods recounted by Lomaśa in the story of Agastya refer to Vāmana as banishing Bali from the three worlds-*vāmanaṁ vapur āśritya trai-lokyād bhraṁśitas tvayā* (3.100.21), while Bhīṣma refers to the three paces with the words *trivikrama-gatiḥ* (6.63.13). In his prayers to Kṛṣṇa in Chapter 13 of the *Vana,* Arjuna refers only to the Vāmana *avatāra.* He mentions that as the son of Aditi, in the form of a child-*śiśur bhūtvā*-he covered heaven, space and earth-*divaṁ khaṁ ca pṛthivīm*-with three steps-*tribhir vikramaṇaiḥ*-and whilst thus situated in the sky outshone the splendour of the sun (3.13.23-25). In the *Śānti,* Yudhiṣṭhira praises Kṛṣṇa as Vāmana (12.43.12), and in his discourse on creation in Chapter 200, Bhīṣma states that Viṣṇu became Vāmana amongst the Ādityas and expanded the opulence of the gods, vanquishing the Daityas with his stride-*tasya vikramaṇād eva devānāṁ śrīr vyavardhata* (27).

The *Nārāyaṇīya* devotes three verses to Vāmana in its list of *avatāras,* 12.326.74-76, stating that when Bali drives Indra from his kingdom Nārāyaṇa will appear as the twelfth son of Aditi, restore sovereignty to Indra and cast Bali down into the nether regions of the cosmos, *patāla-loka.* 12.337.36 mentions Vāmana specifically, but gives no further details, and the *Sahasra-nāma-stotram* includes Vāmana in its list of names (13.135.30). In Chapter 220 of the *Śānti,* we find Bali, having lost all he possessed, delivering a discourse to Indra on the impermanence of material success. Verse 7 refers to the steps of Viṣṇu recovering the worlds-*viṣṇu-krānteṣu lokeṣu*-but does not mention the Vāmana *avatāra.* Thus the epic appears to know the story of the dwarf *avatāra* in substantially the same form as the Purāṇic version but refrains from imparting any detailed narration.

6. Varāha, Viṣṇu's appearance as a boar, is described in Book

3 of the *Bhāgavata Purāṇa.* Shortly after creation the earth sinks below the waters. Viṣṇu then takes the form of a boar to return it to its original position and at the same time kills the *asura* Hiraṇyākṣa who has gained universal dominion. In the *Ādi,* when Kadru and Vinatā are walking by the ocean it is described as being agitated as it was at the time when Viṣṇu took the form of a boar to raise the earth from its depths (1.19.11). Pulastya's account of the places of pilgrimage includes a site known as Vārāha-tīrtha, where Viṣṇu previously stood in the form of a boar–*viṣṇur vārāha-rūpeṇa pūrvaṁ yatra sthito 'bhavat* (3.81.15). The prayers of the gods in the story of Agastya refer to Viṣṇu raising the earth from the ocean in the form of boar–*vārāhaṁ rūpam āsthāya* (3.100.19); when Indra reveals to Karṇa that Kṛṣṇa is Nārāyaṇa himself he states that those who know the Vedas call him Hari, the unconquerable boar–*yam āhur veda-vidvāṁso varāham ajitaṁ harim* (3.294.28). In Brahmā's prayers for the descent of Kṛṣṇa, he glorifies Nārāyaṇa as *varāhādya,* the original boar (6.61.47) and in the same section Bhīṣma mentions Varāha as one of three *avatāras* he refers to (6.63.13). In his final laudation of Kṛṣṇa, Bhīṣma describes him as the ancient boar of terrible power–*varāho 'yaṁ bhīma-balaḥ purāṇaḥ* (13.143.7).

In Chapter 202 of the *Śānti,* Yudhiṣṭhira inquires from Bhīṣma as to why Kṛṣṇa took birth from the womb of a beast–*tiryag-yoni-gataṁ rūpam* (3). The grandsire then narrates how the earth once became overburdened and weighed down by a host of *asuras* who had vanquished the gods. Viṣṇu then assumed the shape of a boar and slew the *asuras,* roaring loudly all the while. The gods wonder who this creature can be and Brahmā explains to them that it is none other than Viṣṇu, the Supreme Lord of all. This narration reflects the view of *avatāra* displayed in the stories of Rāma and Kṛṣṇa, wherein the earth is overburdened by victorious *asuras* and Viṣṇu appears to vanquish them but it does not mention the Varāha *avatāra* raising the earth from the depths of the ocean.

In the *Nārāyaṇīya,* the Deity states that when the earth is submerged under the ocean he will take the form of a boar and raise it up. In that form he will also slay the Daitya named Hiraṇyākṣa (12.326.72-73). In Chapter 330, Nārāyaṇa explains his names Ekaśṛṅga and Trikakut as being derived from the single-tusked, three-humped boar that raised the earth from the ocean (27-28). In the statement of the doctrine of *avatāra,* Varāha is one of the four referred to (12.337.36), and the *Sahasra-nāma-stotram* includes Varāha as a name of Viṣṇu. Again the version of the epic is substantially in accord with that of the *Purāṇas*, including both the raising of the earth from the ocean and the slaying of *asuras* and in 12.202 we have something approaching a full narration of the *avatāra* myth.

7. The Kūrma, or tortoise, *avatāra* is described in Book 8 of the *Bhāgavata Purāṇa*. Desiring to attain the ambrosia of immortality, the gods and *asuras* churn the Milk Ocean. To assist this endeavour and to assure its success Viṣṇu takes the form of a huge tortoise and acts as the pivot on which the mountain used as a churning rod may rest. This story is narrated in Chapters 16 and 17 of the *Ādi* but there is no indication therein that the tortoise is a form of Viṣṇu. He is referred to merely as Kūrma-rāja, the lord of the tortoises. Elsewhere in the epic there is no reference to the Kūrma *avatāra*.

8. The story of Matsya, the fish *avatāra*, is also narrated in Book 8 of the *Bhāgavata Purāṇa*. At the end of the *yuga* when the world is flooded, Viṣṇu appears on the waters as a huge fish and tows a boat on which Manu and the seven *ṛṣis* find refuge from the flood. In the epic, this story is narrated in a similar form by Mārkaṇḍeya in Chapter 185 of the *Vana*. The major difference, however, comes at the end of the discourse when the fish reveals his true identity as Brahmā and not as Viṣṇu–*ahaṁ prajāpatir brahmā* (48). Nowhere else in the epic is reference made to a fish *avatāra* and it seems that here we have an example of the mythology of Brahmā being usurped and absorbed into the Vaiṣṇava tradition.

9. The story of Kalki, the final *avatāra*, is found in Book 12 of the *Bhāgavata Purāṇa*. At the end of the *Kaliyuga*, when *dharma* has all but vanished from the earth, Viṣṇu appears as Kalki, a warrior *brāhmaṇa* who rides forth on a white steed to destroy all sinners and inaugurate a new *Satyayuga* on earth. This story is narrated by Mārkaṇḍeya in Chapter 188 of the *Vana* but with no indication that Kalki is a form of Viṣṇu other than his also being named as Viṣṇu-yaśas,[13] despite the fact that his role as the destroyer of wrongdoers and restorer of *dharma* is characteristic of *avatāra*. In the *Nārāyaṇīya*, one version of 12.326.94 has Nārāyaṇa stating that he will appear as Kalkin, but this has been omitted from the Critical Edition. Elsewhere there is no reference in the epic to this *avatāra*.

10. Rāma the son of Jamadagni is a prominent figure in the *Purāṇas* and epics. In the *Purāṇas*, he is known as an *avatāra* and his story is told in Book 9 of the *Bhāgavata Purāṇa*. By a confusion of oblations, Rāma is born with a *kṣatriya* disposition in a *brāhmaṇa* family and when his father is murdered by the sons of King Arjuna he exacts vengeance by destroying twenty-one generations of *kṣatriyas*. In the *Mahābhārata*, Rāma Jāmadagnya appears at various points in the narrative; he is the *guru* of Bhīṣma, Karṇa and Droṇa, he speaks in the assembly of the Kurus, he fights unsuccessfully with Bhīṣma on behalf of Ambā and it is his curse that hinders Karṇa in the final conflict with Arjuna. In addition, the story of his destroying the *kṣatriyas* is narrated several times (3.115-117, 12.49, 13.52.56), but in the Critical Edition none of these versions, which conform closely with the Purāṇic accounts, describe him as an *avatāra*. Chapter 115 of the *Vana* contains a typical avatāric introduction with the earth in distress due to the wars waged by King Arjuna and the gods praying to Viṣṇu to rectify the situation. This passage, however, is omitted from the Critical Edition and one suspects that it is an interpolation imitating the other *avatāra* stories. The only reference in the Critical Edition to Rāma's identity with Viṣṇu is in the *Nārāyaṇīya*. In 12.326.77, Nārāyaṇa states that in the *Tretāyuga* he will appear as Rāma in the line of Bhṛgu–*tretā-yuge bhaviṣyāmi rāmo bhṛgu-kulodvahaḥ*–and annihilate the *kṣatriyas* who are proud of their strength–*kṣatraṁ cotsādayiṣyāmi saṁvṛddha-bala-vāhanam.*

11. The sage Kapila, the initial propounder of Sāṁkhya, is presented as an *avatāra* in Book 3 of the *Bhāgavata Purāṇa*, which contains an extensive exposition of his philosophical teachings. The *Mahābhārata* is aware of Kapila as the founder of Sāṁkhya and contains some indications that a divine status is ascribed to him. When the sage Lomaśa asks about Arjuna's exalted position by the side of Indra, he is told that only Viṣṇu or Arjuna is able to defeat the *asuras* and in this discourse it is mentioned that when the Deity appears on earth he is named Kapila–*yo 'sau bhūmi-gataḥ śrīmān viṣṇur madhusūdhanaḥ/kapilo nāma devo 'sau bhagavān ajito hariḥ* (3.45.25). Later, when the same Lomaśa is narrating the story of the descent of the Ganges, he mentions that Kapila is known as Vāsudeva–*vāsudeveti yaṁ prāhuḥ kapilaṁ muni-sattamam* (3.106.2). Yudhiṣṭhira's prayers in Chapter 43 of the *Śānti* eulogise Kṛṣṇa as, *kapilas tvaṁ ca vāmanaḥ* (12). The reference is not conclusive as Yudhiṣṭhira goes on to state that the Deity is several other

renowned personalities, but the proximity to Vāmana is at least suggestive. The *Sahasra-nāma-stotram* includes the name Kapila (13.135.109) and although the *Nārāyaṇīya* does not include Kapila in its list in Chapter 326, in 12.330.30 the Deity asserts that teachers of Sāṁkhya call him Kapila–*kapilaṁ prāhur ācāryāḥ sāṁkhyāḥ.*[14]

12. Vyāsa is both the author and a principal character in the epic. Though the *Purāṇas* almost universally consider him an *avatāra* of Viṣṇu, in the *Mahābhārata* he is known as such only in the *Nārāyaṇīya* and even there he is not included in the list in Chapter 326. In 334.9, Vaiśampāyana states that Vyāsa is Nārāyaṇa–*kṛṣṇa-dvaipāyanaṁ vyāsaṁ viddhi nārāyaṇaṁ prabhum*–and this is elaborated upon in Chapter 337 which describes him as the one son of the expansion Nārāyaṇa–*nārāyaṇasyāṁśa-jam eka-putram* (4)–and that the powerful Nārāyaṇa created him as his son–*sasarja putrārtham udāra-tejā vyāsam* (5). The narration is expanded from verse 38 onwards, explaining that a son named Apāntaratamas was born from the speech of Nārāyaṇa–*apāntaratamā nāma sūto vāk-saṁbhavo vibhoḥ.* This son appears in every age at the behest of the Deity to distribute and arrange the Vedas and in the dark age of Kali–*kṛṣṇe yuge* (44)–he has appeared with a dark complexion as Vyāsa. The name Vyāsa also occurs in the *Sahasra-nāma-stotram* (13.135.74), though here it may mean merely the 'arranger' rather than being a specific reference to the author of the epic.

13. Hayaśiras, the horse-headed form of the Deity, plays a central role in the Vaiṣṇava creation story presented in Chapters 194 of the *Vana* and 335 of the *Śānti.* When Brahmā is preparing to recreate the cosmos two *asuras,* Madhu and Kaitabha, appear from the darkness and steal the Vedas from him. When petitioned by Brahmā, Viṣṇu takes the form of Hayaśiras to kill the *asuras* and recover the Vedas. It is doubtful as to whether the epic views this Hayaśiras form as one of the descents of the Deity referred to elsewhere. Although the *Purāṇas* list Hayaśiras amongst the *avatāras,* the *Mahābhārata* makes this connection in only one reference, found in the *Nārāyaṇīya* (12.326.94).

14. A goose *avatāra,* Haṁsa, is described in Book 11 of the *Bhāgavata Purāṇa* imparting spiritual wisdom to an assembly of sages. In Chapter 288 of the *Śānti,* we find a golden goose teaching the gods known as the Sādhyas though here it is stated to be the unborn, eternal Prajāpati who takes that form, a term more usually applied to Brahmā than to Viṣṇu–*haṁso bhūtvātha sauvarṇas tv ajo*

nityaḥ prajāpatiḥ. Perhaps here again we have an example of the acts of Brahmā being expropriated into the body of Vaiṣṇava lore. Haṁsa is included as a name of Viṣṇu in the *Sahasra-nāma-stotram* (13.135.34) though it is also a term used for the soul and is perhaps intended to equate the Deity with the *ātman.* The *Nārāyaṇīya* mentions the goose avatāra in Chapter 326 as one of the manifestations of the Deity–*haṁso hayaśirāś caiva prādur-bhāvāḥ* (94).

15. King Pṛthu is described as an *avatāra* in Book 4 of the *Bhāgavata Purāṇa* which narrates how he appeared to restore *dharma* and restrain the wicked after the reign of the adharmic King Vena. The story is narrated in the *Mahābhārata* as a part of the *Rāja-dharma* (12.59.97-130). There are two references there that indicate a divine status being attributed to Pṛthu. Verse 118 states, *ātmanāṣṭama ity eva śrutir eśā parā nṛṣu*–the *śruti* states that this most exalted of men was the eighth part of the Self—a somewhat obscure statement. Verse 130 is a little clearer, asserting that because of the king's austerity Viṣṇu entered into him–*tapasā bhagavān viṣṇur āviveśa ca bhūmi-pam.* If these references are intended to indicate the status of King Pṛthu as an *avatāra* then the nature of the divine manifestation is different to what is described elsewhere. Rather than the gods praying for Viṣṇu to descend to rectify problems on earth it appears that in this case the Deity enters and effects the apotheosis of a mortal being who has qualified himself for the transformation. Nowhere else in the *Mahābhārata* is a doctrine of *avatāra* of this kind expounded and indeed nowhere else is King Pṛthu referred to as a manifestation of Viṣṇu.

16. The two *ṛṣis,* Nara and Nārāyaṇa, are referred to frequently in the *Mahābhārata.* The concept of *avatāra* in the epic is complicated by the role of the two divine sages, possibly reflecting two distinct early traditions that have been drawn on. Alongside statements that Kṛṣṇa is a part or *aṁśa* of Nārāyaṇa we find the idea that Kṛṣṇa and Arjuna are Nara and Nārāyaṇa who are themselves a manifestation of the Deity. This is expressed as early in the narrative as the burning of the Khāṇḍava forest in the *Ādi*–*nara-nārāyaṇau devau tāvatau viśrutau* (1.219.15)–and recurs on numerous occasions. The apparent dissonance between the idea of Kṛṣṇa being a descent of Nārāyaṇa himself and Kṛṣṇa and Arjuna being the two divine sages Nara and Nārāyaṇa is never resolved or explained by the *Mahābhārata.*

17. Buddha is not mentioned at all in the Critical Edition. Only the Kumbakonam Edition refers to him as an *avatāra* in a reference that may be discarded as a very late interpolation.

18. Book 8 of the *Bhāgavata Purāṇa* tells of Mohinī, a female *avatāra* who awards the ambrosia gained from the churning of the Milk Ocean to the gods at the expense of the *asuras* and arouses lust in the mind of Śiva. The first part of this story appears in Chapters 16 and 17 of the *Ādi* but the role of Viṣṇu here is as the leader of the Vedic pantheon and the form of Mohinī that he assumes is just a temporary change of appearance to confuse the *asuras.*

19. As an interesting aside, particularly in light of the numerous modern claimants to avatāric status, we may note that the epic also refers to a false *avatāra,* Paundraka Vāsudeva. Describing to Yudhiṣṭhira those kings who are allied to Jarāsandha, Kṛṣṇa mentions him as one he had spared previously–*na mayā hataḥ*–and who, although low-minded, is known as the supreme person–*puruṣottama-vijñātaḥ.* People know him in this world as Ātman and Puruṣottama and out of ignorance he constantly bears the emblem of divinity that properly belongs to Kṛṣṇa–*ādatte satataṁ mohād yaḥ sa cihnaṁ ca māmakam* (2.13.17-18). This story is narrated fully in Book 10 of the *Bhāgavata Purāṇa* but is referred to nowhere else in the *Mahābhārata.*

(iii) The Doctrine of *Avatāra* as Taught in the *Mahābhārata*

It is thus apparent that the epic's idea of *avatāra* is less developed than that of the *Purāṇas* and that the notion of *avatāra* is less central to epic Vaiṣṇavism. It is also noteworthy how little attention the various prayers and glorifications of Nārāyaṇa pay to this aspect of the divine nature. The stress is always on the power, supremacy and all-pervasiveness of the Deity with only occasional mention being made of his avatāric descents. For example, when Bhīṣma in 6.63 and Saṁjaya in 5.67 are requested to describe the nature of Viṣṇu, the ensuing discourses entirely ignore the Deity's descents to earth, as does the extensive praise of Kṛṣṇa offered by Bhīṣma and Yudhiṣṭhira in chapters 43, 47 and 51 of the *Śānti.*

It is thus reasonable to assert that despite the centrality of Kṛṣṇa to the theism of the narrative, in didactic terms the notion of *avatāra* remains a peripheral concept. This assertion notwithstanding, the epic still does espouse a doctrine of *avatāra.* This may be taken as twofold in character or possibly as two separate doctrines contained in the text. The first centres on the notion that the descent of an *avatāra* is related to a particular *yuga*, whilst the other stresses the manifestation of *avatāra* when it is required to assist the purposes of the gods and preserve *dharma* on earth.

(iv) The Doctrine of *Avatāra* in Relation to the Cycle of *Yugas*

This doctrine is set out, or at least referred to, in two places in the epic, both in the *Vana*.

(a) In the discussion between Bhīma and Hanumān, the Pāṇḍava prince inquires about the characteristics of the four *yugas*. As a part of his description of each *yuga*, Hanumān states that in the *Kṛtayuga* Nārāyaṇa, the soul of all beings, is white–*ātmā ca sarva-bhūtānāṁ śuklo nārāyaṇas tadā* (3.148.16), in the *Tretāyuga* he goes forth with a red hue–*raktatāṁ yāti cācyutaḥ* (23), in the *Dvāparayuga* he is yellow–*viṣṇur vai pītatāṁ yāti* (26) and in the *Kaliyuga* he is black–*kṛṣṇo bhavati keśavaḥ* (33). No further elaboration or explanation is given regarding these forms of the Deity and it is unclear as to whether Hanumān's assertions constitute a part of a doctrine of *avatāra* that relates specifically to *yugas*, although this would appear to be the implication.

(b) In Chapter 187, where Nārāyaṇa in the form of a child describes his own nature to Mārkaṇḍeya, the same idea occurs though here it appears in conjunction with the second concept of *avatāra*. Verses 26 to 31 mirror the *Bhagavad-gītā*'s teachings but expand on the *Gītā*'s statement, *saṁbhavāmi yuge yuge* (4.8)–I appear *yuga* after *yuga*.

yadā yadā ca dharmasya glānir bhavati sattama
abhyutthānam adharmasya tadātmānaṁ sṛjāmy aham

daityā hiṁsānuraktāś ca avadhyāḥ sura-sattamaiḥ
rākṣasāś cāpi loke 'smin yadotpatsyanti dāruṇāḥ

tadāhaṁ samprasūyāmi gṛheṣu śubha-karmaṇām
praviṣṭo mānuṣaṁ dehaṁ sarvaṁ praśamayāmy aham

sṛṣṭvā deva-manuṣāṁś ca gandharvoraga-rākṣasān
sthāvarāṇi ca bhūtāni saṁharāmy ātma-māyayā

karma-kāle punar deham anucintya sṛjāmy aham
praviśya mānuṣaṁ dehaṁ maryādā-bandha-kāraṇāt

śvetaḥ kṛta-yuge varṇaḥ pītas tretā-yuge mama
rakto dvāparam āsādya kṛṣṇaḥ kali-yuge tathā

'O best of men, whenever there is a decline in *dharma* and a prevalence of *adharma,* then I manifest myself.

When the Daityas who are devoted to violence and cannot be slain even by the best of the gods, and the harsh *rākṣasas* appear in this world, I will take my birth in the houses of the righteous. Entering a human body, I will vanquish all of them.

Having created gods, men, *gandharvas,* serpents, *rākṣasas* and beings that do not move, I then destroy them by my own potency.

In the time for action, having thought of a particular form, I manifest myself again, having entered a human body in order to preserve the regulations of religious principles.

In the *Kṛtayuga* my bodily hue is white and in the *Tretāyuga* it is yellow. It is red in the *Dvāparayuga* and black in the *yuga* known as *Kali.* (3.187.26-31)

In this passage it is to be noted that the bodily colours of the *avatāras* differ from those given by Hanumān who has red for the *Tretāyuga* and yellow for the *Dvāpara.* The passage seems to be based on 4.6-8 of the *Gītā,* verse 26 above being almost identical to 4.7. The *Gītā*'s phrase *yuge yuge* is accepted here as meaning that in every *yuga,* almost according to schedule, Nārāyaṇa manifests himself to preserve *dharma.* The *avatāras* thus designated are distinctive by their colours but appear to have little or no connection with the Purāṇic *avatāras* such as Rāma, Varāha, Vāmana, or Nara-siṁha, known elsewhere in the text. There thus appears to be a divergent doctrine here according to which *avatāras* appear with the change of *yuga,* rather than as circumstances demand. The passage here attempts, without complete success, to integrate the two concepts.

(v) The Doctrine of *Avatāras* Appearing to Execute a Specific Mission

(a) The *Bhagavad-gītā* provides the best known reference to a doctrine of *avatāra* found in the *Mahābhārata*. Chapter 4 opens with Kṛṣṇa telling Arjuna that in ancient times he imparted the wisdom he is teaching to Vivasvān, the Sun God. When Arjuna asks how this is possible, Kṛṣṇa asserts that they have both lived many times before (4.5), and that he is in fact the supreme lord of all beings (4.6). In the two verses that follow, he presents the *Gītā*'s doctrine of *avatāra*.

> *yadā yadā hi dharmasya glānir bhavati bhārata*
> *abhyutthānam adharmasya tadātmānaṁ sṛjāmy aham*
>
> *paritrāṇāya sādhūnāṁ vināśāya ca duṣkṛtām*
> *dharma-saṁsthāpanārthāya saṁbhavāmi yuge yuge*
>
> 'Whenever there is a decline in *dharma*, O descendant of Bharata, and a prevalence of *adharma*, then I manifest myself.
>
> In order to protect the righteous, destroy the wrong-doers and sustain *dharma*, I take birth *yuga* after *yuga*.' (4.7-8)

The similarities with the passage from Mārkaṇḍeya's teachings in the *Vana* are quite apparent. Here verse 7 seems to stress the appearance of an *avatāra* when circumstances dictate the necessity of such a manifestation. Verse 8 presents the mission of the *avatāra* as being to protect the righteous, destroy the wicked and sustain *dharma*. It is unclear whether the phrase *yuge yuge* indicates a scheduled appearance in each *yuga*, or whether it has a more general meaning to show that the process continues through the eons of time. The *Gītā*, unlike Mārkaṇḍeya, does not go on to mention a different coloured *avatāra* for each *yuga*, but neither does it make any reference to the classical *avatāras* such as Vāmana, Varāha, or Nara-siṁha. Kṛṣṇa himself is black and appears at the onset of *Kaliyuga*, but this alone is insufficient to tie in the *Gītā* with Mārkaṇḍeya's concept of *avatāra* and it is impossible to determine precisely the nature of the manifestations referred to in this passage. The essence of the doctrine is, however, established here. Viṣṇu appears as an *avatāra* to assist the gods and the righteous in their struggles against the *asuras* and wrongdoers and thereby ensure the perpetuation of *dharma* in the world.

(b) In Chapter 48 of the *Udyoga*, where Bhīṣma addresses the assembly of the Kurus to warn them of the might of the Pāṇḍavas, he lays stress on the divinity of Kṛṣṇa and Arjuna and their identity with the *ṛṣis* Nara and Nārāyaṇa who are manifestations of the Supreme Deity. In verse 21, he states that they are born repeatedly at times of conflict–*tatra tatraiva jāyete yuddha-kāle punaḥ punaḥ*. This passing reference to *avatāra* is in accordance with the version of the *Gītā*, reasserting the element of conflict that surrounds the divine manifestation.

(c) In Chapter 61 of the *Bhīṣma*, Brahmā prays for Nārāyaṇa to appear on earth and describes the mission the *avatāra* should fulfil:

> *tatrāsura-vadhaṁ kṛtvā sarva-loka-sukhāya vai*
> *dharmaṁ sthāpya yaśaḥ prāpya yogaṁ prāpsyasi tattvataḥ*
>
> 'There (on earth), having brought about the destruction of the *asuras* to bring happiness to the world, having established *dharma* and having won renown, you will in truth attain *yoga*.' (6.61.68)

(d) After the death of Ghatotkaca in the *Droṇa*, Kṛṣṇa explains that the destruction of this *rākṣasa* son of Bhīma was necessary because he was an enemy of the gods and *brāhmaṇas*. Kṛṣṇa then asserts that he has been born in order to bring about the destruction of all the enemies of the gods–*vadārthaṁ tasya jāto 'ham anyeṣāṁ ca sura-dviṣām* (7.156.22).

(e) At the end of Bhīṣma's extensive teachings to Yudhiṣṭhira that run throughout the *Śānti* and *Anuśāsana*, he concludes with a glorification of Kṛṣṇa that includes an expression of the doctrine of *avatāra*:

> *yadā dharmo glāyati vai surāṇāṁ*
> *tadā kṛṣṇo jāyate mānuṣeṣu*
> *dharme sthitvā sa tu vai bhāvitātmā*
> *parāṁś ca lokān aparāṁś ca yāti*
>
> *tyājāṁs tyaktvāthāsurāṇāṁ vadhāya*
> *kāryākārye kāraṇaṁ caiva pārtha*

kṛtaṁ kariṣyat kriyate ca devo
muhuḥ somaṁ viddhi ca śakram etam

'When *dharma*, (which is the will) of the gods, declines, then Kṛṣṇa takes birth amongst men. Fixed in *dharma* and always pure, he appears in both the higher and lower worlds.

Leaving aside those who should be ignored, he is the cause of both the righteous and unrighteous acts that bring about the destruction of the *asuras*. The Lord acts, he is what is done and he is the action, and you must know that he is also Soma and Indra.' (13.143.11-12)

These verses are obscure, apparently making reference to Kṛṣṇa's use of unrighteous means as an expedient in the discharge of his mission. The familiar elements in the epic's understanding of *avatāra* are, however, to be found here again. Bhīṣma asserts that the Deity manifests himself in this world when *dharma* declines to assist the gods and destroy the *asuras*. No specific *avatāras* are mentioned as illustration but the statement that he appears in both the higher and lower worlds gives some indication that it is the classical Purāṇic *avatāras* that are being referred to.

(f) The most complete statement of the doctrine of *avatāra* is found in the *Nārāyaṇīya*. Chapter 327 of the *Śānti* tells how Nārāyaṇa instructs Brahmā to be the *dhātṛ*, or ordainer, for all beings in this world (84), but when the function of the gods–*sura-kāryam*–becomes difficult to perform–*aviṣehyaṁ bhaviṣyati*–he will bring forth a manifestation of himself–*prādurbhāvaṁ gamiṣyāmi* (85). Chapter 337 enlarges upon this brief statement; after bestowing upon Brahmā the *buddhi*, or intellect, by which he is able to manage the workings of the cosmos, Nārāyaṇa considers how the world may be sustained as he requires it:

sṛṣṭā imāḥ prajāḥ sarvā brahmaṇā parameṣṭhinā
daitya-dānava-gandharva-rakṣogaṇa-samākulāḥ
jātā hīyaṁ vasumatī bhārākrāntā tapasvinī

bahavo balinaḥ pṛthvyāṁ daitya-dānava-rākṣasāḥ
bhaviṣyanti tapo-yuktā varān prāpsyanti cottamān

avaśyam eva taiḥ sarvair vara-dānena darpitaiḥ
bādhitavyāḥ sura-gaṇā ṛṣayaś ca tapo-dhanāḥ
tatra nyāyyam idam kartuṁ bhārāvataraṇaṁ mayā

atha nānā-samudbhūtair vasudhāyāṁ yathā-kramam
nigraheṇa ca pāpānāṁ sādhūnāṁ pragraheṇa ca

'All these living beings, great hosts of Daityas, Dānavas, *gandharvas* and *rākṣasas,* have been created by Brahmā, the leader of the gods. The overloaded earth is now afflicted by this burden.

Many powerful Daityas, Dānavas and *rākṣasas* will appear on the earth, performing penances and thereby attaining the greatest gifts.

The gods and *ṛṣis,* whose wealth is penance, will surely be oppressed by all these beings when they become arrogant because of the boons they are given. At such times it is proper that this burden should be removed by me.

This is to be achieved by various manifestations on the earth in due order, and by the destruction of the sinful and protection of the righteous.' (12.337.29-32)

This passage neglects the element of sustaining *dharma,* but includes the notion of removing the burden of the earth. There is no indication that the manifestation of an *avatāra* is connected to the changing *yugas*; the Deity will appear in this world whenever it becomes necessary because of the increasing power of the *asuras* and *rākṣasas.*

The *Mahābhārata* thus seems to contain, and perhaps attempts to reconcile, two doctrines of *avatāra.* One connects the divine manifestation to the four *yugas* and the other with the triumph of irreligion over *dharma.* The former is found only in two passages, or possibly three if the *Bhagavad-gītā* is included, and it is the latter doctrine that is most prevalent. This idea of *avatāra* is firmly rooted in the *pravṛtti* world view and demonstrates the manner in which *bhakti* is linked to *pravṛtti.* The universal order, *dharma,* is manifest both in terms of the regulated working of the cosmos directed by the gods and in the ordered modes of life in human society. *Dharma* is sustained in heaven by the gods and on earth by righteous kings but is threatened by any rise in power of the enemies of the gods or by a predominance of irreligion on earth, though the two are inextricably linked. At such times, Viṣṇu appears in a particular form to fight on the side of the gods and establish the rule of dharmic kings on earth. The principal *avatāras* known to the epic all execute this function–Varāha restores order to the cosmos by raising the earth and slaying Hiranyākṣa, Vāmana and Nara-siṁha both vanquish powerful *asuras* and restore hegemony to the gods, Rāma kills a *rākṣasa* king who is a threat to the gods and establishes the rule of *dharma* on earth, and Kṛṣṇa annihilates the *asuras* who have appeared as kings and establishes *dharma* on earth through the reign of Yudhiṣṭhira.

The role of *avatāra* in the *Mahābhārata* is thus narrower than that indicated by the *Bhāgavata Purāṇa* which includes teachers and sages such as Kapila, Dattātreya and Buddha within the same concept. In addition, whereas the *Bhāgavata* tends to include all manifestations of Viṣṇu under the heading of *avatāra,* the epic has a narrower definition. Hayaśiras, Mohinī and the *ṛṣis* Nara and Nārāyaṇa are presented as forms of the Deity, but the epic does not include them in any discussion of *avatāra,* whereas the *Bhāgavata* includes these forms in its listings. It is noteworthy that in the *Mahābhārata* the term *avatāra* is never used and the forms in which the Deity appears on earth are referred to either as *aṁśas*–parts–or *prādurbhāvas*–appearances or manifestations. For the epic, these appearances of the Deity are either a feature of the *yuga* manifest with distinctive bodily hue, or else, more prevalently, a divine manifestation with the mission of preserving *dharma* by assisting the gods in their struggle with the *asuras.* The need to remove the burden of the earth, referred to less frequently, may be taken as an additional aspect of the role of the *avatāra* or as a part of the destruction of the *asuras* whose activities typically give rise to the burden.

Much has been written on the relationship between the concept of *avatāra* and the Christian doctrine of incarnation.[15] An essential distinction between *avatāra* and incarnation, and one that is laboriously discussed by Christian commentators, is the non-salvific nature of the *avatāras.*[16] The *dharma* that is sustained by the *avatāra* falls under the purview of *pravṛtti* and *sva-dharma,* rather than *nivṛtti* or *mokṣa-dharma,* and it is hence completely consistent that the principal role of the divine manifestation is not soteriological.

This, however, does not mean that the Deity's manifestation on earth has no understanding of or no imperative towards salvation. Kṛṣṇa's instructions to Arjuna in the *Gītā* focus overwhelmingly on the subjects of salvation and the love of God for the individual, and only touch on the mission of the *avatāra* as it is presented elsewhere in the epic by emphasising that gaining *mokṣa* need not entail abandoning dharmic duty. In terms of soteriology, however, the *avatāra* is not an essential element; salvation may gained through yogic self-transformation or by the grace of the Deity but in neither process is the *avatāra* an essential conduit.

(vi) Kṛṣṇa, the *Avatāra*

The *Mahābhārata* offers a great deal of information about the nature and role of the *avatāra* during his sojourn in this world. In the history of Christian thought the status of the incarnation has repeatedly been a focus for controversy. In Hinduism, the concept of *avatāra* has aroused few such controversies although similar questions regarding the divinity and humanity of Kṛṣṇa have inevitably been raised and addressed by Hindu commentators on both the epics and *Purāṇas*.

(a) The Form of the *Avatāra*: The debate here centres on whether the *avatāra* has a body composed of matter, or whether the body of Kṛṣṇa is some kind of spirit form. Orthodox Christianity has insisted that through the incarnation the Deity accepted the constraints of the flesh, but at times this view has been challenged by docetic groups who held that for God genuine suffering and material constraint are impossible. Vaiṣṇava teachers such as Rāmānuja and the followers of Caitanya held the view that the body of Kṛṣṇa is completely spiritual and never decays and this appears to be the perspective of the *Bhāgavata Purāṇa*. The tenth book of the latter work in particular stresses the docetic nature of Kṛṣṇa's life, constantly reminding the reader of the paradox of the Supreme Lord of creation appearing to act as if he were a mortal inhabitant of this world.[17]

It is true that Kṛṣṇa never appears to grow old or age at all in the epic narrative despite the passing of several decades, but how far this is indicative of his having a non-material form is debatable for the same apparent agelessness applies to all the characters. The elderly remain elderly (though they rarely expire from natural causes) and the younger generation never appear to progress beyond middle age. Overall the *Mahābhārata* tends to take a non-docetic view of the *avatāra* with clear indications that Kṛṣṇa accepts the form if not all the limitations of a body composed of matter. In an explanation of his own manifestation given by Kṛṣṇa in the *Gītā*, he states, *prakṛtiṁ svām adhiṣṭhāya sambhavāmy ātma-māyayā*– 'Situated in my own material energy, I am manifest by my own potency' (4.6). It may be argued that this reference is not conclusive because the word *prakṛti* may be interpreted in various ways but the implication of matter from the term is persuasive when its use throughout the *Gītā* is considered.

In the battle scenes we frequently find Kṛṣṇa apparently subject to the limitations imposed by a material frame. 7.18.21 describes him as exhausted and perspiring–*prasiṣvade kṛṣṇaḥ khinnaḥ*–whilst in the *Karṇa*, he is temporarily incapacitated by a lance that passes through his arm (8.19.13). Perhaps more crucially, the *Mausala* tells of the deaths of both Baladeva and Kṛṣṇa, the latter being slain by the arrow of a hunter. The *avatāra* then returns to the abode of Nārāyaṇa, ascending through the regions inhabited by the gods (16.5.20-25). The passage makes it clear, however, that after his departure from this world a body is left on earth which is later burned by Arjuna in a funeral ceremony (16.8.31).

(b) The Divinity and Humanity of the *Avatāra*: The contradiction and paradox of presenting a being who is both human and divine is manifest in the figure of Kṛṣṇa, for he is the Supreme Deity born amongst men. Early scholars of the epic perceived a historical development in the portrayal of Kṛṣṇa, seeing passages in which he displays human traits as early and those in which he is obviously divine as later, after brahminical editors had attempted to ascribe a divine nature to a previously human character. This analysis has in recent years appeared overly simplistic. If editors were attempting to rework a secular narrative and depict one of the heroes as a manifestation of Viṣṇu, the question must be raised as to why they ignored certain passages in which Kṛṣṇa appears constrained by human limitation. Either they were extremely sloppy in their work or else they found no fundamental contradiction between such passages and the position of Kṛṣṇa as an *avatāra*.

However one attempts to resolve this debate it is apparent that the role of Kṛṣṇa in the narrative is paradoxical. At times he appears identical to the Supreme Deity, omniscient and completely in control of the unfolding episodes, but at others he appears limited by the circumscriptions of mortality and subject to the frailties of the human form he has adopted. The text of the epic does not address this paradox and it has been left to later commentators and to the *Purāṇas* to explain that Kṛṣṇa is always an omniscient being but at times acts as if he were an ordinary mortal simply as a pastime for his amusement or to enhance the renown of his followers.

The stress placed on the divinity of Kṛṣṇa has been noted earlier. Repeatedly the text points out that this character is no ordinary mortal but is Viṣṇu himself, the Supreme Deity who creates and controls the entire cosmos. As the political and military conflict develops, Bhīṣma, Droṇa and other sagacious personalities in the Kaurava camp constantly argue that victory for the Pāṇḍavas is certain because Kṛṣṇa is on their side, and the will of Viṣṇu cannot be thwarted. Alongside such assertions, however, we find instances of Kṛṣṇa's apparent limitation. Examples of physical limitations occurring in the battle have been noted above and at other points in the narrative we find Kṛṣṇa apparently blocked in his endeavours. In Chapter 13 of the *Sabhā*, he tells the Pāṇḍavas of how he was forced to flee from his capital in Mathurā in fear of Jarāsandha and build a fortress at Dvārakā protected by the ocean, and in the eventual slaying of Jarāsandha by Bhīma, Kṛṣṇa acts as if he has no divine potency whatsoever. In Chapter 13 of the *Vana*, Kṛṣṇa says that he would have prevented the dice match but was unable to do so because he was at war with his enemy Śālva. In the course of this war, Śālva produces an illusion showing that Kṛṣṇa's father, Vasudeva, has been slain and at least initially Kṛṣṇa is taken in by the ploy. In his surrender to Śiva, especially in Chapters 13 to 17 of the *Anuśāsana*, Kṛṣṇa appears to be very human in seeking boons from the great Deity and having less wisdom than the Śaivites, Upamanyu and Tandin, from whose instructions he learns the secrets of Śiva-*bhakti*.

On the battlefield Kṛṣṇa is typically described as aloof in his demeanour, smiling slightly and above the events he is controlling. At certain junctures, however, he is depicted as displaying more human traits. In Chapter 102 of the *Bhīṣma*, when it appears that the grandfather of the Kauravas will vanquish the entire Pāṇḍava host, Kṛṣṇa, referred to here as the lord of the universe–*jagad-īṣvara*, dismounts from the chariot and runs towards Bhīṣma, so inflamed with wrath that his eyes are copper-red–*krodha-tāmrekṣaṇaḥ kṛṣṇaḥ* (55). A similar display of anger occurs earlier in the text when he hears of how the Pāṇḍavas were deprived of their kingdom at the dice match (3.13.7), and when he encounters the grief-stricken Dhṛtarāṣṭra and Gāndhārī after the battle, Kṛṣṇa weeps on seeing their distress (9.62.36).

The obvious paradox between the eulogies of Kṛṣṇa's control over all things and his human limitations is epitomised by the assertion of Karṇa that Kṛṣṇa is the creator of the universe–*kṛṣṇaś ca sraṣṭā jagataḥ* (8.22.49)–and yet Śalya is a superior charioteer to him–*śalyo hy abhyadhikaḥ kṛṣṇāt* (8.22.53). Similarly, Yudhiṣṭhira states that Kṛṣṇa is the protector and master of the universe–*goptāraṁ jagataḥ prabhum* (7.85.86)–but still feels that Arjuna may need others to protect him. Such passages tend to undermine the theory of early scholars that passages in which Kṛṣṇa is portrayed with limitations are early and those in which he is divine follow a brahminical revision of the text. The fact that references to his being the Supreme Deity and also to his apparent limitation are found in close proximity is more likely to indicate an undeveloped stage of epic monotheism which has yet to differentiate fully between a Supreme Deity and the prominent members of the Vedic pantheon.

The text itself does not openly address the question of how the statements of Kṛṣṇa's dominance over the cosmos are to be reconciled with his displays of limitation. Similarly, the question of whether Nārāyaṇa can only achieve his mission by appearing as an *avatāra* is not discussed. The view of the *Bhāgavata Purāṇa* and of later Vaiṣṇavism is that there is no absolute necessity for Viṣṇu to appear as *avatāras* and that he does so to sport with his devotees and to attract others to him by his remarkable deeds. Any apparent limitation displayed by the *avatāra* is merely a part of this ploy. Hence when Kṛṣṇa appears as a child it seems that he is dependent on his foster-parents, Nanda and Yaśodā, but the reader of the *Purāṇa* is constantly reminded that this is nothing more than a show to please these devotees, for Kṛṣṇa is always the Supreme Deity.

Such a docetic view of *avatāra* is not found in the *Mahābhārata*, although when an overview of the text is taken, it is clear that more stress is laid on the divine potency of the *avatāra* than on any constraints that might be imposed by his human form. A hint of the later docetism may perhaps be recognised in Chapter 52 of the *Aśvamedhika.* On his return to Dvārakā after the battle at Kurukṣetra, Kṛṣṇa encounters the sage Uttaṅka and is asked by him whether he was able to maintain a state of peace amongst the antagonistic factions in the royal order (13-14). To this Kṛṣṇa replies that despite all his endeavours for peace he was unable to prevent the war from breaking out. Uttaṅka is unimpressed by this claim of Kṛṣṇa's and replies that if it had been his will the outcome would have been different–*tvayā hi śaktena satā mithyācāreṇa mādhava* (22)–and threatens to curse him. Kṛṣṇa responds to this merely by asserting that he is the origin of all things and that if the sage curses him the only result will be a loss of the powers Uttaṅka has gained by his asceticism. The claim of divinity is backed up by the fourth display of the *viśva-rūpa* contained in the epic.

It is clear that the theism of the epic is of a different nature to that of the *Bhāgavata Purāṇa* or the writings of Rāmānuja. The notion of omnipotence has yet to be fully explored, as has the implication of the doctrine of *avatāra* for Vaiṣṇava theology. Hence questions that are addressed later in the Hindu tradition are left here as paradoxes to tax the ingenuity of Hindu commentators and Western critical scholars alike.

(c) The Morality of the *Avatāra*: A further paradox in the character of Kṛṣṇa is that while his mission is to preserve *dharma* on earth, his behaviour and the manner in which he works towards this aim appear on a number of occasions to be immoral and adharmic. Certainly in comparison to Yudhiṣṭhira, Kṛṣṇa is found wanting in terms of adherence to moral principles. In the *Udyoga*, whilst Yudhiṣṭhira displays tolerance and forgiveness towards his foes, Kṛṣṇa is the most strident in his demands that they should be made to suffer for their crimes. On the battlefield it is Kṛṣṇa who argues that they must abandon *dharma* in order to kill Droṇa–*dharmam utsṛjya pāṇḍava* (7.164.68)–and that Yudhiṣṭhira should tell a lie (98f); it is Kṛṣṇa who instructs Arjuna to abandon chivalry and kill Karṇa, when the latter has been forced to dismount from his chariot (8.67.1-5); it is Kṛṣṇa who urges Bhīma to contravene the rules of single combat and slay Duryodhana with a foul blow (9.57.5). Adharmic deeds are not confined to Kṛṣṇa, for Baladeva is referred to as being drunk–*tato baladevaḥ kṣībaḥ* (1.211.7), and the *Rāmopakhyāna* describes Rāma's killing of Sugrīva's brother whilst hiding behind a tree (3.264.36).

The text makes no attempt to disguise the adharmic element in these acts of Kṛṣṇa. In the *Droṇa*, Bhuriśravas states unequivocally that all Arjuna's unrighteous fighting is due to Kṛṣṇa (7.118.4-15). When Kṛṣṇa attempts to justify Bhīma's deed to his brother Baladeva, the text describes his words as, *dharma-cchalam*–deceit under the guise of *dharma* (9.59.22), and in Chapter 49 of the *Karṇa*, it is Kṛṣṇa who argues disingenuously that *dharma* is so fluid that it is impossible to say whether an act is righteous or not.

It is possible to identify two ways in which Kṛṣṇa's adharmic acts may be understood. On the one hand, Kṛṣṇa's use of dubious tactics may be justified in terms of the *rāja-dharma* explained by Bhīṣma in the first part of the *Śānti*. It is apparent from this teaching that a *kṣatriya* is acting in accordance with *dharma* if, under duress, he adopts dishonest means to defeat an adversary. There are clear parallels between the more Machiavellian elements in the *Rāja-dharma* and the way in which Kṛṣṇa argues against respecting moral scruples that may be an obstacle to victory. Yudhiṣṭhira stands in contrast to Kṛṣṇa here, for the *dharma* he pursues is based on morality rather than the prescribed duties of the *varṇas*.

Secondly, it must be recognised that in epic theology the Supreme Deity is a wholly transcendent being from another domain and hence not bound by the rules of this world. As God says to Job after behaving in a manner that appears to offend against morality, 'My ways are not your ways.' Kṛṣṇa has appeared as a man but retains his identity as Nārāyaṇa and hence rules of *dharma* and morality cannot constrain his actions. In 3.21-22 of the *Gītā*, he claims that he performs dharmic acts to set an example to others for in reality he is under no such constraint–*na me pārthāsti kartavyaṁ triṣu lokeṣu kiñcana.*

Despite his mission of preserving the *sva-dharma* that pertains to life in this world, Kṛṣṇa's own position is in the sphere of *nivṛtti* for he is always beyond the bondage of *karma* (4.14). The *Mokṣa-dharma* asserts that *nivṛtti* takes one beyond both *puṇya* and *pāpa*, righteousness and sin, into a realm where such concepts no longer exist. Like the liberated soul the Deity is always beyond this world in the sphere of *nivṛtti.* This is exactly the explanation given by Śukadeva in the *Bhāgavata Purāṇa*;[18] responding to questions about the morality of Kṛṣṇa's consorting with the wives of the herdsmen, he stresses that considerations of what is proper or improper are relevant only for humans and not for the Supreme Deity.[19]

It is hence significant that apart from the speech of Bhuriśravas referred to earlier, nowhere in the text do we find Kṛṣṇa criticised for his immorality. After the battle he is threatened with curses from Gāndhārī and Uttaṅka, but in both cases the anger expressed against him arises not from his acting immorally but because as the Supreme Deity he had the power to prevent the conflict and yet chose not to. After the slaying of Droṇa, there are bitter recriminations between the warriors in the Pāṇḍava camp over the unrighteous way in which this was achieved. Harsh words and even threats are exchanged but at no time is Kṛṣṇa condemned although the text makes it clear that he has been the architect and instigator of all that has taken place.

(d) The Early Life of Kṛṣṇa: In the Hindu tradition Kṛṣṇa appears in a number of different personas. He is known as the hero of the *Mahābhārata* and as the speaker of the *Bhagavad gītā* but also as the youthful and amorous cowherd of Gokula-Vṛndāvana. The epic deals with the conflict in the Kuru royal family and hence Kṛṣṇa appears there in his role as a king. His early life is described in detail only in a later appendix to the *Mahābhārata* known as the *Harivaṁśa*, a work that is probably more correctly viewed as an early *Purāṇa.* The idea that the legends surrounding Kṛṣṇa's early life in a pastoral setting belong to a later post-epic era is, however, countered by several passages in the *Mahābhārata* that refer to this period in his life and to episodes narrated fully in the *Harivaṁśa* and *Purāṇas.*

In the story of Śiśupāla's criticism of Kṛṣṇa, he describes the *avatāra* as the killer of Pūtanā–*pūtanā-ghātaḥ* (2.38.4), a herder of cows–*sangopaḥ* (6), who in his childhood killed a bird, a horse and a bull (7), destroyed a cart just by kicking it (8) and held up the hill known as Govardhana for seven days (9). In the debates prior to the battle the invincible power of Kṛṣṇa is a recurring theme and in one such discourse Vidura refers to two wonderful feats he performed as a boy, the killing of Pūtanā and the lifting of Govardhana Hill to protect the cows–*govardhano dhāritaś ca gavārthe* (5.128.45). Later Dhṛtarāṣṭra refers to the early pastimes in his discussion with Saṁjaya about the greatness of Kṛṣṇa. He states that he was raised in the family of a cowherd, killed a mighty horse in the forest by the Yamunā river, and also a terrible demon who had taken the form of a bull (7.10.2-4). Another resonance of the early life of Kṛṣṇa is in the fact that the army he provides for the

Kaurava forces is said to consist of *nārāyaṇa-gopas*, cowherds, and to come from Gokula (8.4.38).

Thus although the *Mahābhārata* never discusses the early life of Kṛṣṇa at any length, certain passages display an awareness of the pastoral tradition and of a number of the legends contained in that cycle. It may be that these sections of the text are interpolations added at the time of the *Harivaṁśa* when the traditions of the *avatāra*'s early life were more firmly established, but according to the criteria of the Critical Edition they are to be accepted as an authentic part of the epic's understanding of Kṛṣṇa. It appears that the failure to expand these references was recognised as an omission at some later date and as a result the *Harivaṁśa* was added to the epic as an appendix.

4. Non-Vaiṣṇava Theism

(i) Introduction

Purāṇic theism presents a 'trinitarian' theology postulating a Supreme Deity manifest in three features as Brahmā, who is the creator, Śiva, the destroyer, and Viṣṇu/Nārāyaṇa, the maintainer.[20] Despite the position of Viṣṇu, Śiva and Brahmā as the three principal Deities in the epic, Hopkins is correct when he states that, "the union of the three highest gods into a trinity forms no part of epic belief."[21] Brahmā is the creator, but he is only a demiurge empowered by Viṣṇu for his creative acts. Viṣṇu and Śiva are the two principal Deities of the *Mahābhārata* and both are described in terms that establish each individually as the Supreme Deity in a manner that tends towards monotheism rather than trinitarianism.

Despite the apparent overlapping of roles, each Deity has individual characteristics and it is in these that a possible proto-trinitarianism may be found, for Viṣṇu is primarily benign and seeks the sustenance of the cosmic and social orders, while Śiva displays the characteristics of a destroyer, uncontrolled and chaotic, wandering across the battlefield and dwelling in the crematorium. Such tendencies, however, fall far short of the later Purāṇic trinitarianism. What is found in the epic alongside the predominant Vaiṣṇava theism, are passages that emphasise Śiva, and occasionally Brahmā and the Goddess Durgā as the Supreme Deity. It is this non-Vaiṣṇava theism that must now be considered.

(ii) Brahmā

There must be some doubt as to whether the Hindu tradition has ever recognised Brahmā as the Supreme Deity in the way that Viṣṇu and Śiva have been conceived of and worshipped. Brahmā figures prominently in the epic as the leader of the pantheon of gods who calls for the descent of the *avatāra* and as the creator of the cosmos under the direction of Viṣṇu. In addition, he is referred to as the *dhātṛ*, or ordainer, who dictates the destiny of individual beings in accordance with their acts. There are passages in which he appears to be superior or equal to both Viṣṇu and Śiva but such a perspective is exceptional and there are few if any direct statements in the text proclaiming such superiority. Predominantly the *Mahābhārata* casts Brahmā in the role of a demiurge who acts as a secondary creator and ordainer under the direction of his creator, Viṣṇu. He is the leader of the pantheon and superior to all the gods but he is not portrayed as the Supreme Deity who exists beyond this world and manifests it from himself. The *Mahābhārata*'s view of Brahmā is of great interest from a historical perspective but he does not have the same status as that ascribed to Viṣṇu and Śiva and is not the focus of the more developed stages of epic theology.

(iii) Durgā

The position of the Goddess in the *Mahābhārata* is complex and warrants more detailed research. Her position is far less prominent than that of Brahmā and she appears mainly in the later *parvans* in her role as consort to Śiva in passages that are of a Śaivite rather than Śākta tendency. Elsewhere, the Goddess is worshipped as the Supreme Deity in a few short passages, though Hopkins exaggerates the case when he observes that Durgā worship is 'prominent' in the *Virāṭa*.[22] The issue here, however, is textual rather than theological as all these passages have been omitted from the Critical Edition as later interpolations. Pusalker defends this position of the Critical Editors, asserting that the, "spuriousness of every one of these passages has been thoroughly established on indubitable MS evidence,"[23] and Hopkins describes both the major laudations of the Goddess as "awkward inserts."[24] Regardless of the textual debate, the Goddess and Śāktism remain peripheral to epic theism and are never a major concern of the epic's theology.

(iv) Śiva in the *Mahābhārata*

The position of Śiva in the epic's thought is far more central and has been the subject of detailed study, most notably the thoroughgoing research of Jacques Scheuer which has served to demonstrate that the influence of Śiva throughout the narrative is more salient than had previously been supposed.[25] The theism of the narrative is predominantly Vaiṣṇava; nonetheless, Śiva appears in the role of the Supreme Deity in various episodes throughout the text and in certain passages there are clear indications of his superiority over Viṣṇu and the *avatāra*. Earlier epic scholarship concluded that the original secular text, having been revised to make it a Vaiṣṇava work, was subsequently edited once more and interpolations added to sustain the position of Śiva as the Supreme Deity.[26] More recent work by Scheuer, Hiltebeitel and Biardeau has marked something of a return to the syncretistic perspective of Dahlmann[27] and Levi,[28] suggesting that Viṣṇu and Śiva are not alternative Deities in the epic, glorified in sectarian interpolations, but should be taken as complementary features of one Supreme Deity manifest alternately depending upon which divine feature was appropriate. According to Biardeau,

> Les deux divinités sont donc . . . étroitement complémentaires, et ne sont jamais que deux visages (ou de moments de l'action) d'un meme dieu, d'un meme Souverein absolu. C'est la fonction respective de chacun qui commande la primauté de Viṣṇu sur Śiva.[29]

The reasoning presented by these writers is persuasive for it is apparent that the "oppositions and relations between Viṣṇu and Śiva are too thoroughly ingrained in the epic to be explained away as interpolations."[30] In attempting to draw conclusions here one is forced to resort to surmise in the absence of direct statements from the text and one must be aware that such conclusions must remain as no more than conjecture. The indications of the text point in different directions, sometimes suggesting a complementary relationship between Viṣṇu and Śiva and sometimes a sectarian perspective. It appears that Scheuer shares this view when he writes,

> On n'exclut pas qu'il y ait, dans le *Mbh* (et plus précisement à propos de Rudra-Śiva) des éléments "sectaires" . . . . Mais

> on a bien l'impression que de tels éléments, s'ils existent, occupent dans le *Mbh* une place réduite et marginale. Ils n'affectent pas le mythe central auquel ils ne sont pas étroitement liés.[31]

Though here he undoubtedly underestimates the significance of sectarian tendencies in the text.

(v) The Significance of Śiva in the Epic

Scheuer has attempted to demonstrate that Śiva's role in the cosmic drama underlying the narrative is both prominent and pervasive and though he might be accused of seeing Śiva where Śiva is not to be found the point is well taken. It is Śiva who gives a boon to Gāndhārī so that she has one hundred sons; Śiva gives a boon to Śrī and punishes the five Indras so that the Pāṇḍavas come to marry Draupadī; his boons facilitate the birth of Śikhandin who will slay Bhīṣma, enable Jayadratha to kill Abhimanyu, and Bhuriśravas to humiliate Sātyakī. In his quest for divine weapons before going to *svarga-loka,* Arjuna fights with Śiva in the form of a hunter before surrendering to his grace and receiving a promise of the Pāśupāta weapon from him. In the battle, before the conflict with Jayadratha, Kṛṣṇa and Arjuna journey to Kailāsa and obtain both the weapon and Śiva's blessing. At the conclusion of the *Droṇa,* Vyāsa tells Arjuna that Śiva precedes him on the battlefield destroying his adversaries and after the final day it is Śiva who enables Aśvatthāman to destroy the Pañcālas and the sons of Draupadī. In the didactic sections of the epic, Chapters 14 to 17, 127 and 128, and 145 and 146 of the *Anuśāsana* are dedicated to the glorification of Śiva as the Supreme Deity.

(vi) Śiva as the Supreme Deity

In the passages referred to above, the text is forthright in expressing the view that Śiva is the Supreme Deity above all other beings, often in terms similar to those used elsewhere to assert the supremacy of Nārāyaṇa. As was noted with reference to Viṣṇu the text also includes certain myths of the gods in which Śiva is portrayed as one of the leaders of the pantheon and like all the gods subject to certain limitations. Here the stories of the birth of Skanda, and the destruction of the three cities of the *asuras* may be cited as examples (8.24.1-161 and 13.145-146). Such myths, however, are infrequent and are atypical of the epic as a whole in their presentation of the nature of Śiva.

When Arjuna encounters Śiva in the form of a *kirāta*, or hunter, the latter is referred to as *deveśa*, the lord of the gods, and *maheśvara*, the supreme controller (3.39.27-28). In Arjuna's prayers of surrender, (3.40.57-60) he is *sarva-bhūteśa*, the lord of all beings, and *deveśa* once again. When he manifests himself before Ambā, Śiva is referred to as *bhūteśa*, the lord of all beings, and *mahādeva*, the great god (5.188.10-11). Such terms, especially in light of the numerous effusive laudations offered to men and demigods, fall short of establishing Śiva as the Supreme Deity. In the *Droṇa*, however, the idea becomes more firmly established. Here Kṛṣṇa seeks to include Śiva in his mission of destroying the asuric kings and with Arjuna makes a nocturnal visit to Kailāsa. There they both worship Śiva who is presented as the lord of this world.

vāsudevas tu taṁ dṛṣṭvā jagāma śirasā kṣitim
pārthena saha dharmātmā gṛṇan brahma sanātanam

lokādiṁ viśva-karmāṇam ajam īśānam avyayam
manasaḥ paramāṁ yoniṁ khaṁ vāyuṁ jyotiṣāṁ nidhim

sraṣṭāraṁ vāridhārāṇāṁ bhuvaś ca prakṛtiṁ parām
deva-dānava-yakṣāṇāṁ mānavānāṁ ca sādhanam

yogināṁ paramaṁ brahma vyaktaṁ brahma-vidāṁ nidhim
carācarasya sraṣṭāraṁ pratihartāram eva ca

kāla-kopaṁ mahātmānaṁ śakra-sūrya-guṇodayaṁ
avandata tadā kṛṣṇo vāṅ-mano-buddhi-karmabhiḥ

'Having beheld him (Śiva), Vāsudeva, whose very self is *dharma*, along with the son of Pṛthā, bowed his head to the ground whilst reciting the eternal words of the Veda.

"Śiva is the origin of the world, the creator of all things, the unborn, immutable master. He is the supreme source of the mind, he is space, he is the wind and in him all luminaries are contained.

He is the maker of the rains, the ultimate form of

> matter and the object of worship for gods, Dānavas, *yakṣas* and men.
>
> For *yogins* he is manifest as the supreme spirit, *brahman* and he is the very essence for those who know the Veda. He is the creator and destroyer of both moving and non-moving beings.
>
> His wrath is manifest as time which destroys all things; he is the great one who is the origin of the attributes of the gods Indra and Sūrya." Kṛṣṇa then worshipped him with words, mind, intellect and deeds.' (7.57.39-43)

The prayers of Kṛṣṇa which follow mainly glorify the form and activities of the Deity but also affirm Śiva in the position elsewhere ascribed to Nārāyaṇa as the one who creates and also pervades the entire cosmos–*viṣvātmane viśva-sṛje viśvam āvṛtya tiṣṭhate* (54).

The final two chapters of the *Droṇa*, 172 and 173, with their unequivocal view of the superiority of Śiva over Viṣṇu are uncharacteristic of the narrative and their perspective is closer to that of the *Anuśāsana*. The references to *liṅga* worship confirm this view and suggest that this passage has been appended to the *Droṇa* at a later date, and comes from the same source as the Śaivite material in the *Anuśāsana*. Vyāsa's words here repeatedly stress the supremacy of Śiva, who is the creator and controller of all things. The victory of the Pāṇḍavas is assured not only because of the grace of Nārāyaṇa but because Nārāyaṇa gained a boon from Śiva that guarantees their protection. Śiva retains his own unique identity in this passage but has also completely taken on the attributes of the Supreme Godhead more usually associated with Nārāyaṇa in the epic. Thus in the prayers offered by Nārāyaṇa Ṛṣi it is asserted that all things in the three worlds, past, present and future, come from Śiva–*bhūtaṁ bhavyaṁ bhavitā cāpy adṛṣyaṁ tvat-saṁbhūtā bhuvanānīha viśvā* (7.172.70)–and phrases such as this set the theological tone of the passage. This theme, established somewhat incongruously at the conclusion of the *Droṇa*, is taken up once more in the *Sauptika* wherein Aśvatthāman slays the surviving warriors in the Pāṇḍava camp. Again we find the idea that the protection of the Pāṇḍavas came from a boon given to Nārāyaṇa by Śiva and now the boon is withdrawn to allow the carnage that follows.

It is in three passages of the *Anuśāsana*, Chapters 14-18, 127-128, and 145-146, that we find material that lends most weight to the argument for sectarian teachings within the *Mahābhārata.* Here Viṣṇu's *avatāra.* appears in the role of a Śaivite devotee being initiated into the worship of the great god by Upamanyu in order to gain the boon of a son. With this as a context, it is apparent that Śiva is the Supreme Deity here and he is repeatedly glorified as such in all the terms familiar from passages that praise the supremacy of Nārāyaṇa. He is described as the eternal one, the source of all things–*namo 'stu te śāśvata sarva-yone* (13.15.30), the door to heaven and salvation–*dvāraṁ tvaṁ svarga-mokṣāṇām* (16.20), beyond both all that is and all that is not in this world–*viśvāviśva-paraḥ bhavaḥ* (16.24), always concealed from gods, *asuras,* and men–*devāsura-manuṣyāṇāṁ yac ca guhyaṁ sanātanam* (16.29), the soul of all things who sees all things, who is all-pervasive and omniscient–*sarvātmā sarva-darśī ca sarva-gaḥ sarva-veditā* (16.30). Such expressions are typical of the *Anuśāsana.* They do not, however, stand by way of a complete contrast to the perspective offered by passages found earlier in the epic. Rather they exaggerate and expand, for Śiva is always more than a demigod and, like Viṣṇu, takes the role of creator and controller of all things.

(vii) Iconography and Personality of Śiva

Whilst Viṣṇu and Śiva are both presented as the Supreme Deity, and as such have certain identical features, a clear distinction between them is sustained through marked differences of personality and iconography. The restrained nature of Vaiṣṇava iconography has been noted, especially in comparison to the *Purāṇas.* Where Śiva is described, however, this is not the case. The iconographic and mythological detail is pronounced while the stress on supremacy and dominance is somewhat restrained, though by no means insignificant. The concept of an all-pervasive Deity assuming the philosophical characteristics of the Upaniṣadic *brahman* is also a less pronounced feature than is the case with Nārāyaṇa and it may plausibly be argued that it is only present at all as imitation of Vaiṣṇava theism.

Typically, the passages in which Śiva is prominent contain references to, and frequently detailed description of, his form, activities and entourage. In the story of Arjuna's meeting with Śiva, the Deity is referred to as *pinākin,* bearing a trident, *śiti-kaṇṭha,* having a blue throat (3.39.25), *giriśaṁ śūla-pāṇinam,* the lord of the mountains with spear in hand, *saha devyā mahā-dyutim,* appearing in an effulgent form with the Goddess (55), and *kapardin,* having long hair tied in a topknot (56). In the narration of Kṛṣṇa and Arjuna's nocturnal visit to Kailāsa, Śiva is described as situated on the peak of the mountain. He constantly performs penance and his emblem is the bull; his effulgence is like that of one thousand suns; he bears a staff or spear–*śūlinam;* his hair is matted like that of an ascetic–*jaṭilam;* his bodily hue is pale–*gauram,* he is dressed in bark and animal skins–*valkalājina-vāsasam;* he is in the company of Pārvatī and a host of other effulgent beings; his associates are engaged in singing, dancing, laughing, clapping, skipping, leaping about, and shouting joyfully (7.57.32-34).

Chapters 172 and 173 of the *Droṇa* provide extensive descriptions of Śiva, elaborating on his fearful aspect. His anger is fierce and he is loathsome to behold–*durdṛśaṁ tigma-manyum* (172.58); he always dwells in places where bodies are burned–*eṣa caiva śmaśāneṣu devo vasati nityaśaḥ* (173.76); he is known as Rudra because he is fierce and terrible and cuts through flesh, blood and marrow—*māṁsa-śoṇita-majjā-daḥ* (173.98). He carries a celestial bow and two quivers and wears golden armour (172.58). His other weapons include the thunderbolt, trident, axe, club and sword; his brow is fair, his hair is matted and the circle of the moon sits on his forehead—*subhruṁ jatā-maṇḍala-candra-maulim* (172.59); he wears a tiger-skin and carries an iron bludgeon and a staff in his hands–*vyāghra-jinaṁ parighaṁ daṇḍa-pāṇim* (59). He wears beautiful arm bracelets, has a snake for his sacred thread–*śubhāṅgadaṁ nāga-yajñopavītim,* and is surrounded by all types of ghosts, spirits and other living beings–*viśvair gaṇaiḥ śobhitaṁ bhūta-saṁghaiḥ* (60). In the same passage, Śiva is again described as being in the company of Pārvatī, his consort of beautiful limbs–*pṛthu-cārvaṅgyā* (64). It is Śiva whom Arjuna sees going before him in battle afflicting the enemy, for his nature is fierce and destructive–*yan nirdahati yat tīkṣṇo yad ugro yat pratāpavān* (173.98).

The *Anuśāsana* presents a similar picture of Śiva as the fierce ascetic who is kind and gracious to those devoted to him, but offers even more elaborate descriptions. In Chapter 14, verses 110 to 149 form a lengthy passage devoted entirely to describing the appearance of the Deity as he was seen by Upamanyu. He is clad in white garments here and surrounded by associates who dance and sing; he has the moon on his forehead and is decorated with a lotus garland and various gems. His weapons, the bow, *pāśupata,* spear and battle-axe, are described at length. In his entourage are found both Nārāyaṇa and Brahmā singing hymns of glorification. A further description of his form and appearance is given when Śiva manifests himself before the devoted Kṛṣṇa (13.15.6-27). In Chapter 127, Bhīṣma tells of Nārada's description of a conversation between Śiva and Umā, the Goddess. This passage also includes substantial iconographic material. The weird and frightful beings who are associates of Śiva are described as having the heads of various beasts--lions, tigers, elephants, jackals, monkeys, owls and hawks—and they entertain him with their dancing and singing. The assembly also includes sages, ascetics and holy men who, in contrast, recite the hymns of Vedas (11). The Deity himself, at the centre, is referred to as *bhīma-rūpa-dharam,* having a fearsome appearance (12), a phrase repeated twice again in this passage (21, 22).

The fearsome nature and appearance of Śiva is a theme taken up again in Chapter 145 where Kṛṣṇa is the speaker, claiming that his words are the *Śata-rudrīya* prayer (4). In Chapter 146, Kṛṣṇa explains the nature of Śiva as being twofold, mild and fierce–*dve tanū tasya devasya . . . ghorām anyāṁ śivām anyāṁ te* (3). The fierce form is like fire, lightning and the sun, while the auspicious form is found in *dharma,* in water and the moon, and undertakes the ascetic practices of *brahmacārya.* The fierce form destroys the world, it burns, it is harsh and terrible, full of potency–*yan nirdahati yat tīkṣno yad ugro yat pratāpavān* (7)–and is known as Rudra.[32] In his mild form he seeks the welfare of all men and hence he is known as Śiva–*śivam icchan manuṣyāṇāṁ tasmād eṣa śivaḥ smṛtaḥ* (9). The remainder of this discourse dwells mainly on the universal feature of the Deity who contains all facets of creation within himself.

Traditionally and to this day, Śiva has been worshipped in the form of a *liṅga,* or phallus, and this is referred to in several passages of the *Mahābhārata.* In Vyāsa's discourse at the conclusion of the *Droṇa,* he states that sages, gods, *gandharvas,* and *apsarases* worship his upraised phallus–*liṅgam asyārcayanti sma tac cāpyūrdhvaṁ samāsthitam* (173.84), that Śiva is known as Sthānu because his phallus is eternal (92), and that those who worship the phallus gain prosperity thereby (94). In the *Anuśāsana,* Upamanyu tells Indra that Brahmā, Viṣṇu and all the gods worship the *liṅga* of Śiva (14.100-102). In Chapter 146, Kṛṣṇa states that when Śiva's *liṅga* is constantly restrained by the vow of celibacy all the world worships it. One may worship either the form or the *liṅga* of Śiva but one who worships the phallus will attain great wealth (15-16). Verse 17 then repeats 173.84 of the *Droṇa* spoken by Vyāsa and cited above. These references demonstrate that Śaivite *liṅga* worship was known and approved of by some of the authors of the *Mahābhārata.* The fact that they appear only in the final two chapters of the *Droṇa* and in the *Anuśāsana* is perhaps significant in illustrating some distinction between the Śaivite theism of these sections and that found elsewhere in the epic.

Śiva in the *Mahābhārata* is thus typically presented as a monotheistic Deity in terms of epic monotheism. His position thus overlaps with that of Viṣṇu/Nārāyaṇa and it is noteworthy that many of the same terms and theological constructs are applied by the epic equally to both Deities. The iconography of Śiva is, however, markedly more pronounced than that of Viṣṇu. Pārvatī is frequently present as the consort of the Deity, his appearances are often marked by descriptions of his form, entourage and dress, and the laudations have a notable iconographic tendency. The *Anuśāsana* offers the most elaborate descriptions of Śiva's form but there is an essential continuity between these passages and those found elsewhere in the text.

The nature of God presented in the character of Śiva is clearly different from that exhibited by Viṣṇu. The latter appears as almost universally benign; a creator-God who intervenes in his creation to preserve order and promote the well-being of the righteous. He is dominant and awesome in his might and splendour but rarely ferocious and terrible, as Śiva is. Śiva is a different type of Deity, having a chaotic, destructive side generally not found in Viṣṇu. As Scheuer demonstrates, he is involved with Kṛṣṇa in the mission of preserving *dharma*, but his character is unpredictable and in a sense adharmic. The mood of the *Śata-Rudrīya* of the *Yajur-veda* and the *Śvetāsvatara Upaniṣad* in their begging that Rudra withhold his destructive energy is reflected in the epic wherein Śiva appears less closely allied to Indra and the gods than Viṣṇu, a destroyer of *yajña*, of fearsome appearance, dwelling in the inauspicious crematorium and surrounded by a weird entourage of ghosts and spirits. When unleashed, his destructive force reeks havoc on both sides in the war, using both Arjuna and Aśvatthāman as agents in devouring the combatants. His position as a *brahmacārin* is also to some extent adharmic for it is connected to *nivṛtti* and involves a withdrawal from the practices of *sva-dharma* in society.

Thus although Śiva appears in some passages to duplicate the role of Supreme Deity ascribed to Nārāyaṇa, he is more an alternative than a replica. The creation is not always benign; the forces of nature are destructive as well as supportive. In the epic, these facets of nature are reflected in their creator, whose compassion cannot always be relied upon and who must sometimes be appeased in order that the ferocious potency may be restrained.

5. Syncretism of Viṣṇu and Śiva

(i) Introduction

Within the *Mahābhārata* we thus have a monotheism of a unique type, expressed sometimes as if Viṣṇu and sometimes as if Śiva were the Supreme Deity. This apparent dissonance may be understood in two ways, one stressing sectarianism and the other adopting a syncretist perspective. Whilst I accept the objections of Hiltebeitel and others that an explanation based solely on alternating sectarian interpolations is unsatisfactory, the idea of Viṣṇu and Śiva being two contrasting features of one Deity also has major shortcomings. It is apparent that both syncretism and sectarianism are contained in the epic and hence any theory that attempts to establish either perspective whilst ignoring the other becomes impossibly problematic.

Where passages extolling either Viṣṇu or Śiva ignore the other Deity, then the syncretist view is tenable but where the other Deity is referred to and established in an inferior position the obvious inference is that the author is writing from a sectarian perspective. Within the text open assertions of complementarity between Viṣṇu and Śiva are infrequent and hence a syncretist interpretation must rely to a large extent on surmise and exegesis rather than the didactus of the epic itself. There is sufficient material, however, to allow such conclusions a degree of credibility. In pursuit of this debate I propose to examine major passages extolling both Viṣṇu and Śiva to attempt to establish the extent to which sectarianism or syncretism appears to prevail. The criterion employed here will be that stated above—where the passage explicitly refers to the other Deity as being inferior a syncretist interpretation will be deemed inappropriate.

(ii) Passages that Extol Kṛṣṇa or Nārāyaṇa

1. The prayers of Arjuna to Kṛṣṇa (3.13.10-36) refer to Rudra, a name of Śiva. Verses 19 and 20 state that Kṛṣṇa is Nārāyaṇa and also other gods who are listed, including Rudra.

2. The teachings of Mārkaṇḍeya expound extensively on Viṣṇu as the Supreme Deity. The only reference to Śiva is in 3.188.6 where Nārāyaṇa describes all the universe and all the gods as himself. Included in the list of gods are the names of Viṣṇu, Brahmā and Śiva–*ahaṁ śivaḥ* (3.187.6). Nowhere else in this extensive passage is Śiva mentioned.

3. The prayers offered by Uttaṅka to Viṣṇu (3.192.11-19) make no reference to Śiva.

4. The glorifications of Kṛṣṇa as the Supreme Deity in the *Udyoga* by Saṁjaya, Dhṛtarāṣṭra and Vidura make no reference to Śiva.

5. Bhīṣma's instructions to Duryodhana about Nārāyaṇa and his descent as Kṛṣṇa, including the prayers of Brahmā, in Chapters 61 to 64 of the *Bhīṣma*, contain no mention of Śiva.

6. Yudhiṣṭhira's prayers to Kṛṣṇa after the slaying of Jayadratha (7.124.3-18) make no reference to Śiva.

7. In Yudhiṣṭhira's praise of the divinity of Kṛṣṇa in the *Śānti* (12.43.1-16), he glorifies him as the three-eyed Śambhu–*tri-cakṣuḥ śambhur ekas tvam* (7).

8. In Bhīṣma's prayers to Kṛṣṇa before beginning his instructions to Yudhiṣṭhira in the *Śānti* (12.47.10-63 and 51.2-9) he ascribes the role of destroyer of the worlds, usually associated with Śiva, to Viṣṇu in his terrible feature–*tasmai ghorātmane namaḥ* (37). Later he is more specific in praising Viṣṇu as having Śiva, or Rudra, as one of his aspects:

> *śūline tri-daśeśāya tryambakāya mahātmane*
> *bhasma-digdhordhva-liṅgāya tasmai rudrātmane namaḥ*
>
> 'My obeisances to the bearer of the trident, to that great soul with three eyes who is lord of the thirty great gods, who is smeared with ashes and whose phallus is upraised. My obeisances to that one who is Rudra himself.' (12.47.52)

In Chapter 51, Bhīṣma describes Viṣṇu as both the creator and destroyer of the worlds–*namas te bhagavan viṣṇo lokānāṁ nidhanodbhava* (2).

9. In the *Bhagavad-gītā*, Śiva is mentioned only in Chapter 10–*rudrāṇāṁ śaṁkaraś cāsmi* (23), and in light of the statement of 21, *ādityānām aham viṣṇuḥ*, I feel that this is not particularly significant apart from revealing that the *Gītā* is aware of Śiva. The revelation of the *viśva-rūpa* in Chapter 11 does, however, provide some intimations of Śiva. It is notable that the vision of the *viśva-rūpa* manifest in the court of the Kurus includes Śiva–*rudro vakṣasi cābhavat* (5.129.5)–whereas in that beheld by Arjuna, Brahmā and all the gods are within the body of the Deity but Śiva is not mentioned.[33]

Where Arjuna is overwhelmed and terrified by the vision of an all-pervading Deity devouring the worlds–*loka-kṣaya-kṛt*–his prayers for the ferocious energy to be restrained are resonant of the *Śvetāśvatara Upaniṣad*'s and the Vedic *Śata-Rudrīya*'s beseeching of Śiva to show his benign feature. In verse 25, Arjuna refers to the Deity as Śarma, a name generally associated with Śiva, and begs, *prasīda deveśa jagan-nivāsa*–be gracious, O Lord of the Gods, O refuge of the world—a phrase repeated in 45. The violent, destructive feature of the Deity displayed here certainly corresponds to the depiction of Śiva found elsewhere in the epic, though it is to be noted that the vocative *viṣṇo* occurs in verses 24 and 30, and *hṛṣīkeśa* in 36.

10. The nine passages discussed above provide no material that is clearly sectarian for nowhere is Viṣṇu stated as being the creator of or superior to Śiva. This is not the case, however, in the *Nārāyaṇīya.* The fact that sectarian Vaiṣṇava doctrines are found only in this section is significant, particularly in light of Esnoul's assertion that within the *Mahābhārata* the *Nārāyaṇīya* is unique in being a Pañcarātric text.[34] Chapter 321 lists 21 *prajāpatis,* or progenitors, who are the first beings created by Nārāyaṇa and who worship him. The first two in the list are Brahmā and Śiva, referred to here as Sthānu (33). The acts of Kṛṣṇa recounted in Chapter 326 include the vanquishing of the *asura* Bāṇa along with Śiva who was his protector–*śaṁkaraṁ ca mahāsenaṁ bāṇa-priya-hitaiṣiṇam* (86). In Chapter 328, at the beginning of his explanations of the names of Nārāyaṇa, Kṛṣṇa tells Arjuna that Brahmā is born from the grace of Nārāyaṇa and Rudra is born from his wrath–*yasya prasāda-jo brahmā rudraś ca krodha-saṁbhavaḥ* (12). In Chapter 330, he goes on to discuss the manifestation of Śiva on the battlefield described in 172 and 173 of the *Droṇa.*

yas tu te so 'grato yāti yuddhe saṁpratyupasthite
taṁ viddhi rudraṁ kaunteya deva-devaṁ kapardinam

kālaḥ sa eva kathitaḥ krodha-jeti mayā tava
nihatāṁs tena vai pūrvaṁ hatavān asi vai ripūn

'O son of Kuntī, you must know that he who goes before you, situated just in front of you in battle, is Rudra, the god of gods, whose hair is braided like an ascetic.

He it is who was described by me to you as time, born of my wrath. All those whom you killed had previously been slain by him.' (12.330.69-70)

It is possible that these verses are a commentary on Chapter 11 of the *Gītā*, particularly 11.32-35 in which Kṛṣṇa declares himself to be time, the great destroyer of the worlds. If this is so, then it strengthens the suggestion made above that the *Gītā* regards the destructive aspect of Kṛṣṇa's nature as a manifestation of Śiva.

The *Nārāyaṇīya*, especially in its creation stories, is emphatic in asserting that Brahmā is created by Nārāyaṇa and is subordinate to him at all times. Thus the view of the text that Śiva is created by Brahmā has clear sectarian implications, as when Vaiśaṁpāyana states that the husband of Umā who imparts the teachings of the Pāśupata sect is the son of Brahmā–*umā-patir bhūta-patiḥ śrī-kaṇṭho brahmaṇaḥ sutaḥ* (337.62). In the next chapter, Śiva is again referred to as Brahmā's son–*putraḥ śivaḥ* (338.11), as he prostrates himself at the feet of the latter–*vavande cāpi pādayoḥ* (12). In the remainder of Chapter 338 and in Chapter 339, Brahmā acts as the preceptor of Śiva, instructing him in the theistic Sāṁkhya which posits Nārāyaṇa as the supreme *puruṣa* who is the life of all beings. The passage is again clearly Pañcarātric with its stress on the fourfold manifestation of the Deity.

(iii) Passages that Extol Śiva

1. In the early interventions of Śiva in the narrative, there is little discussion of his position as the Supreme Deity and nothing at all that directly compares or contrasts his role to that of Viṣṇu.

2. In the passage that describes Arjuna's fight with Śiva in the form of a hunter (3.39-42), the only reference to Viṣṇu comes at the opening of Chapter 41. There Śiva informs Arjuna that in a previous body he was Nara–*naras tvaṁ pūrva-dehe vai* (1)–the

associate of Nārāyaṇa who performed austerities at Badarī for thousands of years. In both Arjuna and Viṣṇu, the supreme person, great power resides–*tvayi vā paramaṁ tejo viṣṇau vā puruṣottame,* and that power sustains the universe. There are resonances here of the idea found in 7.172 and 10.7 of Nārāyaṇa performing penances to worship Śiva and thereby gaining a boon from him by which the Pāṇḍavas are protected. Here, however, the idea is not expressed openly and while there is a certain implication of Śiva's supremacy, the reference to Viṣṇu as *puruṣottama* and to his sustaining the world mean that the passage cannot be classified as overtly sectarian for no direct comparison of the Deities is made.

3. In the nocturnal visit, the reverence shown by Kṛṣṇa to Śiva is clearly significant. On their arrival at Kailāsa he bows his head to the earth—*vāsudevas tu taṁ dṛṣṭvā jagāma śirasā kṣitim* (7.57.39), and seeks protection from Śiva–*jagmatuḥ śaraṇaṁ bhavam* (44). In verses 49-58, both Kṛṣṇa and Arjuna offer prayers, praising Śiva as the soul and origin of the universe. There is no reference to Viṣṇu but the reverential attitude of Kṛṣṇa, who is elsewhere shown to be the Supreme Deity and identical to Viṣṇu, is sufficient to give the passage a sectarian flavour.

4. The teachings of Vyāsa in Chapters 172 and 173 of the *Droṇa* tell of the penances performed by Nārāyaṇa Ṛṣi to satisfy Śiva. After 66,000 years of such *tapas* Śiva finally manifests himself before Viṣṇu in this form and receives his prayers. Kṛṣṇa's power to protect the Pāṇḍavas and his invincibility on the battlefield are explained here as being the result of a boon given by Śiva (74). This perspective is markedly different from that expressed elsewhere where Kṛṣṇa's dominance is due only to his being a manifestation of Viṣṇu. Furthermore, Kṛṣṇa is described as devoted to Rudra and generated from him–*sa eṣa rudra-bhaktaś ca keśavo rudra-saṁbhavaḥ.* Kṛṣṇa understands Rudra to be the origin of all beings and worships him in the form of his *liṅga–sarva-bhūta-bhavaṁ jñātvā liṅge 'rcayati yaḥ prabhum* (89-90). The contrast here with the interpretation of Śiva's manifestation on the battlefield given in the *Nārāyaṇīya* (as being the wrath of Viṣṇu) is pronounced and indicative of a sectarian perspective incompatible with a syncretist theology.

5. In the *Sauptika,* when Śiva appears before Aśvatthāman his manifestation of thousands of forms of Viṣṇu (10.6.9) seems to be based on a sectarian perspective, implying that Śiva is the origin

of Nārāyaṇa. Within the *Sauptika,* we find reference again to the recurring Śaivite theme that Kṛṣṇa's engineering of the Pāṇḍava triumph was possible only because of the boon he received from Śiva (10.7.20-22). The prayers of Aśvatthāman (10.7.2-12), however, make no claims of superiority for Śiva over Viṣṇu as no mention is made of the other Deity. In the recitation of the story of the destruction of Dakṣa's *yajña* (chs 17 and 18), Śiva's dominance over the gods is stressed but the position of Viṣṇu is ignored completely.

6. In the long passage dedicated to Śiva in Chapters 14 to 17 of the *Anuśāsana,* Kṛṣṇa is the principal narrator, telling in detail the history of his devotion to Śiva. In Chapter 14, when Śiva appears to the devoted Upamanyu, the weapon of the Deity is described as being capable of destroying Brahmā, Viṣṇu or any of the gods (130), and both Brahmā and Nārāyaṇa are in his retinue, chanting the *Śata-Rudrīya* to glorify him (147-148). Later, in praising Śiva, Upamanyu states that he is the creator of Brahmā, Viṣṇu, and Rudra:

> *yo 'sṛjad dakṣiṇād aṅgād brahmāṇaṁ loka-saṁbhavam*
> *vāma-pārśvāt tathā viṣṇuṁ loka-rakṣārtham īśvaraḥ*
> *yugānte caiva saṁprāpte rudram aṅgāt sṛjat prabhuḥ*
>
> 'You are the one who, from your right side, created Brahmā, the creator of the world and, from your left side, for the protection of world, Viṣṇu who is the controller. When the end of the *yuga* comes the Lord creates Rudra from his body.' (13.14.183)

Here it is clear that Śiva alone is to be regarded as the Supreme Deity who is the origin not only of Brahmā and Viṣṇu but also of Rudra. There is possibly a hint of trinitarianism in this idea, with Śiva as the one God who appears in three forms to execute the functions of creation, sustenance and destruction, though it is notable that whereas Viṣṇu and Brahmā come from the left and right side of the Deity, Rudra is created from his body, possibly implying that he is a plenary manifestation.

In Chapter 16, Kṛṣṇa praises Śiva by saying that he is all the gods and includes the names of Brahmā, Viṣṇu and Rudra in his list (22), having earlier asserted (16) that none of the gods, including Brahmā and Viṣṇu, can comprehend him. Again the indication is that Śiva is the Supreme Deity behind all lesser gods, including both Viṣṇu and Rudra; this may be taken as equivalent to the passage from the *Vana* in which Nārāyaṇa tells Mārkaṇḍeya that he is both Viṣṇu and Śiva (3.187.5-6). These apparently sectarian passages could thus also be construed as syncretistic in implying that the Supreme Deity exists behind his overt forms of either Śiva or Viṣṇu, though against this it must be remembered that in both passages the Deities themselves are worshipped in their familiar manifestations. It is also to be noted that the placing of Kṛṣṇa in the role of an aspiring Śaivite devotee is strongly suggestive of a sectarian view.

7. Chapters 127 to 133 of the *Anuśāsana* give a description of Śiva and his entourage and of a conversation between the Deity and his spouse, Umā. There is no reference to Viṣṇu in this passage.

8. In Chapters 145 and 146 of the *Anuśāsana,* Kṛṣṇa is again the speaker who expounds upon the glories and supremacy of Śiva. In 145.4, he tells Yudhiṣṭhira that he recites the *Śata-Rudrīya* prayer daily. The only reference to Viṣṇu here is with regard to his becoming the arrow used by Śiva in the destruction of the three cities, a myth which shows the three Deities working in harmony, without any of them having absolute power. Again the devotional attitude of Kṛṣṇa towards Śiva is significant in indicating a sectarian perspective.

(iv) Indications of Syncretism in the Epic

The syncretist view of *Mahābhārata* theology is based on the understanding that the text as we have it may substantially be taken as a whole, without allowing for historical progression or variations between passages. Hopkins' view, and it is one that has been shared by a majority of critical scholars, is that the epic embodies a variety of works from different sources, pulled together in one literature at different times by different editors. Such scholars argue that the presence of sectarian Vaiṣṇava and Śaivite material is strong evidence in favour of their case. From the above analysis, however, it is apparent that overt sectarianism, wherein the superiority of one Deity over the other is avowed, is by no means the rule in either the Śaivite or Vaiṣṇava passages of the epic.

The fact that sectarian material (and here I am admittedly applying a rigorous criterion) from either side appears in only a few passages indicates that a syncretistic understanding of the roles of Viṣṇu and Śiva in the epic is not wholly unreasonable. This notion is supported by certain passages in the text itself, by later Hindu ideas of a similar type, by iconographic representations of Hari-Hara, Viṣṇu and Śiva, found in religious art, and by Purāṇic teachings that present Viṣṇu and Śiva as complementary.[35] The following passages may be cited as indicating a syncretist view of the two Deities.

1. The significance of passages which glorify one of the Deities and make no mention of the other should not be ignored. There can be little doubt that such passages are aware of the existence and status ascribed to the other Deity and hence the fact that there are no assertions of supremacy provides some indication of a theology based on complementarity.

2. In certain of the prayers offered to both Śiva and Viṣṇu, the Deity in question is referred to by the name and sometimes characteristics of the other, though it must be admitted that the force of this argument is curtailed by the fact that the names of other Vedic gods are frequently included in the laudations. In Chapter 33 of the *Sabhā*, for example, wherein Nārada recognises Kṛṣṇa as Nārāyaṇa, the *avatāra* is referred to as both Nārāyaṇa and Śambhu who is the lord of the universe–*iti nārāyaṇaḥ śambhur bhagavāñ jagataḥ prabhuḥ* (16); Arjuna glorifies Kṛṣṇa as Rudra (3.13.20), though in a list of gods); the child who reveals himself as Nārāyaṇa to Mārkaṇḍeya states that he is all the gods including Viṣṇu and Śiva (3.187.46); Bhīṣma praises Kṛṣṇa as Rudra, refers to Śiva as one of his forms (12.47.52), and later glorifies him as Śiva, Nārāyaṇa, and Acyuta (12.52.2); Yudhiṣṭhira praises Kṛṣṇa as three-eyed Śambhu (12.43.7). It is notable that in each of these passages there is no praise of Viṣṇu that indicates that he is the creator of Śiva or superior to him. In both the *Śiva-* and *Viṣṇu-sahasra-nāma-stotrams* names of the other Deity are included in the listings. Thus Hari and Viṣṇu (13.17.100, 101) are presented as names of Śiva, and Śarva, Śiva, Sthānu and Rudra (13.135.17, 26) are included as names of Viṣṇu.

3. During the nocturnal visit to Kailāsa, Arjuna sees that the items he had earlier offered in worship to Kṛṣṇa are now by the side of Śiva, thus indicating that the *avatāra* is identical to Śiva as well as Viṣṇu (7.57.61).

4. The teachings of Vyāsa in Chapters 172 and 173 of the *Droṇa*

have been noted as having an apparently sectarian perspective. The statement of 172.89 that Kṛṣṇa is a devotee of Rudra and was born of Rudra–*rudra-saṁbhavaḥ*–may also be taken as showing the identity of Rudra with Viṣṇu, for the overwhelming view of the epic is that Kṛṣṇa is a manifestation of Viṣṇu on earth.

5. The *Nārāyaṇīya* has likewise been noted as displaying a sectarian perspective but here also there are references that indicate a complementary and syncretist view of the two Deities. Paradoxically, despite the Vaiṣṇava bias of the text, it contains the clearest statements indicating the complementarity of the two Deities. In Chapter 328, Kṛṣṇa teaches Arjuna that Brahmā and Śiva are born respectively from the mercy and anger of Aniruddha, one of the quadruple forms of Viṣṇu in Pañcarātra doctrines. Verses 18 and 19 give a brief description of Śiva using the typical iconography noted elsewhere. The relationship to Nārāyaṇa given in verse 19 is obscure–*nārāyaṇātmako jñeyaḥ pāṇḍaveya yuge yuge*–but may be best translated as, 'O Pāṇḍava, it is known that he is Nārāyaṇa's very self age after age.'

The passage then continues in a syncretist vein. When Maheśvara is worshipped, Nārāyaṇa is also worshipped (20). Kṛṣṇa is the soul of all the worlds; therefore he especially worships Rudra who is his own self–*tasmād ātmānam evāgre rudraṁ saṁpūjayāmy aham* (21). If he did not worship Śiva, then no-one would worship Kṛṣṇa (presumably because Śiva is his self) for he sets the standards followed by all others. Such ordinances of worship are worthy of reverence and therefore Kṛṣṇa shows them reverence; one who knows Śiva also knows Kṛṣṇa. Verse 24 states the syncretist view quite explicitly, *rudro nārāyaṇaś caiva sattvaṁ ekaṁ dvidhākṛtam*–Rudra and Nārāyaṇa are one truth appearing to be twofold. This one truth sojourns in this world, manifest in all activities–*loke carati kaunteya vyakta-sthaṁ sarva-karmasu.* It was for this reason that Kṛṣṇa worshipped Śiva to get a son, for he was in effect worshipping his own self–*putrārtham ārādhitavān ātmānam aham ātmanā* (25). It must be understood that Viṣṇu worships only his own self and for this reason Kṛṣṇa chose to worship Rudra.

This passage is clearly an explanation from the Vaiṣṇava perspective of the references found in the epic to Kṛṣṇa worshipping Śiva in order to obtain a son. It is interesting that the *Nārāyaṇīya* does not deny or ignore the incident, but seeks to overcome the implication of Kṛṣṇa's (and hence Nārāyaṇa's) inferiority by resorting to a syncretist theology which explains that because Śiva and Viṣṇu are the same, Kṛṣṇa is worshipping his own self. The presence of this syncretism must also cast some doubt as to the extent to which references from the *Nārāyaṇīya* considered earlier can be adjudged to be truly sectarian. It is also notable from a critical perspective that the *Nārāyaṇīya* thus appears to be later than at least some of the Śaivite passages which highlight Kṛṣṇa's devotion to Śiva.

The syncretist tendency of the *Nārāyaṇīya* is revealed again in the description of the conflict between Śiva and the *ṛṣis* Nara and Nārāyaṇa, a passage that stands in marked contrast to Vyāsa's teachings in Chapter 172 of the *Droṇa* which tell of Nārāyaṇa Ṛṣi worshipping Śiva. After the conflict is over, Nārāyaṇa tells Śiva that they are the same being: 'One who knows you know me; one who follows you follows me. There is no difference between us'–*yas tvāṁ vetti sa māṁ vetti yas tvām anu sa mām anu/nāvayor antaram kiṁcit* (64).

When all the passages of the *Nārāyaṇīya* that discuss the relationship between Viṣṇu and Śiva are thus considered, it is apparent that the overall theology can best be described as a type of sectarian syncretism. There is no doubt that the text here wishes to emphasise the precedence of Nārāyaṇa over Śiva but this is achieved not by dismissing Śiva as a lesser god or as merely one of the pantheon. Instead he is presented as a manifestation of Nārāyaṇa with whom he is identified and yet revealed as a lesser form of the Deity. There is also an implication of the idea that a remote cosmic Deity, here Nārāyaṇa, who contains all things within himself manifests his divinity in various ways in this world. Sometimes he is Viṣṇu and sometimes he is Śiva who are both therefore manifestations of a transcendent Deity.

6. Scheuer, whose thesis rests substantially on the complementarity of the two Deities, finds further support for his case in the text. He cites examples such as the cooperation of Śiva and Viṣṇu (though here Viṣṇu is represented by Vyāsa, a dubious link) in the generation of the one hundred sons of Dhṛtarāṣṭra, in Nārāyaṇa's sanctioning the polyandric marriage, and in Śiva's providing weapons for Arjuna to assist in the mission of the *avatāra.* Thereby he urges that the two Deities work conjointly and that the notion of their antagonism is erroneous. In addition, he stresses the significance of the phrase, *śivāya viṣṇu-rūpāya viṣṇave śiva-rūpine,*

'(My obeisances) to Śiva who is a form of Viṣṇu, to Viṣṇu in his form as Śiva', from Arjuna's prayers to the hunter in Chapter 40 of the *Vana*, and his addressing the Deity there as both Hari and Rudra, though both these references are omitted from the Critical Edition on textual grounds.[36]

(v) Overview

It is apparent from the above analysis that various theological strands are represented in the epic and that on the issue of syncretism or sectarianism it is impossible to state that the text has one specific doctrine. Alongside material that displays a sectarian tendency or expresses a sectarian form of syncretism, there are other passages which give credence to the thesis that the epic regards Viṣṇu and Śiva as two equal aspects of the same Deity, though it is important to note that there is virtually no didactic expression of such a doctrine anywhere in the *Mahābhārata.* The actual teachings of the text are indeed paradoxical and hence the bulk of the conclusions arrived at by Biardeau, Scheuer and Hiltebeitel in this regard are no more than surmises based on their interpretations of the text.

The ideas of these writers may be summarised briefly as follows. Whilst sectarian tendencies are recognised in some sections of the epic, the predominant theology of the *Mahābhārata* recognises a Supreme Deity who manifests himself in two features, one essentially benign and the other uncontrolled and destructive. Hence Biardeau refers to Śiva as, 'l'envers terrible de Viṣṇu'[37] and 'la face terrible de Viṣṇu'.[38] According to Hiltebeitel, Viṣṇu is the dharmic aspect of the Deity, while Śiva is adharmic, destructive and chaotic, though nonetheless essential, for the Supreme Deity includes all aspects of existence within himself.[39] There is thus but one Deity, appearing sometimes as Viṣṇu and sometimes as Śiva, depending on whether the role is dharmic or adharmic; this explains why, despite the prominence of both Deities, Viṣṇu and Śiva appear very rarely together on the epic stage.

Such a brief résumé does no sort of justice to the work of these writers and takes no account of their differing viewpoints and interests. Nonetheless, it does present in essence the basis of their view of the *Mahābhārata*'s theology. In support of this view the following points are to be noted:-

(a) The few passages cited from the epic that present more or less precisely a syncretistic view.

(b) The weakness on text-critical grounds of theories based on the notion of interpolations leaves a syncretistic perspective as the only possible alternative. It is a logical surmise from the evidence available.

(c) The alternating supremacy in accordance with the dharmic or adharmic nature of a particular episode in the narrative is persuasive though not conclusive.

(d) The fact that later Hinduism incorporates a syncretistic view of Śiva and Viṣṇu is a factor that should not be ignored for antecedents of almost all the major tendencies in medieval Hindu thought are to be found in the epics.

Against the syncretist view it must be noted,

(a) The presence of sectarianism and outright contradiction in certain passages cannot be denied and hence a syncretist view cannot hold for the text as a whole.

(b) If there is a complex theology contained within the epic based on two opposing and yet complementary features of one Deity it is surprising that it remains unstated in any truly didactic sense.

(c) Although the epic characterises Viṣṇu as primarily benign and Śiva as the destroyer, thus indicating a certain complementarity, it must also be noted that each Deity is described as having both features without any reference being made to the other. In the *Gītā*, Viṣṇu shows himself to be the fierce destroyer of the worlds, whilst Kṛṣṇa describes Śiva as having two features, one fearsome and one benign–*ghorā-manyāṁ śiva-manyāṁ te tanū* (13.146.3).

(d) Medieval Hinduism also embodies conflicts and oppositions of a wholly sectarian nature between votaries of Śiva and Viṣṇu. If we are to look for antecedents within the epic, then this must apply equally to the sectarian as to the syncretist.

The clear indication is that the *Mahābhārata* embodies differing theological perspectives. Certain passages have Viṣṇu as the Supreme Deity with Śiva as his subordinate, whilst in others the roles are reversed. In the narrative there is a strong suggestion that Viṣṇu and Śiva work together through their different divine natures to perpetuate the cosmic order and that they are both manifestations of a less personal God who is all-powerful and all-pervasive. The text is complex and it is often impossible to disentangle the varying nuances of theistic thought that it offers but it is apparent that antecedents for both the sectarian and syncretist tendencies of later Hindu theism may be found in the epic.

6. Epic Monotheism

(i) Introduction

In this section I propose to examine the question of whether epic theology is monotheistic. Again, as a preliminary, one must recall that the text contains expressions of various kinds of theism, with the Supreme Deity sometimes appearing as a leader of the pantheon and sometimes transcending any such role in this world. The question is therefore whether any major strand of epic theism is monotheistic. The problem stems from the fact that the term 'monotheism' has become culture-bound to the extent that it is accepted as referring only to Judaeo-Christian or Islamic theism. If, however, a broader definition is allowed, any form of theism which postulates one Supreme Deity who creates and controls this world whilst remaining aloof and personally transcendent to its fluctuations may be regarded as monotheistic. It is on the basis of this definition that the issue of epic monotheism will be discussed. The question to be addressed is whether the epic teaches the existence of one God who is the creator and controller of all things and yet exists beyond them; if this is found to be the case, then it is surely acceptable to speak of 'epic monotheism' and also 'Hindu monotheism'.

The God of the *Mahābhārata* displays both a personality and a form. The epic teaches that this world is eternal but subject to repeated creations and annihilations. Each of these creations is set in motion by the action of Viṣṇu and the secondary creator Brahmā. The creation myth is recounted several times in the text with only minor variations of detail. During the time of dissolution Viṣṇu lies sleeping on the waters on his snake-bed. To inaugurate a new creation, Brahmā appears from a lotus which grows from the navel of the recumbent Deity, but his work is hindered by two *asuras* who steal the Vedas from Brahmā. In distress, Brahmā prays to his creator who kills the *asuras* and restores the Vedas to him. The process of creation then begins, enacted first by Brahmā and then by the *prajāpatis* he creates.

Elsewhere, numerous references assert that not only does the Deity create the universe but that he is also active in sustaining the order of existence that the creative process sets in motion. As noted earlier, the doctrine of *avatāra* rests on the idea of divine action in this world and on one level the *Mahābhārata* tells the story of the Deity's intervention in history to sustain the cosmic order, acting as both Śiva and Viṣṇu to achieve this end. Mārkaṇḍeya refers to Viṣṇu as Janārdana with broad eyes and yellow garments, before stating that he is the creator, the transformer and the maker of the existence of all beings–*eṣa kartā vikartā ca sarva-bhāvana-bhūta-kṛt* (3.186.14). He is the creator, but he is not created–*eṣa kartā na kriyate* (16). Later he prays to Viṣṇu as the one who is the creator of all types of beings:

> *tvayā deva prajāḥ sarvāḥ sa-devāsura-mānavāḥ*
> *sthāvarāṇi ca bhūtāni jaṅgamāni tathaiva ca*
> *brahma vedāś ca vedyaṁ ca tvayā sṛṣṭaṁ mahādyute*
>
> 'O Lord, all living beings, the gods, *asuras*, and men, the moving and non-moving beings, the divine Vedas, and all things that can be known have been created by you, O radiant being.' (3.192.11)

Instructing Dhṛtrāṣtra, Saṁjaya states that Janārdana, the Supreme Person, the soul of all beings, conducts the movement of the earth, the sky and the heavens as if for sport:

> *pṛthivīṁ cāntarikṣaṁ ca divaṁ ca puruṣottamaḥ*
> *viceṣṭayati bhūtātmā krīḍann iva janārdanaḥ*
> (5.66.10)

The progression of time, and the succession of *yugas* does not go on automatically, for it is Keśava who controls all things.

> *kāla-cakraṁ jagac-cakraṁ yuga-cakraṁ ca keśavaḥ*
> *ātma-yogena bhagavān parivartayate 'niśam*
>
> *kālasya ca hi mṛtyoś ca jaṅgama-sthāvarasya ca*
> *īśate bhagavān ekaḥ satyam etad bravīmi te*
>
> 'By his own potency, the exalted one, Keśava, sustains the wheel of time, the wheel of the cosmos and the cycle of the *yugas* in their constant rotations.

This is the truth that I speak to you; this exalted one is he who alone controls time, death and all moving and non-moving beings.' (5.66.12-13)

Similar expressions of the power of the Deity are found throughout the epic. On the battlefield after Droṇa is slain, Yudhiṣṭhira glorifies Kṛṣṇa as the creator of all the worlds–*sraṣṭāraṁ sarva-lokānām*, who has no beginning or end–*anādi-nidhanaṁ devam.* Only because of his mercy has the universe emerged into light from the darkness of chaos (7.124.12-13). The pronounced theism of the *Bhagavad-gītā* also contains notable expressions of the Deity's complete control over this world.

mattaḥ parataraṁ nānyat kiñcid asti dhanañjaya
mayi sarvam idaṁ protaṁ sūtre maṇi-gaṇā iva

'There is nothing beyond me, O Dhanañjaya. The totality of this world rests upon me, as jewels are held in place by a thread. (7.7)

ahaṁ sarvasya prabhavo mattaḥ sarvaṁ pravartate
iti matvā bhajante māṁ budhā bhāva-samanvitāḥ

'I am the cause of all things; it is from me that all things come into being. Knowing this, living beings endowed with wisdom worship me.' (10.8)

(ii) The Deity's Transcendence of this World

The position of the Deity, be it Śiva or Viṣṇu, as being completely dominant over his creation is thus established by numerous references, only a small fraction of which have been cited above. This control is not like that of a pantheon of gods for it is the prerogative of one being only and his power can never be inhibited by any form of restraint. The crucial point here is that unlike the various lesser gods who appear in the narrative, the Supreme Deity is aloof and totally beyond the circumstances of this world. Chapter 8, 17-22, of the *Bhagavad-gītā* describes the repeated manifestations and withdrawals of the world as being the days and nights of Brahmā. The domain of the Deity, however, remains unaffected,

paras tasmāt tu bhāvo 'nyo 'vyakto 'vyaktāt sanātanaḥ
yaḥ sa sarveṣu bhūteṣu naśyatsu na vinaśyati

avyakto 'kṣara ity uktas tam āhuḥ paramāṁ gatim
yaṁ prāpya na nivartante tad dhāma paramaṁ mama

'But beyond this world that becomes unmanifest there is another unmanifest domain that is ever-existing. At the time when all living beings are withdrawn, that domain is not destroyed.

It is described as unmanifest and unchanging and as the highest goal. Having attained it, one does not appear again. That is my supreme abode.' (8.20-21)

The same point is made in Chapter 9:

na ca māṁ tāni karmāṇi nibadhnanti dhanañjaya
udāsīnavad āsīnam asaktaṁ teṣu karmasu

'And yet all these activities of mine can never affect me, O Dhanañjaya. I am situated as if neutral, unattached to any activity. (9.9)

Although he intervenes in this world, he is not a part of it and hence he is known as the one who is not created. This point, made by Mārkaṇḍeya as noted above (3.186.14), is confirmed by Saṁjaya who describes Viṣṇu as *kartāram akṛtaṁ devam*, and by Bhīṣma who asserts that he is beyond and above the five elements of matter–*pañcānāṁ parataḥ sthitaḥ* (12.47.55), and that although appearing in the three worlds he is beyond them–*namas te triṣu lokeṣu namas te paratas triṣu* (12.51.4). Again in the *Nārāyaṇīya*, the Deity himself instructs Nārada that Vāsudeva, the soul of all beings, is beyond the attributes of this world. He cannot be perceived by the senses (12.326.20) and none of the *guṇas* of which this world is comprised can affect him–*sattvaṁ rajas tamaś caiva na guṇās taṁ bhajanti vai* (21). He is unborn, everlasting and eternal, free from the *guṇas* and indivisible–*ajo nityaḥ śāśvataś ca nirguṇo niṣkalas tathā* (22). The passage here is equating the Deity with the *puruṣa*, or soul within, but by so doing it makes the point that Vāsudeva is beyond the attributes that characterise living beings in this world, including the pantheon of gods.

(iii) The Vedic Pantheon

From a superficial perspective it might appear that epic monotheism is called into question by the designation of both Viṣṇu and Śiva as the Supreme Deity, by the different forms assumed by Viṣṇu and by the acceptance of a pantheon of gods who act to sustain the order of the cosmos. The first two of these points have been discussed earlier and it has been shown that they are congruent with a monotheist perspective. In epic theology the pantheon of gods has been very obviously relegated to a position of subordination to Viṣṇu and Śiva and the henotheism detected by Max Müller in Vedic thought has largely been replaced by epic monotheism, though in certain passages it may still be recognised.

Indra now has to seek the aid of Brahmā, Viṣṇu and Śiva in order to preserve the position of the gods and withstand the *asuras*. This limited potency of the gods is implicit in the *Mahābhārata*'s doctrine of *avatāra* in which Viṣṇu manifests himself when the gods have lost control. Similarly, the subordination of the gods to Śiva is apparent from the stories of the destruction of three cities and of Dakṣa's *yajña*, and the punishment of the five Indras that explains Draupadī's polyandric marriage. Müller's idea of henotheism was derived from the tendency of the Vedic hymns to glorify each of the gods of the pantheon in turn in a manner that seemed to elevate each Deity in succession to a position of supremacy. The *Mahābhārata* represents a clear progression from Vedic theology. The recurring panegyrics constantly stress not just the control of the Deity over this universe but also the absolute distinction of the Supreme Deity from the pantheon and the subordination of all other gods to him. In Chapter 64 of the *Bhīṣma*, wherein Bhīṣma recounts the wisdom of various sages regarding Viṣṇu, this distinction is made apparent. The sages know Viṣṇu as the master of the Sādhya gods, the one who is the lord of the god of the gods (perhaps Brahmā)–*sādhyānām api devānāṁ deva-deveśvaraḥ prabhuḥ* (2), and the one who establishes Indra in his position–*tvaṁ śakraṁ sthāpayitā* (4). According to Yudhiṣṭhira, the conquests of Indra are due only to the grace of Viṣṇu, an assertion that expands upon rather than contradicts the view of the *Ṛgveda*,

tvat-prasādād dhṛṣīkeśa śakraḥ sura-gaṇeśvaraḥ
trai-lokya-vijayaṁ śrīmān prāptavān raṇa-mūrdhaṇi

> 'O Hṛṣīkeśa, it is only by your grace that Śakra, the leader of the host of the gods, who goes before them in battle, became endowed with good fortune and gained conquest over the three worlds.' (7.124.9)

Elsewhere, when Viṣṇu is described as the creator of the cosmos, it is made clear that while he is aloof and beyond it, the gods themselves are a part of the creation. Thus Nārāyaṇa tells Mārkaṇḍeya:

> *sṛṣṭvā deva-mānuṣyāṁś ca gandharvoraga-rākṣasān*
> *sthāvarāṇi ca bhūtāni saṁharāmy ātma-māyayā*
>
> 'Having created the gods, men, *gandharvas*, serpents and *rākṣasaṣ*, I then destroy all moving and non-moving beings by my own potency.' (3.187.29)

In the *Bhagavad-gītā* Kṛṣṇa tells Arjuna,

> *na me viduḥ sura-gaṇāḥ prabhavaṁ na maharṣayaḥ*
> *aham ādir hi devānāṁ maharṣīṇāṁ ca sarvaśaḥ*
>
> 'Neither the hosts of the gods, nor the great sages can know my origin, for I am the source of all the gods and great sages.' (10.2)

In the *Nārāyaṇīya*, the Deity explains his dominion over the gods to Nārada:

> *deva-kāryād api mune pitṛ-kāryaṁ viśiṣyate*
> *devānāṁ ca pitṝṇāṁ ca pitā hy eko 'ham āditaḥ*
>
> 'Rituals performed for the ancestors are superior to those done for the gods, O wise one. From the very beginning, I have been the only father of both- the gods and the ancestors.' (12.326.55)

Citations such as these demonstrate the progression from polytheism to monotheism that epic theology exhibits. Myths displaying polytheistic tendencies persist in the epic but they stand out as being incongruous with the prevailing view of the text. There are certain other passages in which gods from the pantheon are glorified, notably Agni (1.231.22-29, 223.7-19),

Skanda (3.213-221) and Sūrya (3.3.18-33), but detailed comparison between these passages and those extolling Viṣṇu and Śiva reveals notable differences of emphasis. Although the laudations are typically effusive, they fall short of elevating the god to the status of a monotheistic or even henotheistic Deity. This difference of emphasis reveals that whatever the merits of Müller's notion of henotheism in the Vedic hymns, it cannot be applied to the theology of the *Mahābhārata.*

(iv) Śaivite Monotheism

The passages cited above as illustration of epic monotheism have been selected from sections of the text that tend towards Vaiṣṇavism but attention must also be drawn to the monotheism of passages which present Śiva as the Supreme Deity. A few examples must suffice here to demonstrate the point. During the nocturnal visit Kṛṣṇa and Arjuna pray to Śiva as *viśvātmane viśva-sṛje*–the soul and creator of the universe, *bhūtānāṁ prabhave*–the origin of the living beings, *prajānāṁ pataye . . . viśvasya pataye mahatāṁ pataye*–the master of all beings, the master of the universe, the master of all great things (7.57.54-56). At the end of the *Droṇa,* Vyāsa describes Śiva as follows:

> *prajāpatīnāṁ prathamaṁ taijasaṁ puruṣaṁ vibhum*
> *bhuvanaṁ bhūr bhuvaṁ devaṁ sarva-lokeśvaraṁ prabhum*
>
> '(Śiva) is the original generator of living beings, the almighty one who is filled with energy. He is the earth, the heavens and the sky, the Deity, the lord of all worlds, the master.' (7.173.9)

The *ṛṣi* Maṅkaṇaka prays:

> *tvayā sṛṣṭam idam viśvaṁ vadantīha manīṣiṇaḥ*
> *tvām eva sarvaṁ viśati punar eva yuga-kṣaye*
>
> *devair api na śakyas tvaṁ parijñātuṁ kuto mayā*
> *tvayi sarve sma dṛśyante surā brahmādayo 'nagha*
>
> 'The wise say that all this is created by you, and that at the end of the age everything enters you once more.
>
> When the gods themselves are unable to comprehend

> you, how is it possible for me? Indeed, O untainted one, all the gods with Brahmā at their head are to be seen in you.' (9.37.44-45)

These references, characteristic of passages in which Śiva is extolled, demonstrate that epic monotheism has Śiva as well as Viṣṇu as its object.

(v) Conclusion

It is reasonable to assert on the basis of the above discussion that the major strand of epic theism is monotheistic. This assertion rests on a broad understanding of monotheism that is not defined by the notions of Judeao-Christian or Islamic theology. The *Mahābhārata,* despite the differing perspectives of different passages, presents a Deity who is the one supreme being who creates and sustains all aspects of the cosmic order whilst remaining transcendent to its fluctuations and its recurring cycle of creation and dissolution. Because epic theism conforms to this definition it is correct to refer to the text as espousing a monotheistic theology.

7. Additional Features of Epic Theism

(i) The Catur-Vyūha, God in Four Features

The concept of the expansion of the Deity into four features is one that is characteristic of Pañcarātric Vaiṣṇavism, expounded in the *Saṁhitās* that appeared several centuries after the *Mahābhārata.* Within the epic this doctrine is presented in detail only in the *Nārāyaṇīya,* though there are two other references in the Critical Edition; it is notably absent from the *Bhagavad-gītā.* In the *Nārāyaṇīya,* in 12.326, the *kṣetrajña* who is the soul of all living beings, is referred to as Vāsudeva (31). The individual living being, commonly known as the *jīva,* is another form of the Deity, this time known as Saṁkarṣaṇa or Śeṣa (35). The mental faculty in living entities is known as Pradyumna (36), while the form of the Deity from whom the universe comes into being is known as Aniruddha (37). Thus in the creation stories it is Aniruddha who generates Brahmā from his navel and destroys Madhu and Kaitabha. In Chapter 332.13-17, the way salvation is attained is described in terms of passing through each of these four forms before attaining final *mokṣa* by entering into Vāsudeva who is the *kṣetrajña.*

This doctrine of the *catur-vyūha* is a complex theological construct closely linked to the theistic Sāṁkhya of epic Pañcarātra. It is not, however, a prominent feature of *Mahābhārata* thought and is significant only in the *Nārāyaṇīya* which is doctrinally distinct from the epic as a whole. Elsewhere, in the prayers of Brahmā recounted by Bhīṣma to Duryodhana (6.61.42-70), we find a brief reference to the *catur-vyūha*. In requesting that the Deity appear on earth, Brahmā refers to him as Vāsudeva who generates Saṁkarṣaṇa from himself, Pradyumna from Saṁkarṣaṇa and Aniruddha from Pradyumna. Aniruddha is known as Viṣṇu and it is from him that Brahmā is born (64-66). In the *Anuśāsana*, Bhīṣma tells Yudhiṣṭhira that Kṛṣṇa is Vāsudeva who becomes Saṁkarṣaṇa, Pradyumna and Aniruddha, but without elaborating on the idea (13.143.37) and in the *Sahasra-nāma-stotram, catur-vyūha* is included as a name of Viṣṇu. It is thus hard to agree with van Buitenen when he writes concerning the *catur-vyūha* that, ". . . in many places in the epic, also outside the *Mokṣa-dharma* section, references to it may be found."[40] Outside the *Nārāyaṇīya*, which is a part of the *Mokṣa-dharma*, only the two references cited above from the *Bhīṣma* and the *Anuśāsana* are included in the Critical Edition. It is thus reasonable to conclude that this idea lies outside the major themes of epic theism.

(ii) The All-Pervasive Aspect of the Deity

Epic monotheism goes beyond its stress on the supremacy of Viṣṇu and Śiva by attempting to ascribe the all-pervasive nature of the Upaniṣadic *brahman* to the personal Supreme Deity it postulates. Here, however, one must be wary in accepting a simplistic view of the historical progression of ideas. Whilst there can be little doubt that epic theology is based to some extent on Upaniṣadic doctrine, it must also be noted that the notion of Viṣṇu as an all-pervasive god is expressed overtly in the *Ṛgveda*. Gonda stresses that the all-pervasive aspect of Viṣṇu is derived not from his being identified with the concept of *brahman*, but from the Vedic myth of his covering the worlds with three strides.[41] It may well be that the reason why Viṣṇu was elevated to the status of Supreme Deity was this cosmic dimension to the god as he is presented in Vedic mythology.

Within the epic, the Deity is not only described as the creator, destroyer and absolute controller of all existence, but equally it is presented that he is all things; he is the all-pervasive reality. The four displays of the *viśva-rūpa*—to Arjuna in the *Gītā*, to the Kauravas in the *Udyoga*, to Nārada in the *Nārāyaṇīya* and to Uttaṅka in *Aśvamedhika*—illustrate this point in a graphic fashion. The best-known of these is, of course, that contained in Chapter 11 of the *Bhagavad-gītā*. After Kṛṣṇa has explained to Arjuna in Chapter 10 that he is to be recognised in the glories of creation, the latter responds by requesting that this be made manifest before his eyes. Kṛṣṇa assents and grants his friend the divine vision through which he will be able to perceive directly the fullness of the Deity's awesome presence (8).

The manifestation witnessed by Arjuna is described as the supreme, most majestic form–*paramaṁ rūpam aiśvaram* (9)–with numerous mouths, eyes, ornaments, weapons, garlands, articles of clothing and fragrant ointments, spreading unlimitedly in all directions (10-11) with an effulgence as dazzling as a thousand suns (12). The mystery of the entire cosmos being contained within the body of the Deity is revealed in the next verse:

> *tatraika-sthaṁ jagat-kṛtsnaṁ pravibhaktam anekadhā*
> *apaśyad deva-devasya śarīre pāṇḍavas tadā*
>
> 'The son of Pāṇḍu then beheld the entire universe with all its manifold varieties situated in one place within the body of the god of gods.' (11.13)

Chapter 11 is exceptional in the *Gītā* because it contains very little by way of instruction from Kṛṣṇa to Arjuna. For the most part it consists of prayers from the awe-struck Arjuna describing the divine form displayed by Kṛṣṇa. These prayers are significant in revealing that the destruction of the Kauravas is certain because it is the will of the Deity, and also in describing Kṛṣṇa's universal, all-pervasive nature. Immediately, Arjuna proclaims that within the form of the Lord he sees all the gods, including Brahmā, as well as all other living beings–*paśyāmi devāṁs tava deva dehe sarvāṁs tathā bhūta-viśeṣa-saṅghān* (15). The Deity is now revealed as infinite, without beginning middle or end (16.19); hence all the directions of the universe, from the earth to the heavens, are pervaded by him alone–*dyāv āpṛthivyor idam antaraṁ hi vyāptaṁ tvayaikena diśaś ca sarvāḥ* (20).

Arjuna then describes the fear and awe invoked in the gods by this manifestation, impelling them to surrender and pray for mercy (21-22). Arjuna is likewise filled with fear when he perceives within the *viśva-rūpa* all the warriors now assembled on the battlefield being destroyed and consumed by the terrible teeth of the Deity (23-31). He is the ancient, original Deity, the resting place of this world, which is pervaded by him in his unlimited form–*tvayā tataṁ viśvam ananta-rūpa* (38). He is all the gods, he has unlimited energy and immeasurable power; he covers and includes everything and therefore he is indeed all things–*sarvaṁ samāpnoṣi tato 'si sarvaḥ* (40). Arjuna finally repents of his previous familiarity with Kṛṣṇa, when he regarded him as a friend and begs that the *viśva-rūpa* be withdrawn and replaced by the familiar form of Kṛṣṇa.

The drama of Chapter 11 of the *Gītā* indicates that behind the personality of Kṛṣṇa and perhaps the iconographic figure of Viṣṇu which the *Gītā* substantially ignores the Deity is the absolute reality that incorporates all things. That this reality is recognised as the *brahman* of the *Upaniṣads* is indicated by Arjuna in Chapter 10 when he calls upon Kṛṣṇa to reveal himself, describing him as:

> *paraṁ brahma paraṁ dhāma pavitraṁ paramaṁ bhavān*
> *puruṣaṁ śāśvataṁ divyam ādi-devam ajaṁ vibhum*
>
> 'You are the Supreme Brahman, the ultimate abode, the most pure; you are the ancient divine person, the original Deity, unborn and mighty.' (10.12)

Thus Viṣṇu may be referred to both as the origin of all things and also as being or containing all things. A citation from the *Anuśāsana* succinctly demonstrates this:

> *śubhāśubhaṁ sthāvaraṁ jaṅgamaṁ ca*
> *viṣvaksenāt sarvam etat pratīhi*
> *yad vartate yac ca bhaviṣyatīha*
> *sarvam etat keśavaṁ tvaṁ pratīhi*
>
> 'You should know that all this world, the pure and the impure, the moving and non-moving beings, come from the Lord whose powers spread in all directions. And you should know that whatever exists, and whatever will come to be, all this is Keśava himself.' (13.143.41)

Here the references to the Deity in both the ablative and accusative cases are indicative of two theological concepts—everything comes from Viśvaksena and everything is Keśava, the phrase *sarvam etat keśavam* being resonant of the Upaniṣadic *sarvaṁ khalv idaṁ brahma*–everything is indeed Brahman.

The idea of the Deity not only generating but actually pervading and being the entire cosmos is found throughout the *Mahābhārata,* especially where the nature of Viṣṇu is being either praised or expounded upon. Where Nārāyaṇa instructs Mārkaṇḍeya about himself, he appears in the form of a child and reveals to the sage the entire universe with all its varieties contained within his body (3.186.92f). He then describes his own nature indicating that all creation is a part of himself. Fire is his mouth, the earth his feet, the sun and the moon his eyes, the sky spreading in all directions is his body, and the wind is situated in his mind (3.187.7). The stars seen in the sky are his different forms (18), all the sources of jewels, the oceans and the four directions are his clothing, his bed, and his abode (19). Lust, anger, joy, fear and delusion are also different forms of the Deity (20).

Instructing Duryodhana, Bhīṣma refers to the all-pervasive feature of Viṣṇu, citing the words of those who undertake penance:

> *śirasā te divaṁ vyāptaṁ bāhubhyāṁ pṛthivī dhṛtā*
> *jaṭharaṁ te trayo lokāḥ puruṣo 'si sanātanaḥ*
>
> 'You pervade the heavens with your head and support the earth with your two arms. The three worlds are the innards of your body; you are the eternal self.' (6.64.7)

References of this type are common in the epic and clearly represent a prevailing mode of thought regarding the Deity. Exactly how such concepts are to be reconciled into a theological system does, however, present problems that the text does not attempt to work through. Just how it is that Nārāyaṇa is to be recognised as present throughout his creation is a question the text does not explore. Such ideas appear to be based on the notion of the cosmic man presented in the *Puruṣa-sūkta* hymn found in Book 10 of the *Ṛgveda.* The *puruṣa* described therein has been adopted by epic theism and his all-pervasive attributes applied to the Deity Viṣṇu, who was already known to the *Ṛgveda* as the one who covers all the worlds with his three strides. It is also apparent that the Deity is recognised as a personification of *brahman*, the underlying spiritual reality postulated in the philosophical thought of Upaniṣadic Vedānta, as when Kuntī prays to Kṛṣṇa, *tvaṁ mahad-brahma tvayi sarvaṁ pratiṣṭhitam*–you are *brahman*, the supreme; all things rest upon you (5.88.103).

(iii) The All-Pervasive Deity of the *Bhagavad-gītā*

In Chapters 7, 9 and 10, Kṛṣṇa identifies himself with various aspects of the creation:

> *raso 'ham apsu kaunteya prabhāsmi śaśi-sūryayoḥ*
> *praṇavaḥ sarva-vedeṣu śabdaḥ khe pauruṣaṁ nṛṣu*
>
> *puṇyo gandhaḥ pṛthivyāṁ ca tejaś cāsmi vibhāvasau*
> *jīvanaṁ sarva-bhūteṣu tapaś cāsmi tapasviṣu*
>
> *bījaṁ māṁ sarva-bhūtānāṁ viddhi pārtha sanātanam*
> *buddhir buddhimatām asmi tejas tejasvinām aham*
>
> *balaṁ balavatāṁ cāhaṁ kāma-rāga-vivarjitam*
> *dharmāviruddho bhūteṣu kāmo 'smi bharatarṣabha*
>
> *ye caiva sāttvikā bhāvā rājasās tamasāś ca ye*
> *matta eveti tān viddhi na tv ahaṁ teṣu te mayi*
>
> *tribhir guṇamayair bhāvair ebhiḥ sarvam idaṁ jagat*
> *mohitaṁ nābhijānāti māṁ ebhyaḥ param avyayam*

'I am taste in water, O son of Kuntī, and I am the radiance of the sun and the moon. I am the vibration *oṁ* in all the Vedas, sound in space and expertise in men.

I am the pure scent in earth and I am the heat in fire. I am that which gives life in all living beings, and I am austerity in ascetics.

You should know, O son of Pṛthā, that the eternal origin of all living beings is me. I am the intelligence of the intelligent and I am the power of the powerful.

I am the strength of the strong devoid of lust and passion. O mightiest of the Bhāratas, I am also lust in living beings when it does not contravene *dharma*.

> You should know that all these states of being, whether they fall under the *guṇas* of *sattva, rajas* or *tamas* are from me; but I am not in them, they are in me.
>
> Held in delusion by such states of being that rest on the three *guṇas*, all this world does not comprehend me, who am immutable and above all of them. (7.8-13)

This difficult passage appears to express the immanence of the Deity. He is not a remote creator, but is to be recognised as pervading his creation; the energy cannot be entirely distinguished from its energetic source. Here the crucial statement is in verse 12 which reasserts the position of the Deity as the origin out of which all things have come–*matta eveti tān viddhi*; he personally is not within the created manifestations–*na tv ahaṁ teṣu*–but they are contained within his all-embracing existence–*te mayi.*

Chapter 9 takes up the subject once again:

> *mayā tatam idaṁ sarvaṁ jagad avyakta-mūrtinā*
> *mat-sthāni sarva-bhūtāni na cāhaṁ teṣu avasthitaḥ*
>
> *na ca mat-sthāni bhūtāni paśya me yogam aiśvaram*
> *bhūta-bhṛn na ca bhūta-stho mamātmā bhūta-bhāvanaḥ*
>
> 'All of this is pervaded by me whose form is not manifest. All beings are situated in me and I am not situated in them.
>
> And yet the living beings are not situated in me; look upon this as my mystical splendour. My very self is that which sustains and provides for all beings and yet is not situated in that existence. (9.4-5)

Again the passage is obscure, not least because the word *bhūta* may refer either to living beings or more generally to whatever exists or has come into being. I have chosen the former because of the reference to *bhūta-grāma* in 8 which is used elsewhere (8.19) to indicate the host of living beings. The text itself admits to its own paradox by asserting first that all beings are situated in the Deity–*mat-sthāni sarva-bhūtāni*–and then immediately contradicting this statement–*na ca mat-sthāni bhūtāni,* thus telling us that all beings are in Kṛṣṇa and yet at the same time they are not in Kṛṣṇa, explaining this contradiction by reference to his greatness and mystery. Kṛṣṇa states clearly that he pervades all creation through what he describes as his unmanifest form–*avyakta-mūrti*, again an obscure phrase.

It is possible that the notion of an all-pervasive Supreme Being rests on the understanding of the identity of the Deity with the individual soul, discussed below. In Chapter 2, Kṛṣṇa tells Arjuna that the soul is found everywhere–*sarva-gataḥ* (2.24)-and hence if the Deity is identified with the self, then as such he may be considered all-pervasive. It would appear, however, that what is being discussed here extends beyond this and that both the passage from Chapter 9 and that from Chapter 7 are linked to the manifestation of the *viśva-rūpa* and to Mārkaṇḍeya's vision of the cosmos within the body of the Deity discussed earlier. The displays of the *viśva-rūpa* reveal all living beings within the body of the Deity and this is congruent with the statement, *te mayi*–they are in me (7.12)–used by Kṛṣṇa when referring to the states of existence under the three *guṇas*.

In Chapter 9, Kṛṣṇa asserts that all this world is pervaded by him in his *avyakta-mūrti*, unmanifest form. Here I take the phrase *avyakta-mūrti* to refer to the *viśva-rūpa*, unmanifest in that it cannot be perceived unless the Deity chooses to make the revelation by giving divine vision. In 9.6, Kṛṣṇa explains the way in which the living beings are situated in him by using a metaphor:

> *yathākāśa-sthito nityaṁ vāyuḥ sarvatra-go mahān*
> *tathā sarvāṇi bhūtāni mat-sthānīty upadhāraya*
>
> 'As the mighty wind that goes everywhere is always situated in space, so it is, you should understand, that all beings are situated in me.'

The wind, or air, is found everywhere, but still it is kept within the confines of space. In the same way the living beings are omnipresent and yet contained within the *avyakta-mūrti* of the Deity. This concept is revealed directly to Arjuna in Chapter 11, causing him to exclaim, *paśyāmi devāṁs tava deva dehe sarvāṁs tathā bhūta-viśeṣa-saṅghān*–O Lord, I see all the gods in your body, along with all the different living beings (11.15).

In Chapter 10, Arjuna asks Kṛṣṇa to describe his own divine glories–*vaktum arhasy aśeṣeṇa divyā hy ātma-vibhūtayaḥ* (16)–and in what forms of existence he should fix his mind on Kṛṣṇa–*keṣu keṣu ca bhāveṣu cintyo 'si bhagavan mayā* (17). Kṛṣṇa responds to this inquiry by reciting twenty verses[42] in which he states that he is to be recognised in the most outstanding example of any category of existence. A few examples illustrate this:

> *ādityānām ahaṁ viṣṇur jyotiṣāṁ ravir aṁśumān*
> *marīcir marutām asmi nakṣatrāṇām ahaṁ śaśī*
>
> *vedānāṁ sāma-vedo 'smi devānām asmı vāsavaḥ*
> *indriyāṇāṁ manaś cāsmi bhūtānām asmi cetanā*
>
> *rudrāṇāṁ śaṁkaraś cāsmi vitteśo yakṣa-rakṣasām*
> *vasūnāṁ pāvakaś cāsmi meruḥ śikhariṇām aham*

> 'Of the sons of Aditi I am Viṣṇu, of luminous objects the radiant sun. Of the Maruts I am Marīci and of stars I am the moon.
> Of the Vedas I am the *Sāma-veda* and of the gods I am Indra. Of the senses I am the mind and of existent objects I am consciousness.
> Of the Rudras I am Śaṁkara and of *yakṣas* and *rākṣasas* I am the Lord of Wealth (Kuvera). Of the Vasus I am the Fire-god and of mountain peaks I am Meru.' (10.21-23)

These verses are problematic, for if the Deity is everything why does he claim identity only with the great and the glorious? In a similar manner in Chapter 7, he claims to be lust only when it does not contravene *dharma.* It may be that what Kṛṣṇa is teaching Arjuna is not so much a doctrine as a method of conceiving of the Deity. It must be recalled that Arjuna's question, *keṣu keṣu ca bhāveṣu cintyo 'si bhagavan mayā,* is practical rather than doctrinal–"How should I conceive of you?", rather than, "What is the nature of your existence?"–and to this Kṛṣṇa replies by saying, "Whenever you see any of the exceptional glories of this creation, then recognise me in them."

The theological doctrine underlying this recital is clarified to some extent at the conclusion of Chapter 10 and the beginning of Chapter 11. The connection between Chapters 10 and 11 is clear, for the display of the *viśva-rūpa* is in response to Arjuna's request to behold an actual manifestation of the glory of the Deity imparted verbally to him in Chapter 10. Therefore the recitation of Chapter 10 must be taken as a description of the all-pervasive feature of Viṣṇu revealed in the *viśva-rūpa*. The final verses of Chapter 10 also provide some elucidation of what has gone before:

> *yac cāpi sarva-bhūtānāṁ bījaṁ tad aham arjuna*
> *na tad asti vinā yat syān mayā bhūtaṁ carācaram*
>
> *nānto 'sti mama divyānāṁ vibhūtīnāṁ parantapa*
> *eṣa tūddeśataḥ prokto vibhūter vistaro mayā*
>
> *yad yad vibhūtimat sattvaṁ śrīmad ūrjitam eva vā*
> *tat tad evāvagaccha tvaṁ mama tejo 'ṁśa-sambhavam*
>
> *athavā bahunaitena kiṁ jñātena tavārjuna*
> *viṣṭabhyāham idaṁ kṛtsnam ekāṁśena sthito jagat*
>
> 'And I am that which is the seed of all beings, Arjuna. There is no being, moving or non-moving, that can exist without me.
>
> There is no end to my divine glories, O scorcher of the foe. Whatever has been described by me about my glory should be taken as examples just for instruction.
>
> Whatever glorious, opulent or mighty existence there is, you should understand that it arises from a part of my energy.
>
> But what purpose is there, Arjuna, in your knowing of these things at such length as this. I am fixed as the one who holds in place this entire universe through a single part of myself.' (10.39-42)

It is significant that here Kṛṣṇa returns to describing himself as the source of emanations in relation to the living beings. In the preceding verses he has referred to himself as being the glories of creation, using the words *asmi* and *aham*, but in verse 38, he says he is the origin–*bījaṁ mām*. This dual understanding of the Deity as being both the source of the emanation and the emanation itself is found throughout the epic, indicating that the energy and the energetic are in one sense identical. The identity is not absolute. Verses 41 and 42 make it clear that all creation comes into being from a part of his energy and hence is identical with him, but equally the existence of the Deity includes and goes beyond the creation. This I take as the explanation of the paradox in 9.4-5. All beings are Kṛṣṇa but he is not circumscribed by that assertion; the circumscription applies only to the living beings and to creation which are nothing but the Deity.

The concept of the identity of the Deity with creation is not confined to passages that extol the divinity of Viṣṇu, and the same idea in relation to Śiva is expressed in virtually identical terms in 7.172.61, 13.14.154f, 13.15.41 and 13.146.12-19. Epic monotheism thus offers a Deity who is both beyond this world and yet immanent within it. It is a monotheism that incorporates the monist notions of the *Upaniṣads* in a manner that is substantially alien to Western theism, with the possible exception of certain medieval Islamic theologians.[43] God is not a watchmaker remote from his work; as the doctrine of *avatāra* reveals he is continually active restoring the harmony of creation and he is also present as the creation itself which, as Rāmānuja urges, is both metaphorically and in reality the body of the Deity.

(iv) The Identity of the Deity with the *Ātman*

Where *bhakti* is associated with the values of *nivṛtti* its doctrines are closely linked to those of Sāṁkhya as is evident from both the *Gītā* and the *Nārāyaṇīya.* Epic Sāṁkhya defines the individual self, or *ātman,* in terms of its distinctiveness from the elements of which matter is comprised, usually designated as being twenty-four in number. Theistic Sāṁkhya takes the step of identifying the twenty-fifth element with the Supreme Deity. Whereas stress on the all-pervasive feature is found throughout the epic, the concept of the identity of the Deity with the soul within is found only in passages where theistic doctrines are combined with Sāṁkhya. Thus, for example, in Uttaṅka's prayers to Viṣṇu (3.192.11-19), in the glorification of Kṛṣṇa by Saṁjaya and Dhṛtarāṣṭra in the *Udyoga,* in Bhīṣma's teachings to Duryodhana (6.61-64), in the prayers of Arjuna and Draupadī (3.13.10-36, 42-53), and in those of Yudhiṣṭhira (7.124 and 12.43), there is no reference that equates the Deity with the *ātman.*

Outside of the major didactic tracts in which Sāṁkhya is prominent, there are only a few references that equate the Deity with the soul within. In the story of Śakuntalā, narrated by

Vaiśaṁpāyana in the *Ādi*, when King Duḥṣanta pretends to have no knowledge of the heroine she replies by saying that though he thinks no-one else knows of their marriage, all sins are known to the Lord within the heart:

> *eko 'ham asmīti ca manyase tvaṁ*
> *na hṛc-chayaṁ vetsi muniṁ purāṇam*
> *yo veditā karmaṇaḥ pāpakasya*
> *yasyāntike tvaṁ vṛjinaṁ karoṣi*

'You think, 'I am alone', but you do not know of that ancient seer residing within the heart who knows all the deeds of the sinful, and in whose presence you discharge your iniquity.' (1.68.27)

At the time of the destruction of the Khāṇḍava Forest, Kṛṣṇa is referred to as *sarva-bhūtatmanaḥ* (1.219.8)–the self of all beings, but the term is used only as a title and no explanation is given. When Bhīma encounters Hanuman lying across his path he is reluctant to step over him for fear of offending the supreme soul, free of the *guṇas,* who pervades the monkey's body–*nirguṇaḥ paramātmeti dehaṁ te vyāpya tiṣṭhati* (3.147.8). Speaking to Mārkaṇḍeya, Nārāyaṇa gives further insight when he states, *evaṁ praṇihitaḥ samyaṅ mayātmā muni-sattama*–O best of seers, the *ātman* is thus directly contacted by me. Unfortunately, the term *praṇihitaḥ,* the participle of *praṇidhā,* is obscure and does not allow for an easy understanding of the relationship between Nārāyaṇa and the *ātman.* The same verse then states, *sarva-bhūteṣu viprendra na ca māṁ vetti kaścana*–O lord amongst *brāhmaṇas,* nobody knows me within all beings (3.187.35).

In Bhīṣma's prayers to Kṛṣṇa in the *Śānti,* he refers to him as the one known as the *kṣetrajña,* the transcendent soul, by the followers of Sāṁkhya:

> *yaṁ taṁ vyakta-stham avyaktaṁ vicinvanti maharṣayaḥ*
> *kṣetre kṣetra-jñam āsīnaṁ tasmai kṣetrātmane namaḥ*
>
> *yaṁ dṛg-ātmānam ātma-sthaṁ vṛtaṁ ṣoḍaśabhir guṇaiḥ*
> *prāhuḥ sapta-daśaṁ sāṁkhyās tasmai sāṁkhyātmane namaḥ*

'Great *ṛṣis* seek out that unmanifest one situated in the manifest, the *kṣetrajña* situated in the body. Obeisances to the one who is the soul of the body.

He is the perceived self situated in the self, marked as separate from the sixteen elements of matter. The followers of Sāṁkhya call him the seventeenth. Obeisances to that one who is known as the self in Sāṁkhya thought.' (12.47.33-34)

In this chapter, Bhīṣma refers to various doctrines such as Sāṁkhya and Yoga, and praises Kṛṣṇa as the one at whom all of them aim. It is significant that the idea of the *ātman*'s identity with the Deity is discussed in relation to the followers of Sāṁkhya, indicating once again that the notion is primarily derived from, or stands in relation to, the Sāṁkhya doctrine of the transcendent self. It is also interesting to note, though not particularly related to the present discussion, that the Sāṁkhya referred to here posits matter as consisting of sixteen elements and the self as being the seventeenth.

In the *Mokṣa-dharma*, Sāṁkhya is predominantly non-theistic and only occasionally refers to the concept of a Supreme Deity. There are, however, a few passages in which the transcendent *ātman* is referred to as *īśvara* and thereby identified with the Deity. Vyāsa's teachings, for example, use the nominatives *kṣetrajñaḥ* and *īśvaraḥ* to refer to the self that is apart from matter (12.241.1), though no attempt is made to expand upon the idea of *īśvara* or equate it with Nārāyaṇa. Later Vasiṣṭha refers to the twenty-fifth element in his Sāṁkhya exposition as Viṣṇu–*pañca-viṁśatimo viṣṇur nistattvas tattva-saṁjñakaḥ* (12.291.37)–but again goes no further in explaining the connection with the Deity Viṣṇu found elsewhere in the epic.

Despite their differing theistic perspectives, the *Nārāyaṇīya* and the *Bhagavad-gītā* both extensively employ Sāṁkhya concepts in their discourses. The *Nārāyaṇīya* directly asserts that the Deity it describes is none other than the *kṣetrajña*. In the opening chapter, 12.321, Nārada asks the *ṛṣis* Nara and Nārāyaṇa which Deity it is that they are worshipping. The *ṛṣis* reply that it is the indwelling self of all beings, known as the *kṣetrajña*, whom they worship–*sa hy antarātmā bhūtānāṁ kṣetrajñaś ceti kathyate* (29). There is no god or ancestor greater than he who is known as the *ātman* and it is he whom they worship–*ātmā hi nau sa vijñeyas tatas taṁ pūjayāvahe* (31).

It is he who originally ordains the duties and correct ways of life to be followed by all men. All the rites by which the gods and ancestors are worshipped come from him (32-37). Those who have gone beyond the seventeen elements of matter, and the fifteen elements that comprise the body are known as *muktas*, the liberated ones (38). They attain *brahman* which is known as the *kṣetrajña–muktānāṁ gatir brahman kṣetrajña iti kalpitaḥ*–found in all places, untouched by the three *guṇas* (39). He can be perceived by the *yoga* of knowledge, and the two divine *ṛṣis* have issued from him–*dṛśyate jñāna-yogena āvāṁ ca prasṛtau tataḥ*;. having gained knowledge of that one who is the *ātman*, they now worship him constantly–*evaṁ jñātvā tam ātmānaṁ pūjayāvaḥ sanātanam* (40). The Vedas and the different *āśramas* (of various religious practices) all worship him and it is he who gives the results. Those, however, who are devoted to him exclusively are able to enter into him (41-42). Nārāyaṇa is not mentioned by name in this chapter, but it is apparent from the narration that follows that he is the *kṣetrajña* referred to. After receiving this instruction Nārada departs for Śvetadvīpa and there offers prayers to the great soul who is all things and is untouched by the *guṇas–stotraṁ jagau sa viśvāya nirguṇāya mahātmane* (325.3). After this recital which stresses that the Deity is everything manifest in this world, the *viśva-rūpa* is displayed to Nārada very much in accord with the prayers he has offered.

In verses 20-97 of Chapter 326, the great Deity teaches Nārada about himself. He is beyond the range of the senses, beyond the *guṇas*, beyond the fluctuations of matter, and is unchanging (20-23). He is the twenty-fifth element known as the *puruṣa*, and, as Vāsudeva, is the one into whom the liberated souls enter (24-25). When all the world is withdrawn nothing remains except the *puruṣa* who is Vāsudeva (28-32). There then follows a discourse on the *catur-vyūha* in which the form of the Deity known as Saṁkarṣaṇa is equated with the *jīva* or individual soul–*sa jīvaḥ parisaṁkhyātaḥ seṣaḥ saṁkarṣaṇaḥ prabhuḥ* (37)–and the Deity, speaking to Nārada, again asserts his identity as the *puruṣa*, the twenty-fifth element of Sāṁkhya philosophy–*ahaṁ hi puruṣo jñeyo niṣkriyaḥ pañca-viṁśakaḥ* (41).

It was observed earlier that virtually no attention is devoted to Vaiṣṇava iconography in the *Nārāyaṇīya*, for the Pañcarātric view is closely tied to Sāṁkhya. The Deity known as Nārāyaṇa is identified with the *kṣetrajña*, the indwelling *ātman* found in all beings. As such he is a universal God who exists everywhere, though not devoid of personal traits through which he accepts different forms to preserve the order he has established. The manifestation of the *viśva-rūpa* to Nārada may well be an imitation of the *Gītā*, as Esnoul suggests,[44] but it is interpreted differently. Here Sāṁkhya thought predominates; the *viśva-rūpa* is essentially an illusion displayed for the benefit of Nārada. The Deity is the personification of the *kṣetrajña* of Sāṁkhya and as such he is beyond all form and limitation, existing in all beings at all times and in all places. There is thus little doubt that the Pañcarātra of the *Nārāyaṇīya* is a form of theistic Sāṁkhya.

The influence of Sāṁkhya on the teachings of the *Bhagavad-gītā* has already been discussed extensively under the heading of soteriology. There are clear differences, however, between the Sāṁkhya of the *Gītā* and that of the *Nārāyaṇīya* and in the way that the theism of the two texts interacts with Sāṁkhya concepts. The *Nārāyaṇīya* embodies the Sāṁkhya of the *Mokṣa-dharma* with its notion of twenty-four elements of matter and the self as the twenty-fifth, and then identifies that *puruṣa* as the universal Deity, Nārāyaṇa. The Sāṁkhya of the *Gītā* is somewhat removed from and is probably earlier than that of the *Mokṣa-dharma*. It is less systematic and concentrates primarily on the differentiation of the self from matter. The Deity of the *Gītā*, as the speaker of the text, is much less remote than that of the *Nārāyaṇīya*, and personal traits are more pronounced.

Nonetheless, here also Kṛṣṇa asserts that he is present within the hearts of all beings. Following the discourse in Chapter 6 on the *yoga* techniques which lead to perception of the transcendent self, he concludes:

sarva-bhūta-stham ātmānaṁ sarva-bhūtāni cātmani
īkṣate yoga-yuktātmā sarvatra sama-darśanaḥ

yo māṁ paśyati sarvatra sarvaṁ ca mayi paśyati
tasyāhaṁ na praṇaśyāmi sa ca me na praṇaśyati

sarva-bhūta-sthitaṁ yo māṁ bhajaty ekatvam āsthitaḥ
sarvathā vartamāno 'pi sa yogī mayi vartate

> 'One who is resolute in *yoga* practice views all things equally, seeing the self situated in all beings and all beings in the self.
>
> For one who sees me everywhere and sees all things in me, I am never lost and he is never lost to me.
>
> Such a person who worships me situated within all beings despite all differing conditions remains a *yogin* fixed on me.' (6.29-31)

The idea expressed here would appear to be identical to that of the *Nārāyaṇīya* in identifying the Deity with the *ātman*, though it is stated only that Kṛṣṇa is within all beings, not that he is the individual soul, and later passages of the text indicate that the *Gītā* has a different perspective, more closely related to that of the *Śvetāśvatara, Kaṭha,* and *Muṇḍaka Upaniṣads*. The *Śvetāśvatara* (4.7) and *Muṇḍaka* (3.1.2) refer to two selves within the body that are like two birds in a tree, one tasting the bitter and sweet fruits, the other observing his companion. When the bird that is enjoying and suffering sees the other, who is the Lord, and recognises his greatness he becomes free from misery–*juṣṭaṁ yadā paśyatya anyam īśam asya mahimānam iti vīta-śokaḥ.*

Here a distinction is being drawn between the individual self and the universal self, and it is this view that the *Gītā* appears to reflect. Chapter 10.8-11 discusses the way in which devotees worship Kṛṣṇa after recognising him as the one from whom all things come. He gives to them the *yoga* of intelligence–*buddhi-yoga*–through which they come to him and he is able to do this because he is situated within every living being.

> *teṣām evānukampārtham aham ajñāna-jaṁ tamaḥ*
> *nāśayāmy ātma-bhāva-stho jñāna-dīpena bhāsvatā*
>
> 'Out of compassion, I who am situated in the very existence of the self, destroy with the blazing lamp of wisdom the darkness born of ignorance.' (10.11)

Here again the implication is that the Deity is intimately connected with the individual self but is essentially separate, acting as a guide, very much in accordance with the Upaniṣadic model discussed above. This view is found again towards the end of the *Gītā*:

īśvaraḥ sarva-bhūtānāṁ hṛd-deśe 'rjuna tiṣṭhati
bhrāmayan sarva-bhūtāni yantrārūḍhāni māyayā

'The Lord of all beings is situated in the heart, O Arjuna, and through his mystical power he directs the wanderings of the living beings who are fixed on the revolving machine of this world.' (18.61)

The *īśvara* is in the hearts of all beings but the distinction is that while they are carried on the cycle of *saṁsāra*, he is the director of the process.

The relationship between the *īśvara* within the heart and the living being is explored and elucidated most fully, however, in Chapter 15. This opens with the metaphor of the inverted banyan tree to which the entanglement of material existence is compared. One must break free by abandoning illusion and attachment and thereby attain the eternal position beyond this world (5-6). In verse 7, the relationship between the individual *jīva* and the *īśvara* is described:

mamaivāṁśo jīva-loke jīva-bhūtaḥ sanātanaḥ
manaḥ ṣaṣṭhānīndriyāṇi prakṛti-sthāni karṣati

'In this world, the eternal living being, who is certainly a part of me, draws to himself the six senses including the mind that rest on material nature.' (15.7)

Here the key phrase is *mamaivāṁśaḥ* which indicates that the *jīva-bhūtaḥ*, or living element, is not identical with the Deity in an absolute sense for it is only an *aṁśa*, a part that has come from the whole. Elsewhere in the epic the word *aṁśa* is used to refer to the way in which the *avatāra* is expanded from the Deity and hence the term implies that the living beings are energetic expansions from the *īśvara* who has his own existence beyond his identity with the energy.[45]

Verses 8 to 11 discuss the transmigration of the soul, and in 12 to 14 Kṛṣṇa asserts that he is the controller of the entire cosmic system. In 15, he returns once more to the subject of his existence within each living being.

sarvasya cāhaṁ hṛdi sanniviṣṭo
mattaḥ smṛtir jñānam apohanaṁ ca

vedaiś ca sarvair aham eva vedyo
vedānta-kṛd veda-vid eva cāham

'And I am situated in the hearts of all; from me comes the gaining of memory and wisdom, and also their loss. It is I who am to be known from all the Vedas; I am the compiler of Vedānta, and I am the knower of the Vedas.' (15.15)

It is the first two lines that are of particular relevance to the present discussion for they deal specifically with the position of the Deity in the hearts of all beings. The absolute identity of Kṛṣṇa with the individual *jīva* soul appears here to be an unlikely exegesis. Again, though situated within the living being, Kṛṣṇa acts in a position somewhat apart as the guide and controller, as in 18.61 and 10.11, sometimes bestowing wisdom and sometimes withdrawing it.

In verse 16, two *puruṣas* are referred to–*dvāv imau puruṣau loke kṣaraś cākṣara eva ca*–one that is destined to pass away and one that is imperishable. All living beings are destroyed–*kṣaraḥ sarva-bhūtāni*– but that one who is superior is known to be imperishable–*kūṭa-stho 'kṣara ucyate.* This is slightly obscure, but I take it at face value as a simple restatement of the basic Sāṁkhya premise of the difference between the material body and personality and the transcendent self, both of which are referred to here as *puruṣa.* Verse 17 is significant:

uttamaḥ puruṣas tv anyaḥ paramātmety udāhṛtaḥ
yo loka-trayam āviśya bibharty avyaya īśvaraḥ

'But there is yet another, the supreme *puruṣa* who is known as the Paramātman. He is the Lord, the immutable one who, having entered the three worlds, then sustains them.' (15.17)

The word *anyaḥ*–other–clearly relates to the two *puruṣas* referred to in 16, and thus indicates that the *īśvara* within is identical neither with the changing body and personality nor the individual soul, for he is *anyaḥ puruṣaḥ,* a separate being. This verse would also appear to refute the conventional Advaitic interpretation of the metaphor of the two birds which urges that they represent the conditioned self and the pure self, apparently separate but in fact the same being. The idea here is that the *īśvara*, the Supreme Deity, expands himself so as to sit in the heart beside the individual self, guiding its progress through the cycle of *saṁsāra*. This concept is made even more explicit in the next verse that effectively concludes the teaching of the chapter:

> *yasmāt kṣaram atīto 'ham akṣarād api cottamaḥ*
> *ato 'smi loke vede ca prathitaḥ puruṣottamaḥ*
>
> 'Because I am above that which decays and also that which does not decay and because I am the highest of all, therefore in both the world and in the Veda I am renowned as the Supreme Being.' (15.18)

That which is referred to in this chapter as *akṣara*, the undeteriorating, is almost certainly the individual self. Hence here again we have Kṛṣṇa asserting that he is the *puruṣa* who is higher than the self and is therefore known as Puruṣottama, the Supreme Person, thereby drawing a distinction between himself as the Deity and the individual soul.

Chapter 13 marks an interesting contrast to this perspective and comes closer to the ideas of the *Nārāyaṇīya*. This chapter stands out as expressing the most developed form of Sāṁkhya found anywhere in the *Gītā*. The teachings here are much closer to those of the *Mokṣa-dharma* and particularly noteworthy is the use of the terms *kṣetra* and *kṣetrajña* to express the distinction between the self and matter. This terminology is repeatedly employed throughout the *Mokṣa-dharma*, but in the *Gītā* it is confined to Chapter 13. Furthermore, the listing of the elements of matter in 13.5 adds up to the typical Sāṁkhya number of twenty-four, though the significance of this is diminished somewhat by the addition of further elements in 13.6 and there is no designation of the soul as the twenty-fifth.

This more developed form of *Gītā* Sāṁkhya includes the notion that the *kṣetrajña* is identified with the Deity and here the *īśvara* is presented not as a witness and guide but as the *ātman* itself. This is not the central theme of the teachings which concentrates on the distinction between the self and matter, but is made apparent in several verses. In 13.2, Kṛṣṇa states quites explicitly, *kṣetrajñaṁ cāpi māṁ viddhi sarva-kṣetreṣu*–'And know me as the *kṣetrajña* in all bodies.' In verse 22, he defines the *puruṣa* as the entity who experiences the different *guṇas* whilst transmigrating from body to body. In 22, he expounds further:

> *upadraṣṭānumantā ca bhartā bhoktā maheśvaraḥ*
> *paramātmeti cāpy ukto dehe 'smin puruṣaḥ paraḥ*
>
> 'He is the witness and the permitter, the sustainer, the enjoyer and the supreme controller. He is known as the *paramātman*, the supreme *puruṣa* in this body.'

This verse could be taken as confirmation of the ideas of Chapter 15, but the definition of the *puruṣa* given in 21 makes this unlikely, and the idea appears to be closer to the theistic Sāṁkhya of certain *Mokṣa-dharma* passages and of the *Nārāyaṇīya*. Verses 27 and 28 again stress the identity of the self with the Deity by referring to the indestructible Supreme Lord situated equally in all beings–*samaṁ sarveṣu bhūteṣu tiṣṭhantaṁ parameśvaram*. It thus appears that the *Gītā* expresses two views of the identity of the self with the Deity, possibly derived from different sources. In one the Deity is within each being, but is separate from the self and acts as a witness and guide through the cycle of rebirth. The other is linked to the more developed Sāṁkhya typical of the *Mokṣa-dharma* and appears to postulate a more complete identity of the self with the Deity. Here the actual *ātman* that undergoes rebirth is designated as the Supreme Lord who, though he is in truth one being (13.16), appears to be manifest in a multiplicity of different forms and identities.

Thus both the *Gītā* and the *Nārāyaṇīya* have an understanding of the Deity being present within each individual being, though their doctrines are not always identical. Furthermore, the passages of the *Anuśāsana* which extol Śiva also refer to the identity of the Deity with the soul within. Upamanyu praises the Deity he worships by saying, *ātmā ca sarva-bhūtānāṁ sāṁkhye puruṣa ucyase*–you are the *ātman* of all beings; in Sāṁkhya you are called the *puruṣa* (13.14.154). Kṛṣṇa says of Śiva, *hṛdayaṁ sarva-bhūtānāṁ kṣetrajñas tvam ṛṣi-ṣṭutaḥ*–you are praised by *ṛṣis* as *kṣetrajña*, the heart of all beings (13.15.40), while Tandin describes him as the *antarātman*, the soul within (13.17.84). Unlike the *Nārāyaṇīya* and the *Gītā*, however, Sāṁkhya is not central to these passages and consequently the identity of the Deity with the individual soul is not a major theme of the Śaivite didactus, and is perhaps referred to there only in imitation of the doctrines of either the *Nārāyaṇīya* or other Vaiṣṇava works.

Overall it may be concluded that the notion of the identity of the Deity with the soul within each being is one that is referred to only occasionally in the epic outside of certain specific passages. The Sāṁkhya teachings of the *Mokṣa-dharma* refer to the transcendent self as *īśvara* and even Viṣṇu, but do not proceed to demonstrate the link with the Deity Viṣṇu who appears in the narrative. The identity of the Deity with the *ātman* is discussed at length only in the *Nārāyaṇīya* and the *Bhagavad-gītā* and in both these passages there is a clear connection between this idea and Sāṁkhya. The theism of the *Nārāyaṇīya* has clear links with the Sāṁkhya of the *Mokṣa-dharma.* Nārāyaṇa reveals himself as the one referred to as *kṣetrajña,* the twenty-fifth element manifest in all beings and hence formless and universal except when appearing as an *avatāra.* The theology of the *Gītā* is less closely connected with the *Mokṣa-dharma.* In tracing the development of Sāṁkhya up to its classical form of the *Sāṁkhya-kārikā,* Larson identifies the *Śvetāśvatara* and *Kaṭha Upaniṣads* in particular as containing the earliest expressions of Sāṁkhya concepts.[46] It is with this Upaniṣadic proto-Sāṁkhya that the theism of the *Gītā* displays the closest links, though Chapter 13 is an exception to this rule.

In contrast to the *Nārāyaṇīya,* the *Gītā* does not always accept the identity of the Deity with the individual self. The *jīva* is an expanded part of Kṛṣṇa's energy and is thus identical with him as the energy to the energetic. The Deity resides within the heart of each being apparently as a separate entity, guiding the *jīva* soul through the wheel of life and death. It may be concluded that we find within these two theistic tracts different perspectives on the nature of the Deity within, one linked closely to the Sāṁkhya of the *Mokṣa-dharma,* and the other to the proto-Sāṁkhya of certain *Upaniṣads.*

8. The Existence of God in Relation to Humanity

(i) Introduction

The Supreme Deity of the *Mahābhārata* creates this world in accordance with a specified order that is both cosmic and social. Thus Kṛṣṇa states that it is through his energy that the sun and moon give light and the earth is sustained in its position (Bhg 15.12-13), and also that he is the creator of the four *varṇas* into which society is divided (4:13).[47] Within the epic the main purpose behind the action of the Deity is to sustain the order that the creative process has set in motion. The central narrative tells of the intervention of the Deity to restore the socio-cosmic order, removing the burden that is distressing the earth, assisting the gods to destroy the *asuras* and ensuring that the rule of *dharma* is kept in place through the actions of righteous kings.

The relation of God to humanity in the epic must be understood in this context. The values of *pravṛtti* stress that man's role in life is to act in harmony with *dharma*, for *dharma* is vital to the order of creation and to act against it is to introduce a chaotic element. The world exists eternally through unending cycles of creation and destruction without any apparent ultimate purpose. There is no sense of 'salvation history' in creation which would give it a purposeful beginning working through the eons of time to a preconceived final goal. The cycles of existence are unending and where *bhakti* is connected to *pravṛtti* the will of the Deity is expressed in terms of sustaining the order that each creation sets in place. The quest for salvation falls under the purview of *nivṛtti* and is thus outside the purpose of creation. The *Gītā* argues that gaining salvation can be reconciled with the pursuit of *dharma*, while the *Nārāyaṇīya* stresses that both *pravṛtti* and *nivṛtti* originate from Nārāyaṇa (12.321.32-40), but the epic does not indicate that the Deity intervenes in this world to lead man towards salvation. The pursuit of *mokṣa* is essentially an individual concern beyond the Deity's purpose for the creation as a whole.

(ii) God and Individual Destiny

One of the great debates running throughout the *Mahābhārata* centres on the question of why events turn out in the way they do, with the perspectives of determinism and individual free will both eloquently and persuasively presented. Is the suffering of the righteous Pāṇḍavas the result of destiny or can it be overcome by endeavour? Will victory fall to the party that destiny decrees will triumph or is the outcome determined by the prowess and valour displayed by the combatants? The different answers to these questions offered by the text are discussed fully elsewhere and in this section only the issue of the Deity's connection with destiny will be addressed.

The classical Hindu view, shared by virtually all philosophical perspectives, centres on the idea of *karma*; success and failure here and now are dependent on the degree of piety displayed by the individual in previous lives. Thus destiny dictated by previous acts is the crucial factor. Both Zaehner[48] and Biardeau have noted that the *Mahābhārata* ascribes a central role to the Deity in the process in a manner that makes him the true controller of destiny.

> Le seul responsable est le *daiva* divin dont Kṛṣṇa est pour le moment le grand acteur sur terre. A l'automisme du *Karman* se substitue la confiance de la *bhakti*.[49]

This view of the Deity, referred to in this role as *īśvara, dhātṛ* or *vidhātṛ*, as the controller of individual destiny is sustained throughout the epic. In the furious debate between Draupadī and Yudhiṣṭhira at the beginning of the exile the Pāṇḍava queen rails against the ordainer who manipulates all beings in the manner of a capricious puppeteer. Because the righteous Pāṇḍavas have met with such discomfiture it is clear that the *dhātṛ* acts according to his whim, like a child playing with toys, and disregards justice (3.31.1f). Yudhiṣṭhira rejects his wife's opinion as *nāstikya*, atheism, but only because of her criticism of the way the Deity acts. In the *Udyoga*, he confirms her view that all destiny is controlled by God:

> *uta santam asantaṁ ca bālaṁ vṛddhaṁ ca saṁjaya*
> *utābalaṁ balīyāṁsaṁ dhātā prakurute vaśe*
>
> *uta bālāya pāṇḍityaṁ paṇḍitāyota bālatām*
> *dadāti sarvam īśānaḥ purastāc chukram uccaran*
>
> 'O Saṁjaya, the righteous and the wicked, the child and the aged one, the weak and the strong—the ordainer has all of them under his control.
>
> Whether it be wisdom given to a child, or childishness bestowed upon a wise man, it is the Controller, the one who in the beginning emits the seed of life, who awards all things.' (5.31.1-2)

At the beginning of the *Śānti*, Vyāsa assures the guilt-ridden Yudhiṣṭhira that he is not to blame for the terrible loss of life that has taken place. He points out the differing opinions on the subject of causality which stress the *īśvara*, the individual, or previous acts. Vyāsa himself urges that the Supreme Being is like the wieldier of an axe in cutting down a tree while the individual is like the axe itself; always it is the axeman who is responsible when a tree is cut down and never the axe. (12.32.11-24). A similar idea is found in Chapter 217, wherein Bali tells Indra that he does not lament for his misfortune for he knows that he is completely under the control of the creator–*evaṁ me niścitā buddhiḥ śāstus tiṣṭhāmy ahaṁ vaśe* (31). At the commencement of the *Aśvamedhika* we find Vyāsa once again comforting a depressed Yudhiṣṭhira with the same argument that all the destruction has been brought about by the will of the Controller, not his own actions:

> *yudhiṣṭhira tava prajñā samyag iti me matiḥ*
> *na hi kaścit svayaṁ martyaḥ sva-vaśaḥ kurute kriyāḥ*
>
> *īśvareṇa niyukto 'yaṁ sādhv-asādhu ca mānavaḥ*
> *karoti puruṣaḥ karma tatra kā paridevanā*
>
> 'Yudhiṣṭhira, to my mind your wisdom is limited. There is no mortal who ever performs deeds by his own power.
>
> Engaged by the Controller, a man performs righteous and unrighteous deeds. It is the *puruṣa* who performs acts, so what need is there for lamentation.' (14.3.1-2)

Here Vyāsa appears to be teaching a doctrine of complete determinism, with the individual having no responsibility whatsoever for his own deeds. A mortal being cannot perform any act by his own power, for he is completely under the control of God in executing righteous and wicked actions. When he understands this, Yudhiṣṭhira should realise that lamenting as if he was the cause of death and destruction is inappropriate, for all things come to be through the will of God and not the endeavours of man. This argument is particularly relevant in connection with the *Mahābhārata* narrative in which it has been made clear that the *īśvara* has appeared on earth specifically to manipulate the course of history in accordance with his will, but there is no indication here that Vyāsa is referring to this circumstance alone.

The *Gītā*'s idea of the *īśvara* within each being acting as the controller and guide has previously been noted. In Chapter 11,

Kṛṣṇa reveals that the slaughter of the Kauravas will take place because of his will, whilst Arjuna, the apparent killer, will be only an instrument–*mayaivaite nihitāḥ pūrvam eva nimitta-mātraṁ bhava savyasācin* (33), an assertion which is confirmed by Arjuna's vision of Śiva at the end of the *Droṇa* and which conforms to Vyāsa's comparison to the axeman and the axe.

In his role as the executor of prescribed destiny the Deity is referred to as *dhātṛ, vidhātṛ, īśvara,* or *īśāna,* terms which relate to his being the Ordainer and Controller. These terms, and the divine role they imply, are applied at different times to Viṣṇu (3.22.6, 3.187.53, 5.149.36) to Śiva (13.16.32, 13.18.22) and also to Brahmā. At other times, as in the debate between Draupadī and Yudhiṣṭhira, no particular Deity is linked to the term *dhātṛ*. Where the role is accepted by Brahmā, he is acting in that capacity as the agent of Viṣṇu, as the *Nārāyaṇīya* makes clear:

> *loka-kārya-gatīḥ sarvās tvaṁ cintaya yathā-vidhi*
> *dhātā tvaṁ sarva-bhūtānāṁ tvaṁ prabhur jagato guruḥ*
> *tvayy āveśita-bhāro 'haṁ dhṛtiṁ prāpsyāmy athāñjasā*
>
> (Nārāyaṇa said), 'You should consider all the proper duties to be performed in this world in accordance with injunctions. You are the *dhātṛ* for all beings, you are the master and guide of the world. Having placed this burden upon you, I shall then find satisfaction.' (12.327.84)

The theistic description of creation given in the *Mokṣa-dharma* also refers to Viṣṇu's giving the *dhātṛ,* here again presumably Brahmā, control over all beings–*adhyakṣaṁ sarva-bhūtānāṁ dhātāram akarot prabhuḥ* (12.200.33). The point here is that although the ordainer of destiny may sometimes be taken as Brahmā, this does not contradict the understanding that the Supreme Deity acts in this world to control the destiny of all beings; it merely implies that he acts through the agency of a demiurge to execute this purpose—according to the *Nārāyaṇīya* to relieve himself of the burden of doing so.

(iii) The Relationship of Love between God and Humanity

The above discussion reveals a Deity who creates and destroys a universal system at scheduled intervals of cosmic time and sustains its structured order during the time when creation is manifest. He controls all things in the world, ascribing individual destinies to the living beings in accordance with their previous acts. The Deity in this conception is personal in a limited sense, but remote and detached from this world. Commentators such as Parrinder,[50] Manimala[51] and Shideler,[52] who have a polemical Christian agenda, have seized on this divine remoteness to demonstrate the distinction between Christ and *avatāra.* The intervention of God in this world described by the *Mahābhārata* is not an expression of the Deity's love for humanity but merely the creator tinkering with his creation to ensure that the order he has generated is maintained.

The Hindu understanding of a reciprocal loving relationship between God and man appears in the *Purāṇas* and flowers in the works of the *ācāryas* of the *bhakti* sects. Hardy is correct in the distinction he draws between the philosophical *bhakti* of the *Mahābhārata* and the emotional expressions of love found in the *Bhāgavata Purāṇa* and the works of the *alvars* of South India.[53] The idea of God's love for man is not a prominent theme of epic theology or an aspect of the nature of God that is stressed. The major passages of the text which discuss the nature of the Deity generally reveal little or nothing indicative of such love. It is noteworthy that while the two *Sahasra-nāma-stotras* give many names that refer to the iconographies and mythologies of Viṣṇu and Śiva, the only expression of reciprocated love is in the names *bhakta-vatsala*–affectionate to the devoted, and *loka-bandhu*–friend of the world (13.135.91).

The epic does, however, contain some indications of the Deity's attachment to his devotees though only of a limited and restrained nature. Regarding the descent of the *avatāra,* whilst the mission is undoubtedly to restore *dharma* and assist the gods, Kṛṣṇa also states that it is to be understood that in doing so he is acting for the welfare of the world. Addressing Uttaṅka, he says that he repeatedly appears to sustain *dharma,* the essence of which is mercy to all creatures:

> *viddhi mahyaṁ sutaṁ dharmam agra-jaṁ dvija-sattama*
> *mānasaṁ dayitaṁ vipra sarva-bhūta-dayātmakam*
>
> 'O best of the twice-born, you should know that *dharma* is my first-born son. It is dear to the mind, O *brāhmaṇa,* and its essence is compassion for all beings.' (14.53.11)

Thus the descent of the Deity does contain some element of attachment for the living beings in this world; because *dharma* has at its heart compassion for all beings, the act of sustaining *dharma* is executed for their benefit.

In the *Vana,* Mārkaṇḍeya tells of how Nārāyaṇa was pleased with him (3.187.41) and as a result offered him different gifts; Mārkaṇḍeya concludes by stating that Nārāyaṇa is the father and mother of all beings and that the Pāṇḍavas should therefore seek refuge with him:

> *sarveṣām eva bhūtānāṁ pitā mātā ca mādhavaḥ*
> *gacchadhvam enaṁ śaraṇaṁ śaraṇyaṁ kauravarṣabhāḥ*
> (3.187.55)

According to Saṁjaya, if Kṛṣṇa is worshipped contentment will be the result but if he is not worshipped there will be no happiness–*pūjito hi sukhāya syād asukhaḥ syād apūjitaḥ* (5.83.7). In Chapter 69, the blind Dhṛtarāṣṭra expresses his longing to behold the Deity directly in his form as Kṛṣṇa and decides that he will seek shelter with him now that he is assailed by great difficulties–*paraṁ parebhyaḥ śaraṇaṁ prapadye* (5.69.6).

The penance executed by Uttaṅka is said to be pleasing to Viṣṇu–*tasya prītaḥ sa bhagavān* (3.192.10), and when he is pleased all the world finds pleasure as it finds fear in his wrath–*tvayi tuṣṭe jagat-svasthaṁ tvayi kruddhe mahad-bhayam* (16). Yudhiṣṭhira speaks in a similar vein in the *Droṇa:*

> *pṛthivī-vijayo vāpi trai-lokya-vijayo 'pi vā*
> *dhruvo hi teṣāṁ vārṣṇeya yeṣāṁ tuṣṭo 'si mādhava*
>
> *na teṣāṁ vidyate pāpaṁ saṁgrāme vā parājayaḥ*
> *tri-daśeśvara-nāthas tvaṁ yeṣāṁ tuṣṭo 'si mādhava*
>
> 'O descendant of Vṛṣṇi, O Mādhava, both conquest of the earth and conquest of the threefold universe is certain for those with whom you are pleased.
>
> For those with whom you are pleased, O Mādhava, there can be no evil and no defeat in battle, for you are the Lord of the master of the master of the thirty great gods.' (7.124.7-8)

In passages that teach devotion to *Śiva* a similar mood is found. Śiva is also recognised as a Deity who is affectionate to his devotees and gives them happiness when he is satisfied:

> *pūjyamāne tatas tasmin modate sa maheśvaraḥ*
> *sukhaṁ dadāti prītātmā bhaktānāṁ bhakta-vatsalaḥ*
>
> 'The Supreme Lord (Śiva) is delighted by such worship and, pleased with his devotees, he who is naturally affectionate to his devotees gives them happiness.' (13.146.18)

Accepting various difficulties, he would even give up his own breath to set free those who look to him for shelter (24-25).

These few passages are typical of the epic's understanding of the relationship between the Deity and humanity. He is pleased with those who worship him and in return offers them boons of various kinds including salvation. There is, however, no concept of a loving Deity—and here a distinction must be drawn between loving and benign. The Deity is presented in the manner of a remote potentate, pleased by surrender and ready to reward those who satisfy him but without any indication that he reciprocates with a mood of love. Indeed, it is noteworthy that the *Mahābhārata*'s idea of *bhakti* is predominated by awe and contrition and hence there is little in the way of love for the Deity to reciprocate. This austere mood is in marked contrast to the emotional outpourings found in later *bhakti* sects worshipping Śiva, Viṣṇu and Kṛṣṇa.

(iv) The *Nārāyaṇīya*

Theologically, the principal concerns of the *Nārāyaṇīya* are to establish the majesty and all-pervasive supremacy of the Deity, and to reveal his identity with the *puruṣa* of Sāṁkhya thought. It is stated that he is pleased by acts of devotion–*tenaikāgramanastvena prīto bhavati vai hariḥ* (12.323.32), *tato 'sya tuṣṭo bhagavān bhaktyā* (324.29)–and that he can be perceived only by devotion, but expressions of reciprocal love between man and God are notable primarily for their absence from the text. Only occasionally do there occur expressions indicative of any form of emotion with regard to Nārāyaṇa. In Chapter 331, Nārada uses the terms *bhāgavata-priyaḥ* and *bhakta-vatsalaḥ* (43) to refer to the Deity, meaning the one who is loved by the devotees and is affectionate towards them. He concludes his speech here by asserting that no-one in the threefold universe is more beloved of Nārāyaṇa than the awakened one who is devoted to him alone (51).

In the creation story, after being robbed of the Vedas, Brahmā implores his maker to assist him, urging that he and Nārāyaṇa share a relationship of mutual attachment–*priyo 'haṁ te priyo 'si me* (12.335.42). Of course it cannot be overlooked that Brahmā is the divine demiurge and not truly a being of this world but nonetheless the reference does indicate the capacity for reciprocated love between Deity and supplicant. Again in Chapter 336, it is indicated that Viṣṇu feels love and affection for those devoted to him–*aho hy ekāntinaḥ sarvān prīṇāti bhagavān hariḥ* (1)–and that his favour is manifested in the form of salvation which is granted to them (66-69).

The significance of these references should not be underestimated in revealing antecedents for the later ideas of emotional reciprocated love, so prominent in the Hindu *bhakti* tradition. Nonetheless, within the context of the *Nārāyaṇīya,* they must be regarded as exceptional and not representative of the pervading mood of the text in which God is portrayed as essentially benign, but awesome in his glory, remote from human experience and a Deity before whose wondrous manifestation one should humbly prostrate oneself. As the *kṣetrajña* of all beings, the Deity of the *Nārāyaṇīya* is presented as devoid of personality, a philosophical concept as much as an individual being. Although it is stated that he has affection for devotees, philosophically he is equal to all as he is the self of all beings–*samaḥ sarveṣu bhūteṣu īśvaraḥ* (12.333.25)–and this image of God inevitably works against any emotional element in the devotion expressed.

(v) The *Bhagavad-gītā*

It is in the *Gītā* that we find the most notable expressions of divine love within the entire *Mahābhārata,* and probably the most legitimate antecedents for the expressions of later Hindu devotion. The *Gītā* also illustrates the contradiction between the intimate mood of loving devotion and the concept of a remote cosmic Deity who is the self of all beings. In Chapter 11, the revelation of the *viśvarūpa* by Kṛṣṇa convinces Arjuna that his previous attitude of intimacy and friendship was inappropriate:

sakheti matvā prasabhaṁ yad uktaṁ
he kṛṣṇa he yādava he sakheti
ajānatā mahimānaṁ tavedaṁ
mayā pramādāt praṇayena vāpi

yac cāvahāsārtham asat-kṛto 'si
vihāra-śayyāsana-bhojaneṣu
eko 'tha vāpy acyuta tat-samakṣaṁ
tat-kṣāmaye tvām aham aprameyam

'Presumptuously regarding you as my friend, I have addressed you, "O Kṛṣṇa, O Yādava, my dear friend," not understanding this greatness of yours because of carelessness and affection.

Whilst we were walking together, lying down, sitting or eating, alone and in company, you were not shown respect by me as I sought my own amusement, O infallible one. Now I seek forgiveness from you who are immeasurable.' (11.41-42)

Here Arjuna highlights the distinction between the cosmic Nārāyaṇa and his manifestation as Kṛṣṇa. With the *avatāra* Arjuna has maintained a relationship of intimate friendship and there is no indication that this is resented by Kṛṣṇa who refers to Arjuna as his devotee and friend–*bhakto 'si me sakhā ca* (4.3). When the cosmic nature of the Deity is revealed, however, this intimate mood cannot be sustained. This is surely significant, especially in light of the fact that overwhelmingly the later expressions of emotional Vaiṣṇava *bhakti* are related to the *avatāras* Rāma and more especially Kṛṣṇa, rather than Viṣṇu/Nārāyaṇa.

The love of God for his devotee is expressed first in Chapter 7. There Kṛṣṇa states that those who surrender to him are able to cross beyond his energy that consists of three *guṇas* (14). Four types of person worship him (16), but of these the one who does so because of wisdom is the best, above those who seek reward in this world. Such a *jñānin* has great love for Kṛṣṇa and Kṛṣṇa has love for him–*priyo hi jñānino 'tyartham ahaṁ sa ca mama priyaḥ* (17). In Chapter 9, the equality of the Deity to all beings is indicated, as it is in the *Nārāyaṇīya* (12.333.25), but here there is a difference:

samo 'haṁ sarva-bhūteṣu na me dveṣyo 'sti na priyaḥ
ye bhajanti tu māṁ bhaktyā mayi te teṣu cāpy aham

'I am equal to all beings; no-one is hated by me and no-one is beloved, but those who worship me with devotion are in me and I am in them.' (9.29)

As the soul of all beings it is assumed that the Deity views all from an equal perspective. The general rule is, *na priyaḥ*, but it is apparent from 7.17 and from Chapter 12 that the worshippers are outside this rule and hence the phrase–*sa ca mama priyaḥ*. Again in Chapter 10, we find the assertion that it is compassion–*anukampā*–that motivates Kṛṣṇa to destroy from within the barriers to salvation (10.11).

It is in Chapter 12, however, that we find the most overt expressions of God's love for humanity found anywhere in the epic. Following the revelation of the *viśva-rūpa* and the statement that such a vision is possible only through devotion–*bhaktyā tv ananyayā śakya aham evaṁ vidhaḥ* (11.54), Arjuna asks who is superior in *yoga*, the *bhaktas* who worship Kṛṣṇa or those who seek the undecaying, unmanifest feature (12.1). To this Kṛṣṇa replies unequivocally that the devotees are superior in *yoga–te me yuktatamā matāḥ* (2), though those who seek the all-pervasive feature also attain him, albeit by a path fraught with difficulty (3-5).

Kṛṣṇa himself is the saviour of those who worship him, delivering them from the ocean of birth and death, and Arjuna is urged to follow this path (6-8). The different ways in which acts of devotion may be performed are then outlined (9-12), and the remaining eight verses discuss the personal characteristics of one who is so engaged. What is relevant to the present discussion is the statement of Kṛṣṇa, given as the last line of 14, 15, 16, 17, 19 and 20, that those devotees who possess these characteristics are the objects of his love and affection. The exact wording here is, *sa me priyaḥ* (14,15,16,17), *bhaktimān me priyo naraḥ* (19), and, *bhaktās te 'tīva me priyāḥ* (20).

Such expressions of love from the Deity for his votaries are virtually unique in the *Mahābhārata* and represent one of the distinctive features of the theology of the *Bhagavad-gītā*. In the final analysis, Shideler and other polemical Christian writers are wrong. Shideler in particular makes glaring textual errors in his analysis of the *Gītā*, and seems to have missed Chapter 12 completely. His statement, 'Kṛṣṇa does not save' is gainsaid by Kṛṣṇa's assurance in 12.7 that he is the deliverer from birth and death; his assertion that Kṛṣṇa's '. . . attitude toward men is neutral', citing 9.29, ignores the second line of the verse as well as the verses cited above that show that the words *na priyaḥ* do not apply to the devotees; and his argument that, 'there is no slightest hint that he will be either disappointed or overjoyed at the response of any person' seems wilfully to ignore the statements of reciprocated love–*priyo hi jñānino 'tyartham ahaṁ sa ca mama priyaḥ* (7.17)–that are clearly indicative of an emotional response from the Deity to the devotional mood.[54] It is true that the specific mission of the *avatāra* is to restore *dharma*, but clearly this does not preclude Kṛṣṇa's expressing love for his devotee. In the *Gītā* that love is openly asserted and in a manner that reveals its links with the notion of salvation through grace.

9. Conclusion

Classical Pañcarātra postulates a Deity manifest in five features known as *vibhūtis*, defined by Rāmānuja in his *Śrī Bhāṣya* (1.1.1.8). These are, 1. The all-pervasive, inconceivable aspect. 2. The four forms in the *catur-vyūha*. 3. The *avatāras*. 4. The *antaryāmin*, the self within. 5. The *arcā*, the image of the Deity worshipped in temples. This complex understanding of the nature of God is matched by the various strands of epic theism, though it is noteworthy that whilst the Deity is recognised as being all-pervasive, present within each being, and manifest in this world in different forms, the *catur-vyūha* is mentioned infrequently and the divinity of images of the Deity not at all.

This complexity is enhanced by the fact that different forms of theism are combined in the epic in creating a depiction of the Deity who is active in its narrative. Hence Viṣṇu/Nārāyaṇa appears sometimes as the leader of a pantheon of gods in their conflict with the *asuras*, in the manner of a Vedic deity, and sometimes as the all-embracing cosmic Deity who manifests all existence from within himself and is identified as being the entire creation and the self of all beings. This dissonance of perspective with regard to the divine nature is based to a large extent on the fact that *bhakti* is connected to both *pravṛtti* and *nivṛtti* and thus reflects two divergent religious tendencies. When *bhakti* is in combination with *pravṛtti* the Deity is portrayed in his Vedic role, supporting the gods, opposing the forces of chaos and endeavouring to preserve the dharmic order that each creation sets in place. Where *bhakti* is linked to *nivṛtti,* however, we encounter a different form of theism, with the Deity assuming his cosmic dimension far beyond the constraints imposed on lesser gods by the conditions of material existence.

The predominant form of theism in the text has been designated as 'epic monotheism' on the basis of its understanding of a Supreme Deity who periodically creates, sustains and withdraws this world whilst remaining personally unaffected by its changing nature. Epic monotheism is uniquely a part of the Hindu tradition and has its own characteristics that render it distinct from Western forms of monotheism. Not only is God the creator of the universe but he is also identified with the creation in his all-pervasive aspect and also with the individual soul within each being.

The Deity is referred to as both Viṣṇu/Nārāyaṇa and Śiva by the text in a manner that reveals both a sectarian and a syncretistic view of the two Deities. Both have specific natures and iconographies, though the personal features of Śiva are more pronounced in the epic than are those of Nārāyaṇa. In order to sustain the order of creation, Viṣṇu appears in the world in various forms and in the *Mahābhārata* he is Kṛṣṇa, the Deity born amongst men. For this reason much of the devotional material in the epic is directed at Kṛṣṇa but the text repeatedly makes it clear that Kṛṣṇa and Viṣṇu are one and the same. It is quite possible that the entire notion of *avatāra* in Hinduism is derived from the necessity of explaining the identity between the personal Kṛṣṇa and the remote cosmic Nārāyaṇa.

Neither the ideals of *pravṛtti* nor those of *nivṛtti* look for a close relationship of reciprocated love between humanity and the Deity. *Pravṛtti* understands the world as being based on a divinely ordained order which is reflected on earth as *dharma.* God is the creator and sustainer of this order and man's role is to ensure that he lives in accordance with its dictates. Those who conform to the ways of *dharma* are hence supporters of the will of the Deity but there is little hint of intimacy or personal interaction in this relationship. The imperative of *nivṛtti* is always towards absolute salvation from this world. The Deity is here presented as existing in the transcendent sphere sought by the *mokṣa-dharmin* but the process of liberation is primarily one of self-transformation. Where recourse is made to the Deity and his grace invoked the interaction is generally presented as a further technique of breaking free from the bondage of this world rather than being based on a personal relationship. It is thus perhaps surprising that in the *Bhagavad-gītā* we find expressions indicative of a loving relationship between man and the Deity. Although the emotional content of these expressions is notably restrained, they may provide a legitimate antecedent within the Sanskrit tradition for the later expressions Hindu devotion.

Notes

1. Bhandarkar, R.G. *Vaiṣṇavism, Śaivism and Minor Religious Systems,* New York, 1980, p. 4.
2. Bhandarkar argues that in the *Mahābhārata* three types of devotion—to the Vedic Viṣṇu, to the cosmic Nārāyaṇa, and to Kṛṣṇa—have been drawn together and loosely united (Bhandarkar 1980, p. 35).
3. Brockington, J.L. 'The Epic View of the Gods', *Shadow,* Vol 9, 1992, p. 9.
4. See, for example, 3.82.107, though Viṣṇu is here referred to as *tri-lokeśa* and *avyaya,* the eternal lord of the three worlds.
5. Hiltebeitel, A. *The Ritual of Battle, Krishna in the Mahābhārata,* Ithaca, 1976, pp. 147-160.
6. Ibid, pp. 144-145.
7. A possible exception is Chapter 11 of the *Anuśāsana* in which Śrī tells Rukminī, the wife of Kṛṣṇa, of the places where she is to be found. The central idea is that Śrī represents worldly prosperity and as such manifests herself amongst the righteous. At the conclusion of the chapter (v19), she states, *nārāyaṇe ekamanā vasāmi sarvena bhāvena śarīra-bhūtā*—"In all ways, with my mind fixed on one object, I reside in a bodily form on Nārāyaṇa." This is probably a reference to the *śrīvatsa* and an indication that as Nārāyaṇa is the embodiment of *dharma* she is always with him, rather than meaning that she is his consort in the Purāṇic sense.
8. The *Nārāyaṇīya,* however, indicates that all displays of a form by the Deity are an illusion created for the benefit of man's inferior perception. Nārāyaṇa himself tells Nārada after displaying the *viśva-rūpa:*
   nirguṇa niṣphalaś caiva nirdvandvo niṣparigrahaḥ
   etat tvayā na vijñeyaṁ rūpavān iti dṛśyate
   icchan muhūrtān naśyeyam īśo 'haṁ jagato guruḥ
   māyā hy eṣā mayā sṛṣṭā yan māṁ paśyasi nārada
   sarva-bhūta-guṇair yuktaṁ naivaṁ tvaṁ jñātum arhasi
   '(I am) without qualities, I have no reactions to my deeds, I am beyond all duality and I have no sense of possession. This is inconceivable to you and thus a form has been seen. If I desire it, this can be withdrawn in an instant; I am the Lord, the instructor of the world.
   This is an illusion created by me which you see as me, Nārada, endowed with the attributes of all living beings. You cannot comprehend this. (12.326.41-42).

9. *Liṅga Purāṇa, Uttarārdham* 48.31-32, cited by Bharadvāja, K. *A Philosophical Study of the Concept of Viṣṇu in the Purāṇas,* New Delhi, 1981, p. 33.
10. *Garuḍa Purāṇa,* 2.30-37, cited by Matchett, F. *The Avatāra Myth in the Harivaṁśa, the Viṣṇu Purāṇa and the Bhāgavata Purāṇa,* Doctoral Thesis, Lancaster, 1990, p. 14.
11. *Songs of the Vaiṣṇava Ācāryas,* translated by AC Bhaktivedanta Swami Prabhupada, Acyutananda Swami and Jayasacinandana dasa, Bhaktivedanta Book Trust, Los Angeles, 1979, pp. 97-98.
12. Though not with the *Viṣṇu Purāṇa* as Freda Matchett makes clear (Matchett 1990).
13. 3.188.19 refers to, *kalkir viṣṇu-yaśā-nāma.* Gonda sees this as indicative of a connection between Kalki and Viṣṇu and states that *viṣṇu-yaśas* means, ". . . being, representing Viṣṇu's glory or dignity, i.e. an essential element in the total divine personality known as Viṣṇu (Gonda J. *Aspects of Early Viṣṇuism,* Delhi, 1969, p. 149).
14. A further reference in Mārkaṇḍeya's account of the different types of fire equates Kapila, the teacher of Sāṁkhya, with the fire known as Kapila (3.211.21).
15. See, for example, Parrinder G. *Avatāra and Incarnation,* London, 1970.
16. Bharadvāja cites the *Padma Purāṇa* (6.269.53) as giving five functions of the *avatāra* (Bharadvāja 1981, p. 324), the first four of which are familiar from epic teachings:- 1. To protect the righteous, 2. To destroy the wicked, 3. To restore *dharma,* and 4. To benefit the gods. The fifth, however–to grant salvation to devotees–introduces a new element that is nowhere referred to in the epic, although it might possibly be construed from 4.9 of the *Gītā* and from Kṛṣṇa's delivering teachings on the subject of salvation.
17. The *Padma Purāṇa, pātāla-khaṇḍa.* 77.43, explicitly states that *avatāras* do not have bodies of matter, and in his *Vedānta-saṁgrahaḥ Pṛṣṭam,* Rāmānuja offers the same conclusion–*devādi-rūpeṇāvatareṣv api na prākṛto dehāḥ* (Bharadvāja 1981, p. 329).
18. *kim utākhila-sattvānāṁ tiryaṅ martya-divaukasām/īśituś ceśitavyānāṁ kuśalākuśalānvayaḥ* (10.34.33).
19. One may also note 12.283.28 of the *Mahābhārata* in which Paraśara asserts that *dharma* and *adharma* are found amongst men, but not other beings:
    mānuṣeṣu mahārāja dharmādharmau pravartataḥ
    na tathānyeṣu bhūteṣu manuṣya-rahiteṣv iha
20. As, for example, in the *Viṣṇu Purāṇa,* 1.2.63-66, which states that Janārdana takes the forms of Brahmā, Viṣṇu and Śiva to create, maintain and destroy the world.
21. Hopkins, E.W. *Epic Mythology,* Strassburg, 1915, p. 231.
22. Ibid, p. 224.
23. Pusalker, A.D. *Studies in the Epics and Purāṇas of India,* Bombay, 1963, p. 128.
24. Hopkins 1915, p. 224.
25. Scheuer, J. *Śiva dans le Mahābhārata,* Paris, 1982, p. 31.
26. See, for example, Hopkins, E.W. *The Great Epic of India,* Calcutta, 1969, and more recently, Dumézil, G. *Mythe et Épopée, L'Idéologie de Trois Functions dans les Épopées des Peuples Indoeuropéens,* Paris, 1968.
27. Dhalmann, J. *Genesis des Mahābhārata,* Berlin, 1899.
28. Levi, S. 'Tato Jayam Udirayet', L.G. Khare trans, *Annals of the Bhandarkar Oriental Institute,* No. 1, 1918-1920.
29. Biardeau, M. and Péterfalvi, J. *Le Mahābhārata,* Volume 2, Paris, 1986, p. 150.

30. Hiltebeitel 1976, p. 174.
31. Scheuer 1982, p. 16.
32. 13.145.7 is identical to 7.173.98, referred to above, adding weight to the suggestion of a connection between the two passages.
33. 11.22 mentions *rudrādityā-vasavaḥ*, but the reference here is almost certainly plural and indicates the gods known as the Rudras rather than Śiva.
34. Esnoul, A.M. *Nārāyaṇīya Parvan du Mahābhārata,* Paris, 1979, p. 3.
35. See, for example, *Viṣṇu Purāṇa* 1.2.63f, Chapter 11 of the *Īśvara-gītā* of the *Kūrma Purāṇa,* and Chapters 24 and 25 of the *Vāyu Purāṇa.*
36. Scheuer 1982, p. 218.
37. Biardeau, M. and Péterfalvi, J. *Le Mahābhārata Livres* 1-5, Paris, 1985, p. 39.
38. Biardeau 1986, p. 149.
39. Hiltebeitel 1976, p. 332.
40. van Buitenen, J.A.B. *Studies in Indian Literature and Philosophy,* Ludo Rocher Ed, Delhi, 1988, p. 197.
41. Gonda, J. *Aspects of Early Viṣṇuism,* Delhi, 1969, pp. 40-54.
42. A corresponding passage dedicated to Śiva is found in 13.14.154f. This is almost certainly a Śaivite imitation of the *Gītā.*
43. Perhaps most notably Muhyi al-Dīn ibn al-'Arabi, d1240CE.
44. Esnoul 1979, pp. 20-23.
45. This understanding explains the merging of the soul of Śiśupāla into the body of Kṛṣṇa described in the *Sabhā* (2.42.22-23).
46. Larson, G.J. *Classical Sāṁkhya, An Interpretation of its History and Meaning,* Delhi, 1969, p. 85.
47. See also 12.200.33.
48. Zaehner, R. *Hinduism,* Oxford, 1962, p. 106.
49. Biardeau 1985, p. 71.
50. Parrinder, G. *Avatāra and Incarnation,* London, 1970, pp. 60-62.
51. Manimala, V. 'Bhagavad-Gītā and the Gospel', *Indian Journal of Theology* 24, 1975, pp. 32-44.
52. Shideler, E. 'The Meaning of Man in the Bhagavad-gītā', *Journal of the Bible and Revelation* 28, 1960, p. 315.
53. Hardy, F. *Viraha Bhakti, The Early History of Kṛṣṇa Devotion in South India,* Delhi, 1983, p. 9.
54. Shideler 1960, p. 315.

Chapter 6

EPIC ESCHATOLOGY

1. Introduction

The term eschatology, literally "knowledge of the end", has two distinct meanings when applied to religious traditions other than Christianity, for it describes both the end of the world and also the fate of the individual after death. In traditional Christian thought both of these have been considered as one topic because it is believed that at the end of the world the dead will be raised up and subjected to judgement. Hence knowledge of the future destination of the individual is a part of knowledge of the end of the world and both are included under the heading of eschatology.

Where the word is applied to other religious traditions its meaning is ambiguous for frequently knowledge of the future of the individual has to be distinguished from knowledge of the future of the world. Thus when different writers refer to the eschatological ideas of the *Mahābhārata,* we find that they may be discussing completely different subjects, sometimes the movement of the soul after death and sometimes the repeated destructions of the universe. Thus there are two quite distinct subjects to be discussed under the heading of eschatology that only marginally overlap one another. These may designated as cosmic and individual eschatology and with occasional exceptions may be considered separately.

2. Cosmic Eschatology

(i) Periods of Cosmic Time

The *Mahābhārata* views the material universe as being eternal but subject to an unending progression of manifestation and withdrawal. It thus considers vast periods of time when the world is active, referred to as *kalpas* or days of Brahmā, and equal periods when it is withdrawn and inactive. There is apparently no beginning and no end to this cycle of existence and therefore no 'last day' in a final sense, for the annihilation or *pralaya* is just the ending of one cycle.

The epic displays a lack of consistency in its consideration of the time span of each manifestation and also in the terminology it employs. The *Bhagavad-gītā* (8. 17-19), Mārkaṇḍeya (3.186.33), Vyāsa in the *Mokṣadharma* (12.224.28-31, 225.16), and the *Nārāyaṇīya* (12. 326. 66-70, 329. 3) all refer to the period of manifestation as a day of Brahmā and designate its duration as being 1,000 *yugas.*[1] The four *yugas,* or cosmic ages, Kṛta, Tretā, Dvāpara and Kali, revolve in cycles one after the other and in these passages we are informed that the universe exists for 1,000 of these cycles before it is withdrawn once more. This idea is confused by the fact that the epic also uses the word *yuga* to mean a day of Brahmā, the complete period of manifestation. In the opening chapter, Sūta refers to the destruction occurring at the end of the *yuga–punaḥ saṁkṣipyate sarvaṁ jagat-prāpte yuga-kṣaye* (1.1.36); in the *Mokṣa-dharma,* the *guru* tells his disciple that after the annihilation the creation takes places at the beginning of the *yuga–pralaye prakṛtiṁ prāpya yugādau sṛjate prabhuḥ* (12.203.14); and just before he recites the *Viṣṇu-sahasra-nāma-stotram,* Bhīṣma asserts that it is Viṣṇu into whom the universe is merged at the end of the *yuga–yasmiṁś ca pralayaṁ yānti punar eva yuga-kṣaye* (13.135.11). Although neither Monier-Williams nor MacDonnell offer this meaning for the word *yuga,* it appears from these references that it is occasionally used in the sense of the complete period of creation as well as the periods of time into which each creation is divided.

The word *kalpa* is that most commonly used in Purāṇic literature to designate the period of a creation and is synonymous with the day of Brahmā. It is also used in this sense in the *Mahābhārata,* as in the *Bhagavad-gītā, prakṛtiṁ yānti māmikām/kalpa-kṣaye punas tāni kalpādau visṛjāmy aham* (9.7), and the *Nārāyaṇīya, etāṁ sṛṣṭiṁ vijānīhi kalpādiṣu punaḥ punaḥ* (12.326.70). In the *Mokṣa-dharma,* however, Yājñavalkya refers to the day of Brahmā as being composed of 10,000 *kalpas–pañca kalpa-sahasrāṇi dvi-guṇāny ahar ucyate* (12.299.1)–and a few verses later gives a duration of 3,000 *kalpas* for the day in which living beings are manifest—*trīṇi kalpa-sahasrāṇi eteṣām ahar ucyate* (14). In a previous treatise we find yet another version offered by Vasiṣṭha. He asserts that the fourfold cycle of *yugas* lasting for 12,000 years is a *kalpa–yugaṁ dvādaśa-*

sāhasraṁ kalpaṁ viddhi catur-guṇam–and that 1,000 of such *kalpas* comprise the day of Brahmā—*daśa-kalpa-śatāvṛttaṁ tad ahar brāhmam ucyate* (12.291.14).

These differences of terminology probably reflect the different *āśramas* and schools of thought from which the different sections of the *Mokṣa-dharma* are derived. What is consistent, however, is the concept of the vast periods of time that each creation covers. According to Mārkaṇḍeya, one cycle of the four *yugas* lasts 12,000 years and as the day of Brahmā is 1,000 of such cycles then the total duration of each creation may be calculated as extending for 12,000,000 years. According to Vyāsa in the *Śukānupraśna,* however, the 12,000 years given for the duration of the four *yugas* are years of the gods and therefore 360 times longer than earth years. If this version is accepted then the creation must be understood as existing for a total of 4,320,000,000 earth years.

It is this latter concept that is accepted by the *Purāṇas*[2] which generally offer a more precise analysis of the divisions of time than is found in the epic. The *Purāṇas* also locate the present time in the progress of the *kalpa* in terms of the number of *yuga* cycles that have already passed. This information is not offered by the *Mahābhārata,* but the epic is clearly aware of the vastness of the eons of time that roll on towards the final destruction and there is no indication that we are approaching that distant point in the future.

(ii) The *Pralaya*

After this time has elapsed the world is completely destroyed, a process generally referred to as *pralaya.* Just as the word *sṛṣṭi,* meaning creation, has the sense of emission, so *pralaya* literally means merging, in the sense that the manifest world is taken back into its unmanifest source. In Purāṇic thought it is Śiva who is the principal agent in the universal annihilation. Although the *Mahābhārata* recognises the destructive side of Śiva's nature and makes reference to his being the destroyer of the worlds,[3] it is noteworthy that in none of the descriptions of the *pralaya* found in the epic does Śiva play a major role.

As with teachings on creation, there are two perspectives in the epic on how the destruction of the world takes place, one mythic and the other based on the Sāṁkhya concept of a reverse evolution of elements. Descriptions of the *pralaya* occur far less frequently in the text than do those of creation and it is only in the teachings of Mārkaṇḍeya that anything like a complete annihilation myth is found. This is given in Chapter 186 of the *Vana.* After 1,000 *yugas* have passed, there is a drought that lasts for many years (56). Weak and afflicted, all beings on earth then meet with destruction (57). The water in the oceans and rivers is dried up by seven blazing suns and all wood and grass is burned to ashes (58-59). Then the Saṁvartaka fire and fierce winds spread across the earth which has previously been scorched dry by the suns (60). Having burned through the earth down into Rasātala, that fire terrifies the gods, Dānavas and *yakṣas* (61). Burning Nāgaloka and all things on earth, in an instant the fire consumes everything here below (62). The blistering wind and the Saṁvartaka fire burn everything for hundreds and thousands of *yojanas* (63). That blazing master of the world consumes all things including the gods, *asuras, gandharvas, yakṣas, uragas,* and *rākṣasas* (64).

There then arise clouds like elephants, streaked with lightning, and wonderful to behold, all of different shapes, sizes and colours (65-68). Those clouds, terrible in both form and sound and full of water, fill the entire sky (69). The whole earth, covered with mountains and forests, is engulfed in a rushing flood of water (70). Impelled by the Supreme Lord–*coditāḥ parameṣṭhinā*–those terrible roaring clouds immediately pour down torrents of rain over all directions (71). Pouring down vast amounts of water and flooding the earth, the clouds extinguish that dreadful blazing fire (72). Impelled by the Great Soul–*mahātmanā*–the clouds with their showers cause floods to cover the earth for twelve years (73). The ocean then overreaches its shores, the mountains are cast down and the earth disappears (74). After covering everything, the clouds are dispersed by the force of the wind and disappear (75). After consuming that ferocious wind, the Self-Created God–*svayaṁbhūḥ . . . devaḥ*–who resides on the original lotus, then falls asleep (76).

Mārkaṇḍeya goes on to tell of his experiences as the only survivor of the universal cataclysm and of his meeting with Nārāyaṇa in the form of a child. The destruction myth told by the sage is straightforward. There is first an expansion of the sun into seven which causes the worlds to burn and then a flood caused by twelve years of torrential rain which extinguishes the fire. Finally the clouds are dispersed by strong winds which Brahmā consumes before going to sleep for the duration of his night. All that is left is one vast ocean devoid of all life. This provides the setting for the Vaiṣṇava creation myth in which Viṣṇu is lying asleep on the ocean before sprouting the lotus from his navel. Although the Deity is involved in the process, he has a relatively minor role in providing the impetus for the clouds to appear before the flood. This may be because Mārkaṇḍeya is a teacher of Vaiṣṇava *bhakti* and does not wish to emphasise the position of Śiva, the Deity generally associated with the *pralaya.*

(iii) The Destruction of the World According to Sāṁkhya

The *Mokṣa–dharma* contains two descriptions of the withdrawal of the universe, narrated by Vyāsa to Śuka and by Yājñavalkya to Janaka.

1. Vyāsa: At the end of Chapter 224 of the *Śānti,* following his teachings to Śuka on the subject of creation, Vyāsa announces that he will now speak about the destruction of the world–*pratyāhāram*– when the Deity makes this world his own self in a subtle form– *yathedaṁ kurute 'dhyātmaṁ susūkṣmaṁ viśvam īśvaraḥ.* Seven suns appear in the sky burning the world with their rays so that all things are consumed by flames (74-75). All living beings are first dissolved back into the earth, and after all forms of life have vanished the earth is left bare like the shell of a tortoise (12.225.1–2). When water takes back aroma which is the quality of earth, then, devoid of its quality, earth moves towards a state of dissolution–*tadā bhūmiḥ pralayatvāya kalpate* (3). Then water remains with its waves roaring and swirling, filling all the world (4). When light takes back the qualities of the waters, then, without qualities, the waters enter the light and become still–*āpas tadā āttaguṇā jyotiṣy uparamanti ca* (5). When the flames of the fire within it conceal the sun, then all this world and the sky is scorched by the flames (6). When air takes back form, which is the quality of fire, the fire disappears and a great wind begins to blow (7).

Having reached the source from which it arises–*mūlam āsādya vāyuḥ saṁbhavam ātmanaḥ*–the wind blows up, down and across in ten directions (8). When space seizes touch, the quality of air, the wind then disappears and the sky remains in silence (9). Mind which is the essence of all manifestation–*abhivyaktātmakaṁ manaḥ*– then absorbs sound, the quality of space; through the mind the manifest becomes unmanifest and of the nature of *brahman* into which all things are absorbed–*manaso vyaktam avyaktaṁ brāhmaḥ sa pratisaṁcaraḥ* (10). When it has entered its own quality, the moon devours (eclipses) the mind–*tad-ātma-guṇam āviśya mano grasati candramāḥ*; after the mind disappears the self remains in the moon–*manasy uparate 'dhyātmā candramasy avatiṣṭhate* (11).

After a long time it is brought under the control of the will–*saṁkalpaḥ kurute vaśe*, one's personal will seizes the mental process and that is the highest wisdom–*cittaṁ grasati saṁkalpas tac ca jñānam anuttamam* (12). Time, according to the *śruti*, devours wisdom and strength also; time devours strength but the wise man brings time under his control–*balaṁ kālo grasati tu taṁ vidvān kurute vaśe* (13). The man of wisdom then draws within himself that sound from space; that is the supreme, the unmanifest, *brahman*, which is eternal and the highest of all; thus it is *brahman* which absorbs all beings (14). This subject has now been described fully and properly, as it has been seen and made known by the great souls who practise *yoga–yogibhiḥ paramātmabhiḥ* (15). This is how the repeated expansion out from and withdrawal into the divine unmanifest takes place; both the day and the night last for 1,000 *yugas* (16).

The description of the destruction of the world presented in this chapter by Vyāsa is far from straightforward. It is made clear that this version is that which is taught by the practitioners of *yoga* and verses 10 to 14 are concerned more with the *yoga* process than with the end of the world. It appears that the sequential withdrawal of the material elements at the time of the annihilation is recognised as being in some way equivalent to the *yoga* system that dissolves the material covering of the self so that *mokṣa* may be gained. This distraction apart, the passage displays several interesting features. The central theme is the withdrawal of each element of matter into its predecessor, as its principal quality or *guṇa* is taken from it, in a manner that is the reverse of the evolutionary notion of creation. Here, however, there is a very obvious attempt to reconcile this idea with the *pralaya* myth narrated by Mārkaṇḍeya in the *Vana*. At the end of Chapter 224, it is mentioned that the withdrawal of the world is set in motion by the Deity–*īśvara*–and that seven suns appear in the sky to destroy the earth by fire. This element of the myth is equated with the first stage of the Sāṁkhya idea of withdrawal when earth is reabsorbed into fire. Similarly the next stage, in which fire is withdrawn into water, is equated with the mythic account of the coming of the flood which extinguishes the Saṁvartaka fire and the withdrawal of water into air is represented by the arrival of winds which drive away the rainclouds.

The passage is theistic, although the Deity is referred to only at the end of Chapter 224 as causing the creation to become himself. This ties in with the statement of the *Nārāyaṇīya* that when the universe is destroyed Nārāyaṇa makes all beings a part of himself–*kṛtvātma–sthāni bhūtāni sthāvarāṇi carāṇi ca* (12.326.66). In Chapter 225, all beings are finally withdrawn into the unmanifest, the Supreme Brahman, which is therefore equivalent to Nārāyaṇa in the understanding of the *Nārāyaṇīya.* It is also noteworthy that although the Deity is here seen as instigating the destruction of the universe, there is no indication of Śiva playing a part in the myth that is made use of.

2. Yājñavalkya: The teachings of this sage to King Janaka begin from Chapter 298 of the *Śānti,* first presenting a description of creation in a manner that integrates the Sāṁkhya notion of the evolution of elements with the myth of the birth of Brahmā.[4] At the beginning of Chapter 300, Yājñavalkya tells his student that having revealed to him the stages of creation and the divisions of time, he will now speak about the destruction–*saṁhāram api me śṛṇu.* Brahmā, who is eternal and undecaying, destroys and creates all beings again and again (2). When his day ends and he becomes inclined to sleep, the unmanifest Deity brings forth an arrogant man–*codayāmāsa bhagavān avyakto 'haṁkṛtaṁ naram* (3). Impelled by the unmanifest one, the sun with its thousands of rays blazing like fire then makes itself into twelve (4). By its power it quickly burns all the different types of living being; they are destroyed in an instant leaving the earth as bare as a tortoise shell (5–6). Having burned the world, he of unlimited power then quickly fills the universe with surging water (7). The water is dispersed when it reaches the cataclysmic fire–*kālāgniḥ*–and that great fire continues to blaze (8). A mighty wind, eightfold in nature–*vāyur aṣṭātmakaḥ*–moving up, down and across, extinguishes the ferocious fire which has seven types of flame and is the heat in all beings (9–10).

Space then takes the wind into itself; mind comes forth and absorbs space which spreads beyond all sound–*ākāśam apy atinadan mano grasati cārikam* (11). Prajāpati who is self-awareness and the self of all beings takes the mind and that Great Soul who knows past, present and future takes self-awareness (12). Śambhu, the master of all beings, then takes that Supreme Soul which is all things–*tam apy anupam ātmānam viśvaṁ śaṁbhuḥ prajāpatiḥ*; he is the unfading light, the lord of the mystic perfections, *aṇimā, laghimā,* and *prāpti* (13).[5] His hands, feet, eyes, heads and faces spread everywhere and his hearing is all-pervasive (14). He is the heart of all beings, measuring the size of a thumb; that Great Soul, the Lord who is all things, finally takes up the unlimited–*anugrasaty anantaṁ hi mahātmā viśvam īśvaraḥ* (15). There then remained only he who is all things, undecaying, unchanging and untouched, the one who is faultless, the creator of the past and present of men (16).

This passage, like the version of Vyāsa, appears to be an attempt to unify several different strands into one semi-coherent understanding of the destruction of the world. Again there is the integration of the Sāṁkhya idea of withdrawal with Mārkaṇḍeya's annihilation myth, but Yājñavalkya gives the theistic element more prominence. Initially it is Brahmā who sets the process in motion when he recognises that his day is ending. The egotistical man he creates–*ahaṁkṛtaṁ naram*–may well be Rudra who is his agent in devouring the world, but the final transcendent principle into which all creation returns is known as Śambhu, another name for Śiva. This remote almost impersonal Deity, however, possesses the characteristics of Nārāyaṇa the all-pervasive spirit, who is the *kṣetrajña* of Sāṁkhya, the *viśva-rūpa,* and the *puruṣa* described by Kṛṣṇa in the *Bhagavad-gītā.*[6] In fact verse 14 here which describes Śambhu is virtually identical to 13.14 of the *Gītā* in which Kṛṣṇa discusses the nature of the Deity who is the all-pervasive *kṣetrajña.*

Yājñavalkya's discourse in effect has three different strands worked together into one version of the *pralaya*:–1. The idea of the Deity or *brahman* expanding all beings and all creation out from himself and then withdrawing them back into his own nature. 2. The *pralaya* myth as narrated by Mārkaṇḍeya. 3. The Sāṁkhya idea, presented concisely in 14.42.4, of each element being withdrawn back into that from which it emerged, and all existence merging finally back into the unmanifest. If Biardeau[7] and van Buitenen[8] are correct and Sāṁkhya was originally theistic, then 1 and 3 are essentially the same with the Deity and the unmanifest being identical principles. 2 and 3, however, do not seem to be naturally consistent and are almost certainly derived from traditions that were originally distinct. A major problem faced by both Yājñavalkya and Vyāsa is that in the myth the great fire destroys the world before the flood, so that during the period of dissolution there is nothing but a vast ocean which is known to be the resting place of Viṣṇu who sets the new creation in motion. According to Sāṁkhya, however, the withdrawal of the elements runs earth-water-fire-air-space.

The result is that there are anomalies in both Yājñavalkya's and Vyāsa's discourses. Vyāsa says that the earth is first scorched by fire from seven suns and then dissolves into water. The element fire, however, makes a second appearance as light–*jyotis*–to take its place in the Sāṁkhya analysis and take water back into itself (225.5). Yājñavalkya likewise has to have two appearances of fire, one before and one after the flood in order to balance the Sāṁkhya and mythic elements in his narration.

There is a further major point of discord: according to Sāṁkhya and the theistic traditions linked to it, all the elements of creation and all living beings are withdrawn into the Deity, *brahman,* or the unmanifest when the universe is wound up and nothing at all remains, yet according to the myths of destruction and creation, after the universe is destroyed there is a great flood which covers all the world and it is on that vast ocean that Viṣṇu lies sleeping on his serpent bed. It thus appears that, although both may be theistic, the two versions of the beginning and end of the world that are connected in the accounts discussed above originally represent different traditions. The authors of the accounts presented in the *Mokṣa-dharma* have identified points of contact between the two and attempted to weave them together but have been unable to completely disguise the distinctiveness of each perspective.

(iv) The Concept of *Yugas*

As noted earlier the word *yuga* in the *Mahābhārata* has two meanings, sometimes indicating an entire span of the creation, but more commonly referring to one of the 1,000 temporal divisions into which each creation is divided. Even when obviously used in the latter sense the term is still ambiguous for when designating the divisions of the day of Brahmā it specifically means one cycle of ages, each of which is also individually known as a *yuga.* Thus we have the *Kṛtayuga, Tretāyuga, Dvāparayuga* and *Kaliyuga* revolving in cycles 1,000 times throughout the course of creation and each cycle is also known as a *yuga.* There are three major passages in which the four *yugas* are described.

1. Hanumān: Chapters 146 to 150 of the *Vana* tell of a meeting between Bhīma and his half-brother Hanumān and the conversation between them. As Hanumān has been blessed with incredible longevity, spanning vast eons of time, a part of their discussion turns to the different ages and their characteristics. Hanumān's depiction of the four *yugas* is useful because it is concise and contains most of the major elements referred to elsewhere.

In the *Kṛtayuga* men practised the eternal *dharma* and hence specific ritual acts were unnecessary. In that age religious principles do not decline and human beings neither grow old nor die (3.148.10-11). There are no gods, *gandharvas, yakṣas, rākṣasas,* or *pannagas,* no purchasing of goods, no agitation, no Vedas and no ritualistic forms of religion (12-13). There is no disease, no deterioration of the senses and no envy, lamentation, pride, slander, quarrel, exhaustion, hatred, hostility, fear, pain, jealousy or enmity (14-15). In the *Kṛtayuga,* Nārāyaṇa, the supreme *brahman* who is the self of all beings, is white in colour (16). *Brāhmaṇas, kṣatriyas, vaiśyas* and *śūdras* all have excellent qualities in that age, and all beings are satisfied with their own activities (17). They have the same *āśrama,* the same conduct and the same deep wisdom; all *varṇas* in that age have the same duties (18). There is one Veda, one *mantra,* one rule of conduct and one mode of action; people of different natures follow the same Veda and all adhere to the same religious vows—*pṛthag dharmās tv eka-vedā dharmam ekam anuvratāḥ* (19). They attain the supreme goal by following the duties of the four *āśramas* of life without attachment to results (20). The *dharma* of the *Kṛtayuga* is *yoga* for realising the true self; in this age all *varṇas* possess the full four parts of virtue (21).

In *Tretāyuga, dharma* decreases by one-fourth part, Acyuta (Viṣṇu) is red and men are truthful and attached to acting in accordance with *dharma* (22-23). In that age, *yajñas* come into being along with different religious systems and charity and rituals for gain and reward (24). In *Tretāyuga* people never deviate from *dharma,* are devoted to penance and charity, and perform their duties according to *sva-dharma* (25). In the *Dvāparayuga* only two parts of *dharma* remain, Viṣṇu is yellow, and the Veda is made into four parts (26). Some people know all four Vedas, some three, some two and some one, while others do not know any of the hymns (27). With the scriptures thus divided, various types of rituals are followed; in executing penance and charity, people are dominated by passion (28). Because of ignorance of the one Veda, they create many Vedas, and because truth in this age is declining they concentrate on being truthful—*satyasya ceha vibhraṁśāt satye kaścid avasthitāḥ* (29). Because of this deviation from truth, many diseases become manifest as well as different types of lust and then natural disasters (30). Afflicted by such occurrences, men undergo penance desiring different objects of pleasure and heaven, while others perform *yajñas* (31).

Thus in *Dvāparayuga,* people start to live by adharmic means and in *Kaliyuga,* only one part of *dharma* remains (32). When the dark *yuga* comes, Keśava is black–*kṛṣṇaḥ;* then the ways prescribed by the Vedas, *dharma, yajña* and ritual acts all disappear (33). Calamities, plagues, exhaustion and bad qualities all become prominent (34). As the *yugas* progress, *dharma* declines and as *dharma* declines, people perish; as people decline, their natures which shape the world deteriorate and religious acts performed at the end of *Kaliyuga* produce a result different to that sought (35-36). This *Kaliyuga* will soon commence and even those who have huge life-spans are forced to change as the *yugas* change (37).

This chapter provides an excellent summation of the *Mahābhārata*'s understanding of the four *yugas,* reflecting a decline in both righteousness and living conditions as the cycle progresses. Although the information offered about each *yuga* is relatively brief, it is sufficient to convey the characteristic idea of different ages changing and revolving through time. Furthermore, the portrayal of human society in a state of perfection in *Kṛtayuga* provides an interesting insight into the epic's view of the various tendencies reflected in its corpus. At this time, because all people were naturally righteous, there were no distinctive duties for the four *varṇas* and no need for ritualised religion. The implication here is that this type of religion is inferior and is required only because human imperfection renders the higher spiritual practices unattainable. This view is significant in the light Yudhiṣṭhira's repeatedly-stated aversion to the principles of *sva-dharma.* Yudhiṣṭhira constantly displays the characteristics of those who lived in the *Kṛtayuga,* being a person in whom virtue exists by nature. Hence he finds the ritualised *dharma* of the *Dvāparayuga* in which he lives inappropriate and unwanted, for it is intended for men inferior to himself.

It is also apparent that righteousness and the nature of life on earth are closely linked. It is not only *dharma* that deteriorates as the ages move forward, but also the nature of human existence. As humanity moves further away from its *Kṛtayuga* status of inherent virtue, so disease, natural calamities, ageing and death increasingly blight the happiness of life. Finally, the relationship between the change of *yuga* and the manifestation of Viṣṇu is to be noted. This feature is mentioned without any explanation in this passage, but is probably connected to Kṛṣṇa's statement in the *Gītā* that he manifests himself in this world *yuga* after *yuga*–*sambhavāmi yuge yuge* (4.8).

2 Mārkaṇḍeya: Mārkaṇḍeya's exposition later in the *Vana* provides further details on the subject, though the understanding of *yugas* is essentially the same as that presented by Hanumān. Like Hanumān, Mārkaṇḍeya has an extraordinary lifespan, having apparently survived even the universal annihilation, and has thus experienced all the *yugas.* At the beginning of Chapter 186, the sage is asked by Yudhiṣṭhira to tell them of his experiences during the huge periods of time through which he has lived. We then learn the duration of each *yuga,* information not provided by the previous discourse. *Kṛtayuga* extends for 4,800 years, *Tretā* for 3,600, *Dvāpara* for 2,400, and *Kali* for 1,200, making a complete cycle of 12,000 years (3.186. 18-22). 1,000 of such cycles constitutes a day of Brahmā. Mārkaṇḍeya then moves on to a lengthy discussion of the nature of human life in the *Kaliyuga,* especially of the period towards its conclusion when the degradation is virtually complete. Here we are presented with many more details both of the wicked behaviour of the people and also of the terrible conditions on earth which they are forced to endure (23-55).

At the beginning of Chapter 188, Yudhiṣṭhira asks to hear more about the decline of *dharma* in the *Kaliyuga* and how a new cycle of the four ages begins. Mārkaṇḍeya then presents another lengthy account of the horrors of *Kaliyuga* which includes new information about the end of that age and the beginning of a new *Kṛtayuga* (14-84). By the end of *Kaliyuga* terrible conditions prevail on earth. The kings are no more than powerful thieves, and murder and robbery are commonplace. At the end of the *yuga,* impelled by time, a *brāhmaṇa* named Kalki will appear, acting like a true king and waging war in order to restore *dharma* (91). Surrounded by other *brāhmaṇas* he will seek out and destroy the miscreants who dominate the world (93). With his host of *brāhmaṇas* he will conquer all lands, destroying the robbers and establishing a new *Kṛtayuga. Dharma* will be restored, the *varṇas* will execute their proper duties, crops will grow in abundance, and ritual acts, *yajñas,* charity and penance will all be performed once more (3.189.1-13).

Mārkaṇḍeya's description of the *yugas* shows no major incongruity with that of Hanumān, but has different points of emphasis. Both accounts stress the concept a continually revolving cycle of four ages, the progression of which is marked by a deterioration in both the virtue of mankind and the conditions of life on earth. In addition, Mārkaṇḍeya gives the duration of each *yuga,* a more detailed account of life in *Kaliyuga,* and a description of how the cycle is renewed with the inauguration of a new *Kṛtayuga.*

There is a predestined inevitability about the progression of *yugas* and the influence they have over human behaviour. There is no explanation as to how and why the nature of the world is repeatedly transformed in this way, but it is clear that humanity is subject to all-powerful cosmic forces over which it can have no control. Hanumān states that even those remarkable individuals whose lives span more than one *yuga* are transformed in their nature by the changing of the ages. Elsewhere, we are told that by the nature of his government a king is able to determine the particular *yuga* that prevails in his domain. It would appear, however, that such statements are figurative for in the passages considered above it is very apparent that the *yuga* makes man, not man the *yuga.*

3. References to the Yugas in the Moksa-dharma: In the *Mokṣa-dharma,* the *Śukānupraśna* contains a brief description of the *yugas* (12.230. 14–20 and 12.224. 16–28, 62–69). In Chapter 224, verses 16 to 20 give the same durations for the *yugas* as given by Mārkaṇḍeya, though here it is made clear that the 12,000 year cycle is in years of the gods. There then follows a brief description of the deterioration of living conditions as the *yugas* progress and of the changes of religious practice made necessary by the change of *yugas.* Verses 62 to 69 similarly discuss the differences in *dharma* between *yugas,* indicating again that the ritualised forms of religion

came into being only because of humanity's declining spirituality. This point is reasserted in Chapter 230 (7–8), perhaps being stressed here in the *Mokṣa-dharma* to emphasise the superiority of *nivṛtti* over the path of *pravṛtti.* As the *yugas* move forward religion deteriorates until in *Kaliyuga* the Vedas and *dharma* disappear.

In Chapter 327 of the *Śānti,* in the *Nārāyaṇīya,* there is an account of Nārāyaṇa instructing the gods as to how they should manage the universe in which he refers to the four *yugas* (73–76). The same basic idea is presented in this short passage which describes the *Kṛtayuga* as the perfect age in which *yajñas* are performed without violence and that as each new age arrives one fourth part of *dharma* is lost until it disappears altogether at the end of the *Kaliyuga.*

(v) Conclusion

The cosmic eschatology taught by the epic is reasonably straightforward and not a subject which appears to be the focus of doctrinal tensions. The world is eternal but subject to repeated periods of manifestation and withdrawal. Each period of manifestation, known as a *kalpa,* a *yuga,* or a day of Brahmā, is divided into 1,000 sub-periods which are also referred to as *yugas.* Each of these *yugas* is further divided into four ages, known as the *Kṛtayuga, Tretāyuga, Dvāparayuga* and *Kaliyuga,* during the progression of which the righteousness of humanity and also the conditions of life on earth steadily deteriorate until the end of *Kaliyuga* when everything is restored and a new *Kṛtayuga* inaugurated.

The *Mahābhārata* clearly draws upon two distinctive eschatological traditions which it attempts to reconcile into one syncretised version. One of these is completely mythic and is intimately connected with the epic's creation myth. The second version is based on Sāṁkhya, which is sometimes theistic and sometimes non-theistic. Here the dissolution of the universe is described in terms of its being an exact reversal of the evolutionary process of creation in which each element emerges from its predecessor. Thus when the world comes to an end, each element is withdrawn back into that from which it came and eventually all aspects of creation are withdrawn back into the unmanifest, or back into the Deity. Despite the clear differences in perspective between the two versions, there is no evidence of any tension between them. The principal tension of the text as a whole, between *pravṛtti* and *nivṛtti,* is absent from the epic's discussion of cosmic eschatology and therefore the different traditions are reconciled and brought together.

3. Individual Eschatology

(i) Introduction

In his discussion of this subject, van Buitenen has pointed out the different types of individual eschatology that the *Mahābhārata* presents.[9] In his opinion the oldest notion is that of *svarga-loka,* referred to by the Vedas, where the righteous and the followers of ritual *dharma* are able to gain a place amongst the gods after death. Further to this we have the concepts of *saṁsāra,* the transmigration of the soul from body to body, and *mokṣa,* the attainment of complete salvation from this world. It is apparent that the different notions of existence after death represent aspects of the tension between *pravṛtti* and *nivṛtti. Pravṛtti* teaches that the execution of *sva-dharma* and ritual acts such as charity, fasting and penance is rewarded by elevation to *svarga-loka.* The ideas of Sāṁkhya and Yoga, however, reject the validity of this type of religious practice, arguing that even life among the gods is temporary and that one should instead endeavour for absolute salvation.

(ii) Svarga-loka

The *Mahābhārata* contains several detailed descriptions of *svarga-loka* and certain portions of the narrative drama take place in that domain. Notable here is the episode in the *Vana* in which Arjuna resides with his true father, the lord of the gods, and also the *Svargārohana,* in which the Pāṇḍavas reach the realm of the gods and are reunited with those slain at Kurukṣetra.

In the *Vana,* Chapters 43 to 45 describe Arjuna's sojourn in heaven. Chapter 43 tells of the arrival of Indra's charioteer, Mātali, to take Arjuna to his father and verses 28 to 38 describe their arrival in *svarga-loka.* Whilst entering the realm of the gods Arjuna sees thousands of amazing flying machines–*adbhūta-rūpāni vimānāni* (28). Neither sun nor moon shines there, for those worlds are self-luminous and are seen in the sky from earth as stars–*tāra-rūpāṇi yān iha dṛśyante* (30). Great sages reside there along with those who have gained perfection and warriors who died in battle. There are also *gandharvas,* celestial musicians whose bodies shine like the sun, and *guhyakas, ṛṣis* and *apsarases.* Arjuna asks Mātali about the luminous planets he can see and is told that they are in fact righteous persons now fixed in their proper positions–*ete sukṛtinaḥ pārtha sveṣu dhiṣṇyeṣv avasthitāḥ*–and seen from earth as stars in the sky (35). Arjuna then sees the city of the gods, Amaravatī, with his father's elephant, Airāvata, standing at the gate.

Chapter 44 gives a description of the city. It is full of sweet-scented flowers and trees, the aroma from which is carried in all directions by gentle breezes. This domain of the gods is seen only by those who perform great penances or *yajñas,* fight bravely in battle, study the Vedas, or bathe at many *tīrthas.* Above the city there are aerial chariots which move at the will of the driver. Arjuna is welcomed by *gandharvas* and sages before being escorted to the palace of Indra to meet his father. Different gods and heavenly beings are seen there, as well as great *ṛṣis* and righteous kings who ruled in the past. Verses 28 to 32 provide a short description of the palace of Indra in which *gandharvas* sing and play beautiful music, while voluptuous *apsarases* dance in a manner that arouses the desires of all who watch.

The *Svargārohaṇa-parvan* actually contains very little by way of description of *svarga-loka.* Its main subject is Yudhiṣṭhira's reaction to seeing sinners enjoying the delights of heaven simply because they died bravely in battle. There is reference again to the delightful performances of the *gandharvas* and *apsarases* (18.3.22), and it is apparent that in *svarga-loka* one is able to meet and recognise departed loved ones. In Chapter 4, Yudhiṣṭhira sees all those allies and kinsmen who fell in battle now with effulgent celestial forms seated in positions of honour.

The *Anuśāsana,* in discussing the rituals and pious acts that enable one to gain a desirable position after death, also contains descriptions of the heavens to which one may be elevated. Chapter 70 describes the meeting of Nāciketas with Yama, famous from the *Kaṭha Upaniṣad,* in the course of which Yama reveals to his guest the abodes gained by the righteous–*lokān sarvāṁs . . . puṇya-kṛtām* (20). Those who reach this heaven inhabit golden palaces bedecked with jewels and bells, surrounded by beautiful woods and lakes. Within these mansions are all kinds of delicious foods, soft beds and luxurious garments, and outside there are trees which yield any fruit one may desire–*sarva-kāma-phalāṁś caiva vṛkṣān* (24).

There are rivers, streets, assembly halls, lakes, chariots, rivers of milk, hills of butter and also pure drinking water, all of which are shown to Nāciketas by the God of Death.

In Chapter 105, Bhīṣma narrates the story of the testing of Gautama by Indra, who appears as a king and steals the sage's pet elephant. As Indra is taking the elephant away Gautama vows that he will follow him wherever he goes, and the remainder of the story contains a series of descriptions of the various celestial domains through which the pursuit proceeds. It is clear from this description that there are many heavens in *svarga-loka*, each of which an individual may attain depending upon the duration and significance of his pious acts. The depictions are similar to those which have been encountered before — singing and dancing by *gandharvas* and *apsarases* (18), and delightful woods and mountains adorned with fragrant flowers and trees (20–22).

There Indra satisfies all desires–*yatra śakro varṣati sarva-kāmān*, women and men enjoy sexual pleasures without restriction, and there are no feelings of jealousy between the sexes–*yatra striyaḥ kāma-cārāś caranti yatra cerṣyā nāsti nārī-narāṇām* (26). Each of the heavens is presided over by one of the gods, Indra, Kuvera, Sūrya, or Varuṇa, who have their assembly halls there. These are described in stereotypical fashion, in a manner similar to that found in Chapters 5 to 11 of the *Sabhā*. Like tribal lords the various gods hold court in their bejewelled halls, though the only details given consist of long lists of celestial beings present there to serve the deity.

The *Anuśāsana* also contains references to a heaven of cows, mentioned by Gautama in the above passage, in verse 42 of Chapter 105. A more detailed description is provided by Chapter 80. From this passage we learn that the heaven of cows is gained by those who make acceptable gifts of cows to worthy persons. There is no actual mention of cows living in this heaven, although the setting is suitably rural. There are beautiful trees, flowers and fruits, while along the river banks the sand is of pure gold. There is no mud or dust there; lotuses flower on fresh streams and lakes of pure water. The major point of interest in these descriptions is their providing a possible antecedent for the Purāṇic portrayal of the spiritual domain of Kṛṣṇa as a world of cows, Goloka, in which he enjoys an idyllic pastoral existence with his devotees.

The status of life in *svarga-loka* is generally one that is attained after death, although there are exceptions where mortals are able to dwell amongst the gods even in this life. *Svarga-loka* is not a transcendental world and in many ways it appears similar to earthly kingdoms. Despite the claim by Nārada (18.1.11) that in heaven all enmities cease, we learn from stories such as that of Nahuṣa (5.9-18) that in fact there may be political intrigue there, accompanied by envy and the desire for power. The delights of heaven are very obviously material and descriptions characteristically focus on the sensual pleasures to be derived from beautiful palaces, soft beds, opulent foods and beautiful women with large hips. This stands by way of contrast to the perspective of *mokṣa-dharma* which teaches a total renunciation of all such pleasures.

Numerous writers have referred to the incongruity between the idea of an afterlife in heaven and the concept of metempsychosis. The epic itself attempts to harmonise these beliefs by presenting existence in heaven or hell as an interim state before rebirth for those who have acted with an excess of either virtue or sin. The crucial distinction, and the key to the incongruity, is the fact that existence in heaven is not rebirth in the sense understood by the doctrine of *saṁsāra.* One elevated to *svarga-loka* after death lives there in a celestial form, but retains the same identity as when living on earth. It is not that one is reborn as a god or *gandharva* in order to experience the delights of heaven, but rather that one is able to live amongst the gods after death as the same individual with the same personality. In 18.3. 27–29, Yudhiṣṭhira bathes in the Ganges, which also flows through *svarga-loka,* in order to give up his human body and gain a divine form. Nonetheless, he retains his identity as Yudhiṣṭhira the Pāṇḍava king, as do Nahuṣa and Yayāti who rise up to heaven and fall down again, but are still recognised as the ancient kings who once ruled the earth.

The *Āśramavāsika* describes how the Pāṇḍavas and others are able to meet on earth those slain at Kurukṣetra who are now living with the gods. In verses 6 to 13 of Chapter 40, we are told of how the dead heroes emerge from the *Gaṅges* (presumably a route from heaven to earth) dressed in effulgent celestial attire, with the same standards and chariots that they displayed during their earthly existence. They are now free from hostility, egotism, anger and pride–*nirvairāḥ nirahaṁkārā vigata-krodha-manyavaḥ* (15)–but clearly have the same identities as they had before death. In Chapter 41, they meet with their old friends, apparently in continuation of earthly relationships but with previous enmities now dissolved.

After hearing this narration, Janamejaya asks Vaiśaṁpāyana how those whose bodies had been destroyed could be seen again on earth in the same forms–*kathaṁ sa tyakta-dehānāṁ punas tad-rūpa-darśanam* (15-42-2). Vaiśaṁpāyana's reply centres on the argument that bodily forms are created by previous acts–*karma-jāni śarīrāṇi*–and that the two remain intimately connected. Although the body has been destroyed, the acts that led to its generation have not–*avipranāśaḥ sarveṣāṁ karmaṇām* (4)–and hence the form persists even in *svarga-loka* as a reflection of those acts.

The passage is interesting for the manner in which it shows how Sāṁkhya teachings based on the notion of a transcendent self were seen as compatible with the idea of elevation to heaven after death. Sāṁkhya teaches that whilst the body is temporary and is destroyed at death, the true self is eternal and survives death by adopting another physical and mental identity. Here, however, we have an explanation in terms of acts creating the physical form of how this rule may be avoided when an individual truly survives death and is able to continue with his same identity into the afterlife. The celestial body is of a different substance and the character flaws of one's earthly nature are moderated, but essentially the individual remains as the same person in *svarga-loka* and is able to carry over relationships formed in this world into a sphere beyond death.

(iii) The Epic's View of Hell

Just as there is a place of reward for the righteous, so there is also a place of punishment after death for those who deviate excessively from *dharma.* References to this hell, designated usually as *naraka-loka* or *niraya,* are found throughout the Mahābhārata most frequently as an antithesis to the idea of adherence to *dharma* carrying a person to heaven. In the *Droṇa,* when the Trigartas take a vow to kill Arjuna on a particular day of the battle (7.16.11f), they swear that the worlds of those who commit sins will be theirs if they do not keep their promise. A similar oath is made by Arjuna when he vows to kill Jayadratha after Abhimanyu has been slain (7.54.1f). In the *Rāja-dharma,* it is stated that kings who misrule their kingdoms have to dwell in hell for many years; the *Anuśāsana* gives a list of different types of sinners using the refrain, *te vai niraya-gāminaḥ,* to indicate that they are consigned to hell (13.24.59-80); in the *Gītā* both Kṛṣṇa and Arjuna talk of hell as the destination for wrongdoers (1.43 and 16.16, 21).

The *Purāṇas* contain graphic descriptions of a variety of hells presided over by the God of Death, in which sinners are tortured in various horrific ways, depending upon the type of sin they have committed.[10] The *Mahābhārata* offers far less detail on the subject, but what references it does contain appear to be in line with the Purāṇic view. The most notable description of *naraka-loka* comes at the very end of the epic in the *Svargārohana.* Having reached the realm of the gods, Yudhiṣṭhira is surprised to see Duryodhana and his allies there, all in exalted positions, whilst his brothers and comrades cannot be seen. Demanding to be shown where they are, he is conducted to hell by a servant of the gods along an impure path which is hard to traverse (18.2.16). It is a terrible place, covered in darkness, with hair and damp slime as its grass; it is filled with the smell of sinners and made muddy under foot by flesh and blood (17). Everywhere there are biting insects, crickets, bees, mosquitoes and rotting corpses; hair and bones are strewn around covered in worms and insects, and blazing fires add to the torments (18-19).

That region is infested with ravens and vultures with beaks of iron, as well as evil spirits with needle-like mouths (20). Scattered everywhere are dismembered limbs, entrails, hands and feet (21). Through that inauspicious place of horror the righteous king proceeded, his mind deep in thought (22). He then saw a river filled with hot water and a forest of trees with leaves razor-sharp like swords (23). There was an expanse of blazing sand with rocks of iron, and copper jars filled with boiling oil (24). There were *Kūṭa-sālmalika* bushes, painful to touch because of their sharp thorns, and Yudhiṣṭhira saw there the torments of those who act sinfully (25).

Yudhiṣṭhira decides to return but hears his brothers crying out to him to stay, for his presence eases their suffering. He complains angrily against the injustice of the Pāṇḍavas being punished like this while Duryodhana and other miscreants are in heaven. At this the gods all appear and hell vanishes; Indra then explains that all kings perform both good and evil deeds and must therefore experience both hell and heaven. Normally the period in hell follows that in heaven, but for the Pāṇḍavas this order has been changed so that they may enjoy their time in heaven without anxiety. Even Yudhiṣṭhira committed one sin in his life in speaking falsely to bring about the death of Droṇa and as a result he also has had to look upon the horrors of *naraka-loka.*

In the *Śānti*, there is a brief description of hell in the story of King Janamejaya's killing of a *brāhmaṇa*. The king is told of the destination that awaits him for this act by the sage Indrota, 'Leaving this world, you will fall head downwards and remain like that for an unlimited number of years. After being afflicted there by vultures and peacocks with iron beaks, you will be born again in a sinful form. If you think that there is nothing but this world, the agents of Yama will remind you of the truth in the abode of the God of Death' (12.146. 16-18). Similarly, in the *Anuśāsana*, Bṛhaspati discusses the fate that awaits sinners after death, mostly in terms of rebirth in animal forms, but also with reference to punishment in the abode of Yama. One guilty of ingratitude is taken after death to Yama's domain and is there afflicted by the cruel servants of the God of Death. He suffers pain from lances, bludgeons, spears and jars heated on fires, as well as a forest of trees with leaves like swords, blazing sand, thorny *Kūṭa-śālmalī* bushes and many other torments. He then returns to the cycle of *saṁsāra* and is reborn as a worm (13.112. 80-83).

These short passages[11] demonstrate the epic's idea that just as a pious individual may be elevated to heaven with the same identity he had on earth, so those who are wicked are carried to hell for a period of punishment before losing that identify through the transmigration of the soul into another bodily form. The *Purāṇas* elaborate upon the idea by describing different hells and various exotic punishments inflicted by the Yamadūtas, but the epic does not carry its consideration that far and the main significance of the idea of hell is as an eschatological concept that provides an antithesis to the understanding of the heavenly rewards bestowed upon the righteous.

4. *Saṁsāra*, the Doctrine of Rebirth

(i) The Transmigration of the Soul

The *Mahābhārata* includes the notions of both heaven and *saṁsāra* and effects a reconciliation between them, as noted above, by taking existence in heaven or hell as an interim status between births. Hence in the teachings of Bṛhaspati in the *Anuśāsana*, it is asserted that a sinner is punished first in hell and then forced to take birth in an animal form to continue the progress of *saṁsāra* (13.112.83). Similarly, in Chapter 16 of the *Gītā*, punishment by hell and by rebirth in a lower species appear to be virtually interchangeable. The same applies to existence in heaven; when Śiva tells Umā of the rewards gained after death by those who execute penances, he speaks both of living in heaven and of birth on earth in a wealthy royal family (13.130).

According to Frauwallner,[12] the ideas on *saṁsāra* and *karma* found in the *Mahābhārata* are identical to those of the *Upaniṣads*, and it thus appears that the compilers of the epic are reflecting in their work a well-established doctrine and have nothing radically different to add on the subject. The doctrine of metempsychosis is common to all parts of the epic, narrative and didactic, and all strands of thought contained within it, be it *bhakti, nivṛtti,* or *pravṛtti.*

Central to epic Sāṁkhya is the distinction between the body and the true self, the *kṣetra* and the *kṣetrajña*. The body is composed of the elements of *prakṛti* and hence is subject to change and decay, but the *ātman* within is eternal and changeless. Thus when the body dies the self remains untouched by death and departs from the body to continue its existence in another form. The first instruction given by Kṛṣṇa in the *Gītā* focuses on this point, as he reassures his distraught comrade that the warriors who are about to die will continue to exist after death. Kṛṣṇa later (2.37) asserts that those who die in battle attain *svarga-loka,* but initially he reassures Arjuna by teaching the doctrine of the transmigration of the self.

> *dehino 'smin yathā dehe kaumāraṁ yauvanaṁ jarā*
> *tathā dehāntara-prāptir dhīras tatra na muhyati*
>
> 'Just as within this body the embodied soul experiences childhood, youth, and old age, so it obtains another body; the wise one is not confused about this.' (2.13)

The idea here is that just as in life the body undergoes progressive change while the self retains the same identity, so it is that when the body is given up, the same self exists in a new bodily form. A few verses later (2.22) Kṛṣṇa compares the process of transmigration to a person's changing his clothes. When one's clothes become worn, one discards them and puts on new ones; in the same way when one's body is exhausted or destroyed it is abandoned and the *ātman* moves on to a new form of embodiment.

A further description of metempsychosis is found in Chapter 15. The self gains a body and then abandons it; having seized a body he moves on, like the wind carrying aromas from their source (8). The verse is a little vague as it is not entirely clear what *etāni* refers to, possibly the succession of bodies the self transmigrates through or else the different senses it uses in a particular form. The simile of the wind and aromas indicates that the effects of experiences in one life are carried over to the next. Almost certainly this refers to the doctrine of *karma* which teaches that acts performed in this life shape the nature of one's future existence, although the point is not elaborated upon here.

Whilst the *Gītā* thus presents a fairly straightforward understanding of the process of transmigration, the narrative as a whole is more concerned eschatologically with heaven and hell. In the didactic interludes in which various sages enter the drama and impart teachings, ideas of transmigration and *karma* are emphasised, but when the main characters consider the fate that awaits them after death it is almost always in terms of heaven and hell. That is not to say that the notion of transmigration and rebirth is wholly absent from the narrative. Occasionally characters do refer to the effects of actions performed in previous lives, as do Dhṛtarāṣṭra and Gāndhārī in the *Strī,* and in the incidents that lead to the death of Bhīṣma the concept of reincarnation is central as Ambā is reborn as Śikhandin. Thus whilst it would be incorrect to assert that the epic narrative is unaware of the doctrines of transmigration and *karma,* it is certainly true that the main eschatological emphasis of these portions of the text lies elsewhere.

As might be expected the major stress on *saṁsāra* is found in passages which present teachings on Sāṁkhya and Yoga. Essentially the ideas presented here are identical to those of the *Gīta,* though occasionally a few more details are added. In Chapter 286 of the *Śānti,* for example, Parāśara briefly discusses the passage of the self through death to rebirth. After the body has been abandoned by the embodied self–*śarīrin*–it becomes inert and devoid of consciousness; the elements of which it is composed return to their own natures and the body becomes earth once more (12.286.16). The body is produced by previous acts and is born here and there and dies in various places; the manifestation of one particular nature or another is understood to be based on previous actions (17). The self, however, is not immediately reborn at the time of death–*na jāyate tu nṛpate kaṁcit kālamayaṁ punaḥ*–but wanders across the sky like a great cloud–*paribhramati bhūtātmā dyām ivāmbudharo mahān* (18). This idea of the soul roaming across the sky awaiting rebirth may be specific to the particular school from which the teachings of Parāśara arose and not a universally held part of the doctrine of transmigration. It is in any case a point of detail and the basic idea remains of the spiritual *ātman* leaving the body at death and accepting a new form. The change of identity is not absolute, for the 'aroma' of the previous life goes with the *bhūtātman* and is the causal factor in determining both the type of body gained and also the fortune experienced in the next life.

(ii) The Doctrine of *Karma*

Parāśara's teachings make it clear that the type of body one is reborn into is determined by actions performed in the previous life. The idea is known as the doctrine of *karma* and has two distinctive features in terms of the type of body the self enters and the individual destiny encountered within that body. There are close connections here, which the *Mahābhārata* is well aware of, with the notion of heaven and hell, for the nature of one's rebirth and the fortune one experiences in the next life may both be seen as punishment and reward for previous good and bad acts.

As with the doctrine of *saṁsāra,* the idea of *karma* is found throughout the epic. The position of the *Bhagavad-gītā* is interesting here, for once again it propounds the Upaniṣadic and Sāṁkhya teachings found only rarely in the central narrative. The *Gītā* does not in fact set out a doctrine of *karma* but clearly takes the notion for granted. Pivotal to Kṛṣṇa's argument is the understanding that actions will have a future reaction and this is the basis of Arjuna's fear. What the *Gītā* teaches is that actions done as a part of ritual duty–*yajñārthaḥ*–or as an offering to the Deity–*mad-arpaṇam*–transcend the law of *karma* because they are performed without selfish desire. In other words the *Bhagavad-gītā* is less concerned with expounding the doctrine of *karma* than with explaining how it may be surmounted.

If a precise exposition of the doctrine of *karma* is difficult to pin down in the *Gītā,* the same is not true of other sections of the *Mahābhārata.* The teachings of Parāśara have already been noted in this context, and in Chapter 174 of the *Śānti,* Bhīṣma presents a complete and succinct discourse dealing specifically with this subject. Yudhiṣṭhira's request here is to be told about charity, sacrifice, penance and service to one's teacher, but Bhīṣma takes this as an impetus to speak about the consequences of sinful actions. When one is improperly engaged the mind indulges in wickedness, and after acting in an impure manner one is placed in a position of great torment (2). Such sinners move from famine to famine, misery to misery, terror to terror, and death to death, while those who act righteously with faith and self-control repeatedly gain festive delights, heaven and happiness (4-5). Unbelievers have to go to inaccessible regions where violent elephants roam and there is fear of snakes and robbers (6). Those men who are not motivated by *dharma* are like blighted grain in the harvest or flies amongst birds (7).

Even if one runs swiftly one's past conduct will follow, being asleep and active at the same time as oneself (8). Like a constant shadow, a man's past conduct remains still when he stops, moves when he moves and acts when he acts (9). However and in whatever way a man's past actions have accumulated, he enjoys accordingly throughout his life (10). Time has complete control over the host of living beings, the results of whose past actions rain down upon them and whose destiny is thus completely circumscribed (11). As fruits and flowers appear without any external impetus, so past actions yield results and the proper time cannot be avoided (12).

Repeatedly, when destiny is exhausted, the progress of life with its honour and dishonour, loss and gain, decay and growth, ceases to be (13). Happiness and distress are acquired because of oneself; having reached the bed of the womb, one enjoys the results of his previous life (14). However one previously acted as a child, a youth or in old age, in a pure or impure manner, one will experience the ensuing results birth after birth in various forms (15). As a calf finds its mother amongst thousands of cows, so actions seek out the one who performed them (16). A cloth which is first moistened is made clean by proper action; through their acts of renunciation there is unlimited happiness for ascetics (17). By performing penance in the forest, all the heart's desires are fulfilled for one whose sins are removed by *dharma* (18). Like the path of birds through the sky or fish through water, the way of those who understand wisdom cannot be seen (19). Enough has been said on this subject through condemnations, glorifications, and disputations in a manner that is artistic, eloquent and beneficial to hear (20).

The doctrine of *karma* as expressed in this chapter contains no substantial advance upon or digression from the ideas of the *Upaniṣads.* Within the *Mahābhārata,* certain sections of the text are less concerned with *karma* than others, as has been noted, but nowhere does it appear to be a subject on which tension arises. This is almost certainly because the tendencies towards *pravṛtti, nivṛtti* and *bhakti* all accept the idea of *karma* as a central element of their world views. The teachings of Bhīṣma in Chapter 174 of the *Śānti* are from the perspective of *mokṣa-dharma,* but his ideas are equally a part of the doctrines of *pravṛtti.* This point is demonstrated by several passages from the *Anuśāsana.* In Chapter 133, Śiva explains to Umā that those who live piously, give charity and engage in public works enjoy the pleasures of heaven and then are born on earth into a wealthy family so that their pleasures may continue (7). Those who never give charity and are indifferent to the sufferings of others go first to hell (13) and then are born into poor families among the lowest of men. In Chapter 112, Bṛhaspati similarly lists the different animal births that are the destination of different types of sinners.

The idea of *karma* and transmigration is an important element in the perspective of *pravṛtti* because it serves to reinforce and legitimate the rigid stratification of society into *varṇas.* One is born into a particular station in the social hierarchy because of one's previous acts; the social order and an individual's position within it are thus not merely conventional, but are ordained by divine dispensation. In Chapters 118 to 120 of the *Anuśāsana,* Bhīṣma tells of a wicked *śūdra* who is reborn as a worm because of his misdeeds. By good fortune he encounters the sage Vyāsa who enables him to rise through various species of life, as one birth follows another, until finally he is born as a *kṣatriya* enjoying the wealth and status of the nobility. Continuing to take instruction from Vyāsa, the *kṣatriya* undertakes various penances and rules his domain in an exemplary fashion. As a result of this piety he is reborn as a *brāhmaṇa* who executes thousands of *yajñas* and thereby reaches the eternal *brahman.*

Although the conclusion of this story, where the worm finally gains the *brahma sanātanam,* appears to indicate that it is based on the ideas of *mokṣa-dharma,* I doubt whether this is the case. The central emphasis of the narration is on the gradual elevation of the soul by means of rebirths in progressively higher positions. 13.119.23[13] clearly makes the point that a righteous *śūdra* next takes birth as a *vaiśya*, a righteous *vaiśya* becomes a *kṣatriya*, a righteous *kṣatriya* is reborn as a *brāhmaṇa*, and for a *brāhmaṇa* the highest eschatological goals are possible, including *mokṣa*. This teaching shows that the tendencies of *pravṛtti* and *nivṛtti* are not absolutely distinct, but more significantly demonstrates how the doctrines of *saṁsāra* and *karma* are integral to the understanding of the *varṇa* system and of the notion of *sva-dharma*.

It is now apparent why all sections of the *Mahābhārata* should present an eschatology in which the self is reborn on earth in a form dictated by previous acts. Although the narrative primarily stresses the idea of heaven and hell, it is also aware of the doctrine of *saṁsāra* as the story of Ambā and other incidents demonstrate. For *mokṣa-dharma*, *saṁsāra* represents the misery of repeated death from which one should endeavour to escape, while the concept of *sva-dharma* is underpinned by the understanding that one's position in the social order is not arbitrary, but is the result of previous actions. Teachings on *bhakti* likewise accept the idea of *saṁsāra* and ascribe to the Deity the role of both controller of and deliverer from the endless cycle.

5. The Concept of *Mokṣa*

(i) Introduction

The schools of Sāṁkhya, Yoga and Bhakti all regard the cycle of continuous rebirth as undesirable for the spiritual *ātman*. Heaven is rejected as being only a temporary relief, for even the position of the gods is ultimately impermanent. Hence Sāṁkhya and Yoga postulate the total and unending release from *saṁsāra* as their goals, and the devotee is assured that he will gain salvation as a result of his worship invoking the grace of the Deity. The processes which these different schools advocate for gaining salvation have already been extensively discussed under the heading of soteriology, but to complete the examination of epic eschatology it is necessary to look at what the state of *mokṣa* actually means.

Whilst the status of existence in *svarga-loka* is made clear by the epic, the state of salvation gained through *mokṣa-dharma* is not, for, as Herman notes, "What one is released from is *duḥkha*, but what one is released to is ambiguous..."[14] The standard pattern found throughout the various treatises is for *mokṣa* to be referred to simply by a single word or phrase, or else in negative terms as being beyond birth or free from all miseries. The teachings on salvation are more practical than philosophical with the emphasis constantly placed on the knowledge that brings release. That which is beyond the twenty-four elements of matter is by definition beyond the range of the senses and thus there are obvious problems if the author wishes to describe it in anything but negative terms.

It is also apparent that *mokṣa* is not understood simply as securing an afterlife in a particular place such as *svarga-loka,* but is more a state of consciousness that may be attained even while the individual remains here. The self is never truly a part of this world and when this is recognised through *sāṁkhya-jñāna* then that self is no longer affected by the material elements, just as much as if it were existing in some transcendental domain. Hence questions of where, when and what is it like are less pertinent, for it is more a matter of existing in a particular state beyond any physical location. One who has attained *mokṣa* no longer sees himself in terms of body, mind, or senses; he exists only as the *puruṣa* and in this state even the question of before or after death loses its relevance. Death does not touch the *kṣetrajña* and one who gains *mokṣa* in this life exists only as the *kṣetrajña.*

(ii) The Teachings of the *Mokṣa-dharma*

Typically the treatises of the *Mokṣa-dharma* discuss the philosophical ideas of Sāṁkhya or occasionally Vedānta, the ethics and lifestyle demanded, and sometimes the *yoga* practices that enable one to directly observe the truths of Sāṁkhya. They frequently conclude by stating that by such means one gains *mokṣa,* usually expressed briefly by a single verse or even a single line with a phrase such as *brahma saṁpadyate tadā* (12.7.35, 12.168.42), *tato brahma samaśnute* (12.66.32), or *brahma-bhūyāya kalpate* (12.154.25). In Chapter 171, Mankin proclaims that he will abandon all desire and attachment and thereby gain the great joy of *brahman–sarvān kāmān parityajya prāpya brahma mahat sukham* (53) — but no more details of the nature of his salvation are given. In Chapter 188, Bhīṣma describes *yoga* practice and in the last line of the chapter states, *gacchanti yogino hy evaṁ nirvāṇaṁ tan nirāmayam*–the *yogins* thereby attain *nirvāṇa* (salvation) from which there is no fall (22) and again the phrase is not elaborated on.

In Chapter 195, Manu teaches that those who reach *mokṣa* attain that which is supreme–*param āpnuvanti* (2). He expands on this statement a little further in the next verse, but only in negative terms. It cannot be perceived by the senses for it contains none of the qualities of touch, taste, sound etc. which the senses are able to perceive. Thus only one who withdraws the senses becomes able to perceive that which is the highest. In Chapter 197, Manu asserts that one who casts off material attributes gains immortality — *amṛtam aśnute* (12) — but does not elaborate, and in 12.199.27, he states that one who follows yogic discipline goes to the body of *brahman–brahma-śarīram eti*–but again there is no explanation of this obscure phrase. In Chapter 207, the *guru* tells his disciple that through celibacy one gains the highest goal–*yānti paraṁ gatim* (7); in 12.208.26 he urges that through *jñāna* one gains immortality–*amṛtaṁ tad avāpnoti,* and in 12.209.19 expands slightly by saying that *brahman* is beyond the gods and *asuras,* and beyond the three *guṇas* that pervade all things material.

These citations serve to illustrate the typical pattern in the *Mokṣa-dharma.* The only fact that is stressed is that in this state there is unblemished joy, though this may also be taken as a negative expression of the freedom that is gained from the miseries of this world. Traditionally there has been a contrast between Sāṁkhya and Vedānta ideas, in that Vedānta teaches the annihilation of the individual *ātman* as it realises its true identity with *brahman,* while Sāṁkhya doctrines set forth the notion of an eternal plurality of souls. Larson is of the opinion that the doctrine of eternal plurality is one of the aspects of Sāṁkhya not found in the *Mahābhārata.*[15] Frauwallner, however, contradicts this view in arguing that plurality is a more obvious and ancient belief than oneness,[16] and also that this doctrine is expressed for the first time in the *Mokṣa-dharma.*[17]

There is little doubt that some of the discourses of the *Śānti* do advocate the notion of eternal plurality of souls, and are also aware of the controversy that the doctrine entails when set against the ideas of early Vedānta expressed in the *Upaniṣads.* In fact the *Mokṣa-dharma* is so catholic a text that the ideas of both Sāṁkhya and Vedānta are found contained within its corpus. In Chapter 212, King Janaka questions the *ṛṣi* Pañcaśikha about the desirability of salvation as he understands it. His speech (2-4) is interesting in that it would appear to represent the perceived inadequacy of *sāṁkhya-mokṣa* from the point of view of Vedānta. If consciousness persists, the king protests, then what is the point of gaining release from this world and why should one undertake severe religious practice to attain such an end.

Hopkins has pointed out that though he is renowned as a teacher of Sāṁkhya with an intimate relationship with Kapila, the proclaimed founder of the system, the doctrines Pañcaśikha expounds are not those usually associated with Sāṁkhya thought.[18] In verses 40 to 44, he expresses the Vedāntic view of salvation, leading Hopkins to conclude that the entire treatise is a 'brahmaist' reworking of an older Sāṁkhya text. Pañcaśikha states that the soul, *kṣetrajña,* is indestructible–*śāśvataḥ*–but that it loses its individuality on gaining *mokṣa,* just as rivers eventually become merged with the ocean:

> *yathārṇava-gatā nadyo vyaktir jahati nāma ca*
> *na ca svatāṁ niyacchanti tādṛśaḥ tattva-saṁkṣayaḥ*
>
> *evaṁ sati kutaḥ saṁjñā pretya-bhāve punar bhavet*
> *pratisaṁmiśrite jīve gṛhyamāṇe ca madhyataḥ*
>
> 'As rivers flowing into the sea lose their names and forms and do not sustain their individuality, so it is for one whose existence disappears. Thus how is it to be understood that in the existence after death when the soul has been taken up and merged its existence in the midst (of *brahman*), consciousness may come to exist once more?' (12.212.42-43)

Verse 43 appears to be a direct response to Janaka's statement in verse 2 regarding the continuance of individual consciousness after salvation, to the effect that this is not the true meaning of *mokṣa* which involves the disappearance of the individual soul.

The same question of whether the soul continues to exist individually after death is raised by Yudhiṣṭhira in Chapter 290. After hearing from Bhīṣma how the followers of Sāṁkhya cross the terrible ocean of life, Yudhiṣṭhira asks whether after attaining the highest position–*sthānam uttamam āsādya*–they are able to recall their birth and death–*ājanma-maraṇaṁ vā te smaranty uta na vā* (76). If the renunciants continue to have conscious awareness in that state–*yadi tatraiva vijñāne vartante yatayaḥ*–then this is a great fault in *mokṣa*–*mokṣa-doṣo mahān eṣa* (78). If that is the case then religion based on pious acts seeking desirable results is superior–*pravṛtti lakṣaṇaṁ dharmaṁ paśyāmi paramam*–for nothing would then be more miserable than to be absorbed in that highest form of knowledge–*magnasya hi pare jñāne kiṁ nu duḥkhataraṁ bhavet* (79). Yudhiṣṭhira's doubt is thus virtually the same as that expressed by Janaka—if individual consciousness persists in the state of *mokṣa,* how can that state truly be free from all miseries?

Bhīṣma replies that even the wise are confused on this issue, but he will attempt to answer according to the version of the followers of Kapila, thus emphasising that the teachings that follow are based on Sāṁkhya. The response he gives, however, does not seem immediately relevant to the inquiry. He instructs Yudhiṣṭhira that the *ātman* is the controller of the senses which cannot function without it. All the qualities and attributes of matter are pervaded by the *sarvātman–sarvātmanā.. vyāpya*–and that is known as the *kṣetrajña.* Having passed beyond matter they go to the unchanging spirit–*prakṛtiṁ cāpy atikramya gacchanty ātmānam avyayam;* this is the supreme Nārāyaṇa himself, free of duality and beyond matter–*paraṁ nārāyaṇātmānaṁ nirdvandvaṁ prakṛteḥ param* (91). Free of both righteous and sinful acts he enters the pure supreme spirit and does not return again. The mind and the senses are left here and only become active when commanded by their teacher, the soul. In a short time it is possible for one seeking this object to find peace–*śakyaṁ cālpena kālena śāntiṁ prāptuṁ guṇārthinā* (94). Thus through the process of knowledge, salvation is gained–*evaṁ yuktena kaunteya yukta-jñānena mokṣinā.* The followers of Sāṁkhya gain the supreme goal through this knowledge and there is no knowledge equal to it–*tulyaṁ jñānaṁ na vidyate.* There should be no doubt regarding the supreme status of *sāṁkhya-jñāna,* for it is fixed and unchanging, imperceptible and complete, the eternal *brahman* itself.

The remainder of the chapter (97-110) consists of a eulogy of Sāṁkhya. The passage as a whole seems unsatisfactory as a response to Yudhiṣṭhira's question about the state of existence after salvation. The most likely interpretation is that the criticism Yudhiṣṭhira articulates–*mokṣa-doṣa*–is of the Sāṁkhya concept of *mokṣa* and is to be recognised as coming from the possibly more orthodox perspective of Vedānta. The Vedānta view is that when salvation is gained individual existence ceases as the *ātman* merges with the totality of *brahman,* the doctrine expressed by Pañcaśikha in Chapter 212.

Verses 70 to 75, which provoke Yudhiṣṭhira's question, express the Sāṁkhya view of *mokṣa* where the self transcends each element of matter until it is free from all aspects of this world, but without any suggestion of merging back into the spiritual totality. The Vedāntist criticism of this notion is that if individual existence continues this state is not truly *mokṣa* for where there is individual consciousness there must also be attachment and suffering. Hence Yudhiṣṭhira's statement that if this is so then *pravṛtti-dharma* is superior, for it accepts the existence of the individual and prescribes acts for its apparent wellbeing. Bhīṣma's reply to this is twofold. In verses 80 to 95, he explains that the self as conceived by Sāṁkhya is not the mind and senses, as in the Upaniṣadic concept of individualism, but is wholly transcendental. Thus individual existence for the soul should not be taken as meaning material existence. Then in verses 96 to 110 he emphasises that Sāṁkhya is the supreme form of knowledge and should never be doubted, thus indicating that Yudhiṣṭhira's question was taken as criticism of Sāṁkhya which he has now refuted.

It may be felt that this reply is inadequate, for whilst it indicates the eternal plurality of souls it does nothing to explain the nature of consciousness or existence in the liberated state. The essential argument is that it is the soul's entanglement with matter that is the cause of suffering and it is the termination of this entanglement that brings relief, not the disappearance of individual existence. Thus Bhīṣma's response to the problem is different from that of Pañcaśikha in that he reasserts the Sāṁkhya understanding of salvation rather than accepting the Vedāntic view that *mokṣa* must involve the loss of individuality. Notable from these two passages is the fact that although both are responses to questions about the nature of existence after *mokṣa*, neither of them offer any form of positive descriptions. The stress is a negative one; in that state the miseries of life and death will cease, and this is sufficient to guarantee eternal bliss in a condition beyond the grasp of the senses and hence presumably impossible to describe.

(iii) Non-Eschatological *Mokṣa*

It is clear from the teachings of the *Mahābhārata* that salvation is not merely a matter of transferring one's existence to some heavenly location. *Mokṣa* can be experienced here on earth by transformation of the individual consciousness through Sāṁkhya and Yoga. When one realises that one is the *kṣetrajña* separate from matter, the miseries of this world no longer have any effect. Thus before death *mokṣa* is achieved and after death there is no rebirth, for one's acts do not produce reactions that require a physical form through which they are enjoyed or suffered.

This is apparent from Chapter 277 of the *Śānti*, wherein Ariṣṭanemi describes to Sagara the characteristics of one who has gained salvation. It is not a description of existence beyond this world, but, using the refrain *mukta eva saḥ*–he is liberated, describes one who lives here without attachment or desire. The first two verses of the passage illustrate the point,

> *kṣut-pipāsādayo bhāvā jitā yasyeha dehinaḥ*
> *krodho lobhas tathā mohaḥ sattvavān mukta eva saḥ*
>
> *dyūte pāne tathā strīṣu mṛgayāyāṁ ca yo naraḥ*
> *na pramādyati saṁmohāt satataṁ mukta eva saḥ*
>
> 'The embodied soul who is resolute in the conquest of hunger, thirst and other states of desire, as well as anger, greed and illusion, is certainly liberated.
>
> The man who is not deluded because of foolishness in the pursuit of gambling, drinking, womanising and hunting, is certainly liberated.' (12.277.25-26)

The passage continues in a similar vein, urging that one who is completely detached from this world has already gained *mokṣa* because his detachment shows that he no longer misidentifies himself with the body and senses. One who has realised this wisdom of Sāṁkhya or has directly perceived the true self through *yoga* practice has attained salvation here and now. Thus in this world he experiences the bliss that this entails without having to wait for the life after death:

> *vikāraṁ prakṛtiṁ caiva puruṣaṁ ca sanātanam*
> *yo yathāvad vijānāti sa vitṛṣṇo vimucyate*
>
> 'One who understands things as they are, that matter is constantly changing but the self is eternal, is completely contented and has gained salvation.' (12.210.35)

6. The State of Salvation According to the Doctrines of *Bhakti*

(i) Vaiṣṇava *Bhakti*

The teachings of the medieval *bhakti* sects and certain of the *Purāṇas* do not see salvation merely in terms of a cessation of the miseries of this world. Their ideas mark something of a combination of the notion of *svarga-loka* with the Upaniṣadic and Sāṁkhya understanding of *mokṣa*. Liberation is understood as the total release from the cycle of rebirth in this world into the heaven of the Deity he or she has worshipped in this life. The devotees of Viṣṇu expect to dwell in Vaikuṇṭha, some of the followers of Śiva long to be his associates in Kailāsa, and the devotees of Kṛṣṇa aspire to join his companions in the forests of Goloka. The *Purāṇas* contain descriptions of these heavens in which liberated souls enjoy eternal existence.

In the *Mahābhārata*, this aspect of devotional thought remains undeveloped. Certain portions of the text make reference to a *viṣṇuloka*, or world of Viṣṇu, but where this occurs the context must be taken into consideration. In the *Vana*, Dhaumya tells the Pāṇḍavas about the numerous pilgrimage sites, and delineates the specific benefits gained from bathing in each one. By visiting some of these *tīrthas* one is promised elevation to *viṣṇuloka–viṣṇulokaṁ ca gacchati* (3.82.105, 107). Here, however, one must bear in mind that the epic displays differing notions of Viṣṇu, so that sometimes he is one god amongst a pantheon as well as being the Supreme Deity. In the description of the *tīrthas* it appears that Viṣṇu is understood in the former position and hence the notion of gaining *viṣṇuloka* is equivalent to gaining the heavens of the gods rather than complete *mokṣa*. Likewise, where teachings on cosmology refer to Viṣṇu or Nārāyaṇa and his domain, the Deity has the role of one god amongst many and his domain is listed as one of the regions of this world presided over by the different gods.[19]

In the *Mokṣa-dharma*, the state of salvation is sometimes referred to as the domain of Viṣṇu.[20] This idea, however, is never elaborated upon to indicate that some kind of eternal heaven is intended. Rather, such references may be taken as indications of the theistic dimension of early Sāṁkhya wherein the Deity is regarded as the totality of all individual beings. Hence the domain of Viṣṇu means a state that is beyond this world in which the *kṣetrajña* exists untouched by any of the material attributes.

In the *Nārāyaṇīya, bhakti* is a technique for gaining *mokṣa* by invoking the grace of the Deity, but there is virtually no suggestion that *mokṣa* means becoming an associate of Nārāyaṇa. The text refers to the inhabitants of Śvetadvīpa as devotees of Nārāyaṇa who worship him constantly. In verses 13 to 15 of Chapter 322 of the *Śānti*, Yudhiṣṭhira asks whether these individuals are ordinary people or *vimuktas*, those who have gained salvation. Bhīṣma's reply, however, does not appear to specifically address the question raised, merely recounting the story of King Uparicara, a great king of the past who worshipped Nārāyaṇa through the Pañcarātra rituals. Again in Chapter 323, the seven sages are able to see the inhabitants of Śvetadvīpa engaged in their worship, but there is no eschatological element in these passages that would imply that a devotee who is liberated by the grace of Nārāyaṇa is given a place in Śvetadvīpa.

The *Nārāyaṇīya* does, however, make frequent reference to salvation, and as, apart from the *Bhagavad-gītā*, it is the *Mahābhārata*'s principal treatise on *viṣṇu-bhakti* these are of particular importance for the present discussion. In Chapter 321, the sage Nārāyaṇa tells Nārada that the one he worships is the *kṣetrajña* within (27-43). All the Vedas and *āśramas* actually worship him and he gives the results they desire, but those fixed solely in worshipping him–*ekāntitatvaṁ samāsthitāḥ*–gain a higher goal–*etad abhyadhikaṁ teṣām*–for they enter into him–*te taṁ praviśanty uta* (42). This idea of entering into the Deity who is the *kṣetrajña* is one that recurs throughout the *Nārāyaṇīya* and can be said to be its principal understanding of the nature of *mokṣa*.

In Chapter 326 of the *Śānti*, when the Deity Nārāyaṇa instructs Nārada, he describes the inhabitants of Śvetadvīpa as not acting through the senses–*ime hy anindriyāhārāḥ*–and not taking any food–*naiṣāṁ vighno bhaved iti* (18). Verse 19 is significant for it implies that they are in a transitory stage between earthly existence and complete salvation:

> *siddhāś caite mahā-bhāgāḥ purā hy ekāntino 'bhavan*
> *tamo-rajo-vinirmuktā māṁ pravekṣyanty asaṁśayam*
>
> 'These blessed perfect beings were previously engaged in undeviating devotion. Free from the lower *guṇas* of *tamaṣ* and *rajas*, they will without doubt enter into me.' (12.326.19)

Here the imperfect tense of *abhavat* followed by the future in *pravekṣyanti* suggests that the inhabitants of Śvetadvīpa were in the past devotees on earth, *ekāntins,* who were elevated to Śvetadvīpa because of their devotion, and in the future will gain complete *mokṣa* by entering into Nārāyaṇa. This is repeated with slight variation in verse 44, with the same verbs and tenses retained; they were *ekāntins–ekāntino'bhavan*–and they will enter into me–*pravekṣyanti ca mām.* Again in verse 117 we find,

> *prāpya śvetaṁ-mahādvīpaṁ bhūtvā candra-prabho naraḥ*
> *sa sahasrācirṣaṁ devaṁ praviśen nātra saṁśayaḥ*
>
> 'Having reached the great white island, and having become a man who appears like the moon, he may without doubt then enter the Lord of a thousand effulgent rays.' (12.326.117)

The implication of these verses is clearly that the *ekāntins,* the devotees on earth, are elevated to Śvetadvīpa where they worship Nārāyaṇa without the disturbance of sensual demands and are thereby able to gain complete salvation by entering into him.

In Chapter 332, the sages Nara and Nārāyaṇa instruct Nārada more fully on how this entering of the Deity takes place. Those who are free from both their righteous and evil deeds leave this world through the gateway of the sun–*ādityo dvāram ucyate* (13). The sun burns all their limbs,or material attributes, so that they become invisible–*āditya-dagdha-sarvāṅgā adṛśyāḥ*–and having become atomic in size they enter the Deity–*paramānu-bhūtā bhūtvā tu taṁ devaṁ praviśanty uta* (14). Being thus liberated, they are situated in the body of Aniruddha–*vinirmuktā aniruddha-tanau sthitāḥ*–and then, being just the mind, they enter into Pradyumna–*mano-bhūtās tato bhūyaḥ pradyumnaṁ praviśanty uta* (15). From Pradyumna the followers of Sāṁkhya who are the best of *brāhmaṇas* along with the devotees enter Saṁkarṣaṇa, who is the *jīva* or eternal soul–*jīvaṁ saṁkarṣaṇaṁ tathā viśanti* (16). Having fully transcended the three *guṇas,* they enter the supreme soul who is the *kṣetrajña,* always beyond material attributes–*paramātmānam añjasā praviśanti dvija-śreṣṭha kṣetrajñaṁ nirguṇātmakam*–and that *kṣetrajña* should be known as Vāsudeva, who is the abode of all things–*sarvāvāsaṁ vāsudevaṁ kṣetrajñaṁ viddhi tattvataḥ* (17). Those who concentrate their minds, are self-controlled, regulate the senses, and are single-minded in their devotion, enter into Vāsudeva.

Although the *Nārāyaṇīya* displays clear links to the thought of both the *Purāṇas* and early Sāṁkhya, eschatologically its ideas correspond with those of the latter rather than the former. A close examination of the text reveals that there is little to suggest an understanding of salvation as being elevation to the abode of Nārāyaṇa to become his associate. The land of Śvetadvīpa is not the final goal of salvation as Vaikuṇṭha is in the *Purāṇas*. In fact the understanding of *mokṣa* is similar to that of Sāṁkhya, centring on the concept of entering the Deity who is equated with the *kṣetrajña* in all beings. What this means specifically, and whether it entails retaining individual identity, is left unclear.

This form of salvation appears to be the goal of the worshippers who inhabit Śvetadvīpa, despite the indications that they have at least partially transcended this world. The only indication that the text may display some tendency towards the Purāṇic concept of *mokṣa* is found in 12.331.41-43. These verses consist mostly of appellations of Nārāyaṇa, but there is some indication here that in Śvetadvīpa he enjoys pleasure in the company of his devotees. The most revealing statement is in verse 42, *te 'rcayanti sadā devaṁ taiḥ sārdhaṁ ramate ca saḥ*–they constantly worship that Deity and he enjoys pleasure in their company. It is apparent that these devotees are able to perceive the Deity directly, but these verses are the only indication in the *Nārāyaṇīya,* and indeed the entire *Mahābhārata,* of the later *bhakti* concept of salvation.

(ii) Śiva *Bhakti*

The passages of the epic concentrating specifically on devotion to *Śiva* are less concerned with the subject of *mokṣa.* It has previously been noted that in the principal passage, Chapters 14 to 18 of the *Anuśāsana,* there is a notable lack of concern with the attainment of salvation. Devotion here is no longer a means to an end or a soteriological technique, but is an end in itself. The devotee, Upamanyu or Tandin, does not even seek *mokṣa,* for his only goal is to remain as a devotee of Śiva. The glorification of Śiva, of which much of this passage consists, stresses that he is the giver of salvation to those who worship him, but the idea is not central and is mentioned only in passing. For the devotee, particularly Upamanyu in Chapter 14, perfection may be gained anywhere in any status of life, so long as he is able to remain fixed in devotion to Śiva. There is no reference to entering into the Deity and no reference to becoming an inhabitant of Śiva's domain in Kailāsa. It appears that as long as the individual can maintain his devotion for Śiva, he is able to disregard the miseries of worldly existence. Thus *bhakti* is *mokṣa,* not a means towards it, and the state gained after salvation can be anywhere in any state of existence so long as the devotion prevails.

7. The State of *Mokṣa* According to the *Bhagavad-gītā*

As elsewhere, the emphasis in the *Gītā* is on how *mokṣa* may be gained rather than on the nature of existence in that state. Thus once again we find explanations given in negative terms, as an antithesis to life in this world, by pithy phrases or by single words. Nonetheless, because the quest for salvation is such a central part of the *Gītā's* teachings, these expressions give some insight into the text's understanding of the nature of *mokṣa.* A detailed analysis reveals not only the extent to which the notion of salvation pervades the various aspects of the *Gītā's* doctrines, but also the ways in which *mokṣa* is conceived.

Different types of expression may be distinguished as follows:

1. At the simplest level a number of references merely assert that salvation is attaining the highest goal or position: 2.51, *padaṁ gacchanty anāmayam*–they go to the position that is faultless; 3.19, *param āpnoti*–he gains the supreme; 6.45, *yāti parāṁ gatim*–he goes to the highest destination; 8.13, *sa yāti paramāṁ gatim*–he goes to the highest destination; 13.29, *yāti parāṁ gatim*–he goes to the highest destination; 8.28, *yogī paraṁ sthānam upaiti cādyam*–the *yogin* reaches the original, supreme position; 9.32, *te 'pi yānti parāṁ gatim*–they also go to the highest destination; 13.29, *yāti parāṁ gatim*–he goes to the highest destination; 13.35, *yānti te param*–they go to the supreme; 16.22, *yāti parāṁ gatim*–he goes to the supreme destination.

2. Another class of statements concentrates on the fact that salvation means freedom from repeated births and deaths: 2.15, *so 'mṛtatvāya kalpate*–he gains immortality; 4.9, *punar janma naiti*–he never takes birth again; 5.17, *gacchanty apunar-āvṛttim*–they go to that position from which there is no return; 8.15, *punar janma ... nāpnuvanti*–they never take birth again; 8.16, *punar janma na vidyate*–birth never takes place again; 13.24, *na sa bhūyo 'bhijāyate*–he never again takes birth; 13.26, *atitaranti . . . mṛtyum*–they cross beyond death; 14.2, *sarge 'pi nopajāyante pralaye na vyanthati ca*–at

creation they do not take birth, and they are not disturbed at the time of destruction; 14.20, *vimukto 'mṛtam aśnute*-being liberated, he gains immortality.

3. Salvation is also described as reaching *brahman* or *nirvāṇa*. These terms are difficult to define from the teachings of the *Gītā* alone, but it should be noted that there is little to suggest the Upaniṣadic concept of the *ātman* merging into *brahman*: 2.72, *brahma-nirvāṇam ṛcchati*-he attains salvation in *brahman*; 4.30, *yānti brahma sanātanam*-they go to the eternal *brahman*; 5.6, *brahma na cireṇādhigacchati*-he soon reaches *brahman*; 5.19, *brahmaṇi te sthitāḥ*-they are situated in *brahman*; 5.20, *brahmaṇi sthitaḥ*-he is situated in *brahman*; 5.24, *brahma-nirvāṇaṁ brahma-bhūto 'dhigacchati*-one existing as *brahman* reaches salvation in *brahman*; 5.25, *labhante brahma-nirvāṇam*-he attains salvation in *brahman*; 5.26, *brahmanirvāṇaṁ vartate*-he exists in a state of salvation in *brahman*; 6.27, *upaiti śānta-rajasaṁ brahma-bhūtam akalmaśam*-he attains the *brahman* state of existence which is unsullied and free of passion; 13.31, *brahma sampadyate*-he achieves *brahman;* 14.26, 18.53 *brahma-bhūyāya kalpate*-he participates in the existence of *brahman*.

4. The idea of being free from repeated birth and death means being free from having to suffer or enjoy the results of previous actions, and several references stress this point: 2.39, *karma-bandhaṁ prahāsyasi*-you will free yourself from the bondage of previous actions; 3.31, *mucyante te 'pi karmabhiḥ*-they are freed from the reactions to their acts; 4.14, *karmabhir na sa badhyate*-he is not held captive by his actions; 4.41, *na karmāni nibadhnanti*-actions do not bind him; 18.49, *naiṣkarmya-siddhiṁ paramām . . . adhigacchati*-he gains supreme perfection, free from reactions to his deeds.

5. Some references emphasise that the state of *mokṣa* is one of tranquillity, in comparison to this world which is full of turmoil and difficulty: 2.71, *sa śāntim adhigacchati*-he attains tranquillity; 4.39, *parāṁ śāntim acireṇādhigacchati*-he soon attains the highest form of tranquillity; 5.12, *śāntim āpnoti naiṣṭhikīm*-he attains unbroken tranquillity; 18.62, *parāṁ śāntiṁ sthānaṁ prāpsyasi śāśvatam*-you will attain that supreme, eternal position of tranquillity.

6. Others stress the unchanging bliss that is experienced when salvation is attained: 5.21, *sukham akṣayam aśnute*-he gains unending joy; 6.28, *brahma-saṁsparśam atyantam sukham aśnute*-in contact with *brahman*, he gains unlimited joy.

7. Two more speak of the purity and freedom from contamination of one who has gained salvation: 4.16, *mokṣyase 'śubhāt*–you will be freed from all that is impure; 6.27, *upaiti śānta-rajasaṁ brahma-bhūtam akalmaśam*–he attains the nature of *brahman*, in which passion is stilled and there is no contamination.

8. Finally, there are a large number of references which introduce a theistic element into the concept of salvation. Here Kṛṣṇa speaks of the devotees coming to him or attaining his nature: 4.9, *mām eti*–he goes to me; 5.29, *māṁ śāntim ṛcchati*–he attains me and tranquillity; 6.15, *śāntiṁ nirvāṇa-paramāṁ mat-saṁsthām adhigacchati*–he attains tranquillity, the supreme salvation which is my position; 8.5, *sa mad-bhāvaṁ yāti*–he attains my nature; 8.7, *mām evaiṣyasi*–you will certainly attain me; 8.8, *paramaṁ puruṣaṁ divyaṁ yāti*–he goes to the supreme divine person; 8.10, *sa taṁ paraṁ puruṣam upaiti divyam*–he attains that supreme divine person; 8.15, *mām upetya punar janma . . . nāpnuvanti*–having reached me they never take birth again; 8.16, *mām upetya . . . punar janma na vidyate* –having reached me he never takes birth again; 9.25, *yānti mad-yājino'pi mām*–my worshippers go to me; 9.28, *vimukto mām upaiṣyasi*–attaining salvation, you will reach me; 9.34, *mām evaiṣyasi*–you will attain me; 10.10, *mām upayānti te*–they come to me; 11.54, *śakyaḥ . . . jñātuṁ draṣṭuṁ ca tattvena preveṣṭum*–one is able to know, to see, and truly enter into (me); 11.55, *sa mām eti*–he goes to me; 12.4, *te prāpnuvanti mām*–they reach me; 13.19, *mad-bhāvopapadyate*–he attains my nature; 14.2, *mama sādharmyam āgatāḥ*–they come to be of the same nature as me; *bhāvaṃ so'dhigacchati*–he attains my nature; 18.65, *mām evaiṣyasi*–you will certainly come to me.

A few phrases stand on their own without falling into any particular category: 5.3, *sukhaṁ bandhāt pramucyate*–he is easily liberated from bondage; 7.14, *māyām etāṁ taranti te*–they cross this illusion; 15.5, *gacchanti . . . padam avyayam*–they go to the unchanging position; 18.55, *viśate tad-anantaram*–he enters that which has no limit; 18.56, *āpnoti śāśvataṁ padam avyayam*–he attains the eternal, imperishable position.

Although this pattern of a single phrase being used to describe the state of *mokṣa* is the usual mode of expression in the *Gītā*, there are two occasions when Kṛṣṇa goes slightly further and provides some elaboration. In verses 17 to 19 of Chapter 8, he describes the days and nights of Brahmā during which the living beings are brought forth and then withdrawn once more. Verse 20 moves on to discuss the domain which is beyond this continuous cycle–*bhāvo . . . sanātanaḥ.* When all the living beings of this world are annihilated, it is not destroyed–*yaḥ sa sarveṣu bhūteṣu naśyatsu na vinaśyati.* That sphere of existence is described as unmanifest and undecaying–*avyakto 'kṣara ity uktaḥ*–and they call it the supreme destination–*tam āhuḥ paramāṁ gatim,* those who attain that supreme abode of Kṛṣṇa's do not return to this world–*yaṁ prāpya na nivartante tad dhāma paramaṁ mama* (21).

In 15.5 Kṛṣṇa states that those who are above the changing fortunes of this world go to the domain that does not change–*gacchanti . . . padam avyayam.* In verse 6 he expands on the concluding line of the previous verse. Neither the sun, the moon, nor fire provides the illumination there–*na tad bhāsayate sūryo na śaśāṁko na pāvakaḥ;* having gone to that supreme abode of Kṛṣṇa's they do not return–*yad gatvā na nivartante tad dhāma paramaṁ mama.*

These verses, however, add little to the information provided by the brief phrases used elsewhere. After *mokṣa* the self is able to exist in a state that is unaffected by the changes of this world in a sphere that is self-luminous, presumably because it is purely spiritual and hence untouched by darkness.[21] It is also described specifically as the *dhāman,* the abode, dwelling-place, or domain of Kṛṣṇa. This statement is suggestive of Vaikuṇṭha, the Vaiṣṇava heaven in which the Deity dwells surrounded by his loving devotees. In the *Gītā,* however, this remains as no more than a suggestion.

As was noted with regard to the *Mokṣa-dharma,* the state of salvation is not always seen by the *Gītā* as one that is to be attained only after death. A number of references, particularly in Chapter 8, lay stress on liberation in the afterlife, using phrases such as *tyaktvā deham, prayāṇa-kāle* or *anta-kāle,* but elsewhere it is indicated that salvation may take place before death occurs. In 5.19, for example, the word *iha* indicates that the cycle of rebirth is overcome here in this life–*ihaiva tair jitaḥ sargaḥ;* those whose minds are controlled and brought to a state of equanimity–*yeṣāṁ sāmye sthitaṁ manaḥ*–are already situated in *brahman–brahmaṇi te sthitāḥ.* Similarly, in Chapter 14, when Kṛṣṇa describes the attributes of one who has transcended the influence of the three *guṇas–guṇātītaḥ*–it is clear that this state of *mokṣa* occurs in this world. The description is not of an individual existing in some other-wordly domain, but of one living in this world unaffected by its circumstances (22-25).

If we attempt an overall review of the *Gītā*'s teachings on the nature of *mokṣa* a natural division is between theistic and non-theistic expressions. Where salvation is referred to in non-theistic terms, the majority of the phrases employed are negative in their emphasis, serving to indicate that above all it is a state where one is unaffected by the unwanted conditions that prevail in this world. The only positive assertion made by the text is that one who attains salvation reaches *brahman,* and Vedāntist commentators have naturally interpreted such statements as indicating the *ātman*'s losing its individuality after *mokṣa* is gained. There is no indication from the *Gītā* alone, however, that this is what is intended by phrases such as *yānti brahma-sanātanam, brahmanirvāṇam ṛcchati,* or *brahma-bhūyāya kalpate.* Such phrases are also found in the Sāṁkhya treatises of the *Mokṣa-dharma* and hence cannot be taken as evidence of Vedāntic teachings in the *Gītā.*

The use of the word *nirvāṇa* is similarly problematic. This term is most commonly associated with Buddhist thought where it is used to designate the state of individual annihilation sought by the Buddhist. Much has been written regarding the *Gītā*'s links with Buddhism and its use of the term *nirvāṇa,* but in truth little can be stated conclusively, with different learned authorities drawing opposite conclusions. A definition of *brahman* is provided by the text but it is hardly enlightening as it merely designates *brahman* as that which does not decay–*akṣaraṁ brahma paramam* (8.3)–or in other words the spiritual nature as opposed to matter. From a doctrinal perspective, it is hard to be dogmatic, and perhaps safest to understand *brahman* and *nirvāṇa* as non-specific terms employed by the *Gītā* to indicate a state of non-material existence.

Despite its drawing on ideas of Vedānta, Sāṁkhya, Yoga, Vedic ritual, and *dharma-śāstra,* the *Gītā*'s principal focus is theistic, and this is clearly reflected in its ideas on salvation. A number of verses speak of going to Kṛṣṇa–*mām eti, yānti mām*–or of attaining his nature–*mad-bhāvam adhigacchati,* but again it is hard to determine precisely the meaning intended, if indeed there be a precise notion underlying these statements. As a result different interpretations are possible, and have been offered by the various commentators. Going to Kṛṣṇa may be taken in a Purāṇic sense of going to the heaven of Viṣṇu or Kṛṣṇa and becoming his associate there. From the perspective of Vedānta, where Kṛṣṇa is taken as a personification of *brahman,* going to Kṛṣṇa is another means of expressing the *ātman's* becoming one with *brahman.* The idea may also be interpreted from the point of view of the *Nārāyaṇīya* which describes the liberated soul as entering the Deity. This latter view must, however, be considered unlikely for the *Gītā* is undoubtedly the work of non-pañcarātric theologians. Along with numerous other differences of doctrine and emphasis, it may indeed be noted that whereas the *Nārāyaṇīya* repeatedly stresses the idea of *mokṣa* as entering the Deity, the *Gītā* has only one reference that in any way corresponds with this notion.[22]

Though the *Bhagavad-gītā* overtly speaks of salvation as being gained through the grace of Kṛṣṇa, and of going to Kṛṣṇa in his domain, precisely what this means is left unclear. Kṛṣṇa speaks of his abode as that which is reached through *mokṣa,* but takes the matter no further and thus leaves the field open for commentary and interpretation. This lack of precision may indeed have contributed to the popularity of the *Gītā* over the centuries, and the superior esteem in which it is held by Hindus and non-Hindus alike over the more dogmatic texts of the tradition.

8. Conclusions

At the outset it was noted that the word eschatology has a dual meaning, denoting both the end of the world and the fate of the individual after death. It is apparent from the above discussion that for the *Mahābhārata* the two subjects are quite distinct. The only exception to this distinction is in the idea that at the end of each creation all of existence, including all living beings, is withdrawn back into the Deity or the Unmanifest wherein it remains in stasis until a new creation is set in motion.

Despite the various strands of religious thought represented in the text, there is a large degree of consensus on the subject of cosmic eschatology. Everywhere it is agreed that the existence of the world is subject to an eternal progression of repeated creation and destruction. In the descriptions of the annihilation of the cosmos, we may recognise mythic and theistic elements, as well as more scientific accounts based on Sāṁkhya. There is no indication, however, that these different approaches are recognised as antithetical, and characteristically the epic's discussions of the destruction of the world attempt to weave together the different elements into one account.

It is noteworthy that the theistic aspects are more prominent in the Sāṁkhya than the mythic accounts. The myth centres on the destructive fire and the great flood that follows it, and the Deity appears in a limited rọle as the urger of these natural forces. In the Sāṁkhya account, however, the Deity is equated with the Unmanifest into which all elements and all beings are withdrawn. Both ideas represent a form of theism, but of a different nature; in one the Deity causes a great flood and then lies down on the water to create again, and in the other He is wholly removed from this world absorbing all things into his very being.[23]

In the teachings on individual eschatology, three main concepts are prominent–heaven and hell, *saṁsāra* and *karma,* and *mokṣa.* Though substantial contradictions have been recognised between these notions, in the epic they are brought together in one system. The tension that exists between them is to be recognised as being at a soteriological rather than an eschatological level. Treatises stressing *mokṣa-dharma,* such as the story of Mudgala or the *Bhagavad-gītā,* may reject the desirability of reaching the heavens of the gods, but they do not attempt to assert that no such heavens exist. Even where heaven is praised as the goal to be striven for, it is accepted that existence there is temporary even for the gods, though one may enjoy fabulous pleasures for vast periods of time. The notion of *mokṣa* is nowhere denied,[24] but where *sva-dharma* is stressed, except in the *Gītā,* the concept is ignored rather than refuted.

The idea of *saṁsāra* and *karma* is accepted throughout the epic, though again it is not an idea that is prominent in the narrative sections of the text. It is most closely linked to the teachings on salvation, as the antithesis to *mokṣa* from which one must aspire to gain relief. *Pravṛtti* also accepts the idea of reincarnation, for it provides explanation and legitimation for the rigid demarcation of society into *varṇas.* Here *saṁsāra* is viewed less negatively than from the perspective of *nivṛtti* which rejects all forms of rebirth as miserable and unwanted. *Pravṛtti* regards rebirth as providing the opportunity for progressive elevation up to life as a *kṣatriya* or *brāhmaṇa* for whom the delights of heaven are available after death.

The impetus towards *mokṣa* is based on a negative view of all forms of life in this world, even those in heaven, because at best they provide only temporary relief from suffering. It is noteworthy that although *mokṣa* is recognised as the principal goal in large sections of the didactus, within the central narrative it is rarely, if ever, a consideration. None of the main characters, not even Kṛṣṇa and Arjuna, the speaker and hearer of the *Gītā*, attain salvation, and all of them are found enjoying the delights of heaven at the conclusion of the epic.

The central focus of the narrative is *dharma*, which is intimately connected with *bhakti*, as the Deity and the gods he leads are dedicated to maintaining *dharma*. Elsewhere, in the *Nārāyaṇīya* especially, but also in the *Gītā*, *bhakti* is linked to *mokṣa*, but this is not the case in the narrative. Viṣṇu as the leader of the pantheon has appeared on earth not with any soteriological intent but to sustain *dharma* and the gods, and his devotees are those who recognise his greatness and assist his mission. The goal of *dharma* is always presented as reaching *svarga-loka* and living amongst the gods; therefore, despite the influence of *bhakti*, the narrative shows little interest in *mokṣa* as a final goal, and, outside of the *Gītā*, Kṛṣṇa does not promise *mokṣa* to those who venerate his divinity.

In those sections of the text where *mokṣa* is stressed, there seems little concern with establishing a detailed understanding of the state of existence attained by those who achieve it. It is sufficient to appreciate that the undesirable circumstances of life in this world will cease. The Vedāntic notion of the merging of the individual self into the supreme spirit is found only rarely in the various teachings contained in the *Mahābhārata*. The predominant system in the passages dealing with salvation is that of Sāṁkhya which stresses the individuality of the soul.

Sāṁkhya-mokṣa is never precisely defined and is referred to primarily in terms of its being a release from misery and rebirth. Even where teachings on the attainment of salvation are linked to the theistic ideas of *bhakti*, there are only the barest hints of the eschatology of the later Vaiṣṇava and Śaivite traditions. The grace of the Deity in bringing release to his votary is seen as a parallel means of salvation to the techniques of Sāṁkhya and Yoga, and the salvation gained is of the same nature. In the *Nārāyaṇīya*, this is described as entering the Deity, and in the *Gītā* coming to the Deity, but in neither is there the concept of a heavenly domain in which the devotee lives eternally in the company of Nārāyaṇa or Kṛṣṇa. The rather vague phrases employed by the texts have allowed them to be interpreted in this Purāṇic sense, but there is no conclusive evidence in the *Mahābhārata* that this is what is intended.

Notes

1. 12.329.3, in the *Nārāyaṇīya*, gives a figure of 4,000 *yugas*, but this must be taken as referring to individual *yugas* rather than complete cycles of the four ages.
2. See, for example, Book 3 of the *Bhāgavata Purāṇa.*
3. See, for example, 12.74.19, 13.146.16.
4. The influence of Yoga on ideas on the creation and destruction of the universe is again apparent here in 12.229.17-18.
5. According to Yoga teachings, magical powers come to the practitioner including *animā*, the ability to make oneself minutely small, *laghimā*, the ability to fly weightlessly, and *prāpti*, the ability to obtain objects just by one's desire.
6. Although the *Gītā* makes no reference to Nārāyaṇa, Kṛṣṇa assumes the cosmic function of that Deity.
7. Biardeau, M. *L'Hindouisme: Anthropologie d'une Civilization*, Paris, 1980, p. 131.
8. van Buitenen, J.A.B. *Studies in Indian Literature and Philosophy*, Ludo Rocher Ed, Delhi, 1988, p. 60.
9. Ibid, pp. 111-112.
10. Apart from the detailed descriptions presented in Chapter 26 of Book 5 of the *Bhāgavata Purāṇa*, similar passages are to be found in the *Garuḍa Purāṇa*, 2.3.41-46, and the *Viṣṇu Purāṇa* 2.6.1-35.
11. And see also 12.309.26-36 for a similar description.
12. Frauwallner, E. *History of Indian Philosophy*, Volume 1, V.M. Bedeker trans, Delhi, 1973, pp. 88-89.
13. *tiryag yonyāḥ śūdratām àbhyupaiti śūdro vaiśyatvaṁ kṣatriyatvaṁ ca vaiśyaḥ/vṛtta-slāghī kṣatriyo brāhmaṇatvaṁ svayaṁ punyaṁ brāhmaṇaḥ sādhu-vṛttaḥ.*
14. Herman, A.L. 'The Problem of Suffering in the Bhagavad-gītā', in *Suffering: Indian Perspectives*, K.N. Tiwari Ed, Delhi, 1986, p. 74.
15. Larson, G.J. *Classical Sāṁkhya, An Interpretation of its History and Meaning*, Delhi, 1969, p. 122.
16. Frauwallner 1973, p. 104.
17. Ibid, p. 114.
18. Hopkins, E.W. *The Great Epic of India*, Calcutta, 1969 (1st Ed. 1901), p. 151.
19. See, for example, 3.16.17-24 and 6.9.15-18. In both these passages Viṣṇu is referred to as the Supreme Deity, but the context seems to place him amongst the pantheon rather than in a transcendent station.
20. See, for example, 12.271.50.
21. This idea of self-luminosity occurs in the descriptions of *svarga-loka*, discussed above; this may indicate a connection between the *Gītā*'s understanding of the spiritual domain and the concept of the heavens of the gods.
22. *bhaktyā tv ananyayā śakya aham evaṁ-vidho 'rjuna*
    jñātuṁ draṣṭuṁ ca tattvena praveṣṭuṁ ca parantapa (11.54).
23. Here again one may detect the transition from belief in a pantheon to a developed form of monotheism.
24. Though the *Bhagavad-gītā* (2.42) refers to ritualists who do assert such a denial.

CHAPTER 7

THE *MAHĀBHĀRATA*'S TEACHINGS ON ETHICS

1. Introduction

The subject of ethics generally deals with questions of right and wrong in a theoretical sense and also modes of conduct that it is proper for human beings to adopt. Before discussing in detail the perspectives of the *Mahābhārata* on such questions some preliminary observations are called for. There is in the West a rather narrow view of what is ethics or ethical, based on a rough mingling of utilitarianism and traditional Judaeo-Christian values, which focuses exclusively on issues of morality. This is, however, only a part of ethics for morality is only one of the criteria by which correct principles and conduct are determined. Even linguistically it can be recognised that the word 'good' has two distinct meanings in terms of expertise and morality. Aristotle considers goodness primarily in the sense of being proficient in the art of being human, and thereby gaining success. A part of this expertise is what we would recognise as moral action, but the point of emphasis is notably distinct from what is normally understood as morality. In Aristotle's thought, to be moral is good because it brings success, but, as the *Mahābhārata* indicates, this may not always be the case and in such circumstances the potential for ideological tension is clear.

The epic contains no specific term for ethics, almost certainly because it is never considered separately from religion as is the case in Western thought. The word *carita* specifically means conduct and is frequently used in discussions of proper behaviour, but what would be understood as ethics is most often categorised under the rather broad heading of *dharma*. The concept of *dharma* is one that has been referred to on numerous occasions and is central to the teachings of the *Mahābhārata*. The question frequently raised and discussed by the text is, "What is *dharma?*" and this may in the broadest sense be understood as, "What is ethical?"

Van Buitenen argues that *dharma* should be translated throughout the epic as 'Law' and understood in a sense similar to that of Law in the Jewish tradition.[1] There are good grounds for this interpretation, for *dharma* is frequently presented as codified rules of conduct, but such a rigid definition is problematic in that it excludes some of the broader senses in which the term is employed. Whereas Law implies a rigid code of conduct, *dharma* is also understood as the inate sense of morality perceived by the righteous person; it is also recognised that *dharma* is not always 'carved in stone', but is subtle and may only be understood by deep contemplation. In addition, the notion of Law would seem to ignore the descriptive aspect of *dharma,* for *dharma* is not only that which a person should do but is also that which a person is by his or her very nature.

Wendy O'Flaherty has offered perhaps the clearest understanding of the structure of the ethical systems propounded by the *Mahābhārata.* She recognises two principal types of *dharma* in Hindu thought, and also the tension that exists between them.[2] The first of these is *sva-dharma,* the specific duties incumbent on each individual in terms of social status. In addition there is *sādhāraṇa* which is a code of morality that every person is expected to adhere to. The didactic sections of the epic present a third type of ethics derived from the ascetic tradition with its other-worldly preoccupations which, though referred to by O'Flaherty as morally neutral, still forms a recognisable ethical code.[3]

This understanding of Hindu ethics in terms of a threefold analysis is useful in considering the ideas of the *Mahābhārata.* One must not, however, lose sight of the fact that this is a Western appreciation of a non-Western thought system, trying to make sense of it in terms that may be more readily comprehended. The text itself never talks in terms of a threefold ethical division, for indeed, as has already been noted, it does not recognise ethics as a specific branch of knowledge.

Furthermore, it is apparent that the three types of ethics are no more than ideological tendencies and are never absolutely distinct. *Sva-dharma* focuses primarily on ritualised action but also includes injunctions based on an appreciation of morality. Likewise, the ascetic ethic involves moral principles many of which are identical to the instructions on morality classified under the heading of *sādhāraṇa.* Hence it is at times difficult to determine what type of ethics is being propounded, and it would be misleading to assert that epic thought embodies three clear and distinctive ethical concepts. These caveats notwithstanding, O'Flaherty's analysis remains valid in considering the teachings of the epic because of the tensions that the text repeatedly and deliberately highlights between differing ideas of right conduct. The point is that where such tensions are recognised, then one is bound to attempt an understanding of the differences between opposing positions and it is here that the different ethical tendencies are brought more starkly into focus.

2. The Ethics of *Sva-dharma*

(i) Theoretical Concepts

Here van Buitenen's understanding of *dharma* as Law is appropriate, for the *Mahābhārata*'s teachings on *sva-dharma* offer a specific code of conduct by which each individual in society must live. These codes are not without a moral dimension, but morality is not the crucial criterion about which they are constructed. Hence Dasgupta is correct when he states that "prescribed duty ought not to be confused with morality in the modern sense."[4] Rigid adherence to *sva-dharma* in the view of the epic constitutes the proper expertise of human existence which delivers an appropriate eschatological reward. Morality is not excluded, but, as we are reminded at the conclusion of the epic, it is the expert as well as the moral person who enjoys the delights of heaven after death.

Central to this ethical tendency is the notion of ritual action. It is useful for an understanding of the epic's concept of ritual to note the Vedic idea that preceded it. In the Vedic ritual of *yajña,* the priests and the king act together in a human performance that is microcosmically in harmony with the ritual progress of the universe which it thereby helps to sustain. The ideas of the epic appear to mark a progression from Vedic thought to the point where the entire conduct of life of both the priest and the king has become a ritual, designated by the term *sva-dharma;* it is, as Biardeau expresses it,". . . comme si toute activité humaine se ramenait au sacrifice, coeur du *dharma.*"[5] One born into the royal order is understood to have inherited the nature of a ruler, and by acting in accordance with that expectation, his conduct of life falls into harmony with both his personal nature and with the harmony of the entire creation. This idea is of crucial significance for the drama of the *Mahābhārata,* as Hiltebeitel recognises in the phrase 'The Ritual of Battle', the title of his major study of the epic. Furthermore, the notion of a ritualised conduct of life is extended to all levels of society, including the *vaiśyas* and *śūdras,* so that each individual acts out a ritual ethic when he or she lives in accordance with dharmic prescription.

This ritual ethic is also of central importance to Kṛṣṇa's teachings in the *Bhagavad-gītā,* as he refers to Arjuna's warlike action as being a part of *yajña* (3.9). Hiltebeitel speaks of the 'horror'[6] with which the epic, including the *Gītā,* regards any mixing of the *varṇas* in terms of both marriage and execution of duty, for action of this type disrupts the smooth harmony of ritual life. It is the threat on earth to this type of *dharma* that is the reason for the appearance of the *avatāra,* for it is not only human society that is threatened but the position of the gods as well. Myths such as that of the suspension of *yajñas* when Agni disappears, and of the destruction of all *yajñas* by the Kālekeya demons illustrate the dependency of the gods on the proper execution of human ritual. In the *Mahābhārata,* Viṣṇu has appeared on earth to maintain the Law which is threatened by the actions of several of the narrative's principal characters—Bhīṣma as a celibate *kṣatriya,* Rāma Jāmadagneya, Droṇa, Kṛpa, and Aśvatthāman as warrior *brāhmaṇas,* and perhaps even Yudhiṣṭhira as a *kṣatriya* who abhors violence. Hence when Kṛṣṇa explains part of his mission in 4.8 of the *Gītā* as *vināśāya ca duṣkṛtām,* the wrongdoers he refers to should probably not be understood as 'the wicked' in a wholly moral sense, but rather as those whose actions contravene the ritual conduct of life amongst men.

According to Wendy O'Flaherty, "The svadharma system of orthodox Hinduism is an ethical system based on the pluralism inherent in the social system of caste (whose goal is the preservation of social and moral balance)".[7] In other words it is a relative rather than an absolute ethical system. That is not to say that each individual has their own unique ethical code, for *sva-dharma* is shared with others of the same *varṇa,* but still there is no one standard of behaviour prescribed for all persons. Whereas, for example, avarice and violence are always wrong for a *brāhmaṇa,* for a king a degree of personal ambition and recourse to warfare are not only allowed but considered essential for effective government.

(ii) Ritual *Dharma*

The previous discussion has centred on the ritual performance of specific *varṇa* duties, and these are undoubtedly the most significant feature of this type of *dharma*. Before looking at these in more detail, however, some note must be taken of ritual practices enjoined by the text in which *varṇa* status is of less significance. The *Anuśāsana* presents numerous instructions on specific ritual acts to be performed by the individual primarily with the aim of securing a favourable position in the afterlife. Thus, for example, Chapters 58 to 86 are devoted to a lengthy description of the giving of charity, specifically of cows, food and gold. Charity is also viewed by the text as a moral act, but here the focus is clearly on its ritual performance and on the reward that will be gained by the giver after death. There are similar discussions in the *Anuśāsana* of the efficacy of penance, fasting and offerings of lamps and flowers to gods and forefathers.

Whilst it is important to recognise the existence of teachings of this type within the *Mahābhārata,* their significance is largely confined to the *Anuśāsana,* of which they comprise a substantial portion. That such ideas fall under the heading of ethics cannot be questioned, but again it is ethics in the Aristotelean sense of acting successfully in the art of being human rather than in terms of morality. When ethical tensions arise in the epic, however, ritual acts such as these are largely ignored as the focus falls repeatedly on morality and *varṇa* duties. Therefore, having noted the presence of such ideas in the *Anuśāsana,* I propose to move on to a more detailed discussion of ritual duties specific to the *varṇas,* for these ideas are clearly central to the thought of the text as a whole.

(iii) Ritual Duties of the *Varṇas*

Although the *Mahābhārata* refers to itself as a *dharma-śāstra* (1.56.21), it is only in the first half of the *Anuśāsana* that the epic attempts any form of detailed exposition on the rules of conduct for the four *varṇas.* There the discussion moves beyond general indications to outline specific rules of marriage and inheritance, but even so falls short of the complex system of regulations found elsewhere in works such as the *Manu-smṛti.* Typically when discussing *varṇa* duties, the epic offers brief lists of occupations that each may undertake along with the characteristic dispositions and general modes of conduct expected from individuals of each designation.

In his teachings to Bhīma, Hanumān gives a brief statement of the occupations appropriate for each *varṇa* — acting as priests in *yajñas* and teaching for *brāhmaṇas,* protecting others for *kṣatriyas,* agriculture for *vaiśyas,* and service for *śūdras.* He then elaborates on *kṣatriya-dharma* for Bhīma's specific benefit, presenting teachings along the same lines as those offered by Bhīṣma in the *Rāja-dharma* (3.150.29-37). At the conclusion of the *Vidura-nīti,* Vidura advises Dhṛtarāṣṭra that regular bathing, performance of *yajña,* wearing the sacred thread, study of the Veda, avoiding unclean food, speaking the truth and working to serve one's teacher ensure that a *brāhmaṇa* never falls from the domain of *brahman.* Having studied the Vedas, kindled sacred fires and worshipped them with *yajñas,* protected his subjects and made himself pure by taking up arms on behalf of cows and *brāhmaṇas,* a *kṣatriya* who falls in battle goes to heaven. Having studied the Vedas, divided his wealth between the *brāhmaṇas, kṣatriyas,* and his dependants at proper times, and having smelled the aroma of the smoke of the three kinds of sacred fire, a *vaiśya* enjoys the delights of *svarga-loka.* Venerating the three higher *varṇas* as is proper for each, a *śūdra* has his sins destroyed by their satisfaction and after giving up his body goes to heaven (5.40.23-26).

The *Mokṣa-dharma* focuses primarily on ascetism and renunciation of the world, but still within its corpus reference is made to the specific modes of conduct for the *varṇas.* In the *Bhṛgu-Bharadvāja-saṁvāda,* Bhṛgu teaches that a *brāhmaṇa* is one who is initiated in rites and ceremonies such as the *Jāta,* who studies the Vedas and is diligent in executing six types of duty;[6] his deeds are pure, he eats the remnants of offerings made to forefathers, pleases his teacher, adheres strictly to vows, and is truthful. Where truth, charity, self-control, non-harming, tolerance, compassion and austerity are seen, then that person is to be known as a *brāhmaṇa* (12.182.2-4). One who wields political power, studies the Vedas and takes pleasure in both giving away and seizing wealth from others is known as a *kṣatriya.* One who is pure and engages in agriculture, tending cows, trade and study of the Vedas is known as a *vaiśya.* One who takes pleasure in any kind of food, performs impure deeds; ignores the Vedas and behaves improperly is known as a *śūdra*. If the characteristics of a *brāhmaṇa* are not found in a *brāhmaṇa*, and likewise the qualities of a *śūdra* are absent from a *śūdra*, then such designations should not be applied to those individuals (12.182.5-8).[9]

The *Rāja-dharma* deals specifically with proper conduct for kings but because a part of that duty is to ensure that the members of the four *varṇas* in society are engaged in the ways of life appropriate to their status, it includes a fuller discourse on exactly what those ways of life should be. This information is provided by Bhīṣma at the beginning of his teachings in Chapter 60 of the *Śānti*. A *brāhmaṇa* fulfils his duty by self-control, recitation of the Vedas and imparting instructions to others (9). If he gains wealth thereby, he should not indulge in any forbidden action but should remain peaceful and satisfied with wisdom alone (10); the wealth should be used to raise children, give charity and perform *yajñas* (11). A *brāhmaṇa*, whether or not he does anything else, fulfils his duty by studying the Vedas (12).

A *kṣatriya* should give but never receive charity and execute *yajñas* though not as the priest (13). He should learn the Vedas but not teach them, protect his subjects, be active in suppressing robbers and show heroism in battle (14). Learned rulers who have performed *yajñas* and conquered in battle are the best of those who reach heaven (15). Those with knowledge of the ancient traditions do not praise a *kṣatriya* who returns from battle without a wound on his body (16). His highest *dharma* is the affliction of other warriors and there is no conduct superior to destruction of miscreants (17). Suitable undertakings for a king are study of the Vedas, *yajñas* and charity; therefore he seeks battle (perhaps to finance ritual ceremonies) (18). He must ensure that all subjects follow the proper ways of life appropriate for them according to the prescribed rules (19). Even if he performs no other duty, a king is to be known as equal to Indra if he properly enacts the duty of protection (20).

Charity, study of the Vedas and making money by honest means comprise *vaiśya-dharma* (21). A *vaiśya* should protect all animals like a father and thereby become joyful; any other course of action is wrong for him (22). After creation, Prajāpati entrusted the animals to the *vaiśya* and entrusted all beings to the *brāhmaṇa* and *kṣatriya* (23). If a *vaiśya* tends six cows, he may take the milk of one and if he tends 100 cows, he may claim two as his own (24). When a cow dies he may claim a half share of the horns and hoofs, and the same is his share of the crop from the seeds he sows (25). A *vaiśya* should never be averse to protection of animals and no other person should take up this duty (26).

Prajāpati created the *śūdra* as the servant of the other *varṇas,* and by such service the *śūdra* gains great happiness (27-28). He should render this service without envy and never accumulate riches in any way, for with such wealth he might sinfully make those of the higher *varṇas* subject to him; only with permission from the king may he satisfy his desires in accordance with *dharma* (29-30). The *śūdras* should be completely maintained by the other *varṇas;* old umbrellas, turbans, seats, shoes and fans should be given to a *śūdra* who renders service (31-33). If a *śūdra* approaches anyone from the higher *varṇas* and offers his service, he should be engaged; *piṇḍa*[10] should be offered on his behalf by his employer and he should be maintained when he grows old or frail (34). A *śūdra* should never leave a master who falls into difficulty, and should maintain him if he becomes poverty-stricken; he may not have wealth of his own, for whatever he possesses belongs to his master (35).

These passages serve to illustrate ethical ideals in a system that is clearly distinct from morality as the term is understood in a modern context. Morality argues that an action should be performed because it is good, and 'good' in the moral sense is understood as providing benefit to others. Here ethics is underpinned by different notions of what is good, which may be recognised as threefold:

1. Eschatological: The notion of 'good' in the ethics of *sva-dharma* is to be equated primarily with 'expert'. One who adheres strictly to his ethical duties as dictated by *varṇa* is a successful human being, and this success is manifested eschatologically by the position gained after death. It is very apparent that Duryodhana, for example, is morally despicable but because his death on the field of battle is the ideal enactment of *kṣatriya sva-dharma,* he is a 'good' man in the sense of good at being human, and at the conclusion of the epic we find him rewarded accordingly with an exalted position amongst the gods. Hanumān's discussion of *sva-dharma* concludes with his making this very point:

tapo-dharma-damejyābhir viprā yānti yathā divam
dānātithya-kriyā-dharmair yānti vaiśyāś ca sad-gatim

kṣatraṁ yāti tathā svargaṁ bhuvi nigraha-pālanaiḥ
samyak praṇīya daṇḍaṁ hi kāma-dveṣa-vivarjitāḥ
alubdhā vigata-krodhāḥ satāṁ yānti salokatām

'As *brāhmaṇas* go to heaven through austerity, accepting the duties of their *varṇa,* self-control and sacrifices, and *vaiśyas* go to the domain of the righteous through charity, serving guests and ritual actions, so *kṣatriyas* go to heaven by punishing and protecting in this world. Having properly inflicted punishment, being devoid of lust and hatred, never greedy and controlling their wrath, they go to the same abode as those who are righteous.' (3.149.51-52)

2. Social: Another understanding of 'good' action stresses the contribution to society as a whole. Society functions effectively when order prevails, and social order is dependent upon the system of *varṇas.* Thus the individual in executing his *sva-dharma* is engaged in right action because his behaviour contributes to social stability and hence the welfare of all. Again Hanumān points out this justification for *sva-dharma*:

sā ced dharma-kriyā na syāt trayī-dharmam ṛte bhuvi
daṇḍa-nītim ṛte cāpi nirmaryādam idaṁ bhavet

vārtā-dharme hy avartantyo vinaśyeyur imāḥ prajāḥ
supravṛttais tribhir hy etair dharmaiḥ sūyanti vai prajāḥ

'If there was no performance of the duties of *sva-dharma,* no Vedic rituals on earth and no punishment of wrong-doers, then this world would become devoid of moral restraints.

When professions are not executed in accordance with *dharma,* the population is ruined. Living beings become blessed by the proper execution of these three types of *dharma* (*yajña,* government, and commerce).' (3.149.32-33)

3. Ritual: The ritual nature of *sva-dharma* is discussed fully elsewhere with its clear links to the cosmic aspects of Vedic ritual. The gods are nourished by *yajñas,* and in the epic the notion of

ritual is broadened to include all prescribed social duties. Hence *sva-dharma* not only brings eschatological reward and preserves social stability, but also sustains the gods and the harmony of creation. Hanumān thus prefaces his short discourse on dharmic duties by stressing their ritual dimension:

> *ācāra-sambhavo dharmo dharmād vedāḥ samutthitāḥ*
> *vedair yajñāḥ samutpannā yajñair devāḥ pratiṣṭhitāḥ*
>
> *vedācāra-vidhānoktair yajñair dhāryanti devatāḥ*
> *bṛhaspaty-uśanoktaiś ca nayair dhāryanti mānavāḥ*
>
> '*Dharma* arises from proper conduct, and the Vedas have arisen from *dharma. Yajñas* take place through the Vedas, and the gods are maintained by *yajñas.* The gods are sustained by the *yajñas* described by the Vedas in their injunctions on proper conduct; men are sustained by the rules of life laid down by Bṛhaspati and Uśanas.' (3.149.28-29)

Here there is a clear connection drawn between the *varṇa* duties that Hanumān goes on to describe and the ritual of *yajña* with its cosmic function of sustaining the gods. This understanding of *sva-dharma* is significant in Kṛṣṇa's urging Arjuna that he must face his enemies in battle. At the outset of the *Gītā,* Arjuna takes the position of a *kṣatriya* desiring to abandon warfare. In expounding his doctrine of desireless action, Kṛṣṇa, like Hanumān, asserts the ritual nature of the *sva-dharma* his cousin wishes to eschew.

This point is stressed especially in Chapter 3 wherein Kṛṣṇa makes it clear that he considers the execution of *kṣatriya-dharma* to have a ritual status equal to the performance of *yajña.* Arjuna's action, according to 3.9, should not be for personal gain, but the act of a priest performing a ritual–*yajñārthaḥ.* Prajāpati created this ritual so that mankind might gain all things needed for life; it nourishes the gods and they in return provide for life on earth (10-11). Here Kṛṣṇa is presenting a simple restatement of the Vedic understanding of *yajña,* but the ritual he is thereby urging Arjuna to undertake is not a sacrifice as such, but the ritual of battle, the *sva-dharma* of a *kṣatriya.*

(iv) Ritual Ethics and Human Nature

It is important to recall that ritual *dharma* is regarded as descriptive as well as prescriptive. It is not just a code of conduct in the sense of the Law but is also a recognition of the inherent natures of different groups of individuals. Whereas a modern discussion of ethics will consider the question of human nature, for the epic it is instead *brāhmaṇa* nature or *kṣatriya* nature that ethical concepts must recognise. Hence ritual ethics cannot be absolute and instead present an ethical hierarchy in which different standards of behaviour are demanded from different groups of individuals to harmonise with the inherent nature with which they are born. For this reason to act against the Law is not merely a moral offence, but is an unnatural act defying the harmony of creation.

3. Ethics and Morality

(i) *Sva-dharma* and *Sādhāraṇa*

The previous discussion demonstrates that Dasgupta is correct in stressing the distinction between the ethics of *sva-dharma* and morality as it is understood in the modern sense. That is not to say that morality has no place in *sva-dharma*, for a study of the *Rāja-dharma* shows that there is a moral dimension to the execution of dharmic duty, but despite this overlapping a clear distinction is apparent. The *Mahābhārata* does, however, have a prominent notion of morality running alongside and interacting with the understanding of *dharma* as Law. This idea is set down didactically in a number of passages, but perhaps the clearest exposition comes from the narrative itself through its depictions of the major characters, most notably Yudhiṣṭhira and Duryodhana. The text recognises the distinction between *sva-dharma* and morality, and explores the question at length both as a doctrinal issue and also as a literary device to enhance the drama of its story.

As noted earlier, O'Flaherty refers to these two tendencies in Hindu ethics as *sva-dharma* and *sādhāraṇa*, duties that are specific and those that are general to all members of society. The epic is aware of these terms and the distinction they denote, though it does not always express it in a manner recognisable as duty and morality. Hanumān sees *sādhāraṇa* as no more than elements of *sva-dharma* that are applicable to all four *varṇas*. He says, *yajñādhyānana-dānāni trayaḥ sādhāraṇāḥ smṛtāḥ–yajña,* study of the Vedas and charity are recorded as the three duties for all people (3.149.34)–a statement that ignores any moral aspect to the concept of *sādhāraṇa.*

In the *Mokṣa-dharma,* however, the distinction O'Flaherty refers to becomes apparent. According to Parāśara,

> *ānṛśaṁsyam ahiṁsā cāpramādaḥ saṁvibhāgitā*
> *śrāddha-karmātitheyaṁ ca satyam akrodha eva ca*
>
> *sveṣu dāreṣu saṁtoṣaḥ śaucaṁ nityānasūyatā*
> *ātma-jñānaṁ titikṣā ca dharmāḥ sādhāraṇā nṛpa*
>
> 'Renouncing cruelty, not injuring, diligence, allowing others what is due to them, performance of the *śrāddha* rite for one's forefathers, serving guests, truthfulness, never giving way to anger, being satisfied with one's own wives, purity, never being envious, understanding the spiritual self within and tolerance–these, O king, are the aspects of *dharma* that apply to all people.' (12.285.23-24)

Here the practices designated as *sādhāraṇa* are primarily of a moral rather than a ritual nature, although the distinction is blurred somewhat by the inclusion of reference to the *śrāddha* rite. At the very beginning of the *Rāja-dharma,* Bhīṣma lists restraining anger, truth in speech, allowing others what is due to them, patience, begetting offspring by one's own wives, purity, freedom from malice, honesty and maintaining the members of one's household as nine elements of *dharma* to be adhered to by all *varṇas–navaite sārva-varṇikāḥ* (12.60.7-8).

Thus there is a destinction recognised by the epic's didactus between aspects of *dharma* all sections of society must respect and those specific to a particular *varṇa.* O'Flaherty identifies this division as resting on the distinction between ritual and moral ethics and goes on to assert that, "the two forms of morality cannot be resolved."[11] There is certainly a greater emphasis on morality in the ethical codes designated as *sādhāraṇa,* and the epic as a whole is very concerned with the tensions between the ethics of *sva-dharma* and morality. This problem is explored primarily, however, in the narrative accounts of the life of Yudhiṣṭhira, and I am not convinced that the text recognises the tension it explores as being between *sva-dharma* and *sādhāraṇa.* The crux of the question is whether *sādhāraṇa* is identified as the morality espoused by Yudhiṣṭhira or simply as duties that all *varṇas* must fulfil and which therefore tend to be the moral aspects of *sva-dharma.* My feeling is that the latter is the more likely and certainly the text of the epic never designates Yudhiṣṭhira's morality, with which he opposes aspects of *sva-dharma,* as being the ethics of *sādhāraṇa.*

(ii) The Epic's Moral Perspective

The recurring tension in the narrative between Yudhiṣṭhira's moral sense and the dharmic duties imposed upon him is a theme that will be discussed later, but first I wish to examine the nature of the moral position depicted through the character of the Dharmarāja. Although they are never mere two-dimensional personalities, there is a clear sense in which Yudhiṣṭhira and Duryodhana, described by van Buitenen as "the dark contrast to Yudhiṣṭhira,"[12] are designed to represent what is worthy and what is unworthy in humanity and thereby present a moral treatise in narrative form. It is noteworthy that although we are constantly aware of the superiority of Yudhiṣṭhira's character over that of Duryodhana, this is based on moral and not ritual ethics. In the execution of *kṣatriya-dharma* Duryodhana may even be regarded as Yudhiṣṭhira's superior, for he is always keen to do battle and gives up his life in the ideal *kṣatriya* manner, while Yudhiṣṭhira is often timid and has no taste for warfare or punishment. Thus the epic's repeated stress on Yudhiṣṭhira's excellence is to be recognised as a stress on the importance of moral ethics.

The good character of Yudhiṣṭhira is emphasised throughout the narrative, with a number of passages specifically listing his qualities and others demonstrating them by descriptions of his behaviour. When urging his son to make peace in the *Udyoga,* Dhṛtarāstra describes Yudhiṣṭhira as true to his word, always diligent, devoted to the words of scripture, obedient to his family, loved by his subjects, kind to his friends, in control of his senses, and a protector of the righteous. In addition, he displays forbearance, tolerance, self-control and honesty; he is always truthful, accepts good advice, is compassionate to all beings and attentive to precept (5.147.32-33).

In the *Vana,* we are given Kṛṣṇa's view of Yudhiṣṭhira's virtues and here it is notable how the *avatāra* emphasises the latter's adherence to *sva-dharma* as well as his moral excellence. Kṛṣṇa praises Yudhiṣṭhira as follows, "*Dharma* is greater than the winning of a kingdom and they describe the execution of it as a penance. By executing the duties of *sva-dharma* with truth and honesty, you have conquered both this world and the next. In the beginning you engaged in study, following various vows, and absorbed the complete science of warfare; having gained possessions and wealth through *kṣatriya-dharma,* you have executed all the traditional sacrifices. You take no delight in licentious pleasures and you do not strive in any way after the objects of enjoyment. You never abandon *dharma* because of greed, and thus, because of your nature, you are the *dharma-rāja.* Having won lands, riches and objects of pleasure, your greatest delight is always in charity, truthfulness, austerity, faith, tranquillity, determination and tolerance." (3.180.16-19)

These and other similar passages give some insight into the qualities that the epic regards highly in its view of morality. The view is one that is common to moralists of most cultures, emphasising truthfulness, honesty, loyalty, kindness, tolerance, self-control, and restraint of lust, avarice and anger. The teaching is presented far more effectively, however, by the portrayal of the life of Yudhiṣṭhira in which he is shown as the paragon of all the virtues that are universally admired. Throughout he is portrayed as being of a gentle disposition with constant goodwill towards other living beings. He is kind and forgiving, tolerant and forbearing, and always anxious to avoid conflict of any kind. He is also notably non-competitive in his attitude to others, transcending such wordly preoccupations by the strength of his virtue.

Following Jayadratha's assault on Draupadī, Bhīma urges that the offender should be slain for such a gross misdemeanour, but Yudhiṣṭhira exhibits the virtues of mercy, tolerance and avoidance of anger in ordering that he be set free, punished only by humiliation and admonition (3.256.7). His powers of forgiveness are similarly demonstrated by his attitude to Dhṛtarāṣṭra after the battle, again in marked contrast to that of Bhīma. Whilst the latter continues to bear a grudge against the old king for the wrongs he has done them, Yudhiṣṭhira displays no ill will whatsoever and provides for all his uncle's needs and wishes (15.3). Only on rare occasions, in the heat of battle, does Yudhiṣṭhira fall prey to anger and as a general rule he is able to withstand even the most extreme provocation, as at the conclusion of the dice match and in the kingdom of Virāṭa when Kīcaka insults Draupadī. His truthfulness is likewise renowned; he will not deviate at all from the terms of their exile because he has given his word, and when he announces on the battlefield that Aśvatthāman is slain, Droṇa cannot doubt that it is so. This is the only untruth that he speaks in his life, and, according to the *Svargārohaṇa,* his only sin (18.3.14).

In the opening chapter of the *Vana,* we are shown the quality of humility in Yudhiṣṭhira. As the Pāṇḍavas are departing for their exile, the citizens of Hastināpura glorify them with extravagant words of praise, but Yudhiṣṭhira disclaims these eulogies. Similarly, after the battle he repeatedly condemns himself as a great sinner for causing the suffering that has taken place and will not accept any of the speeches from his comrades which exonerate him from blame. As a king he demonstrates his compassionate nature and his concern for others. After his victory at Kurukṣetra he ensures that provision is made for the welfare of the women who have been widowed as well as for the poor and the blind (12.42.10-12). This characteristic is further demonstrated by his behaviour at the very end of his life when he refuses to abandon a dog, considered by Hindus an impure creature, and go to heaven alone, because it has followed him for many miles and looks to him for shelter (17.3.7).

Though born a *kṣatriya,* he repeatedly expresses his loathing for violence, and displays little of the desire for power that besets most kings (3.253.21). Though he wages war to regain the kingdom which has been stolen from him, he does so only because he is persuaded that it is a matter of principle and because Kṛṣṇa is the main advocate of conflict. He takes up arms not because of a desire for riches or vengeance, but because it is his duty; for himself he is shown as being delighted by the simple life in the forest during the exile without any form of opulence.

The characterisation of Duryodhana forms an equally important aspect of the narrative's moral directives in indicating the traits and behaviour that are to be avoided by the righteous. He is never mild in his disposition, never gentle in his thoughts, words or deeds, and never forgiving of any offence, real or imagined. He burns with envy over the success of the Pāṇḍavas, he is avaricious for power and opulence, and whenever his will is opposed he is consumed by unrestrained wrath. He has no misgivings about the suffering he will cause through waging war. He is vindictive rather than forgiving and has no remorse; he has no real sense of right and wrong and he and Karṇa construct specious arguments that convince no-one in order to justify their misdeeds (5.21.9-15). Even after the humiliation of the Pāṇḍavas at the dice match, his vindictiveness is such that he wishes to further relish their discomfiture by seeing them suffering in exile in the forest (3.226).

Unlike Yudhiṣṭhira, he shows scant respect for the elders of the family, rejecting the counsel of Gāndhārī, Vidura and others, frequently with a haughty irreverence. He is untruthful and dishonest, as when he lies to his father about the purpose of their journey to Dvaitavana to mock the Pāṇḍavas, and his obstinacy is such that he is never seen to alter his resolve in light of superior advice. Whilst Yudhiṣṭhira is typically portrayed as contented with his lot, Duryodhana is beset by desires over which he has no self-restraint. He is a believer in the value of competitive endeavour and pursues this course with ruthless vigour. Yudhiṣṭhira is ready to compromise rather than fight, even if it means an inequitable division of the kingdom but Duryodhana not only refuses this course but states his belief in the value of competition as an impetus to success. In Chapter 50 of the *Sabhā*, he makes an interesting speech in which he presents himself as a true follower of *kṣatriya-dharma*, arguing that competition is inevitable, and anyone striving for the same goal must be recognised as one's enemy (22). He further urges that dissatisfaction with one's lot is a positive quality, for such a state of mind is the root of prosperity– *asaṁtoṣaḥ śriyo mūlam* (18).

This characterisation of the righteous man and his inimical antithesis is a prominent feature of the epic narrative, and serves to make the work a powerful moral treatise preaching an ethical code that has had a major influence on Hindu culture over countless generations. This moral perspective on life is not confined to the characterisations of the epic narrative, but is also set forth didactically in numerous incidents scattered throughout the *Mahābhārata* in which the central protagonists encounter various purveyors of wisdom.

A few brief examples must serve to illustrate this feature of the epic's teachings. In the story of King Yayāti presented in the *Ādi,* we have Yayāti himself relating to Indra the good instruction that he gave to his son Puru. These stress first not injuring others through harsh words, and secondly not retaliating if others seek to cause distress to oneself:

> One who is abused and afflicted should remain tolerant and not return the abuse; he thereby scorches the abuser and takes from him the merit of his pious deeds.
>
> One should neither cause pain to others nor speak harshly; when deprived of an object, one should not seize it from another; one should not utter mortifying words that belong in the worlds of the damned through which another person is tormented.
>
> That person of rough speech which causes pain has words that pierce men like thorns. Who can be more unfortunate among men than one who bears such a covering of evil within his mouth.
>
> Words spoken by the righteous should be revered to one's front and preserved behind; one should always tolerate the insults of the wicked; a virtuous man should take up the conduct of the righteous.
>
> Arrows in the form of words fly forth from speech, and one who is struck laments both day and night. They strike the other person's most sensitive parts; a learned man never discharges such arrows at others.
>
> There is nothing in the three worlds that engenders goodwill to the same degree as do benevolence to all, charity and sweet words.
>
> Therefore one's speech should always be gentle and never insulting in any way. One should honour those who are worthy of respect; one should give but never beg from others (1.82.7-13).

In the story of Sāvitrī, the heroine delights the God of Death by her learned speeches, several of which are on the subject of morality:

> Not offending any living being with actions, thoughts, or words, along with goodwill and charity is the eternal *dharma* of the righteous.
>
> Even such (as my dead husband) is the nature of this world, where men are of delicate constitution. A virtuous person, even amongst enemies he has made, still manifests compassion (3.281.34-35).

In numerous passages of the *Anuśāsana* particular stress is laid on non-injury, compassion and empathy. In Chapter 5, the story of the parrot and the tree is narrated. The tree in which the parrot lives withers after being struck by the poisoned arrow of a hunter, but out of compassion and loyalty the bird refuses to abandon its roost. Eventually Indra becomes delighted with the parrot's conviction and revives the tree, asserting, "Amongst the virtuous, the great feature of *dharma* is compassion–*anukrośo hi sādhūnāṁ sumahad-dharma-lakṣaṇam*–and compassion always pleases those who are virtuous" (13.5.23).

In Chapter 116, Yudhiṣṭhira asks Bhīṣma why it is that although he has stated many times that not harming is the highest *dharma*–*ahiṁsā paramo dharma ity uktam bahuśas tvayā*–offerings of meat are to be made as a part of *śrāddha* ritual. In chapters 116 and 117, Bhīṣma then eulogises the practice of abstaining from eating flesh and describes the rewards after death that await those who accept such a compassionate vow. He reasons as follows: "The wise praise this as the highest *dharma,* to cherish the breaths of life of other living beings as much as one's own. Acts are performed towards others by great souls of keen intellect, as they would have them done towards themselves, and death is a source of fear; this is the view of the wise who desire prosperity" (13.116.21-22).

Two chapters previously, in an interlude in which Bṛhaspati joins the discussion, Yudhiṣṭhira asks which aspect of virtue is the highest, not harming, Vedic rituals, meditation, subjugation of the senses, austerity, or serving one's teacher. To this Bṛhaspati replies that all of these are worthy, but one who practises not harming is successful in life–*ahiṁsāpāśrayaṁ dharmaṁ yaḥ sādhayati vai naraḥ* (13.114.3). That person who considers all creatures to be as important as himself, who does not chastise others and controls his anger gains true happiness (6).

The *Anuśāsana* also stresses positive community action as a virtue to be pursued with its corresponding reward in the world to come. Chapter 99 urges wealthy individuals to construct lakes, and Chapter 100 emphasises hospitality to guests and the provision of food for animals. Other passages give lists of the great virtues that are considered to be the pillars of morality. Vyāsa teaches that the greatest religious vow has three limbs, never causing pain, giving charity and speaking the truth (13.121.10). When questioned by Umā, Śiva gives not harming, speaking the truth, kindness to all creatures, equanimity and charity as the topmost *dharma* for those who have not renounced the world (13.128.25-27). Bhīṣma defines the eternal *dharma* as being fourfold, not harming, truthfulness, charity and avoiding anger (13.147.22-24). There is no attempt in the *Anuśāsana* to distinguish between moral and ritual acts, for both are recognised as efficacious in securing for the individual a desirable position in the afterlife. The moral perspective that emerges from the above discussion shows a high degree of consistency between the teachings of the didactic portions of the text and the ideal of virtue presented by the characterisations of Yudhiṣṭhira and Duryodhana.

It is notable, at least for those schooled in Western concepts of morality, that very little attention is paid to sexual behaviour in these teachings. The ascetic tradition, considered below, places great value on celibacy for the practitioners of *yoga*, but in the morality espoused by the narrative, sexual restraint is emphasised less than other virtues, notably not harming and restraint of anger. Adultery is condemned and a man is urged to be satisfied with his own wives, but Bhīṣma's vow of celibacy is regarded as awesome rather than virtuous. Although Yudhiṣṭhira is certainly no philanderer, the praises heaped upon him rarely if ever draw attention to his sexual restraint. Indeed there is a notable incident in the *Sabhā* where the Pāṇḍavas are welcomed to Hastināpura for the dice match and entertained at night by women provided for their pleasure, without this being regarded as any form of moral laxity on their part (2.52.36-37).

The overall notion of morality that becomes apparent from studying the text in detail is one that has been criticised by Western commentators and Indian Marxists alike for its quietism and its negative concept of virtue. The passages considered in the above review undoubtedly urge a passive attitude in the face of provocation. Value is placed on not harming, not speaking harshly or dishonestly, keeping one's anger in check, and tolerating insults without retaliation. Despite the stress that is also placed on charity, the predominant emphasis does appear to be a negative one in terms of avoiding doing wrong or causing harm rather than positively striving to do good.

The criticism that epic morality is quietist is therefore perhaps valid to some degree, although it would be wrong to argue that the virtues it teaches place no value whatsoever on positive action. It is rather a question of emphasis. In any case the distinction between positive and negative virtue is in many ways an artificial one, constructed by Western polemicists, both Christian and humanist, to demonstrate the superiority of their own positions and doctrines. The saintliness and civilization of a form of moral ethics that stresses never causing pain, never yielding to anger, not retaliating when wronged, forgiveness, charity and kindness, can never be doubted and matches all that is best in Western thought. The criticisms of quietism and negativity should not be allowed to disguise the true worth of the epic's moral instruction, for it must be recognised that positive virtue rests substantially on the restraint of negative tendencies. The Marxist criticism is no absolute condemnation, but rather serves to highlight two distinctive responses to injustice, one seeking to overthrow the oppressors through revolutionary violence and the other taking the approach of non-cooperation and passive resistance. The debate as to which of these is the more appropriate response is one that will continue to tax moral philosophers.

4. The Ethics of the Ascetic Tradition

In addition to the ritual and moral codes, we can identify in the doctrines of *mokṣa-dharma* a third ethical tendency based on renunciation and world denial. It must be recognised from the outset, however, that this ascetic ethical view is in many ways identical to the notion of morality that has just been reviewed. The argument for identifying it as a distinctive ethical perspective is based on certain notable divergences from the moral ethic, the tension that may be recognised to exist between them, and the contention that despite the severe limitations it places on particular modes of conduct, it is in essence morally neutral. In my own view the third of these is highly questionable but the first two provide a legitimate basis for identifying a distinctive ethical view.

Before considering these questions in more depth, a review of the ethics of the ascetic tradition is called for. The ideas of Sāṁkhya and Yoga dictate a process of withdrawal from the world, in terms of both social involvement and also seeking sensual forms of satisfaction, and its ethical concepts rest substantially on this imperative towards renunciation. Within the *Mokṣa-dharma* and the corresponding teachings of the *Aśvamedhika,* the manner in which an ascetic should conduct his life is frequently discussed, showing that even if the system as a whole is judged to be morally neutral it is still concerned with the manner in which an individual practitioner should behave.

It is impossible to review every passage in these portions of the text which offers guidance on the conduct of a renunciant, especially as there is a high degree of consistency throughout. Chapter 222 of the *Śānti* is fairly typical of this type of material and provides sufficient illustration of the teachings here under review. At the beginning of Chapter 222, Yudhiṣṭhira asks Bhīṣma about the conduct and characteristics of those who attain the *brahman* position, and in reply Bhīṣma recounts a discussion on this subject between Devala and Jaigiṣavya. Such persons have an equal disposition towards those who praise and those who condemn them; they conceal their righteous acts and the vows they undertake (8). In conversation the wise never seek pleasure in arguing with another speaker, and they never strike back at an assailant (9). They do not lament over things yet to come and act only with regard to present occurrences; they never lament over the past and no longer even recall such things (10).

In terms of who is to be honoured or things that may be gained, those mighty ones who accept religious vows act at their own pleasure as each event arises (11). Those whose knowledge is mature, whose wisdom is vast, and who have conquered their anger and their senses, never cause offence in any way with thoughts, deeds or speech (12). Free from jealousy, they never harm one another in any way; being steadfast, they are never unhappy at another's prosperity (13). They never speak exaggerated words in praise or condemnation of others, and are never affected by praise or condemnation (14). They are peaceful in all their dealings and find pleasure in the welfare of others; they do not become angry, do not rejoice and do not give any type of offence. Having loosened the knots that bind the heart, they joyfully go on their way (15). No-one regards them as a particular companion, nor are they an intimate friend of anyone else. Likewise, no-one is their enemy and they do not see anyone else as an enemy (16).

This short passage provides a typical example of the ethics of the ascetic tradition. The stress is clearly upon withdrawal and non-involvement; one should not compete with others, envy them, or harm them in any way, but at the same time affectionate contacts and close interactions with others are also to be shunned. It is likely that conquest of the senses, referred to in verse 12, involves sexual restraint for elsewhere stress is placed on avoiding intimate contact with women. This point is particularly highlighted by the teachings of the *guru* to his disciple in Chapters 206 and 207, and also referred to by the *Gītā* which asserts that celibacy is a part of the *yoga* process–*brahmacāri-vrate sthitaḥ* (6.14).

Another significant feature of the ethics of *mokṣa-dharma* is the importance attached to not harming other living beings. Throughout the *Mokṣa-dharma* and the *Aśvamedhika* we find stress being laid on this point of conduct. Thus, for example, we have Vyāsa, *yadā na kurute bhāvaṁ sarva-bhūteṣu pāpakam/ karmaṇā manasā vācā brahma sampadyate tadā*–when he causes no hardship to any living being with deed, thought or word, then he has reached *brahman* (12.243.6), Bhīṣma, *na cakṣuṣā na manasā na vācā dūsayed api*–not by his glance, his thoughts, nor by his words, should he harm anyone (12.269.4), a Bhārgava sage, *bhūtānāṁ pratikūlebhyo nivartasva*–refrain from things that cause distress to living beings (12.297.5), Nārada, *ānṛśaṁsyaṁ paro dharmaḥ*–benevolence is the highest form of *dharma* (12.316.12), and Kṛṣṇa, *ahiṁsālakṣaṇo dharmo hiṁsā cādharma-lakṣaṇā*–*dharma* is characterised by not harming, causing harm is characteristic of *adharma* (14.43.19).

Such an ethical tendency stressing non-involvement, emotional withdrawal and world indifference clearly corresponds to the dualism and transcendentalism of the wider scheme of Sāṁkhya thought. The indication of commentators such as O'Flaherty[13] and Hacker[14] is that such teachings are essentially amoral; modes of behaviour are dictated not on the basis of consideration of right and wrong, but, as with Aristotelean ethics, because they bring success to the practitioner, in this case in the form of release from the misery of worldly existence. Hence the ethical code presented is not an appreciation of moral rectitude but simply a part of a soteriological technique.

The behaviour recommended in the treatises on salvation is not only a path to *mokṣa,* but also a symptom of one who has reached that goal. Entanglement in this world is caused by *ajñāna,* ignorance, the failure to comprehend the *ātman* as the true self. Because the individual misidentifies himself with the body, mind and senses, his actions are inevitably based on this ignorance and hence take the form of lust, anger, and greed as he seeks to experience pleasure through the perceptual senses. Hence Parāśara tells Janaka,

> *ekaḥ śatrur na dvitīyo 'sti śatrur*
> *ajñāna-tulyaḥ puruṣasya rājan*
> *yenāvṛtaḥ kurute saṁprayukto*
> *ghorāṇi karmāṇi sudāruṇāni*
>
> 'There is but one true enemy and no other; that enemy of every person is identical to ignorance, O king. One fully absorbed in that ignorance and covered by it performs cruel and horrible deeds' (12.286.28).

One acts wickedly only because of a misunderstanding of what is the true self that leads one to seek pleasure through satisfaction of the senses. Abandonment of this type of action is recognised as a symptom of having realised one's true identity as the *ātman,* but the regulated withdrawal from the pursuit of sensual pleasure is also a part of the technique of gaining that realisation. Hence Vyāsa, in describing the *yoga* process to his son, says that the first step is to regulate his conduct by conquering anger, lust, greed, fear and sleep (12.232.4), and Nārada teaches that acting properly by controlling lust and anger leads to *mokṣa* (12.316.10).

Ethical behaviour in the ascetic tradition is thus both a symptom of one who has gained *mokṣa* and also a part of the technique by which *mokṣa* is gained. In stressing the amorality of the ascetic tradition it may further be argued that world-indifference is concomitant to a dualist doctrine which emphasises the transcendence of the self. Furthermore, recognition in the teachings on *mokṣa-dharma* of the absolute supremacy of destiny over endeavour inevitably minimises the force of moral arguments. It is not good or bad acts that create joy and suffering for others, for all such fate is preordained and hence the imperative towards moral action is minimised. Thus one seeking salvation is urged to abandon his family to their fate, understanding that whatever misfortune befalls them comes not from his action but from unassailable destiny (12.277.14-18).

Clearly there is a conflict between a complete emotional withdrawal from the world and the compassion and concern for others which lies at the heart of the moral perspective. Philosophically, epic Sāṁkhya teaches that notions of right and wrong, pious and wicked, pertain only to this world and are causes of rebirth. The state of transcendence aspired to by the practitioner of Sāṁkhya has no such duality, and hence morality is to be transcended along with all other aspects of this world. Asita defines the body as *puṇya-pāpa-mayam,* embued with piety and sin which must be transcended by the self to reach the *brahman* level (12.267.37).[15]

On this basis Wendy O'Flaherty concludes that the ascetic ethic is "morally neutral" and Paul Hacker argues that Vedānta is "non-ethical". Clearly the argument is a strong one, but nonetheless is not to be accepted without reservation. First, one must not lose sight of the fact that the distinction drawn between morality and ritual or between morality and spiritual techniques is an imposition based on a Western perspective. For the *Mahābhārata,* the fact that a code of conduct is a part of a soteriological discipline does not necessarily distinguish it from moral action, and it is notable that the term *dharma* is used for both. Here Hopkins provides a valuable alternative insight when he argues against the view that because a philosophy postulates a final state beyond moral duality it must therefore be non-moral in its ethical stance: "Only the philosophers imagine an unmoral principle of life; but even they insist that in this world man must lead a moral life and that there is a vital distinction between ethical and unethical behaviour."[16] Although there is a clear strand of world-indifference in ascetic ethics, it is questionable as to whether this indicates that it lacks any moral dimension whatsoever.

Undoubtedly sin is recognised as a concept, and understood as a barrier to salvation. A sinner cannot break free of bondage because sin is the outward manifestation of *ajñāna;* only one who misidentifies the twenty-four elements as his true self will follow the dictates of lust, anger and greed which impel him to perform unrighteous acts. In effect *mokṣa-dharma* provides an alternative approach to the question of morality. Beyond merely identifying right and wrong actions and ordering their prosecution or proscription, it seeks to identify the root causes of sinful intent, which it recognises as ignorance and desire, and then recommends techniques by which this basis of sin may be removed. This is certainly a different approach to the question of morality, but hardly one that ignores moral issues altogether.

Within the teachings of the *Śānti,* the stress on not harming is particularly significant because of the way in which it is approached as a moral question. Teachers of Sāṁkhya such as Tulādhara (12.253-256) and Kapila (12.260-262) are not at all indifferent to the sufferings of the animals they witness being brought for slaughter in *yajñas*. Rather than withdrawing and concentrating on their personal salvific technique, they approach the priests and criticise their actions on the grounds that it is wrong to cause another living being to suffer, trying thereby to dissuade them from a ritual act of violence. Passages of this type, of which there are several, along with the repeated stress placed on the behaviour of a *mokṣa-dharmin* lend support to the view that the ascetic tradition does include a moral dimension. Furthermore, the actions of the Sāṁkhya teachers in campaigning against the cruelty of animal slaughter may be cited as a counter to Hacker's view that all forms of social and political action based on Vedānta are inventions of neo-Hindus who do not understand their own tradition.

5. The Tensions Between the Different Ethical Tendencies

(i) Introduction

The three ethical tendencies discussed above are identified and distinguished primarily not by overt statements of the text, but by the tensions between them that the epic highlights and explores. As three ethical views have been identified so the tensions between them fall into three categories, though of these two are prominent and one is secondary. As will have been noted from the foregoing discussion, the ethics of the moral and ascetic tendencies involve similar codes of conduct, though with certain distinctions based on world-involvement and world-indifference. Therefore the principal ethical tensions considered by the text are between ritual and moral and ritual and ascetic ethics.

(ii) The Tension Between Ritual and Moral Ethics

This is a prominent theme explored and employed dramatically throughout the central narrative. Here again the character of Yudhiṣṭhira is of principal significance, though occasionally, as in the *Gītā*, Arjuna is cast in his role. Yudhiṣṭhira is a *kṣatriya* and hence from the point of view of ritual *sva-dharma* is expected to be a heroic man of action, eager to wage war, proud of his martial prowess, intolerant of insults, and competitive in seeking and maintaining power. This indeed exactly matches the behaviour and attitudes of Bhīma who may be recognised as the exemplar of *kṣatriya-dharma* just as Yudhiṣṭhira is of moral *dharma.*

The tensions occur principally because of Yudhiṣṭhira's repeated insistence on placing moral ethics above those of *sva-dharma,* in spite of the criticisms of his family members, to the extent where we have the paradox of the *dharma-rāja* accused of being a *nāstika,* or non-believer. The conflict of ideology is best understood by reference to the text itself in which it recurs on numerous occasions in various shapes and guises:

1. In the *Sabhā,* after the dice match, whilst Bhīma wishes to take immediate revenge on the Kauravas for their insults, Yudhiṣṭhira tolerates all provocation and accepts the terms of exile imposed upon them.
2. In the forest Bhīma and Draupadī both urge Yudhiṣṭhira that a *kṣatriya* should never brook the insults and humiliations that have been heaped upon them and that he should therefore immediately take up arms. Yudhiṣṭhira, however, values the moral qualities of tolerance and truthfulness over *kṣatriya-dharma* and rejects their arguments.
3. After the defeats of Duryodhana and Karṇa by the *gandharvas* and of Jayadratha by the Pāṇḍavas, Bhīma is in favour of taking advantage of the discomfiture of their enemies, displaying the competitive attitude of a *kṣatriya.* Yudhiṣṭhira, however, has compassion for those in distress and orders that they be set free.
4. In the *Virāṭa,* when Draupadī is harrassed by Kīcaka, Yudhiṣṭhira urges tolerance of the situation and is bitterly condemned by his wife for his lack of *kṣatriya* vigour (4.20.28). Again Bhīma disagrees with his brother, and this time takes action to remedy the situation.
5. In the *Udyoga,* Kṛṣṇa, Sātyakī and other warriors are keen to wage war in revenge for the mistreatment of the Pāṇḍavas and to win back their kingdom. Yudhiṣṭhira, by contrast, has no thought of revenge and displays his tolerance and forbearance by being prepared to go to almost any length to compromise. In these debates Kṛṣṇa urges that because Duryodhana is a

thief, it is Yudhiṣṭhira's *kṣatriya* duty to punish him (5.29.28), but still Yudhiṣṭhira is unwilling to take up arms, regarding war as immoral and productive only of further distress (5.70.6-78). In this passage he makes his strongest denunciation of *kṣatriya-dharma,* stating that such *dharma* is wickedness–*pāpaḥ kṣatriya-dharmo 'yam* (5.70.46)–and comparing it to the behaviour of dogs fighting over a piece of meat (5.70.71-72).

6. At the beginning of the *Śānti,* Yudhiṣṭhira is mortified by the death and suffering the war has brought to all the royal families, and initially refuses to accept the throne they have won. His brothers and Draupadī argue that in waging war he was acting properly in accordance with his *sva-dharma* and that the performance of a *yajña* will atone for any sin he may be guilty of. Yudhiṣṭhira, however, will not accept this view and condemns his ambition as the cause of the misery he now sees.
7. At various places in the *Rāja-dharma,* Yudhiṣṭhira responds to Bhīṣma's teachings by saying that he cannot accept the concept of *dharma* that is being set forth. This occurs specifically when Bhīṣma urges that aggressive warfare and recourse to unrighteous conduct in emergency are a part of the duties of a *kṣatriya* (12.98.1, 12.140.1-2).
8. After peace is restored and the Pāṇḍavas resume their reign, the different attitudes towards Dhṛtarāṣṭra are striking. Yudhiṣṭhira can think of nothing but forgiveness, sympathy and respect for an elder of his family, whilst Bhīma, the *kṣatriya,* recognises a foe who has wronged him deeply and cannot accept his elder brother's tolerant disposition (15.3-4).
9. The previous incidents have all served to illustrate the conflict between morality and *kṣatriya-dharma,* but in the *Aśvamedhika* we find that it may also clash with the ritual of *yajña.* After Yudhiṣṭhira has executed his expiatory *aśvamedha-yajña,* the god Dharma appears in the form of a mongoose and asserts that the single act of a starving *brāhmaṇa* couple in giving away the last of their food to a beggar was a far more significant act of *dharma* than the ostentatious ceremony that has just been completed (14.92-93).
10. Finally, in the *Svargārohaṇa,* we have Yudhiṣṭhira complaining against the heavenly rewards bestowed upon Duryodhana for his exemplary *kṣatriya* behaviour, although he was a man devoid of moral worth.

All these passages from different portions of the epic illustrate the tensions between the ethics of morality and those of ritual action that the text seeks to explore. The *Mahābhārata* is clearly aware of the difficulty in reconciling the two, but it does not attempt to give a definite decision as to which path is superior. In effect its message is that *dharma* has two aspects, both of which are valid, and that complex questions arise when they come into conflict; it does not seek to go beyond such an observation by making any definitive judgement. One senses, albeit subjectively, a sympathy on the part of the authors for the goodness of Yudhiṣṭhira, and the statement that the ritual type of *dharma* came into being only after the *Kṛtayuga* when men became degraded by lust and anger adds weight to this intuition. Set against this, however, are other occasions when Yudhiṣṭhira's failure to pursue *kṣatriya-dharma* appears to be at fault. We are attracted by his mercy to Jayadratha and his forgiveness of Dhṛtarāṣṭra, but when he tolerates the aggressions of the rapist Kīcaka and shows lack of resolve and petulance on the battlefield, we are drawn to the more robust attitude of Bhīma.

Similarly, in the final *parvan*, when Yudhiṣṭhira voices his objections to wicked persons gaining heavenly rewards, it is unclear whether his view is the one that should be taken as correct. Certainly his statements on *dharma* must carry weight, but can it be that universal laws are based on injustice? Perhaps the message of this passage is that though it is accepted that moralists will find it objectionable, the fact remains that ritual actions produce results, sometimes in defiance of an individual's moral worth. The epic here seems to explore the subtleties of *dharma*, using them to enhance the interest of the story it is telling, rather than accepting the role of absolute arbiter of contentious doctrinal issues. In the end the hearer is given various indications, but is ultimately left to reach his or her own conclusion. *Dharma* is subtle, and the more it is discussed the more contentious it becomes; therefore to attempt to resolve it with simplistic statements of dogma is a folly that the epic renounces.

(iii) The Tension Between Ritual and Ascetic Ethics

The ritual form of religion, based to some extent on the teachings of the Vedas, has many points of tension with that of the more mystical and other-worldly ascetic sects whose teachings had a profound effect on the doctrines of the epic. Whilst the enactors of ritual sought prosperity and order in this world and the joys of heaven in the next, the ascetics rejected both as diversions from the true quest for salvation and as symptoms of ignorance about the true nature of the self.

In terms of prescribed conduct, the ascetic tradition argues that there is no need to perform ritual duties for they pertain only to this world which is to be transcended. Particularly the question of violent actions is one on which ideological differences centre. The ritual duties of both *brāhmaṇas* and *kṣatriyas* involve acts of violence in sacrificing animals and in opposing enemies, whilst the ascetic tradition stresses not harming as the highest virtue. It is noteworthy that the criticism in this tension comes primarily from the proponents of ascetic values who repeatedly argue against the ethics of those who persist with ritual beliefs and ceremonies. The performers of ritual action respond with the accusation that their critics are *nāstikas* who reject the traditional Vedic system, but their position is essentially a defensive one. This, one feels, must reflect the historical context of the epic period in which the Buddhists and other sects were in conflict with the established orthodoxy. It is clear from the epic that it was not only from the Buddhists that the Vedic religion was under attack, but that the same rejection was coming in varying degrees from the ascetic schools teaching Sāṁkhya and Yoga. The crucial difference, as is apparent from the text of the *Mokṣa-dharma,* is that the teachers of Sāṁkhya and Yoga did not deny the revealed status of the Vedas, but instead argued that the religious practices of the priests were based on a misunderstanding of their true meaning. Hence Sāṁkhya and Yoga have remained within the body of Hinduism while the Buddhists and Jains have emerged as adherents of separate faiths.

It is also to be noted that these conflicts are referred to exclusively in those parts of the epic's didactus in which the tenets of *nivṛtti* are expounded. The central narrative and the dharmaśāstric portions show little concern with the ascetic tradition and rarely if ever seek to criticise its teachings. The rejection of some of the beliefs, practices and goals of ritual religion is, however, a significant element in the teachings on *mokṣa-dharma.* Thus within the *Mokṣa-dharma* we find a number of passages in which teachers of Sāṁkhya criticise performers of *yajña* on the grounds that their behaviour is unethical.

1. In Chapters 253 to 257 of the *Śānti,* we have a discussion between Jājali, a *yogin* and ascetic proud of his austerities, and Tulādhara a shopkeeper who has imbibed the wisdom of Sāṁkhya. The conversation is lengthy and involved, but Tulādhara's main point is that not harming and goodwill is the eternal *dharma*; therefore both meat eating and cruel forms of animal husbandry must be given up. Jājali replies that husbandry provides food and also animals for sacrifice and therefore Tulādhara is a *nāstika* for objecting to such practices-*yato yajñaḥ prabhavati nāstikyam api jalpasi* (12.255.3). Tulādhara refutes this accusation and says that he does not deny the Vedas because in ancient times sacrifice did not involve animal killing and was performed with plants and herbs as the offerings.
2. Chapters 260 to 262 describe a conversation between Kapila and Śyumaraśmi, who has taken the form of a cow awaiting slaughter. Kapila, famous as the original propounder of Sāṁkhya, condemns the killing of animals and the debate that follows focuses primarily on whether the ascetic or ritual lifestyle is superior. Again we find Kapila condemned (12.260.9-11) for ignoring the Vedas, and, like Tulādhara, he denies the accusation, arguing that the Vedas advocate different paths, some demanding the performance of ritual acts and some calling for the renunciation of such acts. Here the disagreement over not harming animals is no more than the starting point for a debate over whether ritual action or renunciation is the superior path, at the end of which Kapila emerges victorious and Śyumaraśmi accepts his teachings.
3. In Chapter 264, Nārada tells of a *brāhmaṇa* named Satya who both performs *yajñas* and undergoes religious austerities. A sage named Parnada takes the form of a deer and offers to allow himself to be sacrificed in one of Satya's *yajñas.* The *brāhmaṇa* is tempted by the heavenly pleasures he may win by offering a deer and therefore agrees to perform the ritual. At this point the god Dharma appears and instructs that sacrifice without animal killing is a superior form of ritual.
4. In Chapter 265, Bhīṣma recounts the speech of King Vicakhnu who is disgusted on seeing the corpses of cows in the sacrificial arena. The king insists that such slaughter is praised only by men who go beyond the bounds of morality, are fools, atheists,

doubters, or immature (4). According to Manu, the essence of *dharma* is not harming in all one's deeds, for causing harm to animals arises from lust and desire (5).

5. In the *Nārāyaṇīya*, Chapter 324 of the *Śānti* tells the story of King Vasu and his arbitration of a dispute between the *ṛṣis* and the gods. The gods argue (3) that when the Vedas say that sacrifice should be performed using an *aja* the word *aja* should be taken as meaning a goat, but the *ṛṣis* contend that *aja* must mean seeds, for the *dharma* of the righteous, especially in *Kṛtayuga* cannot involve the killing of animals (4-5). The dispute is referred to King Vasu, a devotee of Viṣṇu, for arbitration. Vasu, however, is partial to the gods and therefore falsely rules in their favour. Angered by his duplicity, the *ṛṣis* curse the king to dwell in a pit, where he remains until set free by Garuḍa.
6. In Chapter 28 of the *Aśvamedhika*, Kṛṣṇa recounts a conversation between a priest and a renunciant (*adhvaryu* and *yati*). Seeing a goat about to be slaughtered in a *yajña*, the *yati* condemns the priest by saying, "This is an act of violence" (7). To this the priest replies that the goat will not cease to exist and will benefit from being offered; this is the version of the Vedas which approve of the ritual he is about to perform. The ascetic responds by sarcastically asking whether, as the whole performance is for the goat's benefit, he has the support of the animal's parents and relatives (12-15). He then asserts that not harming is the highest of all types of *dharma*, before moving on to an exposition of Sāṁkhya philosophy.
7. In Chapter 94 of the *Aśvamedhika*, there is another telling of the story of the dispute between the gods and *ṛṣis* over sacrificing animals and King Vasu's false arbitration. The sympathy of the narrator, here Vaiśaṁpāyana, is clearly with the view of the *ṛṣis* who are described as *tattva-darśins*, knowers of the truth, while Indra in refusing to accept their view is referred to as controlled by pride and ignorance (17), and Vasu's reply is described as *vitatha*, false or untrue (23).
8. Chapter 259 of the *Śānti* contains a debate between King Dyumatsena and his son Satyavān, both of whom are characters in the story of Sāvitrī, over whether it is proper to execute thieves or whether non-violence is the higher principle. The previous instances cited have focused on the tension between

ascetic ethics and the ritual acts of *brāhmaṇas*, but here it is the righteous violence of *kṣatriya-dharma* that is being called into question by ascetic values. It is clearly recognised that the duties of a king are had to reconcile with the ascetic world-view, a point stressed also by Sulabhā to Janaka in Chapter 308. The distinction between the two ethical codes is here recognised and highlighted through the discussion between the king and his son.

There is no doubt that the view of the writers of these passages is that the ritual code of ethics is flawed, is based on a misunderstanding of the Vedic tradition, is materialistic in its orientation, and ideally should be replaced by a new form of ethics based on non-materialistic aspirations. The rejection of the violence of both *kṣatriyas* and *brāhmaṇas* stands in marked contrast to the general view of the epic in which battle and *yajña* are accepted practices for the two branches of the social élite. It is apparent that the *Mokṣa-dharma* represents the ideas of a different religious perspective which openly challenges the beliefs and ethics of the older Vedic system.

(iv) The Tension Between Moral and Ascetic Ethics

The major ethical tensions of the epic are between the moral and ritual and the ascetic and ritual codes, discussed above. There is substantial congruence between the anti-materialist ascetic ethics and the morality of Yudhiṣṭhira expressed in the narrative and hence the tension between them is not pronounced. The two are not identical, however, for the moral code takes far more account of the welfare of others in this world, whilst ascetic ethics is primarily concerned with withdrawal from the world, and it is on this basis that tension does occasionally occur between the two.

1. In the debates following the battle, Yudhiṣṭhira's stated abhorrence for warfare and his abject remorse for the slaughter that has taken place are critiqued from the perspectives of both the two other ethical tendencies. Whilst his brothers and Draupadī argue that he should have no regrets for acting in accordance with *kṣatriya-dharma,* Vyāsa argues from both perspectives, urging at some points that warfare is righteous for a *kṣatriya* (12.23, 25), and at others, from the ascetic perspective, that all things are controlled by destiny and thus one's acts can make no difference to an individual's fate (12.26, 28). In the

latter instances he is opposing Yudhiṣṭhira's moral repugnance for warfare with the ascetic view that all outcomes are predestined, and that misery does not touch the true self.

2. In the teachings of the *guru* in the *Mokṣa-dharma*, the disciple is urged to abandon even compassion, an essential feature of moral ethics, as it represents continued attachment to this world (12.208.4).
3. The ethics of the *Bhagavad-gītā* are discussed in detail below, but at this point it is worth noting that as with Yudhiṣṭhira, Arjuna's compassion representing a moral stance, is criticised by Kṛṣṇa from the perspectives of both the other two ethical tendencies. In 2.30-37 he argues that renouncing violence is contrary to *kṣatriya-dharma* but predominantly he rejects Arjuna's view on the basis of Sāṁkhya, stressing that because the true self is beyond this world, one should be indifferent to bodily concerns and not lament for the suffering that has to be endured both by oneself and by others.

These three types of ethical tension are significant for an appreciation of the doctrinal issues that the text as a whole is confronting; they are also the principal means by which the three ethical tendencies may be identified as shaping the thought of the epic. Stated simply, the conflict between the duties of *sva-dharma* and morality based on virtue has been recognised and emphasised by the text; the subsequent entrance of ascetic ideals, reflected in the *Mahābhārata* by various didactic interludes, challenged both these ethical codes, though most especially that of *sva-dharma* to which it is fundamentally opposed. What is perhaps most remarkable is that despite a conflict of doctrine equal to that embraced by the Buddhists, the teachings of Sāṁkhya and Yoga were accepted within the orthodoxy of Hindu thought represented by the present form of the text of the epic.

6. The Ethics of the *Bhagavad-gītā*

(i) *Pravṛtti* and *Nivṛtti*

At its most basic level the *Bhagavad-gītā* is an ethical debate of a strictly practical nature. Arjuna faces the dilemma of deciding whether it is proper to kill social superiors and family members who have opted to oppose him in battle. The questions raised by this dilemma and the ideas set forth to resolve it are, however, a contiguous part of the ethical debates that run throughout the

Mahābhārata and it is thus very difficult to properly understand the *Gītā* without its being set in its epical context. Hence the previous consideration of the ethical perspectives of the *Mahābhārata* is of the highest significance in attempting to comprehend the teachings of the *Gītā.*

The opening chapter focuses on *Arjuna's* unwillingness to fight and the arguments he presents to justify this course of action. This is the initial ethical argument of the text, though it is one that is swiftly dismissed. Essentially, Arjuna makes two objections to fighting the war. In 1.36-44 and 2.4-8 he argues very much as Yudhiṣṭhira does elsewhere that to shed blood for personal gain is a wicked act in any circumstances. Duryodhana and his party are prepared to do this but they are known to be sinners, and in making war on them the Pāṇḍavas will be equally unrighteous. Secondly, stationed in the opposing army are his teacher and his grandfather who are the leaders and moral guides of the family. If they are killed their guidance will be lost, and hence to oppose in battle those who are his superiors is an unrighteous act.

This position of Arjuna's may be identified as being derived from the moral code of ethics repeatedly asserted by Yudhiṣṭhira throughout the epic. When the *Gītā* is reviewed in its epic context, it becomes apparent that this debate parallels those found at the beginning of the *Śānti* with Arjuna here adopting the position of Yudhiṣṭhira, and Kṛṣṇa's initial teachings being aimed at rejecting this type of ethics. His first argument is that Arjuna's position is not a genuine one. He identifies an emotional response to a situation in which one's ethical duty is extremely difficult to follow. Arjuna's duty is to adhere to his *sva-dharma* and wage war against wrongdoers, and his recourse to the ethics of morality is a ploy to legitimate what is essentially an emotional response to the deed he is dutybound to perform. Hence Kṛṣṇa's initial statement in Chapter 2 condemns Arjuna not for propounding a misguided doctrine, but for a weakness of resolve which prevents his accepting the proper course of action (2.2-3).

Despite his dismissal of Arjuna's position as being based only on lack of resolve, Kṛṣṇa still confronts the question he has raised, asserting the supremacy of both the ritual and ascetic ethics over the moral position espoused here by Arjuna and elsewhere by Yudhiṣṭhira. In 2.11-29, he stresses the ascetic perspective of world indifference over that of emotional compassion. He argues that because the true self is transcendent to all material conditions, lamentation based on compassion over the material situation is misguided. The true self does not die, nor does it undergo any form of hardship or transformation; therefore one who is distressed by conditions here, and follows an ethical code that focuses primarily on confronting those conditions, does not have true knowledge.

In 2.31-37 and 3.9-16, he asserts the primacy of *sva-dharma* over Arjuna's notion of morality. The views expressed by Arjuna in favour of non-violence cannot be sustained because he is a *kṣatriya* and therefore his *dharma* is to fight (2.31-37). Warfare is a ritual act for a warrior, intimately connected with the execution of *yajñas–yajñaḥ karma-samudbhavaḥ* (3.14)–which nourish and sustain both the gods and the earth. Hence, in terms of the previous discussion, Kṛṣṇa in the opening chapters of the *Gītā* rejects Arjuna's moral view by stressing the ascetic and the ritual ethics just as Vyāsa does to Yudhiṣṭhira in the debate that follows the battle. It is for this reason that Edgerton[17] asserts that morality is underplayed in the *Gītā*, a view confirmed by Dasgupta who states, "the Gītā does not rise to the ideal of regarding all beings as friends or to that of universal compassion",[18] and, "the Gītā has no programme of universal altruism, and is never a handbook of good works."[19]

Thus from an early stage the *Gītā* proceeds to consider the ritual and ascetic ethics, having dismissed on the basis of both Arjuna's moral arguments. According to Wendy O'Flaherty, ". . . the bhakti philosophies deny the validity of the caste system in favour of a more universalistic and apparently more individualistic ethical system, whose goal is salvation,"[20] indicating that the devotional elements of Hindu thought prescribe common practices through which all sections of society may worship the Deity, as referred to by 9.32 of the *Gītā*. This trend, however, becomes fully established only in later devotional thought, and in the *Gītā, bhakti* is related to *sva-dharma*, to the gods, and to Viṣṇu as their leader who descends to protect the institution of *sva-dharma*.

O'Flaherty also points out the *Gītā*'s attempt to reconcile two types of ethics: "Theological texts such as the *Gītā* offer sophisticated and not altogether satisfactory answers to the problem [of two ethical codes]."[21] Here she is referring to *sva-dharma* and *sādhāraṇa*, which is understood as a moral code for all sections of society. It is apparent, however, that the *Gītā* does not attempt to reconcile *sva-dharma* with morality, which it dismisses at an early stage, but rather with the ascetic code of ethics referred to by O'Flaherty[22] as a third way that is morally neutral.

Hence the path taken by the *Gītā* in considering the three major ethical tendencies of the *Mahābhārata* is firstly to establish the superiority of ritual and ascetic ethics over morality, in line with the arguments against Yudhiṣṭhira in the *Udyoga* and *Śānti*, and then to attempt to reconcile the two tendencies it thereby acknowledges. The tensions between ritual and ascetic ethics relate, as has been noted, both to eschatological goals and to modes of conduct. Eschatologically, the *Gītā* is more or less unequivocal[23] in its support of the ascetic view that reaching the heavens of the gods is not a true solution to the problem of rebirth, and that one must therefore follow the path of Sāṁkhya towards complete salvation.[24] In terms of conduct, the ascetic view is that all worldly actions, whether they are in accordance with or contrary to *sva-dharma*, are to be shunned because they fall within the purview of *karma* and thereby perpetuate the process of rebirth. Acts of violence in particular, by both *brāhmaṇas* and *kṣatriyas*, are singled out by the ascetic teachers as an especially repugnant feature of *sva-dharma.*

Kṛṣṇa attempts to overcome this tension by moving the moral focus away from the act and its consequences towards the motivation of the actor. It is this which gives rise to Arjuna's confusion, expressed in 3.1-2 and again in 5.1 as to how Kṛṣṇa can recommend both types of ethics when one argues for the execution of dharmic duty and the other stresses renunciation of acts. Kṛṣṇa argues that killing in the ritual of either battle or sacrifice is not in itself a wrong act, but it is the selfish desire underlying it that makes it wrong. Thus if one kills in the execution of ritual, but without desire to gain thereby, no sin has been committed (4.21). By shifting the ethical focus in this way from the action to the motive, Kṛṣṇa is able to argue that one who has true wisdom can perform his worldly duty provided he is not motivated by desire. Therefore ritual acts may be performed for the sake of the earth, human society and the cosmos without breaching the principles of ascetic ethics.

The *Gītā* is hence more consistent with Sāṁkhya and its world-denying ethos than are those passages of the *Mokṣa-dharma* wherein the opposition to violence has a clear moral and hence world-affirming dimension. If the tenets of Sāṁkhya are accepted, and the self is absolutely transcendental, there is no reason whatsoever to abandon ritual actions even where these entail acts of violence, provided one is not motivated by any form of worldly desire. Thus there appears to be little substance to Edgerton's accusation that Arjuna's question as to how Kṛṣṇa can recommend both renunciation and acts of violence is "shamelessly dodged".[25] The answer presented by the *Gītā* is that ritual actions should be performed by all because they nourish the gods and maintain the social order, and provided they are executed without desire they do not inhibit the pursuit of *mokṣa* through renunciation.

Here some note must be paid to the work of Kaveeshwar which explores the ethics of the *Bhagavad-gītā* in detail.[26] His central thesis is that while utilitarians emphasise only the consequences of action in defining morality, and Kant refers only to the motive, the *Gītā* establishes its ethics on both principles. Thus while the notion of desireless action emphasises motivation, it is not to be construed that the *Gītā* espouses the antinomian concept that all actions are permitted if they are performed without desire. Along with *niṣkāma-karma* the *Gītā* also places stress on *kāryam,* duty, so that it is only right action that is to be executed without desire. Hence *niṣkāma-karma* corresponds to Kant's stress on motive, and *kāryam* emphasises right action which leads to desired consequences.

Kaveeshwar's work highlights a principal concern of the *Bhagavad-gītā* in its attempt at the seemingly impossible task of reconciling ritual action with world renunciation, the former as *kāryam* and the latter as *niṣkāma-karma.* This reconciliation appears initially to be unsatisfactory. The reasons Kṛṣṇa gives, even in their cosmic dimension, for continuing to execute *kāryam* are entirely to do with the welfare of this world. Therefore although one may be convinced that desireless action is not an obstacle to renunciation, there is still no reason why such action should be performed by one who aims at completely renouncing this world. It may uphold the social order and it may even sustain the gods, but from the pure Sāṁkhya perspective all such considerations have nothing at all to do with the true self.

The fact is that there is a fundamental inconsistency between ritual and ascetic ethics which even the sophisticated thought of the *Gītā* cannot conceal. One is concerned completely with this world, both socially and eschatologically, whilst the other, at least ideally, renounces all worldly concerns. Here perhaps some attempt at deconstructing the text of the *Gītā* may be worthwhile. As Kaveeshwar points out there is undoubted emphasis placed on performing right action as well as doing it without desire. The *Gītā* recognises and propounds the ascetic doctrines of Sāṁkhya and Yoga, but at the same time displays concern that the spread of such ideas may lead to the wholesale rejection of the traditional religion on which social stability depends. Therefore it seeks to demonstrate that the execution of ritual *dharma* is not incompatible with ascetic goals and values. Such a view may genuinely be based on a concern for the wellbeing of society, or, as Biardeau suggests,[27] on the fears of *brāhmaṇas* that their source of livelihood from executing ritual ceremonies might be undermined by the spread of new religious ideas. The use of an amoral stance based on world-denying ethics to justify ritual violence may then be recognised as a counter to the ascetic arguments against such violence by employing a logical continuation of their own philosophy.

(ii) The Significance of *Bhakti* in the Ethics of the *Gītā*

Up to this point we may trace the argument as follows. Arjuna's morality is overruled on the strength of both the ritual and ascetic understandings of the world. A reconciliation of these two codes is attempted on the basis that *sva-dharma* undertaken without desire is no obstacle to renunciation. The objection then arises that as *sva-dharma* pertains exclusively to worldly concerns, why should one aspiring for *mokṣa* care whether or not it is performed. It is at this point that the *Gītā* brings in a new element, that of *bhakti*. The initial concept of *niṣkāma-karma* merely explains how the duties of *sva-dharma* are not necessarily incompatible with the quest for salvation, but the devotional teachings of the *Gītā* go further and argue that when it is performed as an offering to the Deity, the execution of such duty is one of the *yoga* techniques with which Sāṁkhya is characteristically associated.[28]

Thus the *Gītā*'s devotional attitude provides a further step in the process of reconciling ascetic and ritual ethics. One seeking *mokṣa* does not have to abandon his social duty because when performed without desire it is not an obstacle. In truth, the highest form of *yoga* is that of devotion to the Supreme Deity, and the technique of that *yoga* is to undertake the requirements of *sva-dharma* as an act of supplication to him. It is thus through the ideas of *bhakti* that the final reconciliation of the ritual and ascetic ethics is attained, by presenting ritual duties as a *yoga* technique through which one may gain release from endless rebirth.

(iii) The Question of the *Gītā's* Non-Moral Perspective

Despite Kṛṣṇa's initial rejection of Arjuna's moral arguments, the *Gītā* is not wholly non-moral in its view. Dasgupta[29] argues that there is no moral dimension to the *Gītā's* teachings, but this is primarily because he is anxious to show that there is no Buddhist influence, and he has therefore overstated the case. As was noted earlier in the general review of ascetic ethics, Hopkins[30] is correct in arguing that such codes do exhibit a moral dimension, and this is reflected in the devotional Sāṁkhya taught by the *Gītā*. Kṛṣṇa expresses the same view as the *Mokṣa-dharma* in urging that sin is the inevitable concomitant of desire. In Chapter 3, when Arjuna asks why one is impelled towards sin even though one does not wish to act in such a way, Kṛṣṇa declares that desire and anger are irresistible impulses, arising from the second of the three *guṇas*–*kāma eṣa krodha eṣa rajo-guṇa-samudbhavaḥ* (3.37)–and desire is the real root, for anger arises from desire–*kāmāt krodho 'bhijāyate* (2.62). Hence the teachings on curbing sensual desire through Sāṁkhya, Bhakti and Yoga involve recognition of wrong action and conquering any tendencies in that direction. A wrongdoer cannot gain success in these disciplines if he persists in his behaviour, for wrongdoing is a part of desire and ignorance.[31]

In several passages Kṛṣṇa outlines the proper mode of conduct for one seeking salvation in a manner that shows the moral dimension to the *Gītā's* *mokṣa-dharma*. In Chapters 5 and 6, it is stated that a *yogin* never seeks pleasure through the senses but finds joy in the self within, tolerating the impulses towards desire and anger (5.22-24). He takes pleasure in the welfare of all beings (25), accepts joy and pain with equanimity, and is equally disposed towards allies and foes (6.7-9). Chapter 12 lists the qualities of the *yogins* who are worshippers of Kṛṣṇa. They have no ill-will towards any living being, they are kindly and well-disposed towards all, have no sense of proprietorship or pride, are equal in happiness and distress, and are forgiving (13). They disturb no-one and are not disturbed by the actions of others; they are free from the anxiety that arises from joy, distress and fear (15). Other verses stress the detachment of the devotees from the changing fortunes of this world, but it is clear that because they have no desires they never offend against others in a way that is sinful.

Chapter 13 lists the qualities and modes of action that are the constituents of wisdom, and here again there is a clear moral dimension to the teachings. Freedom from arrogance and pride, not harming, tolerance, honesty, respect for one's teacher, purity, steadiness, and self-control; renunciation of sensual enjoyments, lack of egotism, and awareness of the miseries of birth, death and disease; not being attached to sons, wives or home, always maintaining one's equanimity in the face of desired or unwanted circumstances; being devoted to Kṛṣṇa through constant *yoga* practice, resorting to solitary places, and not finding pleasure in the company of the common people; being fixed constantly in awareness of the self, and seeing the object of true wisdom (13.8-12).

Chapter 16 focuses specifically on two different types of conduct found amongst men, which it designates as that of the gods–*daivīm*–and that of the *asuras*–*āsurīm,* and of all the passages of the *Gītā* comes closest to being a moral treatise. Verses 1-3 list the godly endowments as fearlessness, purity of nature, adherence to wisdom and *yoga,* charity, restraint, *yajña,* study of the Vedas, austerity and honesty; not harming, truthfulness, not becoming angry, renunciation, tranquillity, not criticising, mercy to other living beings, not being greedy, gentleness, modesty and steadfastness; energy, forgiveness, fortitude, cleanliness, not being inimical, and not seeking honour.

The strength of the passage in teaching morality is diminished somewhat by indications that it is descriptive rather than prescriptive. The list is referred to as being of endowments that one is born with–*bhavanti sampadaṁ daivīm abhijātasya bhārata*–and Arjuna is assured in 16.5 that he is of the godly type rather than being urged to aspire for such a position. The remainder of the chapter discusses the asuric nature in detail, elaborating on the six qualities listed in 16.4–deceitfulness, pride, holding a conceited view of one's own worth, anger, offensiveness and ignorance. Āsuric persons follow neither the path of religious action nor that of renunciation, they are impure, improperly behaved and mendacious (7). They are atheists who say there is no God and the creation has no cause, and on that basis commit wicked acts that cause harm to the world (8-9). They are motivated by desire and follow impure practices, possessed by pride, arrogance and conceit (10). Such persons have limitless schemes to enjoy sensual pleasures and are bound by hundreds of desires. Overwhelmed by lust and anger, they thirst for the objects of pleasure and seek to accumulate them by unrighteous means (11-12). Verses 13 to 15 present a sketch of this type of miscreant scheming to destroy anyone who is an obstacle in his striving after wealth and pleasure, and even planning to execute *yajñas* and give charity in order to enhance his prestige.

Chapter 16 in particular shows that the *Gītā*'s thought does have a moral dimension, as does much of the epic's teachings on *mokṣa-dharma.* It has been argued that the *Gītā* seeks to establish the compatibility of two types of ethics, ritual and ascetic, and its emphasis on right action may likewise be understood along two distinctive paths. First Kṛṣṇa urges Arjuna to undertake *kāryam,* his dharmic duty as a warrior, and secondly he imparts instructions regarding the moral conduct which is a part of *mokṣa-dharma.* There is clearly the potential for contradiction between the two; in Chapter 16, Kṛṣṇa has depicted the sinner as one who is so ardent in seeking to fulfil his desire that he will destroy those who stand in his way. This is of course precisely the basis on which Arjuna and Yudhiṣṭhira have argued that they should refrain from fighting, recognising it as a sin to attack others simply because they are blocking personal ambition. The contradiction is resolved by Kṛṣṇa's recourse to motive as the basis for ethical distinctions. The sinner is wicked because he kills others for selfish gain, but if Arjuna kills as a matter of duty or as a part of the technique of devotional *yoga,* then he is not a sinner because although his act is identical his motive is distinct.

(iv) Conclusions

When set in their context within the *Mahābhārata,* the ethical perspectives of the *Bhagavad-gītā* become clearer. The above discussion has highlighted the following points on which the ethics of the *Gītā* are centred.

1. Arjuna's morality is first dismissed by Kṛṣṇa's asserting the superiority of both ritual and ascetic ethics.

2. A reconciliation of ritual and ascetic practices is then sought through the argument that when performed without desire, dharmic duties are not a barrier to the pursuit of *mokṣa.*

3. Such duties are then presented not merely as being no barrier to *mokṣa,* but as a part of the path to *mokṣa* in the technique of devotional *yoga,* thus completing the reconciliation.

4. Moral instructions found in the *Gītā* appear to mirror the view initially expressed by Arjuna against warfare, but are to be understood not as expressions of the moral ethic, but as the moral dimension of the ascetic ethic.

7. Overview and Conclusions

Ethics or right conduct is an issue of central importance to all sections of the epic, and in many ways is the major topic considered by the text as a whole. It is impossible in the space available here to thoroughly review all the nuances and intricacies of ethical conjecture followed and explored within the *Mahābhārata.* Instead I have sought to identify and examine the major themes of ethical speculation focused upon by the text.

Firstly, there are acts that are recommended primarily because they bring success to the individual. Here particular attention is to be paid to the *Anuśāsana* which offers numerous ritualised types of action in the form of charity, fasting, or pilgrimages which bring prosperity to the practitioner in this world and after death the possibility of living amongst the gods. In considering the epic's central ethical themes, I have followed O'Flaherty in recognising three underlying tendencies, designated as the ritual, the moral, and the ascetic. It must be noted that to some degree this categorisation is an imposition, and that the text's ethical teachings generally do not recognise such designations and allow an overlapping of tendencies. The threeforld division is nonetheless a legitimate approach to the subject primarily because it is highlighted by the text itself through the tensions between them that it overtly explores.

In the narrative's consideration of moral virtue and ritual action, there is no definitive conclusion offered as to which is superior, although one is aware of a profound sympathy for the morality of Yudhiṣṭhira who is after all the embodiment of Dharma, the god of righteousness. The audience's sympathies are drawn towards Yudhiṣṭhira's position, and yet at times one is made to feel that he is misguided in his constant resolve to place virtue above duty. In effect the epic does not attempt an axiomatic resolution, but rather explores the dramatic possibilities of the tensions between different ethical tendencies in the lives of individuals. The question of ascetic ethics is somewhat different, and here the historical context is significant. It is well known that at a time roughly parallel to the composition of the epic the Buddhists launched an acrimonious ethical assault on the beliefs, practices and values of the followers of the traditional Indian religious systems, particularly the *brāhmaṇas.* By nature ascetic ideas are substantially incongruent with the ritual elements of religious belief, and in the *Mahābhārata* such tendencies are represented by the doctrines of Sāṁkhya and Yoga expounded by various teachers.

These are openly in conflict with the ritual forms of religion which are this-worldly in their aspirations and recognise the legitimacy of selfish desire in their ethical concepts. The criticism of the traditional Vedic religion is, however, significantly different from that of the Buddhists. Whilst mirroring the Buddhist abhorrence of ritual violence, they stop short of denying the revealed status of the Vedas. Instead they seek to demonstrate that their own teachings are truly Vedic, whilst the doctrines urging animal sacrifice and ritual acts for material gain are later perversions arising from the deterioration of human nature after the *Kṛtayuga.* It is also noteworthy that the criticism of *yajña* in the *Mokṣa-dharma* is not aimed at priests but rather at ascetics like Jājali who still persist with *yajña.*

The ethical teachings of the *Mahābhārata* have made a major contribution to Hindu culture, and in particular the character of Yudhiṣṭhira shines forth as a role model for all who seek the path of virtue. The *Bhagavad-gītā* is likewise of crucial significance for the way it has opened up the values of the renunciant sects to people who remain active in the world. Any realistic appreciation of the text must lay to rest once and for all the frequently encountered claims of Western thought, both Christian and secular, to ethical superiority over that of India. The qualities of gentleness, tolerance and compassion shine through with a power that is enhanced by their expression through the human Yudhiṣṭhira rather than the divine Kṛṣṇa. There may be validity to the accusation of quietism leveled against Yudhiṣṭhira's and the ascetics' morality, but quietists rarely cause the atrocities that afflict our world and are generally most able to distance themselves from the self-interest that underlies them. Hacker has argued that neo-Hindus misrepresent their own tradition in using the ethics of Vedānta to justify political and social action. This may be so as far as ascetic ethics are concerned, but in the moral *dharma* that is so prominent in the epic, Gandhi and his close followers have found authentic role models within their own tradition.

In present times when competition is so frequently advocated as the cure for any type of social problem it is worth reflecting that in the epic this is the way that is vehemently urged by the demonic Duryodhana, while the saintly Yudhiṣṭhira always seeks cooperation and compromise. A detailed study of the epic leaves one compelled to agree with Hopkins that the whole world might benefit from the wider dissemination of the moral principles it espouses.[32]

Notes

1. van Buitenen, J.A.B. *Mahābhārata, Volume* 1, *The Book of the Beginning,* Chicago, 1973, p. xxviii.
2. O'Flaherty, W. *The Origins of Evil in Hindu Mythology,* Berkeley, 1976, p. 95.
3. Ibid, p. 97.
4. Dasgupta, S. *A History of Indian Philosophy,* Vol 2, Cambridge, 1973, p. 493.
5. Biardeau, M. 'Etudes de Mythologie Hindoue 4, Bhakti et Avatāra', *Bulletin de L'Ecole Francaise d'Extréme Orient,* Tome 63, 1976, p. 167.
6. Hiltebeitel, A. *The Ritual of Battle, Krishna in the Mahābhārata,* Ithaca, 1976, p. 281.
7. O'Flaherty 1976, p. 378.
8. Ganguli lists these as, 1. Morning and evening ablutions, 2. Silent recitation of *mantras,* 3. Pouring libations on the sacrificial fire, 4. Worshipping the Deities, 5. Providing hospitality for guests, and 6. Offering food to the Viśvedeva gods (Ganguli, K.M. *Mahābhārata,* Delhi, 1976, Vol 9, p. 34).
9. *śūdre caitad bhavel lakṣyaṁ dvije caitan na vidyate.*
na vai śūdro bhavec chūdro brāhmaṇo na ca brāhmaṇaḥ (12.182.8).
10. *Piṇḍa* is the offering that all men must make to please and sustain their forefathers.
11. O'Flaherty 1976, p. 95.
12. van Buitenen 1973, p. 15.
13. O'Flaherty 1976, p. 97.
14. Hacker, P. *Kleine Schriften,* Wiesbaden, 1978, p. 594.
15. See also the teachings of Vyāsa in 12.228.5-6.
16. Hopkins, E.W. *Ethics of India,* Port Washington, 1968, p. 69.
17. Edgerton, F. *The Bhagavad-gītā Translated and Interpreted,* New York, 1964, p. 183.
18. Dasgupta 1973, p. 461.
19. Ibid, p. 501.
20. O'Flaherty 1976, p. 378.
21. Ibid, p. 96.
22. Ibid, p. 97.
23. Though 2.32 and 2.37 might be cited as offering an alternative view.
24. The two ethical tendencies stressed by Kṛṣṇa in the *Gītā* are closely associated with their alternative eschatologies. Thus it is in Chapter 2 when he overrules

Arjuna's position by emphasising *sva-dharma* that we find Kṛṣṇa referring to *svarga-loka* as the eschatological goal, whereas elsewhere when the ascetic ethic is pursued, eschatological statements are always presented in terms of absolute salvation.

25. Edgerton 1964, p. 162.
26. Kaveeshwar, G.W. *The Ethics of the Gītā*, Delhi, 1971.
27. Biardeau, M. and Péterfalvi, J. *Le Mahābhārata, Livres* 1-5, Paris, 1985, p. 29.
28. See 9.27, 18.46, 11.55, 9.24, 3.30.
29. Dasgupta 1973, p. 501.
30. Hopkins 1968, p. 69.
31. 4.36 and 9.30 might appear to offer an alternative view. The most likely interpretation of these verses, however, is that past sins which would be expected to lead to future rebirth do not prevent one who has knowledge from gaining salvation.
32. Hopkins 1968, pp. 219-220.

CHAPTER 8

THE *MAHĀBHĀRATA*'S UNDERSTANDING OF HUMANITY

1. The Distinction Between the Self and Matter

In the discussion of epic soteriology, the dualistic understanding of the individual was clearly apparent. A central feature of the Sāṁkhya doctrines of the *Mokṣa-dharma* and the *Bhagavad-gītā* is the distinction drawn between the true self–the *ātman, puruṣa,* or *kṣetrajña*–and the material body and matter as a whole. It also appears that this view is accepted by at least portions of the narrative, for at several junctures the idea of metempsychosis is incorporated into the plot.

It might be argued that the notion of reincarnation does not automatically imply belief in a transcendent self, for the Buddhists accept the former but reject the latter of these doctrines. It is extremely unlikely, however, that the epic shares the Buddhist view and indeed in Chapter 211 of the *Śānti,* Pañcaśikha dismisses such an idea as ridiculous. It would appear that the only viable alternative to dualism found in the epic is derived from a previous form of eschatology. Within the narrative, we frequently encounter the idea that at death righteous kings are elevated to the realm of the gods apparently in exactly the same forms as those in which they lived on earth. Here the examples of Yayāti (1.76-78) and Nahuṣa (5.9-18) may be cited, as well as the warriors slain at Kurukṣetra who reappear in Chapter 40 of the *Āśramavāsika* having been elevated to *svarga-loka* without transmigrating into a different identity.

One must suspect that such beliefs are derived from a different tradition to that which teaches the transmigration of the self, but by the time of the *Mahābhārata* a degree of integration has occurred by which birth amongst the gods is considered not eternal salvation, but one stage in the cycle of repeated rebirth.

Whilst recognising the potential incongruence of these two notions, it is still reasonable to assert that the existence of a transcendent self that survives the death of the body is a doctrine of the epic. This teaching is found throughout the didactic passages, and here, apart from the *Gītā* and *Mokṣa-dharma,* I would draw attention to the instructions of Nahuṣa (3.178.9-15), the direct teachings of Mārkaṇḍeya (3.181.9-41), and those of the same sage through the mouth of the pious hunter (3.199, 200).

An exposition of this doctrine comprises Kṛṣṇa's initial instructions to Arjuna in Chapter 2 of the *Gītā*. Responding to his cousin's lament that he cannot bear to slay those who are dear to him, Kṛṣṇa asserts that such grief is due to lack of wisdom; those who are wise never grieve in this way (2.11), because in truth we are all eternal:

> *na tv evāhaṁ jātu nāsaṁ na tvaṁ neme janādhipāḥ*
> *na caiva na bhaviṣyāmaḥ sarve vayam ataḥ param*
>
> 'Never at any time did I not exist, nor you, nor these lords of men; and there will never be a time in the future when we do not exist' (2.12).

The *Gītā* follows up this statement of the eternality of the self by describing the process of transmigration. The self is here referred to as *dehin*–the embodied–which accepts another body–*dehāntara-prāptiḥ* (13). In verse 16, the body and self are referred to as the *asat* and the *sat* respectively–*nāsato vidyate bhāvo nābhāvo vidyate sataḥ*. Here *bhāva* must be taken as permanence rather than existence, for nowhere in the *Gītā* do we find the idea that the existence of matter is illusion; Kṛṣṇa is continuing with his previous theme by saying that the body is never permanent while the self is never temporary.

Verse 17 elaborates by asserting that that by which all things are pervaded–*yena sarvam idaṁ tatam*–is unchanging and never destroyed; bodies have a beginning and an end but the embodied self–*śarīrin*–is unlimited and indestructible (18). Verse 20 reasserts the eternality of the embodied self (the word *ayam* here must refer back to *śarīrin* of 18); it is never born and never dies–*na hanyate hanyamāne śarīre.* Knowing this, how can one think, as Arjuna is doing, in terms of killer and killed (21). Just as one changes one's clothes, so the *śarīrin* casts off the old body and moves on to a new one; it is never cut by weapons, burned by fire, moistened by water, or dried by wind. It is eternal, all-pervasive, unchanging, immovable and constant (22-24). The embodied self in the bodies of all beings cannot be killed and therefore you should not grieve (30).

The dualism of the doctrine taught here is made apparent by the terms *dehin* and *deha, śarīrin* and *śarīra,* used by the text to distinguish between the body and the self. The transcendent nature of the self is brought out especially in verses 23 and 24 in which Kṛṣṇa emphasises that the elements of this world — water, air, fire, and earth in the form of weapons — can never touch it, because it exists beyond the constraints of this world. The *Anugītā* stresses the same point in a succinct manner, arguing that because the self is subtle and unmanifest by nature it never integrates with any other substance–*saukṣmyād avyakta-bhāvāc ca na sa kvacana sajjate* (14.18.6). In the more developed forms of Sāṁkhya found in the *Mokṣa-dharma,* the same distinction is central to the soteriological purpose of the treatises. The self is the twenty-fifth or seventeenth element, of a completely different nature to the twenty-four or sixteen of which matter is comprised. The self is the *kṣetrajña,* the knower of the *kṣetra,* which includes all forms of matter. Despite the emphasis on heaven and hell in certain parts of the text it is reasonable, on the basis of references to transmigration, to accept that the version presented in these verses (2.11-30) of the *Gītā* reflects the view of the epic as a whole.

As with many of the doctrines discussed in the *Mahābhārata,* it is apparent that the actual relationship of the self to the body and mind was a subject on which the authors were aware of differing views. In Chapter 48 of the *Aśvamedhika,* Kṛṣṇa imparts to Arjuna teachings that Brahmā had previously presented to an assembly of *ṛṣis.* Chapter 48 divides itself into two parts; in verses 1 to 12, Brahmā speaks about *yoga* practice which aims at perceiving the self, and then says that some who are wise–*manīṣinaḥ*–assert the unity of *puruṣa* and *sattva.* There is a problem of terminology here for while *puruṣa* clearly refers to the transcendent self, *sattva* is more difficult. Van Buitenen[1] points out the dual use of the word as meaning both the first of the three *guṇas* and also material nature as a whole. In this passage it appears to be used in both senses. The wise argue for the unity of *sattva* and *puruṣa–sattvaṁ ca puruṣaś caikaḥ* (8), *kṣetrajña-sattvayor aikyam* (9)–because the qualities associated with *sattva-guṇa* are those called for in the *yoga* process that leads to the self—patience, determination, non-injury, equanimity, truth, honesty etc.–*kṣamā dhṛtir ahiṁsā ca samatā satyam ārjavam* (7).

Brahmā goes on to refute this doctrine by reasserting the distinctiveness of the self from *sattva* (10). Unity is allowed only to a very limited degree, as is made clear by the three examples given to elucidate the teachings—the fly living in the Udumbara fruit, the fish in water and the drop of water on the lotus (11-12). There is contact between *puruṣa* and *sattva* but any real form of integration between self and matter would appear to be ruled out by these illustrations.

The second part of Chapter 48 consists of complaints from the assembly that there are so many different doctrines and opinions about spiritual wisdom and practice that everybody is confused. They therefore request that Brahmā should make his meaning absolutely clear (13-29). In Chapter 49, after stressing non-injury (1-6), Brahmā announces that he will speak again about the union and separation–*saṁyogo viprayogaś ca*–of *kṣetrajña* and *sattva* (7). Here the meaning of *sattva* must be taken as matter, which is contrasted to the spiritual being, and not as the first of the *guṇas*.

Brahmā once more stresses the distinction between *puruṣa* and *sattva,* for the former is the enjoyer and the latter the sphere of action–*viṣayī puruṣo nityaṁ sattvaṁ ca viṣayaḥ smṛtaḥ* (8). He reminds them of the example of the fly and Udumbara fruit, urging that *sattva* is not conscious and is to be enjoyed, while that which enjoys it possesses consciousness (9). *Sattva* is not eternal, is filled with dualities and consists of the three *guṇas,* while the *kṣetrajña* is eternal, free from duality and above the *guṇas* (10). Although he enjoys *sattva,* he is not touched by the *guṇas–na lipyate* (12)–like a drop of water on a lotus; *sattva* is the property of the *puruṣa* just as an object is of its maker (13).

Up to this point it is clear that *sattva* is the material nature that is contrasted with the eternal self, and thus it is described as *guṇātmakam* (10), an inappropriate expression if just one of the *guṇas* is intended. In verse 14, however, the use of the term seems to change; here it is stated that just as one uses a light when entering a dark place, so the best of seekers–*paramaiṣiṇaḥ*–go forth with the light of *sattva–sattva-pradīpena gacchanti.* The light shines as long as object and quality exist–*yāvad dravya-guṇas tāvat pradīpaḥ samprakāśate*–but when object and quality cease to be the light becomes invisible–*kṣīṇa-dravya-guṇaṁ jyotir antardhānāya gacchati* (15). This statement is obviously a continuation of the metaphor, indicating that *sattva-guṇa* and its qualities are of use to the *yogin* so long as he is still striving, but when he attains success it may be discarded along with all features of matter. Thus *sattva-guṇa* is the manifest world, whilst the *puruṣa* is known as the unmanifest–*vyaktaḥ sattva-guṇas tv evaṁ puruṣo 'vyakta iṣyate* (16). The discourse changes direction at this point as Brahmā proceeds to instruct the *ṛṣis* on the practice of *mokṣa-dharma*.

This passage is interesting for its indication that the Sāṁkhya teachers whose works are contained in the epic were aware of others who taught a modified form of dualism which placed more stress on the unity of the self with its physical and psychical embodiment. It is also noteworthy that whilst there is no indication that such a view should be accepted, those who adhere to it are still referred to as learned or wise. The doctrine here espoused is that of the relationship between soul and body being like that between the fly and Udumbara fruit, first presented in Chapter 48. I take this metaphor as being clearly dualist, for although the fly lives within the fruit and lives off it there remains a marked distinction between the two that overrides any concept of unity. Chapter 49 stresses this dualism further by noting the separation between the cognizant and the inert, the experiencer and the experienced, the possessor and the possessed. A further metaphor, that of the drop of water trembling on the lotus leaf, reminds us that whatever unity may appear to exist is tenuous and at any moment may be severed as the self departs from its present confines. Thus although the question of unity is raised here, the conventional Sāṁkhya wisdom is emphatically reaffirmed in terms of *kṣetra* and *kṣetrajña;* the self is separate by nature and function from the material faculties with which it is temporarily in contact.

2. The Divine Nature of the Self

The doctrines that seek to identify the individual *ātman* with the Supreme Deity have been discussed at some length under the heading of the nature of God and I do not propose to repeat that discussion here. It is evident, however, that consideration of the *Mahābhārata*'s understanding of the nature of humanity would be incomplete without some reference to the idea of the divinity of the self within. In the teachings of the *Upaniṣads* perpetuated in the Vedānta system of philosophy, emphasis is laid on the oneness of the individual *ātman* with the supreme *brahman,* encapsulated in aphorisms such as *tat tvam asi*–you are that–and *so 'ham*–I am he. The epic bases its mystical doctrines more on Sāṁkhya than Vedānta, and hence such ideas are found only occasionally, as in the teachings of Sanat-sujāta (5.43.34 and 5.45. 1f) and those of Pañcaśikha (12.212.40f). It is noteworthy that despite its drawing on the *Upaniṣads* at specific junctures, the *Gītā* generally avoids such monistic tendencies.

Regarding the Sāṁkhya of the *Mokṣa-dharma,* one cannot ignore van Buitenen's assertion that, "there is no-one at present who seriously doubts that Sāṁkhya began by being theistic."[2] There is a clear line of thought in the *Śānti* which not only distinguishes the self from matter but goes on to equate the *kṣetrajña* thus identified with the Supreme Deity, on occasion using the proper name Viṣṇu to stress the identity. It is in the *Nārāyaṇīya* that this doctrine is pressed to the furthest extent with repeated assertions that the Deity Nārāyaṇa is the *kṣetrajña* in the hearts of all beings. It is important, however, to notice where the emphasis lies in such teachings. Nārāyaṇa is the self, but nowhere is this presented as an injunction to consider oneself to be Nārāyaṇa as the *Upaniṣads* urge the enlightened ones see themselves as *brahman.* Nārāyaṇa is the *kṣetrajña* but the *kṣetrajña* is no more than a small spark of the Deity's divinity.

Similarly, in the *Bhagavad-gītā,* Kṛṣṇa says, *kṣetrajñaṁ cāpi māṁ viddhi*–know that the *kṣetrajña* is me, but at the same time distinguishes between the *ātman* and *puruṣottama* (15.18-19), claiming that the living being in this world is just a part of himself–*mamaivāṁśo jīva-loke jīva-bhūtaḥ sanātanaḥ* (15.7). These passages urge worship and adoration of the Deity who is the self, but never meditation upon oneself as the Deity. The interchanging themes of Sāṁkhya and devotional theism found in the epic didactus are generally quite distinct in this respect from Vedāntic monism. The self is a transcendent spark of the Deity, but never the Deity himself in the fullness of his glory.

3. The Epic's Understanding of Human Psychology

(i) The Senses, Mind and Intellect

The question of the history of the *ātman*'s contact with matter is not addressed by the epic and it may be argued that this question is precluded by the understanding of the eternality of this world. The creation exists in cycles of manifestation and non-manifestation stretching forwards and backwards into eternity, and with it the association of the individual soul with matter in the form of ceaseless transmigrations through the cycle of *saṁsāra.*

The *ātman* is distinct from the personality, the sense of 'I' that we would recognise. It is not that I, as I know myself, will carry on living in another form after death, for the *ātman* is beyond psychological as well as physical characteristics and if I am reborn as a god, I will assume both the psyche and physique of a god. In technical terms the epic refers to the psychological makeup of the individual as being composed of *indriyāṇi, manas, buddhi* and, in some passages, *ahaṁkāra.* Broadly translated, the *indriyāṇi* are the five senses through which perceptions are relayed to the *manas* or mind, while the *buddhi* is the intellect which assesses the information. Chapter 239 of the *Śānti* attempts to explain the functions of the different psychological features. Here Vyāsa is the speaker imparting wisdom to his son Śuka.[3] He first explains how the gross body is comprised of the five principal elements, and in verse 13 goes on to discuss the psychological components. He presents a triad of *manas, buddhi* and also *bhāva,* an imprecise term probably meaning character or personality, and possibly included to make up the triad, a favoured scheme in Hindu thought.

There are five senses in a man, and the sixth is known as the mind - *indriyāṇi nare pañca ṣaṣṭhaṁ tu mana ucyate;* they call the seventh the *buddhi* and the eighth the *kṣetrajña* (14). The function of the eyes is to see, and the *manas* manifests doubt–*cakṣur ālocanāyaiva saṁśayaṁ kurute manaḥ;* the *buddhi* is for determining or discriminating, while the *kṣetrajña* is simply a witness–*buddhir adhyavasānāya sākṣī kṣetrajña ucyate* (15). The idea here seems to be that the *manas* perceives through the five senses, the *buddhi* analyses and draws conclusions from sensory impressions, while the *kṣetrajña* is aloof from the mental process.

Vyāsa speaks on the same subject at the beginning of Chapter 240. The *manas* manifests one's inherent nature, presumably in terms of one's birth–*manaḥ prasṛjate bhāvam*–whilst the *buddhi* is that which discriminates and determines–*buddhir adhyavasāyinī.* The heart comprehends what is attractive and repellent–*hṛdayaṁ priyāpriye veda*–and thus there is a threefold impetus towards action–*tri-vidhā karma-codanā* (1). The objects of perception are greater than the senses and the *manas* is superior to these objects; *buddhi* is superior to *manas* and the *ātman* is beyond the *buddhi* (2). The first line of verse 3 is obscure as the word *ātman* is used in different senses–*buddhir ātmā manuṣyasya buddhir evātmano ''tmikā*. Here I take the first use of *ātman* in the sense of personality and the second as the transcendent self, thus giving the meaning, 'The *buddhi* is the personality of a man and is like the *ātman* in nature.' When it interacts with the manifest world it is the *manas*–*yadā vikurute bhāvaṁ tadā bhavati sā manaḥ*. This phrase indicates that the distinction between *buddhi* and *manas* is functional rather than substantial. When the mental faculty is gathering information through the senses it is known as *manas*, but when it is reviewing that information and working discriminatively it is understood to be *buddhi*, the personality of an individual.

The *buddhi* becomes transformed depending upon which sense is being employed for perception, appearing in different forms as sight, hearing etc. to execute different functions; residing in those senses, the *buddhi* exists in three different natures, sometimes attaining what is dear to it, sometimes lamenting, and sometimes finding neither joy nor grief (5-7). This mental capacity which is one's own personal nature–*seyaṁ bhāvātmikā*–has mastery over these three dispositions, just as the ocean masters the currents of rivers flowing into it (8). When it desires anything it is the *manas*; this has awareness–*saṁsmaret*–of the active senses which exist with the *buddhi* and which must all be controlled (9).

As is typical of the *Mokṣa-dharma*, the discussion then moves on to self-regulation through *yoga* in order that the self may be perceived. There is no exact doctrine of the human psyche found throughout the epic as it is a topic that is of concern only to the Sāṁkhya theorists of the *Mokṣa-dharma*, and hence is primarily a feature of *nivṛtti*. The principal ideas expressed therein are, however, fairly consistent. The *manas* embodies the perceptual process utilising five senses, and the *buddhi* is equated with what we would recognise as our personality, reviewing information it receives and becoming the *manas* when it perceives an object of desire and hankers for it.

Other elements such as *ahaṁkāra*, personal identity or ego, are included in certain passages such as, for example, the *Bhagavad-gītā* (7.4), and Vyāsa refers to *hṛdayam*, the heart, which is mentioned once only in terms that seem to connect it to the emotions. Throughout all such passages, however, the dualist view remains consistent. In Chapter 240, it is notable that although the *buddhi* is mentioned in terms of its relation to the self, still it is subject to grief and rejoicing while the *kṣetrajña* remains completely aloof. It is the *buddhi* that we generally perceive as our self, suffering and enjoying the vicissitudes of fortune, but this is not the true self that survives death. Transmigration involves assuming not only a new bodily form, but also a new personality acting through different senses. Hence only one who comprehends his true self can in reality escape from death.

(ii) The Influence of the Three *Guṇas*

A further concept prominent in both the *Gītā* and the *Mokṣa-dharma* is that of the three *guṇas*, the strands or attributes that control the psyche of an individual and dictate the personality type. These are *sattva*, roughly translated as 'goodness' which gives rise to such traits as tranquillity, honesty, and righteousness, *rajas*, or 'passion', which impels an individual towards endeavour, desire and attachment, and *tamas*, 'darkness' or 'ignorance', which gives rise to characteristics such as sloth, indolence, illusion and dirtiness. There are frequent references to the *guṇas* in the *Bhagavad-gītā*, which describes them as pervading all of the material sphere. In Chapters 17 and 18, Kṛṣṇa explains that the nature of an individual's faith, worship, taste in food, ritual acts, penance, charity, wisdom, mode of action, understanding of the world, intellect, determination and pleasure are all determined by the way the *guṇas* combine to construct a particular personality type. This applies to all creatures, for there is no being in this world free of the influence of the *guṇas* (18.40).

The Sāṁkhya of both the *Gītā* and the *Mokṣa-dharma* regards the *guṇas* as always intermixed and fluctuating in influence as an individual either elevates or degrades himself towards a higher or lower spiritual status. Thus the *Gītā* asserts that those in whom *sattva* predominates are elevated–*ūrdhvaṁ gacchanti sattva-sthāḥ*–those predominated by *rajas* remain in the middle–*madhye tiṣṭhanti rājasāḥ*–whilst those overwhelmed by *tamas*, and fixed thereby in abominable behaviour, go downwards–*jaghanya-guṇa-vṛtti-sthā adho gacchanti tāmasāḥ* (14.18). No individual, however, is ever situated solely under the influence of one *guṇa*, but rather, as 14.10 makes clear, each person is influenced by all three to different degrees.

(iii) Conclusions

The individual is thus defined as a transcendent being untouched by material conditions, never ageing nor decaying and moving on to another state of existence when death comes. The human being is the *ātman* existing within a body composed of five elements, operating through mental faculties which absorb information through sensory perception and discriminate on the basis of that information. It is this psyche, enjoying and suffering on the basis of sensory perception, that man commonly regards as himself, though the true self is beyond both the psychic and the physical and can only be perceived through *yoga* practice. The psychological faculties which dictate personality are shaped by the fluctuating influences of three great qualities, or *guṇas,* which combine to different degrees in each individual and thereby create one's unique character and personality. This in essence is the epic's answer to the question, "What is Humanity?"

4. The Presence of the *Ātman* in the *Prāṇa*, and as a Manikin in the Heart

The above discussion reflects the predominant view of the epic didactus, based on the speculations of the early Sāṁkhya schools. The encyclopaedic nature of the text, however, means that other ideas derived from the *Upaniṣads* are also represented, though less prenouncedly. Hindu physiology recognises different airs within the body that are vital for its physical and mental functioning, and an important element in *yoga* practice entails bringing the movements of these airs under voluntary control. One branch of *yoga* speculation insists that the *ātman* is located in the outward breath known as *prāṇa.* This view is represented occasionally in the didactic passages of the *Mahābhārata,* though it is by no means a prominent doctrine.

Chapter 178 of the *Śānti,* a portion of the *Bhṛgu-Bharadvāja-saṁvāda* in the *Mokṣa-dharma,* and the second half of Chapter 203 of the *Vana,* a part of Mārkaṇḍeya's account of the teachings of the pious hunter, are interesting from a critical perspective because they are both clearly derived from a common source. I do not wish to pursue such critical implications in any detail, beyond noting that the relationship between the two passages highlights the fact that didactic elements found more intimately woven into the epic narrative, as are the teachings of Mārkaṇḍeya, cannot necessarily be taken as more integral to the work as a whole than those found in the *Mokṣa-dharma* which have been branded as 'pseudo-epical' by Hopkins.[4] Bhṛgu's scientific analysis of material nature includes a discourse on anatomy, a portion of which discusses the various airs and breaths, while the hunter uses the same teaching in response to a question about the existence of fire and air in the body. Most relevant to the present discussion is the statement of Bhṛgu in verses 4 and 5 of Chapter 178. The *prāṇa,* which exists in the head and in the fire element, activates the limbs–*prāṇo mūrdhani cāgnau ca vartamāno viceṣṭate* (12.178.3). That is the living entity itself, the soul of all beings, the eternal *puruṣa–sa jantuḥ sarva-bhūtātmā puruṣaḥ sanātanaḥ* (5). Elsewhere, occasional references are found, usually in discourses on *yoga,* as in the *Gītā,* 8.12, which speaks of *ātmanaḥ prāṇam,* and the *Anugītā* which describes the *jīva* as *prāṇa-sthāneṣv avasthitaḥ,* having its position in the places of the breath (14.18.7). It would appear that this idea stems from the *yoga* techniques in which the breathing process is suppressed and regulated, and outside of this specific context the notion of the *ātman* existing within the *prāṇa* is only occasionally encountered in the epic.

Another early doctrine, referred to only in a few instances in the *Mahābhārata,* is that which regards the true self as a manikin the size of a thumb located in the region of the heart. This is not an idea that is stressed by any of the Sāṁkhya schools and is found only rarely in the *Mokṣa-dharma.*[5] In the story of Sāvitrī, narrated by Mārkaṇḍeya to the Pāṇḍavas, we find that when Satyavān dies his soul is drawn from his body by the God of Death in this manikin form–*aṅguṣṭa-mātraṁ puruṣaṁ niścakarṣa yamo balāt* (3.281.16). Such a view would appear to be at odds with the teachings of the *Gītā* and the *Mokṣa-dharma* which insist that the *ātman* is formless, all-pervasive and completely imperceptible to the senses.[6]

5. The Uniqueness of Humanity

(i) Introduction

The dualist perspective of the epic didactus clearly impinges to some degree upon the notion of human uniqueness, for in essence all creatures, and even all plants, have life because of the existence of an identical *ātman* within the corporeal frame. Hence the *Gītā* instructs that the *paṇḍitas* look equally upon a *brāhmaṇa*, a cow, an elephant, a dog and an eater of dogs (5.18 and also 12.231.19). Furthermore, human beings are by no means the highest form of life in the universe. In other worlds and even on earth there are gods, *gandharvas, vidyādharas, yakṣas* and other celestial beings all of whom are greater than man in terms of power, opulence, intelligence and longevity. Such a view of the world notwithstanding, the epic still manifests a degree of anthropocentrism in ascribing a unique position to humanity in the creation.

(ii) Humanity as the Sustainer of the Gods

In the Vedic religion humanity had a central role in sustaining the order of the cosmos through the performance of *yajñas* and rituals. The sacred sounds of the liturgical chants reflected the process of creation, and the gods themselves were dependent upon the ritual acts performed on earth. Nature would only sustain life so long as man enacted this microcosmic ritual of creation. According to Heestermann,

> In the classical system of the ritual, as presented in the brāhmaṇas and the sūtras, the pivot of the ritual is the *yajamāna*, the patron at whose expense and for whose sole benefit the ritual is performed. He is supposed symbolically to incorporate the universe—he is identified with the cosmic man, Prajāpati. The ritual culminates in his ritual rebirth, which signifies the regeneration of the cosmos.[7]

By the epic period religious ideas have been transformed. In the *Mahābhārata*, religious practice is not conceived of as centring exclusively on the ritual enactment of *yajña*, but the orthodoxy and orthopraxis taught by the text as a whole ensures that it does not wholeheartedly reject *yajña* as a legitimate element of religious activity. Vedic beliefs remain a significant factor in epic thought; in the *Gītā*, 3.9-15, we find the idea of men and gods mutually sustaining one another through performing *yajña* and supplying rainfall respectively. In the story of the Kālakeya Dānavas, told by Lomaśa (3.100), when the Dānavas prevent the performance of *yajña* by terrorising the priests, the whole universe, including the gods in heaven, becomes afflicted as a result. Later in the same *parvan*, Hanumān instructs Bhīma that the gods are sustained by *yajña*–*yajñair devāḥ pratiṣṭhitāḥ* (3.149.28).

Despite such evidence of the persistence of belief in the importance of Vedic ritual, it is clear from the epic that the doctrines underlying the performance of *yajña* have undergone considerable modification and are seriously challenged by the schools of Sāṁkhya and Yoga represented in the didactus. The performance of *yajña* has a central position in the narrative, but it is interesting to note how the perspective has changed from that of the Vedas. The first half of the *Sabhā* centres on the execution of the *Rājasūya-yajña* by Yudhiṣṭhira, but the function of the ritual is to establish his personal hegemony over the other kings and there is no reference to any cosmic significance. Similarly, towards the conclusion of the narrative attention centres on Yudhiṣṭhira's performance of an elaborate *Aśvamedha-yajña*, but here the purpose is to gain expiation from sin and for the practitioner to be elevated to *svarga-loka* after death; again the cosmic function of human ritual is virtually disregarded.

Certain passages of the *Mokṣa-dharma* are openly critical of the performance of *yajña*. In Chapter 261 of the *Śānti*, Śyūmaraśmi is forced to defend the violence of ritual practices against a verbal assault from Kapila. Significantly, this defence is based not on the necessity of *yajña* for the sustenance of the natural order, which is referred to only briefly in v11, but on the fact that the ritual is based on Vedic injunction and ensures the elevation of the practitioner to the sphere of the gods. In another *Mokṣa-dharma* discourse, Bhīṣma informs Yudhiṣṭhira that one who has wisdom can abandon all *yajñas* and rituals for they do not lead to salvation (12.306.101-108). Here it is clear that the original cosmic function of the *yajña* has been either forgotten or else ignored.

The central role ascribed to humanity in the Vedas is not, however, necessarily diminished thereby as it is the nature rather than the fact of the ritual that has been changed. Whilst the teachings on *mokṣa-dharma* generally encourage renunciation of ritual acts, the *Bhagavad-gītā* seeks to avoid this outcome by defining a path of *yoga* based on the performance of such duties. The *Gītā* recognises that if religious duties are abandoned, both the social and cosmic orders will be threatened. The fact that this threat applies to the cosmic as well as the social order is apparent from 3.9-15, a passage which according to van Buitenen, "is devoted to ritual."[8]

The idea of human religious practice sustaining the natural

order is therefore preserved but it is no longer confined to one particular type of ritual performed only by *brāhmaṇa* priests. Rather it is indicated that the performance of dharmic duties by all sections of the community has the same function. Thus it is that when Arjuna contemplates giving up his *dharma* of warfare, Kṛṣṇa argues against this on the grounds that the gods are nourished by ritual acts (3.11). We may also note a passage from the *Virāṭa* in which Bhīṣma indicates to Duryodhana the place where the Pāṇḍavas will be found during their year in hiding. Wherever Yudhiṣṭhira resides there will be no misfortune, the people will be righteous, rituals will be properly executed, *dharma* will be adhered to and the clouds will pour down abundant rainfall (4.27.15). The crops will have a good flavour, fruits will be of the highest quality and the flowers will be aromatic (16). The winds will feel pleasant (17), cows will flourish and produce sweet-tasting milk (18), and the people of the realm will be righteous, contented and followers of *dharma*.

This speech parallels that of Kuntī in Chapter 140 of the *Udyoga* wherein she urges that it is the qualities of the king that create a particular *yuga* on earth, and the teachings of Bhīṣma in the *Rāja-dharma* to similar effect.[9] We may note also the story of the sage Ṛṣyaśṛṅga in which a sin on the part of the king leads to years of drought, and the description of the reign of the Pāṇḍavas in Indraprastha during which their righteousness ensured that sufficient rain fell in their kingdom (2.12.11). It is not merely that the monarch's administrative expertise generates prosperity in his domain, but his righteousness and adherence to *dharma* now takes on the function of the Vedic *yajña* in nourishing the earth and sustaining the cosmos. *Yajña* remains as an element in the overall ritual of dharmic life, but it has clearly lost its exclusive status.

It is thus apparent that the epic's understanding of *dharma* to some extent perpetuates the salient position of humanity in the order of the world. The text, however, embodies several doctrinal strands that serve to undermine this view. The world-denying teachings of Sāṁkhya see little significance in ritual acts and the world of *bhakti* in its more developed form cannot logically ascribe the role of cosmic sustainer to humanity. In a sense the view of the *Gītā* is anachronistic when it seeks to integrate the Vedic view of ritual action with *bhakti*, and it is significant that only in the passage already noted (3.9-16) does the text highlight the cosmic rather than the social significance of ritual *dharma*.

A closer look at the third chapter will emphasise the point. After stating that one who gives up ritual duties and lives simply for pleasure is a sinner whose life is useless (16), Kṛṣṇa admits that for one who has found satisfaction by awareness of the *ātman*, there is no obligation to perform such acts–*tasya kāryaṁ na vidyate* (17). According to verses 20 and 21 the reason that dharmic duty is not to be renounced is so that an example may be set to other sections of society, for whatever standard is set by the best of men is followed by all the world (21). I take this as a fairly obvious reference to concern for maintenance of the social rather than cosmic order. The next three verses (22-24) are significant in their indication of the *bhakti* view of how the universe is sustained, for here we find that it is Kṛṣṇa himself, rather than humanity, who maintains the stability of the worlds which would fall into ruin if he did not act–*utsīdeyur ime lokā na kuryāṁ karma ced aham* (24).

The doctrines of *bhakti* assert that there is one Supreme Deity who creates and controls the world, and the pantheon is understood as a part of this world and its order. Hence both men and gods may be seen as working in harmony to sustain the creative equilibrium, but the Deity of *bhakti* is far more of a controlling God whose own existence is beyond the functioning of this world. Where such doctrines prevail there is clearly less scope for humanity to take such a central role in maintaining the world. Viṣṇu and Śiva are Deities of such power that the role of humanity is transformed from participant to supplicant, as indeed is that of the gods in the *Mahābhārata* narrative. Thus as the Vaiṣṇava and Śaivite doctrines develop in the post-epic period, the cosmic necessity of human ritual acts fades from view as the universal order is recognised as being held in place by the power of the Deity alone.

(iii) Humanity as the Generator of *Karma*

The human form of life also holds a unique position in terms of epic eschatology for only the acts of human beings dictate the course of destiny. Existence in the celestial sphere is a reward for righteous acts on earth, and though gods such as Indra may sometimes be afflicted by the results of their misdeeds and kings such as Yayāti and Nahuṣa cast down for misbehaving in heaven, it is primarily human life that is structured so as to bring a positive future destiny. Hence Parāśara states that *dharma* and *adharma* exist among men but not other beings–*mānuṣeṣu mahārāja dharmādharmau pravartataḥ/na tathānyeṣu bhūteṣu* (12.283.28). Conversely, birth as a beast is equated with hell[10] and presented as the result of deviation from *dharma.* The beasts, however, cannot act righteously or sinfully to create a new destiny and the *ātman* must return to a human incarnation before acts are effective in shaping destiny.

(iv) Human Life as the Gateway of *Salvation*

From the perspective of *nivṛtti,* human life is recognised as the most significant for it is only via the human status that the transcendent *puruṣa* can attain *mokṣa.* This idea cannot be taken as absolute for certain passages of the *Mokṣa-dharma* present non-human figures, celestial sages and *asuras* such as Bali, Vṛtra and Prahlāda, as engaging in the quest for salvation. In Chapter 286 of the *Śānti,* however, we find Parāśara instructing King Janaka about the uniqueness of human life. A human being should not degrade himself towards birth in a lower species by indulging in sensual pleasures, for human birth, even as a *caṇḍāla,* is very difficult to obtain–*caṇḍalatve 'pi mānusyaṁ sarathā tāta durlabham* (12.286.31). Human birth is the best that one can gain–*iyaṁ hi yoniḥ prathamā yāṁ prāpya*–for in this state the *ātman* can deliver itself by pure actions–*ātmā vai śakyate trātuṁ karmabhiḥ śubha-lakṣanaiḥ* (32). Therefore one should follow the *śruti* and not risk losing human status which is difficult to gain (33). The indication here is that human life is the most valuable because the *dharma* that leads to deliverance can only be practised by humans.

(v) The Full Potential of Human Life

In discussing the contact between Hindu and Islamic thought, van Buitenen points out that in the Hindu tradition not only is man able to gain salvation by the strength of his own endeavours, but also to attain the power and status of the gods by similar means.[11] This point is illustrated by various characters in the *Mahābhārata,* not least the Pāṇḍavas who, despite being born as men, are able to vanquish hosts of *asuras, gandharvas* and *rākṣasas.* Sages such as Agastya, by dint of their penance and extreme renunciation, come to possess such power that they can execute miraculous feats beyond the potency even of the gods (3.95).

In his teachings about the nature of the world, Mārkaṇḍeya instructs that in the *Kṛtayuga* at the beginning of creation human beings sojourned with the gods–*sarve devaiḥ samāyānti* (3.181.13)–in pure bodily forms–*nirmalāni śarīrāṇi viśuddhāni* (11). They had control over their own life and death (14), could visit any of the gods or great *ṛṣis* they desired to see (15), and lived for thousands of years (16). The indication here is that the relatively degraded status of humanity witnessed at present is not to be taken as an unchanging circumscription of human potential, but is a condition that can be overcome individually by particular codes of practice and generally as the course of time progresses from *yuga* to *yuga*.

The *brāhmaṇas* in particular are singled out as being gods in human form. In the *Anuśāsana*, following Yudhiṣṭhira's question as to whom he should worship (13.136.1), Bhīṣma launches into a laudation of the *brāhmaṇas* that extends over seven chapters. He first praises their wisdom, renunciation and potency, through which they equal and even excel the gods:

> *adaivaṁ daivataṁ kuryur daivataṁ cāpy adaivatam*
> *lokān anyān sṛjeyuś ca loka-pālāṁś ca kopitāḥ*
>
> 'When angered they can make those who are not gods into gods, and deprive the existing gods of their status; they can create other worlds and other gods to rule those worlds.' (13.136.16)

They are in fact the gods of the gods, and the cause of that which is the cause–*devānām api ye devāḥ kāraṇaṁ kāraṇasya ca* (18); even an unlearned *brāhmaṇa* is a god–*avidvān brāhmaṇo devaḥ* (20).

Bhīṣma then tells Yudhiṣṭhira of a conversation between the wind god, Vāyu, and King Kārtavīrya Arjuna in which the god narrates several stories to illustrate the fact that the power and status of *brāhmaṇas* exceeds even that of the gods. Such passages are not unique to the *Anuśāsana,* though clearly its preoccupation with ritual is linked to an exaltation of the priestly hierarchy, and the epic repeatedly seeks to confirm and enhance the status of the first *varṇa.* This may be dismissed as polemic from the authors seeking to enshrine their own status with the authority of scriptural dogma, but at the same time it must be recognised that the view expressed in this passage is fully congruent with the epic's general perspective on humanity and human potential.

The manner in which the *brāhmaṇas* are glorified here is also noteworthy. It is entirely in terms of their divine potency which enables them to control the forces of nature and no reference is made to their priestly functions as enunciators of the sacred sounds that underly the cosmic ritual. The stress here is on asceticism, renunciation and penance which bring spiritual elevation and on their *tejas* or mystic potency which is equal to that of the gods. Hence although humanity is generally fixed in a position below that of the celestial denizens, this hierarchy is less than absolute. Just as man has within himself the power to throw off the bondage of ignorance to attain *mokṣa,* he also possesses the potential to transcend the limitations that the human condition generally imposes. Thus as a *brāhmaṇa* he may have the power of a god, and is to be recognised and worshipped as such.

6. The Hierarchy of Humanity

The above discussion leads naturally to a consideration of another important feature of the *Mahābhārata*'s understanding of humanity. Despite the statement of the *Mokṣa-dharma,* noted earlier, that human life even as a *caṇḍāla* is hard to attain and most exalted, within the broad span of humanity rigid demarcations are drawn. There is a hierarchy that necessitates different lifestyles, practices and even beliefs for different groups. Thus although *brāhmaṇas, śūdras, caṇḍālas* and women are all forms of human beings, the distinctiveness of each type is at least as significant as the commonality. The type of human form within the hierarchy that one is born into is dependent upon acts performed in the previous life; hence one's social position is not arbitrary and flexible, but a divinely ordained niche in the order of the world.

Each section of society has its own *dharma* in accordance with which its members must live. As we have seen, the prescriptions of *dharma-śāstra* are more than social standards, but are accepted as ritual acts related to the order of the universe. For an individual to abandon his own duty and attempt to live out the role of another is as disruptive to the ritual as would, for example, be the case in *yajña* if one of the chanting priests suddenly decided that he would rather offer the ghee into the fire instead. Hence the *Gītā* asserts that to take up the duties of another is a source of fear—*para-dharmo bhayāvahaḥ* (3.35).

Not only is a particular code of conduct what is 'right' for the members of each *varṇa,* it is also what is natural for the disposition they have been born into. Hence to abandon dharmic duties is not only to contravene scriptural injunction, but also to oppose the order of creation. The influence of the three *guṇas* over an individual's psychological nature has already been discussed, but at this point it is pertinent to note that the characteristics of the *varṇas* are seen as being linked to the *guṇas* in dictating the predetermined dispositions of individuals born into a particular *varṇa.* According to the *Bhagavad-gītā,*

> *brāhmaṇa-kṣatriya-viśāṁ śūdrāṇāṁ ca parantapa*
> *karmāṇi pravibhaktāni sva-bhāva-prabhavair guṇaiḥ*
>
> 'O scorcher of the foe, the proper activities of *brāhmaṇas, kṣatriyas, vaiśyas* and *śūdras* are made distinct by the *guṇas* from which their individual natures arise.' (18.41)

Thus a *brāhmaṇa, kṣatriya, vaiśya* or *śūdra* has the disposition to act in a certain manner because each group is influenced by a mixture of the *guṇas* in a distinctive way, the *brāhmaṇas* primarily by *sattva* and the *śūdras* primarily by *tamas* and *rajas.*

It is thus apparent that questions on Hindu ethics such as, 'Do Hindus believe in non-violence?' or 'Do Hindus believe it is wrong to eat meat?' cannot be answered by the epic with simple 'Yes' or 'No' answers. Neither humanity nor the Hindu community is to be taken as a homogeneous mass, but is so rigidly stratified as to require what Wendy O'Flaherty calls a 'hierarchy of morality'[12] which sets limitations on what is possible for individuals of different types to attain in terms of spiritual elevation. Concomitant to such an understanding is an acceptance of a hierarchy of goals that should be striven for in terms of heaven for the higher sections of society and merely an improved rebirth for those lower down the scale.[13]

The hierarchical view of humanity is axiomatic to the *pravṛtti* tendency in epic thought, but where the doctrines of *mokṣa-dharma* and *bhakti* are prominent, we may recognise a movement towards a more absolutist view of humanity. A key issue here, and one on which the epic offers diametrically opposed views, is whether one's *varṇa* is determined by birth or by qualities and propensities. In the *Anuśāsana,* Chapter 28, when Yudhiṣṭhira asks how a person from one of the lower *varṇas* may become a *brāhmaṇa,* Bhīṣma replies that it is possible only after many rebirths of gradual elevation. Elsewhere, however, we find an opposite view; exchanging words of wisdom with Nahuṣa, Yudhiṣṭhira states that one is to be designated as a *brāhmaṇa* or *śūdra* on the basis of visible qualities–*lakṣyam*–alone (3.177.20). The righteous hunter asserts that he considers a *śūdra* fixed in self-control, truth and *dharma* to be a *brāhmaṇa*–*yas tu śūdro dame satye dharme ca satatothitaḥ/ taṁ brāhmaṇaṁ manye* (3.206.12)–and in the *Bhṛgu-bharadvāja-saṁvāda* (12.182.8), we find Bhṛgu reciting almost the same verse as that spoken by Yudhiṣṭhira in 3.177.20.

In the teachings on *mokṣa-dharma,* there are several injunctions to the effect that this superior wisdom should not be imparted to one who is unqualified.[14] It is apparent, however, that the way to salvation is not barred to anyone simply on the basis of birth. Only a few may possess the attributes required but, in contrast to the perspective of *pravṛtti,* it is accepted that a person may emerge from any status of life to display the qualities that make he or she eligible to receive the wisdom of *mokṣa-dharma.* Thus we find the clear statement from Yājñavalkya that the wisdom which brings salvation may be received from a person of any of the four *varṇas,* or even one who is regarded as the lowest of all–*prāpya jñānaṁ brāhmaṇāt kṣatriyād vā vaiśyāc chūdrād api nīcād abhīkṣṇam* (12.306.85). The point is confirmed by the fact that amongst the teachers of Sāṁkhya we find individuals from the lower strata of society–an unnamed hunter (3.198-206), Tulādhara, a shop-keeper or investor–*bhāṇḍa-jīvana* (12.253) and Sulabhā, a female ascetic (12.308).

I would also argue that the *bhakti* of the epic manifests the beginnings of the challenge to the hierarchical view of humanity that became prominent in the medieval period, when even Muslims and outcastes became *ācāryas* of devotional sects. Here again the *Bhagavad-gītā* is crucial in understanding the devotional ideas of the epic. The *Gītā* is clearly concerned to preserve the traditional social hierarchy from the challenge of other-worldly ideas, yet the central teaching of the text focuses on the attainment of salvation through *yoga* and *bhakti.*[15] I have already expressed the opinion that despite the indications of 3.9-15, the *Gītā*'s primary concern in stressing *sva-dharma* is social and not cosmic. I would also argue that the *bhakti* of the *Gītā* goes some way towards opposing the hierarchy of religious belief and practice. At the conclusion of Chapter 9, Kṛṣṇa says that any person can gain salvation by surrendering to him:

māṁ hi pārtha vyapāśritya ye 'pi syuḥ pāpa-yonayaḥ
striyo vaiśyās tathā śūdrās te 'pi yānti parāṁ gatim

'Those who have taken a lower birth because of previous sins, women, *vaiśyas* and *śūdras,* can also attain the supreme goal, having sought shelter with me.' (9.32)

The following verse retracts slightly from the egalitarian position, but does not disavow the principle that from the perspective of *bhakti* there is one religion for all, regardless of the status ascribed by one's birth. Bhāskara, the earliest known commentator on the *Gītā,* understood the text to indicate that only *brāhmaṇas* can gain salvation, but it is apparent that this is the view of an entrenched orthodoxy and does not accurately reflect the teachings of the *Gītā* itself. Despite its emphasis on the importance of performing the duties of *sva-dharma,* the *bhakti* doctrines of the *Gītā* override the understanding of the hierarchy of religion by making all acts of *sva-dharma* acts of devotion leading to the same goal of salvation through the grace of Kṛṣṇa.

Overall it may be concluded that the *Mahābhārata* recognises humanity not as a homogeneous group, but as being significantly stratified into different social and psychological types, each preordained by a differing configuration of the three *guṇas.* On the basis of this differentiation there are varying dharmic duties, varying ethics and varying goals to be sought in the next life. Against these rigid distinctions the ideas of Sāṁkhya, Yoga and *bhakti* embody a tendency towards a more universal religious perspective for all types of human being, from which no-one is debarred simply because of birth and social position. With regard to *bhakti* in particular, the inclusivist tendency noted in the teachings of the *Gītā* is of great significance when set in the context of the development of the Hindu tradition, for a notable feature of later *bhakti* thought was the manner in which the devotional mood is accepted as overriding caste distinctions.

7. The Question of Human Perfectibility

Fred Huber notes that Paul Devanandan considered the major distinction between the doctrines of the *Gītā* and the Christian gospels to rest on the question of human perfection. Human fallibility is axiomatic to orthodox Christianity, whilst Devanandan understood the *Gītā* to teach that through *yoga* practice an individual could remove all faults and contaminations of the soul.[16] Whilst not denying this distinction, I would urge that the issue is as much about soteriology as it is about the nature of humanity. Where salvation is gained by means of 'self-help' rather than by grace, a state of perfection is undoubtedly implied and concomitant to any soteriology of that type. The point is made even more apparent when the Sanskrit word for perfection, *siddhim,* is considered. The root of this word is the verb *sidh,* meaning 'to succeed' or else 'to hit the target', so that one who succeeds in yogic endeavour is declared to be perfect both linguistically and philosophically.

The concept of human perfection, therefore, is linked to those portions of the epic didactus which expound the techniques of Sāṁkhya and Yoga. Chapter 6 of the *Bhagavad-gītā,* for example, describes a technique of self-restraint and meditation aimed at perception of the self. The process is slow and difficult (25, 26, 33, 34), but through persistent endeavour the final stage is reached and one attains the *brahman* position when all passions are stilled and no fault remains–*upaiti śānta-rajasaṁ brahma-bhūtam akalmaśam* (6.27). The word *akalmaśam* is particularly significant here, for it specifically means free from any dirt or contamination, an idea repeated in 28–*yogī vigata-kalmaśaḥ.* Also to be noted is Arjuna's scepticism about the possibility of attaining such a state of perfection as he argues that conquering the self is as hard as controlling the wind (6.33-34). In the next two verses, however, Kṛṣṇa confirms that success in this endeavour is certainly possible by strict adherence to *abhyāsa* and *vairāgya,* repeated practice and renunciation.

It is thus apparent that one strand of thought in the epic, represented by the above passage from the *Gītā,* embodies the notion of man being able to attain purity by his own efforts. It must be recognised, however, that this viewpoint is closely linked to the ideas of *mokṣa-dharma,* with their stress on salvation through self-transformation, and that where such a soteriological perspective is not pronounced, the concept of human perfection is absent. Three areas in particular may be noted:

1. The teachings on *bhakti,* as in the *Gītā, Nārāyaṇīya,* or *Anuśāsana* 14-18, lay stress on the attainment of salvation through grace, a doctrine that clearly precludes any necessity for individual perfection. Later texts went so far as to stress the sinful natures of those saved by the Deity, in order to emphasise the extent of

his grace.[17] The epic does not go this far in its thought; those presented as devotees of Viṣṇu or Śiva are generally high-minded sages, and the *Gītā*'s picture of the devotee (12.13-19) is similar to its view of the *yogin* who gains *mokṣa* through meditation. It may be noted, however, that the essential element in the winning of salvation through grace is whole-hearted surrender to the Deity as exemplified by the Śaivites Upamanyu and Tandin in the *Anuśāsana*. Where such surrender is found, personal imperfection is not an insurmountable obstacle:

> *api cet sudurācāro bhajate mām ananya-bhāk*
> *sādhur eva sa mantavyaḥ samyag vyavasito hi saḥ*
>
> 'One who worships me, devoting himself to no other, fixed in his determination, is to be considered a saint even if he is a perpetrator of the most wicked deeds.' (9.30).

The next verse goes on to reassure us that his wrongdoing will quickly cease; nonetheless it is apparent that this verse represents a genuine antecedent to the Purāṇic view of *bhakti* referred to above.

2. The *Mahābhārata* narrative contains no indication of the possibility of human perfection. Several of the central characters– Duryodhana, Duḥśāsana, Śakuni — are obviously to be taken as wrongdoers, but what makes the story so interesting is the manner in which righteous individuals are portrayed not merely as two-dimensional paragons of virtue, but as true characters subject to temptation and weakness. Bhīṣma, the wise grandsire, is present at the humiliation of Draupadī and does not intervene; the sages who practise renunciation are prone to angry outbursts and vindictive behaviour; amongst the Pāṇḍavas themselves, the character of Bhīma is obviously flawed in his excessive greed, violent nature and thirst for power; Arjuna is shown as envious of Ekalavya's prowess as an archer (1.123), and proud of his own ability. Even Yudhiṣṭhira is seen on occasion to fall short of perfection. During the battle he is exposed as lacking in courage and his fear of his enemies (as in 6.46.1f) leads to excessive lamentation (6.103.13f). He agrees to speak a falsehood in order to overcome Droṇa (7.164.98-107), he falls prey to anger directed against his enemies (8.20.1-10), and he expresses hatred for Karṇa because he fears his prowess (8.46.17). That fear of Karṇa leads

him to succumb to a bitter and unjust outburst against Arjuna, who is virtually single-handedly winning the battle for him.

3. Where the epic slips into dharma-śāstric mode, as in the *Rāja-dharma* and the *Anuśāsana,* a mood of realism prevails. Human limitations are recognised, and, in the case of the lower *varṇas* and of women, over-stressed. The duties of each group are based on pragmatism and the curtailing and regulation, rather than complete eradication, of the human tendency towards the selfish pursuit of pleasure. Even the *brāhmaṇas* are not without blemish and they too must be restricted, not by the royal order but by the regulations of *dharma-śāstra* that apply to them. The very existence of a system of rules to regulate behaviour implicitly suggests human imperfection, for the perfect need no regulation to keep them on the straight and narrow.[18]

The epic's view of human perfectibility must thus be understood in relation to the various religious tendencies contained in the text. Only in the teachings on *mokṣa-dharma* is such a view prominent and here the context of a soteriology based on self-transformation is clearly crucial. Elsewhere, the characterisations of the narrative demonstrate how even the righteous can be corrupted by the exigencies of the human condition with a seeming inevitability. In the *Aśvamedhika,* we have the *Kāma-gītā,* a short passage (14.13.10-20) in which the God of Desire states that no man can be completely free of his power. In the teachings stressing *sva-dharma* and *bhakti,* human perfection is not presented as a goal, for the former works within a context of imperfection and the latter allows those who fall short to find salvation through the grace of the Deity.

8. Summary and Conclusions

The *Mahābhārata* teaches a dualist view of the human being. The mind and body are no more than coverings for the spiritual entity that is the true self or *ātman* which is eternal and transmigrates to another body at death. For epic Sāṁkhya this distinction between soul and body is a fundamental doctrine and all its philosophy and practice are aimed at realising this truth. Hence the dualist perception of humanity is integral to *nivṛtti.* The *bhakti* of the epic didactus incorporates Sāṁkhya doctrines into its concept of humanity, but takes the dualist view a step further by identifying the *ātman* with the Deity which is the object of its veneration.

The view of humanity from the perspective of *pravṛtti* is less clear cut. The sections of the didactus teaching *sva-dharma* confirm the dualist view by stressing the idea of the transmigration of the soul to higher or lower *varṇas*. The narrative, however, only occasionally refers to reincarnation and eschatologically is more concerned with elevation to heaven and punishment in hell as the result of following or neglecting *dharma*. As the same identity is retained in these existences, a dualist view of human life appears somewhat at odds with such ideas. It is probable that the narrative is closer to the Vedic idea of human existence which does not include a rigid distinction between soul and matter, but that latter portions of the text have been influenced by Vedānta and Sāṁkhya and incorporate such distinctions into their teachings.

Sāṁkhya is preoccupied with analysing the elements of which an individual is comprised and distinguishing the soul from all material components. It thus offers an analysis of the physical and psychological attributes of the human being. The body is composed of the five great elements and the psyche is divided functionally into senses, mind and intellect which perceive objects, hanker after them, discriminate on the basis of desire and experience the resulting joy and misery. The psychological makeup of an individual is shaped by the three *guṇas* which define a personality type in accordance with previous actions. This analysis of human nature is uniquely a feature of Sāṁkhya in the epic and hence of *nivṛtti*.

From the perspective of *pravṛtti*, humanity holds a unique position in creation, for human actions and ritual lifestyles form a vital element in the cosmic *dharma* which sustains the gods and the order of the universe. Human life is also unique in being able to generate *karma* and shape the future existence of the individual in heaven or hell and in the various forms of life. Animals, gods and the inhabitants of heaven and hell are all suffering or enjoying the results of actions performed in a human form, for only human beings perform the actions that shape one's future destiny. *Nivṛtti* and *bhakti* share this view of humanity and furthermore stress that human life is especially significant as the status of existence from which *mokṣa* may be gained.

The hierarchy of human types, indicated by the four *varṇas*, is stressed particularly in *pravṛtti*'s understanding of humanity. Each *varṇa* has a specific *sva-dharma* unique to its members and for an individual to take up the duties of another *varṇa* is always condemned. *Nivṛtti* challenges the rigidity of this *varṇa* structure, arguing first that the designations should be based on quality rather than birth and, secondly, that the élite group qualified to practice *mokṣa-dharma* may be drawn from any of the *varṇas* or even the most degraded castes. *Bhakti,* likewise, does not deny the stratification of humanity, but urges that all *varṇas* should share the duty of worshipping the Deity.

The possibility of human perfection is allowed from the perspective of *nivṛtti* because the 'self-help' soteriology of Sāṁkhya and Yoga demands that one who gains success through their techniques be freed from all forms of contamination and sin. As far as *pravṛtti* is concerned, perfection is not a consideration and all human beings are destined to enjoy and suffer in the future as a result of their righteous and adharmic acts. As an 'other-help' form of soteriology, *bhakti* does not require perfection for deliverance, for the grace of the Deity overcomes human shortcomings.

It is thus clear that the epic's view of humanity is shaped by the major doctrinal tendencies of *pravṛtti, nivṛtti* and *bhakti* that dominate its religious ideas. The Vedic notion is here being supplanted by the mystical speculations of Sāṁkhya and Vedānta which postulate a transcendent soul and it is this idea that comes to dominate all forms of later Hinduism with their emphasis on the transmigration of the true self. Human life is thus a transitory stage in the progression of *saṁsāra* and is never to be regarded as one's absolute identity.

Notes

1. van Buitenen, J.A.B. *Studies in Indian Literature and Philosophy,* Ludo Rocher Ed, Delhi, 1988, p. 75.
2. Ibid, p. 60.
3. Chapter 239 of the *Śānti* is clearly derived from the same source as Chapter 189.
4. Hopkins, E.W. *The Great Epic of India,* Calcutta, 1969 (1st Ed 1901), p. 46.
5. See, for example, 12.283.17 and 12.300.15.
6. For Upaniṣadic references to the soul as a figure the size of a thumb, see Howe, *Thirteen Principal Upaniṣads,* Oxford, 1934, p. 583.
7. Heesterman, J.C. *The Inner Conflict of Tradition, Essays in Indian Ritual, Kingship and Society,* Chicago, 1985, pp. 26-27.
8. van Buitenen 1988, p. 173.
9. See, for example, 12.70.7.

10. See, for example, 12.316.25.
11. van Buitenen 1988, pp. 135-143.
12. O'Flaherty, W. *The Origins of Evil in Hindu Mythology,* Berkeley, 1976, p. 289.
13. Though verses such as 5.40.26 indicate that the members of all four *varṇas* may aspire for elevation to *svarga-loka.*
14. See, for example, 12.238.15-20.
15. The three references to the contents of the *Gītā* found elsewhere in the *Mahābhārata* all recognise it as a treatise on salvation–the *Anugītā,* a stated recapitulation, in the *Nārāyaṇīya* 12.336.49, and in 1.2.156.
16. Huber, F. 'The Relevance of the Bhagavad-gītā According to Paul David Devanandan', *Religion and Society* 34, 1987, pp. 55-56.
17. See, for example, the story of Ajāmila in 6.1.3 of the *Bhāgavata Purāṇa* and also 2.1-40 of the *Śiva-mahātmya.*
18. As Yudhiṣṭhira indicates in his claim that the righteous naturally adopt practices that are virtuous (1.187.28-30).

CHAPTER 9

THE CONTROL OF DESTINY OVER HUMAN EXISTENCE

1. The Role of Destiny in the Epic

According to Robin Zaehner, the *Mahābhārata*, "stresses time and again the primacy of fate over human endeavour."[1] Although this statement cannot be denied, the epic's view of this matter is far from straightforward, and, as I hope to demonstrate, reflects once more the underlying tension between *pravṛtti* and *nivṛtti*. In considering the basis for Zaehner's assertion, it must be recalled that the narrative operates on two levels. Behind the human history that is recounted, the reader is constantly reminded that Viṣṇu is at work through the agency of the human protagonists to sustain the position of the gods and uphold the existence of *dharma*. Thus the endeavours of human beings are subordinate to the divine will which is decisive in determining the outcome of events. Throughout the narrative a continuous commentary is sustained to the effect that events are turning out the way they do because of destiny, and that no course of action could have affected a preordained outcome. A few examples from many must serve to illustrate the point.

Droṇa agrees to teach Dhṛṣṭadyumna the art of combat, knowing that he will be slain by him, because one's destiny cannot be avoided–*amokṣaṇīyaṁ daivaṁ hi bhāvi matvā mahāmatiḥ* (1.155.52); in criticising the treatment of Draupadī by the Kauravas, Vidura recognises that destiny is directing events towards war–*daiverito nūnam ayam* (2.63.16); when Maitreya curses Duryodhana for refusing to make peace he is described as impelled by fate–*vidhinā saṁprayuktaḥ* (3.11.31); before the battle Śalya tells Yudhiṣṭhira that the suffering and joy he experiences are not of his own making, for destiny is supreme–*nātra manyus tvayā kāryo vidhir hi balavattaraḥ* (5.9.35); seeing the armies assembled at Kurukṣetra,

Baladeva states that none of this could have been avoided for destiny is supreme–*diṣṭam etad dhruvaṁ manye na śakyam ativartitum* (5.154.24); after he is shot down from his chariot, Bhīṣma tells Karṇa that destiny cannot be overcome by human endeavour–*daivaṁ puruṣa-kāreṇa na śakyam ativartitum* (6.117.18); when criticised for killing Bhuriśravas, Sātyaki defends himself by saying that whatever destiny decrees must come to pass–*bhavitavyaṁ ca yad bhāvi daivaṁ ceṣṭayatīva ca* (7.118.47); even while boasting of what he will achieve as a general, Karṇa still admits that he cannot overcome destinv–*diṣṭaṁ na śakyaṁ vyativartituṁ vai* (8.26.54); and in comforting Yudhiṣṭhira, Vyāsa tells him that a man attains all things in life due to the progress of time–*kālena sarvaṁ labhate manuṣyaḥ* (12.26.5).

In such passages several words are used to denote fate and destiny, the two most common of which are *diṣṭam* and *daivam. Diṣṭam* is the participle of the verb *diś* meaning to order or command, and therefore *diṣṭam* is literally that which is ordained. *Daivam* is a derivative of the word *deva* and hence is literally that which is bestowed by the gods. The word *vidhi* is more commonly used in the sense of a command or rule, implying that destiny is that which is imposed on the individual by external injunction. *Kāla*, meaning time, is also occasionally used in the sense of fate, or what inevitably comes to pass when the preordained moment arrives. The word *diṣṭi* is somewhat different because it is not generally used in the sense of destiny, but to mean good luck or good fortune. Most frequently used in the instrumental form of *diṣṭyā*, by good fortune, it is often found as an exclamation from those who have achieved success, as, for example, by Yudhiṣṭhira when Karṇa is slain (8.69.19,33) and by the assassins of the *Sauptika* who cry out *diṣṭyā diṣṭyā* when their bloody work is done. Finally there is *bhāgadeyataḥ* used infrequently in this sense, but found in the refrain to Dhṛtarāṣṭra's speech on the events at Kurukṣetra–*kim anyad bhāgadeyataḥ,* what can it be but destiny (9.2.29-40). The literal translation indicates a portion or allocation, and here it has the English meaning of 'just one's lot.'

The words *daivam* and *diṣṭam* are frequently used in the narrative to mean the fate which has been ordained. We are powerless to alter events, and our endeavours only appear to be the controlling factor in the progression of history. This is confirmed by the two visions of Arjuna, the first of which is described in Chapter 11 of the *Bhagavad-gītā.* Here Arjuna sees within Kṛṣṇa's *viśva-rūpa* the warriors assembled at Kurukṣetra being destroyed by the teeth of the Deity. When Arjuna asks him to reveal his true identity, Kṛṣṇa asserts that he is time, the great destroyer of worlds. Arjuna is not the true slayer of his foes; their pre-ordained time has come and he is but an instrument in the action of time. Similarly, at the end of the *Droṇa,* Arjuna sees Śiva going before him on the field of battle destroying those who fall before his arrows, a vision which according to Scheuer confirms a teaching found throughout the epic, "nous ne sommes que des instruments."[2]

The concept of destiny in the epic is presented in several different ways; sometimes it is the inevitable progression of time, sometimes the will of the gods or the Deity, and sometimes the result of previous acts. For Wendy O'Flaherty there is a clear distinction in Hindu thought between these different ideas, "*Karma* is clearly distinguished from fate (*daiva*); the latter is often used to explain otherwise inexplicable occurrences which even karma is regarded as inadequate to justify."[3] It is hard to discover, however, where in the *Mahābhārata* such a clear distinction is to be found; *daivam,* as has been noted, is frequently used as an explanation for an individual's success or failure, but there is no indication that its course is not dictated by previous acts.

Scheuer similarly detects different "niveaux de causalité" and cites time, destiny, and *īśvara.*[4] In the text, however, *kāla* appears to be used interchangeably with *daivam* and *diṣṭam.* Time progresses and events unfold as destiny ordains, with individuals enjoying and suffering in accordance with their previous acts. *Īśvara,* or God, is the enactor of the system, who rewards and punishes individuals. It is understood that the results individuals receive from the *dhātṛ* are in accordance with the nature of their previous acts, and only at rare instances in time, as in the events described by the *Mahābhārata,* does the Deity intervene directly to adjust the course of events for a specific purpose. Thus it is doubtful as to how accurate it is to describe these various factors as different levels of causality, for previous acts and the actions of the Deity may be taken as contributory elements in the unfolding process of destiny, without any conceptual contradiction.

This view is confirmed by the opening chapter of the *Anuśāsana* which tells the story of the death of a young boy, the son of

Gautamī, a female ascetic. A hunter named Arjunaka captures the serpent that has killed the child and brings it to Gautamī, offering to assuage her grief by killing the creature before her eyes. She replies that it is pointless to kill another living being, for it will not bring her son back to life. The hunter is not to be dissuaded, however, and so the snake speaks out, absolving himself from blame by stating that he was acting under the impulse of the God of Death and that if any siṇ has been committed it is by him (28). Eventually the god Mṛtyu appears (42) and, whilst admitting that he despatched the serpent to kill the boy, contends that he is under the control of time, as indeed are all things in this world (43-50). The hunter's response to this is that both the god and the serpent should die. Kāla, time personified, then appears (62) and states that he is not to blame and neither is Mṛtyu nor the serpent, for none of them are the true cause–*prayojakaḥ*–of the tragedy. What then is the cause? It is the previous acts of the child that are the only true cause of his premature death; everything else is secondary. Gautamī accepts this verdict, concluding that she too must have sinned in a previous life and is now being forced to grieve for her son as a result.

Essentially this story is a reassertion of the doctrine of *karma*, revealing that present suffering is the result of sins performed in a previous life. In terms of the present discussion, it shows clearly that the various factors referred to above are not to be taken as representing different theories of causation. Nor is it necessarily the case that we face here, "the disquieting ability of Indians to believe several seemingly contradictory tenets at once."[5] To the question, 'What caused the death of my child?' four answers may be given (i) the sinful deed of the serpent, or in other words the endeavour of an individual, (ii) the will of the gods, here Mṛtyu, (iii) it was destined to take place at a certain time, here represented by the figure of Kāla, and (iv) previous acts producing their result. It is clear that these different answers do not necessarily amount to a doctrinal contradiction, except possibly between the first and the other three. The snake is the instrument of the *dhātṛ*, here personified as Mṛtyu, who decides that the child must die because the proper time for this event has arrived as dictated by destiny, which here is Kāla. Destiny, however, is not a blind force but is shaped by the previous acts of an individual.

This, I would urge, is the prevailing doctrine of destiny in the

Mahābhārata, which, though not confirmed in every passage, is contradicted only by the perspective represented here by the hunter. His view is that the extreme determinism of Gautamī and the others removes all forms of condemnation for evil deeds. If this view is logically pursued then there is no meaning to sin and righteousness and no purpose to any endeavour, for all things are preordained and determined externally. This critique of absolute fatalism indicates the major tension in the epic on the subject of destiny, and will be discussed in more detail below.

2. The Predestined Nature of Humanity

Up to this point, destiny has been considered in terms of the fortunes that befall an individual, his success and failure and the happiness and misery that come to him in life. A further aspect of the nature of destiny is highlighted by 3.33 and 18.59-60 of the *Bhagavad-gītā* which indicate that the inherent nature of an individual forces him or her to act in a particular way. One born as a *brāhmaṇa* is endowed with the appropriate psychological and physical disposition which impel him towards a certain course of behaviour. Clearly this view amounts to a different and in some ways separate aspect to the question of destiny, for the issue here is not the fortune that befalls one, but one's inherent nature. At birth one is endowed with a particular disposition, inherited from the parents and conditioned by the mixture of the *guṇas* in one's personal nature, as 18.41 of the *Gītā* makes clear. A *brāhmaṇa* is thus predominantly under *sattva-guṇa* and a *kṣatriya* predominantly under *rajas,* and this acquired nature virtually compels the individual to follow a certain pattern of behaviour.

For this reason religion, *dharma* and ethics are all modified so as to be appropriate for the nature of the different types of individual. Thus not only is Arjuna told that his refusal to fight cannot save those destined to die at Kurukṣetra, but also that he will be unable to prevent himself from fighting because his own nature, based on his *kṣatriya* disposition, will impel him towards acts of violence:

> *svabhāva-jena kaunteya nibaddhaḥ svena karmaṇā*
> *kartuṁ necchasi yan mohāt kariṣyasy avaśo 'pi tat*

'O son of Kuntī, bound by your own type of action which

> arises from your very nature, without being able to resist, you will perform those acts that because of illusion you do not wish to perform.' (18.60)

Elsewhere the same point is confirmed by the manner in which the warlike nature of the *brāhmaṇa* Rāma Jāmadagneya is explained by the confusion of potions that brings about such an unnatural occurrence, and the repeated response to Yudhiṣṭhira's desire for renunciation that such behaviour is unnatural for a *kṣatriya.*

This intensely determinist feature of the epic's view of humanity is not absolutely binding. Yudhiṣṭhira's disavowal of *kṣatriya-dharma* has already been noted, and the *Gītā* remains ambivalent on the subject. Immediately following 18.60, Kṛṣṇa goes on to instruct that Arjuna must now decide for himself what course to follow, as if he does in fact have free will. Aśvatthāman, Droṇa and Kṛpa engage in warfare despite their *brāhmaṇa* birth, and Bhīṣma accepts the renounced lifestyle of a *brāhmaṇa* by taking a vow of celibacy. According to the *Mokṣa-dharma,* men and women from any background can accept the ascetic lifestyle normally associated with *brāhmaṇas* in order to pursue the search for salvation (12.232.32). The idea that an individual's nature is predetermined at birth is clearly linked to the notion of *varṇas,* and as such is to be recognised as a feature of the tendency towards *pravṛtti* and at least partially dismissed by doctrines on salvation.

3. The Conflict of Opinion over Destiny

(i) *Pravṛtti* and *Nivṛtti*

The deterministic view, prominent throughout the text, is clearly problematic in terms of practical application, for if the snake is innocent in the story from the *Anuśāsana* then this view must be applied to all wrongdoers. It is also noteworthy that in the narrative the character who most frequently ascribes all calamities to destiny is Dhṛtarāṣṭra, and one cannot help but suspect that he is thereby trying to obscure his own culpability.[6] In Chapter 156 of the *Udyoga,* there is a notable speech from Saṁjaya in which he specifically refutes his master's claim that the disaster about to occur at Kurukṣetra is due only to destiny, stating quite bluntly that one whose misconduct brings distress can blame neither destiny nor time for his plight.[7] The self-interested recourse to philosophy by the blind king illustrates the difficulties that arise from the determinist view of life which are recognised and highlighted at various junctures by the epic.

Two aspects of the teachings on destiny have previously been discussed relating to one's fortunes and one's nature and the degree to which they are preordained. It is significant to note the way in which these two relate to the doctrinal axis of *pravṛtti* and *nivṛtti*.

1. The view that an individual's nature is predetermined is stressed by the teachings on *pravṛtti*, and to some extent minimised by the doctrines of *nivṛtti*. The acceptance of such an idea is integral to the concept of *sva-dharma*, for the duties of *dharma* are those that are in harmony with one's nature. The notion of *dharma* is both prescriptive and descriptive, indicating both how an individual should act and also the nature of an individual with which the prescribed duties are thought to harmonise. The doctrines of *mokṣa-dharma* cannot accept such a rigid imposition, for they urge that any individual can renounce his or her *sva-dharma* in order to transcend this world and seek salvation.

2. The view that an individual's fortune is preordained is stressed by the teachings on *nivṛtti* and criticised in other passages which urge adherence to *sva-dharma*. The *Mokṣa-dharma*'s teachings on renunciation lay stress on developing an attitude of tolerance and acceptance of life's changing fortunes without aspiration for worldly prosperity. One must recognise that all circumstances arise from destiny and therefore give up striving to improve one's material position. The point is emphasised by examples of great leaders who have been cast down and yet do not lament for their loss, understanding that all things take place because destiny decrees it, as in Chapter 217 of the *Śānti*, and the sage who follows the way of life of a python referred to in Chapter 172.

(ii) Passages which Deny the Absolute Dominance of Destiny

Although such determinism is a prevalent strain of thought in the epic, the problems it involves on a practical level are clearly recognised by the authors. Thus at several points it is challenged in passages which provide a significant counter to the perspective found elsewhere.

1. At the beginning of their exile in the forest Draupadī criticises Yudhiṣṭhira's conduct. Yudhiṣṭhira has accepted the terms

of his defeat in the gambling match and is determined to tolerate the thirteen years of exile imposed upon him. Draupadī and Bhīma disagree with this course of action and urge that he should act now to avenge the insults they have suffered. Draupadī seems to assume that Yudhiṣṭhira will not act because he takes the view that all misfortune is due to destiny. She first urges that by their very nature all creatures must act, and that one who simply depends on destiny is the worst of men (3.33.12-13). Here one cannot but be reminded of Dhṛtarāṣṭra who seeks to cover his own character weaknesses by attributing the results of his misdeeds to destiny.

Although all things are controlled by God (23), one's own actions are also a factor in process of causality. Men have the expertise to build cities, extract oil from sesame seeds and milk from cows, and to cook different types of food; all of this is achieved through acts (24.26). The view that all outcomes are determined by destiny alone is then dismissed as Draupadī argues that only an expert craftsman can produce good work (27). If acts are not effective then what is the point of religious rituals, and why does a disciple learn from a *guru* (28). Because acts are effective people may be praised or blamed for the way they behave (29). Some people say it is the inevitable–*haṭha,* some say it is destiny–*diṣṭa,* and some say that it is individual exertion–*puruṣa-prayatna*–that is effective in producing results (31-35). There are in fact three causes and all three must be taken into account; Manu therefore urges action, for those who endeavour are likely to succeed while the idle always fail (36-39). Persons free from doubt regard those who do not act as purposeless and doubting, but those who do act as resolute (40). Hence Yudhiṣṭhira must now take action. He may not succeed if the other factors, *diṣṭam* and *haṭha,* are against him but if this is the case no-one can blame him, and without taking action there is no possibility of success (41-48).

In an earlier speech in the same discussion, Draupadī criticises the Ordainer for injustice and then retracts, admitting that she was speaking without due consideration. Here, however, there is no evidence that her point of view is to be regarded as incorrect. There is no response from Yudhiṣṭhira, as at this point Bhīma joins the debate in support of Draupadī, and it appears that her views are left to stand as an alternative understanding that at least merits due consideration. It is clear that she does not wholly reject determinism, but urges only that personal endeavour is one factor in the complete structure of causality that interacts with the preordaining force of destiny. What she specifically objects to is absolute determinism which allows no significance whatsoever to individual exertion, arguing that such a doctrine renders human life meaningless. My own understanding of the text is that the author recognised the weight of such arguments as a valid counter to the deterministic doctrines expressed frequently throughout the epic. It is noteworthy that Draupadī here cites the well-known authority of Bṛhaspati to support her opinions (57), and also that the ideas she expresses, especially from verse 50 onwards, correspond closely with the teachings of Bhīṣma in the *Rāja-dharma*, teachings which Yudhiṣṭhira finds equally difficult to accept.

2. After hearing a message from the Kauravas urging Yudhiṣṭhira to give up his military preparations, Kṛṣṇa addresses the Pāṇḍava captains, in Chapter 29 of the *Udyoga*, stressing the efficacy of exertion in producing the desired outcome. In verse 5, he states that various theories about causality are taught by the *brāhmaṇas*. Some say action is effective, some urge giving up action and some say that success is gained only through wisdom; it is known amongst *brāhmaṇas*, however, that even a wise man who does not eat cannot enjoy food. Only those teachings which urge action bear fruit, for the results of action are self-evident, as one who drinks has his thirst relieved (6-7). The gods flourish, the sun rises, the moon moves through the heavens, fire burns, the earth sustains its creatures and rivers carry water, all through actions (8-9). Indra, Bṛhaspati and all the other celestial beings gained their exalted positions by accepting vows of celibacy (10-13).

Here Kṛṣṇa's argument is aimed at demonstrating that exertion by an individual is effective in gaining the desired result, implicitly denying the view that everything comes about because it is preordained to be so. He cites both experience and the position of the gods to demonstrate his point. It is plainly observed that a man is relieved from thirst not because destiny decrees such a fate for him, but because he has taken the action of drinking water. Similarly, the gods have not attained their status through the blind force of time but because in the past they underwent severe austerities, the rewards of which they are now enjoying.

3. In Chapter 75, Kṛṣṇa returns to the same subject in urging Bhīma that he must not give up his resolve to fight. He first points out that the debate over destiny and endeavour is never resolved–

paryāyaṁ na vyavasyanti daiva-mānuṣayor janāḥ (5). One may act under the most learned counsel, but still the outcome is as uncertain as the wind (6-8). At the same time, that which is decreed by destiny can be thwarted by appropriate actions, as with hunger or excessive heat–*daivam apy akṛtaṁ karma pauruṣeṇa vihanyate* (9). That which occurs not as the result of destiny is created by man himself–*yad anyad diṣṭa-bhāvasya puruṣasya svayaṁ-kṛtam*–and hence such circumstances may be averted by actions (10). For people in the world there is no way to live apart from the way of action–*lokasya nānyato vṛttiḥ pāṇḍavānyatra karmaṇaḥ;* one should seek one's goal knowing it will come from a combination of destiny and endeavour–*ubhayānvayāt*–without excessive lamentation or rejoicing over the outcome (11-12).

It is interesting to note how the author of this passage is aware of Kṛṣṇa as the speaker of the *Gītā* and includes a hint of *Gītā* philosophy in verse 12, urging Bhīma to take action whilst remaining unaffected by success or failure. Here Kṛṣṇa accepts that there are two schools of thought on the subject of causality, which may denote the division between *pravṛtti* and *nivṛtti*, and, as in the *Gītā*, seeks to establish a synthesis between them. His conclusion is that some circumstances cannot be avoided because destiny decrees them, whilst others are created by the acts of man alone. Even when one is thrust into a particular plight by destiny, still one's actions may be effective in alleviating the situation, as in a state of hunger one may take action to find food or when oppressed by heat one may seek out a cool place. Therefore, in any situation, the proper course is to act to the full extent of one's ability, for even though destiny does influence our lives its control is never absolute.

4. Whilst the *Mokṣa-dharma* stresses the control of destiny, the *Rāja-dharma* presents an alternative perspective which emphasises the effect of individual exertion. At the outset of his teachings, Bhīṣma stresses that a king should always endeavour strenuously to achieve his goals. He tells Yudhiṣṭhira that he should be active in his exertions, for without such endeavour destiny alone will never satisfy the aspirations of kings (12.56.14). Destiny and exertion are equally effective, but exertion is superior because the nature of destiny is dictated by the acts one performs (15). If one's plans are thwarted one should not lament but endeavour with all one's power to surmount the obstacles to success; this is the highest

duty for kings (16). The view that personal exertion should be regarded as more significant than destiny predominates in the *Rāja-dharma* and is stated specifically in the glorification of endeavour–*utthāna*–by Bhīṣma in 12.58.14-18, and in 12.120.43, 12.128.29, and 12.131.9, as well as by the bird Pūjanī in a fable narrated by him in 12.137.50-53, 78-79.

5. Chapter 6 of the *Anuśāsana* opens with Yudhiṣṭhira directly asking Bhīṣma which is the more significant, destiny or human endeavour–*daive puruṣa-kāre ca kiṁsvic cheṣṭhataraṁ bhavet.* In reply Bhīṣma tells of a conversation between Brahmā and Vasiṣṭha on the same subject. Destiny and endeavour may be compared to a field and the seed planted in it; a field may be ploughed but without seed no crop can grow, and similarly without exertion there can be no success through destiny alone–*tathā puruṣa-kāreṇa vinā daivaṁ na sidhyati* (5-7). In verse 8, the metaphor is inverted and it is stated that acts are the field and destiny is the seed–*kṣetraṁ puruṣa-kāras tu daivaṁ bījam udāhṛtam*–working interactively to produce results. Happiness and pain are the result of past pure and sinful deeds (9-10). Even though wounded by fate, one who takes action will attain his goal, but one who is inactive meets with ruin and rubs salt on the wound (11). The point of this metaphor seems to be that destiny brings unwanted circumstances, but if one is inactive and does not attempt to alleviate the problem then it becomes even worse, just as a caustic substance will aggravate a wound.

One who performs penances will gain beauty, good fortune and wealth, but one who does not will gain nothing through destiny alone, for the kingdom of the gods and all pleasures are gained by personal exertion–*puruṣa-kāreṇa* (12-13). All who dwell in heaven gained their positions by appropriate actions; riches and good fortune likewise come only to those who make the proper exertions, and even Viṣṇu is known to have executed penances (14-18). If acts did not produce results then all action would be pointless; depending on destiny alone, everybody would become indifferent–*udāsīnaḥ* (19). One who gives up exertion and depends on destiny is like a woman with an impotent husband, for there is no chance of success (20).

Even the slightest amount of righteous or unrighteous action causes fear in heaven, far more so than in the world of men (21). Destiny follows the acts people perform–*kṛtaḥ puruṣa-kāras tu daivam evānuvartate*–and without acts there is nothing that destiny can bestow–*na daivam akṛte kiṁcit kasyacid dātum arhati* (22). When the position of the gods is impermanent, how will destiny continue to exist or cause any condition to stand (23). In this world the gods do not act for anyone else's benefit; they incite strong passions in some only out of concern for their own predominance (24). Between the gods and *ṛṣis* there is constant discord; who can describe a state of no destiny acting, out of which destiny came into being?–*kasya vācā hy adaivaṁ syād yato daivaṁ pravartate* (25). And what is the origin of this state of no destiny from which destiny came into being? Thus even in the realm of the gods many types of deceit exist (26).

The self is the friend and enemy of the self, and also the witness in what is done and what is not done (27). When actions are performed they are successful when done righteously; improper action does not achieve its purpose (28). Piety–*puṇya*–is the refuge of the gods and all things are attained through piety; how can destiny affect a man who is righteous by nature?–*puṇya-śīlaṁ naraṁ prāpya kiṁ daivaṁ prakariṣyati* (29). Verses 30 to 41 consist of a list of well-known figures who according to the teachings here have gained success through their endeavours. It is to be noted that this list includes the Pāṇḍavas (40) despite numerous statements elsewhere that their victory was predestined. Similarly, a comparison may be drawn between the assertion that curses take effect because of the power of the sage who casts them (41), and the passage in the *Vana* where Maitreya curses Duryodhana and is said to do so because he is impelled by destiny–*vidhinā saṁprayuktaḥ* (3.11.31).

I have examined this passage in detail because it specifically addresses the question under discussion, although it must be recognised that its perspective is not shared by all sections of the epic. The aphoristic style in which certain verses are composed and the possible corruption of the text of others renders its meaning obscure at times, but nonetheless its overall teaching is clear and certain points are worthy of specific note. Destiny is referred to throughout by the term *daivam,* and there is a clear relationship between the word as it is used here and its root. Linguistically, one may note the use of the unusual *daivatāḥ* to refer to the gods rather than the more conventional *devāḥ.* The intent appears to be to emphasise the links the chapter draws between destiny and the control of the gods. Hence it argues that endeavour is superior to destiny by pointing out that even the gods, the enactors of fate, are themselves temporary and limited (23). This passage also employs the argument of Draupadī against absolute determinism by pointing out its practical difficulties. If people believed that every outcome was predetermined, all actions would be pointless and everyone would be completely indifferent (19). It is noteworthy that the term used in this context, *udāsīnaḥ*, meaning the quality of indifference, is recognised in the *Gītā* as a desirable attribute for *yogins* and devotees dear to Kṛṣṇa (12.16).

The main line of argument in this passage does not, however, centre on whether actions here and now can produce results or whether all things are preordained, but on the relationship between destiny and previous acts. The stress here is on the fact that destiny is not a force on its own, but is shaped by the actions one performs. The message is very clear that one must not merely hope that destiny will bring future satisfaction, but must act now in the prescribed manner in order to ensure future happiness. If one executes the proper rituals then the *puṇya*, or merit, one gains guarantees such a future, for the gods who are the architects of *daivam* are delighted by *puṇyam* (45-47).

Here, at the risk of jumping ahead of the discussion, attention must be drawn to the context of this chapter within the *Mahābhārata*. Large sections of the *Anuśāsana* are devoted to descriptions of ritual acts which assure the practitioner a future existence in heaven. One of the purposes of the discussion in Chapter 6 is to demonstrate that the winning of such a desirable afterlife is by no means just a matter of destiny but depends on the undertaking of appropriate ritual action here and now. Bhīṣma's teachings here also serve to present an alternative view to that of the *Mokṣadharma*, which in the final arrangement of the *Mahābhārata* immediately precedes the *Anuśāsana*. The emphasis there is on the renunciation of rituals and ritualised behaviour and accepting whatever fate may bring. The opening chapter of the *Anuśāsana* demonstrated that fate is dictated by previous actions, and here again the essential point is that destiny is not blind but is bestowed by the gods in accordance with the type of actions executed by the individual.

4. Conclusions

My aim in this discussion has been to demonstrate that whilst the *Mahābhārata* undoubtedly stresses the dominance of destiny over human existence, this view is tempered by a recognition of the impracticality of absolute determinism and of the efficacy of action in attaining results. Following Hopkins, the critical scholar may recognise here another example of the fragmentary nature of the epic in which different ideas are placed together in one inflated work with little consideration of doctrinal or literary continuity. Such views are not without weight, but fall short of providing a complete understanding of the epic's thought.

The question of destiny and free will in any doctrine is always complex, and can never be resolved by simplistic formulae that seek to define reality in terms of rational absolutes. The above examination of key passages makes it clear that the authors were fully aware of the antithesis and incongruity between acceptance of destiny and positive action, both of which the text recognises as effective in producing results. Repeatedly it has been noted that the religious teachings of the *Mahābhārata* are unlike those of Western faiths in that they do not demand rigid absolutes of doctrine or practice. Different religious tendencies are accepted and propounded on the basis that human nature is so diverse that an absolute religion for all people at all times is impractical.

Regarding the antithesis between destiny and endeavour, it is apparent that the emphasis found in particular passages is largely determined by the religious tendency stressed in that section of the epic. Destiny is stressed particularly in the epic narrative, and in the teachings on *mokṣa-dharma,* though in the former case with notable examples of dissent. *Mokṣa-dharma* is concerned with renunciation of the world, transcending the goals it has to offer, and being equal-minded in success and failure. The deterministic acceptance of whatever destiny brings accords easily with such a world view, and hence is repeatedly emphasised where the religious imperative is towards salvation.

The narrative is somewhat different, for its emphasis is predominantly on this world, and absolute salvation is rarely considered. The key to understanding its emphasis on destiny is to be found in the *Bhagavad-gītā,* in Arjuna's vision which reveals that the true destroyer and controller of events is the all-powerful Deity appearing as Kṛṣṇa. This is the world of *bhakti* which predominates in the epic narrative, as we are repeatedly reminded that whatever is taking place on earth is being conducted and controlled by Viṣṇu, Śiva and the pantheon of gods subordinate to them. Human beings may try as hard as they like, but will only be successful if their endeavour is blessed by the supreme Deity, and it is the will of this *deva* that the narrative recognises as *daivam*, the force controlling and directing all events.

When considering passages that present the alternative view that human exertion can resist destiny, their position in the text must equally be noted, bearing in mind the antithesis between *pravṛtti* and *nivṛtti*. In Draupadī's debate with Yudhiṣṭhira, her arguments focus throughout on the idea that warfare is an essential element of *kṣatriya-dharma*. The basis of the ideological differences between them is Yudhiṣṭhira's refusal to accept that the tenets of *sva-dharma* are binding upon him as an individual, just as *mokṣa-dharma* rejects this obligation. Hence Draupadī's arguments against absolute determinism may be seen as a part of the argument against renunciation from the perspective of *pravṛtti*, or else as a feature of the ethical tension between *sva-dharma* and morality.

It was noted earlier how the speeches of Kṛṣṇa in the *Udyoga* contain deliberate hints of the *Bhagavad-gītā*, and his role as the *avatāra* provides the context against which these speeches should be considered. Kṛṣṇa's mission on earth is to oversee a conflict of massive proportions and to preserve the institution of *sva-dharma*. Hence even when he gives teachings on *mokṣa* and *bhakti* in the *Gītā*, he demonstrates how the execution of dharmic duties may become a part of these paths. Kṛṣṇa requires the Pāṇḍavas to execute their warlike *sva-dharma* in order that the destructive aspect of his mission may be fulfilled, and he also seeks the perpetuation of *sva-dharma* in general. Thus his voice, like Draupadī's, when emphasising the primacy of exertion over destiny is to be recognised as speaking primarily from the perspective of *pravṛtti*.[8]

The *Rāja-dharma* specifically teaches the details of *kṣatriya sva-dharma*. As such its teachings are clearly from the perspective of *pravṛtti* and incorporate its emphasis on the power of exertion in shaping events. The *Anuśāsana* represents the perspective of a different religious tendency to that found in the *Mokṣa-dharma*. Salvation is rarely mentioned as the goal to be sought, and instead emphasis is placed on reaching the world of the gods through the performance of ritual acts. Concomitant to such teachings is the view that future happiness and distress are not the result of blind destiny but can be shaped by acts performed in the present. It is noteworthy that in Chapter 149, Yudhiṣṭhira challenges all Bhīṣma's teachings in the *Anuśāsana* on the very basis that actions do not always bring the result one seeks because destiny may or may not be favourable.

I have thus attempted to establish a broad congruence between *pravṛtti* and stress on the efficacy of exertion, and between *nivṛtti* and stress on the control of destiny. I am aware that such a view may be criticised on the grounds that it recognises only two levels of causality, while several are referred to in the text. In reply it may be argued that there is only one principal division, and where more numerous levels of causality are referred to this constitutes a more detailed analysis of one or the other, or of both. Some examples will illustrate the point more clearly.

The straightforward twofold division of causation is presented in 10.2.2-3, where Kṛpa states that results come from endeavour and destiny together and in 12.137.78, where Bhīṣma tells of a queen named Pūjanī urging her defeated son to take up arms again because both destiny and endeavour are mutually dependent. In a well-known passage of the *Gītā*, however, Kṛṣṇa offers five elements that produce results according to the teachings of Sāṁkhya. These are the place, the doer, the instruments used, the various types of exertion entailed, and destiny–*daivam* (18.13-14). This is not, however, a different view from the idea of a twofold basis of causation, but rather an elaboration of the same idea. Here the first four components are the factors that constitute individual exertion, and these interact with destiny to produce a final outcome.

An apparently different teaching is found in the *Udyoga*, in Saṁjaya's discussions with Dhṛtarāṣṭra (5.156.14f). The discourse follows the line typical of the narrative to the effect that man is not the real doer of activities, but is like a wooden doll acting under the volition of a puppeteer who is the real controller. Here again it may be noted how this simile highlights the link between the *bhakti* view of the world and the determinist notion of all things being brought about by destiny. In verse 15, Saṁjaya presents three different opinions as to what is the controlling force in the progression of time–*īśvara-nirdiṣṭāḥ*, the directions of the Deity, *yad-ṛcchayā*, that which befalls one, and *pūrva-karma*, previous acts. Thus the individual is pulled like a plough in a threefold manner.

This threefold doctrine of causation again does not challenge the dual antithesis fundamental to the text as a whole. Here the possibility that exertion may influence the outcome of events is ignored. Instead the nature of destiny is discussed in the context of destiny alone being the controlling factor. All things arise because destiny ordains it, but the nature of destiny may be understood as the will of the Deity, blind fate, reactions to previous acts, or else, as discussed earlier, the three combined in one process. The point is that although various passages may seek to define and refine an understanding of the complexities of both exertion and destiny, such discourses do not undermine the idea of a dual antithesis in the basic understanding of the nature of causality.

The use of the phrase *kecid . . . kecid . . . anye* (5.156.15) reminds us again of the epic milieu where, in the absence of a rigid orthodoxy, various perspectives might be presented and debated. The indication is that the nature of causality was a subject on which respected authorities might differ in their final assessments. This view is confirmed and illustrated by a short passage from the *Mokṣa-dharma,* 12.224.50-52. Here Bhīṣma is recounting the teachings of Vyāsa to his son Śuka. From verse 50, the discourse changes direction as Vyāsa states that some speak of exertion, while others stress destiny, and those who understand the living beings refer to their inherent nature. Exertion, destiny and previous acts are separate factors that produce results but there are some who say there is no distinction between them (51). They assert, "It is this factor", or, "No, it is this other which keeps the world in motion," but those who are fixed in *sattva,* have equal vision and perform their duties say that this subject is hard to comprehend (52). This brief passage reveals that though the notion of destiny was a subject of much discussion there was no prevailing orthodoxy dictating a true creed on whether destiny or free will was predominant. Different views were put forward in the attempt to reach a feasible understanding to a problem of doctrine which even the wise recognise as difficult for the powers of human comprehension to grasp.

At the beginning of this chapter Zaehner's view that the epic is dominated by the understanding that all things are controlled by destiny was noted and confirmed. Now it can be recognised that the answer to this problem presented by the text is complex and to some extent paradoxical. The problems of a deterministic world view are recognised by the authors and expressed at various junctures where the presentation of an alternative perspective is appropriate. Though it is clear that different schools of thought are represented within the text, to dismiss it as no more than a mass of contradictions is shortsighted. There can be no simple solution to the problem of destiny and free-will, and the stature of the epic is surely raised by the fact that when viewed as a work in its entirety it makes no such attempt. Rather it offers different perspectives from different religious tendencies each of which contributes to the development of the reader's comprehension. The roles of both destiny and exertion are recognised, and also the tension between them which was a feature of the debates of the epic period. Just as different religious tendencies are accepted to meet the spiritual needs of different personality types, so either destiny or exertion may be stressed as is deemed most appropriate. For the Western mind, accustomed to absolute creeds, this approach may be disquieting, but it is surely simplistic to conclude that it must therefore represent an inferior level of thought.

Notes

1. Zaehner, R. *Hinduism*, Oxford, 1962, p. 106.
2. Scheuer, J. *Śiva dans le Mahābhārata*, Paris, 1982, p. 282.
3. O'Flaherty, W. *The Origins of Evil in Hindu Mythology*, Berkeley, 1976, p. 19.
4. Scheuer 1982, p. 285.
5. O'Flaherty 1976, p. 26.
6. See, for example, 6.49.2, 6.58.1. Dumézil discusses at length Dhṛtarāṣṭra's use of the notion of *daivam* as an excuse for his own misdeeds (Dumézil, G. *Mythe et Épopée: L'Idéologie de Trois Functions dans les Épopées des Peuples Indoeuropéens*, Paris, 1968, pp. 162-177).
7. *ya ātmano duścaritād aśubhaṁ prāpnuyān naraḥ*
   enasā na sa daivaṁ vā kālaṁ vā gantum arhati (5.156.9).
8. This principle cannot, however, be extended to Kṛṣṇa's teachings to Arjuna in the *Aśvamedhika*, beginning from the *Anugītā*, which are based on Epic Sāṁkhya and display no interest in the preservation of *sva-dharma*.

CHAPTER 10

CREATION: THE EPIC'S TEACHINGS ON THE ORIGINS OF THIS WORLD

1. Eternality and Repeated Creations

(i) Introduction

Within the *Mahābhārata* as in the *Purāṇas* two currents thought regarding the creation of the world may be identified. According to Macdonell, "The one regards the universe as the result of mechanical production, the work of carpenter's and joiner's skills, the other represents it as the result of natural generation".[1] Hopkins similarly notes the sharp distinction between these two views of creation, with one positing the acts of a personal creator and the other seeking a scientific and philosophical explanation of the world.[2] The bulk of this chapter will be devoted to an examination of these two perspectives and discussion of the relationships between them.

One central doctrine, however, that is common to all teachings on creation is the assertion that it is an eternally repeated process. There is not one creation that sets the universe in motion but a cycle of creation and destruction, manifestation and withdrawal, that has no beginning and will never end. Nowhere in the epic is there evidence of this view being challenged by a doctrine expounding an original creation out of nothing. The doctrine of repeated creations is set out specifically in the *Bhagavad-gītā*, the *Mokṣa-dharma* and the *Nārāyaṇīya.*

(ii) The *Bhagavad-gītā*

In a short passage in Chapter 8, the *Gītā* refers to the periods of time when creation is manifest as the days of Brahmā, and the periods of non-manifestation following universal destruction as his nights. One thousand *yugas* together is called the day of Brahmā and the same period constitutes the night which follows it (17). From the unmanifest, or a state of non-manifestation, all manifestations come into being at the start of the day–*avyaktād vyaktayaḥ sarvāḥ prabhavanty ahar-āgame*–and when the night comes they disappear once more; this is known as the non-manifest state–*rātry-āgame pralīyante tatraivāvyakta-saṁjñake* (18). Again and again having become manifest, all living beings are again withdrawn–*bhūta-grāmaḥ sa evāyaṁ bhūtvā bhūtvā pralīyate.* This happens when the night comes, and they have no power over the situation; when the day comes they emerge once more–*rātry-āgame 'vaśaḥ pārtha prabhavaty ahar-āgame* (19).

The *Gītā* presents no detailed doctrine or myth of creation, though both the idea of creation by the Deity, and that of the generation of the elements are referred to (10.6-8/14.3-4 and 13.21 respectively). In Chapter 9, the period when the creation is manifest is designated as a *kalpa.* At the end of the *kalpa* all beings, or possibly the elements of matter–*sarva-bhūtāni*–enter into the original substance of matter, which belongs to Kṛṣṇa–*prakṛtiṁ yānti māmikām*–and at the beginning of the *kalpa* he creates them–*tāni kalpādau visṛjāmy aham* (7). After being merged back into *prakṛti,* they are created by Kṛṣṇa again and again–*prakṛtiṁ svām avaṣṭabhya visṛjāmi punaḥ punaḥ.* They are powerless in this process for they are fully under the control of the material energy–*bhūta-grāmam imaṁ kṛtsnam avaśaṁ prakṛter vaśāt* (8). Here the phrase *punaḥ punaḥ* clearly indicates that the process of creation is continually repeated as the cycle of *kalpas* stretches on into eternity.

Thus for the *Gītā* there is no question of creation *ex nihilo. Prakṛti,* the basic matter from which all creation is formed, as well as *puruṣa,* the soul which is the element of life, are both without beginning (13.20). The process of creation and annihilation is that by which these eternal realities are activated and again made still in a state of non-manifestation.

(iii) The *Mokṣa-dharma* and the *Nārāyaṇīya*

That this view is not confined to the *Gītā* is apparent from several passages in the *Mokṣa-dharma* and the *Nārāyaṇīya.* In 12.203, the *guru* instructs his disciple that after the destruction Viṣṇu creates once more, though here it is stated that this takes place at the beginning of the *yuga* rather than the *kalpa* (14). In Chapter 224, Vyāsa refers to the repeated periods of manifestation and withdrawal in identical terms to those used by Kṛṣṇa in the passage cited above from Chapter 8 of the *Gītā* (30). The account of creation given by Vasiṣṭha in Chapter 291 begins with reference to the universal destruction (13). This night of Brahmā is of the same duration as his day and when it has passed Brahmā awakens and begins to create again (14). In Chapter 300, Yājñavalkya refers to creation and annihilation as a process that is enacted time after time–*yathā saṁharate jantūn sasarha ca punaḥ punaḥ* (2).

In the *Nārāyaṇīya*, the creation of the cosmos by Nārāyaṇa is referred to in Chapter 326 of the *Śānti*. There the Deity tells Nārada that at the end of 1,000 *yugas* he will withdraw the universe once more–*saṁhariṣye jagat punaḥ* (66). He will remain alone with wisdom, and then create the universe again by means of that wisdom–*tato bhūyo jagat sarvaṁ kariṣyāmīha vidyayā* (67). Here the word *bhūyaḥ*, meaning again or once more, is strongly indicative of creation as a repeated process. In Chapter 329, Kṛṣṇa tells Arjuna that after 4,000 *yugas* all beings merge into the unmanifest. After a period of non-manifestation, the process of generation begins once more with the appearance of Brahmā (2-11).

Such passages[3] reveal that for the *Mahābhārata* creation is not *ex nihilo* but is a cyclic process of repeated generation and withdrawal stretching forwards and backwards into eternity. There are obvious differences between the passages regarding the duration of each manifestation and also variance in the terminology employed. Such differences do not, however, affect the basic premise that the stuff of which the cosmos is made is eternally existent.

2. The Mythic Understanding of Creation

(i) Narrations of the Creation Myth

Having established this common doctrine of the epic, I will now examine the two predominant perspectives on creation found in the text referred to in the quotation from Macdonell cited above. I propose first to look at the main passages in which creation is described as being the work of the Supreme Deity. The idea that the principal Deity of the epic, Viṣṇu, is the creator of the universe is clearly central to the *Mahābhārata*'s view of this world. Not only is a Vaiṣṇava creation myth narrated in several places, but repeatedly Viṣṇu, Kṛṣṇa, and occasionally Śiva are glorified as the creator of the cosmos. A few examples from many will serve to illustrate the point–*parāvarāṇāṁ sraṣṭāram,* creator of the exalted and degraded (1.1.21, Viṣṇu); *sraṣṭāraṁ sarva-bhūtānām,* the creator of all beings (3.13.43, Kṛṣṇa); *tvaṁ naḥ sraṣṭā* and *tvayā sṛṣṭam idaṁ sarvam,* you are our (the gods') creator, and, by you all this is created (3.100.18, Nārāyaṇa); *kṛṣṇaś ca sraṣṭā jagataḥ,* Kṛṣṇa is the creator of the world (8.22.49); *viśvakarman namas te 'stu,* obeisances to you who are the maker of all things (12.43.5, Kṛṣṇa); *namas te bhagavan viṣṇo lokānāṁ nidhanodbhava,* obeisances to you, O worshipful Viṣṇu, who are the beginning and end of the worlds (12.51.2); *mahādevo jagat sṛṣṭvā carācaram,* the Great Lord created the world with its moving and non-moving beings (13.14.185, Śiva); *bhavān visṛjate lokān bhavān saṁharate punaḥ,* you create the worlds and you destroy them again (13.126.26, Śiva).

These references are expanded upon in several passages which recount either the creation myth in full or else principal elements of the myth. I do not propose to go through the exact wording of these narrations in detail, for to do so would not contribute greatly to the present discussion. Instead I will concentrate on noting the major elements of the story which individual passages serve to highlight.[4]

1. The Vaiṣṇava creation myth forms a part of the story of the killing of the *asura* Dhundhu by King Kuvalasva told by Mārkaṇḍeya to Yudhiṣṭhira in Chapters 194 and 195 of the *Vana.* When asked about the origin of Dhundhu, the sage tells Yudhiṣṭhira of the time of dissolution when there was nothing but one terrible mass of water (8). On that water Viṣṇu, the creator of the world–*loka-kartā*–sleeps on his serpent bed (9-10). From his navel grows a radiant lotus flower and on that flower the mighty Brahmā appears–*utpannaḥ pitāmahaḥ* (11-12). After some time two Dānavas named Madhu and Kaiṭabha see Viṣṇu lying there on his vast bed, with his crown, Kaustubha gem and yellow garments (13-15). Seeing Brahmā on the lotus they are astonished, but Brahmā fears them and his trembling shakes the lotus and causes Viṣṇu to awaken (16-17). He offers Madhu and Kaiṭabha a boon, but they laugh and offer him a boon instead (18-20). Viṣṇu accepts this offer and for the good of the worlds–*loka-hitāya*–says that he desires their destruction (21-22). They reply that they have never spoken falsely and possess all noble qualities; overcome by time, or destiny, they

now face great danger. In return for the boon they have offered they ask to be killed in a place that is uncovered–*anāvṛte 'sminn ākāśe*–and to become his sons (23-27). Viṣṇu agrees to these requests, but there is no uncovered space at this time either on earth or in heaven. Seeing his own thighs uncovered, he then kills them there with his *cakra* weapon (28-30).

In Chapter 195, the story moves on to tell how Dhundhu was the son of Madhu and Kaiṭabha. The narration in Chapter 194 centres only on one aspect of the creation story, that of the killing of the two Dānavas, for this is what the context demands. The idea of the generation of the demiurge from a lotus growing from the navel of the Deity is mentioned only as it relates to this conflict, and there is no reference to the subsequent acts of creation that follow the killing or even how it is that the Dānavas act to impede the work of creation.

2. In 5.128.49, Vidura refers to the killing of Madhu and Kaiṭabha, though without mentioning creation. Here an alternative element is introduced by his statement that Viṣṇu kills them in this horse-headed form, Hayagrīva.

3. As a part of Bhīṣma's teaching to Duryodhana about the greatness of Nārāyaṇa, a rather vague account of creation is given in which he cites Mārkaṇḍeya, the speaker of the passage from the *Vana* discussed above, as his source (6.63.1-2). Vāsudeva, the Supreme Person, created–*akalpayat*–water, air and fire, and after creating earth, lay down on the waters in yogic slumber (3-4). He created fire from his mouth, air from his breath, speech and the Vedas from his mind (5). In the beginning he created the worlds, the gods and *ṛṣis*, along with the destruction and death of all beings (6). He is his own master, the creator and the creative act–*eṣa kartā ca kāryaṁ ca* (7). He created all that was, is and will be, the twilight, the directions, the sky and its limits–*khaṁ ca niyamaṁ ca* (8). He created the sages and their penances and also the one who creates the world–*sraṣṭāraṁ jagataś cāpi* (9). He created Saṁkarṣaṇa, the first-born, and he created Śeṣa, known as Ananta, who upholds the earth, and is perceived through *yoga* meditation (10-11). From his ear came the fierce *asura*, Mạdhu, who terrified Brahmā and was slain by the Lord, who is therefore renowned as Madhusūdana; he also appears as a boar, lion, and the one who takes three strides (12-13). He is the mother and father of all beings, no being is higher than him; from his mouth he created the *brāhmaṇas*, from

his arms the *kṣatriyas,* from his thighs the *vaiśyas,* and from his feet the *śūdras* (14-15).

The central theme of Bhīṣma's discourse is the tremendous power of Nārāyaṇa against which Duryodhana is contending in the battle, and the description of creation has this as its main focus. Hence Brahmā has virtually no role in the creative process, and is introduced only to provide a cause for the Deity's destruction of a powerful adversary. Here only Madhu is referred to, without Kaiṭabha, and we are now told that the *asura* is born from the ear of Viṣṇu. There is also some connection between this passage and the Sāṁkhya view of creation, in that Nārāyaṇa is described as personally creating the basic elements of matter, fundamental to the Sāṁkhya view of the universe and its generation. There is also a passing reference to the cosmic man of the *Puruṣa-sūkta* from whose body the creation was formed, though here it is spoken of only in terms of the four *varṇas.*

4. In the midst of the *Mokṣa-dharma,* Yudhiṣṭhira suddenly asks Bhīṣma to tell him about Nārāyaṇa, Viṣṇu (using both names), who is the uncreated creator–*kartāram akṛtam* (12.200.2). Bhīṣma replies by saying he will present teachings on this subject as he has learned them from several sages, including the four mentioned by Arjuna in the *Gītā* (10.13) — Nārada, Asita, Devala and Vyāsa — as well as the familiar figure of Mārkaṇḍeya and also those who are knowers of the *Purāṇas.*

The Supreme Person created–*anvakalpayat*–the great elements, air, fire, water, sky and earth, and then lay down on his bed on the waters (8-9). Whilst lying down, filled with potency, he thought of Saṁkarṣaṇa, the first born who gives shelter to all, who is known as the mind, who supports the universe, and is the soul of all beings (10-11). After the appearance of that great one, an effulgent lotus grew from the navel of the Lord on which Brahmā appeared (12-13). Then, from the darkness, Madhu the first-born *asura* was born. He was fierce in all ways and terrified Brahmā; the Lord slew him and hence is known as Madhusūdana (14-16).

From his mind Brahmā created seven sons, Marīci, Atri, Aṅgiras, Pulastya, Pulaha, Kratu and Dakṣa, and Marīci created Kaśyapa from his mind, while Dakṣa begot thirteen daughters the eldest of whom was Diti, and these became wives of Kaśyapa (17-21). Dharma married ten other daughters of Dakṣa and begot the gods known as the Vasus, Rudras, Viśvedevas, Sādhyas and Maruts

(22-23). Soma married twenty-seven daughters of Dakṣa, and the others begot *gandharvas*, horses, birds, cows, *kimpuruṣas*, fish, plants and trees (24-25). Aditi begot the Ādityas, the highest of the gods, of whom Viṣṇu in the form of Vāmana became the master. He increased the prosperity of the gods, vanquishing Dānavas, Daityas and *asuras* (26-27). Danu begot Vipracitti and other Dānavas, while Diti begot the mighty *asuras* (28). Madhusūdana created day and night, time, the seasons, morning and evening, water and clouds, all moving and non-moving beings and the entire earth (29-30). From his mouth Kṛṣṇa created 100 *brāhmaṇas*, from his arms 100 *kṣatriyas*, from his thighs 100 *vaiśyas* and from his feet 100 *śūdras* (31-32). He made Dhātṛ, the Ordainer for all beings (33). The chapter concludes (33-46) by mention of the *yugas* in which sex became necessary for procreation and a list of sinful tribes. In Chapter 201, Bhīṣma again lists the *prajāpatis* who were sons of Brahmā, and the names of their various descendants.

Again in this passage we have the idea that the principal elements of matter were generated by Viṣṇu himself before he lay down on the waters and manifested the lotus from his navel. Here also Madhu appears alone to threaten Brahmā, but this time he is stated to have been born from the darkness rather than the ear of the Deity. Brahmā's role in creation is limited to being the original procreator; he produces offspring from his mind and they give birth to the different species of living beings that populate the universe. There is no indication that Brahmā creates the different worlds and after verse 29, which marks a clear change of emphasis, it becomes apparent that Viṣṇu himself does most of the creative work, though little detail is given. There appears in fact to be some dissonance between the understanding of Brahmā as the original procreator and the statement of verse 30 that Viṣṇu himself created all beings, possibly indicating that two separate creation traditions have been combined in this passage.

5. In Chapter 298 of the *Śānti*, Yājñavalkya gives a version of creation based on Sāṁkhya. Chapter 299 opens with a discussion of the duration of the time over which each creation extends. After the dissolution, the Unmanifest first creates plants, for they provide life for all beings–*sṛjaty oṣadhim evāgre jīvanaṁ sarva-dehinām* (2). He then creates Brahmā from a golden egg, which is called the form of all beings–*sā mūrtiḥ sarva-bhūtānām ity evam anuśuśruma* (3). After living for a year in the egg, Prajāpati emerges

and creates the earth in one place and the heavens in another with space in between; the Vedas–*vedeṣu paṭhyate*–are cited as authority for this statement (4-5). The *ṛṣi* then creates self-awareness which is the most wonderful thing–*sṛjaty ahaṁkāram ṛṣir bhūtaṁ divyātmakaṁ tathā.* Previously he created four other sons from his body who are known as the fathers of the ancestors–*pitṛbhyaḥ pitaraḥ* (7). The gods are the sons of the ancestors, and it is heard that all the worlds were covered by them with moving and non-moving beings (8). Self-awareness, the supreme factor–*parameṣṭhī tv ahaṁkāraḥ*–created the five elements, earth, air, space, water and light (9). The day of this *ahaṁkāra* is said to last for 5,000 *kalpas* (10).

This short passage presents a very different version of the creation story, weaving mythic elements into an essentially philosophical discourse. Viṣṇu is not mentioned by name but may be identified as the Unmanifest which is the creator of Brahmā. Brahmā is generated from an egg rather than a lotus, but he still acts as the original progenitor from whom all living beings are descended. I propose to consider the whole passage in more detail later and examine the relationship between the protagonists of the myth and different features of the Sāṁkhya analysis, but at this point it is sufficient to note this short discourse as an interesting variant on the familiar creation story.

6. The *Nārāyaṇīya* contains two brief and one longer account of the creation by Nārāyaṇa. In Chapter 326, in six verses, the Deity tells Nārada of his creative acts. After 1,000 *yugas* he withdraws the universe once more, taking all creatures back into himself (66). After remaining alone he again manifests this world through his wisdom–*vidyayā* (67). He then creates Śeṣa, his fourth form, who is Saṁkarṣaṇa, and from him Pradyumna arises (68). From Pradyumna comes Aniruddha, and it is he who repeatedly creates the world; from Aniruddha, Brahmā is born on the lotus (69). From Brahmā come all living beings; this creation takes place again and again at the beginning of each *kalpa* (70).

This short passage describes the generation of the creative demiurge, Brahmā, who is born from a lotus that grows out of the navel of Viṣṇu. Here, as in 12.200, there is reference to the creation of Śeṣa who supports the Earth on his head, and also an interpretation of the myth in terms of the Pañcarātric concept of the *caturvyūha,* the four forms of Nārāyaṇa. In line with this doctrine, the Viṣṇu form who inaugurates the creative process is named as Aniruddha, the fourth expansion from the Deity.

7. In Chapter 329, responding to a question from Arjuna about the birth of Agni and Soma, Kṛṣṇa gives a short recitation of the creation myth. During the period of non-manifestation darkness spread everywhere and all that existed was one expanse of water. From this darkness the eternal Viṣṇu appears. From Viṣṇu, Brahmā appeared taking his birth on a lotus flower and, desiring progeny, he generated Agni and Soma (2-14). This short account contains the basic idea of Brahmā taking birth from a lotus and generating offspring to populate the world. The theme of the birth of Agni and Soma has Vedic antecedents and this connection is reinforced by a citation from the Vedas regarding the chaos prior to creation.

8. Chapter 335 contains the most substantial narration of the creation myth found in the epic. It begins with Janamejaya asking Vaiśaṁpāyana about Hayaśiras, Nārāyaṇa's horse-headed form. In reply Vaiśaṁpāyana refers to a conversation between Yudhiṣṭhira and Vyāsa on the subject of why the Deity assumes this form. Vyāsa begins by stating that all things in this world come from a combination of five basic elements, which are born from the intellect of the Deity–*īśvara-buddhi-jāḥ* (10). The Deity is Nārāyaṇa the soul of all beings, giver of gifts, and creator of the cosmos (11). At the time of destruction the elements merge into the unmanifest and darkness covers everything (12-14). From the darkness *brahman* arises, for the darkness is the origin and is immortal. That *brahman* is known as the existence of all things–*viśva-bhāva-saṁjñātam*–and, when taking a body, as the *puruṣa* (15). He is Aniruddha, the original essence–*pradhāna,* known as the unmanifest which consists of the three *guṇas* (16).

He is Lord Hari who with his wisdom creates all things, and who lies on his bed on the waters considering the creation of the world (17). He thus recalls the Mahat, his personal attribute–*mahān ātma-guṇaḥ*–and then self-awareness–*ahaṁkāra*–is born as the pure one, Brahmā, who has four faces, on a lotus with 1,000 petals that comes from Aniruddha. Seeing the worlds covered in water, he begins to create different living beings (18-20). Previously on a petal of the lotus two drops of water had been made by Nārāyaṇa. The Lord saw that one of these was beautiful like honey, and from this by his desire Madhu appeared, while from the other, which was very hard, came Kaiṭabha (21-23). Endowed with the qualities of *rajas* and *tamas,* these two inspected the lotus stalk and saw Brahmā creating the Vedas (24-25). They seized the Vedas from Brahmā and took them to the depths of the ocean (26-27). In despair Brahmā prayed to the Lord, lamenting that with the Vedas lost it was impossible for him to create the world (28-33).

In verse 34 to 43, Brahmā offers further prayers to Nārāyaṇa referring to his previous births from the mind, eyes, speech, ears and nose of the Deity, and from an egg. His present appearance from the lotus is the seventh. Nārāyaṇa then assumes his vast form of Hayaśiras with a horse's head and some characteristics of the *viśva-rūpa* such as the sun and moon as his eyes (44-48). Hayaśiras enters the water and fills all directions with his vibration of the sacred sound *oṁ* (49-51). Madhu and Kaiṭabha, leaving the Vedas in the lower regions, go to search out the source of the sound and Hayaśiras takes the opportunity to recover the Vedas and return them to Brahmā (52-53). On finding the Vedas gone, the *asuras* search for them outside the water and discover Aniruddha lying on his snake bed (54-58). Amazed by the sight they laugh at him and accuse him of having taken the Vedas from them (59-61). Nārāyaṇa then sets his mind on battle and kills Madhu and Kaiṭabha in order to please Brahmā and end his grief (62-65). The work of creation is then resumed by Brahmā who creates all the worlds, while Viṣṇu vanishes back whence he came (66-67).

This lengthy recitation comes not in response to an inquiry about creation, but about Nārāyaṇa's form as Hayaśiras. In fact it is only here and in 5.128 that we are told that Madhu and Kaiṭabha were slain by the Deity in this form. Here also we get more detail about the exact nature of the obstruction to creation presented by the two *asuras*. Other versions state that they terrified Brahmā, but here we learn that they stole the Vedas which apparently are essential for the creative act. There is considerable difference of detail from 3.194, the other main description of the killing of the *asuras*, and no mention of the offering of boons which is central to that version.

The process of creation is only briefly described here, as most attention is focused on overcoming the obstacles, but Brahmā does appear to be the actual creator of worlds rather than the mere progenitor as in 12.200, whilst Viṣṇu does no more than generate the demiurge and overcome the obstacle presented by Madhu and Kaiṭabha. The influence of Sāṁkhya and Pañcarātra is apparent here in verses 10 to 16. The dissolution is described in terms of the elements merging back into each other and finally into the unmanifest, and the form of Viṣṇu from whom Brahmā appears is explained in terms of the Pañcarātric *catur-vyūha* as being Aniruddha, an aspect of the story found only in the *Nārāyaṇīya.* Aniruddha is the *puruṣa* who generates first the Mahat, or great quality, and then the element known as *ahaṁkāra* which is here equated with Brahmā.

(ii) Overview

The above survey reveals that the epic's teachings on creation draw on a central myth which is retold in different versions at different points in the text. Into this basic story the different reciters have woven other elements that reflect their individual concerns. In 6.63 and 12.200, the Sāṁkhya doctrine of the elements of matter appears, so that Viṣṇu generates these elements prior to the commencement of creation proper and only lies down on the waters after bringing them into being. This version may also serve to resolve the difficulty of how the great ocean could exist before creation, as well as presenting a creation story that is to some extent in harmony with Sāṁkhya doctrines.

Hopkins[5] and other scholars have suggested on the basis of several myths in the epic that originally Brahmā was recognised as the Supreme Deity, while the trinitarian ideas of later Hinduism grant him a position equal to that of Viṣṇu and Śiva, with the function of creation. In the *Mahābhārata,* his links with the creative process are clearly established, though he also acts in the role of sustainer by assisting the gods in times of trouble. In some versions of the creation myth, Brahmā's role is no more than that of the first progenitor, with Viṣṇu as the actual creator, while in others he retains the latter function. Nowhere in the creation narratives, however, do we find any indication that Brahmā is the Supreme Deity and his position is always subordinate to that of Viṣṇu.

(iii) The Myth of Creation from an Egg

By way of postscript I would like to touch briefly on the debate within the epic on the idea of creation from a primeval egg. Chapter 138 of the *Anuśāsana* contains a conversation between Vāyu and Kārtavīrya Arjuna in which the wind god demonstrates the superiority of *brāhmaṇas* over *kṣatriyas.* As an example he refers to the power of Brahmā, who is apparently a *brāhmaṇa,* by whom the entire world was made (15). Some who are fools–*apaṇḍitāḥ*–

try to say that Brahmā was born from an egg and that when the egg is divided it forms the mountains, directions, water, earth and heaven (16). None of this was seen by anyone, for if it was how could Brahmā then be the eldest? It is known that space is an egg and it was from this that Brahmā took birth (17). It may be asked where he could situate himself, for nothing existed at that time; but *ahaṁkāra,* the Lord, full of all potency was there (18). There is no egg, but there is Brahmā, the creator of the world–*loka-bhāvana* (19).

This passage offers a fleeting glimpse into the debates taking place in the epic period. It is impossible to fully reconstruct the controversy over creation reflected here, but it is apparent that different theories existed side by side. The *Mahābhārata* itself reflects more than one perspective, acting as a compendium to include a range of views. Thus we may note that 1.1.27, 12.298.3 and 12.335.39 all refer to the idea of the generation of Brahmā from an egg so roundly condemned here. Finally, it is again interesting to note the way in which this passage combines a mythic description of creation with Sāṁkhya concepts. Here there is no reference to Viṣṇu generating Brahmā, so the author recognises the problem of Brahmā appearing from nothing into nothing (18). In the myth this is explained by the figure of Viṣṇu lying on the waters, but here this role is taken by the Sāṁkhya principle of *ahaṁkāra,* self-awareness, referred to as *prabhu,* the master, who contains all potency within himself–*sarva-tejo-gataḥ*.[6]

3. The Sāṁkhya Concept of Creation

The passages discussed above present different versions of a central creation myth. The *Mahābhārata,* however, also includes a different view of creation which moves away from a mythic understanding towards a more scientific view based on Sāṁkhya theories. The concept of matter being divided into enumerated elements is central to Sāṁkhya thought, and this involves a doctrine of the original generation of these elements from the primary material substance. This is clearly a form of scientific analysis, and, according to Frauwallner, "The characteristic of these texts is striking. It is the spirit of natural science which here governs, the attempt to create a picture of the external world based on observation and experience."[7] One should not, however, lose sight of the fact that the primary aim of Sāṁkhya was to realise the self as separate from matter and thereby attain salvation, thus extending the system far beyond natural science as it is understood today. The generation of the elements is described in several passages of the epic, most of which are found in the *Mokṣa-dharma.*

1. Chapter 224 of the *Śānti* marks the beginning of the *Śukānupraśna,* in which Vyāsa instructs his son, Śuka. The first inquiry (9) requests instruction about the creator of living beings, the divisions of time and the duties of a *brāhmaṇa.* Vyāsa replies by saying that in the beginning only *brahman* existed, and giving the divisions of time from the wink of an eye up to a *yuga.*[8] He then discusses the four *yugas,* before describing the periods of creation and destruction (11-31).

All the world comes from the energetic *brahman*; from this one element comes a second and this consists of all beings (32). Awakening at the beginning of his day, he creates the world through his wisdom; at first there is the great element, mind, which is the very essence of the manifest world–*vyaktātmakaṁ manaḥ* (33). Predominating over all things here like the sun, it then creates seven expansions of the mind, for the mind goes far away following paths of reflection with doubt and desire as its essence (34). Creation arises from transformations of the mental factor which produce space which has sound as its quality (35). From space comes wind, the bearer of aromas, of which touch is the quality, and when air is modified, light comes into being with form as its quality (36-37). From a modification of light comes water with the quality of flavour, and from water comes earth with the quality of aroma; all this is the original creation–*pūrvaiṣā sṛṣṭir ucyate* (38).

Each element absorbs the qualities of its antecedents and thus possesses those qualities as well as its own, so if one detects aroma in water it should be known to arise from contact with earth (39-40). These seven elements–*puruṣāḥ*–exist separately, and without mixing cannot produce offspring, but when they are united and in contact with the self this is called the person (41-42). Thus there arises the body with a form of sixteen elements which the living beings enter with their previous acts (43). Along with the living beings the original creator, Prajāpati, also enters the material energy to establish the paths of austerity and ritual (44). The unborn Brahmā, that supreme person, creates gods, *ṛṣis,* ancestors, men, the different worlds, rivers, ocean, directions, mountains, trees, *kinnaras, rākṣasas* and different animals, who resume their activities as in the previous creation in terms of violence or gentleness, mildness or aggression, righteousness or irreligion, according to the way that the Ordainer conceives (45-49).

The remainder of the passage contains a discussion of the dominance of destiny over endeavour and a description of each of the four *yugas*. Both Larson[9] and Frauwallner[10] are of the opinion that epic Sāṁkhya has no theory of an evolution of elements. This passage, however, confirms van Buitenen's view[11] that this conclusion is incorrect for what we have here is clearly based on an evolutionary concept of creation. The origin of creation is referred to as *brahman* and the original substance from which the elements progressively emerge is the mental faculty, *manas*. Each of the elements appears in the creative process from a transformation or modification–*vikurvāṇāt*–of its predecessor, and there can be little doubt that such an idea does indeed amount to a theory of evolution of elements. It is also interesting to note the pervasive Sāṁkhya preoccupation with salvation through realisation of the transcendence of the self. Thus although the subject here under discussion is creation, the focus is on the constitution of the body rather than the total cosmos, for it is this understanding that leads to *mokṣa*.

The passage as a whole clearly presents a different understanding of the creative process to the myths discussed earlier. Nonetheless, a close examination of the text reveals that there is no direct conflict with the mythic versions. It was noted that both 6.63 and 12.200 state that prior to the generation of Brahmā, Viṣṇu creates the five elements of which matter is comprised. Vyāsa's theory of creation may thus be taken as an expansion of such teachings, explaining in more detail how the Deity executes this preliminary task. Viṣṇu is not mentioned by name here, but his mythic function is filled by the concept of *brahman* which acts through its wisdom, *vidyayā* (33), the same term that is used in 12.326 and 12.335 in relation to the creative acts of Nārāyaṇa. Here also Brahmā begins his creation of the various objects and species only after the elements appears, a process referred to as *pūrva-sṛṣṭi* (38), the prior or original creation. Hence it is quite plausible to see this passage and the creation myths not as alternative doctrines but as complementary descriptions of the same process, each with its own centre of emphasis.

2. An interesting and possibly alternative view is found in

Chapter 267 of the *Śānti,* which tells of a discussion between the sages Nārada and Asita. At the outset Nārada asks, 'From whence has this creation arisen and into what is it withdrawn?' (3). Asita then begins his discourse. The objects from which time, under its own impulse, generates living beings are known as the five great elements; one who says there is anything more than this speaks falsely (4-5). Water, sky, earth, air and fire are eternal and unchanging and possess great energy, while time which is known as the sixth is self-existent–*kāla-ṣaṣṭhān sva-bhāvataḥ*; undoubtedly the idea that there is anything beyond these elements is imperfect–*asiddhiḥ param etebhyo bhūtebhyo mukta-saṁśayam* (6-7). Neither by demonstrable reason nor proper argument could such an assertion be true; all manifestations come from these six (8). These five eternal elements, time, the totality of existence and non-existence making the eighth, are the beginning and end of the living beings (9). They come into being through these factors out of a state of non-existence and even when the five no longer exist the living being continues (10).

Although Nārada's question–*kutaḥ sṛṣṭam idaṁ viśvam*–is about creation, Asita's response does not amount to a description of the creative process. What is notable, however, is the insistance on non-theism or even atheism which seems to dismiss the epic's creation myths. The five elements are not generated by Viṣṇu or *brahman* for they exist eternally and creation takes place under the impulse of time alone (5). Thus there is a strong implication that creation is an automatic process, instigated only by the progression of time. The idea of a creator seems to be specifically denied by the assertions of 5, 7 and 8 that anyone who teaches that there is any existence beyond the elements of matter is a fool who is unable to provide any evidence to support his dogma. Here again we are granted a glimpse into the debates of the epic period. The full doctrine of the speaker, and more especially his opponent, cannot be established precisely but a reasonable surmise is that here the *Mahābhārata* is displaying its most eclectic tendency by including a treatise from a school of atheistic Sāṁkhya which rejects the notion that the universe exists as the work of a creator God.

3. Chapter 291 of the *Śānti,* consisting of instructions given by Vasiṣṭha to Janaka, has been referred to earlier with regard to its description of the periods of creation and destruction as days and nights of Brahmā (13-14). The account of creation which follows

is obviously based on Sāṁkhya, but the role ascribed to the Deity in the process reveals at least a limited commitment to theism. Creation begins with an act of Śambhu, usually a name of Śiva, the self-born who has no form–*amūrtātman*, who creates the totality known as Mahat,[12] which has form and is endowed with unlimited acts–*sṛjaty ananta-karmāṇaṁ mahāntam* (15). This Mahat is spread throughout the cosmos entering all things; he is Hiranyagarbha, Mahat, and Viriñci (usually a name of Brahmā). The Sāṁkhya texts–*sāṁkhye ca paṭhyate śāstre*–know him by many names as the indestructible soul of all beings; all the cosmos is covered by this *ātman* who is known as the *viśva-rūpa* because he has many forms. Undergoing various modifications he creates the self through himself–*vikriyāpannaḥ sṛjaty ātmānam ātmanā*–and this self is self-awareness; it has great potency, is conscious of itself and is known as Prajāpati–*ahaṁkāraṁ mahā-tejāḥ prajāpatim ahaṁkṛtam* (16-20).

The text then describes the different stages of creation and numbers them accordingly:- 1. The wisdom creation of the manifest from the unmanifest. 2. The ignorance creation of the Mahat and *ahaṁkāra*. 3. The creation of the elements from *ahaṁkāra*. 4. The elements air, light, space, water and earth then manifest sound, touch, form, taste and aroma. 5. Centring on these objects come the senses of intellect and action–ears, skin, eyes, tongue and nose, then speech, hands, feet, anus and genitals which arise at the same time as the mind (21-27). These twenty-four principles make up the different bodies of all living beings. These are what is known as the manifest, and because they pass away day by day they are called the destructible. That which is indestructible is the twenty-fifth element and that is Viṣṇu (28-37).

There can be little doubt that the teachings expressed here reflect the doctrines of one school of Sāṁkhya, with the characteristic analysis of matter as being comprised of twenty-four elements. The passage is sometimes obscure and its logic difficult to follow but certain points are clearly made and worthy of note. This is not a non-theistic view of creation as the previous passage appeared to be, for there is reference to the creator Brahmā awakening and also to a remote formless Deity, referred to as Śambhu, who institutes the process from afar. Brahmā is equated with the Mahat, the original principle of matter, which when transformed is known as *ahaṁkāra*. Again the main focus of interest is on the bodily forms in which the transcendent element is contained. There is no reference to the generation of mountains, rivers and other natural features, or of the various worlds in which the living beings exist. It is also noteworthy that this passage displays no theory of the evolution of the elements as was noted in 12.224. The teaching indicates that they are generated simultaneously from the principle of *ahaṁkāra* along with their related sense organ and object of perception.

4. The teachings of Yājñavalkya in 12.298-300 present the lengthiest treatise on creation contained in the epic. Responding to a series of questions from Yudhiṣṭhira, Bhīṣma recalls a conversation between the sage Yājñavalkya and King Janaka, a character encountered frequently in the *Mokṣa-dharma* as a seeker after wisdom. Here Janaka is asking about the number of senses and elements, *brahman*, creation and destruction, and the divisions of time (298.5-6).

Yājñavalkya begins by identifying the teachings to come as derived from Sāṁkhya and Yoga, and then runs through the twenty-four elements of matter (8-15). The discourse turns to creation from verse 16, again enumerating the different stages of the process. 1. The conscious self, the Mahat, arises from the unmanifest–*avyaktāc ca mahān ātmā samutpadyati*. 2. *Ahaṁkāra* arises from the Mahat. 3. From *ahaṁkāra* comes the mental faculty which embodies the primary elements. 4. From the mental faculty the primary elements come into being. 5. The sense objects, sound, touch, form, taste and scent then arise. 6. Next ear, skin, eyes, tongue and nose become manifest. 7. All the senses such as hearing arise. 8. That which goes upwards and across next comes into being.[13] 9. Then there is that which flows across and downwards. Thus there are nine creations–*etāni nava sargāni*–which produce the twenty-four factors spoken of in scripture–*yathā śruti-nidarśanāt* (16-25).

In the final verse of Chapter 298, Yājñavalkya says that he is now moving on to describe the divisions of time, *kāla-sāṁkhyām* (26). Thus 299 opens with a discussion of the duration of the days and nights of the unmanifest, and the creation by the Deity who awakens at the end of the night, a passage discussed earlier in the context of creation myths (1-8). From verse 9, the text moves back to the non-mythic teachings of the previous chapter, with the statement that *ahaṁkāra* created the five elements, earth, water, fire, air, and sky; this is designated as the third creation (10). It is these elements that enshroud the living beings, giving rise to attachment, competitive striving, murderous assaults and their movements through different species (11-13). The day and night of these elements both last 3,000 *kalpas* (14). The mind perceives through the senses; in fact the senses do not truly perceive, for only the mind can do this. Thus the mind is known as the lord of the senses (15-18). Chapter 300 describes the previous chapters as discourses on *sarga-sāṁkhya* and *kāla-sāṁkhya*, the divisions of creation and the divisions of time. Brahmā, who is eternal and undecaying, creates the living beings again and again. The remainder of this chapter describes the destruction of the world under the direction of Śambhu as each element is reabsorbed into its predecessor.

This passage divides itself evenly between the three chapters; 298 is the *sarga-sāṁkhya*, the divisions of creation, and explains the generation of the elements of the body according to Sāṁkhya; 299 is designated by the somewhat inappropriate title of *kāla-sāṁkhya*, the divisions of time, and gives a brief version of the creation myth with Brahmā as the creator; 300 moves on to the destruction of the cosmos instigated by the Deity Śambhu. Again we may note how the Sāṁkhya view of creation focuses above all on the composition of the body in which the self exists, with apparently little concern for the way in which the universe itself came into being. Here nine creations are described and all of them relate to the composition of the body. In this passage there is no doctrine of the emanation of elements one from the other. The great elements appear simultaneously, as do the senses and their objects of perception. Only in the beginning stages, in the first, second and third creations (298.16-18), do we find the creative process expressed through ablatives–*avyaktāt, mahataḥ* and *ahaṁkārāt*– which indicate the concept of coming out from.

The major point of interest here, however, is the way in which the Sāṁkhya and mythic versions of creation are placed side by side and to some extent syncretised. The text of Chapter 299 makes no reference to Viṣṇu, but uses the terms *avyakta* and *mahān ātmā*, the unmanifest and the Great Soul, to indicate the origin of Brahmā, and thereby in terms of the Vaiṣṇava Sāṁkhya of the *Nārāyaṇīya* ascribes to them the mythic functions of Nārāyaṇa and Viṣṇu/Aniruddha. Verse 9 equates Brahmā with the principle of self-awareness, *ahaṁkāra*, which it also refers to as Parameṣṭhin.

The text is not explicit on this point, but the idea that *ahaṁkāra* is identified with Brahmā is strongly implied by the context. In any case the inclusion of a form of the creation myth within a Sāṁkhya discourse indicates that the author does not view his teachings as moving between two separate or conflicting views of creation. Rather he sees the creation myth either as taking place after the elements of matter are generated from the unmanifest source, or else takes the divine protagonists in the myth as personifying the primary elements in the Sāṁkhya analysis.

5. A similar passage to the teachings of Yājñavalkya is found in two short chapters of the *Aśvamedhika*, 40 and 41. The first creation is here described as the great soul of deep wisdom appearing from the unmanifest–*avyaktāt pūrvam utpanno mahān ātmā mahāmatiḥ* (1). This great soul is known as Viṣṇu and Śambhu and he is all things — intellect, wisdom, perception, insight, steadiness and memory. When he is known one becomes free from illusion (2-3). His hands, feet, eyes, ears and faces are spread everywhere as he pervades the world, for he is in the hearts of all beings, the Lord–*īśānaḥ*, the unfading light. The great renunciants and *yogins* all go to that great one (4-7); those who know the great soul are never subject to illusion. He is the self-born Viṣṇu, the master in the primary creations; one who knows that Lord concealed in the heart, the ancient person, the *viśva-rūpa*, reaches a state beyond the intellect (8-9).

Chapter 41 describes the second creation as the appearance of the original great element[14] known as self-awareness–*ya utpanno mahān pūrvam ahaṁkāraḥ sa ucyate*–that exists as the sense of 'I'–*aham ity eva saṁbhūtaḥ* (1). *Ahaṁkāra* is the original element which becomes transformed–*ahaṁkāraś ca bhūtādir vaikārika iti smṛtaḥ*; he is full of potency and conscious, the original basis–*dhātuḥ*, the creator and master of all beings (2). He is the Deity who is the source of the gods and the mind, the maker of the three worlds, the sense of 'I' known as the point of reference for all things–*tat sarvam abhimantā sa ucyate* (3). This is the eternal domain for sages constantly absorbed in knowledge of the self and for those who gain success through study and *yajña* (4). The origin and creator of all beings thus creates the different qualities. Becoming transformed, he sets all this in motion and through his potency the universe is activated (5).

This passage has clear similarities with the teachings of Yājñavalkya in 12.298-299. The first two creations, the only ones discussed here, are described in a similar way to 12.298 though here the original element is identified as *ahaṁkāra.* The first creation is the manifestation of the *ātman,* the transcendent self which is referred to as Viṣṇu and Śambhu. In the second creation, the original element, *ahaṁkāra,* appears and it is from the transformations of *ahaṁkāra* that all the other elements come into being. There are also parallels that may be drawn with the epic's creation myth. I would suggest that the Viṣṇu referred to here corresponds to the figure of Aniruddha in the *Nārāyaṇīya*'s account. He is the manifest form of the Deity who emerges from the formless Nārāyaṇa, here mentioned in 40.1 as the unmanifest. Thus the first creation is when Aniruddha, known philosophically as the *ātman,* appears in the world. The second creation is of *ahaṁkāra* and I would suggest that this corresponds to the generation of Brahmā from Viṣṇu. This would be in accordance with the version of 12.299.10 which presents the creation of the five elements from *ahaṁkāra parameṣṭhin* as the third creation.

Explicit confirmation of this view is absent from this passage, though it is found in the *Bhṛgu-bharadvāja-saṁvāda* discussed below. It does appear, however, that this account contains a philosophical equivalent to the creation myth with the Deities who act in that account functionally represented by elements in the Sāṁkhya analysis. Such an understanding of the text clearly lends weight to the view that Sāṁkhya was originally a theistic system.

6. One of the first treatise presented by the *Mokṣa-dharma* is the *Bhṛgu-bharadvāja-saṁvāda,* the discussion between Bhṛgu and Bharadvāja (12.175-185), the first two chapters of which deal with the subject of creation. Bhṛgu's exposition begins with the familiar concept of the Mahat being generated from the unmanifest, which is also referred to as *mānasa,* mental energy, and the Mahat producing the five elements (175.11-14). At this point the text introduces the creation myth by stating that the self-born one generates a lotus on which Brahmā was born. This section is of particular interest for it directly equates the Sāṁkhya principle of *ahaṁkāra* with the god Brahmā–*ahaṁkāra iti khyātaḥ* (16). Viṣṇu is then described in terms of the cosmic man of the *Puruṣa-sūkta* with the different parts of the universe comprising his body, and he is also stated to be the creator of *ahaṁkāra,* just as in the myth he is the creator of Brahmā (21).

The remainder of the chapter includes a discussion of the dimensions of the universe, and a question from Bharadvāja as to how Brahmā can be the eldest in the world when the lotus came before him (35). To this Bhṛgu replies that it is the *mānasa* taking a form that became Brahmā; the lotus, which is in fact the Earth, was created as a seat for him, and the pericarp of that lotus is Mount Meru, the pivotal centre of the world in Hindu cosmology.

Chapter 176 opens with Bharadvāja asking how Brahmā, situated on Mount Meru, creates the living beings. Bhṛgu replies that in order to arouse the living beings, the *mānasa* through mental energy–*manasā*–first created water, for it is water that sustains life (2-4). Bharadvāja then asks how water and the other great elements came into being and in reply Bhṛgu cites the teachings of a divine voice revealed to an assembly of *ṛṣis* (5-8). Before creation there was only darkness, and then water arose like another darkness in the darkness–*tataḥ salilam utpannaṁ tamasīvāparaṁ tamaḥ*–and the pressure of the water created wind (9-10). The manifestation of wind brought sound into being, and the friction of wind and water produced light (11-14). Fire in conjunction with air moved down from space to the water and because of contact with water it became solid (15). As it falls through space its liquidity gradually becomes solid and thereby the quality of earth comes into being and earth is the basis for the existence of tastes, scents, liquids and living beings; within it all things are produced (16-17). In Chapter 177, Bharadvāja asks why amongst all things in creation–*bhūtāḥ*–the five elements are referred to as *mahā-bhūtāḥ*, the great elements. In response, Bhṛgu explains that these five pervade the bodies of all beings and are found throughout creation.

In this passage we find an explicit statement from the text that the principle of *ahaṁkāra* is to be identified with Brahmā. There is a scientific feel to the discourse in Chapter 176, with the generation of wind being explained as displacement caused by the entry of water, friction of water and air generating fire and the falling of fire through space into water causing solidification into earth. There is no recourse to a creating Deity here and the way in which one element emerges from the interaction of the others is explained in a rational fashion, with the sudden appearance of water into the darkness acting as a kind of 'big bang' that sets the process in motion. There is no hint, however, that such a view is recognised as being in conflict with the theistic version. Also noteworthy here is the manner in which the creation myth is made compatible with Hindu cosmology by the assertion that the centre of the lotus is Mount Meru, the hub of the universe, an idea unique in the epic to this passage.

4. Conclusions

At the beginning I referred to Macdonnell's view that the Hindu epics and *Purāṇas* had two concepts of creation, one through the work of a creator God and the other by the generation of matter from an original substance. The ensuing discussion has shown that in the case of the *Mahābhārata* this view is substantially correct, for two distinctive approaches to the subject of creation have been recognised. In one Viṣṇu brings this world into being through the demiurge, Brahmā, who creates the universe, generates progeny, and establishes the cosmic order. The second is based on the Sāṁkhya view of existence and seeks to identify the manner in which the twenty-four elements of which all bodies consist came into being. Classical Sāṁkhya expresses the idea of evolution and emanation, with each element emerging from a modification of its predecessor. This idea is found in the epic only to a limited extent, most notably in 12.224, and in a manner that falls short of the fully developed theory.

Although two distinct perspectives on creation can be identified, there is a lack of uniformity within the two types. The myth is narrated differently by different speakers, and the Sāṁkhya discourses betray different philosophical perspectives and possibly different schools of thought from which they arose. Furthermore, the distinction between them is not absolute. The versions of the creation myth presented in 6.63 and 12.200 include passages in which the principal elements of matter are generated, while the Pañcarātric recital of the story in the *Nārāyaṇīya* displays the characteristic connection between that branch of Hindu theism and Sāṁkhya. Similarly, frequent references are made to the creation myth in the Sāṁkhya discourses, and only in 12.267 does there appear to be a direct refutation of mythic version.

There are strong indications that the teachers of Sāṁkhya have attempted to harmonise their doctrines with the theistic view by equating principles of their analysis with the deities of the myth, with Viṣṇu as the *avyakta* and Brahmā as *ahaṁkāra*. How far the authors of the theistic story are aware of Sāṁkhya ideas is unclear, but it is apparent that the teachers of Sāṁkhya knew the creation myth and did not view it as incompatible with their own doctrines. The theism of the Sāṁkhya accounts is, however, clearly distinct from that of the myth and again reveals the movement away from the Vedic understanding of a pantheon of gods. In the myth Viṣṇu and Brahmā are depicted as Vedic-style gods seeking to promote the harmony of creation and overcoming the forces of chaos to do so. Sāṁkhya theism, however, presents the Deity as a remote cosmic being who is the unmanifest source out of which all the elements of creation emerge. There are thus two concepts of Viṣṇu, one as a god who lies on the waters and with Brahmā creates the world, and the other as the unmanifest source out of which all beings and all elements of creation emerge and into which they are reabsorbed at the time of universal distruction.[15]

Western thought has come to recognise a dichotomy between science and religion, particularly in consideration of the origins and purpose of the physical universe. It is tempting to identify a similar dichotomy in Hindu thought with the creation myth representing the view of the religious orthodoxy and the teachings of the Sāṁkhya schools as a quasi-scientific perspective. Such an analysis would be both superficial and misleading, for it is clear that in the epic no such dichotomy exists. It has been noted that only in one passage does Sāṁkhya teaching appear to refute the theistic understanding of the world, and that typically the teachings recognise both views of creation as integral to the process as a whole. Sāṁkhya is not a scientific mode of thought in anything like the modern sense, for it is essentially a spiritual and arguably a mystical system aiming above all at realising the transcendent nature of the self. Typically, epic Sāṁkhya recognises the position of the creation myth in its understanding of the world. Indeed one cannot ignore the possibility that the two distinctive approaches to creation that I have followed Macdonnell in recognising were not seen as separate by the authors of the epic, and that such an apparently obvious alternation of perspectives would be recognised as such only by one whose logic had been thoroughly conditioned by Western culture.

5. Theodicy: The Problem of Suffering in Creation

(i) Introduction

The problem of theodicy is one that has taxed Western theistic thought for thousands of years. In essence the problem is a simple one; if the creating Deity is all-powerful and all-good, then why is there so much suffering built into his creative work. Max Weber[16] has urged that the doctrine of transmigration and *karma* successfully resolves the question by making man solely responsible for his own destiny. Herman[17] has rightly pointed out, however, that Weber was too quick to accept the doctrine of *karma* as a solution, for the idea of an unbreakable universal law begs questions about the nature of the Deity's omnipotence. True solutions to the problem must accept that the Deity is either not omnipotent or not all-benign, or else try to explain how suffering somehow has a positive, if incomprehensible, purpose for the overall good of humanity. Western theism has traditionally looked to the third of these options though with questionable degrees of success, for it is desperately difficult to demonstrate that the miseries wrought by wars, famines and natural disasters are in fact a mysterious display of divine benevolence.

In the *Mahābhārata* the question of whether the Deity is benign is answered essentially by the affirmative, but this view is not unmixed. God acts in this world to sustain *dharma* and to protect those who follow *dharma*, but those who oppose his will are destroyed utterly without any sense of compassion. Thus the *asuras* are massacred by both Viṣṇu and Śiva because it is the divine will that the gods should pr evail; the Kauravas and most of the warriors in the Pāṇḍava host are slain in droves at Kurukṣetra without any concern being shown by Kṛṣṇa, and, when it suits his purpose, even the Yādavas, Kṛṣṇa's own family, are brought to a violent and humiliating end.

Viṣṇu is typically portrayed as benign in the epic, acting for the good of the world, but the Deity also has a destructive and frightful aspect, usually manifest through the person of Śiva but also made apparent in the *Gītā* in the revelation of the *viśva-rūpa*. This point is emphasised by Heesterman who writes, "The transcendent does not submit to any system, to any order but its own. In its unpredictability, it is full of terror for man, as the theophany of the *Bhagavad-gītā* — to take just one example — shows us."[18] Chapters 172 and 173 of the *Droṇa*, and the whole of the *Sauptika*, reveal that the Deity is not just a benign protector of humanity, but is also a ferocious destroyer, as the typical iconography of Śiva indicates. The Deity of the epic is hence not fully benign in his attitude towards humanity. *Dharma* and the cosmic order must be sustained and to some extent humanity benefits from this, but in order to maintain this *status quo* neither Viṣṇu nor Śiva display much hesitation in besetting mortal beings with terrible afflictions.

Although the epic contains numerous assertions that both Viṣṇu and Śiva are the complete controllers of all existence, the stress on divine omnipotence is moderated by the fact that creation is not ex nihilo. Even in the recountings of the creation myth in which Viṣṇu is clearly the controlling Deity, there is a sense in which he appears to be playing a role in what is in effect an automatic process. In the revolving progression of time the point of creation comes around according to schedule and it is not specified as to whether creation takes place because God wills it to be so at that point, or whether he enacts the creative process because the appropriate juncture has been reached in the inevitable progression of time.

Similarly, the entrance of evil into human society, the fall from a primeval state of human perfection, is described in terms of the progression of *yugas*. The question of why the Deity allows this evil to become manifest does not arise because it appears that he works in this world within the strictures imposed by cosmic time. Again if we look at the myth of the origin of death, narrated in Chapters 248-250 of the *Śānti*, we find the omnipotence of the controlling Deities, Brahmā and Śiva, to be compromised. It is recognised that death is a great cause of suffering in the world, to the extent that when she is created she is unwilling to execute her duty. Nonetheless, Brahmā insists that death must strike down all beings for there is no other way to counteract the burden to the earth due to excessive population. In other words it is accepted that death is a terrible thing, but the Deity can find no other way for his creation to function effectively. Implicitly the notion of divine omnipotence is thereby drawn into question.

Clearly the fact that epic theology does not stress the all-good and all-powerful nature of the creator God to the extent characteristic of Western theistic thought diminishes the force of the imperative towards a solution of the problem of theodicy. Nonetheless, the prevailing doctrines of the *Mahābhārata* still present a Deity who controls all things and is essentially well-disposed towards the living beings who inhabit his creation, to the extent that his motivations for intervention in this world include the protection of those who are righteous–*paritrāṇaḥ sādhūnām* (Bhg 4.8). Therefore an explanation of divine justice would still appear to be called for to explain the misery of the creation the Deity has set in motion. Following the standard pattern of epic thought such an explanation may be found along two fronts, one under the heading of *pravṛtti* or *sva-dharma,* and the other related to *nivṛtti* or *mokṣa-dharma.*

(ii) The Problem of Suffering from the Perspective of *Pravṛtti*

Weber writes, ". . . the most complete formal solution of the problem of theodicy is the special achievement of the Indian doctrine of *karma,* the so-called belief in the transmigration of souls."[19] Obeyesekere further argues that the question of theodicy is one that does not exist in Hinduism because, "In a culture which possesses a theory of suffering like that of *karma* the problem of explaining unjust suffering simply cannot arise".[20] Clearly the doctrine of *karma* switches the onus away from the Deity by making the individual entirely responsible for his own suffering, but it also begs the question of whether the Deity is under the control of the law of *karma.* As Herman contends, Kṛṣṇa must either be powerless to alter an individual's *karma,* in which case he is not omnipotent, or else unwilling to do so, in which case responsibility for suffering is thrust back onto the Deity.[21]

With these points in mind I wish now to explore how the question of suffering is related to an understanding of the effects of previous acts in the text of the *Mahābhārata.* The epic shares the view of Vedānta and Sāṁkhya that the transcendent self moves from one body to another at the time of death, transmigrating through different bodily forms. The suffering and pleasure one experiences in the present life are the direct result of pious and wicked acts performed in a previous existence. This teaching can be found explicitly laid out in the discourse of the pious hunter narrated by Mārkaṇḍeya to Yudhiṣṭhira in the *Vana* (ch 200). It is not exertion that brings success or failure, happiness or distress, but previous acts. When the individual is afflicted by diseases this is likewise to be understood as the result of some earlier contravention of *dharma* (14). All people are overwhelmed by illusion and grief, carried away by the incessant flow of actions and reactions (18). If one was able to control his own destiny by exertion, no-one would die and no-one would suffer. This is not the case because suffering arises as previous acts produce their fruits (19-20).

This philosophical perspective is not confined to the didactic passages of the epic, but is equally apparent from the attitudes and behaviour of the characters in the narrative as the tragedy unfolds and overwhelms them. The *Strī* stands out as the *parvan* of lamentation in which the major protagonists meet together on the field of battle and express their sorrow over the miseries that have arisen from the conflict. In the beginning, we find Dhṛtarāṣṭra bewailing the suffering that will dominate the remainder of his life now that his beloved sons as well as his dearest friends and advisors have been butchered in the carnage at Kurukṣetra. He first regrets ignoring the counsel he received from Kṛṣṇa, Nārada, Vyāsa and Rāma, and says he cannot recall any great wickedness he has performed in this life that would bring such misery as a result (11.1.17). Therefore he must have performed many sinful deeds in previous lives–*pūrveṣu janmasu*–and is now suffering because the Ordainer is bestowing upon him the appropriate result (18-19).

Later we find Gāndhārī's lamentation following a similar course. Seeing her sons' widows grieving over the corpses of their slain husbands, she demands of Kṛṣṇa what could possibly make her existence more miserable than seeing these women in such a plight (11.16.58). Hence she concludes that in previous lives she must have committed some grave fault–*nūnam ācaritaṁ pāpaṁ mayā pūrveṣu janmasu*–the result of which is compelling her to look upon her sons, grandsons and brothers now lying here lifeless.

References such as these provide some form of an answer to the question of divine justice. God is not responsible for the sufferings of people in this world for whatever fate they are forced to endure is entirely of their own making. If the Deity is not bound by such universal laws of action and reaction, and verses such as 12.7 of the *Gītā*–*teṣām ahaṁ samuddhartā mṛtyu-saṁsāra-sāgarāt*– would indicate that he is not, then it may be argued that he is responsible because he allows the suffering to take place. To this objection, the response must be that the Ordainer permits the suffering to descend upon the individual because it is a proper reward for evil deeds, just as in other traditions he uses eternal damnation or fire and brimstone to chastise those who have offended against his laws. John Bowker therefore contends that there can be no Hindu Job complaining that the righteous and unrighteous are both made to suffer: ". . . the problem of Job cannot arise, because it must always be the case that occurrences of suffering are a consequence of activities, not simply in this existence, but in previous ones as well."[22]

It is clear, however, that the epic does at several junctures encounter the 'problem of Job', when the suffering of the righteous is discussed. In the telling of the story of Rāma Jāmadagneya by Akṛtavraṇa to Yudhiṣṭhira (3.115-118), we find Rāma agonising and questioning how it is possible for his father, who has been murdered by the sons of Kārtavīrya Arjuna, to meet such a death when his adherence to *dharma* was so constant, when he was always truthful, and when he never injured any living being,

> *dharma-jñasya kathaṁ tāta vartamānasya sat-pathe*
> *mṛtyur evaṁ-vidho yuktaḥ sarva-bhūteṣv anāgasaḥ*
> (3.117.2)

In a similar manner Rāma the brother of Kṛṣṇa, on seeing the Pāṇḍavas forced to live in the forest, questions whether following *dharma* does bring good fortune (3.119.5-8). One of limited intelligence–*alpa-buddhiḥ*–would conclude from seeing the exaltation of Duryodhana that *adharma* is superior to *dharma*, and on seeing the way events have turned out all people are now perplexed as to how to conduct themselves.

The prime candidate for the epic Job, however, must surely be Draupadī who in Chapter 31 of the *Vana* rails against the Ordainer for his injustice in allowing the wicked to prosper while the righteous Yudhiṣṭhira is overwhelmed with discomfiture. In verses 1 to 20 she challenges the idea that adherence to *dharma* brings prosperity; Yudhiṣṭhira has never once swerved from *dharma* and yet behold the plight in which he now finds himself — humiliated, exiled, and doomed to years of unbearable poverty. She then asserts the control of the Deity, referred to as *dhātṛ* and *īśānaḥ*, over the enactment of the law of *karma*; it is he who bestows happiness and misery on the individual, controlling all people absolutely like a puppeteer with dolls or a herdsman with a bull that is roped through the nose (21-26). Ignorant and powerless in making his own happiness and distress, each soul goes either to heaven or to hell under the direction of the Lord–*īśvara-preritaḥ* (27). The particular body bestowed on a living being is the means through which the *dhātṛ* causes suffering and enjoyment and he uses one individual as an instrument in bringing death to another, enacting his will through various agents (30-35).

Having thus described the way in which the Ordainer operates the law of *karma*, Draupadī then challenges his sense of justice, comparing his bestowal of rewards and punishments to the capricious play of a child (36). He does not act towards the creatures of this world as would a mother or father, but is impelled by anger and ill-will–*roṣāt* (37). She is troubled at heart seeing how the righteous suffer and the irreligious prosper, and therefore reproaches the Ordainer–*dhātāraṁ garhaye*–for his ignorance of scripture, his cruelty, greed and opposition to *dharma* (38-40). If it is true that the results of a deed come to its doer, then certainly the Controller will suffer for such unjust acts, and if this is not true then might alone will prevail and one can only lament for the plight of the weak (41-42).

This is a remarkable speech by Draupadī, and somewhat difficult to locate in terms of overall epic doctrines. Clearly she cannot accept the straightforward logic of the sins of previous lives causing the righteous to suffer, as Dhṛtarāṣṭra and Gāndhārī do, and it is interesting to note that nowhere in this debate with Yudhiṣṭhira is such a solution suggested. The overall context makes it apparent that the ideas expressed in Chapter 31 are not to be taken as doctrinally sound. In the *Bhūridatta Jātaka*, a Buddhist text cited by Wendy O'Flaherty,[23] the concept of a divine Ordainer is dismissed with arguments very similar to those expressed by Draupadī, and it may be that the *Mahābhārata* is using this incident to show how such a perspective may arise under duress. At the start of Chapter 32, Yudhiṣṭhira replies by condemning his wife as a *nāstika*, an atheist, just as the authors of the epic would almost certainly have condemned the Buddhists, and in Chapter 33 she relents and admits that she was talking wildly (1-2).

One who knows the outcome of the narrative is also aware that the triumph of Duryodhana and the humiliation of Yudhiṣṭhira are both temporary. The sinner will be vanquished by destiny and the follower of *dharma* will prevail. The point seems to be that in times of adversity even a righteous persons such as Draupadī may waver and doubt the justice of *karma*, but one must remain constant in faith, aware that all positions are temporary. Thus the version of

Draupadī is rejected and we are reassured that there is justice in the world. Nonetheless, the passage does serve to show that Obeyesekere and Bowker are not entirely correct, for the question of theodicy does arise here in the Hindu tradition, and the voice of Job may be heard, albeit with less stridency than that of the Old Testament patriarch. Clearly the sight of the wicked prospering and the good suffering raised questions for the authors of the epic, but the response they come back with is that it is temporary and that either in this life or in a future incarnation justice will undoubtedly prevail.

The case of Yudhiṣṭhira is of particular interest in taking the discussion on to its next phase. Greg Bailey points out that suffering in the epic can be due either to transgression of *dharma* or else simply because it is a part of existence in this world.[24] This division again reflects that between *sva-dharma* and *mokṣa-dharma,* for whereas the former urges that the righteous person who correctly follows his duties will be rewarded with happiness and good fortune, the latter takes the view that even the righteous must suffer and hence both *dharma* and *adharma* must be transcended. Yudhiṣṭhira displays many of the characteristics of the impetus towards *nivṛtti,* for even amongst the gods in heaven he is dissatisfied. His virtue, even when rewarded does not bring pleasure and thus it is he above all others who learns the alternative view of suffering which in turn incorporates an alternative theodicy.

(iii) The Problem of Suffering Viewed from the Perspective of *Nivṛtti*

Both the Sāṁkhya and the Vedānta teachings presented in the *Mahābhārata* argue that suffering is experienced only because of illusion based on ignorance. This illusion consists principally of misidentifying oneself as a part of matter and hence accepting self-interest as the satisfaction of the senses. It is this desire based on a lack of comprehension of the true nature of the self that is the root of misery. The *Gītā* teaches that the quest for pleasures derived through the senses is the very womb of suffering (5.22), and this concept is a dominant theme in the teachings on *mokṣa-dharma* expounded in the epic.

At the very beginning of the *Mokṣa-dharma,* Yudhiṣṭhira opens with an inquiry as to how grief may be overcome (12.168.6). Bhīṣma then tells him of a discourse delivered by a *brāhmaṇa* to

King Senajit explaining that suffering arises out of desire and attachment for the things of this world. The same point is reiterated constantly through the various passages of the *Mokṣa-dharma,* and at the end, as at the beginning, we find Nārada instructing Śuka along the same lines. In 12.316.26, he tells Śuka to hear how the living being is constantly roasted–*pacyate*–by the miseries of death and old age. It is all due to illusion,

> *ahite hita-saṁjñas tvam adhruve dhruva-saṁjñakaḥ*
> *anarthe cārtha-saṁjñas tvaṁ kim arthaṁ nāvabudhyase*
>
> 'You consider that which is harmful to be beneficial, that which is temporary to be constant, and that which is worthless to be of value. How is it that you are unaware of the true significance of things.' (12.316.27)

The living beings of this world are like worms wrapped in cocoons created by their own acts, unaware of their true identities. The cocoon is not the worm and the body and senses are not the true being, but because of this misapprehension the living being is forced to experience hardship and suffering.

Thus from the standpoint of *nivṛtti,* when the question is asked as to why this world is full of misery, the reply is that the suffering is unreal and is only perceived to exist because of ignorance of one's true nature. As a deranged persons suffers because of delusions that have no substance, so all people in this world undergo distress; this must be tolerated and by the therapeutic process of *yoga* the ignorance will be destroyed and true vision will reveal that there is no misery at all. On this basis the epic teaches that *mokṣa* is gained in this world and that for one who thus transcends illusion there is no suffering. This point is illustrated in the *Mokṣa-dharma* by the examples of Prahlāda (12.216-217), Bali (12.217.220), Namuci (12.219) and Vṛtra (12.270) who are presented as great adversaries of the gods who have been vanquished but do not suffer in adversity because they are endowed with the wisdom that takes them beyond misery. Similarly, 12.168 presents the example of Piṁgalā the courtesan, and 12.172 the *brāhmaṇa* encountered by Prahlāda, both of whom are free from suffering because they have transcended attachment to the fluctuating fortunes of this world.

Thus the epic embodies an explicit line of though that connects suffering with the ignorance that prevents salvation, and presents wisdom as the panacea that brings unimpeachable joy. Addressing the lamenting Yudhiṣṭhira at the start of the *Śānti*, Vyāsa points out the ignorance that underlies grief, again citing the example of King Senajit. Grief arises from the loss of wealth, wives, children or parents (12.26.17), but such grief is inappropriate for even one's body and personality are not truly related to oneself (18-19). In Chapter 243 of the *Śānti*, Vyāsa asserts that one who has knowledge of the self enjoys pleasure that never fades–*sukham avyayam*–and that pleasure such as this can be gained only through *yoga* (15-16). Even though hungry and devoid of wealth, the *yogin* is satisfied for he experiences the joy of self-knowledge–*ātma-ratiḥ* (17-18). Having gone beyond desire–*kṣīna-kāmam*–he finds happiness everywhere expanding like the waxing moon, and having transcended the realm of the three *guṇas*, he experiences a sense of joy that removes all sorrow–*sukhenāpohyate duḥkham*–just as the sun dispels the darkness, and he is no longer touched by old age and disease–*jarā-mṛtyū na vindataḥ* (19-21).

The teachings on *mokṣa-dharma* thus provide an alternative perspective on the causes of suffering. Here the premise is different. Suffering is no longer considered in terms of its arising solely because of prior irreligious behaviour, but is taken as an inevitable part of material existence, however strictly one adheres to *dharma*. In a sense Draupadī's challenge to the justice of the Ordainer is precluded in this understanding, for suffering only exists because of illusion symptomised by attachment. When one gains *jñāna* the illusion fades away and with it all forms of grief and misery. Even death, old age and bereavement cannot touch such an enlightened one because he recognises his true self-identity with the eternal *ātman* and not the transient physical frame. Here the challenge of theodicy is minimal, first because the systems of Sāṁkhya, Yoga and Vedānta do not have a creator God at the heart of their doctrines, and secondly because suffering itself is only an illusion. The question, 'Why is there so much misery in this world?' is answered by the assertion that it is simply because of ignorance that one perceives this to be so and one with true vision sees that there is nothing but joy in all directions.

(iv) The Teachings of the *Bhagavad-gītā* on Suffering

Examining the doctrines of the *Gītā*, Herman urges that the problem of suffering is resolved in the text entirely by the concept of *karma.*[25] Kṛṣṇa does have the power to change individual destinies, but except in the case of his devotees he chooses not to. He is not to be blamed for this because a person encounters suffering as a result of previous acts, and hence in the final analysis receives the joy and grief he deserves. In all probability this is the doctrine of the *Gītā,* although there is no clear statement that previous acts produce good and bad fortune.[26] Though Kṛṣṇa moves rapidly form his original starting point still the *Gītā* has much to say on the subject of suffering, for it begins its teachings from the point of Arjuna's lamentation over the fact that his *dharma* and his circumstances dictate that he must slay those whom he both respects and loves.

With this context in mind, it is interesting to note that the response from Kṛṣṇa rests not on the assumption of universal justice in the law of *karma,* which he virtually ignores, but on the perspective discussed above which argues that suffering must be recognised for the illusion that it is. Thus his immediate response to Arjuna's tearful proclamation that he will not fight is to argue that death should not be grieved over because it is unreal. We are all eternal and the true self continues after death by obtaining another bodily form–*dehāntara-prāptiḥ* (2.11-13). Hence it appears that the solution offered by the *Gītā* to the problem of suffering is that is arises only because of the ignorance manifested by Arjuna. The *paṇḍita* feels no grief because his wisdom reveals the true self beyond the fluctuating conditions of matter. Therefore Kṛṣṇa indicates as the conclusion to his teachings on the transcendent self the practical result of such an understanding, *na tvaṁ śocitum arhasi*–you should feel no sorrow (2.25, 26, 27, 30).

The point I am trying to draw attention to in this brief look at the *Gītā* is that its response to the problem of suffering follows the view of *nivṛtti* rather than *sva-dharma,* for despite its insistence on the performance of duty it is essentially a soteriological treatise.[27] The suffering confronted by the *Gītā* is of the most acute nature, for not only does it involve the deaths of loved ones, but circumstances have conspired to compel Arjuna to play the central role in their slaying. Kṛṣṇa responds to this predicament by attempting to convince Arjuna that his misery exists only because he sees himself and others in terms of body and senses, and not in terms of their true eternal nature. When the truth is perceived there is no misery or grief, and hence the *yogin* who has perceived his true spiritual identity enjoys a unique pleasure that is never impinged upon by any form of distress.

(v) Conclusions

Is it therefore correct to argue that the *Mahābhārata* offers a solution to the problem of theodicy? There is no clear answer to this question for despite what has been stated above, Obeyesekere is correct when he urges that for the Hindu the problem does not exist in the way that it has loomed so large in Western theism. It is important to observe that amongst all the array of inquiries presented in the epic from seeker to teacher, nowhere is the problem of theodicy directly raised as needing doctrinal clarification. Thus it is clear that the problem is not one that the authors of the epic recognised as arising from their teachings.

According to Obeyesekere, Weber, Hermàn and others it is the doctrine of *karma* that renders to so; because the problem is solved so obviously it is irrelevant to raise it. The weight of this view cannot be denied, but I am in agreement with Wendy O'Flaherty in seeing the issue as a little more complex than such a unidimensional view might suggest. It would appear that the problem of theodicy is so prominent in Western theism because of the glaring dissonance between the nature of the Deity postulated by orthodox theology and the nature of the creation we confront day by day. It is significant to note how this dissonance is avoided in the epic, wherein the character of the Deity more closely resembles the nature of the manifest creation. The bountifulness, fertility and beauty of the world is reflected in the benign nature of the Deity, generally personified as Viṣṇu, but at the same time the fierceness and wanton cruelty of earthquake, flood, famine and drought is also reflected in the nature of God, most usually in his personification as Śiva. Thus in a Hindu context the notion of a Deity who is 'all-good' falls short of being axiomatic.

Furthermore, the understanding that creation is a continuously repeated process serves to constrain the emphasis on divine omnipotence, and also to reduce the sense of purposiveness. Where the Deity manifests a world that has never existed before in any shape or form the demand for explication of the divine motive is far more pressing than where a doctrine presents the notion of continuously repeated creations without beginning or end. Where creation is *ex nihilo* it is presumed that the Creator acts on a particular idea and hence the suffering that is evidently concomitant to that idea is more directly attributable to his will. In the *Mahābhārata*, the Deity plays a crucial role in the creative process and yet there is clearly less of a sense of his being the absolute determiner and controller.

Thus in summation I would urge that the imperative towards a resolution of the problem of theodicy is obviated in the epic by the following factors:- 1. The notion that the Deity is all-good is not axiomatic. 2. The notion that the Deity is all-powerful is pressed in a manner that is less than absolute. 3. The law of *karma* places the responsibility for suffering very obviously with the individual. 4. The doctrines of Sāṁkhya, Yoga and Vedānta dictate that suffering is in any case an illusion that vanishes as soon as true *jñāna* is realised.

Notes

1. Macdonell, A.A. *Vedic Mythology*, New York, 1974, p. 11.
2. Hopkins, E.W. *The Great Epic of India*, Calcutta, 1969 (1st Ed 1901), p. 187.
3. And see also 1.1.27-36 at the very beginning of the epic.
4. For a discussion of the Vedic antecedents to the epic's creation myth, see Gonda, J. *Aspects of Early Viṣṇuism*, Delhi, 1969, p. 89.
5. Hopkins 1969, p. 184.
6. The functional identity of *ahaṁkāra* is more usually with Brahmā, but here it appears that *ahaṁkāra* is in the role of Viṣṇu.
7. Frauwallner, E. *History of Indian Philosophy*, Volume 1, V.M. Bedeker trans, Delhi, 1973, p. 101.
8. This passages is virtually identical to 1.66-70 of the *Manu-smṛti*.
9. Larson, G.J. *Classical Sāṁkhya, An Interpretation of its History and Meaning*, Delhi, 1969, p. 143.
10. Cited by van Buitenen who states that Chapter 187 of the *Śānti*, "gives the lie to a primitive 'Sāṁkhya' without evolution, as Frauwallner construes." (van Buitenen, J.A.B. *Studies in Indian Literature and Philosophy*, Ludo Rocher Ed, Delhi, 1988, p. 48).
11. Ibid, pp. 45-48.
12. The word *mahat* may be translated as 'The Great Element', but I have chosen to accept van Buitenen's opinion: "I have taken more and more to putting this *mahān* within quotes because it becomes increasingly clear that the word is not to be taken in any literal sense but as a proper name which is still in search of an identity." (Ibid, p. 218).
13. This is probably a reference to the airs in the body, as is No. 9.
14. Here it may be that Mahat is identified with *ahaṁkāra*, but I take it in a general rather than specific sense as the original great element.
15. The verb *sṛj*, used for creation, has the more literal meaning of discharge

and has sexual overtones. This sexual metaphor in the theistic understanding of creation is made explicit in 14.3-4 of the *Bhagavad-gītā.* The Word *pralaya,* used for destruction, likewise literally means a 'merging' or 'absorption.'

16. Weber, M. *The Sociology of Religion,* Ephraim Fischof trans, London, 1963.
17. Herman, A.L. 'The problem of Suffering in the Bhagavad-gītā', in *Suffering: Indian Perspectives,* K.N. Tiwari Ed, Delhi, 1986, p. 62.
18. Heesterman, J.C. *The Inner Conflict of Tradition, Essays in Indian Ritual, Kingship and Society,* Chicago, 1985, pp. 83-84.
19. Weber 1963.
20. Obeyesekere, G. 'Theodicy, Sin and Salvation in a Sociology of Buddhism', in *Dialectic in Practical Religion,* Edmund Leach Ed, Cambridge Papers in Social Anthropology No. 5, 1968, pp. 7-40.
21. Herman 1986, p. 81.
22. Bowker, J. *Problems of Suffering in the Religions of the World,* Cambridge, 1970, p. 215.
23. O'Flaherty, W. *The Origins of Evil in Hindu Mythology,* Berkeley, 1976. p. 5.
24. Bailey, G. 'Suffering in the Mahābhārata: Draupadī and Yudhiṣṭhira', in *Suffering: Indian Perspectives,* K.N. Tiwari Ed, Delhi, 1986, pp. 38-60.
25. Herman 1986, pp. 86-88.
26. Although in Chapter 16 Kṛṣṇa is explicit that the wicked will suffer after death for their misdeeds and throughout there is a presumption that rebirth is the result of *karma.*
27. As is stated in 1.2.156:
    kaśmalaṁ yatra pārthasya vāsudevo mahāmatiḥ
    moha-jaṁ nāśayāmāsa hetubhir mokṣa-darśanaiḥ

CHAPTER 11

THE *MAHĀBHĀRATA*'S TEACHINGS ON GENDER

1. Introduction

Contemporary religious debate has increasingly recognised the importance of gender issues, and modern religious thought has been forced to face the problems raised by this debate. The problem may be summarised as follows. Modern liberal ideology pushes strongly for gender equality in terms of economic and social position and also of ascribed conjugal roles. Despite persisting discrimination against women in society, the debate in favour of gender equality has been won in the West and also amongst a substantial section of the westernised intelligentsia in India. To argue now for a retention of or return to a state of normative inequality is to be branded as both ultra-conservative and as a supporter of oppression. For the adherents of religious traditions in societies where Western values predominate this relatively rapid shift in social values is problematic. The scriptures recognised as revealed by such traditions substantially reflect the value systems of the cultures and societies from which they arose. The notion of gender equality is almost uniquely modern and hence the cultural perspectives enshrined and legitimated in the scriptures of the world's religions invariably include ethical codes which regard women as inherently inferior to men.

The problem for the modern apologist of religious traditions in such societies is that he or she must either reaffirm the orthodox view of scripture, and thereby risk marginalisation and rejection by the mainstream culture, or else seek to reinterpret the tradition and bring it into closer harmony with contemporary perspectives. The latter of these two options may appear more attractive, but there are clear difficulties to be overcome if it is to be successfully pursued. Reinterpreting the direct statements of scripture inevitably involves a revision of the tradition's view of its scripture, relativising the status of the texts and raising questions about their authenticity as the revealed word of God. In addition, religion sees its function as imparting the divine will to humanity, dictating thereby the proper standards of social morality. When it is seen to fall in with contemporary trends, this role as dispenser of divine injunctions is seriously called into question and the religious system becomes no more than one institution amongst many in the social fabric.

Contemporary Hindu thought has been substantially influenced by Western liberal ideas. As such this neo-Hinduism has little sympathy with the statements of its religious literature consigning women to a position of constitutional inferiority. In considering the *Mahābhārata*, writers have drawn a distinction between the statements of the epic *dharma-śāstra* and the manner in which women are portrayed in the narrative. Krishna Moorthy entirely ignores the teachings on the social status of women found in the *Śānti* and *Anuśāsana* and on the basis of what he sees as the society depicted in the narrative feels able to assert, "The status of women, especially those belonging to the ruling class, was in no way unequal to that of men."[1] Shakambari Jayal in her well-researched study of the subject[2] recognises a historical progression from the age of the composition of the narrative portions to that of the composition of the dharma-śāstric teachings. During this period, she contends, the position of women in society became increasingly degraded to the point where they were little more than possessions of men. Her view is that whilst the narratives of both the *Mahābhārata* and *Rāmāyaṇa* provide role models that all women may follow without fear of oppression, the didactic passages prescribe a social structure in which women are deprived of liberty and all opportunities for self-improvement.

Jayal implicitly denigrates the value of the epic's dharma-śāstric material in comparison to the narrative sections of the text. This attitude is understandable, but does of course raise questions about the status of the epic as scripture. Effectively what is taking place here is the representation of specific sections of the text as more authoritative than others on the basis of how closely their view corresponds with contemporary values. This type of approach is characteristic of the neo-Hinduism discussed by Paul Hacker,[3] where values are projected back onto a reinterpreted tradition, rather than the tradition speaking as an authoritative voice to the present day.

2. Passages Offering Teachings on Gender

(i) Introduction

In attempting to outline the epic's view on gender issues I am aware that Jayal has preceded me with admirable thoroughness, drawing on both the epics for her material. It would be impractical for me to repeat such an exhaustive study; instead I will examine a few of the most significant passages which present direct teachings on how a woman should live and behave, and then consider the role and character of the female figures in the narrative.

(ii) The *Draupadī-Satyabhāmā-saṁvāda*

Chapters 222 and 223 of the *Vana* tell of a discussion between Draupadī and Satyabhāmā at the time of a visit of the latter's husband, Kṛṣṇa, to the Pāṇḍavas in the forest, a passage known as the *Draupadī-Satyabhāmā-saṁvāda.* The conversation begins with Satyabhāmā asking how Draupadī behaves as the wife of the Pāṇḍavas, keeping them submissive to her will and yet never causing them to be angry with her (3.222.4-7). In reply, Draupadī presents her view of how a wife should conduct herself in relation to her husband.

Draupadī claims that she devotedly serves her husbands and their other wives without pride, anger or desire (18). With affection and self-restraint she waits attentively on their wishes without any selfish thoughts. She works hard to manage the home, never speaks harshly, never laughs loudly, never causes offence and is never idle. She never cooks food her husbands do not like, and she is dutiful in performing the offerings to the ancestors and in serving guests (19-33). Even though they are gentle by nature, she treats her husbands as if they were venomous snakes, always prone to anger (34). The eternal *dharma* for a woman is to serve her husband in this way, for he is her god and she has no object in life other than his service (35). She never disregards the instructions of her husbands over her sleeping and eating, nor with regard to the ornaments she wears; she never speaks ill of her mother-in-law and always defers to her opinion (36-37).

When Yudhiṣṭhira was king in Indraprastha, he ruled with magnificent opulence, keeping a huge household retinue and feeding many *brāhmaṇas* and sages. All this was overseen with scrupulous care by Draupadī, including keeping account of income and expenditure. She alone knew the extent of the kingdom's wealth, taking this burden away from her husbands. By relieving them of the anxiety of managing the royal exchequer, she has made her husbands favourably disposed towards her (38-57). For a woman there is no god other than her husband. When he is satisfied she gets everything she desires — clothes, perfumes, bedding, furniture and even rebirth amongst the gods — but if he is angered then all things will be lost to her. Only by overcoming difficulties can happiness be won; therefore a woman must be prepared to suffer in the service of her husband so that her wishes may be fulfilled. She must be attentive to his desires and serve him dutifully, even accepting the role and demeanour cf a serving maid (3.223.1-7). A wife should never gossip about matters her husband has disclosed to her; she should be amicable towards his friends and cold towards those who are inimical to him (8-9). She should never talk privately with other men and should make friendships only with women who are respectable (10-11). Such behaviour leads a woman towards rebirth in *svarga-loka.* Draupadī therefore advises Satyabhāmā that she should dress and perfume her body with care and then devote herself to the worship of her husband.

In this passage, the speech of Draupadī focuses specifically on conjugal relations between husband and wife. There is no hint of ambivalence; it is accepted that power and dominance in the relationship rests in the male partner and that the female should never act in a way that challenges this situation. There is no sense whatsoever of equality between marital partners and it is clear that the speaker does not recognise such equality as desirable or possible. Male dominance is to be accepted, embraced and acted under as an unchangeable constant. The successful and prosperous woman is one who accepts her subservience and proves herself to be diligent and faithful. In response to this behaviour the contented patriarch will bestow upon her the things she hankers for. The view of a woman's trivial nature is demonstrated by the goals she is thought to aspire after. Items like clothing, jewellery and perfumes are seen as sufficient to satisfy the female mind. Within the household, and in Draupadī's case this extends to the entire kingdom, the wife is given considerable responsibility. It cannot escape notice, however, that all such duties are performed as service by the wife to her spouse, without independence or proprietorship. It is the husband's domain that she tends, and she can exercise only such authority as is granted by him.

The ideas expressed in the *Draupadī-satyabhāmā-saṁvāda* relate only to the conjugal aspect of gender roles, but are clearly important to the text as a whole in embodying the essence of a woman's *sva-dharma.* This view of marriage relations is replicated elsewhere in the parable of the pigeons and the hunter (12.143), the instructions of Śāṇḍilī (13.124), and those of Umā (13.134.31f), all of which insist that a woman's *dharma,* through which *svarga-loka* is attained, is to do everything possible to satisfy one's husband, regarding him as a god on earth.

(iii) Bhīṣma's Teachings in the *Anuśāsana*[4]

Chapter 38 of the *Anuśāsana* opens with Yudhiṣṭhira saying to Bhīṣma that he now wishes to hear about the nature of women, who are by nature petty-minded–*laghu-cittāḥ*–and the root of all faults. In his reply, Bhīṣma confirms Yudhiṣṭhira's view by citing the words of the *apsaras* Pañcacūḍā spoken to the *ṛṣi* Nārada (11-30). The major fault found in even beautiful, well-born and married women is that they will not accept the restrictions imposed by *dharma.* They are the source of all faults and always prone to sin, for even when married to a good husband they are still attracted to other men. They cannot resist one who courts them with flattering words and if they do remain true to their husbands it is due only to physical restraint, watchful relatives or lack of opportunity. Even the wife of a noble husband may be attracted by an ugly man who has no good qualities if he pays her attention, for women are always restless, anxious for new companions and never satiated.

In Chapter 39, Yudhiṣṭhira asks how a husband can protect his wife when women are so expert in the arts of deceit, especially in speaking false words. Even when worshipped and treated with respect, they still prove to be unfaithful, so how can they be protected? In Chapter 40, Bhīṣma agrees that women are as dangerous as a blazing fire, illusion, a razor's edge, poison, a serpent and death itself (1-4). He then explains why this is so by recounting the story of the creation of women by Brahmā. In the beginning, all people were righteous and by gradual elevation attained the realm of the gods which became overpopulated as a result. In distress the gods then approached Brahmā who resolved the problem by creating a new type of woman.

In the original creation women were virtuous, but these women were by nature unchaste (8) for the creator filled them with carnal desires which impelled them to constantly seek new male companions. They have no dharmic duties, according to the *śruti* they lack resolve and energy, they have no access to the Vedas and are to be known as falsehood itself (11). After creating them, Prajāpati gave these women bedding, seats, jewellery, food, drink, unrighteousness, slander and sexual pleasure as objects of enjoyment (12). Hence it is impossible for anyone to restrain them by words, by threat of death, by bonds, or by various afflictions; by nature they remain unrestrained and prone to sin (13).

From the outset, where Yudhiṣṭhira designates them as *laghucittāḥ*, this passage offers a strikingly negative stereotype of the female disposition. Jayal sees the *Anuśāsana*'s misogyny as being derived from the ascetic tradition with its stress on celibacy,[5] but such a conclusion seems unlikely. For one thing teachings on asceticism and *mokṣa-dharma* are found only rarely in the *Anuśāsana*. The *dharma-śāstric* elements of the epic, as represented in this passages, are concerned primarily with the regulation of society, whilst the ascetic tradition aims at salvation through renunciation of the world. What we have here is different from the Buddhist expressions of revulsion for women stemming from a monastic culture, and is derived more from the paranoia of husbands and fathers over the chastity of wives and daughters. It is not the rejection of all contact with women that is being urged, but rather consideration of how one may keep one's women under safe control.

The principal feature of the female nature emphasised here is the tendency towards infidelity which leads women to seek a succession of lovers. For this reason they are a threat to men not because they will break a man's vows of celibacy, but because he will find it difficult to keep them as his personal objects of enjoyment. The stereotype of the feminine nature depicts women as both deceitful and trivial, interested only in petty adornments. The story of the creation of women by Brahmā demonstrates that the negative qualities of the female nature are inherent to the gender; hence they can never be expected to reform themselves or to be reformed by good instruction, but must be compelled by force to behave in a manner that accords with *dharma.* The implication of such negative stereotyping is obvious, for it provides justification for repressive behaviour towards women on the grounds that if such steps are not taken their nature will inevitably impel them towards sin. Such repressive injunctions are found in the *Anuśāsana* in the chapters of *dharma-śāstra* that relate to the behaviour of women.

In Chapters 40 to 43, Bhīṣma goes on to narrate the story of Vipula to illustrate the tendency of women towards marital infidelity, though at the conclusion he does admit that there are two types of women, the righteous and the wicked, rather than condemning women as a whole (13.43.19). In Chapter 44, he discusses different types of marriage in response to a question from Yudhiṣṭhira about the root of the various forms of *dharma.* Bhīṣma cites different opinions on the question of polygamy; some condemn the practice whilst others allow three wives for a *brāhmaṇa,* two for a *kṣatriya* and one for a *vaiśya,* in addition to one wife born a *śudra* (10-12). A man aged thirty years should wed a girl aged ten and a man aged twenty-one should wed a girl aged seven, whilst nobody should marry a girl who has no father or brother (13-14). If a girl is not married before puberty, then after three years she should seek a husband for herself (15).

Bhīṣma then discusses the subject of dowries, expressing the opinion that one may marry a girl even though a dowry has been paid to her kin by another man, for Manu does not approve of a wife being forced into a marriage against her will (20-26). Even if a marriage has been arranged, it is not to be considered binding until the ceremony has taken place. The practice of selling one's daughter to the suitor who offers the highest sum is condemned as sinful; a widow whose marriage was not consummated may become the wife of her dead husband's younger brother (31-58).

In Chapter 45, Bhīṣma moves on to discuss female inheritance rights. If a man has paid a dowry before marrying a girl, she should not be deceitfully married to another whilst he is absent (1-4). Sāvitrī chose her own husband (this story is narrated by Mārkaṇḍeya to the Pāṇḍavas in Chapters 277-283 of the *Vana*) but few who are experts in *dharma* approve of such a practice. King Sukratu expressed the following opinion on this subject, "How can one win-renown on the path of unrighteous conduct, and how can the righteous have doubts or questions about this. Such neglect of *dharma* is unrighteous, is of the nature of the *asuras*, and was never heard of in ancient times" (5-10).

At this point Yudhiṣṭhira interjects with a question about female inheritance, asking how a father's wealth is divided and expressing the view that a daughter is equal to a son (11). Bhīṣma agrees with this opinion. A daughter is the same as a son and nobody should prevent her from inheriting her share which is designated as the private wealth of her mother or else the dowry given by her mother's father. If a man has no sons then his inheritance goes to the sons of his daughters; a man who has no sons may make his daughter his heir, and any subsequent male offspring, born or adopted, must share the inheritance with her. No inheritance is to go to the sons of a daughter if that daughter has been sold to her husband, for this is a wicked practice and any man who acts in this way will go to the same hell as those who violate maidens by force.

In the fourteen verses of Chapter 46, Bhīṣma discusses the treatment of a married woman in the home of her husband's kin. The husband and family receiving his bride should always be kind to her, treat her gently, show her respect and please her with gifts, for if she is unhappy the whole family will suffer. The gods are always pleased with those who treat women well and curse those houses where they are mistreated. Manu has instructed that women should be cared for by men for they are mostly weak, easily seduced, soft-hearted and lovers of honesty. Some women are harsh, stupid, and malevolent, but still men should honour them for when the women are satisfied society is peaceful. According to Janaka there are no set rituals for women to perform and their only duty is to serve their husbands; this is sufficient to guarantee elevation to *svarga-loka*. Females should be under the care of their fathers as children, their husbands in youth and their sons in old age, but should never be independent (13). When women are cherished in society, there is prosperity and good will for all.

In Chapter 47, Bhīṣma returns to the subject of inheritance, discussing the share of a father's wealth that should be given to each son in accordance with the *varṇa* of his mother. After verse 22, he speaks once more about female inheritance. A wife may be given a sum no greater than 3,000 coins which she may use at her pleasure in addition to whatever gifts she has received from her husband; none of this should be taken from her (23-24). Whatever wealth is received by a woman from her father is inherited by her daughters, for they are equal to sons (25). The discourse now moves away from the inheritance rights of women to consider the status of persons born of parents of different *varṇas*.

These four chapters (44-47) contain the epic's principal *dharma-śāstra* concerning women. Based on the stereotype of the feminine nature presented in chapters 38-43, they demand that strict limits be placed on the freedom of women in society. In marriage there is no question of equal partnership and undoubtedly such a concept was alien to the *dharma-śāstra-kāras*. For the three higher *varṇas* polygamy was acceptable, reinforcing the unequal status, and the notion of a girl choosing her own husband is roundly condemned. The problem of a girl being forced to marry a man she dislikes is recognised, but still it is considered ideal if the father chooses a husband for his daughter and she is married while still a child of seven or ten. Inevitably, as Jayal forcefully argues, child marriage must lead to a status of marked inferiority for women both socially and conjugally. It is interesting to note how the compilers of this passage were aware of examples found elsewhere in the epic that contradict their views. Here the case of Sāvitrī who was allowed by her father to travel the world and choose her own husband is mentioned (13.45.5), and then authority is cited to show that such practice is not in accordance with *dharma*.

Regarding wealth and inheritance, which constitute a real basis of social independence, women are not completely disenfranchised though it is clear that primary inheritance passed from father to sons rather than daughters. Almost certainly this reflects the view that women had less need of independent wealth because their husbands were the providers of maintenance. A woman could inherit up to 3,000 coins from her husband and if the wife had any private property this went to her daughters. It is difficult to say how effective such injunctions would be in freeing a woman from a state of dependence, but with the primary inheritance passing through the male line and with women having no acceptable means of earning their own income one suspects that their position of subordination was ensured by economic constraints as well as the socio-religious notion that a woman must never be granted freedom at any stage of life.

The repressive nature of the dharma-śāstric literature is tempered somewhat by the denunciation of harsh treatment of women by husbands and society as a whole. Despite the obvious disparity of status between the genders, within her prescribed station the woman is to be admired and treated with respect and kindness. Here one recognises a perspective which takes the subordination of women for granted and is able to be magnanimous in the implementation of that inferior status. It also reflects the genteel tone of the epic as a whole, for whatever distaste the modern mind may feel for the discrimination against women embodied in the text, one cannot deny that it is the work of civilised men of largely compassionate intent.

A disturbing exception to this principle is the recommendation that windows commit suicide. It is clear that not all widows were expected to take this extreme measure of conjugal devotion, but still it is recognised as a meritorious act in keeping with a woman's *dharma.* This course is adopted by Mādrī, Pāṇḍu's second wife, and in this she is envied by Kuntī who remains alive only to care for her sons (1.116). In a story narrated by Kuntī, Bhadrā the wife of King Vyuṣitāsva states that without her husband a woman's life is no life at all and therefore a widow should follow her spouse into the afterlife (1.112). In Chapter 41 of the *Āśramavāsika,* the widows of the slain warriors are urged by Vyāsa to drown themselves in the Ganges and after the death of Vasudeva, Kṛṣṇa's father, his widows commit suicide on his funeral pyre and thereby accompany their husband to realm of the gods (16.8.24). There is no suggestion that social pressure was exerted upon widows to take their own lives, but the indication that such an act was pious and was rewarded in the afterlife is clearly open to abuse and has undoubtedly contributed to practices that have brought the Hindu tradition into disrepute in the eyes of the world.

In addition to the passages examined above there are numerous brief references to the status of women found throughout the epic, all of them along similar lines. In marriage, it is the woman's *dharma* to serve her husband faithfully and several stories, such as those of Sāvitrī, Damayantī, and Sukanyā are inserted into the text to illustrate the point. In society women have a status subordinate to men; polygamy is acceptable but not polyandry (1.146.34, 14.79.14-15, it is made very clear that the case of Draupadī is exceptional); women should not be the proprietors of their own wealth (5.33.57); and they are restricted from taking an effective role in politics (12.84.53). The picture presented throughout the didactic portions of the epic is thus consistent with the *dharma-śāstra* found in the *Anuśāsana.*

3. Female Characters in the Epic Narrative

Jayal points to a distinction between the status and demeanour of women portrayed in the *Mahābhārata* narrative and that recommended in the dharma-śāstric didactus. With regard to marriage, she notes two views of the institution from the female perspective, *pativratā,* in which the wife sees herself as no more than a submissive servant of her husband, as is urged by *dharma-śāstra,* and *saha-dharminī,* where the wife is a co-partner to her husband in executing dharmic duties, offering support, advice and assistance, as portrayed in the narrative especially through the character of Draupadī.[6]

There is no doubt that the women described in the narrative passages behave in a manner that is notably different from that prescribed by the teachings of the *Anuśāsana,* but the question remains as to how far this portrayal represents a radically alternative view of the social status that women may aspire towards. The three most prominent female characters are Draupadī, the wife of the Pāṇḍavas, Kuntī, their mother, and Gāndhārī, the mother of the Kauravas. Attempting to establish doctrine from narrative portrayals is inevitably problematic, for one can never be absolutely certain of the authors' attitude to individual characters. It appears, however, that all three of these women are to be viewed in a positive light, though there are hints that each of them is to be understood as prone to feminine weakness.

With regard to marriage, it is to be noted that whilst the *Anuśāsana* recommends that girls be married before puberty this does not appear to be the practice of the society described in the narrative. Kuntī has already born a son before she is married to Pāṇḍu, as has Satyavatī prior to her marriage to Śaṁtanu. After her rejection by Bhīṣma and Śalya, Ambā is able to wander the earth and make her own decisions in a manner that indicates an adult level of maturity. Draupadī likewise was not a child bride; she is the twin sister of Dhṛṣṭadyumna who at the time of her wedding plays an adult role in the affairs of state, and the beauty of Draupadī, referred to at the time of her *svayaṁvara,* is clearly of an adult nature giving rise to feelings of lust in all who behold her. Though the age of girls at the time of their marriage is rarely specified, there is no indication in the narrative of girls being married before puberty.

There is a very obvious disparity between the instructions imparted to Satyabhāmā by Draupadī about how a wife should serve her husband and the actual behaviour of the heroine in her personal dealings. Throughout she is depicted as a woman of strong emotions and developed opinions, well-educated and never afraid to express her point of view in predominantly male assemblies. In the *Vana*, she directly confronts Yudhiṣṭhira about his course of action and also about his understanding of *dharma*, citing relevant authorities in support of her arguments. It is noteworthy that Yudhiṣṭhira responds to his wife by putting forward his own view of the course that *dharma* dictates but without condemning her opposition to his will as inappropriate for a woman.

This scene in particular characterises the female role of *sahadharminī*, for when the husband behaves in what she sees as an improper manner it is the partner's duty to speak out to correct him. Throughout the *Mahābhārata* we find Draupadī prepared to criticise her husbands' behaviour if she thinks their actions are ill-advised. In Chapter 17 of the *Virāṭa*, she complains at length to Bhīma about the conduct of Yudhiṣṭhira in a manner completely at odds with the advice she has previously given Satyabhāmā. Here she blames her eldest husband for the insults to which she has been subjected and criticises his weakness for gambling. Later, after victory has been won and Yudhiṣṭhira is proposing to abandon the kingdom for a life of religious penance, she goes so far as to brand him an atheist opposed to *dharma* and urges that the other Pāṇḍavas ignore their brother and rule the kingdom without him (12.14.33).

It may be that Draupadī is a unique case of a particularly independent female who will not accept the strictures conventionally placed on those of her sex. Nonetheless, her displays of independent thought are not unique amongst the epic heroines. Kuntī never opposes her husband to the extent that Draupadī does, but she is never provoked to the same extent. She is, however, able to debate with Pāṇḍu about what course should be pursued in order to secure an heir after the curse of lifelong celibacy has been placed upon him (1.112-113). She is devoted to her husband and the satisfaction of his wishes, but still appears as far more of an equal partner than is dictated by the epic's didactus, to the extent that she feels able to disagree with Pāṇḍu on certain principles and urge an alternative course of action.

The one fact regarding Gāndhārī known to all Hindus is her constant wearing of a blindfold out of consideration for Dhṛtarāṣṭra. There is little doubt as to the significance of this gesture; recognising that her sight renders her superior to her blind husband, she acts to prevent this and preserve his superiority in all respects. Here she is behaving in a manner that accords absolutely with the views of *dharma-śāstra*. On the other hand, she is an individual who warrants respect from all and when she recognises that the kingdom is on the verge of catastrophe she does not hesitate to condemn her husband for his folly in favouring his own sons and failing to exercise proper control over their behaviour (5.127.11f).

The relationship between the two mothers, Kuntī and Gāndhārī, and their grown sons who have positions of political power is also enlightening. Despite the fact that both the Pāṇḍavas and Kauravas have come into their own estates and are the rulers of flourishing kingdoms, both groups remain deferential to their mothers, worshipping them with reverence and listening to their advice in both personal and political matters. The difference is that the righteous Pāṇḍavas always act on the order of their mother as if it were a divine injunction, whereas the deviant Kauravas ignore that of Gāndhārī and are destroyed. It is apparent that it is in the role of mother that a woman enjoys the highest prestige in epic society. Though she may be subject to the will of her husband and socially disenfranchised, within the home the matriarch is a figure of authority and to disrespect that authority is to stray dangerously into the sphere of *adharma*.

The *Anuśāsana* allows polygamy for the three higher *varṇas*, and in the narrative this practice is adopted by most of the main characters, though not strictly in accordance with the rules laid by the *dharma-śāstra-kāras*. The rule given in 13.44.10-12 is that a *brāhmaṇa* may take three wives plus a *sūdra* woman, whilst a *kṣatriya* may take two plus a *śūdrī*, but the narrative presents Arjuna as having four wives and Kṛṣṇa with several thousand, whilst none of the *brāhmaṇas* appears to practise polygamy at all. The impression gained from the narrative is that polygamy amongst the royal order was commonplace and restricted by practicality and desire rather than religious injunction. *Brāhmaṇas* display more of a tendency towards renunciation and hence generally accept only one wife. The narrative text virtually ignores the lower orders and therefore gives little or no indication of the status of the marriage institution amongst them.

A woman's selecting her own spouse is frowned upon by the epic's *dharma-śāstra* and there is little in the narrative passages to indicate that a different standard prevailed. Again the information we obtain relates overwhelmingly to the royal families where marriages had political implications and were hence less likely to be permitted merely on the basis of a girl's personal preference. The marriages of both Kuntī and Gāndhārī were arranged by their fathers, and even though Draupadī was allowed a *svayaṁvara* it was a "self-choice" in name only, for her husband was to be the winner of an archery contest designed specifically to facilitate her marriage to Arjuṇa, the man selected by her father. This interpretation of *svayaṁvara* as a contest to win the hand of an eligible young woman is found frequently in the epic and in Chapter 173 of the *Udyoga*, we find Ambā condemning her father for adopting such a practice in which martial prowess is the dowry. Overall it would appear that the depiction of marriage in the narrative matches the view expressed in the *dharma-śāstra.* The ideal method recommended there is that adopted by Virāṭa on behalf of his daughter Uttarā, whereby the father selects an eligible and qualified person and offers his daughter to him as a bride.

It has been noted that in the narrative the relationship between husband and wife appears more equitable than is recommended by the didactus. There is no indication, however, that a respectable woman might live independently, and the view of 13.45.13 that a woman is to be protected by her father, husband and son throughout her life is substantially confirmed by the narrative. Such an arrangement in society is not entirely repressive, for protection clearly involves responsibility and guarantees that women will not be lift destitute at any stage of life. As a widow, Kuntī is maintained by her sons, but she retains her influence over their actions and is always shown reverential respect.

From a negative point of view it is also apparent that women are constantly in a position of dependency, unable to break free from unhappy situations in a male-dominated society. The unfortunate plight that such dependency may lead to is graphically illustrated by the story of Ambā. Having been rejected as a bride by Vicitravīrya, Bhīṣma and Śalya, she is regarded as unmarriageable, for no *kṣatriya* will accept her as a wife after she has offered herself to others. Her only recourse is to return to her father, but she cannot bear the thought of the contempt in which she will be held by her relatives (5.174.9-13). As a result there is no opportunity open to her and she abandons everything except the single-minded pursuit of vengeance against those who have wronged her. There is no indication that outside of disreputable professions — actresses and courtesans — a woman may live independently in society and the narrative offers no examples of any women who seek this course.

The central story of the epic deals primarily with the warrior culture of the royal order, with politics and warfare as the major preoccupation. It is evident that women are substantially excluded from the political sphere and that the councils that direct affairs are places for men only. As Sally Sutherland points out, the women of the epic are powerless victims of the weaknesses and foibles of men; they suffer the effects of these shortcomings but lack the influence to direct events towards a more favourable outcome. This does not amount to an absolute exclusion as on a number of occasions the principal women are seen to intervene in the affairs of state. Satyavatī takes an active role in ensuring the continuance of the dynasty on the death of her husband Śaṁtanu; Draupadī always makes sure her voice is heard in the debates over peace or war in the *Udyoga;* Kuntī acts as an advisor to her sons when they are considering what course of action they should adopt; Gāndhāri is occasionally summoned to the assembly of the Kauravas to add her weight to the arguments against Duryodhana's intransigence. Thus it is not entirely correct to assert that women are excluded from the political and military affairs on which the *Mahābhārata* focuses so much attention, but they rarely play a central or dominating role. They may offer opinions and advice, but in the end the major decisions are taken by men and the womenfolk have to suffer the consequences as powerless bystanders.

In Chapter 40 of the *Anuśāsana,* we find Yudhiṣṭhira and Bhīṣma discussing the existential nature of women which renders them low-minded, petty in their aspirations and constantly seeking new male companions. This view of the feminine disposition is not reflected in the female characters portrayed in the narrative. Draupadī, Kuntī and Gāndhārī are noble and high-minded individuals, well-educated, compassionate, and as devoted to *dharma* as any of the men. Nowhere are they seen as unchaste or unfaithful to their husbands; indeed Draupadī strenuously resists two flattering admirers, Kīcaka and Jayadratha, in a manner entirely at odds with that suggested by the *Anuśāsana* as the inherent nature of women. Though frequently forced to endure hardship because of their husbands' folly, they remain loyal, if not uncritical, throughout. Thus when reflecting on the discussion between Bhīṣma and Yudhiṣṭhira, it is hard to identify what experiences from their own lives could have led them to such a negative conception of the female disposition.

4. Conclusions regarding *Dharma-śāstra* and the Narrative

It is clear that Jayal is correct in noting the dissonance between the view of women presented in the epic's *dharma-śāstra* and that illustrated by the female characters of the narrative. There would also appear to be some inconsistency between the two views of a woman's role and status in society. In the narrative we find no reference to child brides, and wives are allowed a more equal status in marriage. They are more than mere servants, able to advise their husbands and present their own views which are frequently found to be more noble and more intelligent than those of the male protagonists.

It would be wrong, however, to push the point too far, as is the temptation for a number of modern Hindu writers. The crucial element lacking, essential for any true notion of equality, is that of independence. In both the society prescribed by *dharma-śāstra* and that depicted in the narrative, a woman's social status is delineated in relation to men, either as daughter, wife, or mother, and hence the typical question for any man encountering a female alone is "To whom do you belong?" Independent women are found in the epic only when they have fallen below respectable society, as prostitutes or actresses, or else when they have transcended it as ascetic practitioners of *yoga*.

5. The Ascetic Tradition

(i) Introduction

The dualist view of life in which the true self is rigidly distinguished from the corporeal frame is frequently characterised by expressions of disgust at all forms of material indulgence. In Indian religious thought both the Buddhists and the Jains place great stress on those aiming at perfection completely renouncing all the pleasures of the flesh, and Buddhist texts contain numerous expressions of revulsion for the female form and women in general. It is interesting to note, therefore, the extent to which the teachings on Sāṁkhya and Yoga propounded in the *Mahābhārata* mirror such tendencies.

A close study of the *Mokṣa-dharma* and the *Bhagavad-gītā* reveals that they only rarely stray into this type of condemnation, and more typically urge indifference with regard to physical enjoyment. The *Gītā* clearly teaches that *mokṣa* is attained through the renunciation of material desires, but its view of renunciation does not include a loathing of the world. Equanimity rather than revulsion is the key to the *Gītā*'s ideal view of material life, as expressed, for example, in the fifth chapter:

> *jñeyaḥ sa nitya-sannyāsī yo na dveṣṭi na kāṅkṣati*
> *nirdvandvo hi mahā-bāho sukhaṁ bandhāt pramucyate*
>
> 'One who does not loathe and does not hanker is known as always renounced. Free from such duality, O mighty one, he is joyfully liberated from bondage.' (5.3)

The treatises of the *Mokṣa-dharma*, though they place great emphasis on renunciation and asceticism, again only rarely contain expressions of revulsion for women and the female form. The teachings of the unnamed *guru* to his disciple may be noted as an exception to this rule, though it must be born in mind that his specific topic in Chapter 206 is the practice of *brahmacārya* by a young celibate student. According to the *guru*, it is women who keep the soul bound in this world, forcing it to endure horrible conditions in the womb, covered in excrement, urine and blood, and then to live a life of subjection to wrath and passion (6-7). Women are like the *kṣetra* that binds the *kṣetrajña*, keeping a man trapped in this world and therefore a wise man does not seek women (8). Woman is a sorceress of feartul form–*kṛtyā hy etā ghora-rūpā*–who beguiles foolish men; she is absorbed in passion–*rajasy antarhitā*–the very embodiment of the senses (9). From contact with women children are born, but they should be abandoned just as one casts off worms found on the body without regard for their wellbeing (11-12).

The use of terms such as *kṣetra* and *kṣetrajña* indicates that this passage is based on Sāṁkhya, but the misogyny expressed here is untypical of the Sāṁkhya teachings of the *Mokṣa-dharma.* The attitude here is more akin to the dharma-śāstric view of women found in the *Anuśāsana,* for it expresses not only loathing but also fear of the female nature which is viewed as dangerous and enticing, dominated by sensuality, and able to exert an almost mystical power over the unfortunate male. Such a perspective is rare in the *Mokṣa-dharma,* however, and the above citation from Chapter 206 is the most vehement expression of this type.

Chapter 207 continues to impart teachings on how the practice of celibacy may be successfully executed, but here the *guru* concentrates entirely on the male response to sexual arousal without any vilification of women. Celibacy, he asserts, is hard to sustain and hence one should never hear the talk of women nor see them unclothed, for any sight of them arouses passion in the weak (11-12). One who feels sexual desire should perform the *kṛchram* vow to accept various fasts, and immerse himself in water for three days; if desire arises during sleep, the *brahmacārin* should recite three *aghamarśana* hymns (13-14).

More typical of the *Mokṣa-dharma* than the ideas expressed in Chapter 206 is the perspective from which Bhīṣma speaks a few chapters later in 215. Here a more moderate form of asceticism is recommended in line with the view that the greatest penance is renunciation and humility–*tyāgaś ca sannatis caiva śiṣyate tapa uttamam* (4). Thus a married *brāhmaṇa* who approaches his wife only at a time when she is likely to conceive is considered equal to one who is completely celibate (5). In Chapter 277, Ariṣṭanemi takes a similar line when he instructs Sagara that the true secret of renunciation, including giving up attachment to sex, is detached indifference. Stepping back from the world, one should observe the interactions of life from afar, without passion, attachment or disgust. It is this perspective, corresponding closely with the teachings of the *Gītā,* that is the characteristic view of epic Sāṁkhya, standing as a notable contrast to the expressions of extreme revulsion frequently found in other world-denying religious traditions.

(ii) The Liberal Force of *Nivṛtti*

It must also be noted that *mokṣa-dharma* involves abandoning the rigidly demarcated duties ascribed to all persons as their *sva-dharma*, and recognising that all beings are equal in essence. The adept in Sāṁkhya does not view others in terms of their bodily designation as *brāhmaṇa* or *śūdra*, man or woman, for he perceives the eternal *ātman*, which is the same spiritual entity in the hearts of all. The dharma-śāstric tenets that insist that women are inferior to men are taken in the same light as those which designate the hierarchical stratification of society in terms of the four *varṇas*. From the point of view of the mystical thought of the *Bhagavad-gītā*, the *Mokṣa-dharma* and other passages of the epic, all beings are equal regardless of bodily designation. This point is clearly defined by the *Gītā* in verses such as 5.18 and 6.32 which stress the importance of those who have wisdom viewing equally all human beings and all creatures.

The point here, and it is one that has been utilised by modern Hindu reformers,[8] is that the basic concepts of Sāṁkhya and Vedānta tend towards a form of mystical egalitarianism. The social rules which divide humanity into specific types, including those define gender roles, are all transcended by one who has true wisdom. At this level no being is to be regarded as higher or lower though, according to the *Gītā*, worldly conventions may still be observed for the sake of social stability. It has been noted that there is no place for an independent woman in the society depicted by the *Mahābhārata* and it can be no coincidence that it is only amongst the ascetics who exist outside or on the fringe of society that women are portrayed as existing without any form of male jurisdiction over their lives. Just as there are *ācāryas* of *mokṣa-dharma* born of a lower *varṇa*, so there are female sages who have renounced the world and live independently, pursuing their own spiritual goals. Undoubtedly there are more men than women amongst such *ṛṣis*, but women are encountered frequently enough to demonstrate that such behaviour was not viewed as particularly exceptional. We may note here those referred to by the *Mahābhārata*.

1. In Chapter 111 of the *Udyoga*, in the story of Gālava's search for a gift of horses for his *guru* Viśvāmitra, Gālava and Garuḍa encounter Śāṇḍilī, a *brāhmaṇa* woman, engaged in penances on the peak of Ṛṣabha Mountain. Although in this passage it is clear

that she lives alone, it is interesting to note that this same Śāṇḍilī appears in Chapter 124 of the *Anuśāsana* instructing Sumanā that she has won the right to enter heaven not through her austerities but by attentive service to her husband. Perhaps we have here an example of the revision of previous traditions by *dharma-śāstra-kāras* in order to bring them into harmony with their own views.

2. In the same story, Mādhavi, the daughter of King Yayāti, is traded three times with different kings to make up the gift of horses from the dowry each of them gives for her. This in itself reflects a very unusual attitude towards women and marriage explained only by her great beauty which distracts the kings from the question of propriety. Finally, she is invited to select her own husband from a great assembly of princes but chooses instead the forest life, living on grass and water and accepting celibacy in preference to marriage (5.118.6-11).

3. On his pilgrimage tour, Rāma, the brother of Kṛṣṇa, visits an *āśrama* which was the abode of a *brāhmaṇa* woman who gained perfection in life–*brāhmaṇī siddhā.* This was achieved through vows of celibacy, *yoga* and austerity, following the course adopted by the daughter of King Śāṇḍilya, presumably another reference to the above-mentioned Śāṇḍilī (9.51-52).

4. In the story of Aṣṭāvakra's search for a bride, narrated by Bhīṣma to Yudhiṣṭhira, he encounters an elderly woman who wishes to have sexual relations with him, saying that he need have no fear of *adharma* because she is independent–*sva-tantrāsmi* (13.21.11). To this Aṣṭāvakra responds by asking how such a position is possible, for a woman is always under the protection of either her father, husband or son (18-19). The woman replies that this regulation does not apply to her because since her youth she has lived the life of an ascetic.

5. In the first chapter of the *Anuśāsana,* Bhīṣma tells of a discussion on the subject of destiny following the death of the son of Gautamī, a woman who is referred to as fixed in tranquility–*śama-saṁyutā* (13.1.10.). In the course of the narration it becomes apparent that Gautamī possesses the wisdom of *mokṣa-dharma*; she is not disturbed by the afflictions that beset her and is unmoved in her conviction that all things arise due to destiny.

6. The most notable example in the *Mahābhārata* of a female teacher of Sāṁkhya is that of Sulabhā, presented in the *Mokṣa-dharma.* In response to Yudhiṣṭhira's question as to whether anyone

has gained salvation whilst remaining with his family, Bhīṣma describes a meeting between Sulabhā and Janaka, the King of Mithilā. The discussion between them is interesting because it appears to refute the teachings of the *Bhagavad-gītā* to the effect that one may practise *yoga* without renouncing one's position in society. Janaka is cited on a number of occasions in the epic, including the *Gītā,* 3.20, as an example of a person who attained perfection by transforming his consciousness without abandoning his royal position, but here we find this notion effectively challenged.

Sulabhā herself is described as a *bhikṣukī,* a renounced mendicant, who is fixed in *yoga-dharma* and roams the earth at will, evidently independent of any male guardian (12.308.7). Doubtful of Janaka's proclaimed transcendence of worldly attachment, she uses her magical powers to enter the mind of the king and examine him (16). In the ensuing debate Janaka claims that despite his regal opulence he remains unattached and then criticises Sulabhā for entering his mind. She is a young women and hence such intimate contact with a man constitutes a breach of *dharma.* Moreover, she is a *brāhmaṇa* by birth and a renunciant, whilst he is a *kṣatriya* living with his family; therefore the contact between them was even more adharmic because it was of a *pratilomā* nature between different *varṇas* and *āśramas* (59-60). If she is married then adultery has taken place, but if she is independent then she is still at fault for it is contrary to *dharma* for women to live in such a state (the same wording, *sva-tantrāsi,* is used in v64 as in the story of Aṣṭāvakra, referred to above). Finally, Janaka accuses Sulabhā of making contact with him in a deceitful manner because she is proud of her yogic power (65-75).

The lines of the debate are laid out by this opening speech of Janaka, for despite his claims to freedom from attachment, his criticism of Sulabhā is entirely from the standpoint of *pravṛtti.* Hence he is concerned with both the correct conduct of a woman in society and also the regulated interactions of persons of different *varṇas.* The response that follows is to be recognised as representing the critique of *sva-dharma* typical of *nivṛtti,* and it is interesting that the speech has been placed in the mouth of a woman. Having denied Janaka's accusation of deceitful conduct, Sulabhā then presents a Sāṁkhya analysis of the elements of matter. The conclusion drawn is that all products of matter, and concomitantly all bodily forms, are comprised of identical elements, for in essence all are *prakṛti* (96-115). From the point of insemination, bodies develop from embryo to child to adult and because the body is constantly changing it cannot be the true self (116-126). Therefore the questions he has addressed to her — "Who are you?" and "To whom do you belong?" — are inappropriate (127). When he still draws such distinctions between himself and others, friends and enemies, how can the king claim to be liberated (128)? A liberated person–*mukta-lakṣaṇam*–views all beings equally but at the time of their meeting Janaka did not display such knowledge (129-130).

Sulabhā then argues that one whose wisdom is pure, based on the Sāṁkhya taught by Pañcaśikha, can never rule as a king for it is impossible to execute the duties of kingship whilst viewing the world with the equal vision that Sāṁkhya demands (131-175). There is no possibility of a mixing of *varṇas* from the contact between them, because the true self has no *varṇa*; it is transcendent to all such designations (176-180). She concludes the speech by telling of her personal background. She was not born in a *brāhmaṇa* family, as Janaka had presumed, but is a princess. When no suitable husband was found for her she renounced the world and now wanders the earth alone, following the vows of *mokṣa-dharma*. She never speaks falsely or engages in intellectual wrangling, and had come to Mithilā with a genuine desire to hear spiritual wisdom from its king. When Sulabhā ends her discourse Janaka is left silent, unable to reply to the points she has made.

The teachings of Sulabhā provide a valuable insight into the perspective of *nivṛtti* on the question of gender distinctions. Sulabhā here presents a Sāṁkhya critique of the rigid differentiation of individuals according to both gender and *varṇa*. Janaka's objections to the mental contact she makes with him are based on the dharma-śāstric world view with its preoccupation with *sva-dharma*. This provides the impetus for her rejection of this perspective and her denial of his claim that a king can be a *mukta*, free of the illusion that binds one to rebirth, a claim that is a major theme of the *Bhagavad-gītā*.

The wisdom of Sāṁkhya taught by Pañcaśikha reveals that all bodies are composed of the same *prakṛti* and all selves are the spiritual *ātman*. Therefore the arguments of Janaka, based on distinctions of gender and *varṇa*, display a false perception of reality. Here we are confronted by the recurring debate between *nivṛtti* and *pravṛtti*. The words spoken by Sulabhā reveal that passages which ascribe an inferior status to women in society and argue that the female nature is inherently flawed are based on the perspective of *pravṛtti.* The Sāṁkhya view she articulates presents a different understanding, arguing not only that teachings based on *pravṛtti* are derived from a faulty observance of the world, but that the entire understanding of reality on which that observation is based is a product of ignorance. This response is certainly very different from that to be expected from the modern critic, but is equally effective in undermining the dogma of female inferiority.

6. Overview

I began this discussion by referring to the problem faced by religious traditions in the modern world in reconciling the contemporary liberal consensus towards gender equality with the perspective of their own scriptures on this issue. It is thus interesting to look at the response of modern Hindus to the misogynous tendencies of the *Mahābhārata.* Krishna Moorthy takes Hopkins's line that the didactic passages of the later *parvans* are adjuncts to the epic and not truly a part of the text; hence their teachings on the subject may be disregarded. In looking at the narrative, a selective review of specific passages which appear to support his argument enables him to conclude that the women of the epic are not presented as inferior to men. Thus by a creative reinterpretation of the text he is able to satisfy modern sensibilities without diminishing the authoritative status of the *Mahābhārata.*

Jayal's approach to the epics entails too thorough a textual analysis to permit such latitude in drawing conclusions. She stresses the difference between the society prescribed by the didactus and that portrayed in the narrative passages, and has no hesitation in condemning the epic *dharma-śāstra* for its attempts to create a social environment that represses the natural talents of women. What she seeks to establish is that there is an ancient Vedic form of Hinduism which predates the repressive ideas expressed in certain portions of the epics. This original Hinduism allowed women a social status of some equality, a situation reflected in the society depicted in other sections of the text. With the passage of time, however, this early religious tradition became degraded and a part of this process is seen in the oppression of women in society.

Such a view of the history of the Hindu tradition can only be regarded as conjecture for there is insufficient evidence on which to base definite conclusions. What is significant is that it calls into question the scriptural status of the epics, for in this view of the Hindu tradition only the *śruti* is truly canonical and the later *smṛti*, including the epics, is reduced to a status in which it can no longer be regarded as fully authoritative. This, of course, accords perfectly with the views of the Brahmo-samāj and certain other neo-Hindu groups, but it is questionable as to how far it matches the conceptions of the Hindu mainstream. There is no doubt that from the viewpoint of Western liberal thought the ideas expressed in the *Mahābhārata* regarding gender distinctions will be seen as oppressive and pernicious in their giving legitimation to a patriarchical social structure. Such criticism is certainly valid, but for a proper appreciation of the epic's approach to questions of gender it is essential to consider the overall context.

The epic's view of society stresses order above all else, for a breakdown of the social order meant poverty, starvation and a state of chaos in which criminals flourished and everyone else suffered. To preserve social order every individual was ascribed a rigidly demarcated position in a hierarchical structure, generally based on the family of birth. The criticism of such a rigidly stratified society is that it is repressive to the individual, be it a *śūdra* who is designated as inferior to the higher *varṇas* or a woman who is designated as inferior to men. Modern liberal thought regards the rejection of such a social structure as axiomatic; nonetheless, it remains problematic for us to judge such a society, for clearly its intellectual élite took the view that individual freedom should be sacrificed for the sake of what was seen as communal prosperity based on the rule of law. For the modern commentator there are obvious difficulties in making any judgement as to whether this view was correct. It must also be borne in mind that women in the epic period must have spent long periods of their adult lives bearing and nursing children, for effective contraception was unknown and large families were socially and economically desirable. In such an environment it is hard to see how the question of gender equality would arise in any form comparable to the modern debate. The problem, of course, becomes pronounced when ancient *dharma-śāstra* is regarded as absolute authority that must be rigidly enforced in all ages.

Many contemporary interpreters of religious traditions have found it comparatively easy to accept the relative status of injunctions from the ancients about social issues. It is accepted that such social horizons may have been desirable for earlier societies, but now circumstances have changed scriptural teachings on such subjects can quite legitimately be revised or reinterpreted. What is more problematic, however, and what represents a fundamentally repressive aspect of epic thought, is the idea that the social order prescribed is not conventional but reflects the inborn nature of individuals. Women are condemned to an inferior status not because society appears to function more efficiently through this arrangement, but because the inherent female disposition renders her inferior. The teachings here are not merely a recommendation for an efficient social structure but are a view of humanity that provides a universal underpinning for gender-based oppression. This perspective, arguing that the social inferiority of women is justified because it reflects the natural distinction between the genders, will instantly be recognised as characteristic of much traditional Western thought on the issue and it is one that feminism has fought long and hard to counteract.

The *Mahābhārata* does, however, include an alternative view of humanity which has a very different focus in its preoccupation with the spiritual identity of all beings. In this world view, the commonality of life overrides the temporary, and therefore illusory, distinctions conventionally drawn on the basis of class, race and gender. Clearly, as Sulabhā points out to Janaka, it is impossible to live one's life entirely on this basis, for the individual cannot avoid making distinctions between child and adult, male and female, man and beast. Nonetheless, it is legitimate to regard the philosophy of *mokṣa-dharma* as providing the basis for an egalitarian understanding of humanity and not just the beliefs of scattered mystical sects on the fringe of society.

In terms of contemporary beliefs, it may be noted how the traditions of Sāṁkhya and Vedanta have been utilised by modern Hindus to legitimate opposition to colonial, social, sexual and economic oppression. Paul Hacker is quite correct when he points out that this adoption of the tenets of *mokṣa-dharma* for political purposes is a deviation from the original intent which is world-indifferent.[9] Nonetheless, there is no absolute orthodoxy or consistency of doctrine on how one should conduct one's life having once absorbed the realisation of true *jñāna*. Some teachers urge the renunciation of all contact with society, but the *Bhagavad-gītā* expresses a radically different opinion, and one may recall how Sulabhā employs the doctrines of Sāṁkhya to dismiss Janaka's question as to whom she belongs to and his criticism of her independent status.

Notes

1. Moorthy, K. 'Socio-Cultural Milieu of the Mahābhārata', in *Mahābhārata Revisited,* R.N. Dandekar Ed, New Delhi, 1990, p. 147.
2. Jayal, S. *The Status of Women in the Epics,* Delhi, 1966.
3. Hacker, P. *Kleine Schriften,* Wiesbaden, 1978, pp. 580-608.
4. These passages are in many places identical to teachings on the same subject in the *Manu-smṛti.*
5. Jayal 1966, p. 230.
6. Ibid, p. 102.
7. Sutherland, S. 'Sita and Draupadī: Aggressive Behaviour and Role Models in the Sanskrit Epics', *Journal of the American Oriental Society* 109, 1989, p. 72.
8. Vivekananda stated, "I shall not rest till I root out this distinction of sex. Is there any sex-discrimination in the Ātman? Out with the differentiation between man and woman — all is Ātman! Give up the identification with the body and stand up! Say, *asti, asti,* 'Everything is!' — cherish positive thoughts." (*Teachings of Swami Vivekananda,* Calcutta, 1976, p. 137).
9. Hacker 1978, p. 594.

Chapter 12

CONCLUSION: THE SIGNIFICANCE OF THE *MAHĀBHĀRATA*'S TEACHINGS

1. Introduction

The *Mahābhārata*, whatever else it might be, is a didactic literature which seeks to educate and enlighten those who hear its message. Much of this teaching is clearly specific to the time and culture in which the authors lived and to the issues that confronted them. Nonetheless, it would be wrong to judge on this basis that the modern world has nothing to learn from a text of this type and numerous writers have pointed out the ongoing contribution that such literature can make. Ninian Smart discusses the way in which ancient beliefs retain a meaning in the modern context, referring to this as 'compatability',[1] Wendy O'Flaherty argues that the myths of Śiva reveal general and universal truths which have a message for the modern world,[2] and David Tracy presents the concept of the 'religious classic' which speaks to all peoples in all times.[3]

For the modern Hindu, the *Mahābhārata*, and the *Bhagavad-gītā* in particular, is one of the most authoritative scriptures of his or her tradition, and its teachings are hence a vital source of inspiration in confronting the ethical and religious dilemmas of life. The same, of course, does not apply to the West where the *Mahābhārata* is recognised as coming from an alien and perhaps exotic tradition, and in any case the notion of religious authority is becoming an increasingly archaic concept. The collapse of religious orthodoxy, however, and its replacement by the 'heretical imperative'[4] means that Western thought should be more open to hearing from and reflecting upon the ideas of other cultures. In this section I wish, therefore, to consider briefly some of the ways in which epic thought may contribute to contemporary considerations, both secular and religious.

2. The Question of Right Action

Western society in the twentieth century has been profoundly influenced by 'social-Darwinist' ideologies based on competitive action. Nazism and contemporary fascist and nationalist movements emphasise the notion of races striving against one another in violent competition for land, wealth, power and scarce resources of all types. Free market capitalism is concerned more with the individual than with nation or race, but still stresses selfish aggrandisement as the primary motivation for human activity and as the natural stimulus for human achievement. Such world views argue that competitive endeavour reflects the essence of human nature, and that ethics must be in line with that human nature rather than working against it. This ethical view has not prevailed unopposed, and moral philosophies and religious beliefs continue to urge that right action must be based on morality rather than a demeaning view of human nature. In the last two decades, however, the tendency towards unfettered competition in market economics and the rise of aggressive forms of nationalism have pushed moral ideologists onto the defensive.

There is no doubt that the *Mahābhārata* opposes the view that factional and individual competition are inherent to human nature and should therefore be accepted and embraced. In his writings on the epic, Krishna Chaitanya sees within the text a rejection of this 'scientism' which he believes to be derived from the works of Bentham, Hobbes and Adam Smith which urge that man is motivated by hedonism alone.[5] In contrast, it preaches a moral view of life opposing the cruelty and search for power and wealth that characterise the mechanistic view of humanity. The prevailing ideology preached by the *Mahābhārata* is concerned specifically with sustaining virtue in opposition to selfish and hedonistic ways of life. This notion of virtue is a familiar one involving honesty, being true to one's word, generous, forgiving, kind-hearted and tolerant. Yudhiṣṭhira, the apogee of virtue, denies tribalism and is equal to friend and foe alike to a degree where it enrages many in his own party. He also rejects the competitive mentality of Duryodhana who can see no further than the notion of personal gain at the expense of those who are perceived as rivals.

The portrayal of the character and ambitions of Duryodhana makes a significant point that is too often overlooked today. Dramatically in the narrative and didactically in Chapter 16 of the

Bhagavad-gītā, the argument is forcefully asserted that personal and factional ambition leads to immorality and dishonesty, and that competition produces hatred, enmity, conflict and the violent abuse of others. At a time when various strands of contemporary ideology are urging that materialism and even greed are positive qualities, eulogising the effectiveness of competition for realising human potential, the alternative perspective presented by the epic makes an important contribution to such debates.

The *Mahābhārata* attempts to highlight the petty-mindedness that is a concomitant of selfish ambition, setting it in stark contrast to the wisdom of one who is able to judge the changing fortunes of this world in their true perspective. The criticism of quietism has been levelled at the epic's ideology, but Yudhiṣṭhira ultimately is not a quietist, for he wages war with all the means available to him when no option beyond absolute surrender remains. He more than any other character refuses to submit to social and familial pressure, always trying to put principle above self-interest. His final recourse is to accept violence as necessary, but only after every other possibility has been explored and only then with reluctance.

The message of the epic is one of restraint; Duryodhana displays the opposite characteristic, readily taking offence at insults real and imagined and then immediately considering ways in which he may retaliate against those he takes to be his enemies. Against this, the apparent quietism of Yudhiṣṭhira is an example from which all can learn, for too often we see petty differences elevated into deep-seated hatred, enmity and quarrel. The tolerance and ability to forgive seen in Yudhiṣṭhira thus teaches a valuable lesson and it is perhaps this above all that Vyāsa finally cries out that his readers should learn from,

ūrdhva-bāhur viraumy eṣa na kaścic chṛṇoti me
dharmād arthaś ca kāmaś ca sa kim arthaṁ na sevyate

na jātu kāmān na bhayān na lobhād
dharmaṁ tyajej jīvitasyāpi hetoḥ
nityo dharmaḥ sukha-duḥkhe tv anitye
jīvo nityo hetur asya tv anityaḥ

'With arms raised, I cry cut, but no-one hears me. From virtue come both wealth and pleasure, so what is the purpose in not following it?

> One should never abandon virtue for the sake of pleasure, out of fear or because of greed, nor even for the sake of life itself. Virtue is everlasting, but joy and misery are not; the living being is eternal, but the cause of his existence here is impermanent.' (18.5.49-50)

3. Ritual and Virtue in Religious Belief

The recurring dichotomy between ritual acts and acts of virtue will remain a question to tax theologians as long as any form of organised religion exists. Is religion to be understood as a system of divinely ordained ritual acts, which may or may not be based on morality, or is it the impetus towards individual virtue and personal upliftment through a collective comprehension of the divine will? Here also the *Mahābhārata* makes a significant contribution. A major theme of the epic narrative is the will of the Deity being enforced to ensure that ritual *dharma* is sustained, yet at the same time we have the paradox of Yudhiṣṭhira, *dharma* personified, expressing constant misgivings about the execution of ritual conduct where it conflicts with his understanding of individual virtue.

As always the attitude of Yudhiṣṭhira carries weight in the text, but the epic does not go so far as to teach that individual virtue can stand alone as the pure form of religiosity. It recognises the need for custom, tradition and ritual, and perpetuates the Vedic belief that ritual acts are necessary for the sustenance of the cosmic order and the gods who preside over it. Thus the text presents its hearer with a dramatic interplay which stresses the necessity of both ritual and virtue, but recognises the tensions that arise between them and explores the dramatic possibilities of human responses to such tensions. In the end we are presented with an eschatological conclusion in which both those who pursued virtue with little regard for ritual action, and also those who ignored virtue but followed the ritualised conduct of life are rewarded in heaven with an exalted position amongst the gods.

The view of the epic thus emerges that the social and socialising function of religion must exist alongside the individual's personal commitment to virtue. Tradition, custom, ritual and practice are not to be abandoned, for society depends upon stable institutions; and yet interacting within this contingency, individuals must seek the path of 'goodness' which is more than mere adherence to the traditional rules of conduct that religion and society prescribe for them. The text accepts that tension will emerge as a part of this process of interaction, but rather than offering a simplistic solution it illustrates the tension dramatically as if seeking to do no more than make the hearer aware that such situations are a part of religious belief.

4. The Yoga View of the World

Several writes, notably Greg Bailey[6] and Madeleine Biardeau,[7] in reasserting a more synthetic view of the *Mahābhārata*, have argued that the extensive teachings found in the *Śānti, Anuśāsana,* and *Aśvamedhika* present in a more codified form ideas that are identical to those explored by the narrative. This is true perhaps of the *Rāja-dharma,* but the teachings on Yoga and renunciation mark a perspective that is distinct from anything found elsewhere in the text. The narrative is rarely if ever concerned with absolute salvation nor with the philosophy and techniques through which release from this world is sought, and yet the didactus devotes several hundred chapters almost exclusively to this subject.

Acceptance of such teachings demands a commitment of faith of a religious nature. One must believe in the self as an entity distinct from the body and believe further that the Yoga techniques described by the *Mahābhārata* can lead the self to a state of absolute freedom and unadulterated joy. Where the individual is unable to make that faith commitment, however, there is still much to be learnt from the epic's teachings on Sāṁkhya and Yoga. Whilst belief in a transcendent soul is clearly a commitment of religious faith, the concept of detachment in the sense of easing the more intense forms of emotional involvement is one that can be of great psychological value. Epic philosophy here urges us towards taking at least a first step back from worldly preoccupations, limiting the hold of the selfish and egotistical state of mind, and thereby finding the capacity to assess each situation from a position that is less distorted by an egocentric world view. The more detached attitude stressed by Sāṁkhya thus helps us to confront reality from a more balanced perspective.

The fact is that so many of the anguishes we endure, so many of the sources of frustration, anger, enmity and hatred, are trivial affairs and can be seen as such if one is able to withdraw somewhat from the egocentricity that perverts rational judgement. Although this psychological adjustment is not the main thrust of Sāṁkhya thought, which is always soteriological, the teachings here may be of value in allowing an individual to develop a more dispassionate and hence less self-centred view of the world.

5. Understanding of the Nature of God

The *Mahābhārata* is a predominantly theistic text, reflecting several stages between the worship of a pantheon of gods and the acceptance of an all-powerful principal Deity. By their very nature such ideas can substantially influence the thought only of those who are non-atheists, but those who consider the existence of God a possibility may find within the epic much to ponder in attempting to comprehend how the divine nature could interact with the world. Furthermore, those who claim for their own traditions a supremacist or exclusivist position will find their ideas challenged by the epic's sophisticated theism, which is hard to dismiss as primitive or inferior.

Epic theism is characterised by the different aspects of the nature of God that it portrays. We have Viṣṇu taking the role of the Vedic Indra, leading a pantheon of gods into a conflict of cosmic dimension against the forces of chaos and evil. The Deity and the demigods who follow him are shown as directly intervening in the history of mankind, for human affairs and the stability of the cosmic order are interrelated. The nature of the Deity manifest on earth reveals both his otherness and his immediacy. The narrative portrays righteous persons, wicked persons and those who are mixed, and there is also Kṛṣṇa who is beyond such assessments. His actions, unlike those of men, cannot be subjected to tests and judgement,[8] for as God says to Job, "My ways are not your ways."

Viṣṇu is characteristically a benign Deity, or perhaps, as Biardeau and Scheuer would argue, the benign aspect of the Deity. This is not his only feature, however, for he also displays a ferocious side to the divine nature in which the awesome power of God overwhelms the lesser concerns of human beings which are far outstripped by the vastness of his time and his dimensions. To meet this divine power human beings must rise above the mundane, for, as the epic repeatedly stresses, the mundane will be carried away by god who as time is the mighty destroyer of worlds. This uncontrolled and destructive feature of the Deity is also portrayed by the text as Śiva, who iconographically is an ascetic, a *yogin*, and a magician whose fierce energy cares nothing for the ways of men or even the ways of *dharma.*

The *Mahābhārata* also teaches a complex philosophical understanding of the nature of God. There is no wholesale dichotomy between the philosophical and mythic perspectives, for the Deity is still Nārāyaṇa who is known as Viṣṇu and Kṛṣṇa, but here the nature of God is removed from the anthropomorphic notions of the mythic theology. This is the inconceivable and incomprehensible Deity, especially as described in the *Gītā* and the *Nārāyaṇīya,* who has his own mystic identity and yet is all things, is the self within all living beings, and is the 'unmanifest' in whom all things rest when the creation is withdrawn. Thus the epic offers an understanding of God which includes a Deity who is present and involved in the progression of worldly events and yet is also remote, inconceivable and far beyond anything the human mind can absorb.

The text urges that this God should be worshipped with devotion, and that the life of the believer should be dedicated to such surrender. It is the Deity who is the controller of destiny and therefore in all our acts and endeavours it must be accepted that success will come only if the Ordainer wills it to be so. One should thus surrender personal ambition and accept whatever he bestows. The *Gītā* in particular propounds the notion of divine reciprocation, through which the worshippers are protected by God and by his grace attain the salvation that is reached with great difficulty by the followers of Sāṁkhya and Yoga.

The understanding of the divine nature thus represented by the epic is one that provides a valuable contribution to the debates focusing on the notion of a global theology. This is the process that Hebblethwaite refers to when he writes,

> It is important at some stage to try to press back from the more specific notions fastened in particular theistic traditions to more philosophical and more general notions, which do not presuppose alleged self-revelations of a personal creator. This is necessary if there is to be dialogue between, say, the Hindu theologian and the Christian theologian.[9]

All too often one encounters works which seek only to find differences between traditions and then proceed to demonstrate the inferiority of that which is divergent from the doctrines to which the particular writer subscribes. Alternatively, it is sometimes argued that the distinctiveness of individual cultures and traditions renders any form of cross-cultural dialogue meaningless. It is surely apparent, however, that despite the uniqueness of different cultural identities, there is much to be learned by listening to the teachings of others and allowing the ideas offered to broaden the understanding of the divine nature within one's own culture.

6. Political and Social Action

Activists in the Indian nationalist movement of the first half of this century and other political idealists have sought to find legitimation for their actions from within their own tradition, as well as inspiration and guidance for the continuation of their struggles. There are obvious problems in this attempt, for Vedānta, Sāṁkhya and Yoga are other-worldly philosophies that seek complete detachment from the activities of human society. The same is not true, however, of much of the ideology of the *Mahābhārata* which portrays the forces of good and evil in narrative form, and sets the struggle between them in a political as well as a cosmic context. The nature of power is a central theme in the epic; the proper use of royal authority is an essential part of *dharma*, and yet the evil consequences of excessive attachment to power are repeatedly portrayed as we hear of the wickedness of Duryodhana and the weakness and corruption of the potentially righteous Dhṛtarāṣṭra.

The warning against the corrupting influence of power is very stark; those who seek positions of authority easily become seduced by the sweetness of the power they wield and under the influence of such intoxication lose their regard for virtue. Their sense of proper values is gradually undermined to the point where the attachment to power becomes like a drug and any principle may be sacrificed in order to keep and expand its influence. Hence a clear warning is sent out by the epic that although the execution of power is an absolute necessity; one should be aware of its degrading influence on those who wield it. Their reason may become disturbed to the extent that like lunatics they would sooner plunge the world into a state of catclysm and horror than relinquish the power they hold. For this reason Vyāsa holds up his arms and cries out for humanity to listen to him and not allow lust to overcome our instincts for virtue.

Power must therefore be allowed to reside only in those whose addiction to righteousness is such that it will not be undermined by the impulses of personal ambition. The ideal leader is first of all one who does not aspire for power for personal reasons, but accepts it as a duty it would be delinquent to avoid. It is this absence of personal ambition that characterises an effective leader, for his or her judgement will then be able to recognise right action without being perverted by selfish considerations. The text also recognises, however, that selfish motivation is a powerful incentive to leadership and that the ideal leader will frequently avoid the competitive struggle for power. Hence there is an ever present danger of society being controlled by persons who are not worthy of the responsibility. The lesson that one should be wary of those who ardently seek power is one that has clear resonances for contemporary society in which leadership so often seems to be reposed in persons rendered unfit for the responsibility by either ineptitude or selfish ambition. Political leaders are today regarded as one of the least trustworthy groups in society and the epic indicates that this is to be expected because ambition for power is a great destroyer of virtue.

To the modern political thinker ancient ideas on the art of kingship may appear to be of little contemporary relevance, but it is apparent that modern political institutions are not as dissimilar from those depicted by the epic as might be imagined. All societies are effectively controlled, politically and economically, by élites. Marxist ideology talks in terms of class dictatorships and seeks a 'dictatorship of the proletariat', but in reality this means at best the dictatorship of an élite sympathetic to the interests of the proletariat. Capitalist democracy progagandises that its political system represents government of the people by the people, but the extent to which real power truly devolves down to those without economic influence is questionable. It is the economic rather than the political institutions that are the true repositories of power in capitalist democracies and the political systems are substantially controlled by an economic élite. It is also questionable as to how far the vicissitudes of the electoral process involve any substantive transference of power, leaving the élite to dominate the state and, in the modern context, the world.

The *Mahābhārata* has no illusions about power. It recognises and endorses the right of an hereditary ruling élite to dominate society, with its power based on military strength and expertise. The epic view is that domination by such an élite is essential for social stability and no theoretical transference of power to a broader base is contemplated. The modern mind will inevitably view such a perspective as inherently repressive, for there is no scope within it for any form of mass political action; politics is a field reserved for a tiny minority of individuals. To such objections the argument of the epic is that whilst a concentration of power may lead to tyranny, this danger is a necessary evil that must be tolerated so that order may prevail over chaos.

In any case it may be argued again that all societies are dominated by élites and that all such élites are prone to oppression. The advocates of liberal democracy may congratulate themselves on having at least limited oppression and extended basic political rights to all citizens. They must not forget, however, that in today's global economic system the affluence of Western capitalist states is made possible only by the economic and, where necessary, military oppression of poorer nations, the majority of whose citizens are condemned to a life of grinding poverty as a result.

It is thus not wholly unreasonable to take the view that élites always dominate societies and élites always exploit and oppress. In defence of epic teachings it may be said that legitimation was given to the notion that the ruling élite had a religious duty to protect the citizens from misfortune, crime and poverty, and that it was a sin leading to hell to allow personal lust to dictate oppressive economic policies. The capitalist ethos, especially where the freedom of the market is stressed, is completely different. Here a social-Darwinist type of world view has come to predominate in which there is no absolute right or wrong and no heaven or hell as reward or punishment. Instead the ethos of competition prevails with winners and losers, and inevitably suffering and poverty must be the lot of the losers.

On a global scale the poorer nations are the permanent losers in the competition and their peoples suffer poverty as a result, but the capitalist world view places no moral imperative upon the winners to abandon their self-interest and assist the poorer nations. The essential difference is in terms of morality. Free market capitalism is amoral in a Darwinist sense, and hence contains no moral argument or religious curtailment limiting the severity of the competition it upholds. The *Mahābhārata* concept is fundamentally different for it is based on the notion of *dharma*, an absolute unchallengeable morality. In a manner distinct from the modern liberal perspective, oppression is to be curtailed not because it is counter-productive, as the Brandt Report argued, but because it is wrong and falls under the heading of *adharma*. As to how effective such ideas were in restraining oppression we can only speculate, but the very existence of the religious legitimation of restraint is a significant factor.

7. Approach to Establishing Doctrine

Finally, the very manner in which the *Mahābhārata* approaches the question of doctrine provides a valuable lesson that today is more relevant than ever. In the history of Western religion there are numerous instances of strict creedal formulae being enforced in response to subtle metaphysical and ethical questions, and these rigid creeds have then been defended with unyielding vigour in bitter conflicts with those whose own axioms digress from them only in the slightest manner. This approach is not confined to the field of religion and it is arguable that the traditional Christian insistence on a formulaic orthodoxy as well as the somewhat simplistic demarcation drawn between good and evil, saved and damned, has had a profound and negative effect on the entire progress of Western thought.

It is apparent that science, the source of truth statements for Western culture, has a tendency to follow a similar course in establishing unchallengeable dogmas and vilifying anyone who attempts to pursue an alternative course. In truth, in all academic fields one frequently observes the delight with which one scholar seizes upon perceived shortcomings in the work of another and scornfully dismisses their theories and methods. Projects which reflect upon the most profound issues related to human existence are thus seen at times to deteriorate into petty squabbling between scholars whose primary aim seems to be to enhance their own reputations at the expense of any perceived rival.

The contradictions apparent in the doctrines expounded by different portions of the epic have been noted by many writers. Wendy O'Flaherty refers to, "the disquieting ability of Indians to believe several contradictory tenets at once,"[10] and according to Edgerton, we find in the *Gītā*, "expressions which, in strict logic, contradict its most cardinal doctrines."[11] To the Western mind this apparent lack of precision is a serious limitation of the epic's function as teacher of religious doctrine, for it seems to be the result of woolly thinking that cannot stand up to the examination of hard logic. The critical scholar gains inspiration from such contradictions, seeing in them evidence of different accretions to an original text.

The *Mahābhārata* must, however, be recognised as a work which explores as much as it dictates religious ideas, and when this is recognised the variety of perspectives it embodies is less of a problem. It is this complex approach to religious truth, using contradictions in a dialectical manner, which Peter Brook stresses in discussing the dramatic content of the epic:

> Because the basic story of the *Mahābhārata*–and this was one of the main reasons I was drawn to it in the first place–is very different from almost any other epic in the sense that *everything* in it creates contradiction: all the characters and all of their actions are such as to smash any single moral idea . . . The essence of all religious thought is that it can't be captured in ordinary intellectual terms . . . it can only be experienced.[12]

There is surely a lesson to be learned here for those who seek to reduce ethical and metaphysical ideas to simplistic codes which contribute little towards a deepening of human wisdom. According to Frances Young, a Christian theologian,

> Eusebius of Caesarea signed the creed of Nicaea for the sake of church unity, but he was clearly embarrassed about it. What we need is not new creeds, but a new openness which will allow manifold ways of responding and elucidating that response.[13]

The *Mahābhārata* does of course make numerous overt statements of doctrine, but it does not allow its teaching to be completely circumscribed by doctrinal logic. It recognises and explores the complexities, contradictions and tensions that reality places before us—the way in which belief systems conflict with real life. Dramatically and didactically the epic explores these issues, but frequently in a manner that regards the hearer as more than a passive receiver of creeds, offering instead the possibility of deeper reflection on questions where creeds alone can provide only the most restricted form of comprehension.

Thus through its complexity, its contradictions, and the variety of perspectives it embraces, the epic indicates an approach to knowledge that avoids some of the pitfalls of over-dogmatising. It urges that different views should be heard with respect, but with the understanding that they do not necessarily provide the final word. *Dharma* is subtle and the more one considers it the more its complexity becomes apparent. This understanding of knowledge is a great lesson that warns us to be cautious of any form of dogmatic or absolute view of reality. The truth is not simple and will not always comply with the unidimensional reasonings of scientific or religious truth statements. If the truth is to be known at all, then the view of the epic is that it is perceived not by logicians, creedists, or experimenters, but only by those who place virtue above all else.

8. Conclusions

Each chapter of this study provides specific conclusions regarding the teachings of the *Mahābhārata* as they pertain to a particular topic. There are in addition certain general points about the nature of the epic and of epic studies that have become apparent and it is appropriate that these should be highlighted as a final note.

1. A significant point regarding the study of Purāṇic material is made by Freda Matchett in her study of the *avatāra* myth in the *Harivaṁśa, Viṣṇu Purāṇa* and *Bhāgavata Purāṇa.*[14] She points out that the numerous structuralist studies that have appeared in recent years have used individual *Purāṇas* as "quarries" from which to extract material relevant to the author's theorising. The great weakness of this approach is that it ignores and obscures the specific focus of individual works. Matchett's study demonstrates that passages taken from any of these three works can be properly understood only by reference to its context, for each has specific doctrinal and theological preoccupations influencing, shaping and structuring the material it employs.

When Matchett's view is applied to the *Mahābhārata*, it is clearly more problematic for the epic is a far more diverse and complex work than any of the *Purāṇas*. Nonetheless, I would contend that one of the principal results of the present study is to enhance the integrity of the *Mahābhārata* as a unitary text. Whilst no single, cogent line of thought can be detected throughout the various sections of the epic, it is apparent nonetheless that there are specific preoccupations addressed by the text to the extent where it is legitimate to speak of a style of 'epic thought' distinctive to the *Mahābhārata.* I am not arguing here for any form of restatement of Dahlmann's synthetic view,[15] but rather seeking to confirm the opinion of van Buitenen,[16] Fitzgerald[17] and others that it is possible to identify specific themes which comprise a distinctive epic perspective.

2. These central preoccupations may be identified as being firstly, the concern over the nature and execution of *dharma,* defined as one's duty to God, to human society and to the entire cosmic order. Specific aspects of this question confronted by the epic include how *adharma,* especially in the form of violent action, may become a necessity for preserving *dharma,* the relationship of *dharma* to the gods and above all their leader, Viṣṇu, how the man who accepts *dharma* thereby joins the faction of the Deity, how *dharma* leads to heavenly rewards and prosperity on earth, and how *dharma* interacts with virtue and at times comes into conflict with it.

We then encounter a second phase of epic thought which reflects the impact of the ideas of the ascetic sects on the established ritualism of society and also the conflict between individual spirituality and the hierarchical structure of a social belief system. This offers a more advanced dualistic notion of the individual, a more world-denying ethos, an alternative soteriology and eschatology, and a more philosophical notion of the nature of God as a Deity beyond the pantheon, beyond this world altogether, and identified with both the Unmanifest reality and the self in all beings. These two major themes lie at the heart of 'epic thought', corresponding to the tendencies referred to by the text as *pravṛtti* and *nivṛtti.* Not only are both explored by the epic, but at its heart lies the *Bhagavad-gītā,* its doctrinal essence, in which the attempt is made to find a synthesis between these two major religious tendencies and the ideas of devotion to the Deity that interact with both of them.

3. It is essential to stress that I do not regard the present study as being a complete exposition of epic thought. It provides one channel of understanding concentrating primarily on the overt statements of the text, but there is much more that could be said from this perspective, and various other angles from which the

subject can be approached. One drawback, in my opinion, to the work of Dumézil, Biardeau, and to a lesser extent Hiltebeitel, is their view of the text as being a kind of encoded message to which they have finally found the key. With this discovery now made, the true meaning tumbles forth as a subtext lurking beneath the chapters and verses.

I do not wish to deny the validity of such studies, for they frequently display accurate and detailed analysis of the text and offer many valuable insights, but merely to point out that this approach is just one line among several along which epic studies may be pursued, and not the absolute method of analysis which is the only means by which the text can be properly understood. Thus when Hiltebeitel criticises Otto's work on the *Mahābhārata* for concentrating too much on theology and ignoring the mythic aspect of the text,[18] a valid response would be that Hiltebeitel's own work is equally incomplete for dealing only with myths and making virtually no reference to epic theology. There are clearly various perspectives from which the text may be understood, and it would be unrealistic for me to claim that I have made a complete study of the epic. The different chapters provide insights into its thought and its teachings, but only from one perspective and even then without completely covering all aspects of doctrine discussed by the *Mahābhārata*.

4. It is perhaps inappropriate to attempt an evaluation of the *Mahābhārata*, for any such judgements are inevitably subjective and culturally conditioned. Christian commentators[19] and writers such as Hopkins[20] and Edgerton[21] are critical of the epic for its logical inconsistencies and its lack of genuine historicity. It must recognised, however, that any such evaluation comes from a particular perspective. Traditional Christianity has a deep-seated interest in denegrating the ideas and practices of other traditions in order to establish the uniqueness of its own revelation, whilst post-enlightenment Western thought regards sequential reasoning as the absolute key to knowledge, and judges pejoratively any work that does not mirror this view. Hence any evaluation of the epic from the West, however closely reasoned, is almost inevitably an ethno-centric judgement based on culturally derived preconceptions. Perhaps it is sufficient to recognise the *Mahābhārata* as a great classic of religious literature and I hope the present study has served somewhat to demonstrate an aspect of this greatness

by highlighting its potential contribution to a global theology, and the profundity of its reflection on the deepest questions that humanity faces generation after generation.

Here one can reasonably argue that more than any other authoritative text, the *Mahābhārata* is the single work which comes closest to presenting a full expression of Hindu belief, a point recognised by Zaehner whose general work on Hinduism[22] is little more than a study of the ideas of the epic. Chronologically, it stands at a point of immense significance in the development of the tradition, when the Vedic ideas on ritual worship of the gods through *yajñas* are still central, but are facing the influence of ascetic mysticism, and possibly non-Aryan beliefs which combine to set in motion the monotheistic and devotional ideas that are of such significance in later Hinduism.

It would be inaccurate to argue that all strands of Hindu thought are represented in the epic; devotion to the Goddess plays only a minor role, and there is virtually no expression of the emotional forms of *bhakti* or of Tantric ideas. The fact remains, however, that Hinduism in all its manifold forms has been profoundly influenced by the *Mahābhārata* and virtually all facets of the tradition will be found to have some connection with material contained in the epic. Therefore, when considering the different branches of Hindu thought that the text touches upon, one is reminded of the words spoken by Arjuna when he first beholds Kṛṣṇa as the universal Deity–*pasyāmi devāṁs tava deva dehe sarvān.*

Notes

1. Smart, N. *The Science of Religion and the Sociology of Knowledge: Some Methodological Questions,* Princeton, 1977, p. 101.
2. O'Flaherty, W. *Asceticism and Eroticism in the Mythology of Śiva,* London, 1973, p. 1.
3. Tracy, D. *Blessed Rage for Order, The New Pluralism in Theology,* New York, 1975, p. 156.
4. Berger, P. *The Heretical Imperative, Contemporary Possibilities of Religious Affirmation,* London, 1980.
5. Chaitanya, K. 'The Mahābhārata: Epic of Universality and Human Concern', In *Mahābhārata Revisited,* R.N. Dandekar Ed, New Delhi, 1990, pp. 163-167.
6. "What is implicit in the narrative material is made explicit in the didactic mode." (Bailey, G. 'Suffering in the Mahābhārata: Draupadī and Yudhiṣṭhira', in *Suffering: Indian Perspectives,* K.N. Tiwari Ed, Delhi, 1986, p. 39).
7. Biardeau, M. and Péterfalvi, J. *Le Mahābhārata,* Volume 2, Paris, 1986, p. 326.

8. This is attempted in the epic by Gāndhārī and Uttaṅka, but is shown to be a pointless exercise.
9. Hebblethwaite, B. *The Problems of Theology*, Cambridge, 1980, p. 7.
10. O'Flaherty, W. *The Origins of Evil in Hindus Mythology*, Berkeley, 1976, p. 19.
11. Edgerton, F. *The Bhagavad-gītā Translated and Interpreted*, New York, 1964, p. 109.
12. Cited in Cott, J. 'A Forest Without End: Peter Brook on the Mahābhārata', *Parabola* 12, 1987, p. 88.
13. Cited in Wilson, I. *Jesus: The Evidence*, London, 1984, p. 162.
14. Matchett, F. *The Avatāra Myth in the Harivaṁśa, the Viṣṇupurāṇa and the Bhāgavata Purāṇa*, Doctoral Thesis, Lancaster, 1990, pp. 483-486.
15. Dahlmann, J. *Genesis des Mahābhārata*, Berlin 1899.
16. van Buitenen, J.A.B. *Mahābhārata, Volume 1, The Book of Beginning*, Chicago, 1973, p. 16.
17. Fitzgerald, J.L. 'The Great Epic of India as Religious Rhetoric: A Fresh Look at the Mahābhārata', *Journal of the American Academy of Religion* 51, 1983, p. 615.
18. Hiltebeitel, A. *The Ritual of Battle, Krishna in the Mahābhārata*, Ithaca, 1976, p. 125.
19. See, for example, Shideler, E. 'The Meaning of Man in the Bhagavad-gītā', *Journal of the Bible and Religion* 28, 1960.
20. Hopkins, E.W. *The Great Epic of India*, Calcutta, 1969 (1st Ed 1901), pp. iv. x.
21. Edgerton 1964, pp. 108-109.
22. Zaehner, R.C. *Hinduism*, Oxford, 1962.

BIBLIOGRAPHY

I. Sanskrit Texts and Translations, in alphabetical order by title of text.

Aitareya Upaniṣad	Sanskrit text and trans Swāmī Śarvānanda, Madras, 1973
Bhagavad-gītā	trans and ed R.C. Zaehner, Oxford, 1973
Bhagavad-gītā	*The Bhagavad-gītā in the Mahābhārata,* trans and ed J.A.B. van Buitenen, Chicago, 1981
Bhagavad-gītā	*Bhagavad-gītā As It Is,* Sanskrit text, trans and commentary A.C. Bhaktivedanta Swami Prabhupada, Los Angeles, 1983
Bhāgavata Purāṇa	Sanskrit Text, Goṛakhpur, Gīta Press
Bhāgavata Purāṇa	*Śrīmad-Bhāgavatam,* trans and commentary A.C. Bhaktivedanta Swami Prabhupada, New York and Los Angeles, 1979-1991
Bhāgavata Purāṇa	*The Śrīmad-Bhāgavatam* trans J.M. Sanyal, 2 Vols, New Delhi, 1973
Brahma-Sūtras	trans S. Radhakrishnan, London, 1960
Harivaṃśa	ed P.L. Vaidya, 2 Vols, Poona 1969-1971
Harivaṃśa	trans M.L. Dutt, Calcutta, 1897
Kaṭha Upaniṣad	Sanskrit text and trans Swāmī Śarvānanda, Madras, 1981
Mahābhārata	ed V.S. Sukthankar et al., 19 Vols, Poona, 1933-1959
Mahābhārata	ed V.S. Sukthankar et al., 4 Vols, Poona, 1971-1975
Mahābhārata	trans J.A.B. van Buitenen, 3 Vols completed, Chicago, 1973-1978
Mahābhārata	trans K.M. Ganguli, 12 Vols, Delhi 1981 (first published 1883-1896)
Manu-Smṛti	*The Laws of Manu,* trans G. Buhler, Sacred Books of the East Vol XXV, Delhi, 1982, (first ed Oxford, 1886)
Nārāyaṇīya	*Nārāyaṇīya Parvan du Mahābhārata,* French trans by A.M. Esnoul, Paris, 1979

Rāmāyaṇa — *Śrīmad Vālmikī Rāmāyaṇa,* Sanskrit text and English trans, 3 Vols, Gorakhpur, 1974

Ṛg Veda — *The Ṛg Veda, An Anthology,* trans W.O'Flaherty, Harmondsworth, 1981

Śvetāśvatara Upaniṣad — Sanskrit text and trans Swāmī Tyāgiśānanda, Madras, 1979

Upaniṣads — *The Principal Upaniṣads,* Sanskrit text and trans S. Radhakrishnan, London, 1969

Upaniṣads — trans P. Olivelle, Oxford, 1996

Viṣṇu Purāṇa — Sanskrit text, Gorakhpur, Gītā Press

Viṣṇu Purāṇa — *The Viṣṇu Purāṇa: A System of Hindu Mythology and Tradition,* trans H.H. Wilson, Calcutta, 1972 (first ed 1840)

II. Works in European Languages, in alphabetical order by author

BAILEY, G. — *The Mythology of Brahmā,* Delhi, 1983

BAILEY, G. — 'Suffering in the Mahābhārata: Draupadī and Yudhiṣṭhira' in *Suffering: Indian Perspectives,* K.N. Tiwari Ed, Delhi, 1986, pp38-60

BEDEKAR, V.M. — 'Studies in Sāṁkhya: The Teachings of Pañchśikha in the Mahābhārata', *Annals of the Bhandarkar Oriental Research Institute,* 38, 1957, pp233-244

BEDEKAR, V.M. — 'The Mokṣa-dharma Studies: The Place and Functions of the Psychical Organism', *Annals of the Bhandarkar Oriental Research Institute,* 40, 1959, pp262-288

BEDEKAR, V.M. — 'Śukrācārya in the Mahābhārata: A Composite Personality', *Poona Orientalist,* 24, 3-4, 1959, pp91-103

BEDEKAR, V.M. — 'The Dhyāna-yoga in the Mahābhārata, XII 188: Its Similarity with the Jhāna of Early Buddhism', *Bharatīya Vidyā,* 20-21, 1960-61, pp 116-125

BEDEKAR, V.M. — 'The Doctrine of the Colour of Souls in the Mahābhārata: Its Characteristics and Implications', *Annals of the Bhandarkar Oriental Research Institute,* 48-49, 1968, pp329-338

BEDEKAR, V.M. — 'Yoga in the Mokṣadharmaparvan of the Mahābhārata', *Wiener Zeitschrift fur die Kunde*

Sud-und Ostasiens und Archiv fur Indische Philosophie, 12-13 1968-69, pp43-52

BEDEKAR, V.M. 'The Sanatsujātīyam: A Fresh Study', *Annals of the Bhandarkar Oriental Research Institute,* 58-59, 1977-78, pp469-477

BALVALKAR, S.K. 'The Cosmographical episode in the Mahābhārata and Padmapurāṇa', *The New Indian Antiquary,* Extra Series 1, 1939, pp19-28

BALVALKAR, S.K. 'Saṃjaya's "Eye Divine"', *Annals of the Bhandarkar Oriental Research Institute,* 27, 1946, pp310-331

BALVALKAR, S.K. 'The Origin and Function of the State According to the Rājadharmaparvan', *Annals of the Bhandarkar Oriental Research Institute,* 29, 1949, pp293-301

BHANDARKAR, R.G. *Vaiṣṇavism, Śaivism and Minor Religious Systems,* New York, 1980

BHARADVAJA, K. *A Philosophical Study of the Concept of Viṣṇu in the Purāṇas,* New Delhi, 1981

BIARDEAU, M. 'Some More Considerations About Textual Criticism', *Purāṇa,* 10, 2, 1968, pp115-123

BIARDEAU, M. 'Etudes de Mythologie Hindoue 4, Bhakti et Avatāra', *Bulletin de L'Ecole Francaise d'Extreme Orient,* Tome 63, Paris, 1976, pp111-263

BIARDEAU, M. 'Etudes de Mythologie Hindoue 5, Bhakti et Avatāra', *Bulletin de L'Ecole Francaise d'Extreme Orient,* Tome 65 Fasc. 1, Paris, 1978, pp87-237

BIARDEAU, M. *L'Hindouisme: Anthropologie d'une Civilization,* Paris, 1980

BIARDEAU, M. 'Etudes de Mythologie Hindoue, Tome 1, Cosmogonies Purāṇiques', *Publications de l'Ecole Francaise d'Extreme Orient,* Tome 128, Paris, 1981

BIARDEAU, M. and MALAMOUD, C. *Le Sacrifice dans l'Inde Ancienne,* Paris, 1976

BIARDEAU, M. and PETERFALVI, J. *Le Mahābhārata, Livres* 1-5, Paris, 1985

BIARDEAU, M. and PETERFALVI, J. *Le Mahābhārata,* Volume 2, Paris, 1986

BROCKINGTON, J. *The Sacred Thread: Hinduism in its Continuity and Diversity,* Edinburgh, 1981

BROCKINGTON, J. 'The Epic View of the Gods', *Shadow,* Vol 9, 1992, pp3-12

van BUITENEN, J.A.B. *Mahābhārata, Volume 1, The Book of the Beginning,* Chicago, 1973

van BUITENEN, J.A.B. 'A Reply to Goldman', *Journal of Asian Studies,* 35, 3, May 1976, pp470-473

van BUITENEN, J.A.B. *The Bhagavad-gītā in the Mahābhārata,* Chicago, 1981

van BUITENEN, J.A.B. *Studies in Indian Literature and Philosophy,* Ludo Rocher Ed, Delhi, 1988

CHAITANYA, K. *The Mahābhārata: A Literary Study,* New Delhi, 1985

CHAITANYA, K. 'The Mahābhārata: Epic of Universality and Human Concern', in R.Ṇ. Dandekar Ed, *Mahābhārata Revisited,* New Delhi, 1990, pp159-167

DAHLMANN, J. *Genesis des Mahābhārata,* Berlin, 1899

DANDEKAR, R.N. 'The Mahābhārata: Origin and Growth', *University of Ceylon Review,* 12, 1954, pp65-85

DANDEKAR, R.N. 'The Mahābhārata and its Critical Edition', *Indo-Asian Culture* 11, 1962, pp39-53

DASGUPTA, S. *A History of Indian Philosophy,* vol 2, Cambridge, 1973

DASGUPTA, S. *A History of Indian Philosophy,* Vol 4, Delhi, 1975

DUMEZIL, G. *Mythe et Epopee: L'Ideologie de Trois Functions dans les Epopees des Peuples Indoeuropeens,* Paris, 1968

EDGERTON, F. *The Bhagavad-gītā Translated and Interpreted,* New York, 1964

EDGERTON, F. 'The meaning of Sāṃkhya and Yoga', *American Journal of Philosophy* XLV, No 177, 1924, pp1-46

ESNOUL, A.M. *Nārāyaṇīya Parvan du Mahābhārata,* Paris, 1979

FITZGERALD, J. 'The Great Epic of India as Religious Rhetoric: A Fresh Look at the Mahābhārata', *Journal of the American Academy of Religion,* 51, 1983, pp611-630

FRAUWALLNER, E. *History of Indian Philosophy,* Volume 1, V.M. Bedekar trans, Delhi, 1973

GOLDMAN, R.P. 'India's Great War', *Journal of Asian Studies,* 35, 3, May 1976, pp463-470

GOLDMAN, R.P. *Gods, Priests and Warriors, The Bhṛgus of the Mahābhārata,* New York, 1977

GONDA, J. *Aspects of Early Viṣṇuism,* Delhi, 1969

GONDA, J. 'Dumezil's Tripartite Ideology: Some Critical Observations', *Journal of Asian Studies,* 34, 1, 1974, pp139-149

HACKER, P. *Kleine Schriften,* Wiesbaden, 1978

HARDY, F. *Viraha Bhakti, The Early History of Kṛṣṇa Devotion in South India,* Delhi, 1983

HEESTERMAN, J. C. *The Inner Conflict of Tradition, Essays in Indian Ritual, Kingship and Society,* Chicago, 1985

HELD, G. *The Mahābhārata, An Ethnological Study,* Amsterdam, 1935

HERMAN, A.L. 'The Problem of Suffering in the Bhagavadgītā', in *Suffering: Indian Perspectives,* K.N. Tiwari Ed, Delhi, 1986

HILTEBEITEL, A. 'The Mahābhārata and Hindu Eschatology', *History of Religions,* 12, 1972-73, pp95-135

HILTEBEITEL, A. *The Ritual of Battle, Krishna in the Mahābhārata,* Ithaca, 1976

HILTEBEITEL, A. 'The Two Kṛṣṇas on One Chariot: Upaniṣadic Imagery and Epic Mythology', *History of Religions,* 24, 1984-85, pp1-26

HILTEBEITEL, A. 'Toward a Coherent Study of Hinduism', *Religious Studies Review,* 9, 1983, pp206-212

HILTEBEITEL, A. 'Purity and Auspiciousness in the Sanskrit Epics', *Journal of Developing Societies,* 1, 1985, pp41-54

HOPKINS, E.W. 'Yoga Techniques in the Great Epic', *Journal of the American Oriental Society,* 22, 1901, pp333-379

HOPKINS, E.W. *Epic Mythology,* Strassburg, 1915

HOPKINS, E.W. *Ethics of India,* Port Washington, 1968

HOPKINS, E.W. *The Great Epic of India,* Calcutta, 1969 (first ed 1901)

HUBER, F. 'The Relevance of the Bhagavad-gītā According to Paul David Devanandan', *Religion and Society,* 34, 1987, pp53-65

IYENGAR, K.R.S. 'The Mahābhārata: An Epic of Universality and Deep Human Concern', in R.N. Dandekar Ed, *Mahābhārata Revisited,* New Delhi, 1990

JAYAL, S. *The Status of Women in the Epics,* Delhi, 1966

KANE, P.V. *History of Dharma-Śātra,* Vol 1, Part 1, Poona, 1971

KARVE, I. 'Kinship Terms and the Family Organization as Found in the Critical Edition of the Mahābhārata', *Bulletin of the Deccan College Research Institute,* 5, 1943-44, pp61-148

KARVE, I. *Yuganta: The End of an Epoch,* New Delhi, 1974

KAVEESHWAR, G.W. *The Ethics of the Gītā,* Delhi, 1971

KAWTHEKAR, P.N. 'Fables in the Mahābhārata', *Felicitation volume Presented to Mahamahopadhyaya Dr. V.V. Mirashi,* 1965, pp122-129

KEITH, A.B. 'The Brahmanic and Kshatriya Tradition', *Journal of the Royal Asiatic Society,* 1914, pp118-126

KHAIR, G.S. *Quest for the Original Gītā,* Bombay, 1969

KLAES, N. *Conscience and Consciousness: Ethical Problems of the Mahābhārata,* Bangalore, 1975

LAINE, J.W. 'Hinduism and the Mahābhārata: A Review Essay', *Wiener Zeitschrift fur die Kunde Sudasiens und Archiv fur Indische Philosophie,* 30, 1986, pp73-81

LAINE, J.W. '*Visions of God: Narratives of Theophany in the Mahābhārata,* Doctoral Thesis, Vienna, 1989

LARSON, G.J. *Classical Sāṃkhya, An Interpretation of its History and Meaning,* Delhi, 1969

LATH, M. 'The Concept of Ānṛśaṃsya in the Mahābhārata', in R.N. Dandekar Ed, *Mahābhārata Revisited,* New Delhi, 1990, pp113-119

LONG, J.B. 'The Concepts of Human Action and Rebirth in the Mahābhārata', W.O'Flaherty Ed, *Karma and Rebirth in Classical Indian Traditions,* Berkeley, 1980

MACDONNELL, A.A. *Vedic Mythology*, New York, 1974

MATCHETT, F. *The Avatāra Myth in the Harivaṃśa, the Viṣṇupurāṇa, and the Bhāgavatapurāṇa,* Doctoral Thesis, Lancaster, 1990

MOORTHY, K. 'Socio-Cultural Milieu of the Mahābhārata', in R.N. Dandekar Ed, *Mahābhārata Revisited,* New Delhi, 1990, pp140-150

NARAHARI, H.G. 'Karma and Reincarnation in the Mahābhārata', *Annals of the Bhandarkar Oriental Research Institute,* 27, 1946, pp102-113

OBERHAMMER, G. *Philosophy of Religion in Hindu Thought,* Delhi, 1989

O'FLAHERTY, W. *Asceticism and Eroticism in the Mythology of Śiva,* London, 1973

O'FLAHERTY, W. *The Origins of Evil in Hindu Mythology,* Berkeley, 1976

OLDENBURG, H. *Das Mahābhārata: Seine Entstehung, Seine Inhalt, Seine Form,* Gottingen, 1922

PANDE, G.C. 'The Socio-Cultural Milieu of the Mahābhārata: An Age of Change', in R.N. Dandekar Ed, *Mahābhārata Revisited,* New Delhi, 1990

PARGITER, F.E. *Ancient Indian Historical Tradition,* London, 1922

PARRINDER, G. *Avatāra and Incarnation,* London, 1970

PUSALKER, A.D. *Studies in the Epics and Purāṇas of India,* Bombay, 1963

RUBEN, W. 'The Beginning of Epic Sāṃkhya', *Annals of the Bhandarkar Oriental Research Institute,* 37, 1956, pp174-189

SCHEUER, J. *Śiva dans le Mahābhārata,* Paris, 1982

von SCHROEDER, L. 'Indiens Literatur und Cultur', in *Historischer Entwicklung,* Leipzig, 1887

SHARMA, A. 'The Role of the Anugītā in the Understanding of the Bhagavadgītā', *Religious Studies,* 14, 2, 1978, pp261-267

SHARMA, A. 'Fate and Free Will in the Bhagavad-gītā', *Religious Studies,* 15, 1979, pp531-537

SHARMA, A. 'The Bhagavad-gītā and the Hindu Epics: A Study in Comparative Devotional Theology', *Indian Journal of Theology,* 32, 1983, pp43-44

SHARMA, A. 'Suffering in Hindu Theism', in K.N. Tiwari Ed, *Suffering: Indian Perspectives,* Delhi, 1986, pp26-37

SHIDELER, E. 'The Meaning of Man in the Bhagavad-gītā', *Journal of the Bible and Religion,* 28, 1960, 308-316

SUKTHANKAR, V.S. 'Epic Studies 6: The Bhṛgus and the Bhārata, a Text-Historical Study', *Annals of the Bhandarkar Oriental Research Institute,* 18, 1, 1936-37, pp1-76

SUTHERLAND, S. 'Sita and Draupadi: Aggressive Behaviour and Role Models in the Sanskrit Epics', *Journal of the American Oriental Society,* 109, 1989, pp63-79

WEBER, M. *The Sociology of Religion,* Ephraim Fischoff trans, London, 1963

WIKANDER, S. 'Le Legende des Pāṇḍava et la Substructure Mythique du Mahābhārata', Georges Dumezil trans, in *Jupiter, Mars, Quirinius* IV, *Explication de Textes Indiens et Latins,* Paris, 1948, pp37-53

WILLIAMS, C. 'World Negation and World Maintenance: Some Hindu Perspectives', *Scottish Journal of Religious Studies,* 8, 1987, pp85-102

WINTERNITZ, M. *A History of Indian Literature,* V.S. Sarma trans, 2 volumes, Delhi, 1981-83

ZAEHNER, R. *Hinduism,* Oxford, 1962

INDEX